BRIEF CONTENTS

W9-CCJ-138

the Bedford Book of Genres

a guide & reader

SECOND EDITION

Amy Braziller
Red Rocks Community College

Elizabeth Kleinfeld
Metropolitan State College of Denver

bedford/st.martin's
Macmillan Learning
Boston | New York

For Bedford/St. Martin's

Vice President, Editorial, Macmillan Learning Humanities: Edwin Hill
Senior Program Director for English: Leasa Burton
Program Manager: Molly Parke
Marketing Manager: Vivian Garcia
Director of Content Development: Jane Knetzger
Developmental Editors: Ellen Thibault and Christina Gerogiannis
Assistant Editor: Stephanie Cohen
Senior Content Project Manager: Kendra LeFleur
Assistant Content Project Manager: Emily Bower
Workflow Supervisor: Joe Ford
Production Supervisor: Robin Besofsky
Media Project Manager: Melissa Skepko-Masi
Media Editor: Angela Beckett
Editorial Services: Lumina Datamatics, Inc.
Composition: Lumina Datamatics, Inc.
Photo Editor: Hilary Newman
Photo Researchers: Martha Friedman and Krystyna Borgen
Permissions Editors: Kalina Ingham and Arthur Johnson
Senior Art Director: Anna Palchik
Text Design: Jerilyn Bockorick
Cover Design: John Callahan
Printing and Binding: LSC Communications

Manufactured in the United States of America.

2 1 0 9 8 7
f e d c b a

For information, write: Bedford/St. Martin's, 75 Arlington Street, Boston, MA 02116

ISBN 978-1-319-05847-0

Acknowledgments
Acknowledgments and copyrights appear on the same page as the text and art selections they cover; these acknowledgments and copyrights constitute an extension of the copyright page.

ABOUT THE AUTHORS

Amy Braziller is an English faculty member and former department chair at Red Rocks Community College. She received her BA from Empire State College and her MA from New York University. Amy has presented on teaching writing and new media at numerous national and regional conferences. Her research focuses on the intersections between classroom and personal writing. Amy, who is at work on a series of personal essays related to her punk rock days in New York City, blogs about food, film, music, GLBT issues, and social media distractions at amybraziller.com.

Elizabeth Kleinfeld is the Writing Center Director and Professor of English at Metropolitan State College of Denver. She received her BS from Bradley University and her MS in English and PhD in Composition and Rhetoric from Illinois State University. Elizabeth is a contributing researcher on The Citation Project and has published articles on new media, writing centers, and student source use in various journals and collections, including *Computers & Composition Online* and *Praxis*. Her research interests include disability studies, feminist pedagogies, and teaching for social justice. Her current research focuses on restorative justice models of plagiarism mitigation.

PREFACE FOR INSTRUCTORS

It's a beautiful, multimodal world. It's a gorgeous stream of videos, blogs, ads, radio essays, graphic novels, PowerPoint presentations, editorials, artifacts, profiles, and infographics. It's colorful, chaotic, and fascinating. With so many genres in the world, why limit our students to the written essay (as wonderful a genre as it is)? Why not use multiple genres to teach students how to read and respond to any rhetorical situation?

The Bedford Book of Genres grew out of our wish to help our students with rhetorical analysis—to help them see its value and learn how to apply it in any setting. We were thrilled to see so many colleagues and their students embrace the first edition, and we were gratified by the many stories students themselves told us about engaging with the text. We hope that students using this book will recognize rhetorical analysis as the foundation for reading any kind of text critically and for composing any kind of text persuasively. We hope they'll experiment and take risks while learning to think through their research, composing, and reflecting processes in terms of purpose, audience, and other considerations. We hope they'll create smart, interesting work that's fun and thought-provoking for them to compose—and for you to grade (not to be underrated!).

So why a book about genres? Because working in a variety of genres and modes gets students to invest in what they do in first-year writing. When we began to experiment with multigenre/modal assignments in our own classrooms, we saw that happen. Now our students are excited, curious, and really "into" their projects. They bring fun, imagination, and personality into their academic work. And they see what they do in terms of skills they can travel with, and work they can showcase in their portfolios.

In response to feedback from users of the first edition, the second edition of *The Bedford Book of Genres* adds explicit coverage of the rhetorical situation, discussion and examples from academic and workplace genres, and a reader organized around the themes of identities, body and mind, activism, and creativity. Reviewers helped us understand the need to include more brief writing activities that could be incorporated into the classroom; many chapters now have several marginal writing prompts that can be used as classroom writing activities. Just as in the first edition, this edition includes student work along with detailed analyses of student processes.

A Rhetorical Road Map for Reading & Composing—in Any Genre

In the beginning, we set out to make this book do two things. First, to provide the basics that students need to read any text, to follow any author's rhetorical moves, and to recognize the elements at work in any genre. Second, to offer a framework for analysis and composition to help students understand their own rhetorical situations, to make smart choices as composers themselves, and to select and work in genres that are best for their purposes.

No one is an expert on every genre. But we—you and our students— don't have to be. We can all start from different places, and with any level, or lack, of technical skills. With these factors in mind, we do not cover every genre there is. Instead, we've put together a compendium of common genres. And we present them for students to read and analyze, and for them to use as models or jumping-off points for their own creations.

How This Book Is Organized

GUIDE

This is the heart of the book, where we introduce students to the rhetorical situation and genres, then move them from analyzing the work of others to composing their own texts. The Guide is divided into three parts; the first part is almost entirely new material, providing more instruction for first-year writing students to fully grasp the concepts of the rhetorical situation and how it drives composing choices. The second part builds on the concept of rhetorical situations, delving into many genres that were not covered in the first edition, helping to prepare students for composition situations they will encounter in college and beyond. Users of the first edition requested additional coverage of the Author/Artist's Statement, so we devoted an entire chapter to exploring this genre. The third part includes a totally revised student project with the student's explanation of the composing choices he faced.

Part 1 | Rhetoric, Reading, & Composing

1 Rhetorical Situations & Choices

2 Genres

3 Guided Readings: Rhetorical Situations & Genres Together

4 Composing: Drawing on Experience & Evidence

In Part 1, students learn about rhetorical situations and explore the rhetorical choices that go into composing in genres. Students learn how to read rhetorical situations and to apply a rhetorical lens for analyzing a variety of genre texts so that they can understand authors' choices (with a focus on purpose, audience, rhetorical appeals, modes, and media). At the same time, they learn to identify what makes a genre a genre. Students learn to analyze conventions, to examine the common elements of a given genre and the typical use of style, design, and sources. The Guided Readings, dozens of texts that we've annotated to point out composers' rhetorical situations and how they work with their chosen genre (explained in detail on p. xi), are a big part of how this all happens. Part 1 concludes by following a student's composing process from analyzing the academic assignment she's been given to brainstorming through drafting and revising.

Part 2 | Composing in Genres

5 Composing in College & Beyond

6 The Author's/Artist's Statement: A Genre for Reflection

7 Academic Genres

8 Workplace Genres

9 Public Genres

10 Revising & Remixing

In Part 2, students explore writing processes and some common genres they are likely to encounter in college and beyond. While the first edition organized genres around purpose, based on our own use and feedback from users of the first edition, we restructured our discussion of genres around audience. This allowed us to address more fully the three types of genres students are most likely to produce: academic, workplace, and public genres. Through a variety of Guided Readings, students get a glimpse of the rhetorical situations and choices real writers deal with. Students deepen their understanding of academic genres by examining genres such as researched arguments and critical analyses. Students learn about workplace genres by studying resumes and business memos. Moving beyond college and the workplace, students then explore public genres such as *Wikipedia* entries and editorials. In the final chapter, we return to Gwen Ganow from Part 1 to see how she revised her work based on peer feedback and ultimately remixes her work into a new genre.

Part 3 | Composing with Sources

11 Exploring Topics & Creating a Research Proposal

12 Evaluating & Choosing Sources

13 Integrating & Documenting Sources

14 Composing: Drawing on In-Depth Research: A Student Case Study

15 Assembling a Multigenre Project

Part 3 takes students through the research process, from choosing a topic to doing preliminary research, formulating research questions and writing a proposal. Students are then guided to evaluate and choose sources, and finally how to integrate into their writing, and document them. Students then follow Jasmine Huerta as she begins her research process, and later, they follow Michael Kipp as he assembles multiple researched pieces into a multigenre project.

READER

Part 4 | Reader

16 Identities: We Are Multiple

17 Mind & Body: Connections

18 Activism: Making Your Voice Heard

19 Creativity: It's Complicated

In the Reader, we offer a thematic approach to a variety of topics and genres. The readings offer models for composing, sources to draw upon, and hopefully some moments that are thought-provoking, entertaining, and inspiring too. (For more on this, see pp. xii–xiii.)

Features

Navigable and Flexible—with an Emphasis on the Rhetorical Situation and Elements of Genre

The Bedford Book of Genres is designed to be an accessible guide that supports students as they analyze and compose their own multimodal texts. It also serves as a reference that they can easily refer to as they work on their own or with peers.

We wanted to make this book flexible enough to support a variety of approaches to first-year composition. Whether you ask your students to compose in different genres or not, we hope you will take advantage of the guidelines provided for applying rhetorical analysis, as well as the variety of texts and genres that students can use for practicing rhetorical analysis.

For those of you who like to emphasize visual rhetoric in your class, you might focus on the many visual examples in the book, including maps, photo essays, and infographics.

If your primary focus is on interesting topics and themes, you might want to teach the book through a thematic lens. In addition to the thematic chapters and clusters in the Reader, we have provided an Index of Themes that sorts the rich contents of the book into plenty of relevant and exciting categories that will spark student attention and imagination.

Guided Readings That Help Students Analyze Various Genres

Annotated Guided Readings throughout the Guide highlight the rhetorical moves that writers and composers make in different genres and modes, and point out common genre conventions. We've designed the annotations—presented in the margins of over two dozen texts—to help students see what choices authors make, and what the consequences of those choices are. As students notice what professional writers and composers do, they become more aware of what they can and should do in their own work.

These Guided Readings demystify genres and help students recognize familiar strategies composers make across genres, such as appealing to readers' sense of pathos or logos. They also help students understand aspects of composing in genres and modes they might not be familiar with, and to look at features such as design.

How to find and use a Guided Reading   The Guided Readings are clearly listed in the book's table of contents and in chapter opening brief contents; they are designed with large headings and framed with annotations, and the genre of the reading is named in a tab at the top of the page.

The annotations in the margins of the Guided Readings are structured around two main ideas: (1) the composer's specific rhetorical situation and choices (purpose, audience, rhetorical appeals, modes/media); and (2) the typical conventions of the genre (common elements, style, design, and sources). We see this as a kind of "grid" that students might apply whenever they read or compose any kind of text in their composition course and beyond.

As your students begin to learn about reading genres critically, you may ask them to annotate texts that you or they bring to class (texts not included in the book); they might want to model their analyses on the structure of the annotations that appear in the margins of our Guided Readings. You'll find Guided Readings throughout Parts 1, 2, and 3.

Guided Processes that offer advice about multimodal composing built around interesting student projects   As mentioned on p. ix of this Preface, we follow several of our former students throughout the book, showing work they did in our classes in various stages, from brainstorming to finished project. Allowing students to see how other real students approach composing in genres lets students see that there is no one-size-fits-all way to compose. Seeing, for example, how Gwen Ganow, featured in Chapters 4 and 10, moves from a very early rough draft through a variety of later drafts shows how important revision is and, more important, what revision looks like for a real student writer. Chapter 14 stars Michael Kipp, discussing his multigenre project on the psychology of happiness. In the chapter, Michael unpacks his complete research process; the complete project is available on LaunchPad (launchpadworks.com).

Presenting real students' work also gives us a chance to show that we envision the students who will use this book as interesting and complex, and as desiring a challenge to compose using various techniques for a variety of outcomes.

How to find and use a Guided Process Like the Guided Readings, the Guided Processes (found in Chapter 4 and Chapters 10–13) are easy to locate in the table of contents, in the chapter opening brief contents, and on the page. Guided Processes walk your students through the steps other students have taken to research, compose, and revise, working in genres that were in some cases new and unfamiliar to them. They show that students don't have to begin as experts to research a topic and make a point about it in a new and interesting way.

The Guided Processes also work as reference materials that students can refer back to as they work through their own projects.

Clear Guidance on the Author's/Artist's Statements Students Write

We believe that the Author's/Artist's Statements that students compose—in which they explain how and why they created their specific genre composition(s)—are crucial. And we've found, through our review programs, conference panels, hands-on workshops, and conversations with many of you, that you think the same. These Statements give students a venue in which to discuss their work in terms of choices and intentions and even to make a case for the sources they drew on (we ask our students to include Works Cited pages with their Statements). Most significantly, these reflective pieces give students a place to think critically about their composing processes, about how they worked with (or outside of) a genre's typical conventions, and how they positioned themselves rhetorically in terms of their audience and purpose. Even if, say, a student is not pleased with her genre composition (maybe her collage is less than perfect, or her brief documentary or her video ad is not exactly what she'd hoped, or she didn't plan her time well, or she didn't have ample resources), she can still do the thoughtful work in her Statement that we want to see in a first-year writing course. Being able to reflect on and constructively critique one's own work is a lifelong skill that will serve our students well beyond our classrooms. Due to its importance in helping students develop meta-cognitive awareness, the second edition devotes an entire chapter (Chapter 6) to this genre for reflection.

Thematic Readings—with a Unique Mix of Genres & Modes—for Students to Draw On

While some themes in our Reader are found in other textbooks, the readings themselves take an unusual approach to the topic. For example, in Chapter 16, "Identities: We Are Multiple," we include very current issues, such as Muslim identity and in Chapter 17,

"Mind & Body: Connections," we include pieces on friendship and disability. In Chapter 18, "Activism: Making Your Voice Heard," we include protest signs and activist speeches. Chapter 19, "Creativity: It's Complicated," includes several pieces on the growing acceptance of failure as part of a creative process. When we chose the readings, we made sure to offer a variety of voices and genres, including research-based essays, blog entries, infographics, advertisements, and photographs.

Students can use these chapters to help them hone their critical reading skills, study the rhetorical choices composers make in various genres, and integrate different pieces for research-based writing on these topics. Each chapter begins with an introduction to the theme. Each reading includes both analytical questions and a composing project prompt. Each chapter closes with two long-term projects.

New to This Edition

More Support for Understanding Rhetorical Choices & Genres

In response to instructor feedback—and to align with the theory of rhetorical situations and genre as a social response—Parts 1 and 2 of the book have been reorganized and revised. Two new chapters open the book to give sharp focus to purposes as responses to rhetorical situations. Part 1 also emphasizes for students how they can work with the Guided Reading feature and gets them started with composing by drawing on their own experience. Part 2 now organizes readings and instruction into three categories—academic, public, and workplace genres—to highlight how context shapes writers' choices about genres.

In-depth research coverage in Part 3 includes an up-to-date guide to MLA and APA documentation. A new chapter, guest authored by Michael Kipp, one of Amy Braziller's former students, follows him as he draws on multiple sources to compose. Students will hear from a peer, in his own words, with practical advice for working with multiple sources.

A thoroughly revised Reader.   Two new topics, "Activism: Making Your Voice Heard" and "Creativity: It's Complicated," feature a range of voices on important topics that students will respond to. First-edition Reader chapters, "Identities: We Are Multiple" and "Mind & Body: Connections," are filled with new selections sure to enliven classroom discussion and composing. Post-reading questions and writing activities now follow every selection.

An all-new and accessible design that will motivate students to read and reread. Who doesn't love thumbing through a magazine or a lookbook of swatches for inspiration? The sheer variety of dynamic examples, clean design, and point-of-need instruction in *The Bedford Book of Genres* will inspire students to explore new kinds of writing and find topics they want to research and write about.

Interactive options and activities in LaunchPad. *LaunchPad for Bedford Book of Genres,* Second Edition, includes a complete, interactive e-book that is mobile-friendly and accessible, with customizable, auto-scored multiple-choice reading quizzes for every professional selection in the text. Also available are diagnostic quizzes; an expanded set of LearningCurve adaptive quizzing activities on grammar, argument, source documentation, and other topics; and Exercise Central, a bank of searchable and customizable grammar, punctuation, style, writing, and research exercises.

Acknowledgments

As with the first edition, we could not have written this book without the support and good cheer of many people. Obviously, if our own students hadn't gamely agreed to work on projects in multiple genres and modes, our teaching, and thus the book, would have stalled immediately, and so our first and heartiest thanks go to all the students who have taken our first-year writing classes. We are grateful to all the students whose work appears in these pages, especially to Gwen Ganow and Michael Kipp, whose work is featured in Chapters 4, 6, 10, and 14.

Some of the people who were key to the development of the first edition continued to inspire us in the second. Ellen Thibault, our first editor, helped us re-envision the book for its second edition. Leasa Burton, Molly Parke, and Vivian Garcia asked challenging questions that helped shape the direction of this edition. Christina Gerogiannis, our new editor, showed enormous patience during our sometimes chaotic revision process. Kendra LeFleur expertly managed the production of this edition, including its attractive, functional, and accessible new design. Permissions were ably overseen by Hilary Newman, Kalina Ingham, and Angela Boehler.

We could not have done this without the support of our loved ones. Amy is so thankful for her partner Nan Walker's constant encouragement and support. Elizabeth is grateful to her husband, Tom DeBlaker, and daughter, Lily, for their patience and good humor.

We'd like to thank our reviewers, many of whom generously offered comments through the entire development of the book—and who have become part of the community surrounding this project: Shannon Blair, Central Piedmont Community College; Ron Brooks, Oklahoma State University–Stillwater; Sabrina Chesne, Northwest Arkansas Community College; Michael Cripps, University of New England; Douglas Downs, Montana State University; Nicole Fisk, University of South Carolina; Rebekah Fitzsimmons, Georgia Institute of Technology; Lorena German, Lawrence High School; Elise Green, Longwood University; Maria del Rocio Grimaldo, Florida State University; Brandy Hawkins, Georgia Southern University; Anne Helms, Alamance Community College; Maurice Hunt, Baylor University; Diane Krumrey, University of Bridgeport; Geri Lawso, California State University, Long Beach; Ildiko Olasz, Northwest Missouri State University; Jen Richrath, Illinois Central College; Joseph Rodriguez, University of Texas,

El Paso; Mauricio Rodriguez, El Paso Community College; Allison Russell, Xavier University; Sandra McRae Sajbel, Red Rocks Community College; Courtney Schoolmaster, South Louisiana Community College, Lafayette; Suba Subbarao, Oakland Community College; Cynthia VanSickle, McHenry Community College; and Andrea West, Midlands Technical College.

We want to thank our enthusiastic colleagues, particularly the ones who used the book and gave us classroom-inspired feedback. Their belief in our vision and excitement at the prospect of the second edition helped spur us on.

And most important, we'd like to thank each other for sharing a brain, food, cocktails, and the good fortune to collaborate on this journey.

Amy Braziller
Elizabeth Kleinfeld

We're All In; as Always.

Bedford/St. Martin's is as passionately committed to the discipline of English as ever, working hard to provide support and services that make it easier for you to teach your course your way.

Find **community support** at the Bedford/St. Martin's English Community (community .macmillan.com), where you can follow our *Bits* blog for new teaching ideas, download titles from our professional resource series, and review projects in the pipeline. Also learn more there about our commitment to becoming a carbon-neutral publisher as part of Macmillan Learning. Sustainability is a central factor in all of our business decisions, including our choice to rely on certified paper.

Choose **curriculum solutions** that offer flexible custom options, combining our carefully developed print and digital resources, acclaimed works from Macmillan's trade imprints, and your own course or program materials to provide the exact resources your students need.

Rely on **outstanding service** from your Bedford/St. Martin's sales representative and editorial team. Contact us or visit macmillanlearning.com to learn more about any of the following options.

LaunchPad for *The Bedford Book of Genres*: Where Students Learn

LaunchPad provides engaging content and new ways to get the most out of your book. Get an interactive e-book combined with assessment tools in a fully customizable course space; then assign and mix our resources with yours.

- **Quizzes** for every reading in the book—and key visuals—test students' comprehension and analysis skills.
- The complete version of **Michael Kipp's multimodal project**, as discussed in Chapter 14, allows students to see the end result of his research process.
- **Diagnostics** provide opportunities to assess areas for improvement and assign additional exercises based on students' needs. Visual reports show performance by topic, class, and student as well as improvement over time.
- **Pre-built units**—including readings, videos, quizzes, and more—are easy to adapt and assign by adding your own materials and mixing them with our high-quality multimedia content and ready-made assessment options, such as **LearningCurve** adaptive quizzing and Exercise Central.
- Use **LaunchPad** on its own or integrate it with your school's learning management system so that your class is always on the same page.

LaunchPad for *The Bedford Book of Genres* can be purchased on its own or packaged with the print book at a significant discount. An activation code is required. To order LaunchPad for *The Bedford Book of Genres* with the print book, use ISBN 978-1-319-05033-4. For more information, go to **launchpadworks.com**.

Choose from Alternative Formats of *The Bedford Book of Genres*

Bedford/St. Martin's offers a range of formats. Choose what works best for you and your students.

- *Popular e-book formats* For details of our e-book partners, visit **macmillanlearning .com/ebooks**.

Instructor Resources

You have a lot to do in your course. We want to make it easy for you to find the support you need—and to get it quickly.

Resources for Teaching The Bedford Book of Genres is available as a PDF that can be downloaded from macmillanlearning.com. Visit the instructor resources tab for *The Bedford Book of Genres*. In addition to chapter overviews and suggestions for evaluating student work, the instructor's manual includes a sample syllabus and suggested lesson plans.

2014 WPA Desired Outcomes	Relevant Features of *The Bedford Book of Genres*
RHETORICAL KNOWLEDGE	
Learn and use key rhetorical concepts through analyzing and composing a variety of texts.	*The Bedford Book of Genres* is designed to help students read and compose—in any genre.

The Bedford Book of Genres is designed to help students read and compose—in any genre.

In Part 1, "Rhetoric, Reading, & Composing," authors Amy Braziller and Elizabeth Kleinfeld help students recognize rhetorical situations. Students learn how to apply a rhetorical lens for analyzing a variety of genre texts so that they can understand authors' choices—with focuses on purpose, audience, rhetorical appeals, modes, and media.

The framework of the book—the consistent analysis of rhetorical situations and genre conventions—supports students as they read a variety of texts and create their own work. A wide offering of Guided Readings with annotations point out composers' rhetorical situations and how they work with their chosen genre. Two new chapters open the text to provide sharp focus to purposes as responses to rhetorical situations. Part 1 also emphasizes how students can work with the Guided Reading feature and gets students started with composing by drawing on their own experiences.

In Part 2, "Composing in Genres," the authors use student examples to model research and composing processes and showcase their own students' projects. Part 2 now organizes readings and instructions into three categories—academic, public, and workplace genres—to highlight how context shapes writers' choices about genres.

Highly visual, annotated models called Guided Readings and Guided Processes help students analyze and compose in various genres, in print and online, and in multiple modes. The authors' annotations focus on two main things: (1) a given composer's rhetorical situation (with a focus on purpose, audience, rhetorical appeals, and choice of modes/media); and (2) the conventions of the genre he or she is working in (with a focus on its elements, and use of style, design, and sources). The Guided Processes show student readers how other students approached research and composing. Some examples of Guided Processes include models for how to choose a topic and create a bibliography (Chapter 5), how to preview and evaluate a source (Chapter 6), how to quote from, paraphrase, and summarize a source (Chapter 7), and how to work with sources and compose in multiple genres (Chapters 11–15). Essential to the student work is the reflective analytical piece—the Author's or Artist's Statements that they compose to accompany their genre compositions.

In Part 3, "Composing with Sources," students are guided through the research process, from choosing a topic to doing preliminary research, formulating research questions and writing a proposal. Students are then guided to evaluate and choose sources, and finally how to integrate sources into their writing, and document them.

Part 3 also provides an up-to-date guide to MLA and APA documentation. In addition, a new chapter, guest-authored by student Michael Kipp, follows him as he draws on multiple sources to compose, providing students with a peer example on working with multiple sources.

(Continues on next page)

Gain experience reading and composing in several genres to understand how genre conventions shape and are shaped by readers' and writers' practices and purposes.	A consistent focus on the rhetorical situations of readers and composers—and on how genres function in different scenarios—is central to this book's pedagogy. This focus is built solidly into the framework of the Guided Readings, Guided Processes, checklists, and assignments.
	Additionally, the idea that genres are fluid, and not fixed, is introduced in Chapter 1, "Rhetorical Situations & Choices," and continues throughout the text. Students get a sense that they can adapt a genre, depending on their own rhetorical situations as composers.
	Chapters 2 through 4 on composing in genres give students an overview of how purpose, audience, context, and other rhetorical concepts are interconnected, with guidance on choosing and composing in specific genres. Annotated Guided Readings highlight the rhetorical moves that writers and composers make in different genres and modes, and point out common genre conventions, demystifying genres and helping students recognize familiar strategies composers make across genres, such as appealing to readers' sense of pathos or logos.
	Building on Part 1 is Part 2, "Composing in Genres," which encourages students to work with different genres and rhetorical situations. These chapters follow six student writers and artists as they respond to unique rhetorical situations. Specifically, Chapter 4, "Composing: Drawing on Experience & Evidence," helps students decide which genres will work best for their contexts.
	Additionally, the Guided Readings and the thematic approach feature examples of many genres, including multimodal genres. For more avenues into the book, see the Contents, the Index of Genres, and Index of Themes.
Develop facility in responding to a variety of situations and contexts, calling for purposeful shifts in voice, tone, level of formality, design, medium, and/or structure.	In the Guide section of the book, Guided Readings and Guided Processes highlight the rhetorical situations and genre conventions of a large variety of texts.
	The annotations surrounding the Guided Readings and Processes focus on rhetorical situations with a specific emphasis on *purpose, audience, rhetorical appeals*, and *modes/media*. They also focus on the conventions of the genre at hand with specific emphasis on *elements of the genre, style, design*, and use of *sources*. This provides a type of "grid" that students might apply whenever they read or compose any kind of text, in their composition course and beyond.
	For example, Chapter 4, "Composing: Drawing on Experience & Evidence," follows student Gwen Ganow of Red Rocks Community College as she drafts, annotates sources, chooses a genre, and composes in that genre. Gwen's project-in-progress shows readers how she thought through options for composing and using voice, tone, and other techniques in her work, through multiple revisions.
	Chapter 10, "Revising & Remixing," follows Gwen as she remixes her composition from one genre to another, demonstrating how voice, tone, formality, design, and other elements, may change from one genre to the next.

Understand and use a variety of technologies to address a range of audiences.	In Part 2, "Composing in Genres," the authors encourage students to use a variety of technologies for composing—from creating "low tech" compositions such as print texts or collages made of found objects—to creating more complex digital texts, such as videos and multigenre projects. These chapters give clear guidance on how to use various strategies, tools, and genres to research, compose, review, revise, and share work aimed at specific audiences. For example, coverage of exploring topics and using sources shows students how to work with digital materials and urges them to draw on nondigital sources as well (such as people and cultural artifacts).
	Chapter 10, "Revising & Remixing," guides readers through integrating peer feedback and remixing work into new genres. Students learn to share documents in electronic environments and to use track changes to draft, collect feedback, and revise. In the Guided Process beginning on page 272, student Gwen Ganow remixes her project from an essay into a PowerPoint presentation, giving readers a practical example for how they might use digital media to compose and remix their own work to suit different contexts.
	Chapter 15, "Assembling a Multigenre Project," features Guided Readings of three student projects that address different audiences and use different technologies.
Match the capacities of different environments (e.g., print and electronic) to varying rhetorical situations.	The second edition adds explicit coverage of the rhetorical situation, discussion and examples from academic and workplace genres.
	The Reader is organized around the themes of identities, body and mind, activism, and creativity, which helps students hone their critical reading skills, study the rhetorical choices composers make in various genres, and integrate the different pieces for research-based writing on these topics.
	Attention to rhetorical situations and how composers choose genres, modes, and media to best reach their audiences and achieve their purposes is foundational to *The Bedford Book of Genres*. See the Guided Readings, Guided Processes, assignments, and checklists throughout the text.
	See Chapter 1, "Rhetorical Situations & Choices," especially the introduction to rhetorical situations (pp. 10–11) and academic text conventions (pp. 12–15).
	See Chapter 4, "Composing: Drawing on Experience & Evidence" (pp. 41–65), which follows Red Rocks Community College student writer Gwen Ganow. Ganow has a specific context for composing, and readers can see her process as she chooses the genres and media that will best suit her purposes, audiences, and use of rhetorical appeals.
CRITICAL THINKING, READING, AND COMPOSING	
Use composing and reading for inquiry, learning, thinking, and communicating in various rhetorical contexts.	The purpose of this book is to help students read, analyze, and compose in any genre, and in any context. The authors provide a framework that students can use when reading and analyzing the work of others, and in composing their own. By focusing on (1) the rhetorical situation and (2) the conventions of a given genre, students learn to think critically and compose thoughtfully.
	See especially the annotations surrounding the Guided Readings and Guided Processes, and the structure of all questions, assignments, and checklists.

(Continues on next page)

Read a diverse range of texts, attending especially to relationships between assertion and evidence, to patterns of organization, to interplay between verbal and nonverbal elements, and how these features function for different audiences and situations.	Part 1, "Rhetoric, Reading, & Composing," offers a range of texts that represent various genres, including verbal and nonverbal. The annotations surrounding the Guided Readings in these chapters make clear how composers use rhetorical appeals and draw on evidence and sources, for example. The annotations of the Guided Readings and Processes, as well as the structure of the assignments, questions, and checklists, are structured around two main ideas: (1) the composer's specific rhetorical situation and (2) the typical conventions of the genre.
	See the Reader portion of the book, as well as the Contents, and at the back of the book Index of Genres, and Index of Themes.
	The Reader portion is divided into four sections—identities, mind & body, activism, and creativity—and provides a thematic approach to a variety of topics and genres, as well as offering models for composing and sources to draw upon. Each reading includes both analytical questions and a composing project prompt. Each chapter closes with two long-term projects.
	Two new topics: "Activism: Making Your Voice Heard" and "Creativity: It's Complicated" feature a range of voices on important topics that students will respond to. First-edition chapters "Identities: We Are Multiple" and "Mind & Body: Connections" contain new selections to enliven classroom discussion and composing. Post-reading questions and writing activities now follow every selection.
Locate and evaluate primary and secondary research materials, including journal articles, essays, books, databases, and informal Internet sources.	Students learn to conduct research, evaluate sources, and draw on them as they compose. See Part 2, "Composing in Genres," especially:
	Chapter 11, "Exploring Topics & Creating a Research Proposal," which covers how to use sources to develop and refine a topic idea, a research question, a bibliography, and a proposal for further research. Chapter Readers follow student Jasmine Huerta through her project on diabetes.
	Chapter 12, "Evaluating & Choosing Sources," covers how to locate, preview, and evaluate primary and secondary sources. Readers follow student Emily Kahn as she previews a source for her project on women in comics, and student Calvin Sweet, as he evaluates in depth three different sources for his Hurricane Katrina project.
	Chapter 13, "Integrating & Documenting Sources," shows students how to use parenthetical citations and signal phrases, and how to quote, paraphrase, and summarize a source. Readers follow student Paul Pierre through part of his project on nonviolent protest. The second part of Chapter 13 provides a thorough guide to documenting sources in MLA and APA styles, with models for documenting even the trickiest electronic sources, such as blogs and video games, as well as objects found in the physical world.
Use strategies—such as interpretation, synthesis, response, critique, and design/redesign—to compose texts that integrate the writer's ideas with those from appropriate sources.	The role of sources is highlighted in the book, consistently identified in the annotations surrounding the Guided Readings and Guided Processes. Students are introduced to the rhetorical situations and genres, then moved from analyzing the work of others to composing their own texts.
	See Part 3, "Composing with Sources," where Guided Processes show strategies used by student writers as they research, compose, and revise. For example, in Chapter 13, "Integrating & Documenting Sources," we follow student Paul Pierre as he quotes from a source, paraphrases a source, and summarizes a source during his research for his project on nonviolent protest.

In Chapter 4, "Composing: Drawing on Experience & Evidence," see also the Guided Process that begins on page 48 and follows Red Rocks Community College student Gwen Ganow as she analyzes and integrates sources into her work. Her annotations critically examine each source in terms of the author's purpose, audience, use of rhetorical appeals, and more.

PROCESSES

Develop a writing project through multiple drafts.	Part 2, "Composing in Genres" and, specifically, Chapter 10, "Revising & Remixing," emphasize and demonstrate the importance of drafting and revising multiple times on the way to a final composition.
	Both chapters follow student Gwen Ganow's work-in-progress, beginning with her early drafts and brainstorms and on to her revisions, work with sources, peer review, Author Statement (in multiple drafts), final composition, and even a remix of that composition into another genre.
Develop flexible strategies for reading, drafting, reviewing, collaboration, revising, rewriting, rereading, and editing.	These strategies are built into the framework of the book, most visibly in the Guided Readings and Processes in Chapters 1 through 10. See especially Chapters 7 through 9, which encompass composing in various genres, and Chapter 10, "Revising & Remixing," which provides guidelines for drafting, revising, and remixing a project into a new genre.
	Further, Chapter 10 features sections on Revising Based on Your Own Observations and Revising Based on Peer Review that offer strategies for revision and collaboration.
Use composing processes and tools as a means to discover and reconsider ideas.	Chapter 11, "Exploring Topics & Creating a Research Proposal," makes clear how to use basic research to discover and test ideas.
	The Guided Processes in this chapter follow student Jasmine Huerta as she moves from a research question to a proposal and working bibliography. Huerta is seen moving from an early idea to a revised, more workable idea.
	Chapter 12, "Evaluating & Choosing Sources," follows student Emily Kahn as she previews a source for her women in comics project, and student Calvin Sweet as he evaluates in depth three sources related to his Hurricane Katrina project.
	See also Chapter 4, "Composing: Drawing on Experience & Evidence," which follows student Gwen Ganow as she drafts and revises her project on superheroes, refining her ideas along the way.
Experience the collaborative and social aspects of the writing processes.	Chapter 10, "Revising & Remixing," encourages students to collaborate with peers at different points in their composing processes. See also Chapter 11, "Exploring Topics & Creating a Research Proposal."
	Choosing a Topic through Basic Research in Chapter 11 prompts students to begin a research project by reading for ideas and discussing them with peers. The authors encourage students to use discussion as a way to discover what they want to say about a given topic.
	Guidelines for revising a draft based on peer review appear in Chapter 10, with a checklist of questions and follow-up questions to ask peers responding to a draft. See also the chapter's Guided Process for integrating peer feedback, beginning with a draft and ending with a finished composition.

(Continues on next page)

Learn to give and act on productive feedback to works in progress.	See previous page. Note that the first Guided Process in Chapter 10, Integrating Peer Feedback: Draft to Finished Composition follows student Gwen Ganow as she edits multiple drafts and integrates peer review.
Adapt composing processes for a variety of technologies and modalities.	This book is designed to help students think of themselves as composers—as authors, artists, and academic writers with specific rhetorical situations—and a variety of genres to choose from when they write and create. The all new and accessible design will motivate students to read and reread. Built into the pedagogy (see the Guided Readings, Guided Processes, and checklists, especially) is support for making sound choices about genres, technology, and modality. Students learn to compose any kind of text, by applying a basic framework: (1) look at the rhetorical situation first (What do you want to say? Who is your audience?) and (2) think critically and creatively about which genre(s) and modalities would work best in that situation. This framework can be applied regardless of a student's access to electronic technology, as several of the compositions in the book show (see the student work in Chapter 1, for example).
Reflect on the development of composing practices and how those practices influence their work.	Students reflect on their own composing processes and final works in their Author's/Artist's Statement (see Chapter 6). Students compose these Statements to accompany their genre compositions. In these documents, student composers discuss their processes—how and why they did what they did, how successful they think they were, and even what they might do differently in a future iteration of the project.

KNOWLEDGE OF CONVENTIONS

Develop knowledge of linguistic structures, including grammar, punctuation, and spelling, through practice in composing and revising.	In the Guided Readings and Processes, annotations consistently help students read (and compose) with an eye and ear for style, tone, word choice, and other considerations. This helps them keep multiple audiences in mind. To complement the book's coverage of composing and revising, and to provide help with grammar, punctuation, and spelling, consider packaging *The Bedford Book of Genres* at a discount with a Bedford handbook.
Understand why genre conventions for structure, paragraphing, tone, and mechanics vary.	See the Guided Readings in the following chapters: Chapter 2, "Genres" Chapter 3, "Guided Readings: Rhetorical Situations & Genres Together" Chapter 5, "Composing in College & Beyond" Chapter 7, "Academic Genres" Chapter 8, "Workplace Genres" Chapter 9, "Public Genres" The authors' annotations that surround the Guided Readings point out specific aspects of genre conventions, including the adaptability and flexibility of genres.
Gain experience negotiating variations in genre conventions.	Please see above.

Learn common formats and/or design features for different kinds of texts.	Please see previous page. The annotations surrounding the Guided Readings highlight (1) the composer's rhetorical situations and (2) the conventions of the composer's chosen genre. The conventions of genres that are identified include common elements and use of style, design, and sources.
Explore the concepts of intellectual property (such as fair use and copyright) that motivate documentation conventions.	Research coverage appears in Part 3 (Chapters 11–15), in which the authors and several of their students take readers through steps for exploring a topic, evaluating and choosing sources, and integrating and documenting them. For example, see the Guided Processes for how to preview a source, how to evaluate a source, how to quote from a source, how to paraphrase a source, and how to summarize a source. Students will find advice for how to avoid plagiarism, especially the kind that can happen inadvertently when working with digital sources. Of particular interest in our research material is the section on MLA and APA documentation in Chapter 13, in which the models show students how to cite today's sources, such as videos, games, wiki articles, and artifacts.
Practice applying citation conventions systematically in their own work.	See above. Chapter 13, "Integrating & Documenting Sources" gives students readable guidance on how to use parenthetical citations and signal phrases, how to cite sources at the end of their papers, and also how to safeguard against plagiarism. Guided Processes show how to quote from a source, paraphrase, and summarize, and the guide to MLA and APA styles in Chapter 13 uses a visual, handbook-style approach that takes the mystery out of how to use these styles correctly.

BRIEF CONTENTS

CONTENTS

Preface for Instructors   vii

GUIDE

4 Composing: Drawing on Experience & Evidence 40

7 Academic Genres   103

8 **Workplace Genres** 166

9   Public Genres   201

Contents **xxxiii**

12   Evaluating & Choosing Sources   314

13   Integrating & Documenting Sources   349

14 Composing: Drawing on In-Depth Research: A Student Case Study   411

15 Assembling a Multigenre Project   428

Guide

PART I
RHETORIC, READING, & COMPOSING

1

RHETORICAL SITUATIONS & CHOICES

What is rhetoric? Rhetoric refers to the ability to communicate effectively and with a purpose. So what is a rhetorical situation? It's the context in which you create a composition. To put it simply, as a writer, you have a specific purpose and an audience. You need to know what you want to say; you also need to know your readers' expectations and accommodate them in some way. For example, when you write a review of a restaurant on yelp.com, you know that Yelp readers want to know your opinion of the meal; they also expect specific details about the individual dishes, service, and ambience you experienced.

Thinking about the rhetorical situation before you begin composing can help you make all sorts of important decisions about your composition, including what level of vocabulary to use (simpler words for an audience of middle schoolers than for a college-educated audience), what kinds of examples to use (more technical examples for an audience of experts than for an audience of laypeople), and what kind of color scheme to use (high-contrast color scheme for people who have color blindness if you anticipate they might be part of your audience).

In 1968, Lloyd Bitzer, a communications scholar, first articulated the modern concept of a rhetorical situation. He identified three aspects of rhetorical situations:

- **The exigence:** The motivation for the writer or composer. For example, our exigence for writing this chapter is that we want college students to understand the importance of rhetorical situations in their own reading and writing. In this book, we use the term "purpose" to convey the idea of exigence.
- **The audience:** Whoever will receive the message conveyed by the writer or composer. Our audience right now is you, students in a college writing course.
- **The constraints:** The situational factors that a writer or composer must take into account. One of our constraints is that a textbook relies on the written word, so although we might want to explain rhetorical situations to you through an interpretive dance, we are instead using written words.

You consider rhetorical situations all the time, even if you are not consciously aware of doing so. When you make choices about the way you tell a story about a snowboarding adventure you had—perhaps including more colorful language and slang when you tell the story to your friends and then choosing more formal language when you tell the story to your insurance agent—you are responding to a particular rhetorical situation. There is no one "right" way to tell the story of your adventure; the way you tell the story depends on your audience. Likewise, your purpose in telling the story makes a difference. If you are telling the story to illustrate that you are an adrenaline junky, you may highlight the level of risk or danger involved in snowboarding, but if you are telling the story to convince a nervous friend to try snowboarding, you might emphasize that you avoided injury on your adventure by taking a few precautions and using high-quality equipment.

Already today, you've probably been involved in several rhetorical situations. If you think of rhetorical situations broadly to include any communication event, then any interaction you had this morning with roommates, family, fellow public transportation riders, or the barista at your favorite coffee shop counts. Think about how you communicated differently with these different people. You might have been more polite with some, more direct with some, or more verbose with some. You may not have even realized you were making choices in your level of politeness, directness, or verbosity because you probably understand the concept of rhetorical situations instinctively.

In this book, we will constantly ask you to think explicitly about the rhetorical situations you find yourself in so that you can be more deliberate about the choices you make in your day-to-day interactions and in your writing. As you think about rhetorical situations, we will ask you to consider your purpose, your audience, your use of rhetorical appeals, and your choice of modes and media. In other words, we will ask you to think carefully about rhetorical choices.

Understanding Rhetorical Situations & Choices

Purpose | Why Are You Composing?

Every time you write—or compose anything, in any genre—you do so for a reason. You might be trying to convince someone to change her mind about something or take action. You might be telling a story to build rapport with someone or entertain him. You might be giving someone information to help her make a decision. Or you might have another purpose.

There are many reasons to write, and sometimes these reasons overlap. As writers, we often have several purposes for creating a single text. Let's look at a possible example. Let's assume that you love farmers' markets and want to establish one in your town. Your purpose is to start up a weekly local farmers' market. To make this happen, you need to (1) present your idea to others and (2) persuade them that it's worth acting upon. You expect that some people will object. In this context or rhetorical situation, you have more than one purpose. To persuade others, you need to explain your idea, say what's great about it, provide supporting statistics, and tell a persuasive story about how a similar plan succeeded in a neighboring town. You also have more than one audience. Some people will agree with you 100 percent; others won't be so sure; still others—maybe grocery store owners or city planners—will reject your idea altogether.

Audience | Whom Are You Composing For?

Every time you compose, you do so for multiple audiences: a primary audience, which is your intended reader, and a secondary audience, which is other people who might end up reading what you wrote. For example, we are writing this book for you, students, so you are our primary audience; however, writing instructors and writing program administrators are likely also going to read this book. Audiences are made up of people—and people can be easily bored, pressed for time, or generally disinterested. You need to grab their attention and keep it. Let's look at an example: Imagine you are traveling across the country and want to tell stories of your adventures (your purpose) to your friends, family, and even strangers interested in travel (your audience). You decide that the best way to reach your audience is to create a blog where you can write about your experiences, show maps and photos, and connect to other social media sites. That is what the world-traveling blogger Gilad Hizkiyahu (who also calls himself Giladhiz) decided to do (see p. 8).

Gilad clearly understands his audiences (his primary audience of travelers and a secondary audience of folks like us who happened upon his blog while looking for examples) and wants them to stick with him. To this end, he does the following:

- Provides a photo of himself and an "About the Author" section so that readers can make a personal connection with him
- Addresses his readers directly: "So, dear friends and accidental surfers, allow me to begin with the reasons that brought me to plan and go on that trip"
- Writes in a casual, readable, and humorous style, meant to hook his readers and keep them interested in his ongoing adventures
- Structures his post with subheadings to guide readers, and provides options for navigating content and for e-mailing or connecting by social media

CHECKLIST | Composing with a Purpose

As you begin to compose, ask yourself:

☐ Why am I writing? What do I want to communicate? And to whom?

☐ What do I want my audience to believe or do after reading my composition?

☐ Is what I'm communicating objectionable or controversial to anyone? If so, how will I address this?

☐ If I'm trying to convince someone of something, what are the best ways to do so for my particular readers?

☐ If I'm trying to build rapport with someone, how can I share something about myself or my experiences to help my readers relate to me?

☐ If I'm helping someone make a decision, what information does my reader need, and how can I communicate it clearly?

Rhetorical Appeals | Ethos, Pathos, and Logos

Regardless of what your purpose is, you need to get your audience on board. Even when persuasion is not your primary goal, it is always part of what you're doing, no

WRITE

When you write, do you think of who will read your writing? When you compose a status update on social media, do you think of who will experience what you've created? Write about a time you considered your audience in writing a status update on Facebook, Twitter, or another social media platform.

matter what. We persuade our audiences by using what are called *rhetorical appeals.* Aristotle identified three rhetorical appeals. They are often used in combination:

- *Ethos* is the credibility, authority, and trustworthiness the writer or composer conveys to the audience.

- *Pathos* is an appeal to an audience's emotions or values.

- *Logos* is the logic and connection of facts and evidence to the point being made.

Modes & Media

What do we mean by mode?   When you want to communicate an idea to an audience, you have to decide whether to express it in writing, visually, through sound, or in some other way. Do you want to write down your idea? Express it visually with paint on canvas? Or tell the story orally? Whichever method of expression you choose is the composition's mode.

There are many modes, but for the purpose of this book, we work with three modes: **written** or **text-based, visual**, and **audio**. The term *multimodal* refers to more than one mode used in a composition. For example, a photo essay usually uses two modes (text and visuals), while a TED talk might use three modes (visuals and text on slides and the audio delivery of the speech).

What do we mean by media?   Media is how the composition is delivered to its audience. Will your audience read your piece in a book (print), or will they read it in an e-book (digital)? Will your audience watch your TED talk by going to the TED Talk Web site (digital), watch you deliver it on stage (face-to-face), or read a transcript of it (print)?

For the purpose of this book, we work primarily with three types of media: **print, digital**, and **face-to-face**. Media, though, also includes film, television, software, MP3, and more.

A particular mode can be delivered in multiple media. For example, an audio essay could be recorded either on an old-fashioned tape recorder or digitally. An obituary might be printed in a newspaper or published online.

The modes of Gilad's blog, *Gilad Is Doing South America*, are both written and visual, and the medium is digital. A simple way to distinguish mode from medium is to think of mode as the "how" and medium as the "delivery system." A separate concept is genre, which we will cover in Chapter 2. For now, keep in mind that the genre—in Gilad's case, a blog—is what the composer presents as a final product.

WRITE

Go back to the paragraph you wrote from page 6 about a rhetorical situation you were involved in earlier today. Write another paragraph in which you discuss the mode and media choices you made and why you made them. How might the situation have unfolded differently if you had made different choices?

CHECKLIST | Composing for an Audience

As you begin to compose, ask yourself:

☐ Who is my audience in terms of demographics? How do they identify in terms of gender? What is their age range? Where do they live? What do they like? Do they have particular religious beliefs? Are they from a particular social class? Are they of a particular race or ethnic background?

☐ What is my audience's stake in the issue I'm presenting? Do they care? Why or why not?

☐ What does my audience value? Will my message be in line with—or contradictory to—their values? How can I present my message so that my audience will consider it? And perhaps even be persuaded by it?

☐ What level of education does my audience have? What kind of language will best reach them?

☐ Who is my primary audience, and what do they need to know?

☐ What possible secondary audiences might read this, and how do I need to take them into account?

Reading Rhetorical Situations

In your classes, you might have heard your professors say that the course empha-sizes critical reading. This might even be noted on the course syllabus. Reading the rhetorical situation of a text is an important aspect of critical reading. It allows you to dig beneath what is being said to understand the choices the writer made when composing.

Reading rhetorically is an active way to read. You are interacting with the text, notic-ing and asking questions about the assumptions the composer made. For example, if you are reading a letter to the editor arguing that a homeless shelter should be closed because it is expensive to operate, you might notice that the writer's argument hinges on the assumption that a homeless shelter should not cost the public so much to operate. That means the writer must believe that there is an appropriate amount of money that could be spent on housing the homeless. You might also ask where the writer got his or her information about how much the shelter costs to operate. Are the figures current? You might also ask about other perspectives, such as those of the homeless people who rely on the shelter or the people who are employed by the shelter.

Initially, when you pick up something to read, you probably read it to understand the message the writer is trying to convey. For example, if you read a Yelp review of a nearby restaurant, you might read it to see whether the writer says you should eat there. However, if you were to read this review rhetorically, you would examine how the writer got her point across. You wouldn't only be concerned with whether you want to eat at the restaurant, but you would dig into how the author convinced or failed to convince you to eat at that restaurant. To read something rhetorically, you read to understand not just what the writer is telling you, but also how the writer conveys information and makes her point. When reading rhetorically, you might ask who the composer is, why this is being written (purpose), whom the composer is addressing (audience), and how language is used to convey the message or appeal to the audience.

Reading to Understand Purpose

Knowing why a piece was written helps you understand how you might experience that piece and what you can reasonably expect to get from it. Is the purpose to per-suade you about an issue? Help you make a decision? Provide a constant stream of belly laughs? Share a story? Knowing that a Yelp review about a restaurant is intended to help you make a decision about whether to eat at the establishment keeps you focused on looking at the reasons the writer gives for eating there rather than lingering on a clever turn of phrase.

Reading to Understand Audience

Understanding for whom the piece is written helps you determine what extra information you might need to digest the text. Are you the intended primary audience? If not, how does the piece pertain to you? If the audience of a piece about a landslide is a geologist, you might need to look up some terms to understand the information. What additional resources will you need to understand or relate to the piece?

Reading to Understand Rhetorical Appeals

Consider who the writer is. Is it someone qualified to write about the subject? Is the Yelp reviewer someone who eats out a lot? Once you've determined that the writer is credible (*ethos*), read to see how the writer establishes that credibility. Is credibility established through the level of information or details provided? Through the language used? Is it established because the writer has written numerous pieces about the subject? Another thing to consider is how the writer connects with you (*pathos*). Are you hooked? Is it because of the emotion used to help you feel the situation? Consider your reactions to the text and why you continue to read or view it. Finally, ask yourself how the author makes his case (*logos*). Is it supported with evidence? Are ideas organized in a particular way to help you consider the question at hand?

Reading to Understand Modes & Media

Why has the writer chosen to use text? Is it because that's the most efficient way to convey the information to her intended audience? Did the writer include pictures? Ask yourself why the visuals were included. Perhaps the Yelp review you're examining incorporates a photo of the delicious onion soup dumplings to illustrate the unique qualities of the chef. This might help convince you to try the restaurant more than if just words were used. If you are listening to a podcast about the homeless, you might ask how listening to the story affects you. Did the writer choose to record words so you could hear the voices of the homeless?

In addition to examining the modes used, read to understand the choices made in media. Is the piece available digitally so that it can be accessed anywhere there is an Internet connection? You might want to access a Yelp review from your computer at home when planning a trip or when you land in an unfamiliar city and are starving, seeking some comfort food for dinner.

While reading rhetorically might seem like a lot of work, it ultimately helps you gain a better understanding of the decisions the composer has made. This not only helps you discern the messages in a seemingly difficult text, but it also helps you consider the ways you might deliver your own messages. Throughout the text, you will see numerous guided readings that illustrate ways to read rhetorically.

Reading Academic Texts

You've probably been reading for most of your life and probably read countless texts every day—road signs, text messages, food labels, and more. But reading complex academic texts such as textbooks, peer-reviewed journal articles, and scholarly books requires a special set of skills. When you read road signs, you are simply reading for information. Academic texts, however, usually make an argument of some sort; if you simply read them for information, you might miss the point. For example, if you read the previous material about reading rhetorical situations and just took away that it includes noticing purpose, audience, appeals, and modes and media, you would be missing the point that understanding the rhetorical situation helps you see why a writer made certain decisions.

Here are some strategies you can use to make these complex texts more digestible:

Previewing

Rather than diving in to read from the beginning, it can be helpful to skim through a complex text from beginning to end to get a sense of its organization and purpose. Skimming will help you understand what the topic is and what argument is being made. For example, simply skimming through to read the headings can help you see whether a text will cover both a problem and a solution or only discuss the problem.

Looking for Key Terms

As you preview, you may notice that some technical terms are used in the headings or are in bold or italics in the text. Since these terms are being emphasized, you should make sure you comprehend them or you will have trouble making sense of the text once you begin reading it more closely. Identify key terms and be sure to look up definitions if you are unsure of what they mean. For example, if you see the word *hegemony* several times in your skimming and aren't absolutely certain what it means, you should look it up because it is clearly essential to an understanding of the text.

Identifying Knowledge Claims & Evidence

After you skim the text, you will need to read it at least once, slowly and carefully. As you read, notice the difference between facts and knowledge claims. A fact is something that is uncontested; a knowledge claim is open to debate. For example, it is a fact that millennials spend more time reading on the Internet than reading books; it is a knowledge claim that this is problematic. Once you identify something as a knowledge claim, you want to search for the evidence that supports that claim. For example, in the 1968 article mentioned earlier, Lloyd Bitzer makes a knowledge claim that some rhetorical situations are so dramatic that we "can predict with near certainty" what the response will be.* He then supports that claim with a discussion of the rhetorical response to President Kennedy's assassination.

Considering the Composer's Perspective

Many people have written about farmers' markets, but consider how different an article on farmers' markets written by an economist might be from an article written by a city planner. The economist will likely be considering the economic impact on communities, consumers, large-scale farmers, or small farmers, while the city planner will more likely be thinking about how weekend farmers' markets impact traffic patterns and put pressure on a community's parking options. Understanding the perspective of the composer will help you understand why particular knowledge claims are made and not others.

Annotating the Text

One way to force yourself to read slowly and deliberately is to annotate the text you are reading. Annotating is different from highlighting, which is simply noting important words or sentences in the text. Annotating means making notes directly on the text (this can be done by writing on a hard copy or using software to add notes to a digital copy). With highlighting, you are limited to noting what the author has said; annotating allows you to summarize the writer's ideas in your own words, which is a good way to understand and remember them. Additionally, you might want to ask questions, write down definitions of words you looked up right next to the words themselves, and write down connections or contradictions you notice between the text you are reading and other texts.

Annotated Example | Reading an Academic Text

Following is an example of an academic text: an assignment to create a bibliography that you might get from your instructor. This assignment sheet is from Elizabeth's second-semester composition course. The annotations in the margins (in black) show you how you might read the assignment using the strategies we've described.

---

*Bitzer, Lloyd F. "The Rhetorical Situation." *Philosophy & Rhetoric*, vol. 1, no. 1, 1968, pp. 1–14.

Composition 201
Metropolitan State University of Denver

After you have conducted general research on your topic and have a sense of the issues, subtopics, agreements, and disagreements discussed by people committed to your topic, you are ready to delve more deeply into your topic. Peer-reviewed journal articles are a good place to do research when you are ready to move beyond what the general public knows about your topic and find out what experts are discussing. Showing that you're knowledgeable about experts in the field helps you establish your ethos as a researcher.

1. Find 14 peer-reviewed journal articles on your topic. If you are not sure if your articles have been peer-reviewed, ask me or a librarian for help.
2. For each article, do the following:
   a. Read the entire article. Journal articles are not "quick reads," so be sure you have plenty of time and are in a space where you can concentrate. I highly recommend that you annotate as you read.
   b. Write a bibliographic entry in MLA or APA format.
   c. Write a one-paragraph summary of the main argument or point the article makes and the support offered. This should be a well-developed paragraph of at least five sentences. Journal articles make complex arguments, so you will not be able to do an article's main argument justice in fewer than five sentences. All quotations and paraphrases should include in-text citations.
   d. Write a one-paragraph discussion of how the article aligns with, departs from, extends, or complicates what other sources on the bibliography say. Again, this should be a well-developed paragraph, with some examples to support your assessment. All quotations and paraphrases should include in-text citations. Note that you may not end up using all of these articles as sources in your research paper. That's normal—most researchers consult many more sources than they end up using. You may also end up using or consulting non-peer-reviewed journal articles; that's fine, but ONLY peer-reviewed journal articles should appear on your annotated bibliographies.

Credit: Elizabeth Kleinfeld.

Are you reading an academic text, such as an assignment or a scholarly essay? Keep the following questions in mind.

☐ **Purpose.** Is the writer trying to convince you of something? Is the writer sharing a story? Is the writer giving you information? You might even notice other purposes that we haven't mentioned here, such as entertaining you. Is the writer reporting, telling a story, entertaining, and persuading all at the same time? Don't worry. Sometimes purposes for writing or composing overlap.

☐ **Audience.** Who seems to be the author's primary audience? Secondary audience? How do you know? Why do you think someone would read (view, listen to, etc.) the text? How does the author capture and sustain audience attention?

☐ **Rhetorical appeals.** How does the author use the rhetorical appeals—ethos, pathos, and logos—to reach his or her audience? How does the author convey credibility? What kinds of evidence does the author offer to support the point of the piece?

☐ **Modes & media.** What choices has the writer made about mode (how to convey an idea)? If multiple modes are used, how do they interact with each other? What choices has the writer made about media? For example, has the writer made the piece available in print form or digitally? How do the writer's choices about modes and media reflect his or her purposes and audiences?

PRACTICE

Reading Any Text Rhetorically

Locate three texts you have read today—maybe a text message, an advertisement, and an assignment sheet or other text for one of your courses. For each one, identify the purpose, audience, rhetorical appeals, and mode and media. Is reading these texts through a rhetorical lens different from how you read them in the first place? Write one paragraph for each piece to explain.

2 GENRES

In Chapter 1, "Rhetorical Situations & Choices," we explained that the composition scholar Lloyd Bitzer described a rhetorical situation as a communication event that includes an exigence or purpose, an audience, and constraints or limitations that help shape how the speaker can respond. Bitzer was concerned with describing the rhetorical situation, but he doesn't address how to respond to the rhetorical situation. That's where "genre," the key word in this chapter's title, comes in. Genre is how the speaker chooses to respond to the rhetorical situation.

The concept of genre has existed since the ancient Greeks used it to classify literature, and following the Greeks, today the word is sometimes oversimplified to mean "category" or "type." Scholar Carolyn Miller, however, gives a modern-day definition of genre as a social response to a rhetorical situation. The word "social" highlights that genre is a form of communication between a speaker and an audience; it involves social interaction.

For example, let's say you are working on an assignment for your biology class the night before it is due and you realize you don't understand the assignment. The rhetorical situation you find yourself in involves a purpose (you need to figure out what the instructor wants you to do) and an audience (your instructor). You also need to take into account that it's too late to call your instructor, office hours have been over for many hours, and you know you probably should have read the assignment more closely when you first got it and asked questions then, instead of waiting until the last minute. As you consider your options for communicating with your instructor (genre responses) about this pickle you're in, you are considering *social responses to your rhetorical situation*:

1. You could write an e-mail in which you apologize for waiting until the last minute and ask for clarification.
2. You could text a classmate and hope that she can explain the assignment.
3. You could wait until tomorrow and go to the instructor's office first thing in the morning to ask for clarification.
4. You could make some educated guesses about what the instructor wants, do the assignment as best you can, and keep your fingers crossed.
5. You could just take a 0 on the assignment.

Notice that each of the first four options includes a particular form of communication: an e-mail, a text, an in-person conversation, and an assignment that may or may not have been completed correctly. But even the fifth option, not submitting anything, is a genre of communication: doing nothing in this case is a deliberate choice, and so it counts as a social response to the rhetorical situation.

WRITE

Think of a rhetorical situation you found yourself in recently in which you considered two or more possible responses. Write a brief paragraph in which you describe the two (or more) options you considered and explain why you went with the one you did.

Reading Genres

Why bother thinking about genres? Because they represent possibilities. We wrote this book to acknowledge that in college and beyond there are many more genres available to us besides the five-paragraph essay or the traditional term paper. As respectable and time-honored as those genres are, there are a whole lot of other options out there. We wrote this book to help you understand and create in a variety of genres—and we invite you to produce works that matter to you and enjoy doing so. As an added bonus, paying attention to genre will make you a better writer and artist because you'll be focused on the needs of your audiences and your own purposes as a composer.

The Blog as a Social Response

Because genres are responses to social situations, they are dynamic, changing over time as people and their needs change over time. Before digital composing, writers who wanted to record their thoughts wrote with a pen in a journal or diary, in a physical notebook. Then blogs were created, and since then, blogs have changed. The original blogs were more stream of consciousness and had smaller audiences than many blogs today. Blogs changed because the people using them, both composers and audiences, realized that blogs could be interactive, could be shared, could be multimodal, and more. Thus, the genre of blog continues to change.

The blog *The Dragonfly Woman* is hosted by Christine Goforth, who identifies herself as an "aquatic entomologist with a blogging habit." In her first blog entry, dated May 28, 2009, she explains why she adopted the name "Dragonfly Woman" and how she went from being a kid terrified of insects to a woman obsessed with dragonflies.

The "About DW" page on Christine's blog states that she is now a "bona fide entomologist/scientist" who manages citizen science for the North Carolina Museum of Natural Sciences. She explains her rhetorical situation, speaking directly to her readers. In several paragraphs, she acknowledges her audience and purpose:

> If you arrived here, you probably wanted to learn a little more about the crazy woman who tells strange stories and goes on and on about aquatic insect respiration on this blog. I'd hate to disappoint, so here is everything you ever wanted to know about me or my blog condensed down into a few bullet points.
>
> I am a bona fide entomologist/scientist—I have an undergraduate degree in biology and a grad degree in entomology. I don't know whether that makes me seem any more reliable or trustworthy to my readers or not, but there it is. I study aquatic insects, especially behavior and respiration in giant water bugs and dragonflies. If you've spent any time here in the summer, you'll know I also run a citizen science project called the Dragonfly Swarm Project.

I am NOT a taxonomist, so I *will* get the occasional identification wrong. If you happen to notice a mistake, *please* let me know (use that Contact Me button above). It's frustrating enough to read all the misinformation about insects online without being part of the problem.

I cover a variety of topics, but everything is at least tangentially related to insects. I had originally intended for this blog to be purely educational, but it's evolved into more of a celebration of insects, scientifically, culturally, and personally. I like it better this way.

Christine Goforth, from her blog *The Dragonfly Woman* (thedragonflywoman.com)

By acknowledging that she is not a taxonomist, Goforth makes it clear that her purpose is not to be meticulous with identifying insect species, but rather to use her blog to host a "celebration of insects, scientifically, culturally, and personally." In keeping with the celebratory theme, the tone of the blog is enthusiastic and even a bit folksy, as she tries to entice people who might be more like the scared kid she was into becoming more appreciative and less fearful of insects. By sharing her personal excitement about bugs, she helps her audience see them as beautiful and fascinating. All of this also helps her develop ethos and come across as a credible source.

Goforth uses the genre of the blog because she wants to reach out to many more people than she could through her job at the museum in North Carolina. She can tell museum-goers that her blog is a place for them to pursue their curiosity about insects, and she can also count on getting traffic to her blog from people who Google topics she covers, including "giant water bugs" and "terrestrial insects." Since the blog also includes many links to other blogs and Web sites on insects, it is a rich resource for anyone interested in entomology.

While blogs are no doubt a familiar genre, think for a moment about the different genres you read and compose in each day. As a student, you write research papers and presentations; these are two examples of academic genres. In each case, you know what is expected of you as a writer because you understand certain features of the genre. You know that to write a research paper, you must gather a variety of reliable sources and cite them in a specific way.

▼ BLOG

Christine Goforth, *The Dragonfly Woman*. In her post titled "Well-Nigh Wordless Wednesday: Itty Bitty Wasp," the blogger writes: "I was walking past my back door about a month ago and caught sight of something out of the corner of my eye. I went to inspect and discovered this: [see image] A very tiny wasp! I'm betting it's one of the parasitic wasps, based on the diminutive size and enormous hind legs. I grabbed my iPhone and my "macro" lens and snapped a few photos because it was simply too adorable to pass up. Apparently my glass could do with a bit of cleaning, though." See thedragonflywoman .com.

Credit: Christine L. Goforth.

Itty bitty wasp

A very tiny wasp! I'm betting it's one of the parasitic wasps based on the diminutive size and enormous hind legs. I grabbed my iPhone and my "macro" lens and snapped a few photos because it was simply too adorable to pass up. Apparently my glass could do with a bit of cleaning though...

In other situations, you choose the genre to compose in, depending on what you want to say, who you want to say it to, and how you want to say it. Your choice of genre also depends on your own skills and interests, as well as the materials available to you. For example, your band is playing next week and you need to advertise the event. Your purpose is to persuade your potential audience to come to your show. You might choose to present your ad as a poster. Depending on your supplies and desired effect, you could create a handmade poster to tape up at school or design one to post on Facebook. Alternatively, you might choose to advertise by creating and posting a short music video.

The Memoir as a Social Response

One of the best ways to become a better writer or composer is to read like one—to pay attention to what other writers and composers do, how and why they work in a particular genre, and how they make that genre work for them. Let's look at an example from history. Annie L. Burton (ca. 1858–unknown) was born a slave and as an adult decided to write about her experiences; her 1909 memoir is titled *Memories of Childhood's Slavery Days*. She writes:

> Our clothes were little homespun cotton slips, with short sleeves. I never knew what shoes were until I got big enough to earn them myself. If a slave man and woman wished to marry, a party would be arranged some Saturday night among the slaves. The marriage ceremony consisted of the pair jumping over a stick. If no children were born within a year or so, the wife was sold. At New Year's, if there was any debt or mortgage on the plantation, the extra slaves were taken to Clayton and sold at the court house. In this way families were separated.

While we can't fully know Burton's purpose in writing her memoir, we can assume she wrote to help her readers understand how a formerly enslaved African American woman experienced and resisted expected social and economic roles. What we do know, however, is that she was motivated by her faith. In her memoir, she states:

> For God has commanded me to write this book, that someone may read and receive comfort and courage to do what God commands them to do. God bless every soul who shall read this true life story of one born in slavery.

Thus one purpose of the memoir was to give readers "comfort and courage to do what God commands them to do." Another purpose might have been to help women readers understand what it was like to be a woman and a slave.

Since a purpose of slave narratives is to build empathy in readers, Burton probably intended to reach white people who had not suffered the indignities of slavery. Her audience might have also included literate former slaves, most likely in the North

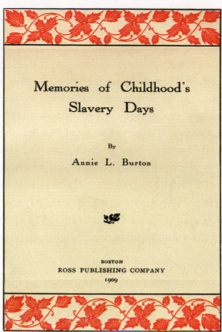

Memories of Childhood's
Slavery Days

By

Annie L. Burton

BOSTON
ROSS PUBLISHING COMPANY
1909

because her book was published in Boston. Her current audience might include students like you, scholars, and historians who want to read a firsthand account of slave life.

Burton likely took into account various constraints and situational factors, including the attitudes of white readers toward African Americans. While she had the education and writing skills to sustain an ambitious writing and research project, she chose to tell her own story simply. As Burton considered her rhetorical situation—she wanted to communicate a message of resistance and faith—and pondered an effective social response, she must have noticed that a very popular genre of the day was memoir. Because memoirs were widely read, Burton could expect a good-sized audience for her piece, and she stood to make some profit from it. The memoir allowed Burton to tell her personal story the way she wanted to tell it, to make her point about resistance, and to set it in a historical context.

So, Burton chose her genre—the memoir—as a social response to her rhetorical situation. If she had been trained in music, she would have written a ballad or an opera, or if she had been born a little later, she might have told her story as a documentary film.

In her memoir, Burton wrote in the first person, portrayed real people, described settings, conveyed conflict, and told stories from her own life. These elements are features of the memoir genre and of any autobiography.

Some Genre Conventions

Do you want to be a great writer or composer? If so, you need to know something about the genre you're composing in; you need to know its basic qualities and agreed-upon conventions, and you need to be familiar with some examples. As Scott McCloud shows in his book *Understanding Comics*, writers and artists who work on comics use visual images and text to convey ideas, balloons to indicate dialogue, and simple but dynamic drawings and design to hold the reader's attention. Let's say you want to tell a story and convey it graphically. You don't need to be McCloud or Picasso or Art Spiegelman, but you do need to understand how artists, graphic novelists, and memoirists work with visuals and text to tell stories. It helps to have some familiarity with the genre (read a few examples!) and perhaps have one example in mind as a model. Or let's say you want to draw an annotated map of your neighborhood. It would help to know some of the established conventions of mapmakers, such as using color to represent specific

▶ **COMIC**

Scott McCloud, from his book *Understanding Comics: The Invisible Art.*

Credit: Excerpt from p. 66; Copyright © 1993, 1994, Scott McCloud. Reprinted by permission of HarperCollins Publishers.

geography, or symbols to identify features or places. If you're using a blog or social media to share your thoughts on specific news items, you will have more authority when you link directly to the material you're responding to. Hyperlinking is a convention of the blog genre.

Keep an open mind as you choose genres to compose in. Consider collaborating with classmates who have more detailed knowledge of the genres that you're less familiar with. Often students in our writing classes will discuss and figure out together the conventions of specific genres and media (e.g., video or PowerPoint) and go from there. Other times they keep it simple but thoughtful, creating scrapbooks, print-based texts, or audio essays.

Common Elements

In this book, we ask you to pay attention to the main features of a given genre: the specific elements that are common to most examples of the genre. For instance, most press release writers try to be as brief and objective as possible and to aim at answering the questions who? what? why? where? and when? For those reasons, we consider brevity, objectivity, and thoroughness to be elements of the press release genre. (For an example, see Paul Henderson's press release on p. 36 about the Wall Arch collapse.)

Style

Style refers to the particular ways we communicate. In this book, we pay attention to the techniques that individual writers use — and to what extent these techniques reflect the style of others composing in the same genre. We look at how much detail writers include and how precise that detail is. We listen for tone (seriousness, humor, etc.) and voice (the presence of the author) and analyze how these qualities affect the overall composition. How a writer uses sources is part of style as well. A writer who has cultivated a serious, academic style will probably use serious, academic sources as evidence. A writer with a more casual, chatty style might depend more on conversations with friends for evidence.

As a writer, you use style when you compose. The trick is to make sure that the style you're using is appropriate to your purpose and accessible and persuasive to your audience. For example, the writer and traveler we mentioned in Chapter 1, Gilad Hizkiyahu, uses a particular style on his blog. Because he is interested in attracting "accidental surfers" to his blog — that is, people who stumble upon his blog accidentally — he takes a casual and funny approach to his travels rather than a serious, scholarly tone. A serious, scholarly tone would probably appeal to an audience interested in the economics or politics of his travels, but because Gilad's purpose is to share his quirky, funny adventures, his casual, humorous style makes more sense.

Just chilling...

But I jump ahead... first of all – thank you all for navigating your browsers to my Blog. If you've read all the way down to this line – I assume you're the "reader" kind of person rather than the "browser" type who's looking for anchor words or just looking at the pretty pictures... so from now on I'll consider my writing as a kind of a monologue, knowing that there's someone out there who actually listens to me babble.

So, dear friends and accidental surfers, allow me to begin with the reasons that brought me to plan and go on that trip.

Reason #1
Coincidence

I still have no idea how it happened. One day I was in a middle of a long term relationship (3 year), living in a rented apartment in Ramat Gan, working at a place I'd rather not mention – while studying for my MBA degree.

Design

Design describes the visual features of a composition, including the use of headings, format, color, and illustration. Design is aesthetic but also functional. As we discuss throughout the book, the design features you and other writers choose can be important in achieving purposes and reaching audiences. Take a look at how Gilad uses images in his blog. Maps show readers exactly where this traveler is, the timeline indicates the duration of his trip, and the photos of Gilad help readers connect with him personally. Gilad's photos documenting his travels let readers see what he saw. Because one of his purposes is to allow others to share in his travels vicariously, the photos are particularly important.

Sources

Sources are the people, conversations, documents, books, journal articles, movies, and other works that we refer to for facts, perspectives, and models as we compose. For example, sources Gilad drew on for his travel blog (see p. 25) include Google Maps, the people he meets, and tourist information, such as brochures from historical sites. In this book, we consider sources because sources shape what writers create.

When you compose in certain genres, such as academic and research essays, you need to document the sources you refer to. In other cases, such as novels, comics, and music lyrics, while you've read and used sources, you're not required to document them formally. Whether or not sources need to be documented depends on the rhetorical situation. Sources referred to in a research essay aimed at academic readers should be documented because readers will want to know where ideas and information came from; the purposes of song lyrics are different, though. Listeners of a song aren't

listening for information, so the sources of information are less important. Throughout the book we look at the conventions of specific genres in this regard, and in Chapter 13, we provide specific guidelines for using documentation styles.

To compose in different genres, you first should be able to identify them, see how other writers use them to achieve purposes and reach audiences, and learn some of the basic features so you can experiment.

CHECKLIST | Reading Genres

Are you looking at a text and wondering what genre it is? Ask yourself the following questions.

- ☐ **Common elements.** What do you know about this genre already? What are some of the typical features of this genre? How is the content organized? How does the author use words, images, or other media to convey a purpose and reach an audience?

- ☐ **Style.** What is the author's tone? How would you describe the language of the piece? How much detail does the author use?

- ☐ **Design.** What does the composition look (sound, feel, smell) like? How do words and visuals and other media work together in the genre, physically? How would you describe the format of the composition? Would the format change if the mode were changed? For example, if a newspaper editorial moves from a print medium to an online medium, what changes occur in the genre?

- ☐ **Sources.** What sources does the author draw on? How do you know? How does the author incorporate and give credit to sources? Is there documentation? Hyperlinking?

Choosing a Social Response

Think back to the opening discussion about identifying different social responses to the situation of being confused about your biology homework. Now write down a challenging situation you've encountered recently. List five different actions you could have taken in response. Which actions would have generated a form of communication? Which would have been most effective? Why?

3

GUIDED READINGS:
RHETORICAL SITUATIONS & GENRES TOGETHER

What Do Rhetorical Situations Have to Do with Genres?

Now that you have an understanding of what constitutes a rhetorical situation and a beginning concept of genres, it's time to examine how they work together. When composing, a writer is always working within a rhetorical situation. That means the writer considers the purpose of her piece, whom she wants to reach, how best to appeal to her reader, and what sources and evidence to use, along with other considerations mentioned in Chapter 1. The next step for the writer is to choose how to best respond to her rhetorical situation. Which genre or genres are the best social response to her situation?

Genres Respond to Rhetorical Situations

If we examine a particular event, we can see that there are numerous ways someone might choose to respond. After the Orlando shooting in the Pulse nightclub on June 12, 2016, people chose to respond in a variety of ways. Former President Barack Obama responded by releasing a press statement that included, "Our thoughts and prayers are with the families and loved ones of the victims." Canadian Prime Minister Justin Trudeau tweeted, "We grieve with our friends in the US & stand in solidarity with the LGBTQ2 community after today's terror attack." Samantha Bee, a comedic television talk show host, used her show *Full Frontal* to issue her response:

> After a massacre, the standard operating procedure is you stand on stage and deliver some well-meaning words about how we will get through this together, how love wins, how love conquers hate. That is great, that is beautiful, but you know what? F--- it.

Many people changed their profile pictures on Facebook to show solidarity. Perhaps you read or posted a blog about it. At the Tony Awards, which took place the evening after the shootings, *Hamilton* playwright Lin-Manuel Miranda chose to respond in a line in his acceptance speech: "And love is love is love is love is love is love is love is love cannot be killed or swept aside."

Consider different ways people might protest against something. They might make signs and march, give a speech, create a public service announcement, circulate a petition, or write a letter to the editor. The genre is chosen based on the rhetorical situation.

There are times, however, when genre is stipulated for you. In academic settings, you are often given an assignment and told to compose a research essay, write a poem, or create a lab report based on an experiment. In business settings, you might need to create a proposal, write a recommendation report, or prepare a presentation. We will discuss academic genres in more detail in Chapter 7.

A Meme Responds to a Rhetorical Situation

An Internet meme is a concept that spreads quickly from person to person via the Internet through blogging, e-mail, or social media. Memes are easily replicated and altered; for example, when Elizabeth sees that a blogger has posted a photo of his ferret wearing a party hat and looking irritated, she can take that concept and post on her Instagram account a photo of her dog wearing a cowboy hat and looking irritated. Amy might then see Elizabeth's meme and post to her Facebook status a photo of her cat wearing a baseball cap and looking irritated.

The rhetorical situation that the original blogger and Elizabeth and Amy are all responding to is simple: They all have pets that they think are just adorable and find their pets' reactions to being anthropomorphized hilarious. They are participating in a long tradition of pet owners sharing the silliness of their own pets (purpose) with other pet owners (audience).

A related example is the *Hipster Llama* meme (see p. 30). *Hipster Llama* appears in many variations online. Like most memes, authorship is not identified. Rather, the meme can be revised, remixed, and shared repeatedly and anonymously online. To unpack this particular meme, let's first consider that a person or persons composed it (or revised an existing version of it). Like all composers, the meme creators worked within a **rhetorical situation**. Let's start by asking: What are the meme creators doing, and why? What are some decisions they have made as composers? Following is a preliminary reading:

- The composers are providing a commentary (**purpose**).
- They are communicating to like-minded readers on the Internet (**audience**).
- They are using humor and satire to connect with their audience (drawing on the **rhetorical appeal**, pathos).
- They are working with both text and imagery (**mode**) and delivering the composition digitally, online (**medium**).

Now, let's think about the composers' **choice of genre**. What are memes? How do they function? What are their typical qualities and conventions?

- Memes often parody or poke fun at something or someone. They take many forms but often feature an image and a brief caption written in informal language (**elements and style**).
- Often an image is prominent, and the words — typically what the subject of the meme is saying or thinking — are presented in a large display font (**design**).
- Memes draw on current topics and popular culture (**sources**).

Here we provide a partial reading of the *Hipster Llama* meme. Notice the structure of the annotations in the margins. This is a "guided reading," a feature we discuss in detail in the next section.

Guided Reading | Meme

Author Unknown, *Hipster Llama*

PURPOSE

The composer of *Hipster Llama* memes poke fun at hipsters, making fun of things hipsters say, their values, and specifically, their haircuts. This particular meme focuses on the stereotype that hipsters are more concerned with exploring their aesthetic sides than on focusing on paid work, and are perhaps more concerned with their personal style than what they produce.

AUDIENCE

Because hipsters are often self-referentially ironic, it's likely that hipsters themselves are an audience. People who make fun of hipsters are also clearly part of the audience.

RHETORICAL APPEALS

The humor in the meme is an appeal to pathos because laughter is considered an emotional response. The composer's knowledge of hipster hairstyles and attitudes is an appeal to ethos.

MODES & MEDIA

Modes = text and visual.
The meaning of the meme depends upon both the text and the visual working together.

Medium = digital.
Memes circulate on the Internet and so are digital.

◀ What is the composer of *Hipster Llama* doing?

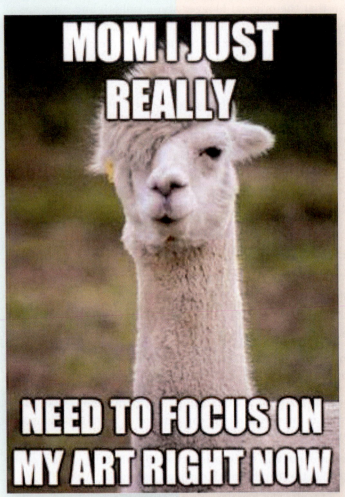

The composer of *Hipster Llama* chose to create a meme. What are the conventions of a meme? To what extent is the composer adhering to them? ▶

ELEMENTS OF THE GENRE

Humor: Memes are designed to be humorous. The composer of the *Hipster Llama* memes use humor to poke fun at a particular group.

Repetition: This meme is part of a series. Viewers can instantly recognize the use of the llama and the fact that this is a part of a larger series.

Social media: Memes are distributed online. They can be sent by e-mail, posted on a blog, or shared on social media sites such as Facebook, Twitter, and Instagram.

STYLE

The text in this meme uses a *conversational tone.* Additionally, the text in a meme is fairly brief, as is the case here.

DESIGN

Visual with text. The llama is the center of focus, with the text complementing it. A meme usually begins with a funny photo and then attaches a caption that amplifies the humor. Here the visual shows the *Hipster Llama* accompanied by words he might say.

Font: The font is usually bold, san serif, and not too flashy.

SOURCES

Memes usually draw on ideas in popular culture, respond to news events, or highlight a celebrity. Memes are often remixes of a visual and a quote that already exist. Here, the meme focuses on the concept of the hipster, a popular culture concept.

Visualizing Rhetorical Situations & Genres

What Is a Guided Reading?

Guided readings throughout this book (such as the one provided on the previous page for *Hipster Llama*) highlight the moves that writers and composers make in different genres and modes, and they also point out common genre conventions. These readings are presented with critical annotations in the margins of the page or screen. The annotations focus on two main ideas:

1. The composer's **rhetorical situation and choices** (purpose, audience, rhetorical appeals, modes/media) and

2. The typical **conventions of the genre** the author chose to compose in (common elements, style, design, and sources).

We've designed the annotations to help you see how authors respond to their rhetorical situations. Seeing the choices and decisions that experienced authors made can help you learn how to think through and respond to the rhetorical situations you will find yourself in.

Guided readings appear in the table of contents at the beginning of the book and in the brief contents that open chapters, and they are also listed in the adjacent directory.

Ways to Apply Guided Readings

As you read in different genres on your own, you might use the headings we've used for the guided readings to remind you of things to notice. We are big fans of annotating, as you might have noticed, and we hope you might try annotating the pieces you read the same way we've annotated the guided readings. We find that annotating a reading helps us articulate our thoughts and move them from being fuzzy, half-formed ideas to concrete observations and analysis.

When you are composing, find a guided reading in the genre you're using (or one close to it), and refresh your mind about the different choices you should consider. Consider your purpose, and as you compose, ask yourself if that purpose will be evident to your reader. Pay close attention to the genre conventions. These will help guide you and remind you of certain stylistic principles you need to consider.

Sample Grid | A Framework for Reading Any Text Rhetorically

When you are reading or composing, consider applying the framework of the guided reading to what you're analyzing or creating. The image below is the grid that we use for the guided readings in this text. It's a grid that you can use for approaching any text and for evaluating your own compositions.

PURPOSE
What is the composer trying to do? Inform? Persuade? Tell a story? Something else? Does he or she have multiple purposes? And how can you tell?

◄ **What is the composer doing?**

**What genre has the composer ►
chosen to work in? To what extent is he or she adhering to that genre's conventions?**

ELEMENTS OF THE GENRE
What are some of the patterns you notice across several examples of this genre? Is there a typical organization pattern or approach? Do sentences or paragraphs seem to be notably short or long? Does one element always seem to appear, such as an anecdote, or an abstract, or notes in the margin?

AUDIENCE
Who is the composer communicating to? Are there secondary audiences?

Place the text that you're reading or evaluating right here in the middle.

Next, read through the annotations in the margins to look more closely at the composer's rhetorical choices and how the composer works within his or her chosen genre.

RHETORICAL APPEALS
How does the composer entice his or her audience(s)? To what extent does the composer establish his or her ethos? Is logos evident in the text? Does the author appeal to readers' emotions (pathos)?

STYLE
Is it in the first or third person? Is the tone formal or informal? What is the level of vocabulary used?

DESIGN
How is formatting used? Are images included? Is color used?

MODES & MEDIA
What is the mode (visual, text, audio)? Why do you think the composer chose that mode? Or perhaps more than one mode is used; if so, why do you think the author made that choice? What is the medium (print or digital)? Why do you think the composer chose that medium?

SOURCES
What kind of source material is used (personal experience, Internet research, interviews, etc.)? How are sources referenced within the piece?

Guided Reading | Advertisement

Following is an excerpt from another guided reading (for the full guided reading and more on advertisements, see Chapter 9, "Public Genres," p. 232). The annotations in the margin to the left of the advertisement for Evian water analyze the rhetorical situation and the rhetorical choices the composers made. The annotations to the right of the ad analyze some typical conventions of advertisements, the genre the composers chose in response to their specific rhetorical situation.

Left: rhetorical situation & choices.   In the analysis of the rhetorical situation and choices, the first thing you'll notice is a discussion of the ad creators' **purpose**. In this case, the composers' intention is to persuade the viewer to purchase Evian. Directly below that is a discussion of **audience**. You will see that the audience is not *everyone*. Instead, the audience is specific, such as "people looking for health benefits." After examining these aspects of the rhetorical situation, the guided reading then presents an analysis of the choices the creators made to **appeal to their audience**. For the Evian ad you will notice that pathos is the central appeal (see Chapter 9, p. 236). Noticing this will help you understand how an advertisement might be motivating you to take action. Finally, the annotations note the composers' choice of **modes and media**. The Evian ad offers an example of the power of a prominent visual with just a bit of text.

Right: genre conventions.   In the guided reading for the Evian ad, we examine the ad's conventions. While we might not note all the **elements**, we do describe the key ones associated with an advertisement (such as it being an argument, having a headline, and having particular ad copy). The next topics are the **style** and **design** of the genre, and finally how **sources** are used (for full annotations, see Chapter 9, p. 236).

Danone/Evian and Havas Worldwide, *Detox with Evian*

RHETORICAL SITUATION & CHOICES

PURPOSE
Havas Worldwide, the creators of this ad (hired by Danone/Evian), hope to persuade consumers to buy Evian water.

AUDIENCE . . .

RHETORICAL APPEALS . . .

MODES & MEDIA . . .
(See p. 235 for the complete Guided Reading.)

◄ What are the composers of the ad, Havas Worldwide, doing?

GENRE CONVENTIONS

How do I know this is an ► advertisement?

ELEMENTS OF THE GENRE
Argument: This ad presents an argument (which is visual and textual) for purchasing a product.

Action: The headline, "Detox with Evian," is brief, direct, and directive. The ad copy, "Return to purity with water from the French Alps that's been naturally filtered for over 15 years," suggests . . .

DESIGN . . .

SOURCES . . .

Responding to One Event: Two Rhetorical Situations, Two Genres

Arch Collapse at a National Park

In this case study, two writers report on a single event. One writes a press release, the other a blog post.

The event.   In August 2008, a rock formation in Utah's famous Arches National Park collapsed.

The writers.   Paul Henderson, a ranger at the park who also wrote press releases, and Shaan Hurley, a blogger and fan of the park who had hiked and photographed it.

The compositions.   **Press Release:** "Wall Arch Collapses" (Henderson); **Blog Post:** "The Wall Arch Collapses in Arches National Park" (Hurley).

As you'll see, Henderson and Hurley provide much of the same information about the arch collapse, but they write in different genres and with different purposes and audiences in mind. The notes in the margins of each piece explain their rhetorical situations and how they work within the conventions of the press release and the blog post.

Guided Reading | Press Release

At the time of the collapse, Paul Henderson was chief of Interpretation and Visitor Services for Arches National Park, which is managed by the National Park Service, part of the U.S. Department of the Interior. When the arch collapsed, Henderson was interviewed by news outlets, including MSNBC, which also quoted from the press release on page 36.

Paul Henderson, *Wall Arch Collapses*

PURPOSE

Henderson, who works for the National Park Service, a government agency, writes to inform readers about the collapse. He reports that there were no injuries and that the area is temporarily closed. He reassures readers that the event is normal, that arches are temporary and "eventually succumb to the forces of gravity and erosion."

AUDIENCE

Henderson's readers want an official statement from park management, rather than one by an outside observer. Readers are mainly members of news organizations—but also park patrons, including hikers and nature photographers, looking for details.

RHETORICAL APPEALS

For Henderson and other press release writers, ethos is crucial. Readers need to trust the authority of the writer and his information, especially because Henderson represents a government agency.

Henderson establishes logos by presenting information in a sensible order, beginning with the event and ending with its effects.

MODES & MEDIA

Mode: Henderson uses text to inform and visuals to show the effect of the collapse.

Media: His press release was posted digitally on the National Park Service's site and was probably also distributed by e-mail to news organizations.

◄ What is the composer, Paul Henderson, doing?

How do I know this is a ► press release?

Wall Arch Collapses

Date: August 8, 2008
Contact: Paul Henderson, 435-719-2140

Subscribe 🔊 | What is RSS

Wall Arch, located along the popular Devils Garden Trail at Arches National Park collapsed sometime during the night of August 4, 2008. Rock has continued to fall from the arms of the remaining portion of the arch necessitating the closure of the Devils Garden Trail just beyond Landscape Arch.

On August 7, 2008, representatives from both the National Park Service Geologic Resources Division and the Utah Geological Survey visited the site and noted obvious stress fractures in the remaining formation. Rock debris has completely blocked this section of the trail. The closure will remain in effect until visitor safety issues can be resolved.

First reported and named by Lewis T. McKinney in 1948, Wall Arch was a free standing arch in the Slickrock member of the Entrada sandstone. The opening beneath the span was 71-feet wide and 33-1/2 feet high. It ranked 12th in size among the over 2,000 known arches in the park.

All arches are but temporary features and all will eventually succumb to the forces of gravity and erosion. While the geologic forces that created the arches are still very much underway, in human terms it's rare to observe such dramatic changes.

No one has reported observing the arch collapse and there were no visitor injuries.

Credit: Courtesy of National Park Service.

ELEMENTS OF THE GENRE

Facts: Henderson explains: *Who* = people at the site of the collapse
What = the arch collapse
When = 8/4/08
Where = specific location of the collapse
Why = gravity and erosion
How = falling debris

Brevity, timeliness: Like most press releases, this is concisely worded, just a few paragraphs long. Henderson wrote it just four days after the event.

Pointedness: Henderson begins with the most crucial information and follows it with significant details.

Contact information: Henderson wants readers, especially the news media (the target audience for press releases), to be able to get in touch.

STYLE

Tone: Henderson is objective in his writing. He doesn't give his opinion and writes in the neutral third person.

Clarity, directness: Henderson provides facts simply and details concisely (e.g., "Rock debris has completely blocked this section of the trail").

DESIGN

Simplicity: Henderson uses a standard press release design, with a headline to summarize and get attention, a dateline, and contact information. There are just two images to support the text.

Navigation: The Web page itself includes the name of the park, an image, and a menu bar for easy navigation.

SOURCES

Draws on official information. Henderson uses facts from the National Park Service and from the Utah Geological Survey, which he credits in the body of his press release.

Guided Reading | Blog Post

Blogger Shaan Hurley has a background in mechanical design and works in the field of technology. Between the Lines (autodesk.blogs.com) is Hurley's personal blog; he also posts on Twitter. He posted the following entry in August 2008.

Shaan Hurley, *The Wall Arch Collapses in Arches National Park*

RHETORICAL SITUATION & CHOICES

◄ **What is the composer, Shaan Hurley, doing?**

PURPOSE

Hurley has a few reasons for writing: to inform readers about the collapse, to share his own experiences and photos of the park, and to persuade readers to enjoy nature now, rather than later, when the opportunity may not exist. He writes: "Now I will not have the opportunity to photograph Wall Arch except the remnants on the ground. It is another example of how things you take for granted may disappear."

AUDIENCE

His readers are fans of the park, other hikers and photographers, and even potential park visitors. His readers are looking for a personal take (rather than an official statement) on the arch collapse.

RHETORICAL APPEALS

Because Hurley's main goal is to urge readers to seize an opportunity, he relies largely on pathos to appeal to emotion. Notice how he describes the beauty and "magic" of the park.

He also establishes ethos, or his authority to write on this topic, by sharing his firsthand experiences and photos of the park.

MODES & MEDIA

Mode: Hurley uses text and visuals to inform.
Media: His blog is digital and embedded with hyperlinks that bring readers to additional information. Readers can also share the link so others can read Hurley's post.

Credit: Courtesy of Shaan Hurley at Autodesk.

GENRE CONVENTIONS

How do I know this is a ► blog post?

ELEMENTS OF THE GENRE

Brevity, visuals, hyperlinks: Like most effective blog posts, Hurley's is just a few paragraphs long, visually interesting, and embedded with links that offer more information without adding length.

Paragraphs: Hurley's concise, chunked text keeps digital readers interested.

Photos: Hurley's images provide context, attract readers, and offer his perspective on the event.

"About" page, comment option: Hurley gives biographical information and a space for readers to offer feedback and share their own views on the park.

STYLE

Directness: Hurley, like many bloggers, offers his own reflections and is present in his writing. He writes in the first person, addressing readers directly.

DESIGN

Clarity, navigation: Like other blogs, Hurley's is designed so users can easily find additional content; they can also access his page on flickr.com.

SOURCES

Draws on official and firsthand information. Hurley credits the National Park Service for some of the photos; he also draws on his own experience (his trip of 2007) and external sources such as *Wikipedia*.

RHETORICAL SITUATION & CHOICES

1. **Purpose.** Reread Henderson's press release and Hurley's blog post. What are the writers' purposes? How can you tell? How do these purposes differ? How might they overlap?

2. **Audience.** Who do you imagine is the primary reader for Henderson's press release? For Hurley's blog post? Explain.

3. **Rhetorical appeals.** How effective are Henderson and Hurley in using ethos, pathos, or logos to reach their audiences? Which appeals do they rely on most effectively, and why?

4. **Rhetorical appeals.** Consider how hyperlinks, photos, and other information can contribute to a composer's ethos. Why do you think Hurley used the National Park Service as a source for information and images? How did this choice affect his ethos?

5. **Modes & media.** Both Henderson and Hurley use a combination of text and visuals. If you were to add audio or video to either piece, what would you add? What meaning or information would the audio or video add?

GENRE CONVENTIONS

6. **Elements of the genre.** As a reader interested in the arch collapse, would you be likely to consult a press release? A blog? Both? Neither? Explain. To what extent is genre important? And in what contexts? When might it not matter?

7. **Elements of the genre.** What are the most significant differences between the press release and blog post as genres? Based on these examples, what conventions of these genres can you identify? How do these conventions affect what the writers say and how they convey it?

8. **Style.** Analyze the language Henderson and Hurley use. What do their words and tone suggest about their different purposes and audiences?

9. **Design.** How does the design of each piece enable readers to quickly find information they want or need?

10. **Design.** Look again at the photos included in the blog post and press release. What purposes do they serve in each? How effectively do the authors use them?

11. **Sources.** How does Hurley use the National Park Service's press release as a source? How does that source contribute to his success in achieving his purpose and reaching his audience?

When you compose, you can refer to the checklist below as well as the blank guided reading grid provided on page 32.

RHETORICAL SITUATION & CHOICES

☐ **Purpose.** Is my purpose to tell a story, inform, or persuade? Do I have several purposes, and if so, which is my primary purpose?

☐ **Audience.** How would I describe my primary audience? Whose attention do I want most? Who are the people I want to persuade? Do I have another, secondary audience? How will I entice this audience?

☐ **Rhetorical appeals.** How will I establish my credibility (ethos)? Will appealing to my audience's emotions help me persuade them (pathos)? How might logic (logos) help me convince others?

☐ **Modes & media.** Do I want to work with written words? Will I present my ideas in person, orally? Will I use visuals? How about audio? Does my idea lend itself to video? Do I want my piece to be available digitally or in print? Will I use some combination of these modes and media?

GENRE CONVENTIONS

☐ **Elements of the genre.** How will I structure my composition? What is the best way to combine elements to convey my purpose—and make my case to my audience?

☐ **Style.** Whatever form my composition takes (visual, verbal, etc.), what is the best tone to use to reach my audience? What voice will I use? How present will I be in my composition? What kind of language will I use? What level of detail will I need to convey my purpose?

☐ **Design.** How do I want my composition to look? How will the layout help me achieve my purpose?

☐ **Sources.** What sources will I draw on for my composition? Do I need to conduct interviews? Do I need to research online or in the library? How will I attribute my sources?

PRACTICE

Analyzing Responses to Rhetorical Situations

Think of a current issue affecting your community and do some quick research to locate two responses to that issue. The responses should represent two different genres. For example, you might look at how the issue is covered in different genres such as a news report, editorial, documentary video, demonstration, or comic strip. Next, using the structure and categories of this book's guided readings (see Arches texts earlier in this chapter), annotate both pieces. Then, write an analysis in which you focus on the rhetorical situations (purpose and audience) and some of the rhetorical choices (rhetorical appeals, modes/media) for both texts. How do the texts function as a social response to the rhetorical situations? What does comparing these two works teach you about genre?

Note: Although both pieces should respond to the same issue, they may not have identical rhetorical situations.

Advanced move: Want to take it a step further? Compose a response to the situation in a third genre.

4

COMPOSING:
DRAWING ON EXPERIENCE & EVIDENCE

Responding to an Assignment

All composing takes place within a rhetorical situation. Remember that genre is a social response to a rhetorical situation. In this chapter, we will follow one of Amy's former students, Gwen Ganow, as she composes in response to the rhetorical situation of an assignment in her writing course. Here is the assignment she was given, along with her annotations. (Note: It's a good idea to annotate an assignment to make sure you understand it and to help you think through the different steps.)

◄ STUDENT AUTHOR PHOTO

Gwen Ganow, a graduate of Red Rocks Community College and Metropolitan State University of Denver, is now a Colorado State Parks Ranger. *Credit: Courtesy Gwen Dalynn Ganow.*

ATTENTION, COMPOSERS

As we follow Gwen's process, and the processes of other composers in this book, keep in mind that there is no one correct or best way to respond to an assignment, do research, or revise your writing. We provide sample processes in order to offer various contexts that you can learn from, adapt, and, if helpful, apply to your own processes.

Annotated Example | Reading an Academic Text

ASSIGNMENT **Amy Braziller,** *"Take a Position,"* with Notes by Gwen Ganow (STUDENT)

English 121
English Composition

Date: November 1, 2016
Assignment: Take a Position

Argue?

Take a position on a topic you care about and have experience with. Then think about who you want to communicate your ideas to and compose in a genre that will allow you to do that.

I get to pick the genre

You may compose in any genre that seems appropriate for your purpose and audience. The length should be appropriate to the genre; in other words, a magazine article will have more words than a poster. Be sure to choose a genre that will allow you to communicate with the audience you have in mind.

For sources, you should primarily draw upon your own experience. If you wish, you can use other source material if it is appropriate to your genre choice and topic.

My experience. For this assignment, research is optional.

Movies, video games, outdoors, comics, animals?

1. Brainstorm potential topics you have experience with and could take a position on.

(Continues on next page)

What do I want to
say? Who do I want to
say it to?

2. Select the topic you are most excited about and take a
   position. You might find freewriting useful to help you
   articulate your position.
3. Consider your rhetorical situation. You know your
   purpose is to take a position and try to convince others of
   its merit. Who are the others you are convincing? That is
   your audience.
4. What genres might that audience encounter? List three
   of them that would allow you to achieve your purpose and
   reach your audience.
5. Analyze and annotate examples of the three different
   genres that you are considering composing in, identifying
   the genre conventions.
6. Draft your genre piece.
7. Revise your genre piece.

The genre I choose
needs to respond
to my purpose and
audience. How will I
figure this out?

Credit: Courtesy of the author and Gwen Dalynn Ganow.

Getting Started

Whenever you write—as a student in a composition classroom or a professional in
a workplace—you focus on a specific topic. In some instances, you may be asked to
address a general theme or a specific topic or issue. For example, your instructor might
ask you to respond to an essay you've read for class, or your manager at work might
ask you to develop and share plans to improve business or increase sales. Other times,
most often in the course of college work, you get to start from scratch and choose a
topic purely out of your experience, interest, and curiosity.

So, how do you choose a topic? Where should you start? One place might be this book.
The Index of Themes, page T-1, organizes every reading in the text by topic, and the
Index of Genres, page G-1, will help you see the relationship between topic choice and
genre choice.

The best way to get started on identifying a topic that is meaningful to you is to get
your ideas flowing. Following are some ways to do that.

Talk to people.　Discuss your topic ideas and questions with classmates, friends, family, and coworkers to find out what others have to say about the topic you're considering.
Often, explaining why you're interested in a topic can help you focus. When others ask
you to clarify your ideas, you will often discover what you really want to say.

Make a brainstorm list.　What do you care most about? Begin by making a list of
things you are passionate about, your pet peeves, things you are curious about, things
you don't understand, or things you'd like to change about the world. From your initial
list, force yourself to double or triple the size of the list. Often the best topic ideas are the
less obvious ones—ideas that will come to you when you push yourself to keep listing.

English 121
English Composition

Date: October 21, 2016
Name: Gwen Ganow
Brainstorm List: Ideas for the "Take a Position" Assignment

What issues, ideas, or practices do I care about most? What topics would I want to take a position on?

PASSIONS

Movies
Comic books
Video games
Hiking
Dogs
Camping

PET PEEVES/CURIOSITIES

Why do people hate?
How to respond to hate?
Why do people drive slowly in the left lane?
Should I major in biology?
Why do people toss their beer cans on the ground at concerts?

MORE IDEAS

Superheroes
Good guys save the world
Gay rights
Winter hikes
How to stay safe on a mountain in bad weather
Summer hikes
Border collies
Animal rescue
Best training methods for dogs
Water conservation
Zombies
Simpsons
How bad are sugary cereals?
Batman and the remakes
Why is black associated with bad guys?
What is the most humane way to keep elk out of your yard if you live outside a city?
Adventure films
Bacteria: what jobs could I get that deal with bacteria?
What kind of training could police departments implement to improve public relations?

Credit: By permission of Gwen Dalynn Ganow.

Mind map.　Like list making, mind mapping gives you a creative format for sketching out your early ideas about a topic. To begin, write the topic or idea you are exploring in the middle of a blank piece of paper (alternatively, you can use mind-mapping software, some of which is available for free online). As you think of details and related ideas, write them around the central topic, connecting them with lines that indicate their relationships.

Freewriting

If you've identified a general topic area, or some of the ideas you've generated in your conversations and brainstorm lists interest you, try freewriting. The goal is to get your ideas written down without judging what you're writing, or editing yourself, or trying to write beautifully. Experiment by making yourself write nonstop for ten to thirty minutes. As you keep your fingers moving, don't worry about making sense or about readers being confused or impressed. No one is going to read this document but you. When you take away the pressure of producing smooth prose, you may be surprised to see the ideas you generate. We like to refer to this as a "shitty first draft."

Advice for Freewriting

As you begin your rough or exploratory draft, remember that it is just for you. No one else ever needs to see it. Think of your draft not as an organized, perfect piece of writing with a clear purpose, but as a messy opportunity for creativity and experimentation.

Don't worry about a thesis or about being logical or eloquent. Instead, focus on quantity rather than quality. That's right: quantity, not quality. Think of words in the first draft as raw materials. You want as much raw material to work with as possible. Imagine an artist beginning a painting. Would she have only the exact amount of paint she needs to create her piece? What if she changes her mind midway through the painting and wants to use more yellow than red? Wouldn't it make sense for her to begin with extra paint in each color to allow her the flexibility to modify her ideas? Writing and other kinds of composing are similar. Beginning with more words than you need gives you more options. Here are some pointers for getting your first draft written:

1. Set a timer for thirty minutes and force yourself to write for the entire time, not stopping for anything. That means no stopping to reread and correct or to refer to sources or models, and definitely no stopping to check Facebook.
2. Don't stop to correct or edit what is on the page.
3. Write until you have five thousand words or you run out of time.

Don't worry about grammar, punctuation, spelling, transitions, topic sentences, organization, titles, and so on. Don't even worry about genre or what the finished piece will look or sound like. Once you have your thoughts down, you can think logically about your purpose, audience, and the points you want to convey.

At this stage, if you're putting pressure on yourself to write flawless, beautiful prose, remind yourself of the term *freewrite*. Take a little more pressure off by thinking of Anne Lamott's phrase "shitty first draft." Everybody, including published authors, writes them. (See Anne Lamott's essay in the Reader section of this book, on pp. 522–25.)

Let's circle back to Amy's student Gwen. Earlier in this chapter, we looked at the "Take a Position" assignment that Gwen responded to, followed by her brainstorm. Her thoughts on the assignment and her brainstorm led her to focus on superheroes and social attitudes. What position could she take on the relationship between the heroes and the values and prejudices of the real world? She began with this question:

> **TOPIC QUESTION FOR "TAKING A POSITION" ASSIGNMENT**
> To what extent do superheroes reflect real-world values and attitudes?

Gwen then moved from that question to a freewrite.

Guided Reading | Freewrite

Gwen began with some exploratory freewriting, a low-stakes method that allowed her to reflect on her experiences and solidify her thoughts about superheroes and social attitudes.

Gwen Ganow (STUDENT), *Topic for the "Take a Position" Assignment: Superheroes and Social Attitudes*

GWEN'S RHETORICAL SITUATION & CHOICES		GENRE CONVENTIONS	

AUDIENCE
At this point, Gwen is writing for herself and her instructor, Amy. They'll go over this draft together to try to pin down a direction. Gwen will later identify her additional audiences—her classmates as well as public audiences.

RHETORICAL APPEALS
Gwen is in exploration mode so is not concerned right now about ethos, logos, and pathos.

MODES & MEDIA
Gwen e-mailed this Word document to her instructor.

◄ What is the author, Gwen Ganow, doing?

What characterizes a ► freewrite?

English 121
English Composition

Date: November 1, 2016
Name: Gwen Ganow
Freewrite: Topic for the "Take a Position" Assignment: Superheroes and Social Attitudes

I've always been fascinated by superheroes. I remember sitting in my bedroom when I was in second grade and paging through a stack of comic books. I became obsessed with them. And my superhero posters, I could stare at them for hours. In a way, superheroes were my first loves.
Man, those superheroes—very, very cool. I loved the power they had.
What kind of power? They faced challenges and obstacles, evil men trying to destroy someone, usually evil men, seldom women. Why? Superheroes protect people. Innocent people

ELEMENTS OF THE GENRE
A freewrite is characterized by free form thought and questions. It is a brainstorming tool to use to reflect on your experiences with your topic, to discover what you already know and think about your topic, and to consider what you want to say about it.

STYLE
Gwen is not worried about style, grammar, or how her freewrite reads. It's not meant to be perfect. Her writing is very casual, as if she's writing in a journal to herself.

PURPOSE

Gwen explores possible angles for her project. "To what extent do superheroes reflect real-world values and attitudes?"

She lets herself be unfocused as she writes about her fascination with superheroes. After her freewrite, she realizes that she wants to cover how superheroes fight intolerance.

Seems that the city was always the setting—not the suburbs. Why is that?

Regardless of challenges, superheroes win. Why can't they die? What would that mean? Losing hope, maybe. Okay, that's a downer. I need them to win.

Superheroes were giant protectors and a way for me to escape. I'd read at night, even after lights out, wanting to see how the superhero would save the day.

Subjected to prejudice or intolerance—superheroes are often seen as different, as outsiders. It causes social problems for them. They worry that their loved ones will be hurt—like Spider-Man and Mary Jane. The superhero is actually a victim of injustice. Many become superheroes because of injustice in their life, like Batman's parents being murdered.

Superheroes are champions fighting discrimination. They defeat evil powers. How do they do that? I'd like to explore that. Do they fight racial injustice? Are there other forms of intolerance? Other areas of intolerance in life: racism, sexism, prejudice against LGBT community?

DESIGN

A freewrite is not designed. It's typically a simple document without formatting.

SOURCES

Gwen does not discuss evidence in this draft, but she could have, depending on her rhetorical situation and whether source material was appropriate for the situation or assignment.

Credit: By permission Gwen Dalynn Ganow.

CHECKLIST | Getting Started on Your Topic with a Freewrite

Keep the following questions in mind.

RHETORICAL SITUATION & CHOICES

☐ **What is my purpose?** What do I want to say—and how do I want to say it? What experiences have shaped my thoughts on this topic?

☐ **Who am I composing for?** Who will my audience ultimately be—beyond myself and my instructor and maybe my classmates?

☐ **How will I connect with my audience?** How will I establish my authority as a composer (ethos) so that my readers will trust me? What is the most logical way for me to present what I have to say? To what extent will I want to appeal to my audience's emotions? For example, if I want to persuade people to take a certain action, how will I cultivate their enthusiasm?

GENRE CONVENTIONS

☐ **As I freewrite, how can I take pressure off myself so I can generate my ideas freely?** I need to remember that freewriting is about quantity over quality. I can refine later.

☐ **What do I already know about my topic?** What intrigues me about this topic? What questions do I still have about it?

☐ **Based on my experience and thinking so far, what arguments am I familiar with about this topic?** Are there some that resonate for me more than others? Do I have an opinion on this topic?

☐ **Is there a way to narrow my topic by time, place, demographics, or something else?** For example, if I write about pets reducing anxiety, do I focus on therapy dogs (narrow by breed) or the acceptance of therapy animals in the workplace (narrow by place)?

Choosing a Genre to Compose In

After reviewing your freewrite, you should have a better sense of what you want to say about your topic. Your next decision is to choose a genre. You may find the checklist on page 54 helpful.

Steps for Choosing a Genre to Compose In

Step 1. Revisit your topic & central idea. Remember that rough draft? Since you've done more reading and analyzed a variety of genres, what's changed for you? How might that affect your focus?

Step 2. Revisit your rhetorical situation. Remember that the piece you are composing is a response to a situation. What has motivated you to communicate these ideas? What are you responding to? What's your stake in this? Why do you care about this?

Step 3. Focus on your purpose. Look over your initial freewrite and highlight some of the main ideas you want to explore. Make a list of four or five of them. Next, choose the idea that you are most excited about. Then, decide on the primary purpose of the piece you are composing.

Step 4. Really think about your audience. Consider your audience. Keep in mind that aspects of your topic that are obvious to you may not be obvious to your audience.

Step 5. Strategize on how you'll use rhetorical appeals. Start thinking about how to appeal to your audience's senses of ethos, logos, and pathos.

Step 6. Consider your mode & medium. Once you have narrowed the scope of your purpose and audience, think about whether you want to work with text, visuals, video, audio, or some combination. Consider the advantages of each, as well as your skills and the tools available to you.

Step 7. Narrow your choices down to three possible genres. Put together a short list of potential genres you want to consider. Remember that there is no perfect genre. Your goal at this point is to choose a genre that will best enable you to respond to your rhetorical situation.

Step 8. Look at examples of the three genres you're interested in. There are many features to consider when looking at genre:

- **Is point of view important for your purpose and audience?** For example, if you need your piece to be first person so that it includes your perspective, make sure you choose a genre that accommodates this point of view.
- **What type of connection do you want to establish with your audience?** If you want to remain at a critical distance, consider choosing a genre that emphasizes ethos in its rhetorical appeal. To make a closer connection by appealing to readers' emotions regarding your topic, consider choosing a genre that emphasizes pathos.

Keep this in mind:
Genre decisions
at this point are
still tentative; as
you draft, you may
stumble upon a
completely different
genre idea that
fits your purpose,
audience, and other
aspects of your
rhetorical situation.
Keep an open
mind as you draft.
Remember that the
drafting process is a
process of discovery.

- **What tone do you want to use in order to achieve your purpose?** If you want your piece to have a certain level of formality (or informality), be sure to choose a genre that demonstrates that.

Step 9. Zero in on how you'll use your experience & evidence. Finally, you'll need to think about how you will use sources in your piece—and how the genre you're considering typically deals with sources. You may realize that you need to do research, talk to experts, or dig deeper. For more on help with research, see Part 3 of this book.

Guided Process | Choosing a Genre

In the following pages, Gwen Ganow decides which genre she'd like to compose in by doing the following.

1. She considers her rhetorical situation and commits to a purpose and audience. Her purpose is to persuade her audience that superhero characters help to fight intolerance. Her audience is both academic and public, including her instructor and peers, as well as fans of comics and superheroes outside her course.

2. She looks at three examples of public and academic genres: an ad, a researched argument, and a film review.

3. She decides how she wants to use her own experience and evidence—and which genre will work best overall. In this section, Gwen moves from brainstorming about a possible genre to compose into making a final choice about which genre will be best for her project. (Spoiler alert: It's a film review.)

Even though Gwen has decided on her purpose and audience, she still needs to work out a few details to choose a genre that best responds to her rhetorical situation and allows her to achieve her purpose.

BRAINSTORM **Gwen Ganow** (STUDENT), *Choosing a Genre for the "Take a Position" Assignment: Superheroes and Social Attitudes*

English 121
English Composition

Date: Nov. 8, 2016
Name: Gwen Ganow
Brainstorm: Choosing a Genre for the "Take a Position"
Assignment: Superheroes and Social Attitudes

RHETORICAL SITUATION & CHOICES

How can I achieve my purpose?
Since I want to persuade my reader that there is a need for
superhero characters to fight intolerance, I might create a

fictional account that illustrates a superhero fighting some evil. I could also create an advertisement that shows a superhero in action fighting injustice.

Who is my audience?
My academic audience already knows something about superheroes. And my public audience, comic book lovers and experts, will expect me to be very well-informed about superheroes. I'll need to draw on evidence and details from comics to support my points. Whatever genre I choose for my composition, something visual and narrative will most appeal to my readers.

How can I connect with my audience rhetorically?
Ethos. As an author, if I want to persuade my audience it's going to be crucial to convince them that my information and argument are credible—and that I am qualified to make the argument. I've grown up with comics and have a good base of knowledge; I'll establish that in my composition.

Logos. I'll need to build a logical case for my audience. I'll need to be methodical and organized.

Pathos. Part of what makes me care about superheroes is my emotional connection to them as people who care—who put themselves "in harm's way" to help and rescue others.

How will I reach my audience through mode and media?
Mode. My composition will probably have more text than visuals. My comics-fan audience may expect visuals, but I'm more comfortable working in text and presenting arguments that way. Also, I might be drawing on evidence. How would I do that in a nontextual medium? I'm a good writer, but I feel less comfortable as an artist. Maybe I can use existing images from comics in my work as evidence to support my points.

Media. If I create a written text for a digital environment, I can embed links. That might be an easy way to bring in my sources. I'd like to build into my work some existing clips from films and animations.

POSSIBLE GENRES

What are three genres that respond to my rhetorical situation?
1. *An advertisement?* I like that I could mix visuals with text if I made an ad. Where would I publish this ad? It would need to be somewhere that comic book fans would see it. If my ad is image centered, then I will be creating a type of visual argument. That may be a good way to reach comic book lovers, a public audience.
2. *A researched argument?* I wouldn't mind doing research and drawing on some evidence. If I choose this academic and

(Continues on next page)

public audience genre, I won't have to worry about length problems and could easily include visuals to make my case. I'm now thinking I could present this online in a magazine, journal, or blog.

3. *Film review?* As an avid film-viewer I do read a lot of film reviews. I could review a film that focuses on a superhero. I'm not sure if I could use visuals with this.

Now that Gwen has narrowed her choice of genre down to three types—an ad, a researched argument, and a film review—she looks at an example of each. She annotates the examples, reading them not only for information about her topic but also to find out more about the genres and their conventions. For example, how did the composers of these works incorporate sources? As she reads these texts closely, she asks herself: Which of these genres should I ultimately choose for my composition?

Gwen analyzes and annotates each piece according to the composer's rhetorical situation and use of genre conventions. Below is her annotation of A. O. Scott's film review: "Iron Man: Heavy Suit, Light Touches" from *The New York Times* online.

Guided Reading | Annotated Sample Film Review

A. O. Scott, *"Heavy Suit, Light Touches,"* with Notes by Gwen Ganow (STUDENT)

RHETORICAL SITUATION & CHOICES		GENRE CONVENTIONS	
Gwen's notes on Scott's review	◀ **What is the composer, A. O. Scott, doing?**	**How do I know this is a film ▶ review? Do I want to write one?**	Gwen's notes on Scott's review

PURPOSE
Scott wants to persuade readers that *Iron Man* is a film to see. He shows readers that it's a "superhero movie that's good in unusual ways." I like that his purpose is extremely clear and that he draws on moments in the film as evidence for his claims.

The world at the moment does not suffer from a shortage of superheroes. And yet in some ways the glut of anti-evil crusaders with cool costumes and troubled souls takes the pressure off of *Iron Man*, which clanks into theaters today ahead of Hellboy, Batman, and the Incredible Hulk. This summer those guys are all in sequels or redos, so Iron Man (a Marvel property not to be confused with the Man of Steel, who belongs to DC and who's taking a break this year) has the advantage of novelty in addition to a seasonal head start.

ELEMENTS OF THE GENRE
In a film review, a writer takes a position about a movie and backs that up by drawing on moments from the film, and even from film history. Here, Scott's first paragraph gets my attention. He identifies the genre of the film and makes

And *Iron Man*, directed by Jon Favreau (*Elf*, *Zathura*), has the advantage of being an unusually good superhero picture. Or at least—since it certainly has its problems—a superhero movie that's good in unusual ways. The film benefits from a script (credited to Mark Fergus, Hawk Ostby, Art Marcum, and Matt Holloway) that generally chooses clever dialogue over manufactured catchphrases and lumbering exposition, and also from a crackerjack cast that accepts the filmmaker's invitation to do some real acting rather than just flex and glower and shriek for a paycheck.

There's some of that too, of course. The hero must flex and furrow his brow; the bad guy must glower and scheme; the girl must shriek and fret. There should also be a skeptical but supportive friend. Those are the rules of the genre, as unbreakable as the pseudoscientific principles that explain everything (An arc reactor! Of course!) and the Law of the Bald Villain. In *Iron Man* it all plays out more or less as expected, from the trial-and-error building of the costume to the climactic showdown, with lots of flying, chasing and noisemaking in between. (I note that there is one sharp, subversive surprise right at the very end.)

What is less expected is that Mr. Favreau, somewhat in the manner of those sly studio-era craftsmen who kept their artistry close to the vest so the bosses wouldn't confiscate it, wears the genre paradigm as a light cloak rather than a suit of iron. Instead of the tedious, moralizing, pop-Freudian origin story we often get in the first installments

Credit: Paramount/Courtesy Everett Collection.

(Continues on next page)

of comic-book-franchise movies—childhood trauma; identity crisis; longing for justice versus thirst for revenge; wake me up when the explosions start—*Iron Man* plunges us immediately into a world that crackles with character and incident.

It is not quite the real world, but it's a bit closer than Gotham or Metropolis. We catch up with Tony Stark in dusty Afghanistan, where he is enjoying a Scotch on the rocks in the back of an armored American military vehicle. Tony is a media celebrity, a former M.I.T. whiz kid and the scion of a family whose company makes and sells high-tech weaponry. He's also a bon vivant and an incorrigible playboy. On paper the character is completely preposterous, but since Tony is played by Robert Downey Jr., he's almost immediately as authentic and familiar—as much fun, as much trouble—as your ex-boyfriend or your old college roommate. Yeah, that guy.

Tony's skeptical friend (see above) is Rhodey, an Air Force officer played with good-humored sidekick weariness by Terrence Howard. The girl is one Pepper Potts (Gwyneth Paltrow, also in evident good humor), Tony's smitten, ultracompetent assistant. His partner and sort-of mentor in Stark Enterprises is Obadiah Stane, played by Jeff Bridges with wit and exuberance and—spoiler alert!—a shaved head.

These are all first-rate actors, and Mr. Downey's antic energy and emotional unpredictability bring out their agility and resourcefulness. Within the big, crowded movements of this pop symphony is a series of brilliant duets that sometimes seem to have the swing and spontaneity of jazz improvisation: Mr. Downey and Ms. Paltrow on the dance floor; Mr. Downey and Mr. Howard drinking sake on an airplane; Mr. Downey and Shaun Toub working on blueprints in a cave; Mr. Downey and Mr. Bridges sparring over a box of pizza.

Those moments are what you are likely to remember. The plot is serviceable, which is to say that it's placed at the service of the actors (and the special-effects artists), who deftly toss it around and sometimes forget it's there. One important twist seems glaringly arbitrary and unmotivated, but this lapse may represent an act of carefree sabotage rather than carelessness. You know this ostensibly shocking revelation is coming, and the writers know you know it's coming, so why worry too much about whether it makes sense? Similarly, the patina of geopolitical relevance is worn thin and eventually discarded, and Tony's crisis of conscience when he discovers what his weapons are being used for is more of a narrative convenience than a real moral theme.

All of which is to say that *Iron Man*, in spite of the heavy encumbrances Tony must wear when he turns into the title character, is distinguished by light touches and grace notes. The hardware is impressive, don't get me wrong, but at these prices it had better be. If you're throwing around a hundred million dollars and you have Batman and the Hulk on your tail, you had better be sure that the arc reactors are in good working order and that the gold-titanium alloy suit gleams like new and flies like a bird.

And everything works pretty well. But even dazzling, computer-aided visual effects, these days, are not so special. And who doesn't have superpowers? Actually, Iron Man doesn't; his heroism is all handicraft, elbow grease and applied intelligence. Those things account for the best parts of *Iron Man* as well.

Iron Man is rated PG-13 (Parents strongly cautioned). It has a lot of action violence, none of it is especially graphic or gruesome. Also, Iron Man has sex, and not with the suit on. But not completely naked either.

Opens on Friday nationwide.
Directed by Jon Favreau; written by Mark Fergus, Hawk Ostby, Art Marcum and Matt Holloway based on the character created by Stan Lee, Larry Lieber, Don Heck and Jack Kirby; director of photography, Matthew Libatique; edited by Dan Lebental; music by Ramin Djawadi; production designer, J. Michael Riva; visual effects by John Nelson; produced by Avi Arad and Kevin Feige; released by Paramount Pictures and Marvel Entertainment. Running time: 2 hours 6 minutes.

With: Robert Downey Jr. (Tony Stark), Terrence Howard (Rhodey), Jeff Bridges (Obadiah Stane), Shaun Toub (Yinsen) and Gwyneth Paltrow (Pepper Potts).

Gwen has decided she wants to write a film review because it allows her to achieve her purpose and is a genre her audience is likely to read. She needs to figure out what movie to review and how that will allow her to make her argument.

Keep the following questions in mind.

RHETORICAL SITUATION & CHOICES

☐ **Purpose.** What is my purpose? Which genres respond to my rhetorical situation best? Which ones do I know the most about? Which ones do I want to try out? Which ones can I get help with? Among the sources I've drawn on in my research, which ones stood out? What are their genres?

☐ **Audience.** How familiar is my audience with my topic? What assumptions might my audience make about my topic? What expectations will my audience have about my piece?

☐ **Rhetorical appeals.** How will I connect with my audience? For example, if I create an ad or an editorial, how will I work within that genre to be as compelling and convincing as possible?

☐ **Modes & media.** What is the best mode for saying what I want to say? If I rely on text only, will anything be lost? And what medium would be best?

GENRE CONVENTIONS

☐ **Elements of the genres.** What features make a particular genre what it is? How would I use (or not use) those features?

☐ **Style.** What are my strengths as a writer or composer? What tone will be most appropriate for my composition, considering the genre I choose to use? What kind of vocabulary will I use? How much detail will be appropriate?

☐ **Design.** Once I choose the genre for my composition, how will it look (or sound)? Will I use a conventional design, or perhaps tailor a standard layout or structure to my own purposes?

☐ **Sources.** What do I already know about my topic? What experiences have I had? To what extent will I need to draw on sources? Will I need to quote from them? Document them?

Composing Your Genre Piece

If you've followed Gwen to this point, we hope you have some solid ideas for your own composition, including a sense of your rhetorical situation and choices—and of the genre or genres that would work best in response.

Steps for Composing

Once you're ready to move from your freewrite to creating a first draft, keep the following steps in mind. As we've mentioned elsewhere, there is not "one process" that will work for everyone, and your own processes will likely vary from project to project. The following guidelines for composing are here for you to draw on as needed.

Step 1. Write a solid draft.   Review the freewrite you created earlier in this process and begin fleshing it out so it has a beginning, middle, and end, or whatever elements are appropriate for your chosen genre. It should include, at least in rough form, the main points you want to make, as well as some examples or evidence you'll use to support your points.

Working from this draft, follow the steps below to evaluate and revise it.

Step 2. Evaluate your use of experience & evidence.   Look at a really good example of the genre you're working in—and compare it to yours. How does that author support claims with evidence? Draw on experience? What kind of evidence will your audience expect and respond to? Will anecdotes and personal stories be convincing to your audience, or will they be more convinced by statistics and references to peer-reviewed studies?

Note: Refer to the sample of your genre as you complete steps 3–7.

Step 3. Confirm the scope of information to provide.   How much coverage of the topic is appropriate for the genre you've selected? Examine the sample of the genre you're comparing your draft to. Does it present an overview of the subject? What is the level of detail?

Step 4. Consider your use of style.   Think about voice, tone, language, and point of view. Is the genre you're composing in characterized by the use of first or third person? How explicit and present will your voice and experience be in the piece? Look at the example you're comparing your piece to. Does that composer use an objective, authoritative tone, or a personal, subjective tone, or something else?

Step 5. Look at how you use rhetorical appeals.   Look at your draft and the sample genre piece you're consulting. To what extent does the other author use ethos, pathos, and/or logos? How effective is his or her approach, and what might you want to adapt for your own work?

Step 6. Look at your organization.   How have you organized your content? Is this the best way, considering who your audience is and what you're trying to achieve? Is it logical? Persuasive? Does the sample you're consulting have anything to offer you in terms of a model for improving your work?

Step 7. Consider your mix of words & images.   This is also a moment to think about design and medium. Are you being as effective as you could be? Again, consult your example.

ATTENTION, COMPOSERS

Wondering about media? What medium will best suit your genre and rhetorical situation? Will you reach your audiences best through a print or physical medium—or in a digital environment? If you're composing online, will you use audio? How about video or animation? What medium will your primary audience respond to best?

Step 8. Make a list of what you want to work on when you revise.   Base your list on what you've determined in steps 2–7.

Step 9. Revise your draft based on your revision list.   After you've revised, reread your work and make notes to address things you want to improve for the next draft.

Step 10. Revise a little more.   Get your work in the best shape you can in the time you have.

Guided Process | Composing a Film Review

At this point in her process, Gwen has a clear sense of her genre—as well as her rhetorical situation. She now gets down to writing. In the following section, she writes a first draft of her film review. She then spends time evaluating it—reading it against a published film review—to see how she might improve her own. In this process, she reviews her work for how well she deals with purpose, audience, and other rhetorical concerns. She also pays attention to how well she works within the genre of the film review itself. After this process, she revises her first draft, creating a second and third draft.

Gwen notes: "I decided to review the film *X-Men*. It's a significant film in the superhero genre that my audience will be familiar with. Following is my attempt at a first draft."

DRAFT 1   **Gwen Ganow** (STUDENT), *"Take a Position" Assignment, Superheroes and Social Attitudes:* X-Men

English 121
English Composition

Date: Nov. 10, 2016
Name: Gwen Ganow
Assignment: "Take a Position" Film Review
Superheroes and Social Attitudes: *X-Men*

The punctuated equilibrium concept of Niles Eldredge and Stephen Jay Gould states that evolution and speciation occur at a rapid rate followed by long periods of stasis. The film *X-Men* explores how a modern American society would react to its own punctuated equilibrium in which a new, superhuman species rises and suddenly integrates with "normal" humans. Through the events and emotions of the movie *X-Men*, our past and current social issues of prejudice and intolerance as an American society become exposed.

   X-Men opens with a powerful image of prejudice and intolerance, a Nazi concentration camp. While unloading a new trainload of Jews, Nazi soldiers rip a young boy from the arms of his parents. He sits in the rain crying and watches helplessly as his parents are herded off to other buildings. His yellow Star of David, his label of difference, is the only color against the dismal backdrop of rain, mud, and hate. The young boy survives his Nazi captors and grows up to be a mutant with the power to move and control metal.

   The movie leaves the scene of war and enters the chambers of Congress where a Senate committee hearing is taking place. Magneto attends this committee hearing of the Senate because he is curious about what the American government is doing about the so-called "mutant problem" in the United States. Senator Kelly, a staunch supporter of the Mutant Registration Act, is debated by Dr. Jean Grey (a mutant herself). Jean Grey argues against the Mutant Registration Act and says, "Mutants who have revealed themselves publicly have been met with fear, hostility, and violence." To this, Senator Kelly responds with the questions, "Are they dangerous? Do you want your children in school with mutants? Do you want your children to be taught by mutant teachers?"

To shield the younger generation from the violence created by the words of intolerance spoken by Senator Kelly, Charles Xavier (a mutant with powerful psychic abilities) creates Xavier's School for Gifted Youngsters and makes it a place for young mutants who have recently discovered that they are very different from their peers and have run away from home. Here he offers these young men and women a place of refuge and sense of inclusiveness. This is a safe environment where they can be taught how to control their developing minds and powers by some of Xavier's finest past students like Storm, Cyclops, and Jean Grey, who become mentors to a new generation of young mutants, afraid of the world around them. Charles Xavier never gives up hope that humanity will come to realize the error of their judgment. He teaches his students that intolerance should not be returned with even more intolerance.

Magneto's view of humanity is radically different from the views of Charles Xavier. Magneto sees nothing wrong with trying to solve the plight of mutants by using violence and fear against humans. He devises a plan using his own powers combined with a radiation-generating machine to change non-mutants into mutants. By doing this, he feels that vengeance will be carried out by putting would-be persecutors into the lives of the people they sought to persecute and chooses Senator Kelly as his first test subject. Magneto tells the senator: "Humankind has always feared what it doesn't understand. You have nothing to fear from God and nothing to fear from me. Not anymore."

The fear, intolerance, and violence toward mutants that is conveyed in *X-Men* closely ties in with the fear, intolerance, and violence endured by the GLBT community today. Sometimes, the reality of the comic book universe resembles our own reality more than we would like to admit. The movie *X-Men* questions whether we as Americans really believe in freedom for all or whether we really mean freedom for some.

Next, Gwen evaluates her film review by comparing it to an example of the genre: A. O. Scott's review "*Iron Man*: Heavy Suit, Light Touches," which she looked at earlier. She evaluates Scott's use of evidence and sources, his scope and use of rhetorical appeals, and his organization and use of visuals. Then she applies this lens to her own review.

Guided Reading | Evaluation of Film Review

DRAFT 1 **Gwen Ganow** (STUDENT), *Superheroes and Social Attitudes: X-Men*

Gwen's notes on sample film review by A. O. Scott

USE OF EVIDENCE & SOURCES

Scott puts *Iron Man* in context with other movies of the same genre. He refers to the director, his other films, and the scriptwriters.

Scott gives plot details but does not give the story away. He supports each claim with a brief snippet from the plot. Whenever he makes a point, he backs it with specific evidence and quotations from scenes.

SCOPE

His scope is in line with his purpose: to evaluate the film and make an argument in favor of it. Scott chooses key details about characters and from specific scenes to support his case.

He summarizes quite a bit: He gives just a snapshot of the plot by providing setting, character descriptions, and parts of the story.

STYLE

I like Scott's writing style. It's almost as if I can hear him speaking. He chooses each word carefully and keeps his language interesting. For example, he uses

---

Heavy Suit, Light Touches
By A. O. SCOTT
Movie review | 'iron man'
Iron Man (2008)

Credit: Paramount/Courtesy Everett Collection.

The world at the moment does not suffer from a shortage of superheroes. And yet in some ways the glut of anti-evil crusaders with cool costumes and troubled souls takes the pressure off of *Iron Man*, which clanks into theaters today ahead of Hellboy, Batman, and the Incredible Hulk. This summer those guys are all in sequels or redos, so Iron Man (a Marvel property not to be confused with the Man of Steel, who belongs to DC and who's taking a break this year) has the advantage of novelty in addition to a seasonal head start. . . .

(For the full version of Scott's review, see p. 50)

English 121
English Composition

Date: Nov. 12, 2016
Name: Gwen Ganow
Assignment: "Take a Position" Evaluation of Film Review: Superheroes and Social Attitudes *X-Men*

The punctuated equilibrium concept of Niles Eldredge and Stephen Jay Gould states that evolution and speciation occur at a rapid rate followed by long periods of stasis. The film *X-Men* explores how a modern American society would

---

Gwen's notes on draft 1 of her film review

USE OF EVIDENCE & SOURCES

In my review, I put the movie *X-Men* in context with the theory of "punctuated equilibrium," which I learned about in a biology class (and cite Eldredge and Gould as my source). I support my claims about the "powerful image of prejudice and intolerance" (paragraph 2) with plot details and specifics from a scene. Like Scott, the evidence I use to support my position includes details from the plot and other aspects of the film and its creators.

SCOPE

I go into way more detail than Scott does, maybe because I am retelling the plot chronologically. Is this a problem? Do I need to pull back from some of my details to give more summary?

STYLE

I'm not sure my voice comes through enough in my review. I think I sound knowledgeable, but I'm not so sure how present I am in the writing in terms of

a variety of terms (film, picture) to refer to the movie. Scott writes in the third person, but I like how he sometimes invites the reader in by using the word "we."

RHETORICAL APPEALS
Scott builds his ethos by drawing on evidence and crediting the film's creators. He also appeals to readers through pathos: He entices readers to go see *Iron Man* through his language and tone.

ORGANIZATION
Scott begins with general comments about superheroes and the popularity of superhero movies before he moves on to Iron Man.

Next, he situates the film within its genre, hinting at his opinion of the movie. He outlines some of his expectations. He makes claims that he supports with details of the plot and characters; he closes with a final evaluation of the film.

USE OF VISUALS
Scott includes a few visuals. The large still featuring Robert Downey Jr., who plays the lead, is pretty striking. There is also a small picture further into the review.

react to its own punctuated equilibrium in which a new, superhuman species rises and suddenly integrates with "normal" humans. Through the events and emotions of the movie *X-Men*, our past and current social issues of prejudice and intolerance as an American society become exposed.

X-Men opens with a powerful image of prejudice and intolerance, a Nazi concentration camp. While unloading a new trainload of Jews, Nazi soldiers rip a young boy from the arms of his parents. He sits in the rain crying and watches helplessly as his parents are herded off to other buildings. His yellow Star of David, his label of difference, is the only color against the dismal backdrop of rain, mud, and hate. The young boy survives his Nazi captors and grows up to be a mutant with the power to move and control metal.

The movie leaves the scene of war and enters the chambers of Congress where a Senate committee hearing is taking place. Magneto attends this committee hearing of the Senate because he is curious about what the American government is doing about the so-called "mutant problem" in the United States. Senator Kelly, a staunch supporter of the Mutant Registration Act, is debated by Dr. Jean Grey (a mutant herself). Jean Grey argues against the Mutant Registration Act and says, "Mutants who have revealed themselves publicly have been met with fear, hostility, and violence." To this, Senator Kelly responds with the questions, "Are they dangerous? Do you want your children in school with mutants? Do you want your children to be taught by mutant teachers?" . . .

(For a full version of Ganow's Film Review Draft 1, see p. 56.)

voice, personality, or humor. My review does not seem as personal or subjective as Scott's. I think my perspective is more objective. Is that a strong point? Or a problem?

RHETORICAL APPEALS
I want to establish myself as an expert on superheroes and film. I'm not sure how well I've conveyed my ethos. I also need to persuade my audience, so I need to appeal to pathos.

MY ORGANIZATION
I move through the plot, giving readers a general sense of the story. I don't discuss the film in terms of a broader context but I probably should. I need to state my position clearly and directly.

MY USE OF VISUALS
I haven't yet added any images/film stills into my review, but I need to. Which characters and key scenes do I want to show?

(Continues on next page)

Composing Your Genre Piece

What to focus on when I revise? ▼

1. **Reorganize my review so it isn't just a chronological plot summary.** I need to identify the points I want to make and then choose supporting details from the plot, much as Scott does.

2. **Establish a clearer sense of voice.** Make sure not to shift between third and first person. Add a little personality.

3. **Make my opinion of the film much clearer.** I need my position about the film to be stronger. Is it worth seeing? Why or why not? Also, I want readers to see the dilemma of the hero as related to that of the GLBT community.

4. **Do more to establish ethos and appeal to readers' emotions.**

5. **Pay more attention to language.** Incorporate visuals—also maybe embed video.

Based on her evaluation of her first draft (see above) and the items she's identified to revise (see list in right column), Gwen rewrites to create her second draft that she titles "*X-Men*: Mutants R Us."

English 121
English Composition

Date: Nov. 14, 2016
Name: Gwen Ganow
Assignment: "Take a Position" Film Review
X-Men: Mutants R Us

As a "hard-core" comic book fan, I always considered the 2000 *X-Men* film the epitome of a true comic book movie. What sets the *X-Men* apart from other comic book films is that the story behind the *X-Men* is not overshadowed by special effects. In *X-Men*, equilibrium is punctured; humans face a sudden and dramatic evolutionary change, one that results in the existence of "mutants." The mutants are humans with superhuman powers, who look human enough to integrate invisibly into society. The movie explores how American society might react to the existence of these mutants, exposing our past and current social issues of prejudice and intolerance. Bryan Singer, best known for 1995's *The Usual Suspects*, directs from the screenplay written by David Hayter.

Created by Stan Lee and Jack Kirby in 1963, X-Men are children of parents who were exposed to atmospheric radiation and became genetically altered. The mutant kids are outsiders in the world, and are envied and feared by "normal" humans. The alienation of the X-Men is similar to that of other groups of people who have experienced prejudice, like African Americans, Jews, Japanese, and homosexuals. Singer makes this parallel explicit with the opening scene.

X-Men opens with a powerful image of prejudice and intolerance, a Nazi concentration camp. While unloading a new trainload of Jews, Nazi soldiers rip a young boy from the arms of his parents. He sits in the rain crying and watches helplessly as his parents are herded off to other buildings. His yellow Star of David is the only color against the dismal backdrop of rain, mud, and hate. The young boy survives his Nazi captors and grows up to be a mutant known as Magneto with the power to move and control metal.

The movie leaves the scene of war and enters the chambers of Congress where a Senate committee hearing is taking place on the Mutant Registration Act, which would require mutants to register with the government and list their special abilities, making it impossible for them to blend in unnoticed with the rest of society. Magneto, played

(Continues on next page)

by Ian McKellen, attends this committee hearing because he is curious about what the American government is doing about the so-called "mutant problem." Senator Kelly, played by Bruce Davison, a staunch supporter of the Mutant Registration Act, is debated by Dr. Jean Grey, a mutant herself, played by Famke Janssen. Kelly supports the Mutant Registration Act, believing that mutants are a danger to "normal" humans and should be locked away, while Grey argues that forcing mutants to register would create the potential for them to be treated as freaks.

The performers share good chemistry, with the one-upmanship between Hugh Jackman's Wolverine and James Marsden's Cyclops bringing humor to their scenes. Patrick Stewart's Charles Xavier seems both fatherly and professorial, and Anna Paquin as Rogue does a fine job conveying fear about her future as a mutant and lovesickness over Wolverine. Rebecca Romijn makes an impression in a role that relies more on physical presence than lines.

In *X-Men*, responses to prejudice by the victims of prejudice are explored through the actions of two important mutants, both leaders of mutant groups. Charles Xavier, a mutant with powerful psychic abilities, creates a school for the gifted for young runaway mutants. Here he offers these young men and women a place of refuge and a sense of inclusiveness. This is a safe environment where they can be taught how to control their developing minds and powers by some of Xavier's finest past students like Storm, Cyclops, and Jean Grey, who become mentors to a new generation of young mutants, afraid of the world around them. Xavier's "turn the other cheek" philosophy links him to the Jesus Christ of the Christian culture. The fact that Charles Xavier provides a safe house for people rejected by humanity also links him to our real-life organizations like NAACP, GLBT (gay, lesbian, bisexual, and transgender) resource centers, and some of our churches.

The other leader is Magneto, who fronts the Brotherhood of Mutants. Magneto's perspective on humanity stems from his experiences as a young boy at a WWII concentration camp, which was captured in the film's opening scene. This experience left Magneto distrustful of humanity and convinced that mutants are bound to suffer the same fate met by the inmates of the Nazi death camps. To preserve the survival of his mutant species, Magneto declares war on humankind. Magneto's view of humanity is radically different from the views of Charles Xavier. Magneto sees nothing wrong with trying to solve the plight of mutants by using violence and fear against humans.

Although the film is worth seeing for the performances and direction alone, the special effects, while relatively low-key for a superhero movie, are stunning. Magneto's spinning contraption, the fight scenes, and Storm's weather conjuring add to the fun. Finally, while there is seldom a clear right and wrong in real life, Singer's film makes it easy for us to take the right side. The heroes of the film are clearly Professor Xavier's X-Men. In this way, Singer allows us to imagine the consequences of violence and anger, as shown by Magneto's band of mutants, and ultimately root for Xavier's more tolerant gang.

Credit: By permission Gwen Dalynn Ganow.

Gwen evaluates her second draft and comes up with a list of items to focus on for her third and final draft. Gwen observes the following.

1. Overall, I've done a better job in Draft 2 in evaluating the film and taking a position about it. It's clear what I think of the movie and why.

2. Draft 2 is also more interesting and readable. I've done more to appeal to my audience of superhero/comic lovers. For example, my first sentence and paragraph are aimed at drawing them in.

3. My writing still seems stiff in places. I want to make the style and tone a little more casual; also, I want to tighten up the wording and do more to make this flow.

4. A final point: This doesn't *look* like a film review yet. I'll need to apply design principles and add an image from the film. I'd also like to embed links to other reviews and to interviews with the director and actors.

When she revises again, she addresses document design, images, and embedded links. She also polishes her writing and continues to evaluate her choice of mode and medium, with thoughts of future iterations of her project. Following is an excerpt from her final review.

English 121
English Composition

Date: Nov. 21, 2016
Name: Gwen Ganow
Assignment: "Take a Position" Film Review
X-Men: Mutants R Us

As a "hard-core" comic book fan, I always considered the 2000 *X-Men* film the epitome of a true comic book movie. What sets the *X-Men* apart from other comic book films is that the story behind the X-Men is not overshadowed by special effects. In *X-Men*, it's the story that matters. In the world of this film, the equilibrium of existence has been punctured; humans face a sudden and dramatic evolutionary change, one that results in the existence of "mutants."

The mutants are humans with superhuman powers, who look human enough to integrate invisibly into society. The movie explores how American society might react to the existence of these mutants, exposing our past and current social issues of prejudice and intolerance.

Bryan Singer, best known for 1995's *The Usual Suspects*, directs from the screenplay written by David Hayter. . . .

The performers share good chemistry, with the one-upmanship between Hugh Jackman's Wolverine and James Marsden's Cyclops bringing humor to their scenes. Patrick Stewart's Charles Xavier seems both fatherly and professorial, and Anna Paquin as Rogue does a fine job.

Hugh Jackman as Wolverine, from *X-Men* (2000).
Credit: Everett Collection.

Credit: By permission Gwen Dalynn Ganow.

CHECKLIST | Composing by Drawing on Experience & Evidence

As you compose, keep the following in mind. (For help with composing from sources, see Chapter 14.)

RHETORICAL SITUATION & CHOICES

☐ **Purpose.** Why am I composing this piece? What do I hope it will achieve? How can I best convey my interest and passion to meet my purpose?

☐ **Audience.** Whom am I composing for? What will they already know about my topic? What will they need to know? What level of detail will my audience want and need? Do I need to consider a secondary audience?

☐ **Rhetorical appeals.** What experiences and evidence can I draw on to establish my credibility? Is it appropriate to emphasize pathos? How can I make the logic of my position or point clear?

☐ **Modes & media.** How should I mix words, audio, and/or images to be effective? Will my audience want something digital or a hard copy? What medium will my primary audience respond to best?

GENRE CONVENTIONS

☐ **Elements of the genre.** Am I using the conventions of the genre appropriately? Do I need to look at more examples of the genre?

☐ **Style.** Have I used a tone that is appropriate for my genre and will it achieve my purpose with my audience? What point of view (first person, second person, third person) will help me achieve my purpose? Have I chosen my words carefully?

☐ **Design.** How have I used design elements to direct my audience's attention? Have I designed my piece according to the design conventions of the genre? For example, if I'm writing a blog, does it look like a blog?

☐ **Sources.** Are the experiences and evidence that I draw on appropriate for my genre? Have I cited them according to the genre's conventions? Is there additional experience or evidence that I need to incorporate to achieve my purpose?

PRACTICE

Taking a Position

Do the same assignment Gwen did: Take a position on a topic you care about and have experience with. Then think about who you want to communicate your ideas to and compose in a genre that will allow you to do that.

You may compose in any genre that seems appropriate for your purpose and audience. The length should be appropriate to the genre; in other words, a magazine article will have more words than a poster. Be sure to choose a genre that will allow you to communicate with the audience you have in mind.

For sources, you should primarily draw upon your own experience. If you wish, you can use other source material, if it is appropriate to your genre choice and topic.

Refer back to Gwen's process and try to mimic it as closely as possible.

PART 2
COMPOSING IN GENRES

5 COMPOSING IN COLLEGE & BEYOND

What Do You Compose in College & Beyond?

As you saw in Chapter 3, a press release and a blog post, both written in response to an event at Arches National Park, show that there is no one right way to write about a particular topic or issue (see Chapter 3, pp. 35–38). How you write about a topic or issue will always depend on the rhetorical situation you find yourself in. This statement applies for all the writing you do, both as a student and beyond college. In this chapter, we will briefly describe some of the types of writing you might expect to do in college and beyond and the types of rhetorical situations you might find yourself in.

Discovering Ideas Through Writing

Whether you are in the classroom beginning an assignment, sitting at work staring at a request from your supervisor, or anticipating standing on the street corner giving a speech at a rally, you need a way to figure out what you want to say and how you want to say it. As we discussed in Chapter 4, one of the best ways to do this is through freewriting. Essentially, when you freewrite, you write for a particular amount of time without stopping, not worrying about whether your ideas make sense. You don't stop to correct spelling, ponder whether you have chosen the best word, or reread what you've written. Instead, you let your thoughts spill onto the page, trusting that through the process you will begin to get some interesting ideas flowing. It is best to freewrite using pen and paper rather than a computer, since there is less chance you will want to go back and correct or reread.

WRITE

Write for ten minutes with a pen and paper. Start with one of the following prompts: "Why I Like to Write" or "Why I Don't Like to Write." Don't let your pen stop. If you get tired of writing, just become Bart Simpson at the board and keep writing the prompt over and over. Eventually, you will start writing something else. Trust the process. After you finish, read over what you wrote and underline or circle anything you hadn't considered when you first heard the prompt.

Academic Genres & Assignments

Any writing you do for the classes you take in college is considered academic writing. Most of this writing is done "on demand," meaning you are not writing because the muse inspired you, but rather because your professor told you to. Most academic writing begins when an assignment is given.

Some of the typical purposes of academic writing are to demonstrate that you can think in ways appropriate for the discipline, to give you practice with writing skills you'll need for other classes, to give instructors an opportunity to guide you as a writer and learner in a fairly personalized way through their feedback, and to give your instructors a chance to assess how well you have grasped the concepts and skills the course focuses on. You may have other purposes as well, such as to learn about the topic you are writing about and to share what you've learned with your reader(s).

In most academic writing, your audience will be your professor and sometimes your classmates. Sometimes your professor might tell you to write for another audience, such as the board of regents, the city council, community leaders, or local business owners. In some cases, your audience might be a wider one. For example, some instructors ask students to create or edit *Wikipedia* entries or to do other composing that will be published online for a public audience. If your assignment doesn't specify whom you are writing for, you should ask.

Genre is often dictated by the assignment itself. For example, academic assignments include the lab report, the annotated bibliography, and the film analysis essay. In these situations, you do not get to choose the genre you want to write in. You might be wondering now if this means that genre is not always a response to a rhetorical situation. It still is: Genre is *always* a response to a rhetorical situation. For example, if your biology professor asks you to write a lab report, that's because when someone in biology finds himself in a rhetorical situation in which the purpose is to report the results of an experiment and the audience is the professor or other biologist, the common social response is to write a lab report. Now, you could write a lyrical poem instead, and frankly, nothing is stopping you from doing so. However, whenever a composer gives her audience something very different from what they were expecting, there are consequences. In this particular rhetorical situation, the consequence could be an F on the assignment. (It's always a good idea if you want to deviate from the assigned genre to talk to your professor first.)

Some typical assignments you might encounter include a position paper in which you take and defend a position on an issue, an analysis of a film or art piece in which you discuss the choices the filmmaker or artist made, a literacy narrative in which you discuss an aspect of yourself as a reader and writer, a research report in which you share what you learned through research about a particular topic, a proposal to conduct research on a particular topic, a presentation to your classmates in which you share your research on a particular topic, and an annotated bibliography in which you summarize and analyze source material you have read in your research. You will find examples of some of these genres throughout the book. (For a list, see the Index of Genres, p. G-1.)

An academic genre that has a somewhat different rhetorical situation is the personal statement. A personal statement is an essay you write when you apply for a scholarship or to graduate school in which you explain to a funder or graduate program (your audience) why you deserve the scholarship or admittance to the graduate program you are applying for.

Below is an example of an academic genre you are probably somewhat familiar with: the academic research paper. Shown here is an excerpt of a paper Chase Dickinson wrote as a student at Weber State University in Utah. For the complete, annotated paper, see Chapter 7, "Academic Genres," page 108.

Guided Reading | Researched Argument

Chase Dickinson (STUDENT), Excerpt from *Are Kids on a One-Way Path to Violence?*

PURPOSE
Dickinson wants to persuade readers that video games do not cause violent behavior in mentally healthy children.

AUDIENCE
His readers are his instructor, his classmates, and the students at Weber State University who read the journal *Weber Writes*.

RHETORICAL APPEALS
Dickinson develops his ethos by stating that he is a gamer himself and that he's even worked in the industry.
By noting that the DC Sniper trained at a shooting range, Dickinson appeals to readers' sense of logos to question the connection between the DC Sniper and his video game experience.

MODES & MEDIA
Mode = written
Medium = print

◄ What is the composer, Chase Dickinson, doing?

Chase Dickinson composed a ► researched argument. What are the conventions of this genre? To what extent does he adhere to them?

ELEMENTS OF THE GENRE
A researched argument:

- States a thesis or makes a clear claim.
- Presents an argument based on research.
- Acknowledges counterarguments.
- Refutes or concedes counterarguments.
- Cites specific examples, synthesizing them into his main argument.

STYLE
A researched argument:

- Features a descriptive title.
- Gets readers' attention in the introduction.
- Closes with a simple, memorable statement.
- Conveys a strong authoritative voice and tone.
- Presents detail.

DESIGN
Dickinson submitted his work formatted in MLA style. For use in *Weber Writes*, it was single-spaced to conform to that journal's design.

In the popular video game *Grand Theft Auto* (GTA), players are thrust into a world without laws, free to do just about anything they want. Stealing cars, killing civilians, and causing general mayhem are common occurrences in the fictitious world of Liberty City (Rockstar Leeds). In fact, GTA is about as lawless as games get. But can a game such as *Grand Theft Auto* actually fuel real-world violence? There are many who believe so, and violent video games have therefore become a hotly debated topic in today's headlines.

If you were to listen to politicians and critics, the relationship between video games and crime is blatantly clear: children who play video games will either become more aggressive or actually commit real-world acts of violence. According to the lawyers of Lee Malvo, the young "DC Sniper," Malvo learned to shoot by playing "very realistic and gory" video games. These games were also said to have "desensitized (him) . . . to train him to shoot human forms over and over" (qtd. in Provan). Another popular argument against violent video games comes in the form of the infamous Columbine shootings in which Dylan Klebold and Eric Harris killed thirteen students and injured twenty-three more before killing themselves. During the investigation that followed, it was discovered that both teenagers enjoyed playing the bloody first-person shooter *Doom*, and that they went on the rampage shortly after their parents took the game away from them. It has also been speculated that the pair created a level in *Doom* with the same layout as their school in order to plan out their attack (Mikkelson). Yet another argument finds Jack Thompson, a leader in the fight against violent video games, blaming . . .

Note from editors: This marks the end of the excerpt of Dickinson's paper. For the full text of this paper, see Chapter 7, "Academic Genres," pages 108–111.

(Continues on next page)

Works Cited

Adams, Duncan. "The Alienation and Anger of Seung-Hui Cho." *The Roanoke Times*, 30 Aug. 2007, www.roanoke.com/vtinvestigation/wb/130177.

Benedetti, Winda. "Were Video Games to Blame for Massacre?" *MSNBC.com*, 20 Apr. 2007, www.roanoke.com/vtinvestigation/wb/130177.

Biggs, John. "Why Video Games Don't Cause Violence." *CrunchGear.com*, 18 Apr. 2007, techcrunch.com/2007/04/18/why-video-games-dont-cause-violence/.

Bungie, developer. *Halo: Combat Evolved*. Microsoft Studios, 15 Nov. 2001, www.halowaypoint.com/en-us.

Entertainment Software Association. *Entertainment Software Rating Board*, www.esrb.org. Accessed 27 Jan. 2001.

Kutner, Lawrence, and Cheryl Olson. *Grand Theft Childhood: The Surprising Truth About Violent Video Games and What Parents Can Do*. Simon & Schuster, 2008, p. 8.

Mikkelson, Barbara. "Columbine Doom Levels." *Snopes.com*, 1 Jan. 2005, www.snopes.com/horrors/madmen/doom.asp.

Musgrove, Mike. "Va. Tech: Dr. Phil and Jack Thompson Blame Video Games." *The Washington Post*, 17 Apr. 2007, voices.washingtonpost.com/posttech/2007/04/va_tech_dr_phil_jack_thompson.html.

Provan, Alexander. "The Education of Lee Boyd Malvo." *Bidouan*, 13 Jan. 2009, www.bidoun.org/magazine/16-kids/the-education-of-lee-boyd-malvo-by-alexander-provan/.

Rockstar Leeds and Rockstar North, developers. *Grand Theft Auto: Liberty City Stories*. Rockstar Games, Capcom, 24 Oct. 2005, www.rockstargames.com/libertycitystories.

Credit: By permission of Chase Dickinson.

SOURCES
Using the MLA style of documentation, the author cites sources in the body of the text and at the end in a Works Cited list. For help with documenting sources, see Chapter 13.

Academic Reflective Genres

When you reflect in your journal, you are writing just for yourself. Unless your journal is meant for consumption by others, you are writing *only* for yourself. In this case, your writing scenario is not a social situation (even if someone snoops in your desk to find your writing). In this section we focus on genres that allow writers to reflect but that are also intended to be shared with an audience.

Reflective genres allow you to contemplate what you think and why, what you did and why, or what you could do and why. Other times, reflective genres are used to describe and reflect upon challenges. Reflective genres depend upon describing thoughts or actions but also move beyond description to analysis.

What are some of the reflective genres you might encounter in college? Your professor might ask you to write a reflection on your writing process and turn in it alongside a research report, or you might be asked to write a reflection on a field experience for your geology class. You will also encounter reflective genres in the workplace; for example, an organization's employee evaluation and review process might involve having employees write self-evaluations. In public life, reflective speaking is often used in self-help groups (e.g., Alcoholics Anonymous, Narcotics Anonymous), such as when a participant stands up and tells his story and reflects on his experience. Another example of reflection in a public setting is when a musician is asked by an interviewer to reflect on his or her influences. However, the stand-alone reflection is usually only seen in academia or the workplace.

The audience for reflective genres is usually either a professor (in academic settings) or a supervisor (in workplace settings). Readers want to gain insight into what you did and why. In the case of someone in a self-help group, the audience is other members of the group and possibly a facilitator, who can respond to the reflection in helpful ways.

Reflective genres also respond to a rhetorical situation. For example, if you have to write a reflective essay to accompany a visual argument you created, your purpose might be to help your professor (your audience) understand why you made particular choices in composing the visual and what overall effect you want the visual to have on its audience.

Some typical genres for reflective writing are portfolio cover letters, in which you describe and reflect on items in a portfolio of writing or artwork; progress reports, in which you describe and analyze the progress you've made toward achieving a particular task or outcome; and self-evaluations, in which you discuss some of your successes and challenges on the job.

The following is an example of an Artist's Statement, an assignment we like to give students in our classes that prompts them to discuss and reflect on the composing choices they've made. Shown here is an excerpt. For Michael Kipp's full-length Artist's Statement, see LaunchPad for *The Bedford Book of Genres* (macmillanlearning.com).

WRITE

Make a list of all the genres you remember writing in when you were in high school or in your most recent education experience. Which ones did you enjoy the most and why? Which ones did you find most challenging and why? Which ones do you think helped you grow the most as a writer and why?

Guided Reading | Artist's Statement

Michael Kipp (STUDENT), Excerpt from *On Composing Happiness: How and Why I Created My Collage* Thank You

RHETORICAL SITUATION & CHOICES	GENRE CONVENTIONS

PURPOSE

Kipp's purpose is to persuade readers that "practicing gratitude can make us happier" and that his collage furthers that goal. He wants readers to know that he made thoughtful decisions when composing the collage.

AUDIENCE

His readers are his instructor and fellow students. They want to know why he created a collage and what research informed it.

RHETORICAL APPEALS

Kipp establishes his credibility, or ethos, in paragraph 1 by including quotes from experts to show he's done research on positive psychology. Kipp appeals to logos by explaining his choices logically.

MODES & MEDIA

Mode = written
Medium = print

◀ **What is the composer, Michael Kipp, doing?**

Michael Kipp created ▶ an Artist's Statement to accompany his collage. What are the conventions of the genre? To what extent does he adhere to them?

"Psychologists have repeatedly shown that perceptions are more important than objective reality" ("Positive Thinking"). That statement embodies the message behind my collage. It ties in with messages from other research I've done on the science of happiness, including my reading of the article "Psychological Research: Gratitude," by Jerry Lopper. In that piece, Lopper quotes psychologist and researcher Dr. Alex Wood as saying: "Gratitude is a life orientation towards noticing and appreciating the positive in the world." What Wood suggests is that feeling grateful requires mental work (Emmons, *Thanks!* 6). Gratitude is a part of our perception, a "life orientation," and without effort that perception will not arise or be maintained. Thus, to have an attitude of gratefulness, we must change our outlook on life. My purpose in creating this collage is to promote the idea that we make choices about how we perceive experience, and that practicing gratitude can make us happier.

My intended audience for my collage is made up of people who like art, psychology, and philosophy, who appreciate the abstract expression of concepts, and who may be persuaded to think about how a grateful attitude could be more important than one's objective reality—and how they may practice that in their own life to be happier.

In my collage I used *pathos* to convey these ideas—I wanted to sway my viewers emotionally, to cause them to feel curious and inspired when looking at the collage. I did this through my choices of composition, colors, and subjects, which are discussed in depth below. I used striking contrast and positioned the objects in ways the viewer might not expect, thereby drawing attention to them. I also used *logos* by putting the piece together in a logical manner, and by grounding my concept in positive psychology research. Furthermore, by connecting my audience with research on

ELEMENTS OF THE GENRE

- Kipp discusses a specific composition and makes an argument about it. He supports claims.
- Kipp addresses readers directly.
- Kipp talks about his rhetorical situation and specific related choices.
- Kipp reflects on his successes and limitations.

STYLE

Kipp uses specific details.

DESIGN

Kipp structures his statement as a traditional researched essay.

SOURCES

Kipp's sources for his statement include the collage itself and the research he conducted on gratitude. He cites his sources per MLA style.

the power of the perception (in para. 1), I ask viewers to think about how the collage illustrates that concept. My goal is that my audience will ponder what each part of the collage represents and come to logical conclusions about . . .

Note from editors: This marks the end of the excerpt of Kipp's Statement. For the full text of this paper, see LaunchPad for The Bedford Book of Genres.

———————

Works Cited

Emmons, Robert A. *Thanks! How the New Science of Gratitude Can Make You Happier.* Houghton Mifflin Harcourt, 2007. Google Books, books.google.com/books?id=tGCcH2l4jUUC.

Emmons, Robert A., and Charles M. Shelton. "Gratitude and the Science of Positive Psychology." *Handbook of Positive Psychology*, edited by C. R. Snyder and Shane J. Lopez, Oxford UP, 2002, pp. 459–71.

Lopper, Jerry. "Psychological Research: Gratitude." *Suite101*, 19 May 2008, www.suite101.com/content/psychological-research-gratitude-a54399.

Martinez-Marti, et al. "The Effects of Counting Blessings on Subjective Well-Being: A Gratitude Intervention in a Spanish Sample." *Spanish Journal of Psychology*, vol. 13, no. 2, 2010, pp. 886–96, www.ucm.es/info/psi/docs/journal/v13_n2_2010/art886.pdf.

Pursuit of Happiness. "Positive Thinking: Optimism and Gratitude." *The Pursuit of Happiness*, www.pursuit-of-happiness.org/science-of-happiness/positive-thinking/. Accessed 26 Nov. 2012.

Rodin, Auguste. *The Thinker.* 1880–81, Cleveland Museum of Art, Cleveland. Bronze sculpture.

Tsang, Jo-Ann. "Gratitude and Prosocial Behaviour: An Experimental Test of Gratitude." *Cognition and Emotion*, vol. 20, no. 1, 2006, pp. 138–148, www.academia.edu/365898/Gratitude_and_prosocial_behavior_An_experimental_test_of_gratitude.

Watkins, Philip C., et al. "Counting Your Blessings: Positive Memories Among Grateful People." *Current Psychology*, vol. 23, no. 1, 2004, pp. 52–67. JSTOR, doi: 10.1007/512144-004-1008-2.

Workplace Genres

Workplace writing is any kind of writing or composing you do in a business or professional setting. Sometimes this is referred to as business writing. Much like academic writing, workplace writing is also produced "on demand." You are usually asked by your manager to compose something specific because of the particular job you are doing.

Workplace writing usually responds to a need that someone has. For example, you write a resume and cover letter in response to a job opening because you need a job and your potential employer needs an employee, or you create a presentation to help pitch a solution for a client's problem. Other typical purposes of workplace genres are to communicate ideas to internal or external audiences, to analyze situations so that you and your colleagues can make informed decisions, to report on the progress of a project, or to persuade your reader to take a certain action.

The readers of workplace genres can be divided into internal or external audiences. Often you create something that is distributed within a company, such as a memo written to members of your team that captures the salient points discussed for an upcoming sales meeting. At other times you direct your message outside the workplace; for example, you might deliver a proposal for a new medical records system to a local hospital.

The types of genres chosen are usually dictated by the situation, the task, and the audience. If you wanted to quickly communicate something to a few coworkers, such as a follow-up communication after a meeting, you would send an e-mail. However, if you needed to communicate something more formally, such as a serious safety or other issue you discovered, you might choose a report to your supervisor that would be delivered in hard copy to emphasize the seriousness of the issue.

Your choice of workplace genres, just like other genres, is always based on the rhetorical situation. You want to determine your purpose and audience, and then choose the best ways to approach and reach that audience. For example, if you were searching for a job on campus and you saw a notice for an open position for a student worker to assist people at the Student Life Desk, you would most likely submit your resume and a cover letter to the person who oversees the desk. Your purpose would be to get the job, and your audience would be the person who is doing the hiring.

Some typical workplace genres are memos, which are internal and generally fairly short informational updates; reports, which can be internal or external and are generally long and complex, giving a rich analysis of a situation, often with recommendations; proposals, which usually outline costs and plans associated with taking a particular course of action; and presentations, in which someone shares information live with an audience, often accompanied by PowerPoint slides or other visuals.

WRITE

You may or may not have experience writing in workplace genres, but you certainly have experience writing in academic genres. How do you think writing in academic genres might help prepare you to write in workplace genres? Imagine you are in an elevator on your way up to a job interview. To your surprise, the person in the elevator with you is your interviewer. She asks you to explain how your experience writing as a student might make you a good on-the-job writer. Turn to a classmate, and answer the question.

Workplace genres often depend to some degree on templates, which provide a standard structure to documents. For example, some companies have templates for trip reports, so that when an employee returns from a business trip, she can simply plug in information about where she went, what purpose the trip had, and what the outcome was.

Below is an example of a cover letter by job applicant Julia Nollen. The letter accompanied a resume that she submitted when applying for a position as a marketing assistant. Shown here is an excerpt of that letter, with abbreviated marginal annotations. For a complete version of the letter and Nollen's resume, see Chapter 8, "Workplace Genres," pages 176–79.

Guided Reading | Cover Letter

Julia Nollen, Excerpt from *Application for Marketing Assistant Job*

RHETORICAL SITUATION & CHOICES

PURPOSE
Nollen writes her cover letter to persuade the director of marketing that her background makes her an ideal fit for a marketing assistant position.

AUDIENCE
Nollen's primary audience is Karen Soeltz, the director of marketing. Secondary readers might be other supervisors and employees who work with the marketing department.

RHETORICAL APPEALS
Nollen establishes her **ethos** by describing the variety of her work experience in the publishing industry. . . .

Nollen appeals to **logos** by making logical connections. . . .

◄ What is the composer, Julia Nollen, doing?

GENRE CONVENTIONS

As a job applicant, Julia ► Nollen wrote a cover letter to accompany her resume. What are some conventions of the cover letter as a genre? To what extent does she follow those conventions?

ELEMENTS OF THE GENRE
Nollen and other writers of cover letters:

- Introduce themselves as applicants. . . .
- Use standard business letter formatting. . . .
- Refer specifically to the position they're applying for. . . .
- Explain why the job and organization are appealing. . . .
- Refer to their resumes. . . .
- Are brief. . . .
- Close with a request for an interview.

STYLE
Nollen and other writers of cover letters:

- Write in the first person.
- Are professional in voice and tone,

July 6, 2017

Karen Soeltz
Director of Marketing
Bedford/St. Martin's
75 Arlington St.
Boston, MA 02116

Dear Ms. Soeltz:

My name is Julia Nollen, and I am writing at the suggestion of Executive Editor Ellen Thibault, who recommended I apply for the open Marketing Assistant position at Bedford/St. Martin's. I am currently attending New York University's Summer Publishing Institute until July 16 but am available to interview in Boston at your convenience. I've been a longtime fan of Bedford's titles and have even contributed to one of your books. Further, during a recent informational interview at your

(Continues on next page)

MODES & MEDIA
Mode = written
Medium = digital

Boston office, I was impressed by the creative energy and commitment of the people working there. I'd love to be a part of that.

What interests me most about Bedford is its mission to publish educational products across several platforms. At NYU I've studied the publishing industry and confirmed that I want to work for a company that blends established practices and innovative technology to create the best educational tools. I've learned that . . .

Note from editors: This marks the end of the excerpt of Nollen's letter. For the full text, see Chapter 8, "Workplace Genres," pages 176–79.

but also indicate something about their personalities.
• Are specific and detailed, while being brief.

DESIGN
Nollen uses single-spaced paragraphs

SOURCES
Nollen draws on her own experiences.

Credit: By permission of Julia Nollen.

Public Genres

When you write for public audiences, consider that there are different degrees of publicness. When you post on Facebook, for example, you might consider yourself to be writing for your friends, but if you don't have your privacy settings configured to keep strangers from seeing your posts, you are actually composing for everyone on Facebook, over a hundred million readers. In general, you are writing for a public audience anytime you expect people you don't know personally to encounter your writing. Composing for public audiences can take many forms, from creating an art exhibit to writing a letter to the editor to posting a flyer on campus or an image on Instagram. Most composing for public audiences is initiated when a composer is moved to share a message with a public group.

Some of the typical purposes of composing for public audiences are to argue for a position on an issue, to share an idea, and to join an ongoing conversation. For example, you might decide to post a Facebook status update that includes a link to an article about a topical issue to show that you agree with the sentiments presented. You are hoping that anyone who reads your post will then also read the article and see your viewpoint.

If a piece is created for a public audience, you don't necessarily have control over who that audience is. For example, while an initial tweet might only have the audience of your followers, one of your followers might decide to retweet and your tweet would then be received by a group of people you've never encountered. Additionally, this same tweet might be randomly found through a search for a hashtag you used. If we look at audience in relationship to visual art, the viewers might be people literally passing by (if the art is a mural painted on the side of a building), people who specifically went to the art gallery because they know the artist, or people who were visiting the museum and were intrigued by a poster they saw for the exhibit.

Genres for public audiences, just like the other genres previously discussed, respond to a rhetorical situation. Consider how many times you learn about something newsworthy via Facebook or Twitter. The composer of the posting has chosen one of these genres because they can reach a wide audience immediately. It is then easy for anyone receiving the information to share that information with others. Another example to consider is a TED talk. When a colleague of Amy shared his approach to a business class that integrated running a marathon during his TEDxYouth presentation, his purpose was to inspire a public audience to be challenged to change their habits by training for a marathon.

Some typical genres for public audiences are posts on social media sites (Facebook, Twitter, Instagram), blog postings, art exhibits, music and theater performances, and presentations designed for a public audience (such as a TED talk).

Below is an example of a presentation titled "The Doodle Revolution," by Sunni Brown, that she gave as an Ignite talk. Shown here is an excerpt of her talk with abbreviated annotations in the margins. The complete presentation, full annotations, and information about Ignite are available in Chapter 9, "Public Genres," pages 207–12.

WRITE

As the discussion makes clear, you are part of a public audience. Have you ever considered yourself a public audience? If so, in what situations? If not, how does thinking about yourself as part of a public audience change the way you think about genres such as editorials and letters to the editor? Jot down your ideas and share with a classmate.

Guided Reading | Presentation

Sunni Brown, Excerpt from *Ignite Talk: "The Doodle Revolution"*

RHETORICAL SITUATION & CHOICES		GENRE CONVENTIONS	
PURPOSE Sunni Brown wants to persuade her audience that doodling, though considered socially unacceptable in many settings, is actually a very effective tool for recording, absorbing, and retaining information. As she seeks to persuade, she also seeks to entertain her audience and hold their interest	◀ What is the composer/ presenter, Sunni Brown, doing?	Sunni Brown created a ▶ presentation to make an argument about the value of doodling. What are some common conventions of the presentation as a genre? To what extent does she adhere to those conventions?	**ELEMENTS OF THE GENRE** Presentation creators do the following: • Provide an ethos-building introduction to their argument. • Write a thoughtful conclusion. • Include interesting visuals. • Write with clear transitions.

"I am what I refer to as a large-scale strategic doodler. So people pay me to track auditory content and display it to them in a visual language format. And I have a series of 'whoa' moments when I do this."

(Continues on next page)

with visuals, humor, focused statements, and brisk pacing.

AUDIENCE
Brown's audience is made up of information geeks, designers, writers, and doodle enthusiasts who appreciate irony, comedy, comics, and pop culture.

RHETORICAL APPEALS
Brown builds ethos as a creator of doodles and expert on visual thinking. As a professional, scholar, and coauthor. . . .

MODES & MEDIA
Mode = audio and visual
Medium = face-to-face and video

"I have a significantly high level of comprehension of the information that I doodle. I also have increased attention and recall of that content, weeks and months later, and I can easily immerse myself back into it. Additionally, I've noticed that when I do strategic doodling, I have increased creativity and I can make solutions to problems that are even surprising to me. And finally, my listening skills are like, ninja-like. I can discern immediately what's relevant and what's not relevant."

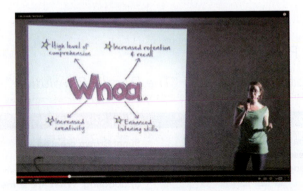

Note from editors: This marks the end of the excerpt of Brown's presentation. For the full version of her talk, see Chapter 9, "Public Genres," pages 207–12.

Credit: Sunni Brown, Infodoodler-in-Chief, Author and Leader of the Doodle Revolution.

- Provide supporting examples.

STYLE
- Smart use of detail. Brown offers just enough. . . .
- Good delivery technique. Throughout her talk, Brown faces the audience. . . .
- Persuasive, friendly voice and tone. . . .

DESIGN
Brown does not use traditional slides with text; rather, she. . . .

SOURCES
Brown's sources are her own experience and background, and information that she's gathered. . . .

Another purpose for public genres is activism. When considering the concept of genres used for activism, perhaps you first think of protests—people carrying signs with their messages. Maybe you think about famous speeches, such as Martin Luther King Jr.'s 1963 "I Have a Dream" speech delivered at the National March on Washington. Have you ever received a phone call from an organization encouraging you to vote a particular way? Perhaps you've been greeted on the street by a person with a clipboard, asking you to sign your name to bring a particular issue to the ballot. All of these situations involve genres used to effect change.

The purpose of composing a genre for activism is usually to encourage change or action. For example, if you posted a tweet after the November 2015 terrorist bombing in Paris and used the hashtag #PrayForParis, your purpose might be to literally have people take a moment to pray for the survivors of the attack. Sometimes it is to bring an issue into focus. For example, you might decide to hold up a sign at a rally for raising the minimum wage that says, "How about a maximum wage?" Here you would want your viewer to understand that you are concerned about the 1 percent having too much wealth.

The audience for these genres is similar to those we discussed under "Public Genres." If you are standing at a rally, you might not know all the people who end up viewing your sign. While most of the viewers are others who share a similar opinion since they are attending the same rally, people who do not agree with you might also see your sign (such as when there are counterprotests across the street). You might also be captured on the news, and then anyone who turns on that night's news sees you and your message. You might also hope that voters or lawmakers will hear about the rally, perhaps on TV or the Internet, and see your sign.

With the rise in social media use and the proliferation of digital devices, participatory or citizen journalism has become a major player when it comes to activism and change. Basically, this means that a public citizen, you, distributes news to an audience. Most often, these acts of individual journalism are designed to highlight an injustice, such as when acts of brutality are videotaped, or to illustrate to a wide audience an event going on, such as the Occupy protests.

Some typical genres for activism and change are similar to those for public audiences, such as posts on social media sites (Facebook, Twitter, Instagram) and blog postings. In addition, genres such as political speeches, protest signs, and petitions are commonly used to call for an action. Although flash mobs were originally created for entertainment, such as when a group of people gather in an airport and break into dance and song to entertain bored travelers, they can also be designed to effect change. In 2009, an invitation for a flash mob to protest Wall Street read, "Bring a pillow to Wall St. & Broad St. at 3:00 pm. Dress in business suits, demand your bailout."

An annotated example of a protest poster is on the next page.

WRITE

Make a list of all the genres you can think of in which you've seen appeals for public action, such as Twitter, Facebook, and signs. Which ones are you most likely to notice? Which ones have you used for composing messages geared toward social activism and change?

Guided Reading | Poster

Norma Jean Gargasz, *Give Bees a Chance*

RHETORICAL SITUATION & CHOICES	GENRE CONVENTIONS

PURPOSE
The composer of this protest sign likely wants to show support for restricting or labeling genetically modified foods.

AUDIENCE
The composer of this protest sign probably has multiple audiences. One is the public who will see the sign and perhaps be persuaded to share the same position. Another is voters or lawmakers who will vote on ballot measures or legislation regarding genetically modified foods.

RHETORICAL APPEALS
The protester's sign appeals to the viewer's sense of pathos. "Give bees a chance" implies that there are environmentally hazardous things in our food that we may not know about.

MODES & MEDIA
Mode = text + art: The sign's composer has chosen to convey the message with text and a visual only at the top, which allows for very large letters on the sign so the words are easily read from a distance.

Media = print: Protest signs must be print because a digital sign would require the protester to carry an open laptop or tablet, which is not practical and would be hard for anyone to view.

◄ **What is the composer of the poster, doing, rhetorically speaking?**

Credit: Norma Jean Gargasz/Alamy Stock Photo.

What are some conventions of the protest poster, as a genre? To what extent does the poster adhere to those conventions? ►

ELEMENTS OF THE GENRE
A short, direct message: You can read the entire text in just a moment and know immediately which side of the issue the protester is on.

Homemade: The sign is clearly made by a person with magic markers rather than by a professional sign maker.

Easy to read from a distance: The letters are very large and take up most of the space on the sign.

STYLE
Because composers of protest signs need to convey their messages quickly, they often write in phrases or pithy sentences. If they can introduce cleverness into the sayings on their signs, viewers may remember them better. In the case of this sign, the slogan is a reference to the Plastic Ono Band's famous 1969 song "Give Peace a Chance."

DESIGN
Because protest signs must be easily read from a distance, composers of protest signs usually keep design very simple so there are minimum distractions from their message. Color is usually high-contrast, again to help with readability.

SOURCES
Protest signs may refer to statistics or facts that quickly convey their message. For example, a sign about fracking could cite a statistic on levels of contamination in water in areas where fracking takes place.

Using Genres to Inform, Narrate, or Persuade

Whether you're writing an academic genre, a workplace genre, or a genre for public audiences, you often need to decide how to make your points. Authors often make their points by giving information, telling stories, and/or persuading.

INFORMING

Purpose: Why share information?

Audience: How do we inform others?

Rhetorical appeals: How do we use them to inform?

TELLING STORIES

Purpose: Why tell stories?

Audience: How do we connect through stories?

Rhetorical appeals: How do we use them to tell stories?

PERSUADING

Purpose: Why write to persuade?

Audience: How do we persuade others?

Rhetorical appeals: How do we use them to persuade?

Giving Information

Information is everywhere, all the time: online, on your phone, in e-mail, on social networking sites, on TV, and on radio. It's on billboards, road signs, and menus. But not all information is equal: some is reliable; some is not. How do we make sense of it all? The trick is to (1) figure out which sources of information are the best, and (2) analyze, use, and share that information according to your needs as a reader or writer.

In daily life, you draw on a variety of sources for information.

- You want to plant tomatoes on your back porch, so you consult a reference book or online guide by the American Horticultural Society on varieties that grow best in your region.

- You want to avoid the flu, so you read the U.S. Department of Health and Human Services' latest recommendations online or stop in at your pharmacy for information about the flu vaccine.

- You need to create a presentation using software you don't know how to use, so you refer to a Microsoft PowerPoint tutorial or ask an experienced colleague for a quick lesson.

- There's something wrong with your car and you don't know what the flashing light on your dashboard means, so you flip through your owner's manual, search YouTube for tutorials, or call a knowledgeable mechanic.

In each of these cases, you've found convenient but also authoritative sources.

- *Authoritative sources of information.* Here's another scenario. Let's say you want to prepare for a disaster. You do a quick search on YouTube and turn up a video by a guy in a gas mask who lives in a desert bunker. His instructions seem to have some merit but overall are rambling and confusing. Though the video may be riveting, it is a poor source of information because the author lacks credibility (or ethos) and logic (logos). A better, if less colorful, source would be a government organization such as Homeland Security, FEMA (Federal Emergency Management Agency), or the American Red Cross. These are considered excellent sources because the organizations are long established and made up of experts. The material they publish is researched, written, and reviewed by authorities in the field of emergency preparation; approved by the government; and tested out in actual emergencies.

- *Author bias.* No author is purely objective. Personal viewpoints, inclinations, and prejudices can creep into any communication, whether it's a recipe or a government document. Bias can show up in the language that writers use. Bias can also be apparent in the writer's tone. For example, imagine that an article appears in your local newspaper about a family lost during a snowmobiling trip. You might expect the reporter to simply present the facts. However, after reading closely, you see the reporter's opinion has subtly found its way onto the page: The family's lack of preparation influenced the writer and affected his or her tone and the use or omission of details. On the other hand, imagine that the reporter thinks the family did the best they could have—they were as prepared as possible, but no one could have survived that avalanche. In that case, the writer would use a more sympathetic tone.

Presenting information is not a neutral activity. All writing has a persuasive quality, and informative writing is no exception. Keep this in mind as you read and compose.

Purpose: Why share information?   When we write with a primary purpose to inform, we share facts and details with our readers. One type of informative writing is instructions. If you've ever purchased a piece of furniture that required assembly, you've probably worked with a set of instructions. The instructions were likely designed by an engineer or technical writer with two goals: (1) to help you put together parts of an object, and (2) to persuade and assure you, through simple images and language, that the task will be easy.

Another example of informative writing is a brochure. You've probably seen these at your doctor's or dentist's office—brochures about how to control asthma or whiten your teeth. Consider the teeth whitening brochure: It may provide facts about various methods; however, it might also offer reasons for whitening, pricing information, and a photo of an attractive model with sparkling-white teeth. Is the material in the brochure presented only to inform, or is there another motive at work? Could the brochure creators also be trying to convince you to whiten your teeth?

When you read informative pieces, notice what else is going on. An author of a scientific report, for example, may present facts, but as a way to influence you to share an opinion or take an action.

Audience: How do we inform others? As writers, we need to know our audiences—who they are and what they want. For example, in Thibault's memo in Chapter 8, she included specific information that her assistant would need to accomplish the tasks. Additionally, she numbers the tasks so that her assistant knows what needs to happen first. Thibault uses very precise language and only includes pertinent information for her audience.

Rhetorical appeals: How do we use them to inform? When we write to inform, how do we get our audiences invested? Whether you're composing a research paper, fact sheet, or flowchart, you will use rhetorical appeals: ethos, logos, and pathos.

- *Ethos*—how you, as an author, are perceived by your audience—is extremely important when informing. That's why it's essential to draw on reliable sources of information in your research and to convey that knowledge with authority and as neutrally as possible. If your audience thinks you are unreliable, or that you have some unstated motive, you will not have established your ethos.
- *Logos*—or your use of logic as an author—is also significant. "How to" or instructional genres, such as recipes, make heavy use of logos. When cooks create recipes, they direct the reader in what to do, in a specific order. Chopping ingredients, mixing them, and cooking them must be presented to readers as logical steps.
- *Pathos*—your appeal to your readers' emotions—is generally not a priority when you're writing to inform. On the other hand, if you want to inform but also persuade your readers, you can appeal to their emotions by using humor, for example. Generally humor is appropriate for less formal informational genres, but you also have to consider your specific purposes and audiences.

Telling Stories

Constructing narratives is a universal impulse; stories help us make sense of our lives and connect with others. Regardless of the specific genres our stories take—and whether they're fact or fiction, comedies or tragedies, or something in between—they generally include real people or made-up characters, a setting, a conflict, and action.

In your composition course, you may be asked to write a literacy narrative: a story about how you learned to read and write. But there are other, less formal ways to share stories. For example, even a single page from a photo album or scrapbook suggests part of the story of someone's life.

An obituary is another narrative genre that tells a story. Writers of obituaries—sometimes the deceased himself or herself (some people write them well in advance), sometimes a friend or family member—tell the story of the deceased through key biographical details. A related genre, the eulogy, is a speech delivered at the funeral or memorial, usually written by friends or family members. Through eulogies, writers share stories about the deceased's life, character, and accomplishments. Even an epitaph, the inscription on a gravestone, can tell a story about a life.

Purpose: Why tell stories?   As we worked on this book, we always began our sessions with an exchange of stories about what happened during the course of the day. Our students do this before class, talking about what happened in other classes or at their jobs. Stories help us reconnect with others.

Stories also help us chronicle events. A story can be true, such as a factual news report or an autobiography, or it can be made up, such as a short story, novel, or other work of fiction. Some stories change history, such as the *Narrative of the Life of Frederick Douglass, an American Slave, Written by Himself*. Douglass's autobiography, which he published in 1845 while living in the North as an escaped slave, helped spark the abolitionist movement in the United States.

Stories also entertain and instruct us. For example, while most well-known fairy tales make for interesting reading, they were actually created to teach children some kind of lesson. Stories can also serve to persuade others. For example, in a job interview, you might tell relevant stories about your previous experience that show you're qualified for the position you're discussing.

Audience: How do we connect through stories?   We write stories in order to explore our experiences and share them with others. For a story to resonate, readers must be able to connect with it personally. As writers, we strive for ways to make that happen. For example, in his memoir, *Dreams from My Father*, Barack Obama shares his experiences growing up as a black American and the struggles he faced as he traced his origins, something many readers can relate to. He tells his story through a series of anecdotes that read like a conversation, beginning with how he heard of his father's death. By beginning with such a universal situation and using an informal tone, Obama gets readers invested in his story.

Rhetorical appeals: How do we use them to tell stories?   Whether your favorite narrative genre is the Facebook status line or the memoir, you'll be most effective if you tap into the rhetorical appeals: ethos, logos, and pathos.

- *Ethos*—how you, as an author or composer, are perceived by your audience—is crucial when you tell a story. For example, if you write an autobiography, deliver a eulogy, or share an oral history, your readers and listeners assume that what you are telling them is true, that the stories have actually taken place. If you create a photo essay, your viewers assume that you have accurately depicted real events. If you create a work of fiction, your ethos as an author is also important. Readers want to trust that you're going to tell them an interesting, worthwhile story, perhaps with a solid, interesting plot and relatable characters they can care about.

- *Logos*—the logic you use as an author or composer—is also significant when you tell a story. For example, a short story, even if it is not told chronologically, usually follows a pattern in which the plot and characters unfold in a logical manner to the reader.
- *Pathos*—your appeal to readers' emotions—can go a long way in connecting readers with your story. For example, when you write a memoir, you identify a moment in your life that has emotional significance and convey it in a way that gets readers to identify emotionally with that experience.

Persuading

Open your Web browser, page through any magazine, scroll through Facebook, or take a walk to the coffee shop, and you will be barraged by texts and media created to persuade you—to think something, do something, like something, or buy something.

Online, advertisers individualize their messages to you. For example, when you log on to Amazon.com, you are greeted with a list of recommendations based on your previous purchases. On Facebook, the ads on your page are generated according to your likes and dislikes, as well as other information you provide in your profile and posts.

While advertising is probably the most pervasive attempt at influence, there are many other kinds of texts that we create at school, in the workplace, or for public audiences to convince others to see things our way. In fact, you could argue that almost every communication—a text message to a friend about what movie to see, a posting of a cute kitten or puppy, a dating profile, an editorial on Fox News, a joke made on *The Simpsons* about Fox News editorials, or even a chapter in a textbook—has persuasive elements built into it.

Purpose: Why write to persuade?   When we write to persuade, we do so because we want to convince our readers to do something—usually to agree with us about a topic, issue, or idea or to take a specific action. As a student, when you write a paper in which you take a stance on an issue or you give a speech in which you ask your audience to do something, you are writing to persuade. As a professional, when you apply for a job, you craft a resume and cover letter and make a convincing case for yourself during your interview to persuade the person hiring that you are the best candidate. A persuasive text can also be as simple as a six-word slogan.

Audience: How do we persuade others?   As citizens of a democracy, we may read persuasive texts such as editorials to help us figure out our own positions on specific issues. As a writer, anytime you want to persuade your audience, you need to lay out your ideas, anticipate possible objections, and support your argument with relevant information. As with informing (see p. 83 of this chapter), accuracy is important when persuading others. Backing up your ideas and claims with correct information, gathered from reliable sources, will make your argument stronger.

Rhetorical appeals: How do we use them to persuade?   Whether you want to convince others to agree with you on an important issue, to date you, to vote for your candidate, or to buy your product, you will be most persuasive if you relate to your audience through the rhetorical appeals—ethos, logos, and pathos.

- *Ethos*—the authority and trustworthiness that you establish as a writer, composer, or speaker—is crucial when you want to persuade others. If your boss asks you to review several possible locations for an important fund-raising event and recommend one, you will want to establish yourself as dedicated to getting a high-quality venue for a reasonable price. To do this, you'll need to demonstrate that you've taken the assignment seriously, studied the options objectively, and weighed your company's needs and priorities carefully.

- *Logos*—the logical chain of reasoning that you provide for readers—is extremely important when you are making any kind of argument. Imagine you are taking a car for a test drive to decide whether you will buy it. You might mention to the salesperson that you are interested in a car that won't be too bad for the environment. The salesperson might then present you with some facts about the mileage the car gets, the measures the manufacturer has taken at the factory to protect the environment, and the paper-free policy the dealership has initiated by conducting as much business as possible electronically. By talking about these factors, the salesperson is creating a chain of reasoning that—she hopes—will lead you to conclude that the car you are driving is an environmentally responsible choice.

- *Pathos*—the appeal that you use when you want to evoke your readers' emotions—comes in handy when you are trying to persuade someone to do something. An appeal to pathos connects you with your audience, and vice versa. For example, when a salesperson asks you about yourself and then tells you a bit about himself and you find some commonalities, that salesperson is appealing to your pathos. When he later tells you that he loves the stereo you are looking at, you're more likely to buy it because you've already identified with him.

As you compose, keep the following questions in mind.

RHETORICAL SITUATION & CHOICES

☐ **Purpose.** What is the purpose of this piece of writing? Is it to demonstrate what I've learned? To respond to a need that someone has? To argue for a position on a controversial issue? Or something else?

☐ **Audience.** Who am I composing for? What is their purpose in reading? Does my audience go beyond the classroom? If I'm composing in the workplace, is my audience internal or external? Do I need to consider a secondary audience or audiences that I may not have intended (for example, if your tweet is retweeted)?

☐ **Rhetorical appeals.** Considering who my audience is, what will I need to do to establish my credibility? To what degree will following established conventions help my credibility? If my purpose is to effect change, how can I use pathos to engage my audience? If I'm trying to persuade my audience to take action or make a particular decision, how can I use logos to emphasize the logic of my position?

☐ **Modes & media.** What limitations does my rhetorical situation impose, such as assignment specifications or workplace expectations? Will my audience want something digital or a hard copy? What medium will my primary audience respond to best?

GENRE CONVENTIONS

☐ **Elements of the genre.** Am I using the conventions of the genre appropriately? Do I need to look at more examples of the genre? Am I taking the assignment or audience expectations into account?

☐ **Style.** Have I used a tone that is appropriate for genre and will achieve my purpose with my audience? What point of view (1st person, 2nd person, 3rd person) will help me achieve my purpose? Have I chosen my words carefully? Have I received any additional instructions about style that I need to take into account?

☐ **Design.** How have I used design elements to direct my audience's attention? Have I designed my piece according to the design conventions of the genre? For example, if I'm creating a protest poster, can it be read quickly from a distance?

☐ **Sources.** Are the experiences and evidence that I draw on appropriate for my genre? Have I cited them according to the genre's conventions? Is there additional experience or evidence that I need to incorporate to achieve my purpose? Are the sources I've used appropriate for an academic, workplace, or public setting?

PRACTICE

Connecting Genres with Social Settings

Look at the list of genres on the book cover. Which ones do you think occur mostly in academic settings? How about workplace settings? Which would you consider to be public genres? Which seem to fit into two or three categories?

Create a chart, diagram, or other infographic that conveys your categorization of the genres, including the ones that span multiple genres.

6

THE AUTHOR'S/ARTIST'S STATEMENT:
A GENRE FOR REFLECTION

BRIEF CONTENTS

Explaining the rationale behind our actions and decisions is an important kind of reflective writing because it makes visible what is otherwise invisible. Amy can see that Elizabeth may have chosen to write an e-mail in Comic Sans font, but unless Elizabeth explains why, the choice may seem mysterious and odd to Amy. Composers and artists of all sorts often write a statement for their audience that explains their inspirations, intentions, and choices in their creative and critical processes. The liner notes that come with a CD, the program you receive at the theater or symphony, the Director's Statement on a DVD, the Artist's Statement pinned to the wall at an art gallery—these are all forms of Authors' or Artists' Statements. We write explanations of our decisions to support many academic, workplace, and public genres. Below, we discuss an academic example and an example from a public setting; a workplace example might be a self-review or part of an organization's annual report.

On page 92, there is an example of a reflective statement written by a chef for the magazine *Cook's Illustrated*. The point of the discussion—or what you could call an Author's Statement, as the chef is the author of the recipe he is explaining—is to explain and discuss what went into the creation of the recipe, what went well, and what could have gone better, as well as to discuss the cooking process. The Author's Statement articulates the different, otherwise invisible, choices and decisions the chef made in the creation of the recipe, from the selection of one ingredient over another to the order in which ingredients are combined and why. The Author's Statement discusses not just what ended up in the final recipe but what was tried but didn't work, and why it didn't work. In this way, the statement helps readers understand the invisible logic behind the finished product, the recipe.

WRITE

What are some examples of Authors'/Artists' Statements that you've seen lately? How does understanding a composer's perspective and intent contribute to how you relate to the composer's work? Write a quick list of movie scenes, lyrics, art pieces, and other creative works you've understood differently once you read or heard about the composer's rationale.

You may wonder why a cook would go to all this trouble—to not just develop a recipe but then to put energy into articulating in writing the process of developing the recipe. The rhetorical situation of writing for *Cook's Illustrated* is that readers are not your typical home cooks who just want to get a meal on the table fast. *Cook's Illustrated* readers are serious foodies who don't mind spending hours on a recipe and they want to understand every decision the chef made so they can learn from the chef's mistakes or maybe even use the recipe as inspiration for their own creation.

In the following discussion of the recipe for Thai Grilled-Beef Salad, recipe writer Andrew Janjigian explains what his goals were and the thought processes behind the decisions he

▲ CHEF PHOTO

Andrew Janjigian.
Credit: America's Test Kitchen.

made as he tinkered with the recipe. Janjigian is an associate editor for *Cook's Illustrated* and also works for *America's Test Kitchen*.

An Author's/Artist's Statement helps the reader understand the process that led to the product. If you've watched a DVD recently, you may have found a Director's Statement included along with the feature film or documentary. In this statement, the director—or an actor, choreographer, or other person associated with the film—talks

---

Thai Grilled-Beef Salad

Our goal was to look no further than the supermarket to replicate this salad's complex range of flavors and textures. Along the way, we learned a neat trick for grilling meat.

⇒ BY ANDREW JANJIGIAN ⇐

In winter when I crave Thai food, it's often a rich, coconut milk–based curry or a wok-charred noodle dish. But in the summer months, I'm more tempted by the country's famous salads, particularly the grilled-beef rendition known as *nam tok*. Served warm or at room temperature, this preparation features slices of deeply charred steak tossed with thinly sliced shallots and handfuls of torn mint and cilantro in a bright, bracing dressing. In the best versions, the cuisine's five signature flavor elements—hot, sour, salty, sweet, and bitter—come into balance, making for a light but satisfying dish that's traditionally served with steamed jasmine rice.

I paged through the test kitchen's stack of Thai cookbooks for some nam tok recipes to try and was pleased to find that both the shopping list and the cooking time—about half an hour from start to finish—were very manageable. The most unusual ingredient was toasted rice powder, which I knew would be easy enough to make at home. Still, the salads that I produced in the test kitchen, while not bad, fell short of the versions that I've eaten in good Thai restaurants. Either the dressing's flavors were unbalanced—too sweet, too salty, too sour—or the beef itself didn't boast enough char to give the salad its hallmark smoky, faintly bitter edge. Clearly, I had some tinkering to do.

High-Steaks Decisions

The obvious place to start my testing was with the beef. Surprisingly, the recipes that I consulted were all over the map. Some specified lean cuts like tenderloin, others more marbled choices like skirt

A scoop of rice turns this steak salad into a meal.

steak or New York strip steak. A few recipes called for marinating the meat before grilling; others suggested simply seasoning it with salt and white pepper (a staple ingredient in Thai cuisine). Most of them didn't even specify a grilling method. As a starting point, I built a standard single-level fire—a full chimney's worth of coals spread in an even layer over the kettle—and seared a variety of beef cuts: New York

strip steak, boneless short ribs, tenderloin, and flank steak, each one sprinkled with salt and white pepper. Once each piece had developed a thick, dark crust, I pulled it off the fire, let it rest briefly (to allow the interior juices to be reabsorbed), cut thin slices, and tossed them in a standard dressing of equal parts fresh lime juice and fish sauce, a little sugar, and a thinly sliced Thai chile.

Just as I had expected, the more marbled pieces of beef fared better than the lean tenderloin, which started out woefully bland and ended up overcooked by the time it developed even the barest crust. Flavorwise, any of these fattier cuts would have been a fine choice, but two came with a caveat. Boneless short ribs vary in quality: Some are evenly marbled and ideally shaped, almost like small strip steaks, while others are misshapen and full of interior fat and connective tissue that requires trimming. Meanwhile, New York strip steaks boast good flavor and pleasantly tender chew but don't come cheap. I settled on flank steak. The uniformly shaped, moderately priced slab was also beefy, juicy, and sliced neatly.

Next decision: whether or not to marinate the meat in a mixture of the dressing ingredients. A quick side-by-side test made my decision easy. Since moisture thwarts browning, the crust on the marinated flank steak was markedly thin and pale compared with that on the nonmarinated sample. Besides, once the slices of grilled steak were tossed with the dressing, they were plenty flavorful.

Five Tastes of Thai Grilled-Beef Salad—and One More

One of the keys to this salad is balancing the signature flavor elements of Thai cuisine. In addition to achieving this, we added one more complementary flavor: the earthiness of toasted cayenne and sweet paprika.

HOT	SOUR	SALTY	SWEET	BITTER	EARTHY
A fresh Thai bird chile creates bright, fruity heat in the dressing.	A generous 3 tablespoons of fresh lime juice adds bracing acidity.	Derived from salted, fermented fish, pungent fish sauce acts as a rich flavor enhancer.	A half teaspoon of sugar tames the dressing's salty-sour flavors without becoming cloying.	Thoroughly charred steak adds both a pleasing textural contrast and a subtle bitter edge.	Though nontraditional, ground cayenne and sweet paprika add earthy flavor without too much heat.

COOK'S ILLUSTRATED
12

▲ **AUTHOR'S STATEMENT**

about the considerations that went into making the film, such as casting, lighting, music, and blocking. The Director's Statement, like an Author's Statement, makes visible, to some extent, the behind-the-scenes work that is invisible in the final product.

When our students create assignments—whatever genre or media they create in—we ask them to write an accompanying Author's/Artist's Statement that can give us insight into what they set out to do, how they did it, and what they might do to further improve the piece.

Falling Water

With the cut of meat decided, I could now focus my attention on the grilling method. The single-level fire had produced decently charred results, but for this salad, the contrast of a crisp, smoky, faintly bitter crust and a juicy center was a must, and I knew I could do better. To get a true blaze going, I turned to the test kitchen's favorite high-heat grill method: a modified two-level fire, in which all the coals are concentrated in an even layer over half of the grill. This way, the meat's exterior would caramelize almost on contact and would cook more rapidly, ensuring that the interior would stay medium-rare.

The recipes that I consulted may have been vague about the fire setup, but they did offer one grilling pointer: As the steak cooks, beads of moisture will appear on its surface—an indication that the meat is ready to be flipped. In fact, the dish is named for this visual cue; "nam tok" translates as "water falling." Grateful for the cue, I flipped the meat as soon as beads of moisture showed up, let it sear another five minutes on the second side, and pulled it off the grill. To my delight, this steak was not only perfectly charred on the exterior, but also spot-on medium-rare within. (For more information on the topic, see "Unbeadable Thai Trick: Knowing When to Flip.")

Well Dressed

With perfectly grilled and subtly, satisfyingly bitter meat in hand, I moved back indoors to address the other four flavor elements: hot, sour, salty, and sweet. Everyone agreed that my initial dressing needed some tweaking—a bit more sweetness, a more balanced (and less heady) salty-sour punch, and more complex heat. The first two requests were easy to fix: I quickly landed on a 2:3 ratio of fish sauce to lime juice, plus ½ teaspoon of sugar and 2 tablespoons of water to tone it all down a touch. But the chile situation required a bit more attention. A fresh chile was a given, and I'd been using a Thai bird chile; when sliced thin and tossed with the other vegetable components, it adds a fruity, fiery blaze to each bite. So why did something still seem to be missing? I found the answer in a recipe from Thai cuisine guru David Thompson: His grilled-beef salad calls for not only fresh Thai bird chile, but also a toasted powder made from the dried pods.

Hoping that regular old cayenne powder toasted in a skillet would suffice, I compared its effects on the salad with that of a powder made with ground, toasted chiles following Thompson's instructions. The consensus was unanimous: The powder made from the dried Thai bird chiles added a deeper, earthier complexity than the hotter, more one-dimensional cayenne. Just ½ teaspoon of cayenne, in fact, overpowered the meat's smoky char. I was about to resign myself to the extra step of grinding my own powder when I spied a jar of sweet paprika in the spice cabinet. Could this give me the earthy, fruity red pepper flavor that was missing from the cayenne? As it turned out, a 50-50 mix of cayenne

and paprika did the trick. I added just a dash of the toasted spice mixture to the dressing and put the rest aside as a seasoning for those who wanted to kick up the heat another notch.

The other condiment that I had to address was the *kao kua*, or toasted rice powder. These days most Thai recipes call for the commercially made product, but it can be hard to find. It was simple enough to make my own by toasting rice in a dry skillet and pulverizing it in a spice grinder. Tossing half of the powder with the salad components gave the dressing fuller body, while sprinkling on the rest at the table added faint but satisfying crunch.

As for the vegetable components, it was really a matter of personal taste. Some salads called for incorporating only the requisite sliced shallots and torn mint leaves and cilantro, while others required adding green beans, cabbage, cucumbers, and lettuce. My tasters and I agreed that any accoutrements should complement—not compete with—the grilled beef. We settled on just one extra: a thin-sliced cucumber, which contributed a cool crispness to this nicely balanced, complexly flavored Thai classic.

THAI GRILLED-BEEF SALAD
SERVES 4 TO 6

Serve with steamed jasmine rice, if desired, although any style of white rice can be used. Don't skip the toasted rice; it's integral to the texture and flavor of the dish. If a fresh Thai chile is unavailable, substitute half of a serrano chile.

- 1 teaspoon sweet paprika
- 1 teaspoon cayenne pepper
- 1 tablespoon white rice
- 3 tablespoons lime juice (2 limes)
- 2 tablespoons fish sauce
- 2 tablespoons water
- ½ teaspoon sugar
- 1 (1½-pound) flank steak, trimmed
  Salt and white pepper, coarsely ground
- 4 shallots, sliced thin
- 1½ cups fresh mint leaves, torn
- 1½ cups fresh cilantro leaves
- 1 Thai chile, stemmed and sliced thin into rounds
- 1 seedless English cucumber, sliced ¼ inch thick on bias

1. Heat paprika and cayenne in 8-inch skillet over medium heat; cook, shaking pan, until fragrant, about 1 minute. Transfer to small bowl. Return now-empty skillet to medium-high heat, add rice, and toast, stirring frequently, until deep golden brown, about 5 minutes. Transfer to second small bowl and cool for 5 minutes. Grind rice with spice grinder, mini food processor, or mortar and pestle until it resembles fine meal, 10 to 30 seconds (you should have about 1 tablespoon rice powder).

2. Whisk lime juice, fish sauce, water, sugar, and ¼ teaspoon toasted paprika mixture in large bowl and set aside.

Unbeadable Thai Trick: Knowing When to Flip

This salad's Thai name, *nam tok* (literally "water falling"), refers to the beads of moisture that form on the surface of the steak as it cooks—an age-old Thai cookery clue that the meat is ready to be flipped. While this method sounded imprecise, during testing I found it to be a surprisingly accurate gauge of when the flank steak is halfway done. Here's why: As this steak's interior gets hotter, its tightly packed fibers contract and release some of their interior moisture, which the fire's heat then pushes to the meat's surface. When turned at this point and cooked for an equal amount of time on the second side, the steak emerged deeply charred on the outside and medium-rare within. (Note: We do not recommend this technique across the board for steaks; since the thickness and density of the meat fibers vary from cut to cut, the time it takes for heat to penetrate and for beads of moisture to be pushed to the meat's surface differs.) –A.J.

TIME TO FLIP
For perfectly cooked meat, flip the steak when beads of moisture appear on its surface.

3A. FOR A CHARCOAL GRILL: Open bottom vent completely. Light large chimney starter filled with charcoal briquettes (6 quarts). When top coals are partially covered with ash, pour evenly over half of grill. Set cooking grate in place, cover, and open lid vent completely. Heat grill until hot, about 5 minutes.

3B. FOR A GAS GRILL: Turn all burners to high, cover, and heat grill until hot, about 15 minutes. Leave primary burner on high and turn off other burner(s).

4. Clean and oil cooking grate. Season steak with salt and white pepper. Place steak over hot part of grill and cook until beginning to char and beads of moisture appear on outer edges of meat, 5 to 6 minutes. Flip steak and continue to cook on second side until charred and center registers 125 degrees, about 5 minutes longer. Transfer to plate, tent loosely with aluminum foil, and let rest for 5 to 10 minutes (or allow to cool to room temperature, about 1 hour).

5. Slice meat, against grain, on bias into ¼-inch-thick slices. Transfer sliced steak to bowl with fish sauce mixture. Add shallots, mint, cilantro, chile, and half of rice powder; toss to combine. Transfer to platter lined with cucumber slices. Serve, passing remaining rice powder and toasted paprika mixture separately.

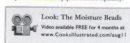

Look: The Moisture Beads
Video available FREE for 4 months at
www.CooksIllustrated.com/aug11

▲ **RECIPE**

Andrew Janjigian. In his article "Thai Grilled-Beef Salad," from *Cook's Illustrated*, July/August 2011, the chef reflects on one of his creations.
Credit: America's Test Kitchen.

Analyzing Authors'/Artists' Statements

Purpose

The purpose of an Author's/Artist's Statement is for an author (or artist or other composer) to discuss the decisions and choices he or she made in composing a specific text or other work. Let's say you've created an ad or a documentary film for your course. By writing an accompanying Author's/Artist's Statement, you can persuade your readers to see your finished piece in a particular way. A successful Statement reflects your understanding of your chosen genre (and the elements, style, design, and use of sources that characterize it)—and of your specific rhetorical situation (your reasons for composing, your audience, how you use rhetorical appeals, and your choice of mode and medium).

If you're writing an Author's Statement in an academic setting, your main purpose is to inform and persuade readers—your peers, your instructor, your audience—of the critical and creative thought you put into your composition. For example, Michael Kipp explains on p. 99 that he "used striking contrast and positioned the objects in ways the viewers would not expect, thus drawing attention to them." Knowing that the "striking contrast" in the collage is deliberate and not merely a happy accident helps the reader understand the thought process that went into arranging the images.

Audience

The audience for an Author's/Artist's Statement is usually a particularly engaged and interested reader or viewer. In an academic setting, your audience is made up of invested and critical readers and viewers, such as your professor and peers, who want to confirm that you've made deliberate choices throughout your composing process. In Kipp's statement, available in his full project on LaunchPad for *The Bedford Book of Genres*, he notes his audience as "those who want to be happier and . . . are open to developing a different mindset."

Rhetorical Appeals

In an Author's/Artist's Statement, writers persuade readers by appealing mainly to logos and ethos.

- *Ethos* The author's credibility (ethos) is particularly important because, as with most persuasive pieces, the writer needs to come across as honest and thoughtful.
- *Logos* Authors can establish ethos through the reasoning (logos) they present in their Authors' Statements. When writers logically present evidence to readers about the choices they made in organizing and presenting their work, readers are more likely to accept the claims they make.
- *Pathos* To persuade, composers may sometimes appeal to their audience's emotions. For example, if a composer wrote a piece of music as a memorial and wanted it performed a certain way, that message would appear in the program.

Modes & Media

Authors choose modes and media for their Statements that are appropriate for those of the work they're discussing. An artist showing work online would probably create a digital Artist's Statement, whereas an artist showing work in a brick-and-mortar gallery would probably print out a text-based statement to hang next to his or her masterpieces.

Elements of the Genre

In their Authors'/Artists' Statements, writers do the following:

- *Discuss a specific composition and make an argument.* In an Author's/Artist's Statement, writers discuss a particular composition—such as an essay, painting, photo, documentary, ad, or other work. They refer directly to that work and provide specific details as they explain the "what, why, and how" of their creation. For example, in the Author's Statement example from *Cook's Illustrated*, Andrew Janjigian explains that he set out to create a dressing that would successfully blend "the four Thai flavor elements: hot, sour, salty, and sweet." He then explains how he did that.

  Writers also make a case for their compositions in order to persuade readers to see their work in a particular way. For example, Andrew Janjigian wants us to see that his beef salad recipe succeeds in blending desired flavors.

- *Discuss their specific rhetorical situation and related choices.* The Author's/Artist's Statement gives you, as a composer, an opportunity to explain to audiences:

  - » **Your purpose:** why you composed the work on that specific topic, in that specific way

  - » **Your audience and use of rhetorical appeals:** what you understand about your readers and how you connected with them through choices regarding ethos, pathos, and logos

  - » **Your mode and medium:** why you chose them and how they benefit your work overall

  For example, if you created a collage—perhaps on the topic of body art and identity—in your Artist's Statement, you could explain to viewers:

  - » Your purpose or main point in creating a collage on the relationship between body art and identity—and what the relationship is

  - » Why you chose specific central images, how they contribute to your message, and how you hope your viewers will read them and relate to the overall collage

  - » How you wanted to connect with your viewers through pathos, logos, and ethos (for example, your arrangement of images might appeal to their logic or emotions)

  - » Why you decided to create the collage, say, in a digital format

- *Answer the question "why."* Readers of Author's or Artist's Statements want to understand all the thinking that went into the creation of the final product. While that thinking is obvious to you, it is invisible to readers. The point of the Author's or Artist's Statements is to make it visible, and that can only be done by providing many specific details about the "why" of decisions that were made. If you write "I decided to create an advertisement," you should follow it up with an explanation of why you decided to create an advertisement.

- *Address readers directly.* Writers use the "I" construction, which allows them to speak plainly to readers about their choices. They also refer to the works they're discussing in the Statement as "my essay" (or "my painting," "my photograph," etc.), indicating their ownership of the composition and the choices they made.

- *Explain their choice of genre and how they worked with its conventions.* The Author's/Artist's Statement is a place for a composer to explain why he or she chose to work in a particular genre. For example, let's say that for your composition course you chose to write an opinion piece on gun control. In a separate statement, submitted with your opinion piece, you might explain to your instructor and classmates why you chose this genre. Pointing out your specific choices builds your ethos and persuasiveness. You might note, for example, that the opinion piece was the best choice of genre because it allowed you to:

  » Clearly present your opinion on the topic of gun control (and write in the first person)

  » Be brief (just a few paragraphs) and lively

  » Deal with potential objections and offer potential solutions

  » Invite readers to respond

- Alternatively, maybe you created a photo essay for your class or a wider audience. An accompanying statement—in which you explain why you found the photo essay to be the best way to communicate your ideas about gun control—would go a long way toward helping your viewers get the most out of your work.

- *Reflect on their compositions, discussing successes and limitations.* Writers use Authors' Statements as an opportunity to look back at a composition and evaluate the extent of their achievement; they might also note what they would have done differently or better. For example, if you created an advertisement showing how marines achieve strength without steroids, you might note in an accompanying Author's Statement that you felt you'd succeeded in providing a captivating visual, an original slogan, and an emotional appeal. On the other hand, don't hesitate to mention places where you could improve your work editorially or technically. Doing your best, reflecting on what you did well, and talking about what you'd like to improve adds to your ethos as a composer and to the persuasiveness of your work.

- *Provide context.* In the Author's/Artist's Statement, it's useful for writers/artists to give some background on their composition, such as how they became interested in the topic, what their inspirations were, or, if they've created a series of related works, how the piece fits in with other pieces. Andrew Janjigian explains in his Author's Statement that he decided to create his own beef salad recipe because he hadn't found one that came close to achieving the quality of beef salads he'd eaten in Thai restaurants.

Style

Statement authors do the following:

- *Use detail.* The persuasive and critical nature of the Statement depends on the use of specific detail. Janjigian, for example, names particular ingredients that he tried and describes the exact result he got, such as in his discussion of what happened when he used cayenne pepper instead of powdered Thai bird chiles: "Just ½ teaspoon of cayenne, in fact, overpowered the meat's smoky char."

- *Write in a tone that builds ethos.* In their Statements, authors use critical, analytical language to make their points. They choose words related to their subject of inquiry to establish themselves as experts. When you write such a Statement, even though you're writing in the first person (I), use a serious, straightforward tone to emphasize that you have made deliberate, thoughtful choices. Kipp establishes himself as an expert on gratitude when he says "the landscape refers to the fact that grateful people experience a positive memory bias," showing that he is familiar with the research on his subject and fluent with the terms (see full text in LaunchPad).

Design

Authors'/Artists' Statements can often look like an academic essay, with indented paragraphs and little or no decoration except for subheadings that offer structure and organization. However, a writer might choose to design a Statement to reflect the genre of the composition. For example, the Statement might take the form of a letter written to a professor, a Director's Statement, or a one-page Artist's Statement.

Sources

The most persuasive authors discuss the sources that informed their composing process. For example, in his Statement, student Michael Kipp mentions specific sources by title or author's name, including page numbers. Depending on the audience, sources may be cited according to MLA or APA or other academic formats, as in Michael Kipp's Statement on page 99. An artist who is inspired by another artist usually names his or her inspiration and cites specific works by that artist.

Guided Reading | Artist's Statement

 As a student at Red Rocks Community College, Michael Kipp became interested in the concept of gratitude and happiness when he took a psychology course and studied positive psychology. In his second-semester research-based composition class, Kipp decided to focus his semester-long multigenre project on the idea of gratitude, looking at research in the field and reflecting on his own experience with feeling gratitude. His entire project is presented in LaunchPad for *The Bedford Book of Genres* (macmillanlearning.com). One of the pieces that Kipp created for the project was a collage illustrating gratitude. Accompanying the collage was his Artist's Statement, which analyzed the choices he made in creating the collage, such as design and organization, and illustrated how his collage achieved his purpose and used rhetorical appeals to persuade his audience.

▲ STUDENT AUTHOR PHOTO & COLLAGE

Michael Kipp and his composition, *Thank You*, the subject of his Artist's Statement on page 99.

Credit: Michael Kipp.

Michael Kipp, (STUDENT), *On Composing Happiness: How and Why I Created My Collage* Thank You

PURPOSE
Kipp's purpose is to persuade readers that "practicing gratitude can make us happier" and that his collage furthers that goal. He wants readers to know that he made thoughtful decisions when composing the collage.

AUDIENCE
His readers are his instructor and fellow students. They want to know why he created a collage and what research informed it.

RHETORICAL APPEALS
Kipp establishes his credibility, or ethos, in paragraph 1 by including quotes from experts to show he's done research on positive psychology. Kipp appeals to logos by explaining his choices logically.

MODES & MEDIA
Mode = written
Medium = print

◀ What is the composer, Michael Kipp, doing?

Michael Kipp created ▶ an Artist's Statement to accompany his collage. What are the conventions of the genre? To what extent does he adhere to them?

ELEMENTS OF THE GENRE
Kipp discusses a specific composition and makes an argument about it. He supports claims. Kipp addresses readers directly. Kipp talks about his rhetorical situation and specific related choices. Kipp reflects on his successes and limitations.

STYLE
Kipp uses specific details.

DESIGN
Kipp structures his statement as a traditional researched essay.

SOURCES
Kipp's sources for his statement include the collage itself and the research he conducted on gratitude. He cites his sources per MLA style.

"Psychologists have repeatedly shown that perceptions are more important than objective reality" ("Positive Thinking"). That statement embodies the message behind my collage. It ties in with messages from other research I've done on the science of happiness, including my reading of the article "Psychological Research: Gratitude," by Jerry Lopper. In that piece, Lopper quotes psychologist and researcher Dr. Alex Wood as saying: "Gratitude is a life orientation towards noticing and appreciating the positive in the world." What Wood suggests is that feeling grateful requires mental work (Emmons, *Thanks!* 6). Gratitude is a part of our perception, a "life orientation," and without effort that perception will not arise or be maintained. Thus, to have an attitude of gratefulness, we must change our outlook on life. My purpose in creating this collage is to promote the idea that we make choices about how we perceive experience, and that practicing gratitude can make us happier.

My intended audience for my collage is made up of people who like art, psychology, and philosophy, who appreciate the abstract expression of concepts, and who may be persuaded to think about how a grateful attitude could be more important than one's objective reality—and how they may practice that in their own life to be happier.

In my collage I used *pathos* to convey these ideas—I wanted to sway my viewers emotionally, to cause them to feel curious and inspired when looking at the collage. I did this through my choices of composition, colors, and subjects, which are discussed in depth below. I used striking contrast and positioned the objects in ways the viewer might not expect, thereby drawing attention to them. I also used *logos* by putting the piece together in a logical manner, and by grounding my concept in positive psychology research. Furthermore, by connecting my audience with research on the power of the perception (in para. 1), I ask viewers to think about how the collage illustrates that concept. My goal is

(Continues on next page)

that my audience will ponder what each part of the collage represents and come to logical conclusions about . . .

Note from editors: This marks the end of the excerpt of Kipp's Statement. For the full text of this paper, see LaunchPad for The Bedford Book of Genres.

———————

Works Cited

Emmons, Robert A. *Thanks! How the New Science of Gratitude Can Make You Happier*. Houghton Mifflin Harcourt, 2007. Google Books, books.google.com/books?id=tGCcH2l4jUUC.

Emmons, Robert A., and Charles M. Shelton. "Gratitude and the Science of Positive Psychology." *Handbook of Positive Psychology*, edited by C. R. Snyder and Shane J. Lopez, Oxford UP, 2002, pp. 459–71.

Lopper, Jerry. "Psychological Research: Gratitude." *Suite101*, 19 May 2008, www.suite101.com/content/psychological -research-gratitude-a54399.

Martinez-Marti, et al. "The Effects of Counting Blessings on Subjective Well-Being: A Gratitude Intervention in a Spanish Sample." *Spanish Journal of Psychology*, vol. 13, no. 2, 2010, pp. 886–96, www.ucm.es/info/psi/docs/journal/ v13_n2_2010/art886.pdf.

Pursuit of Happiness. "Positive Thinking: Optimism and Gratitude." *The Pursuit of Happiness*, www.pursuit-of -happiness.org/science-of-happiness/positive-thinking/. Accessed 26 Nov. 2012.

Rodin, Auguste. *The Thinker*. 1880–81, Cleveland Museum of Art, Cleveland. Bronze sculpture.

Tsang, Jo-Ann. "Gratitude and Prosocial Behaviour: An Experimental Test of Gratitude." *Cognition and Emotion*, vol. 20, no. 1, 2006, pp. 138–148, www.academia.edu/365898/ Gratitude_and_prosocial_behavior_An_experimental_test _of_gratitude.

Watkins, Philip C., et al. "Counting Your Blessings: Positive Memories among Grateful People." *Current Psychology*, vol. 23, no. 1, 2004, pp. 52–67. JSTOR, doi: 10.1007/S12144-004-1008-2.

RHETORICAL SITUATION & CHOICES

1. **Purpose.** How does Kipp convince you that his collage illustrates that "practicing gratitude can make us happier"?

2. **Audience.** Although the primary audience for the piece is Kipp's instructor, are there other audiences that might be interested in reading the piece? If so, who? Why?

3. **Rhetorical appeals.** One of the ways Kipp establishes his ethos is by including research. How else does he establish his ethos?

4. **Rhetorical appeals.** Why would it be inappropriate for Kipp to use pathos in an Artist's Statement? Are there any circumstances where pathos might be appropriate for an Artist's Statement? What circumstances? Why?

5. **Modes & media.** How would including visuals enhance Kipp's Artist's Statement? Where might he incorporate visuals?

GENRE CONVENTIONS

6. **Elements of the genre.** What types of evidence does Kipp use to support his claims? How effective is the evidence? Are there places where he might have included different evidence? If so, where and what?

7. **Elements of the genre.** Throughout the statement, Kipp shows how research influences his choices and motivations. Do you learn anything about Kipp's own personal motivation for exploring this subject? If so, how? If not, what would this add to the Artist's Statement?

8. **Style.** How does Kipp use language to establish his credibility?

9. **Design.** Kipp chose to submit his Artist's Statement in a traditional academic essay form. Would the piece be strengthened if he had used subheads and divided the Artist's Statement into sections? If so, what would be the different sections?

10. **Sources.** What are the different purposes the research serves in Kipp's Artist's Statement?

CHECKLIST | Drafting an Author's/Artist's Statement

Thinking of drafting an Author's/Artist's Statement? Ask yourself the following questions.

RHETORICAL SITUATION & CHOICES

☐ **Purpose.** What is the central claim I want to make about my piece? What particular elements do I need to justify? What choices did I make as I created the piece? What motivated me to create the piece?

GENRE CONVENTIONS

☐ **Elements of the genre.** What persuasive point do I want to make about my piece? How can I support that point with specific examples and details from my composition and process? Are there aspects of the context that readers should know to fully understand and appreciate my work?

RHETORICAL SITUATION & CHOICES

☐ **Audience.** Am I writing this Statement for my instructor? For fellow students? Will my Statement be read by people outside the academic setting? If so, how will this affect what I write?

☐ **Rhetorical appeals.** What makes me a credible writer on this subject? How will I show readers my credibility? How will I organize my information to support my claims?

☐ **Modes & media.** Will I present my Statement only in written form? Is it appropriate to incorporate visuals? If so, what types of visuals? How would the inclusion of audio enhance my Statement? Would it be appropriate to just use audio? Do I want to present my work in print or digital form?

GENRE CONVENTIONS

☐ **Style.** How can I use my tone to convey the seriousness with which I view my work? What details can I use to support the generalizations I make?

☐ **Design.** How will I organize my Statement? What visuals should I include? Should I use subheadings, or is my Statement short enough that subheadings aren't necessary?

☐ **Sources.** Is the piece I composed informed by source material? What inspired me? Where did I get the facts and information that I used? Will my audience expect formal citations?

PRACTICE

Reflecting on a Composition

Look at a composition that you completed earlier in the semester or for another class. It can be any kind of composition: a report, an object, a video, and so on. Reflect on the choices you made as you thought through and created the piece. Where did you put most of your energy, and why? Where did you get your ideas? What did you tinker with? Imagine that your instructor had asked you for permission to use your composition as an example for future students and wants you to write a letter to the students in which you articulate some of the more important choices you made. Then draft a brief statement in which you discuss your process and thoughts.

ACADEMIC GENRES

Researched Arguments

A researched argument is any work in which a writer presents an argument and backs it up with solid sources. Most academic research papers are researched arguments (see also the peer-reviewed journal article discussed on p. 117). Writers of researched arguments do the following:

- Investigate a topic and work with sources
- Make a specific and persuasive case about that topic
- Incorporate in their writing voices of their sources through summary, paraphrase, and quotation
- Cite those sources in the body of the composition
- List the sources at the end

The main purpose of writing a researched argument is to persuade your readers of the merits of your argument. Drawing on and citing your sources builds a case for your argument.

In academic settings, researched arguments appear in the classroom and in peer-reviewed journals. Researched arguments appear beyond academia too—in magazines, and on the Internet in the form of blog entries and other argumentative pieces. Depending on the level of research they've conducted and where they publish their work, authors of this genre may be scholars who are recognized by other scholars as experts on the subject they are writing about, or they may be reporters, bloggers, or other types of experts on their subject. For example, an experienced snowboarder who researches different snowboarding designs and blogs in favor of one would be considered an expert on the subject she's writing about.

At work, researched arguments often take the form of reports or memos. When an employee wants to persuade an organization to change a policy or procedure, he may write a memo or report in which he refers to specific research or to policies at similar organizations.

Analyzing Researched Arguments

Purpose   We write researched arguments because we want to persuade others to share our point of view on a topic. We may be looking for readers to simply agree, or maybe to take a specific action. When you write a researched argument, you begin by conducting research in hopes that the quality and quantity of the data you present will convince readers.

Audience   Authors of researched arguments usually write in response to an assignment for a class. This might be for an English, psychology, biology, or business class. The initial audience for the assignment is your instructor, while the secondary audience might be your peers if they are going to read your paper. Readers may or may not agree with the argument the writer proposes, but they're generally curious enough to read about the perspectives of others. If you're an expert writing a researched argument for a peer-reviewed journal, then your audience is other experts.

Rhetorical appeals   When writing a researched argument, authors can establish *ethos* when they do the following:

- Describe their research methods
- Explain the data they collected and how they analyzed it
- Discuss their findings and conclusions in detail
- Cite their sources appropriately
- Write as directly and persuasively as possible

Writers can establish *logos* when they:

- State their position clearly
- State each aspect of their argument clearly—and in an order that makes logical sense
- Anticipate and address objections
- Support their claims with evidence, including the views of others (drawn from their sources)

Modes & media   Researched arguments published as articles in peer-reviewed journals, as memos, and as reports are text based and may include visuals such as charts, graphs, and images to support and illustrate points. These types of pieces can be available in print or online.

Elements of the genre   To compose a successful researched argument, writers do the following:

- *State a thesis or make a clear claim.* To make a position clear, a writer can (1) indicate the topic at hand and his or her position on it right in the title, (2) provide a clear thesis, doing so right at the beginning, or (3) combine both.

- *Present an argument.* The reasons for the position the author takes need to be clearly stated and explained.

- *Base their arguments on solid research.* All researched writing relies on research of some kind. Most writers support their ideas by drawing on the research of others—of experts and leaders in the field. As a student, unless you do primary research (such as conducting interviews), you most likely draw on the research of others in your researched writing. Some authors—mainly academics writing for peer-reviewed journals—draw on their own research, particularly if they've conducted a study or survey of some kind that brings in data. When Elizabeth and Amy present papers at conferences, they draw on and cite specific research done by academic experts and

ATTENTION, RESEARCHERS & WRITERS

Poorly integrated and cited research casts doubt on you as an author and seriously compromises your ethos—while a smart use of sources does a lot to build it. See Chapter 13 for more on integrating and citing sources.

colleagues to support their arguments. Arguments for peer-reviewed journals are usually written in a formal style using precise language and are reviewed by others in the field for accuracy and reliability. (For more on peer-reviewed journal articles, see p. 113 of this chapter.)

- *Address counterarguments.* To build logos, writers need to acknowledge contrasting or opposing arguments and either (1) refute them by exposing their holes or presenting evidence that outweighs them or (2) concede that they are legitimate and then explain why, despite this legitimacy, the audience should take the author's position.

- *Synthesize and attribute the work of others.* As noted above, citing sources—and specific examples—builds ethos. It's also a good idea to pull information from multiple sources and to synthesize it by showing readers how these sources align and differ. When a writer relies on only one source, the argument looks weak and is therefore much less persuasive. (For more on synthesizing sources, see Chapter 13.)

Style   Authors use style in the following ways to present their researched arguments. They:

- *Title their work to make their position clear.* Readers need a clear sense of the writer's topic and perspective on that topic.

- *Write with authority.* Writers use a strong voice and tone to convey expertise on a topic, support their ethos, and persuade their readers.

- *Gain readers' attention with simple but memorable introductions and closing statements.* For example, a writer may begin with an anecdote or statistic that demonstrates the importance of the topic.

- *Use detail.* The more specific writers are—in terms of both the main point and the research they're drawing on—the better and more persuasive the argument.

Design   Writers of researched arguments design their documents with their readers in mind. They:

- *Provide subheadings.* Dividing a researched argument into sections with subheadings makes a long, complex piece easier to navigate. Subheadings also signal readers that an author is shifting his or her focus.

- *Support their arguments with images.* Photos, charts, and illustrations convey complex information visually—and can serve as sources.

Sources   Because a successful researched argument draws on solid research, authors do the following:

- *Curate sources carefully.* Authors use credible sources that their readers will respect.

- *Cite sources according to genre conventions.* If you've been asked to compose a researched argument in response to an academic assignment, your instructor will most likely require a particular citation system, such as MLA, APA, or *Chicago* style. You would include a bibliographic list at the end of the article and use parenthetical citations throughout.

Guided Reading | Researched Argument

Chase Dickinson, a former student from Herriman, Utah, wrote the following researched argument when he was a freshman at Weber State University, where he studied geoscience. As he mentions in the following essay, Dickinson worked for a video game vendor called Play N Trade, a fact that influences his argument about video games in "Are Kids on a One-Way Path to Violence?" The essay, which he wrote for his English composition course, was also published in Weber State's journal of student work, called *Weber Writes*, edited in 2010 by Scott Rogers and Sylvia Newman.

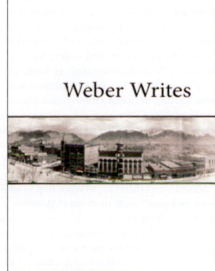

◀ **STUDENT AUTHOR PHOTO, JOURNAL COVER, WEB SITE**

Chase Dickinson; *Weber Writes,* the student journal that published Dickinson's researched essay; and Weber State University's site.

Credits: (top left) Chase Dickinson. (top right and bottom) Weber State University.

Chase Dickinson, *Are Kids on a One-Way Path to Violence?*

RHETORICAL SITUATION & CHOICES	GENRE CONVENTIONS

◀ **What is the composer, Chase Dickinson, doing?**

How do I know that this is ▶ a researched argument?

PURPOSE

Dickinson wants to persuade readers that video games do not cause violent behavior in mentally healthy children.

AUDIENCE

His readers are his instructor, his classmates, and the students at Weber State University who read the journal *Weber Writes*.

RHETORICAL APPEALS

Dickinson develops his ethos by stating that he is a gamer himself and that he's even worked in the industry.

By noting that the DC Sniper trained at a shooting range, Dickinson appeals to readers' sense of logos to question the connection between the DC Sniper and his video game experience.

MODES & MEDIA

Mode = written: Dickinson's assignment specified that he write an essay; however, sometimes assignments allow students the latitude to choose another mode, such as a video or audio essay. Dickinson could have included visuals with his essay, perhaps screenshots of the video games mentioned in the

In the popular video game *Grand Theft Auto* (GTA), players are thrust into a world without laws, free to do just about anything they want. Stealing cars, killing civilians, and causing general mayhem are common occurrences in the fictitious world of Liberty City (Rockstar Leeds). In fact, GTA is about as lawless as games get. But can a game such as *Grand Theft Auto* actually fuel real-world violence? There are many who believe so, and violent video games have therefore become a hotly debated topic in today's headlines.

If you were to listen to politicians and critics, the relationship between video games and crime is blatantly clear: children who play video games will either become more aggressive or actually commit real-world acts of violence. According to the lawyers of Lee Malvo, the young "DC Sniper," Malvo learned to shoot by playing "very realistic and gory" video games. These games were also said to have "desensitized (him) . . . to train him to shoot human forms over and over" (qtd. in Provan). Another popular argument against violent video games comes in the form of the infamous Columbine shootings in which Dylan Klebold and Eric Harris killed thirteen students and injured twenty-three more before killing themselves. During the investigation that followed, it was discovered that both teenagers enjoyed playing the bloody first-person shooter *Doom*, and that they went on the rampage shortly after their parents took the game away from them. It has also been speculated that the pair created a level in *Doom* with the same layout as their school in order to plan out their attack (Mikkelson). Yet another argument finds Jack Thompson, a leader in the fight against violent video games, blaming the Virginia Tech shooting on the first-person shooter *Counter-Strike*, saying that once again the shooter trained for his crime by playing the popular first-person shooter (qtd. in Benedetti).

With video games rapidly gaining popularity, we have to ask ourselves if these crimes are actually caused by the increasing violence in games. While there are many who tend to think so, I believe that it is not the fault of the games themselves, but the lack of parental supervision and interaction with today's youth. Also, preexisting mental

ELEMENTS OF THE GENRE

States a thesis or makes a clear claim: Dickinson's thesis is "I believe that [violent behavior in people who play video games] is not the fault of the games themselves, but the lack of parental supervision and interaction with today's youth."

Presents an argument based on research: He presents his argument in paragraph 3 and develops it in subsequent paragraphs— reasoning that the DC Sniper, Columbine shooters, and Virginia Tech shooter had histories of mental illness, and that is what the crimes should be attributed to. He argues that parents should monitor children's use of games and take mental health into account when deciding what their children can handle.

Acknowledges counterarguments: For example, in paragraph 2, the author mentions that lawyers claimed there were connections between their clients' violence and use of video games.

essay or mug shots of the DC Sniper.

Medium = print: Again, Dickinson was required by his assignment to produce an essay in print form, but researched arguments often appear digitally, on blogs, for example.

disorders have been found to play a huge role in how different people will react to video games.

Take, for example, the DC sniper shootings. *Halo*, the game that Malvo supposedly used to prepare for his crimes, employs the use of unrealistic guns to shoot giant alien bugs (Bungie). Such actions are hardly effective ways to learn how to shoot a sniper rifle at human beings. Malvo even admitted that he trained by shooting a real gun at makeshift targets with paper plates for heads (Provan). Similarly, the claims that the Columbine shooters created a level with their school's layout were never found to be true. In fact, all of the levels they made were later found on their Web site, and all of them were based on fictitious locations on alien planets (Mikkelson). Lastly, no one was ever reported to have seen Seung-Hui Cho, the Virginia Tech shooter, playing any video games. His roommate told *The New York Times* that he would sometimes enter Cho's room and find Cho sitting at his desk, staring into nothingness (Biggs). He wasn't staring at a computer and playing *Counter-Strike*, but was rather staring at nothing at all.

In addition, Seung-Hui Cho had been diagnosed with selective mutism, a severe anxiety disorder, as well as major depressive disorder (Adams). The DC shooter had a long history of antisocial and criminal behavior, including the torturing of small animals (Kutner 8). Similarly, FBI investigations were able to conclude that Klebold was significantly depressed and suicidal, and Harris was a sociopath (Kutner 8).

Ultimately, it falls upon the parents to filter what gets to their kids, and, when a known mental problem exists, parents should be that much more strict on what their kids play. As an avid gamer myself, and as someone who has worked in the industry, I understand the sense of accomplishment received from a well placed shot in *Modern Warfare* just as much as I understand that video games are not real. I was personally raised buying and playing games under the supervision of my parents, and am a strong supporter of such supervision. Even so, according to the anti-video game activist Jack Thompson and others with his mindset, I should be a ball of boiling hatred ready to explode at the slightest provocation (Musgrove).

Contrary to the claims of many naysayers, it is becoming easier to filter what a child does and does not play. A rating system implemented by the Entertainment Software Rating Board (ESRB) provides a fantastic way for parents to monitor what their kids are playing. This rating system issues an age range for each game, disclosing the full contents of the game. The most common ratings include E (Everyone, suitable for everyone age six and older), T (Teen, suitable for ages thirteen

Refutes or concedes counterarguments: For example, in paragraphs 4 and 5, the author discredits the links others have made between specific criminals and video game habits.

Cites specific examples, synthesizing them into his main argument. Rather than being general, the author specifies shooters (DC Sniper, Columbine, and Virginia Tech) and particular games (*Grand Theft Auto*, *Doom*, *Halo*, and *Counter-Strike*).

STYLE

Descriptive title: Dickinson's title makes it clear that his essay deals with kids and violence.

Gets readers' attention in the introduction: Dickinson accomplishes this by stating that players are "free to do just about anything they want" in the game *Grand Theft Auto*.

Closes with a simple, memorable statement: His final sentence reads: "Rather than focusing on trying to ban video games for their so-called influence on violent crime, an emphasis on parental supervision should be implemented in the fight against modern-day crime."

(Continues on next page)

and older), and M (Mature, suitable for ages seventeen and older). The AO rating (Adult Only) is the only one higher than the M rating, and is actually considered to be a death sentence for games because brick-and-mortar stores will not sell them. AO- and M-rated games are the ones that come under the most fire from the media because they contain the most violent and bloody content. However, many people don't realize that in order to purchase an M-rated game from any major retailer, the customer must be at least seventeen years of age. Because of this age restriction, it is harder for young children to get their hands on violent content without parental approval (Entertainment Software Assoc.).

There is no denying that video games have matured since their introduction in the '70s. Back then, games meant playing *Pong* or *Space Invaders* with friends and family. Today, games are becoming more and more complex, with violence playing a large role in almost all modern titles. Still, with parents staying involved in their kids' lives, it is possible to filter violent content and keep it to a minimum, which can prevent any type of aggressive behavior from developing. And with resources such as ESRB, it is becoming easier and easier to keep children from playing games that are not age appropriate. Rather than focusing on trying to ban video games for their so-called influence on violent crime, an emphasis on parental supervision should be implemented in the fight against modern-day crime.

Works Cited

Adams, Duncan. "The Alienation and Anger of Seung-Hui Cho." *The Roanoke Times*, 31 Aug. 2007, www.roanoke.com/vtinvestigation/wb/130177.

Benedetti, Winda. "Were Video Games to Blame for Massacre?" *MSNBC.com*, 20 Apr. 2007, www.roanoke.com/vtinvestigation/wb/130177.

Biggs, John. "Why Video Games Don't Cause Violence." *CrunchGear.com*, 18 Apr. 2007, techcrunch.com/2007/04/18/why-video-games-dont-cause-violence/.

Bungie, developer. *Halo: Combat Evolved*. Microsoft Studios, 15 Nov. 2001, www.halowaypoint.com/en-us.

Entertainment Software Association. *Entertainment Software Rating Board*, www.esrb.org. Accessed 27 Jan. 2001.

Kutner, Lawrence, and Cheryl Olson. *Grand Theft Childhood: The Surprising Truth About Violent Video Games and What Parents Can Do*. Simon & Schuster, 2008, p. 8.

Strong authoritative voice and tone: The author chooses to avoid phrases such as "I think" and "in my opinion" but is still present in the essay.

Uses detail: For example, he names violent criminals and identifies the games they're associated with.

DESIGN

For this brief essay, the author decided that subheadings and explanatory notes would be inappropriate. When he submitted it for class, it was double-spaced. For use in *Weber Writes*, it was single-spaced to conform to that journal's design.

SOURCES

Using the MLA style of documentation, the author cites sources in the body of the text and at the end in a Works Cited list. His sources are varied and include video games, works by scholars and journalists, and the fact-checking site Snopes.com. For help with documenting sources, see Chapter 13.

Mikkelson, Barbara. "Columbine Doom Levels." *Snopes.com*, 1 Jan. 2005, www.snopes.com/horrors/madmen/doom.asp.

Musgrove, Mike. "Va. Tech: Dr. Phil and Jack Thompson Blame Video Games." *The Washington Post*, 17 Apr. 2007, Voices .washingtonpost.com/posttech/2007/04/va_ tech_dr_phil _jack_thompson.html.

Provan, Alexander. "The Education of Lee Boyd Malvo." *Bidouan*, 13 Jan. 2009, www.bidoun.org/magazine/16-kids/ the-education-of-lee-boyd-malvo-by-alexander-provan/.

Rockstar Leeds and Rockstar North, developers. *Grand Theft Auto: Liberty City Stories*. Rockstar Games, Capcom, 24 Oct. 2005, www.rockstargames.com/libertycitystories.

Credit: By permission of Chase Dickinson.

QUESTIONS | Analyzing Dickinson's Researched Argument

RHETORICAL SITUATION & CHOICES

1. **Purpose.** Has Dickinson persuaded you that video games cannot be conclusively linked to violent behavior in players? Why or why not?

2. **Audience.** Besides Dickinson's professor and classmates, who else might be an appropriate audience for this essay? Would Dickinson need to revise his essay to make it accessible for other audiences?

3. **Rhetorical appeals.** What are two techniques Dickinson uses to develop his ethos?

4. **Rhetorical appeals.** Dickinson's appeals to ethos and logos are discussed in the annotations. Can you find any appeals to pathos in the essay?

5. **Modes & media.** How would the inclusion of screen shots of the video games mentioned add to or detract from the essay?

GENRE CONVENTIONS

6. **Elements of the genre.** How effective do you think Dickinson's refutation of the counterarguments is? What other refutations could he have used?

7. **Style.** Dickinson begins his essay by stating that players are "free to do just about anything they want" in *Grand Theft Auto*. What are some other ways Dickinson could have gained readers' attention at the beginning? For example, how could a reference to one of the criminals mentioned in the essay be used in the introduction?

8. **Style.** Dickinson writes in a strong, declarative voice rather than in a tentative "I'm just a student" voice. Find two or three sentences that are particularly strong and analyze the techniques Dickinson uses to come across as authoritative.

9. **Design.** Because this is a short essay, Dickinson opted against using subheadings. If the essay were developed into a longer one, say, fifteen pages, what are some subheadings he might use?

10. **Sources.** Look over Dickinson's Works Cited list. Do some sources appear more reliable than others?

CHECKLIST | Drafting a Researched Argument

Are you thinking of writing a researched argument? Ask yourself the following questions.

RHETORICAL SITUATION & CHOICES

☐ **Purpose.** What topic am I researching that might lend itself to an argument? What are some potential persuasive claims I could make about that topic? Have I discovered something about the topic that would contribute to other scholarly research?

☐ **Audience.** Assuming my readers are my classmates and professor—I need to think about how much they already know about my topic. How much background information will they need? What kind of terminology will they expect? How will they use the information I present?

☐ **Rhetorical appeals.** How will I establish my authority as a writer? How will I build a case for my conclusions using logic? What kinds of sources establish me as an expert and work to build my case?

☐ **Modes & media.** Can some of the information I present be shown with a chart or graphic? Do I want readers to access my article in print or digitally? Or do I want to make both options available?

GENRE CONVENTIONS

☐ **Elements of the genre.** How will I make my thesis clear and declarative? How will I refer to my sources? How can I synthesize my sources to show readers that my sources are in conversation with each other?

☐ **Style.** How can I project an authoritative voice? How much detail will I need to provide so that readers understand the complexity and validity of my research?

☐ **Design.** How will I use design elements to my advantage? Will I use subheadings to organize and chunk information? Will I use images to illustrate points?

☐ **Sources.** Will my readers expect me to cite my sources in MLA, APA, or another format? Will my readers respect the types of sources I've referred to?

PRACTICE

Researching & Making an Argument

Think of a controversial topic you are curious about, even one that you don't feel informed about. Some topics might be the environment and the right to clean water or the future of AIDS research, or perhaps a topic drawn from ideas represented in the Reader section of this book (see Chapters 16 through 19). Ask your instructor, librarian, or other expert to help you find three reliable sources on the subject. Read the sources and then draft an argumentative thesis statement in which you take a position on the topic. Sketch out at least two counterarguments and your refutations of them. Consider how you might integrate your sources. As you sketch out the counterarguments and refutations, indicate what information came from your sources.

Peer-Reviewed Journal Articles

The research paper we have just discussed is a common assignment that often introduces you to the next genre: peer-reviewed journal articles. As you investigate a specific topic—let's say, feral (wild) housecats—you can gather information from primary sources or secondary sources, and sometimes both. A primary source would be your own observations of feral cats, and a secondary source would be someone else's thoughts and observations about feral cats. If the results of your research produce a paper that you think is good enough to publish in a journal, you will send it to a journal and it will be reviewed by certain other scholars on the topic of feral cats and either rejected or accepted for publication. This is the "peer-reviewed journal article."

This section will help you analyze scholarly articles and perhaps give you ideas about writing an article of your own. Authors of peer-reviewed articles are scholars who are recognized as such by fellow experts. Many scholars are college professors; some work in research laboratories. Research labs can be associated with universities, medical facilities (such as the Mayo Clinic), the government (such as the U.S. Naval Research Laboratory), for-profit organizations (such as Pfizer and other pharmaceutical companies), or nonprofit organizations (such as the Pew Research Center). Research labs are sometimes referred to as "think tanks."

Publishers of peer-reviewed journal articles, such as the science journal *Nature*, present the latest research in a given field to a specialized audience. The scholarly authors of these articles might also present them as "papers" or "talks" at academic conferences to audiences of fellow experts. They must cite their sources rigorously; a charge of plagiarism can easily end an academic career. As noted, readers of these articles are usually experts, but sometimes general readers, such as students or other nonexperts, might read them because they are interested in learning more about the topic covered.

Most of the time, you will use peer-reviewed journal articles to support some research paper you are writing for class, so you will use them as secondary sources. After you locate a source, you don't merely report what you've found: You also synthesize, compare, and analyze what has been said. You incorporate the voices of your sources in a systematic way, using quotations, citing sources in the body of your paper (or other composition), and listing them at the end. For some assignments, you might also respond to the work of others by presenting and supporting your own argument. (For more on researched writing, see pp. 104–12 of this chapter.)

Analyzing Peer-Reviewed Journal Articles

Purpose Scholars write articles for peer-reviewed journals in order to share their research results with others in the same field. Sometimes scholarly writers present groundbreaking new research, such as a new drug or an alternative energy source. Other times, they present more subtle findings, such as a different way of looking at existing data.

Another purpose of scholarly writers is to persuade readers to see things the way they do. For example, when presenting data, a scholar may want to argue for his or her own particular interpretation of the data. Most scholarly articles are meant to both inform and persuade.

Audience   Authors of scholarly articles usually write for a fairly narrow primary audience that includes researchers, professors, and other scholars who want to stay up-to-date in their fields. However, they also have secondary audiences in mind. For example, as a student, you might refer to a scholarly journal article as a source for a research paper. Peer-reviewed journals exist in every academic field, including the sciences, humanities, and social sciences. For example, Amy and Elizabeth both read academic journals such as *College Composition and Communication (CCC)*, which focuses on teaching and composition; they use *CCC's* journal articles to deepen their own understanding of writing and teaching research.

WRITE

What scholarly journals are related to your major? To what extent do you relate to them as a reader? Make a list of all the scholarly journals and next to each, indicate how you might relate to it as a reader.

Rhetorical appeals   Scholars who write articles for peer-reviewed journals need to establish ethos by describing their research methods, explaining the data they collected and how they analyzed that information, and discussing their findings and conclusions in detail. They must also cite sources appropriately, taking into account the findings of others. And, because logic is important to scholarship and the writers' audience, writers must appeal to logos by building arguments that rest on tightly organized pieces of evidence and scrupulously researched data. Scholars must keep in mind that their readers will need to be convinced of the legitimacy of their research methods, the accuracy of their data collection, and the logic of their data analysis.

Modes & media   Scholarly articles are text based and may include visuals such as charts, graphs, and images to support and illustrate points. Journals are available in print and, increasingly, online; many articles that originate in print-based journals are available through subscription databases such as *EBSCOhost*, *JSTOR*, and *Project MUSE*. There are also a few scholarly journals that are only available digitally.

Elements of the genre   Peer-reviewed articles are:

- *Based on original research or research of another expert or peer*. In a peer-reviewed journal article, scholars usually write about their own original research.
  - » First, they identify a question that needs to be answered, such as "How does living near a nuclear reactor affect birthrates?"
  - » Next, they design an experiment or research plan that will allow that question to be studied, for example, identifying nuclear reactors, collecting data on birthrates in the surrounding communities over time, interviewing obstetricians who practice in the area, and so on.
  - » Then they perform the research, analyze the data they've gathered, and offer their interpretations in writing. Authors usually refer to related research by other scholars to contextualize their own work.

- *Reviewed by others in the field for accuracy and reliability.* Scholarly articles are written by scholars, for scholars. During the peer review process, other experts in the field review the article to check for clarity and style, but even more important, to make sure the research conducted is a legitimate means of measuring or studying the subject of the article. Peer reviewers might question, for instance, the validity of studying birthrates near nuclear reactors by merely interviewing people who live in the community. They would probably want more rigorous, objective data, such as hospital records documenting pregnancies, fertility rates, and births.

- *Organized around a thesis.* Scholarly authors write to make a point about the research they've conducted—a point that usually has both informative and persuasive elements. For example, if an author's point is "drugs X, Y, and Z alleviate symptoms of condition A," she will go on to inform readers of how she drew that conclusion (how she conducted the research and analyzed the data) and will also—if the article is well researched and written—persuade readers that the drugs discussed in the article should be prescribed more often.

- *Based on sources or works of others.* Scholars who write articles for peer-reviewed journals summarize, paraphrase, and quote from their sources. When writers use other sources (outside of their own original research), they properly document the work of others through in-text citations and Works Cited lists.

- *Syntheses of multiple sources.* Like a student writing a research paper, scholars must synthesize their sources in journal articles. That is, they pull together information across multiple sources to make their points.

- *Formal and precise in their use of language.* Scholarly writers use formal language to convey the seriousness of their ideas and research. They also use precise language to communicate complex information accurately and in detail. In a scientific research study, the difference between .1 and .01 can be crucial.

WRITE

Why do authors of scholarly articles tend to use long, descriptive titles? What are the benefits and drawbacks of such titles? Use these questions to begin a freewrite. Write for at least five minutes.

Style Peer-reviewed journal articles are characterized by the following stylistic elements:

- *Descriptive title.* In scientific fields, the more descriptive the title is, the better, such as "Hospital Mortality, Length of Stay, and Preventable Complications Among Critically Ill Patients before and after Tele-ICU Reengineering of Critical Care Processes" (from *JAMA*). In the humanities, titles often have two parts: an imaginative or creative phrase, followed by a colon, and then a more descriptive phrase, such as "Black, White, and Blue: Racial Politics in B. B. King's Music from the 1960s" (an article by Ulrich Adelt, from *The Journal of Popular Culture*).

- *Strong, authoritative voice and tone.* Authors use voice and tone to establish their ethos. For example, in "Status Struggles: Network Centrality and Gender Segregation in Same- and Cross-Gender Aggression," an article in *American Sociological Review*, authors Robert Faris and Diane Felmlee begin their article in a way that reinforces their expertise and authority:

Aggression is commonplace in U.S. schools: bullying and other forms of proactive aggression adversely affect 30 percent, or 5.7 million, American youth each school year (Nansel et al. 2001). The National Education Association (1995) estimates that each weekday, 160,000 students skip school to avoid being bullied. This aggression has important consequences. Being victimized by bullies positively relates to a host of mental health problems, including depression (Baldry 2004), anxiety (Sharp, Thompson, and Arora 2000), and suicidal ideation (Carney 2000).

Robert Faris and Diane Felmlee, from "Status Struggles: Network Centrality and Gender Segregation in Same- and Cross-Gender Aggression," *American Sociological Review,* February 2011

- *Use of detail.* Authors of scholarly articles use specific details to develop complex ideas. They also use details as evidence to back up their assertions. For example, in the article discussed above, Faris and Felmlee support general statements ("Aggression is commonplace in U.S. schools") with examples and evidence (bullying "affect[s] 30 percent, or 5.7 million, American youth each school year").

Design   Peer-reviewed journal articles feature the following design elements:

- *Subheadings.* Many peer-reviewed articles are divided into sections by subheadings that make a long, complex article accessible. Subheadings also signal to the reader when the writer is about to turn his or her focus to another example or another aspect of the topic.

- *Images.* Many scholarly articles include images, such as photos, charts, and illustrations, to convey complex information visually. Those that are published digitally can include hyperlinks to sources and other materials.

Sources   Scholarly writers must use sources that are authoritative and are appropriate to their topic and approach. Of particular importance are the following:

- *Types of sources used.* Authors must choose sources carefully. For example, in the peer-reviewed article that follows on page 117, the author draws on scholarly research, but also quite heavily on movie reviews. This is appropriate because she discusses many films and their popular reception. Movie reviews would not be used as sources for an article on molecular science, unless, for instance, the essay focuses on how molecular science is portrayed in films.

- *Works Cited list.* Scholarly writers include a bibliography at the end of their articles. They list sources in the format dictated by the journal they're publishing in, or according to the format favored in their discipline's professional organization, such as the Modern Language Association (MLA style) and the American Psychological Association (APA style). For more on documentation, see Chapter 13.

Guided Reading | Peer-Reviewed Journal Article

Sika Dagbovie-Mullins is an assistant professor of English at Florida Atlantic University, where she teaches literature and researches the representation of mixed-race identity in literature and culture. Her article, originally titled "Star-Light, Star-Bright, Star Damn Near White: Mixed-Race Superstars," first appeared in 2007 in *The Journal of Popular Culture*, a scholarly, peer-reviewed journal. The journal, based at Michigan State University and published by the Popular Culture Association, presents the works of scholars in the field as well as in the related areas of literature, film studies, and African American studies. Dagbovie-Mullins's book *Crossing Black: Mixed-Race Identity in Modern American Fiction and Culture* was published in 2013.

THE JOURNAL OF POPULAR CULTURE

Editor: Gary Hoppenstand
Michigan State University, Department of English
625C Wells Hall, 619 Red Cedar Road, East Lansing, MI 48824
Email: tjpc@msu.edu

Submissions | Recent Articles | Editorial Board | FAQs | Subscribe | Advertise | Awards

The JPC is accepting book reviews once more. See the Submissions page for more information.

Why is the JPC published?

The Journal of Popular Culture is a peer-reviewed journal and the official publication of the Popular Culture Association. The popular culture movement was founded on the principle that the perspectives and experiences of common folk offer compelling insights into the social world. The fabric of human social life is not merely the art deemed worthy to hang in museums, the books that have won literary prizes or been named "classics," or the religious and social ceremonies carried out by societies' elite. The Journal of Popular Culture continues to break down the barriers between so-called "low" and "high" culture and focuses on filling in the gaps in a neglect of popular culture has left in our understanding of the workings of society.

How often is the JPC published and where can it be found?

The Journal of Popular Culture is published six times a year and is available in print form in roughly 1400 university libraries worldwide.

The Journal of Popular Culture is also indexed/abstracted in:

Academic Search Elite; Academic Search Premier; America: History and Life; Cambridge Scientific Abstracts Linguistics and Language Behavior Abstracts; Communication Abstracts; Corporate ResourceNet; EBSCO MasterFILE Elite; EBSCO MasterFILE Premier; EBSCO MasterFILE Select; Humanities Abstracts; Humanities Index; International Bibliography of the Social Sciences; Linguistics and Language Behavior Abstracts; Modern Language Association Bibliography; Periodical Abstracts

▲ **PEER-REVIEWED JOURNAL WEB SITE**

The Journal of Popular Culture, where Sika Dagbovie-Mullins published her article.

Credit: Courtesy of The Journal of Popular Culture.

Sika Dagbovie-Mullins, *Mixed-Race Superstars*

RHETORICAL SITUATION & CHOICES	GENRE CONVENTIONS

PURPOSE
As the author of a peer-reviewed journal article, Dagbovie-Mullins aims to inform her readers of how biracial celebrities present their "blackness." She also makes an argument about how American popular culture both accepts and rejects "blackness."

◄ **What is the composer, Sika Dagbovie-Mullins, doing?**

In an episode of *The Chris Rock Show*, comedian Chris Rock searches the streets of Harlem to find out what people think of Tiger Woods.[1] When he asks three Asian storekeepers if they consider Woods Asian, one replies, "Not even this much," pressing two of his fingers together to show no space. This comic scene and the jokes that surround Woods's self-proclaimed identity reveal a cultural contradiction that I explore in this essay, namely the

How do I know that this is a peer-reviewed journal article? ►

ELEMENTS OF THE GENRE
Is based on original research and research by other scholars: Dagbovie-Mullins examines the publicity and representations of three celebrities. She acknowledges that she uses some of the ideas from another scholar, Richard Dyer, as models for her ideas.

(Continues on next page)

simultaneous acceptance and rejection of blackness within a biracial discourse in American popular culture. Though Woods's self-identification may not fit neatly into the black/white mixed-race identity explored in this project, he still falls into a black/white dichotomy prevalent in the United States. The Asian storekeepers agree with Rock's tongue-in-cheek suggestion that Tiger Woods is as black as James Brown, opposing sentiments like "The dude's more Asian than he is anything else" on an Asian American college Internet magazine ("Wang and Woods"). Woods cannot escape blackness (a stereotypical fried-chicken-and-collard-green-eating blackness according to Fuzzy Zoeller), and yet he also represents a multicultural poster boy, one whose blackness pales next to his much-celebrated multi-otherness.[2]

Through advertising, interviews, and publicity, biracial celebrities encode a distinct connection to blackness despite their projected (and sometimes preferred) self-identification. Drawing from Richard Dyer's *Stars*, I read biracial celebrities Halle Berry, Vin Diesel, and Mariah Carey by analyzing autobiographical representations, celebrity statuses, public reception, and the publicity surrounding each of the representations.[3] Dyer writes, "Stars are, like characters in stories, representations of people. Thus they relate to ideas about what people are (or are supposed to be) like" (*Stars* 22). Recognizing that we can never know how much agency stars have in their image, I acknowledge that biographies or interviews are not necessarily "truths." However, the interviews, career moves (e.g., movie roles or music), public reception, and publicity that I examine all play a part in creating a star's image. I argue that the reception of mixed-race celebrities in popular culture reflects a national inclination to define blackness. While laws have historically defined who is black, social laws also attempted to regulate blackness, ensuring that blacks "kept their place." Similarly, in contemporary popular culture, advertisers and media attempt to define blackness. For mixed-race celebrities, this means blackness is deemed acceptable only when it upholds stereotypical white preconceptions and desires.

During and after slavery, many whites thought that mulattos were intellectually superior to "pure" blacks, a notion that confirmed white supremacy. At the same time, some whites believed mulattos were psychologically unstable, suggesting that even one drop of black blood could lead to mental and other deficiencies. Though mixed-race

(See "Infographics:
Visual Instructions"
on p. 190.)

**Medium = print and
digital:** This piece
originally appeared
in both the print and
digital versions of *The
Journal of Popular
Culture.* Subscribers
to the print journal
automatically get
online access to the
digital version of the
journal, enabling
readers to choose
which medium they'd
prefer to read an
article in (there are no
content differences
between the versions).
Some journals have
developed apps
for iPads and other
mobile devices that
allow readers to
access the online
version of an article
on the go.

men were often labeled rapists and murderers, mixed-race
women were seen as lascivious seductresses. Some of these
same stereotypes reappeared in nineteenth and twentieth
century American literature. Sterling Brown was the first
to name the literary stereotype the "tragic mulatto." In
"Negro Character as Seen by White Authors" he describes
the archetype as "a victim of divided inheritance and
therefore miserable" (162). The persistence of this stereotype
has continued in contemporary popular culture, revealing
America's obsession with race mixing and mixed-race
bodies. Like census statisticians, America does not know
what to do with "mulattos." Historically and today, mixed-
race individuals are used to explore, praise, or condemn the
"racial unknown."

Though multiracial identity has become a modish
identity that white Americans seek, desire, and fetishize,
Americans still fear and loathe blackness, marginalizing
and criminalizing black bodies. The fascination with
mixed-race bodies is metaphorically synonymous to racial
slumming in the late 1920s. Kevin Mumford explains,
"The influx of white mainstream urbanites . . . temporarily
participated in the interzones [black/white sex districts],
usually for pleasure, and then returned to their homes
and lives apart from the black/white vice districts" (133).
Similarly, whites' obsession with black/white mixed-race
bodies permits "consumption" of a more palatable form of
blackness while allowing whites to return "home" or stay
distanced from the supposedly less "attractive" aspects of
black identity.

Some mixed-race celebrities are read as black, even
when they distance themselves from blackness. Conversely,
mixed-race celebrities who claim a black heritage often get
labeled as multiracial, not black. In short, the contradictory
desires of the American public and media, manifested in
a simultaneous disavowal and celebration of mixed race,
show both our discomfort and fascination with mixed-race
people and their bodies in particular. In the entertainment
industry, a star's biracial identity may fade, be tucked away,
or even disappear according to audience perceptions and
star construction. On the other hand, a mixed-race identity
never satisfies. Berry may self-identify as black, yet the
media often holds onto her multiracial background. Diesel's
desire not to talk about his racial background unsurprisingly
fuels more interest. Carey proudly asserts a biracial identity
while alternately encoding blackness and "otherness" in
the media. Although Berry is distinct from the two other

STYLE

Descriptive title: The
author uses the title
to grab attention and
present the gist of her
argument.

Strong author's voice:
Dagbovie-Mullins
refers to many sources,
but her voice stays
in control; her voice
doesn't get lost in the
midst of quotations.

**Authoritative and
declarative tone:** The
author states her case
with confidence. She
sometimes uses first
person to present her
ideas as researcher
and scholar.

Use of detail: The
author follows her
generalizations with
specific examples to
back up her claims.
For example, she
states, "The titles of
articles on Berry reveal
a tendency to read her
as a modern day tragic
mulatto" and then
provides evidence:
"'Halle Berry, Bruised
and Beautiful,
Is on a Mission,'
'The Beautiful and
Damned,' 'Am I
Going to Be Happy
or Not?' and even
an unauthorized
biography entitled
*Halle Berry: A
Stormy Life* all
highlight Berry's
troubled personal life,
recalling mixed-race
literary characters
whose beauty was
rivaled only by their
ugly misfortunes."
Details help readers
understand her
research and evaluate

(Continues on next page)

celebrities in her constant embracing of and identification with blackness, the reception of all these celebrities groups them together. The hype surrounding Berry, Diesel, and Carey shows the inconsistencies of America's racial desires over whether to control blackness on the one hand or encourage racial harmony on the other, or perhaps to abandon race altogether.

Claiming Halle Berry: Biracial or Black?

When Halle Berry won the Oscar for Best Actress in 2002, she became more widely recognized as an accomplished black actress. Berry's acceptance speech confirms her racial allegiance: "The moment is so much bigger than me. . . . It's [the Oscar] for every nameless, faceless woman of color that now has a chance because this door tonight has been opened." Despite Berry's claim, competing discourses on her ethnicity consume popular cultural discussions of her. In a 1994 interview with Lisa Jones, Berry makes clear, "I never once announced that I am interracial. I was never the one to bring it up. . . . Yet reporters constantly ask what childhood was like to an interracial person" ("Blacker" 60). Berry consistently identifies as African American, evoking an identity grounded in a black politics. Jones asks Berry if mixed-race children should choose a race. Berry replies, "You've got to identify with one group or the other. It is a political choice" (60). Berry learned this, she claims, from her white mother who advised her to "accept being black, embrace it" (Kennedy 28). Berry's biracial background follows her in her movie roles and public persona, evidenced perhaps in the approval she seems to give to stereotypes of mulatta women. The media's investment in reading Halle Berry within a biracial narrative assures a biracial script both within the movies and in pseudo-liberal discussions of race. She is more easily accepted in a "role," both cinematic and stereotypic, that is familiar to Americans—that of the exotic mixed-race woman.[4]

Donald Bogle's discussion of Dorothy Dandridge is particularly helpful in thinking about Halle Berry. Bogle describes Dandridge as having "the rich golden skin tone that had always fascinated movie audiences, black and white." He continues, "she was a destructive personality, schizophrenic, maddening, euphoric, and self-destructive," all characteristics that define what the tragic mulatta has become: a beautiful, licentious, yet confused and unhappy woman (166). Dandridge's roles in films like *Carmen Jones* (1954), *Island in the Sun* (1957), and *Tamango*

(1957) perpetuated the tragic mulatto stereotype around which her career became centered. Bogle asserts that Dandridge "epitomized the confused, unsatisfied movie star dominated by the publicity and lifestyle that informed her screen image" (174–75). Similarly, *Ego Trip's Big Book of Racism!*, a biting collection of satiric essays and lists, places Berry as number five in its "Top Ten Tragic Mulattos." The media unnecessarily emphasize her biraciality in any description of her misfortunes, including an abusive father and ex-boyfriend, two divorces, and a suicide attempt. The authors of *Ego Trip's* cite Berry's "emotionally wrenching turn as her troubled role model, Dorothy Dandridge" as partial evidence of her "tragic mulatto" status (Jenkins 81).

In an interview with Entertainment Television, Warren Beatty says, "She's a beautiful woman and she's the essence of that biracial thing in America that is so beautiful" ("Halle Berry"). Beatty, who acted with Berry in *Bulworth* (1998), romanticizes mixed-race identity as an American ideal, reducing Berry to the essence of a biracial "thing," no longer an individual but a notion or concept. Praising Berry as a national ideal inadvertently summons the history of black/white mixing in America, namely the sexual abuse of black women by white men during slavery.

However, Beatty's comment also suggests a desire to interpret Berry within a "melting pot" framework, one that depoliticizes identity. This rhetoric abounds in multiracial literary interpretations, such as in Maria P. P. Root's assertion that "the accomplishment of complex identities by racially mixed persons gives us the hope that if individuals have been able to resolve conflicting values, claim identities, synthesize multiple heritages, and retain respect for individual heritages . . . perhaps it is possible for us eventually to do this as a nation" (347). Multiracial activists see a mixed-race Berry in the same way they view Tiger Woods, as an indication of racial harmony or what David L. Andrews and C. L. Cole describe as "racially coded celebrations which deny social problems and promote the idea that America has achieved its multicultural ideal" (70).[5] Reading Berry in a biracial framework falls in line with historical and cinematic representations of mixed-race women and allows a white patriarchal system to prevail under the guise of politically correct rhetoric. In other words, other people define Berry and place her in a category that best satisfies white perceptions of race and mixed race.

The titles of articles on Berry reveal a tendency to read her as a modern day tragic mulatto. "Halle Berry, Bruised and Beautiful, Is on a Mission," "The Beautiful and Damned," "Am I Going to Be Happy or Not?" and even an unauthorized biography entitled *Halle Berry: A Stormy Life* all highlight Berry's troubled personal life, recalling mixed race literary characters whose beauty was rivaled only by their ugly misfortunes (Kennedy; Hirschberg; Haynes; Sanello). Though the media extol Berry's beauty, their accolades always urge references to her tragic life. Films including *The Flintstones* (1994), *Introducing Dorothy Dandridge* (1999), *X-Men* (2000), *Die Another Day* (2002), and *Monster's Ball* (2002) also subtly accentuate Berry's image as tragic or exotic. In the miniseries *Queen (1993)*, Berry plays Alex Haley's grandmother, daughter of a white master and a black slave. The producers stayed "true" to Queen's racial background by choosing Berry for the part and remained loyal to the "tragic mulatress text: Not only does *Queen* drag out mulatto

(Continues on next page)

clichés from every B movie and paperback, it luxuriates in them with eerie aplomb" (Jones, *Bulletproof* 50). Yet even Berry's decidedly "monoracial" characters, like the role of Nina (a pro-black "fly girl") in *Bulworth*, repeat a tragic motif. Patricia Williams writes that Berry's role "never rises above the most ancient of clichés" by bordering "black and white," "hope and despair, good and bad, sane and insane; the positive and negative divided by two, multiplied by sex" (11). In the sci-fi comic-book-turned-movie *X-Men*, Berry's character again occupies an "in-between" space. Lynne D. Johnson asserts that Berry's role as Storm in *X-Men* did not surprise, given her mixed racial background: "Though not a tragic mulatto in the classic sense of the myth, being mixed in both the racial and genetic mutation sense of the word, Storm is representative of this idea." In 2004, Berry played another mutant woman, *Catwoman*, first made famous by biracial actress Eartha Kitt in a 1960s television show. Like Berry's other films, *Catwoman* capitalizes on Berry's reputation as exotic, liminal, and hypersexual.[6]

Berry's casting as Leticia Musgrove in *Monster's Ball* prompted diverse reviews from moviegoers and critics. The reaction from the black community was mixed, mostly due to Berry's casting as a stereotypical black woman in a film that "unfolds like something that was written by Simon Legree, the slave owner in *Uncle Tom's Cabin*. Just hours after they meet, the black woman lustfully seduces the startled white man" (Wickham 15A).[7] While many reviews mention the clichés in *Monster's Ball*, most fail to mention the stereotypical image of black women.[8] Actress Angela Bassett declined the role, she claims, because "I wasn't going to be a prostitute on film. . . . I couldn't do that because it's such a stereotype about black women and sexuality" (Samuels 54). Bassett does not mention the stereotypes of mixed-race women implicit in Berry's portrayal of Leticia, a woman who wants Hank to "heal" her through sex. Here the movie recycles nineteenth-century images of black and mixed-race women as oversexual.[9] More specifically, the movie encourages the myth of mixed-race women "as lewd and lascivious as the men are idle, sensual, and dishonest" (Mencke 102). Though the film does not specifically label Leticia mixed race, her characterization urges such readings. Symbolically, the movie recalls the history of miscegenation yet, more specifically, the movie reinforces general perceptions of Halle Berry as biracial. One reviewer sarcastically claims that the film suggests blacks and whites will get along only when "black women are already half white, already measure up to the white beauty standard," like Halle Berry ("Monster Balls"). Berry's role in *Monster's Ball* speaks to Berry's own tragic mulatto image, and her image never strays far from the "biracial" characters she plays.

As so many viewers and audiences have lamented, Hollywood representations of blackness have been limited and narrow. Movies have historically slighted actors who are "too black" and, simultaneously, shunned those who are "not black enough." Like Dorothy Dandridge and Lena Horne, Berry has been hindered by her lighter complexion, and sometimes deprived of movie auditions and offers for "black" roles. Berry's manager, Vincent Cirrincione, claims that when Berry auditioned for *Strictly Business* (1991), they told her to "get a tan" (Kennedy 28). Conversely, Cirrincione says other executives have told him "milk is milk until you add a little Hershey. It doesn't matter if you add a little Hershey or a lot"

(Kennedy 28). More often than not, Berry does not signify real "blackness." Philip Kerr remarks that in *Monster's Ball*:

> I didn't see a black woman who looked, well, black. Am I the only one to have noticed? Halle Berry—who let's face it, is half-white—made a lachrymose, Oscar-winning thing about being a woman of color, and yet the reality is that she looks no more like a person of color than I do. Is it just me, or do most of the black women cast in Hollywood films, with their straight hair, thin lips and cappuccino-colored skins, look just a little bit white? (44)

Kerr's offensive statement uses biology to classify Berry, relying on crude physical descriptions like "straight hair" and "thin lips" to declare Berry "not black." Though Kerr's criticism rightly addresses the prejudice against darker actresses, his critique also suggests a restrictive and monolithic view of blackness. Such physical stereotypes of African Americans neglect the wide array of physical characteristics and skin color within black communities. Berry cannot pass and does not "look" white as Kerr suggests; her physical markings represent those commonly associated with a person of color. That Berry self-identifies as black makes Kerr's statement particularly insulting in terms of his desire to read her as "half-white." The media criminalizes dark skin, associating darkness with poverty, ignorance, and physical ugliness. Cannot Leticia be poor, desperate, downtrodden, and still light skinned? Aside from presenting narrow-minded views on race, Kerr's description shows that the public and critics invest in Berry's "whiteness."

Public discourses about Berry belabor her looks when referring to her celebrity allure. Charlie Kanganis, who directed Berry in *Race the Sun* (1996), compares Berry with "a double espresso machiatto, a dollop of shapely foam, a shower of cinnamon and cocoa." No other actress in "Cinema and the Female Star," a collection of reflections and tributes to actresses, is so objectified. Warren Beatty claims that people laugh when they first see Berry because "they don't know how else to react. They're not used to someone that beautiful" ("Halle Berry"). Literary descriptions of mixed-race women in early American fiction suggest a similar exceptional, almost unreal beauty. In Charles Chesnutt's novel, *The House Behind the Cedars* (1900), John, not yet recognizing Rena as his sister, describes her as "strikingly handsome, with a stately beauty seldom encountered" (7). These characterizations imply a uniqueness associated with mixed race that persists in popular culture. Lynn Hirschberg claims that Berry's beauty is "actually distracting; the perfection of her face would not seem to allow anything less than a perfect life" (26). Would people review Berry's beauty in the same way if she were "just black" (and not "biracial")? She represents the supposed mystique of mixed-race people, alluring because they symbolize a social taboo. Her image represents "black" and "not black," which unsettles and entices. A *Time* article begins, "Is it a curse to be beautiful?" continuing a familiar rhetoric about Berry's looks, one that intensified after *Monster's Ball* (Corliss 124–25). Descriptions of Berry's beauty intimate what has become a common boasting on numerous multiracial Web sites—that mixed-race people are "prettier." This notion gets directly and indirectly repeated in advertisements and magazines that use

(Continues on next page)

models who physically represent racial mixture. The point here is not to judge or critique Berry's beauty, but rather to examine why it attracts so much attention. Berry cannot be taken out of a historical context of mixed-race beauty images. Her image reflects back the fantasy that makes Americans both anxious and envious.

Multiracial to the Rescue: Vin Diesel

When Tiger Woods gained notoriety, he was proclaimed the new multiracial face of America. Andrews and Cole maintain that Woods represents the "latest in America's imagined realization of its ideals (agency, equality, responsibility, and freedom) and its imagined transformed sense of national self (America has become the world that came to it)" (73). Yet Vin Diesel's recent explosion in Hollywood has introduced an even "better" Tiger Woods, because unlike Woods, Diesel refuses to name himself racially. Diesel, a self-described "mystery man," represents an amalgamation of all races, literally in his racial ambiguity and symbolically in his equally racially vague movie roles. In short, he is "everyman." His image enacts America's desired "other": multiracial, de-politicized, and lacking any serious racial allegiance.

When asked about his background, Diesel firmly describes himself as "multicultural." Diesel's name change from Mark Vincent to Vin Diesel seems to corroborate his racial ambiguity or at least encourage a multiracial reading of this ethnicity as "Vin" is a stereotypical Italian American name. ("Diesel" refers to the slang term, "cock diesel," describing a man's muscular physique.) Diesel explains that this nickname emerged when he worked as a bouncer: "We all had nicknames. It was wonderful to detach a little bit" (Tesoriero 61). As an actor, Diesel appears to detach from any racial group. Rumors abound about his Italian mother and African American father, but he maintains, "I want to keep my mystery" (Kirkland). Diesel denies "hiding anything": "It's not that I don't want people to know anything. It's just that I would rather spend more time talking about more productive things that relate to the film [XXX]" (Kirkland). Diesel's silence seems a strategic response not just to advertisers but also to the broader cultural pattern that advertisers respond to, namely multiculturalism. One advertising executive asserts, "Both in the mainstream and at the high end of the marketplace, what is perceived as good, desirable, successful is often a face whose heritage is hard to pin down" (La Ferla). Diesel confirms what Danzy Senna jokingly calls "mulatto fever," telling one reporter that his "ambiguous, chameleon-like ethnicity" is "cool" (Thrupkaew). His production company, One Race, enforces his raceless image, reminiscent of Jean Toomer's early twentieth century proclamation, "I am at once no one of the races, and I am all of them." Diesel's explanation of his racial background captures how his image reflects America's desire for ethnic homogeneity. He presents no controversy and gives no reminders of black/white miscegenation.

Diesel's relationship with the black community seems dubious considering his reticence to claim any identity. Samuel Jackson, who stars with Diesel in XXX, tells People Weekly, "There's an air of mystery and danger about Vin, but he also has a little bit of the just-like-us quality" (Miller 87). Perhaps "just-like-us" speaks to the African American colloquial belief, "we know our own." Jackson's comments imply Diesel's blackness ("just-like-us") but also suggest his multiracial background ("air of mystery"). Despite claiming a nebulous "multicultural" description, Diesel has been somewhat accepted by the black community, at least superficially in terms of his appearances as a presenter at the 2002 NAACP Image Awards and his inclusion in *Ebony's* 2003 top black moneymakers list. This acceptance is, however, limited. A forum on bet.com (Black Entertainment Television) which posed the following question, "If Vin Diesel has any Black heritage, should he claim it publicly?" and articles such as "Outing Diesel" repeat a familiar resentment with celebrities who do not outwardly claim the black community (Hill). Still, that Diesel's refusal to acknowledge (or disclaim) blackness (or any race) has incited less anger and uproar than Tiger Woods's self-termed "Cablinasian" perhaps speaks to America's desire to forget about racial divisions. Similarly, publicity surrounding Vin Diesel exposes America's desires to be like Diesel, "of no particular place, and at the same time, able to be anywhere and be anything" (Iverem).

Diesel's recent movies, with their over-the-top action and "heroes" of superhuman strength, seem geared toward teenagers. Diesel says he claims a "multicultural" identity because of his young audience: "I support the idea of being multicultural primarily for all the invisible kids, the ones who don't fit into one ethnic category and then find themselves lost in some limbo" (Iverem). Homi Bhabha contends that "the multicultural has itself become a 'floating signifier' whose enigma lies less in itself than in the discursive uses of it to mark social processes where differentiation and condensation seem to happen almost synchronically" (31). Diesel represents Bhabha's explication of the multicultural. The celebration over his fame both depends upon his difference as "Hollywood's new superhero: a self-made man unconfined by racial categories" (Thrupkaew) and his ability to relate to Americans as "multiethnic Everyman, a movie star virtually every demographic can claim as its own" (Svetkey 5). Diesel is a floating signifier, and, as *Boiler Room* director Ben Younger claims, "People seem to make him into whatever they want him to be" (Svetkey 5). Unlike Berry who cannot "pass," Diesel's racially uncertain physical characteristics allow him to pass as various ethnicities in his movies. For example, he plays an Italian in *Saving Private Ryan* (1998) and in *The Fast and the Furious* (2001), and a racially ambiguous person in *Boiler Room* (2000), *Pitch Black* (2000), and *The Chronicles of Riddick* (2004). While critics have charged Diesel with passing, others applaud his savvy marketing skills. Diesel admits, "Being multicultural has gone from the Achilles' heel of my career to my strength." He describes the world as a "big melting pot," deducing that "people are ready for a hero who is more ambiguous" (Thrupkaew).

XXX's advertising refers to its main character, Xander Cage, as "a new breed of secret agent," a seemingly intentional though oblique reference to Diesel's mixed-race background and his emergence in a genre once dominated by now outdated white action stars like Arnold Schwarzenegger, Sylvester Stallone, and Bruce Willis (A. White). Similar descriptions follow Diesel, naming him a new "multicultural hero" (Mora) and the "first truly All-American action hero" (A. White). Director Rob Cohen (*XXX* and *The Fast and the Furious*) maintains, "It has taken America a long time to acknowledge the new face of America . . . and to some degree, Vinny is that new face" (Kirkland). Such descriptions recall *Time*'s 1993 special issue cover, "The New Face of America," featuring a future mixed race, computer-made American woman. Suzanne Bost argues that *Time*'s female creation "charms . . . and yet she is taboo, bloodless,

(Continues on next page)

impure" (1). Lauren Berlant suggests that "new faces" like the *Time* cover respond to "problems of immigration, multiculturalism, sexuality, gender, and trans(national) identity that haunt the U.S." (398). What does it mean that this new representative (noncomputerized) face is a man, a "He-man" no less? Diesel's image, in part created through his movie roles, represents America's assimilation and capitalist impulses. In other words, his image encourages the idea that race is a commodity that people can trade, buy, or sell, virtually "e-racing" national histories of racialization. Henry Giroux writes, "National identity in the service of a common culture recognizes cultural differences only to flatten them out in the conservative discourse of assimilation and the liberal appeal to tolerance" (182). The suggestion that Diesel stands for "everyman" attempts to create a national identity that eliminates difference. Santiago Pozo, CEO of Arenas Entertainment, tells *Time*, "In the past, John Wayne and Jimmy Stewart were the face of America. . . . Today it's The Rock or Vin Diesel" (Tesoriero 61). Such a comparison suggests that biracial celebrities like The Rock or Diesel evoke a "multiracial sameness," a sugar pill oxymoron that ends up surreptitiously recentering white normative American identity.

Mariah Carey as Biracial Fantasy

If Halle Berry is America's prized mulatta, then Mariah Carey is her lascivious tragic sister. Carey's image depends on her exploitation of the mulatta stereotype.[10] On the one hand, she represents the alienated racial outsider in songs such as "Outside" (from the *Butterfly* album) where she bemoans the difficulties of not belonging. On the other hand, she exploits the notion of the racially ambiguous seductress, wearing next to nothing in music videos and publicity photos. Since Carey's self-titled debut album in 1990, she has publicly performed various "roles" including white ingenue, biracial outsider, black hip-hopper, and erotic/exotic "other." Kate Lanier, a scriptwriter for Carey's film, *Glitter* (2002), asserts that "a lot of mixed-race girls and young women . . . hold Mariah up as a hero." Lanier claims this makes Carey "proud" because "for a long time she was encouraged to play up her white side. Since she has been allowed creative freedom, she has related more to black culture" (Beller 13). Carey's image both deflects and confirms blackness, creating an "in-between" status she teases in terms of her racialized sexuality. She wears biracial stereotypes like a blackface "costume," allowing audiences to explore racial and sexual fantasies while maintaining racial stereotypes.

Music reviews and articles have paid close attention to Carey's overt sexuality and racial shifts in a popular culture context. Vincent Stephens observes: "Along with genre changes, Carey has taken on a more sexualized visual persona and has become more outspoken about her multiracial heritage and struggles for artistic freedom" (234). Caroline Streeter sees Carey "transform[ing] from white to black before our very eyes" (311). Indeed, Carey's album covers trace her shifting racial movements from what Lisa Jones calls "a rainbow body of African descent, skin toasted almond and hair light brown" to her current whitewashed blond pin-up look (*Bulletproof* 200). While other ethnic stars such as Jennifer Lopez or Beyoncé sport blond hair, Carey's hair transformation seems particularly racially motivated considering the initial marketing of Carey that concealed her blackness. In 1990, music critics labeled Carey a "white Whitney Houston" until outside pressures prompted her record company to make a statement. Carey cleared up misconceptions at a press conference where she declared, "My father is black and Venezuelan. My mother is Irish and an opera singer. I am me" (Jones *Bulletproof* 197). Following Carey's public disclosure, black publications ran articles such as "Mariah Carey Tells Why She Looks White but Sings Black" in *Jet*, and "Mariah Carey: Not Another White Girl Trying to Sing Black" in *Ebony* (Norment), seemingly attempting to assure black audiences that Carey was not trying to pass or disregard her black ancestry. However, Carey's later physical transformation suggests an effort to depart visually from "black" and to reflect white standards of beauty.

Despite publicly claiming a multiracial heritage, Carey admits that her physical hints of blackness made her self-conscious. Recalling her *Butterfly* (1997) album cover, Carey shares that she felt pressured to cover up her face "because I had been told I looked horrible and too ethnic with my face showing" (Grigoriadis 194). As Carey's hair turns straighter and blonder, she increasingly signifies "whiteness" while contradictorily maintaining a position as ethnic "other" vis-a-vis her public assertions of biracialism. Richard Dyer suggests that "blondeness is racially unambiguous" and "the ultimate sign of whiteness" (*Heavenly* 44, 43). Carey represents a racial anomaly because her image simultaneously projects different racial tropes. These competing discourses establish Carey in a biracial narrative that depends upon her liminality.

Musically, Carey has moved from pop to hip-hop, in some ways a symbolic shift from white to black. After Carey divorced then Sony Music president Tommy Mottola, her music and image changed drastically. Carey claims that her *Butterfly* album symbolizes her feelings of personal and professional freedom impelled by her divorce. As she explained it in 1997, "I feel more free to put more of myself into my music" (Thigpen 113). With *Butterfly*, Carey has worked with more hip-hop artists and producers to tap into her "broad demographic." As she observes, "I have an audience that's urban and one that's Middle America." She continues, "So I have to really be a little bit conscious of the fact that it's broad, and also it's diverse in terms of the racial thing. I am anyway, being a mixed person racially" (Carey, Interview by Ehrlich 338). On *Rainbow* (1999), Carey collaborated with hip-hop artists and rappers including Jay-Z, Usher, Da Brat, Missy Elliott, and Snoop Dogg. Carey's earlier albums *Mariah Carey* (1990), *Emotions* (1991), and *Daydream* (1995) demonstrated her penchant for love ballads and cross-over pop songs, save for Carey's "Dreamlover" remix with Ol' Dirty Bastard on *Daydream*. Earlier albums also feature Carey in her pre-blonde days, suggesting that Carey's physical transformation heightened after she professionally embraced black culture. In a 2002 MTV interview Carey revealed, "Most of my friends and most of the music I listen to and most of my influences are R&B and hip-hop" ("Mariah Carey: Shining"). Still, Carey's most hip-hop albums visually emphasize her whiteness, such as *Charmbracelet* which shows her with platinum streaks.

Carey constructs a stereotypical mulatta trope in public discussions of her biraciality. Inside the *Rainbow* CD liner Carey's message to fans expresses her desire for people of all races and hues to live with one another happily and without conflict. Her words both reveal her vision of racial unity and explain why multiracial organizations herald her as an ideal biracial "spokesperson." In "My Saving Grace," on *Charmbracelet*, Carey positions herself as tragic, discussing how during her childhood she felt confused and suffered from low self-esteem due to her

(Continues on next page)

mixedness. In general, she laments over the media's and public's obsession with her racial identity yet openly discusses her feelings of racial alienation and isolation. She shares always feeling "so separate from everybody, even if I never talked about it" (Udovitch 34). She attributes this alienation to various reasons: "Because my father's black and my mother's white. Because I'm very ambiguous-looking." Carey has claimed multiple descriptors including "person of color" and the glib, "I view myself as a human being" (Farley 75). Yet despite Carey's supposed desires to put the issue of her racial background to rest, she often brings it up in interviews and has appeared on national shows like *Oprah* to discuss such issues. In an *Oprah* show entitled "Mariah Carey Talks to Biracial Teens," Carey announces herself as somewhat of a multiracial nationalist, claiming, "I bond with mixed people" (7). Yet, Carey frequently exploits biracial stereotypes, betraying her role model status. Carey's hypersexuality intensifies as she encodes "whiteness" via her album covers and "blackness" via her music, symbolically evoking the "warring" racial divisions and libidinous nature of the mulatta stereotype. Magazine photos play up her sexuality so that her overall image combines multiple representations: mulatta sex kitten, black performer, and white pin-up. However, Carey and her music are not considered "black" in the same way, for example, that Mary J. Blige represents "blackness." And physically, Carey is too ethnic to be a white sex symbol. The result places Carey in an in-between, mixed-race seductress narrative. For example, the *Rainbow* CD liner opens up to reveal a photo which exploits Carey as a heterosexual male fantasy: she suggestively lies on a bed in white cotton underclothes, wearing stiletto heels and licking a heart-shaped lollipop. A nearby phone lying off the hook may suggest Carey's possible roles as phone sex operator or prostitute. Magazine photos of Carey (as in *Vibe* March 2003) (Ogunnaike) are not just revealing, but border on soft porn. In one photo she wears a trench coat, partly opened to reveal her naked body. Another frames Carey lying on a couch, one hand on her breast, the other suggestively positioned below her stomach. Still another shows Carey in an unzipped miniskirt and unzipped midriff top, suggestively looking downwards at her skirt. While many pop stars like Christina Aguilera and Britney Spears also wear skimpy and sexy clothing, Carey's provocative style of dress is coupled with a publicized troubled multiracial identity, making her sexuality fetishized and tragic. Tellingly, Carey cites Marilyn Monroe, a star whose name virtually equaled sex in the 1950s and who began her career as a pin-up, as the person she most admires.[11] Not surprisingly, Barbara Walters symbolically likens the two, calling Carey "a soldier's pin-up girl come to life" while describing her Kosovo trip to visit U.S. troops (Carey, "Surviving").

Carey's semi-autobiographical box office failure, *Glitter*, confirms her racialized sexuality despite its attempts to critique biracial clichés. In one scene the music video director explains his idea for the main character's video: "She is not black, she is not white, she is exotic, OK?" This same theme follows representations of Carey's public and private life. In July 2001, Carey appeared on MTV's *Total Request Live* (*TRL*) pushing an ice-cream cart in a "Loverboy" (the name of *Glitter*'s first single) T-shirt and heels. She proceeded to perform a pseudo striptease, taking off her T-shirt to reveal a hidden skimpy outfit. Entertainment reporters and tabloids ridiculed Carey for her bizarre behavior and incoherent ramblings to *TRL* host,

Carson Daly. Accordingly, *Ego Trip's Big Book of Racism!* comically named Carey their number one "Tragic Mulatto" for, among other things, "a propensity for 'whorelike attire,' a nervous breakdown, a mocked and derided cinematic debut, and a failed soundtrack" (Jenkins et al. 81). Such descriptions urge the question, what role does Carey have in sexualizing her image? Carey reports feeling "constantly amazed" regarding her portrayal as "very loose morally and sexually," an ironic statement considering that Carey invites such readings in nearly all recent publicity photos and public outings ("Mariah Carey Discusses" 58). Though we can never know how much agency stars exert over their image, Carey seems to perpetuate wittingly an oversexual public persona. She represents a historically comfortable vision of mixed race women. Carey poses little threat to racial hierarchy because she fits a mold that showcases just enough "blackness" to intrigue but not enough to appear definitive or political.

New Faces, Old Masks

The media commodifies biracialism by using "new" celebrity faces: Diesel's movie posters that target a younger, more multicultural and multiracial generation and Carey's seemingly produced and packaged embodiment of the mulatta seductress in videos, albums, and magazines. Despite Berry publicly announcing a black identity, her image still "sells" biracialism through media representations of her life and less obviously via her stereotyped movie roles. In this sense, all three stars symbolically represent the "multiracial neutral" in that their images "sell" the idea of racial pluralism and freedom, and yet their images remain "Other," available for audiences and consumers of all racial backgrounds to "claim" or "own." The popularity of these stars does not reflect a more racially tolerant or progressive America. Like the cliché "some of my best friends are black," which attempts to prove a supposed lack of racism, the multiracial craze only superficially embraces the dark "Other." Liberals and conservatives alike have repeatedly placed idealistic expectations on mixed-race individuals in discussions of racism and multiculturalism. Though expectations differ, this pattern gets repeated in a popular culture context with mixed-race stars. Thus, Tiger Woods is not just a superb athlete of color, but an emblem of racial harmony, the Great Multiracial Hope. When stars' images do not fit our vision, we force them into familiar stereotypes that satisfy other expectations. Halle Berry's image may not represent racial unity, but at least it does not depart from what we have learned to expect from mixed-race women. In a popular culture context, biraciality "works" for people who do not really want to confront racial issues when it exploits difference under the guise of celebrating diversity. The "new" faces of America have no racial responsibilities, loyalties, or obligations. People admire them for their beauty, celebrate them as America's future, and envy their "cool" multiracial status. However, old masks lurk alongside interpretations of what new faces represent, namely racial stereotypes. Until power relations equalize, any celebration of mixed race needs to recognize those who are not celebrating or benefiting from America's longtime fascination. Questioning what it means to be black or part-black allows one to be critical of traditional assumptions about racial identification and realize the urgency of racial responsibility in a society built upon racial inequality.

(Continues on next page)

Notes

1. See *Best of the Chris Rock Show*.

2. In 1997, golfer Fuzzy Zoeller made a racist joke during the 62nd Masters golf tournament in Augusta, Georgia. He reportedly joked that he hoped fried chicken and collard greens would not be served at the next year's tournament should Tiger win and choose the menu.

3. My essay focused on these particular celebrities because they have represented multiple racial tropes in popular culture and in their work. Their immense popularity, I argue, is also connected to their "otherness." These stars differ from other biracial stars, such as Alicia Keys, whose blackness often foregrounds their public image. This essay was written after Mariah Carey's 2002 album and after Vin Diesel's and Halle Berry's 2004 films.

4. In his classic book, *Toms, Coons, Mulattoes, Mammies, and Bucks*, Donald Bogle examines the persistence of these five common stereotypes of African Americans on film. Bogle cites *The Debt* (1912) as one of the earliest film representations of the tragic mulatto. Like the literary stereotype, the mulatta on film was often near white, exceedingly beautiful, exotic, and doomed as a result of her mixed race.

5. Such perceptions abound in Web sites and often show up in online discussions, particularly following Berry's Oscar speech, which angered many people who self identify as multiracial. For example, responding to a post in a "Moms of Biracial Children" forum on Commitment.com, one woman writes, "I didn't watch the awards but it's pretty sad that she had to put a label on the [Black] community she was thanking. . . . It's comments like that continues the separatism of races." Another respondent writes, "My daughter a beautiful little girl loves Halle Berry and couldn't understand why she only said she was black. I think it was a very confusing statement." See "Did Halle Berry Forget Her Mom Is White?" for other postings.

6. Continuing her portrayal of "liminal" characters, Berry says she is preparing for a movie entitled *The Guide*, playing "a spiritual woman—half Native American, half African-American—who guides people through times of crisis" (Ritz 128). Most recently, she portrayed Zora Neale Hurston's mixed-race character, Janie, in Oprah Winfrey's television rendition of *Their Eyes Were Watching God*.

7. See, for example, the online discussion, "Bassett: 'Monster' Role Was Demeaning."

8. For a sample of reviews on *Monster's Ball*, see Roger Ebert, Leslie Felperin, Lisa Schwarzbaum, and Stephanie Zacharek.

9. In *Ar'n't I a Woman?: Female Slaves in the Plantation South*, Deborah Gray White argues that the jezebel stereotype that emerged during slavery was used to justify the sexual exploitation of black women. The stereotype suggested that black women were promiscuous and invited rape and sexual abuse.

10. Ironically, an April 2005 *Essence* article on Mariah Carey begins, "This 'mulatto' is hardly tragic" (121). See Joan Morgan.

11. See "All Mariah" on Carey's homepage (www.mariahcarey.com).

Works Cited

"All Mariah." *Mariah Carey*, www.mariahcarey.com. Accessed 19 Mar. 2004.

Andrews, David L., and C. L. Cole. "America's New Son: Tiger Woods and America's Multiculturalism." *Sport Stars: The Cultural Politics of Sporting Celebrity*, edited by David L. Andrews and Steven J. Jackson, Routledge, 2001, pp. 70–86.

"Bassett: 'Monster' Role Was Demeaning." *The Black Web Portal*, www.blackwebportal .com/forums/. Accessed 28 Mar. 2004.

Beller, Thomas. "The New M.C." *Elle*, July 2001, p. 13.

Berlant, Lauren. "The Face of America and the State of Emergency." *Disciplinarity and Dissent in Cultural Studies*, edited by Carey Nelson and Dilip Parameshwar Gaonkar, Routledge, 1996, pp. 397–439.

Berry, Halle. "Halle Berry Dishes the Dirt." Interview by David A. Keeps, *Marie Claire*, Feb. 2002, pp. 52–59.

Best of the Chris Rock Show. HBO, 1999. DVD.

Bhabha, Homi K. "Culture's in Between." *Multicultural States: Rethinking Difference and Identity*, edited by David Bennett, Routledge, 1998, pp. 29–36.

Bogle, Donald. *Toms, Coons, Mulattoes, Mammies, and Bucks*. Continuum, 2003, pp. 166, 174–75.

Bost, Suzanne. *Mulattas and Mestizas: Representing Mixed Identities in the Americas, 1850–2000*. U of Georgia P, 2005, p. 1.

Brown, Sterling B. "Negro Character as Seen by White Authors." *Journal of Negro Education*, 2 Apr. 1933, p. 162.

Carey, Mariah. "Outside." *Butterfly*, Columbia, 1997.

———. *Rainbow*. Columbia, 1999. CD.

———. Interview by Dimitri Ehrlich, *Interview*, Oct. 1999, pp. 338–39.

———. "My Saving Grace." *Charmbracelet*, Island Def Jam, 2002. CD.

———. "Surviving the Glare: Celebrities Who Prevailed After Scandal." Interview with Barbara Walters, *20/20*, ABC, 9 May 2002.

Chambers, Veronica. "Mariah on Fire." *Newsweek*, 15 Nov. 1999, pp. 80–81.

Chesnutt, Charles W. *The House Behind the Cedars*. 1900. Modern Library, 2003, p. 7.

Corliss, Richard. "Halle Berry: Monster's Ball." *Time*, 21 Jan. 2002, pp. 124–25.

"Did Halle Berry Forget Her Mom Is White?" *Moms of Biracial Children*, 11 Sept. 2000, www.commitment.com/boards/boardMB/MBbrmsgs/142.html. Discussion list post.

Dyer, Richard. *Stars*. British Film Institute, 1979, p. 22.

———. *Heavenly Bodies: Film Stars and Society*. St. Martin's Press, 1986, pp. 43–44.

Ebert, Roger. "*Monster's Ball* Review." Review of *Monster's Ball*, directed by Marc Forster, *Chicago Sun-Times*, 1 Feb. 2002, www.suntimes.com/ebert/ ebert_reviews/2002/02/020101/html.

Farley, Christopher John. "Pop's Princess Grows Up." *Time*, 25 Sept. 1995, p. 75.

Felperin, Leslie. "*Monster's Ball* Review." Review of *Monster's Ball*, directed by Marc Forster, *Sight and Sound*, June 2002, sec. 12, p. 46.

(Continues on next page)

Giroux, Henry A. "The Politics of National Identity and the Pedagogy of Multiculturalism in the USA." *Multicultural States: Rethinking Difference and Identity*, edited by David Bennett, Routledge, 1998, p. 182.

Glitter. Directed by Vondie Curtis-Hall, Twentieth Century Fox, 2001.

Grigoriadis, Veronica. "The Money Honey." *Allure*, Sept. 2001, p. 194.

"Halle Berry." *Road to the Red Carpet*. Entertainment Television, 3 May 2003.

Haynes, Esther. "Am I Going to Be Happy or Not?" *Jane*, Dec. 2003, pp. 126–28.

Hill, James. "'Outing' Diesel." *Black Entertainment Television*, 2 Aug. 2002, www.bet.com.articles/o,,c3gb3453-4121,00.html.

Hirschberg, Lynn. "The Beautiful and Damned." *The New York Times Magazine*, 23 Dec. 2001, p. 26.

Iverem, Esther. "A Monster Love." Review of *Monster's Ball*, directed by Marc Forster, 21 Feb. 2002, *Seeing Black*, www.seeingblack.com/x022102/monstersball.shtml.

Jenkins, Sacha, et al. *Ego Trip's Big Book of Racism!* Regan Books, 2002, p. 81.

Johnson, Lynne D. "Bearing the Black Female Body as Witness in Sci-Fi." *Pop Matters*, 1 Dec. 2003, www.popmatters.com/ columnsjohnson/031218.shtml.

Jones, Lisa. "The Blacker the Berry." *Essence*, June 1994, p. 60.

———. *Bulletproof Diva: Tales of Race, Sex, and Hair*. Doubleday, 1994, pp. 50, 197, 200.

Kanganis, Charlie. "Halle Berry." Cinema and the Female Star: A Symposium, Part 1, *Senses of Cinema*, 23 Dec. 2002, www.sensesofcinema.com/contents/02/23/symposium1.html#berry.

Kennedy, Dana. "Halle Berry, Bruised and Beautiful, Is on a Mission." *The New York Times*, 10 Mar. 2002, pp. 2A+.

Kerr, Philip. "A Shocking Cheek." *New Statesman*, 17 June 2002, p. 44.

Kirkland, Bruce. "Word's Out: Vin's In." *Toronto Sun*, 4 Aug. 2004, www.canoe.ca/JamMoviesArtistsD/diesel_vin.html.

La Ferla, Ruth. "Generation E.A.: Ethnically Ambiguous." *The New York Times*, 28 Dec. 2003, sec. 9, pp. 1+.

"Mariah Carey Discusses Her Sex Life, Race, Career." *Jet*, 31 May 2000, pp. 56–60.

"Mariah Carey: Shining Through the Rain." Interview by John Norris, MTV, 3 Dec. 2002.

"Mariah Carey Talks to Biracial Teens." *Oprah*, ABC, 27 Dec. 1999. Transcript.

"Mariah Carey Tells Why She Looks White but Sings Black." *Jet*, 4 Mar. 1991, pp. 56–57.

Mencke, John G. *Mulattoes and Race Mixture: American Attitudes and Images, 1865–1918*. Umi Research Press, 1979, p. 102.

Miller, Samantha. "XXX Appeal." *People*, 19 Aug. 2002, vol. 58, no. 9, pp. 87–88.

"Monster Balls." Review of *Monster's Ball*, directed by Marc Forster, *Metaphilm*, 29 Feb. 2004, www.metaphilm.com/index.php/detail/monsters_ball/.

Mora, Renee Scolaro. Review of *XXX*, directed by Rob Cohen, *Pop Matters*, 9 Aug. 2002, www.popmatters.com/film/reviews/x/xxx.shtml.

Morgan, Joan. "Free at Last." *Essence*, Apr. 2005, p. 121.

Mumford, Kevin J. *Interzones: Black/White Sex Districts in Chicago and New York in the Early Twentieth Century*. Columbia UP, 1997, p. 133.

Norment, Lynn. "Mariah Carey: Not Another White Girl Trying to Sing Black." *Ebony*, Mar. 1991, pp. 54–58.

Ogunnaike, Lola. "Through the Fire." *Vibe*, Mar. 2003, pp. 113–20.

Pappademas, Alex. "Over the 'Rainbow': A Tale of Two Mariahs." *Boston Phoenix*, 22 Nov. 1999, weeklywire.com/ww/11-22-99/boston_music_2.html.

Prince. "Controversy." *Controversy*, Warner Bros., 1981. CD.

Ritz, David. "Heart to Heart." *Essence*, Dec. 2002, pp. 128+.

Root, Maria P. P. "From Shortcuts to Solutions." *Racially Mixed People in America*, edited by Maria P. P. Root, Sage, 1992, pp. 342–47.

Samuels, Allison. "Angela's Fire." *Newsweek*, 1 July 2002, p. 54.

Sanello, Frank. *Halle Berry: A Stormy Life*. Virgin Books, 2003.

Schwarzbaum, Lisa. Review of *Monster's Ball*, directed by Marc Foster, *Entertainment Weekly*, Issue 639, Feb. 2002, p. 47, *EBSCOhost*, doi: 6056917.

Stephens, Vincent. Review of *Rainbow*, by Mariah Carey, *Popular Music & Society*, Summer 2003, sec. 26, pp. 234–35.

Streeter, Caroline A. "The Hazards of Visibility: 'Biracial Women,' Media Images, and Narratives of Identity." *New Faces in a Changing America: Multiracial Identity in the 21st Century*, edited by Loretta I. Winters and Herman L. DeBose, Thousand Sage, 2003, pp. 301–22.

Svetkey, Benjamin. "Vin at All Costs." *Entertainment Weekly*, 2 Aug. 2002, p. 5.

Tesoriero, Heather Won. "The Next Action Hero." *Time*, 5 Aug. 2002, pp. 61–62.

Thigpen, David E. Review of *Butterfly*, by Mariah Carey, *Time*, 15 Sept. 1997, p. 113.

Thrupkaew, Noy. "The Multicultural Mysteries of Vin Diesel." *Alternet*, 16 Aug. 2002, www.alternet.org/story.html?StoryID=13863.

Udovitch, Mim. "An Unmarried Woman." *Rolling Stone*, 5 Feb. 1998, pp. 30–32.

"Wang and Woods." *Asian American E-Zine*, Stony Brook University, 11 Dec. 2002, www.aa2sbu.org/aaezine/articles/sports/12-WangAndWoods.shtml.

White, Armond. Review of *XXX*, directed by Rob Cohen, *New York Press*, www.nypress.com/15/33/film/film2.cfm. Accessed 4 Mar. 2004.

White, Deborah Gray. *Ar'n't I a Woman?: Female Slaves in the Plantation South*. Norton, 1984.

Wickham, DeWayne. "Bassett Criticism Has Its Merit." *USA Today*, p. 15A.

Williams, Patricia. "Bulworth Agonistes." *The Nation*, 7 June 1998, p. 11.

Zacharek, Stephanie. Review of *Monster's Ball*, directed by Marc Forster, *Salon*, 4 Jan. 2002, archive.salon.com/ent/movies/review/2002/01/04/monsters_ball/.

RHETORICAL SITUATION & CHOICES

1. **Purpose.** Dagbovie-Mullins discusses Halle Berry, Vin Diesel, and Mariah Carey, but how does she make it clear from the beginning that she's not writing about these actors as entertainers? What seems to be her main purpose? Does she seem to have secondary purposes?

2. **Audience.** What features of this paper make it clear that she's writing for other scholars, rather than, say, general readers of *People* magazine, who might also be interested in reading about Halle Berry, Vin Diesel, and Mariah Carey? How would the author need to revise for a *People* magazine audience?

3. **Rhetorical appeals.** How does Dagbovie-Mullins establish her authority on the topic she writes about?

4. **Rhetorical appeals.** How does the author appeal to your sense of logic in presenting examples and details to support her points? What specific details appeal to your sense of logos?

5. **Modes & media.** This particular article does not include any images, although there are thousands of images of Halle Berry, Vin Diesel, and Mariah Carey available. Why do you think the author opted not to integrate images into her article?

GENRE CONVENTIONS

6. **Elements of the genre.** What is Dagbovie-Mullins's thesis? How easy was it for you to locate her thesis? What cues does she use in her introduction to indicate that the thesis is coming?

7. **Elements of the genre.** Do you have to be familiar with the author's sources to understand her point? Explain.

8. **Style.** Celebrities are typically considered more appropriate subjects for gossip magazines than scholarly journals. How does the author present celebrities as appropriate subjects for a researched article?

9. **Design.** Dagbovie-Mullins uses subheadings to break the article into chunks. Did you find these helpful? Did you want fewer or more of them? Why or why not? Also note that some subheadings are questions, while others could be considered thought-provoking statements ("Multiracial to the Rescue: Vin Diesel"). How did these subheadings work on you as a reader? Did they make you want to keep reading? Explain.

10. **Sources.** Note the extensive Works Cited list. Glance through the list of sources and note how many seem to be scholarly sources and how many seem to be other types of sources. How does the use of nonscholarly sources seem appropriate or inappropriate for this article?

Are you thinking of drafting a peer-reviewed journal article? Ask yourself the following questions.

RHETORICAL SITUATION & CHOICES

☐ **Purpose.** What topic have I researched that I could inform other experts about? Have I discovered something about the topic that others like me might find interesting or conducive to their own research? Do I want to persuade readers of something? To effectively persuade readers, what will I need to inform them about?

☐ **Audience.** My readers will be experts on my general topic, but they won't know as much as I do about the aspect I'm writing about. How much background information will they need? What kind of terminology will they expect? How will my readers use the information I present?

☐ **Rhetorical appeals.** How will I establish my authority as a writer? How will I build a case for my conclusions using logic? Will I need to cite sources to establish myself as an expert? What kinds of sources will help me build my case?

☐ **Modes & media.** Can some of the information I present be shown with a chart or graphic? Do I want readers to access my article in print or digitally? Or do I want to make both options available?

GENRE CONVENTIONS

☐ **Elements of the genre.** How can I make sure my thesis is clear and declarative? How will I refer to my sources? How can I synthesize my sources to show readers how they are in conversation with each other?

☐ **Style.** How can I project an authoritative voice? How much detail will I need to provide so that readers will understand the complexity and validity of my research?

☐ **Design.** How will I use subheadings to present my information in chunks? Will I use images to illustrate points?

☐ **Sources.** Will my readers expect sources to be cited in MLA style, APA style, or another format? Will my readers respect the types of sources I've referred to?

PRACTICE

Analyzing a Peer-Reviewed Article

Think about a topic you are researching or have already researched for one of your courses. Then, find a peer-reviewed article related to that topic. If you need help locating a peer-reviewed article, please refer to Chapter 10 or ask your instructor or librarian for help. Once you've found the article, read through it carefully, considering the rhetorical choices and genre conventions. Then, create your own close reading or chart using the model of the Dagbovie-Mullins's article found on page 118. After you finish, write a one-page reflection that conveys how the close reading helped or didn't help you understand the peer-reviewed article.

Researched Poster Presentations

Many scholarly articles are science reports (one could be on feral cats), and they are usually submitted as written papers. Sometimes, however, they take different forms. In the following section, we will discuss and present a researched poster presentation. But first, here is some background on why and where this kind of scholarly work would be presented.

An academic or scholarly conference is an event in which faculty, scholars, and/or researchers formally gather to share and discuss their research. Usually three or four scholars each get fifteen to thirty minutes to present their research orally in what is called a panel presentation. Many conferences, however, include sessions called "poster sessions," where researchers present their research in the form of a poster rather than by doing an oral presentation. Ten to several hundred scholars set up their posters in a large room, and conference attendees walk around the room, stopping to view and read the posters they are interested in. Researchers usually stand by their poster, so they can answer questions. Poster sessions are less formal than panel presentations and give attendees the opportunity to spend as much or as little time as they want lingering over a poster and talking with its creator.

Academic or scholarly conferences are organized and hosted by scholarly organizations. Sometimes conferences are organized around a discipline, such as the American Psychological Association's annual convention; other times, conferences attract researchers from a variety of different disciplines who are interested in a particular topic, such as the League for Innovation in the Community College's annual conference on STEM (science, technology, engineering, and math) technology. Many universities have student research conferences on campus that include poster sessions.

Scholars who want to present their work, whether as part of a panel or in poster form, must submit a proposal that is peer-reviewed.

Analyzing Researched Poster Presentations

Purpose   Scholars create researched posters to share their research and findings with other scholars and experts and to engage in conversation with others who are doing research in the same field. As with peer-reviewed journal articles, poster creators may be sharing work that is highly original and groundbreaking, or they may be sharing work that is a replication or extension of another researcher's work.

Creators of researched posters aim to inform other researchers about their work and also to persuade others of the value or significance of their research.

Because poster sessions allow attendees to interact with the poster creator, poster creators often have several purposes: to discuss their research with others, hear feedback from other researchers on their methods or findings, or to meet potential collaborators for related projects.

Audience   The audience is conference attendees. Generally scholars attend conferences in their discipline or related ones to find out what other researchers are doing. A physicist, for example, would likely attend physics conferences but may also attend conferences on astronomy or engineering or education, depending on her research interests and employment.

Rhetorical appeals   For a scholarly poster, the most significant appeals are ethos and logos. Like authors of peer-reviewed journal articles, poster makers need to establish their credibility by carefully describing their research methods, data collection, analysis strategies, and findings. They must cite sources scrupulously. Logos is important because audiences need to understand the logic of the particular research method that was used and see how the conclusions or findings flow logically from the data analysis.

Modes & media   Researched posters use both text and images to present information. Most posters are created on poster board, but depending upon the conference, posters may also be accompanied by sounds, projected images, or other items. A poster at an archaeology conference, for example, could be accompanied by a vase that was excavated at the site the poster is about. A poster can also be presented digitally at a conference. Digital posters allow for the inclusion of both audio and video files. These posters can be viewed by people who are not able to attend the conference.

Elements of the genre   Researched, scholarly posters are characterized by the following. They are:

- *Based on original research.* Poster makers usually present their own original research. Their posters convey information about the research question or topic they studied, the research methods they used, the data they collected, how they analyzed that data, and the conclusions they drew from the data.

- *Peer-reviewed at the proposal level.* Conferences typically require poster presenters to submit a proposal in which they summarize the research for their poster. Proposals are evaluated by scholars who determine whether the proposed poster is relevant to the conference and whether the research described is ethical, in line with the scientific method, and significant.

- *Concise.* Because all the information must be contained on the poster and easily read by people standing several feet away, text must be concise and to the point.

- *Informative and eye-catching.* To attract attention from attendees who might be wandering around the room, posters usually include color and visuals, including charts and graphs, that can be easily viewed from several feet away.

- *Visually organized.* Information is presented in chunks, such as "methods" and "discussion," that are set off from other chunks with a combination of white space, headings, boxes, borders, and color.

Style   Following are some stylistic elements of researched, scholarly posters. Their composers do the following:

- *Feature a descriptive title.* The title needs to immediately convey the topic and significance of the research presented in the poster.

- *Present concise and precise data.* Research and scholarship rely on precision, so posters give specific amounts, durations, chemical names, and so forth rather than generalizations and abstractions.

- *Use simple, clear language.* Posters must clearly convey precise and accurate information, so they do not use figurative language.

Design   Scholarly posters presented at conferences are characterized by the following. They:

- *Are large.* Some posters are sturdy trifold objects that can be stood up on a table, if the conference provides one. Some conferences provide hanging space for posters that are flat. In either case, posters are large, usually between 2 × 3 feet and 5 × 8 feet.

- *Involve poster board.* Posters typically feature computer-printed text and images glued onto poster board; more commonly these days, the text and images are created using a template and then printed on paper the size of the finished poster.

- *Are made to be viewed from a distance.* Because posters are meant to be seen from several feet away, they usually involve large text, images, and colors that contrast for easy reading.

Sources   Creators of researched, scholarly posters cite their sources carefully, providing bibliographies of sources cited. Sometimes sources are cited directly in the text of the poster or listed at the bottom of the poster. Other times, an accompanying bibliography might be handed out at the session.

Guided Reading | Researched Poster Presentation

Ricky Martinez, Vinson Turco, and Ashleigh Nakata are students at Metropolitan State University of Denver. MSU holds an annual undergraduate research conference in which Martinez, Turco, and Nakata participated in a poster session. This poster represents research that they conducted on bird habitats.

Ricky Martinez, Vinson Turco, and Ashleigh Nakata (STUDENTS)
Reforested Pastures and Plantations as Valuable Habitat for Birds in Costa Rica

---

RHETORICAL SITUATION & CHOICES

What are the ▶
composers, students
Ricky Martinez
et al., doing?

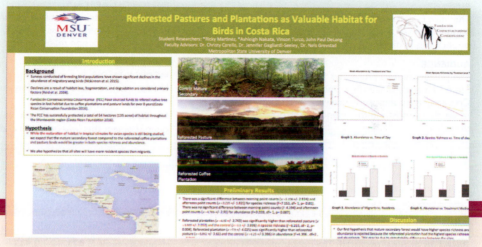

Credit: Used with permission of the authors and creators.

GENRE CONVENTIONS

How do I know ▶
that this is a
researched science
report?

(Continues on next page)

PURPOSE

The main purpose of the poster creators is to share what happened when they tested their hypothesis about bird populations in different climates.

AUDIENCE

The poster creators presented their poster at Metropolitan State University of Denver's Undergraduate Research Conference, so their audience was undergraduate researchers, mostly in the sciences but some from other disciplines.

RHETORICAL APPEALS

The poster creators carefully articulated their methods and results to come across as credible and develop their **ethos.** The discussion relies on logic to explain their results, appealing to **logos.**

MODES & MEDIA

Mode = written and visual: The poster includes both text and images.

Medium = print: The poster was displayed as a professionally printed object that was 36" high and 48" wide.

ELEMENTS OF THE GENRE

Based on original research: The poster presents original research the creators conducted.

Peer-reviewed at the proposal level: The MSU Denver Undergraduate Research Conference requires that all presenters submit an abstract several months before the conference; abstracts are peer-reviewed by a committee.

Concise: Information is conveyed directly, without any extraneous detail. For instance, the poster says, "Surveys conducted of breeding bird populations have shown significant declines in the abundance of migratory song birds."

STYLE

The poster's title clearly indicates the research the poster reports. The poster uses precise language, such as "There were significantly more resident birds (3.365 +/− 1.727) than migratory birds (1.471 +/− 0.943) for species richness for all three treatment groups ($F = 23.686$, $df = 1$, $p = 7.94e\text{-}06$)."

Visually organized: The poster uses color, image, and white space to capture viewers' attention and help them understand how information is organized.

DESIGN

The poster is carefully designed to be readable from several feet away. The poster's creators used a PowerPoint template to create the poster. Chunks of information are clearly defined through the use of boxes and headings.

SOURCES

The poster includes citations.

QUESTIONS | Analyzing the Researched Poster Presentation

RHETORICAL SITUATION & CHOICES

1. **Purpose.** Does the title of the poster make you aware of the purpose of the research that was conducted? If so, how? If not, why not?

2. **Purpose.** One purpose of the poster is to inform viewers/readers about the research the creators did on bird habits. What do you think they are trying to persuade you of?

3. **Audience.** What features of the poster make it clear that the authors anticipated an audience of scientists?

4. **Rhetorical appeals.** How do the poster creators establish their credibility?

5. **Modes & media.** If this poster presentation were being revised into a peer-reviewed journal article, which of the images would you recommend including in the article and why?

GENRES CONVENTIONS

6. **Elements of the genre.** Imagine this poster being 36 inches tall and 48 inches wide and you were seeing it from several feet away. Would the layout, color, and images catch your attention? How is the color scheme of the poster appropriate or inappropriate for the subject of the poster?

7. **Style.** How specific and precise is the "methods" section of the poster? Based on the description of the methods used, do you get a clear sense of what the researchers actually did?

8. **Style.** Can you find any text in the poster that could have been expressed more concisely?

9. **Design.** How do the images in the poster help you understand the information?

10. **Sources.** How do the sources cited add to or detract from the creators' ethos?

CHECKLIST | Drafting a Researched Poster Presentation

Are you thinking of composing a researched science report in poster form? Ask yourself the following questions.

RHETORICAL SITUATION & CHOICES

☐ **Purpose.** What topic have I researched that I could tell others about? How can I persuade others of the significance of my research?

☐ **Audience.** Considering that I will have limited words and space on a poster, what are the key ideas I need to communicate to my audience to capture their interest? What will they already know about my topic? What will I need to explain to them?

GENRE CONVENTIONS

☐ **Elements of the genre.** How can I present my research concisely without leaving out important details? How can I title my poster to efficiently convey its topic? How can I visually organize the information on my poster?

☐ **Style.** How can I make my title descriptive and specific? How can I express the information I want to share as accurately as possible? How can I be as concise as possible?

RHETORICAL SITUATION & CHOICES

☐ **Rhetorical appeals.** How can I establish myself as a credible researcher? How can I make the logical connections between my research and findings clear?

☐ **Modes & media.** What kinds of images can I use? How can I present some of my information through charts and graphs?

GENRE CONVENTIONS

☐ **Design.** What images can I use to help readers/viewers understand the information I am presenting? How can I use color to catch readers'/viewers' attention and help them make sense of the information I am presenting? Which information can I present with charts and graphs?

☐ **Sources.** What sources did I use? Will my readers expect sources to be cited in MLA style, APA style, or another format? Will my readers respect the types of sources I've referred to?

PRACTICE

Remixing Your Research

Think about a research project you recently completed. If you don't have one handy, then find a friend's project or find something on the Web. Consider how you might remix this project into a poster. What kinds of images would you include? What might you use for a descriptive and attention-getting title? Sketch out on paper or on the computer a layout for a poster that would present the information in the original project. Show this to a classmate and get feedback on your concept. Incorporate that feedback as you create the actual poster. Your finished poster can be digital or print.

Critical Analyses

A critical analysis is an evaluation of a particular work. This work might be a piece of literature, a film, an essay, an advertisement, a symphony, or a sculpture. Essentially, the writer does a close reading of the piece and then breaks it down to more fully understand what is being communicated and how. The writer then explains the composer's central points and provides her own evaluation of whether the composer's argument was or was not successful.

Critical analyses are commonly assigned in academia. In literature classes, you often undertake a literary analysis to gain a deeper understanding of literary elements. In a composition class, you might be assigned to read an argumentative essay and then analyze how the writer supports his position in order to help you make your own arguments. In a film studies class, you might be assigned to write a critical analysis of a documentary film to see how a director mediates truth.

The ultimate purpose of a critical analysis is to evaluate and understand how another writer/artist/composer created meaning.

Analyzing Critical Analyses

Purpose Writers critique a work to provide a deeper understanding of how a piece works and to evaluate it. Their purpose is to take a stance on the work and provide evidence from the work to support that stance.

Audience When a critical analysis is written for a school assignment, the audience is usually the teacher and the secondary audience might be peers in the class if they are going to read or peer-review the piece. A critical analysis of a literary work published in a literary journal is written for an audience of scholars wanting to understand more about that particular work.

Rhetorical appeals Writers of critical analyses rely on ethos and logos to make their points. Since a critical analysis is essentially an argument, writers must first establish ethos to gain the reader's trust. For example, to indicate their expertise, they would use terminology associated with the genre they're evaluating. Someone analyzing a poem would use terms such as *meter* and *tone*, while someone analyzing a scientific report might use terms such as *methodology* and *materials*. Writers also rely on logos, supporting their claims with evidence from the text they're analyzing.

Modes & media Critical analyses are most often published as text. When they're part of an academic assignment, they usually must be submitted as written words. They might have visual elements combined with the text if appropriate. For example, if you were analyzing a painting, you might include small visuals that illustrate the part of the painting you are discussing. A critical analysis could also use the mode of audio. The evaluation and analysis could be delivered on the radio as part of a news program or a podcast. Critical analyses are available in both print and digital formats.

WRITE

What types of critical analyses do you enjoy reading, viewing, or listening to? Have you ever composed one outside the classroom (for example, have you posted a review of a business on a Web site like Yelp)? If so, what was it, and what was your purpose? Make a two columned list. In one column included the types of analyses you enjoy reading, viewing, or listening to and in the other column include all the analyses you've composed.

Elements of the genre Critical analyses use the following conventions. Composers:

- *Introduce the work being analyzed.* Since a critical analysis focuses on a particular piece of literature, a film, or something else, the writer always introduces that work to the reader. Sometimes this can be done through the title of the analysis. In addition, an introductory paragraph usually provides the reader with information about the work. If the critical analysis is about a work of art, the writer would provide the reader with the title of the artwork, the name of the artist, the year it was created, and its medium.

- *Provide a summary or description of the work.* The summary is usually brief and only provides the necessary information a reader needs to understand the evaluation.

- *Identify the work's central point or thesis.* What is the central point that the artist, writer, or composer of the piece being analyzed makes? Since an analysis evaluates the success of the piece's argument, it's important to clearly state what the writer believes the composer is attempting to achieve. Besides identifying a central claim, the writer also examines the evidence provided to support this claim.

- *Make a clear evaluative claim.* The writer takes a position about the work being analyzed. It's clear what the writer thinks about the work that is being analyzed. The writer doesn't just restate the work's central point, but judges or evaluates it.

- *Provide evidence from the work to support claims.* Assertions are supported by specific evidence from the text, artwork, or piece being examined.

Style Authors of critical analyses choose titles for their work that make their position clear for readers right away. They also use language that shows their perspective on the piece they are evaluating.

Design Critical analysis papers are formatted like most other academic papers: as text-based essays or researched arguments that follow a specific documentation style, such as MLA, APA, or *Chicago Manual of Style.* Usually these papers have one-inch margins, an introductory paragraph, supporting body paragraphs, a concluding paragraph, and a list of citations because an analysis always draws on at least one other work (the thing being analyzed) and often other sources as well.

Sources Writers of critical analyses provide the following for their readers:

- *Specific examples from the text.* The main source of a critical analysis is the text being analyzed. Sometimes writers include outside research, if appropriate, to help support their claims. For example, in doing a literary analysis, writers might include some analyses by other literary critics that help support their claims about the work.

- *Documentation of the piece they're analyzing.* The piece being analyzed, plus any outside sources, are included in a Works Cited list at the end of the analysis, as well as in parenthetical citations in the body of the essay.

Guided Reading | Critical Analysis

Student Ren Yoshida was given an assignment to find an advertisement on a topic that interests him. He was asked to then compose a critical analysis of that ad. In his analysis on page 146, Yoshida responds to a coffee ad created for a company called Equal Exchange. Before he wrote his analysis, he did a close reading of the ad and annotated it. Take a look at the annotated version of the ad below before you read Yoshida's analysis.

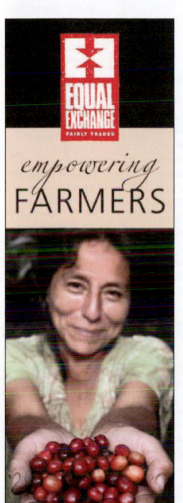

What does "Equal Exchange" mean? What is being exchanged? Is the exchange truly "equal"?

Who is "Empowering Farmers"? Why is "Empowering" presented in a cursive font? Maybe to contrast the "FARMERS," in sturdy all capital letters?

Straightforward design and not much text.

The central image is outstretched hands. Is she giving a gift? Inviting a partnership?

Model's hands held in a heart shape, filled with coffee beans. Angle makes her hands large.

Coffee beans are red, earthy.

Ad text has positive words: consumers choose, join, empower, farmers stay, care, farm, support, plan.

What is the "network"?

How would I know whether buying this coffee will help farmers stay on their land?

◀ ANNOTATED ADVERTISEMENT

Equal Exchange, "Empowering Farmers." Annotations by Ren Yoshida, student.

Ren Yoshida (STUDENT), *Sometimes a Cup of Coffee Is Just a Cup of Coffee*

RHETORICAL SITUATION & CHOICES

PURPOSE
Yoshida takes an evaluative stance regarding the advertisement. He wants to show readers that while the ad succeeds on an emotional level, it fails on a logical level.

AUDIENCE
Since the critical analysis was a response to an assignment in class (to analyze an advertisement), Yoshida's audience is his instructor and peers (unless he chooses to share his work outside the classroom).

RHETORICAL APPEALS
Yoshida establishes his ethos by using specific elements found in advertising. This shows that he is familiar with the genre's conventions, such as by discussing the ad's design elements. He also relies on logos to make his case, providing specific examples from the ad as support for his assertions.

MODES & MEDIA
Mode = text: While Yoshida might have included some specific screenshots from the ad to illustrate his point visually, he instead relies on just text to make his points.

◄ What is the composer, Ren Yoshida, doing?

GENRE CONVENTIONS

How do I know that this ► is a critical analysis?

English 101

Ren Yoshida
Professor Marcotte
4 November 2012

Sometimes a Cup of Coffee Is Just a Cup of Coffee

A farmer, her hardworking hands full of coffee beans, reaches out from an Equal Exchange advertisement (Equal Exchange). The hands, in the shape of a heart, offer to consumers the fruit of the farmer's labor. The ad's message is straightforward: in choosing Equal Exchange, consumers become global citizens, partnering with farmers to help save the planet. Suddenly, a cup of coffee is more than just a morning ritual; a cup of coffee is a moral choice that empowers both consumers and farmers. This simple exchange appeals to a consumer's desire to be a good person—to protect the environment and do the right thing. Yet the ad is more complicated than it first seems, and its design raises some logical questions about such an exchange. Although the ad works successfully on an emotional level, it is less successful on a logical level because of its promise for an equal exchange between consumers and farmers.

The focus of the ad is a farmer, Jesus Choqueheranca de Quevero, and, more specifically, her outstretched, cupped hands. Her hands are full of red, raw coffee, her life's work. The ad successfully appeals to consumers' emotions, assuming they will find the farmer's welcoming face and hands, caked with dirt, more appealing than startling statistics about the state of the environment or the number of farmers who lose their land each year. It seems almost rude not to accept the farmer's generous offering since we know her name and, as the ad implies, have the choice to "empower" her. In fact, how can a consumer resist helping the farmer "[c]are for the environment" and "[p]lan for the future," when it is a simple matter of choosing the right coffee? The ad sends the message that our future is a global future in which producers and consumers are bound together.

First impressions play a major role in the success of an advertisement. Consumers are pulled toward a product, or pushed away, by an ad's initial visual and emotional appeal.

ELEMENTS OF THE GENRE
- In the opening sentence, Yoshida **introduces the advertisement** and its creator, The Equal Exchange.
- Yoshida's opening paragraph **provides a summary and description** of the advertisement. He gives us details about the ad, such as the hands being "in the shape of a heart."
- At the end of his opening paragraph, Yoshida **makes a clear evaluative claim:** "Although the ad works successfully on an emotional level, it is less successful on a logical level because of its promise for an equal exchange between consumers and farmers."
- Throughout the analysis, Yoshida **provides evidence to support his claims.** He discusses the farmer's hands, uses pieces of text from the ad, and incorporates elements of the ad's design.

STYLE
Yoshida's title "Sometimes a Cup of Coffee Is Just a Cup of Coffee" indicates **his position.**

Medium = print:
This assignment was
submitted in print
form.

Here, the intended audience is busy people, so the ad tries to catch viewers' attention and make a strong impression immediately. Yet with a second or third viewing, consumers might start to ask some logical questions about Equal Exchange before buying their morning coffee. Although the farmer extends her heart-shaped hands to consumers, they are not actually buying a cup of coffee or the raw coffee directly from her. In reality, consumers are buying from Equal Exchange, even if the ad substitutes the more positive word choose for buy. Furthermore, consumers aren't actually empowering the farmer; they are joining "a network that empowers farmers." The idea of a network makes a simple transaction more complicated. How do consumers know their money helps farmers "[s]tay on their land" and "[p]lan for the future" as the ad promises? They don't.

The ad's design elements raise questions about the use of the key terms equal exchange and empowering farmers. The Equal Exchange logo suggests symmetry and equality, with two red arrows facing each other, but the words of the logo appear almost like an eye exam poster, with each line decreasing in font size and clarity. The words fairly traded are tiny. Below the logo, the words empowering farmers are presented in contradictory fonts. Empowering is written in a flowing, cursive font, almost the opposite of what might be considered empowering, whereas farmers is written in a plain, sturdy font.

The ad's varying fonts communicate differently and make it hard to know exactly what is being exchanged and who is becoming empowered.

What is being exchanged? The logic of the ad suggests that consumers will improve the future by choosing Equal Exchange. The first exchange is economic: consumers give one thing—dollars—and receive something in return—a cup of coffee—and the farmer stays on her land. The second exchange is more complicated because it involves a moral exchange. The ad suggests that if consumers don't choose "fairly traded" products, farmers will be forced off their land and the environment destroyed. This exchange, when put into motion by consumers choosing to purchase products not "fairly traded," has negative consequences for both consumers and farmers. The message of the ad is that the actual exchange taking place is not economic but moral; after all, nothing is being bought, only chosen. Yet the logic of this exchange quickly falls apart. Consumers aren't empowered to become global citizens simply by choosing Equal Exchange, and farmers aren't empowered to plan for the future by consumers' choices. And even if all this empowerment magically happened, there is nothing equal about such an exchange.

Yoshida uses **language that illustrates judgment.** He uses words like *successful* and *suggests*.

DESIGN

Straightforward academic essay and research paper format: text organized into paragraphs with source citations.

SOURCES

Using the MLA style of documentation, the author cites his source in the body of the text and at the end under a Work Cited heading.

(Continues on next page)

Advertisements are themselves about empowerment—encouraging viewers to believe they can become someone or do something by identifying, emotionally or logically, with a product. In the Equal Exchange ad, consumers are emotionally persuaded to identify with a farmer whose face is not easily forgotten and whose heart-shaped hands hold a collective future. On a logical level, though, the ad raises questions because empowerment, although a good concept to choose, is not easily or equally exchanged. Sometimes a cup of coffee is just a cup of coffee.

Work Cited

Equal Exchange. Advertisement. Equal Exchange. Equal Exchange, n.d. Web. 14 Oct. 2012.

QUESTIONS | Analyzing Yoshida's Critical Analysis

RHETORICAL SITUATION & CHOICES

1. **Purpose.** What stance does Yoshida take regarding the advertisement? Is his claim evaluative? Why or why not?

2. **Purpose.** How does Yoshida provide his audience with a deeper understanding of how the advertisement is constructed and its effectiveness?

3. **Audience.** Even though this piece was written for a class assignment, and thus his audience are his teacher and peers, this analysis might have other audiences. Who might they be? Why?

4. **Rhetorical appeals.** How does Yoshida establish his ethos? Do you find him to be a credible writer? Why or why not?

5. **Modes & media.** How would the piece be stronger if Yoshida had included visuals of the ad throughout? Which visuals might he have included?

GENRE CONVENTIONS

6. **Elements of the genre.** How effective is Yoshida in presenting a balance of summary and evaluation? Are there places where you wanted more summary? More evaluation?

7. **Style.** How does Yoshida use diction to show that his writing is evaluative? Use specific examples from the analysis.

8. **Style.** How does Yoshida's title prepare you for his analysis? Is the title aligned with his purpose? Why or why not?

9. **Design.** Yoshida has clearly designed this piece as an essay for a class assignment. Consider your response to question 3 on audience. How would he need to alter the design to address a different audience?

10. **Sources.** How effective is Yoshida in providing evidence from the text? Are there places where he might have used more evidence? If so, where? What types of evidence?

CHECKLIST | Drafting a Critical Analysis

Are you thinking of writing a critical analysis? Ask yourself the following questions.

RHETORICAL SITUATION & CHOICES

☐ **Purpose.** What is my central evaluative claim I want to make? What is it that I want to understand about the piece I'm analyzing?

☐ **Audience.** What do I hope my audience learns from this piece? Have I described the piece enough for an audience that is unfamiliar with what I'm analyzing?

☐ **Rhetorical appeals.** Have I established my ethos so that my reader trusts my judgments? Have I used terminology that shows I'm familiar with the genre I'm analyzing? Is my logos evident? Have I used enough evidence to build my case?

☐ **Modes & media.** Is text the only way to present my analysis? How would it be strengthened by including any audio? Visuals? Are there advantages to presenting this digitally? Print?

GENRE CONVENTIONS

☐ **Elements of the genre.** Have I properly introduced the work being analyzed? Have I provided a brief summary? Have I examined the writer/composer's central claim? Have I presented my own clear evaluative claim?

☐ **Style.** Does my title indicate the position I'm taking? Am I using language throughout that indicates how I feel about the work I'm evaluating?

☐ **Design.** Have I formatted this to meet the assignment? Have I used proper essay structure? Do I have a clear introductory and concluding paragraph?

☐ **Sources.** Have I included enough evidence from the work to support my claims? Have I properly cited my information? Have I included a Works Cited page for any of the sources used?

PRACTICE

Analyzing the Work of Others

Is there a film you watched recently that was particularly interesting or memorable? Or perhaps a new album has come out by your favorite artist? Maybe you are mesmerized by a particular ad? Or series of tweets? Choose something that captivates you and read/watch/listen to it several times, and very closely. What do you notice about the work upon close examination? Take notes about what the composer's central point is and how she achieves that, perhaps breaking the piece into its parts. Then, draft a critical analysis in which you take a clear stance about the work you're evaluating. Be sure to include specific evidence from the original work.

Literacy Narratives

A literacy narrative tells a story of remembering. In this sense, it is similar to a memoir. Like memoirists, when the writers of literacy narratives tell their own stories, they relate events and also analyze how these events have shaped their identities. However, there is an important difference between the memoir and the literacy narrative: The writers of literacy narratives tell a story specifically about how they learned to read and/or write.

You may be familiar with literacy narratives already; many memoirs include sections about how the authors learned to read or write or important moments in the development of their literacy. Examples include Jimmy Santiago Baca's *Working in the Dark* and Eudora Welty's *One Writer's Beginnings*. Other memoirs focus more on the development of the author's literacy, such as Stephen King's *On Writing* and Anne Lamott's *Bird by Bird*. Sometimes memoirists will use the story of the development of their reading and writing as a context in which other stories are woven, as Azar Nafisi does in *Reading Lolita in Tehran: A Memoir in Books*, in which she tells the story of a secret women's book group in Iran and how the books they read reflected and affected the lives of the women in the group.

WRITE

What was the first book (or sentence or word) you read? What was the context? Where were you, and who was present? What was the experience like for you? Put your pen to paper and freewrite for ten minutes about this experience.

Analyzing Literacy Narratives

Purpose People write literacy narratives because their formative experiences with reading and writing are important to them; they want to share their stories with others, especially if their literacy histories involve obstacles or challenges. Some may also want to make an argument about the importance of literacy.

Audience Literacy narratives are often written in composition classes and other college courses. Instructors assign this genre to help students understand what influences their speaking, reading, and writing. In this case, a writer's main audience is his or her instructor and classmates. Outside the classroom, writers create literacy narratives to help educators, librarians, and other people involved in literacy fields better understand how literacy practices and histories manifest themselves in people's lives. (For examples of narratives in various media—text, audio, and video—see the Digital Archive of Literacy Narratives at Ohio State University.)

Literacy narratives are often published for a wider, popular audience; they may appear in a magazine or journal, or as part of a larger collection of essays, as is the case for the narrative that appears later in this section (the excerpt from Richard Rodriguez's *Hunger of Memory* on p. 153).

Rhetorical appeals Writers of literacy narratives use direct language and real details from their lives to establish credibility (ethos). They also make logical connections (logos) between their narratives and the larger issues of literacy; often these authors write to emphasize and argue about the importance of literacy, which makes the use of logos especially important.

Modes & media   Many writers of literacy narratives use the traditional essay or book form; for example, Helen Keller includes her memoir of learning to understand Braille in her autobiography, *The Story of My Life*. Other literacy narratives appear on the Internet as blog entries or YouTube videos, or are presented in online archives.

Elements of the genre   Literacy narratives can take the form of memoirs, in which writers reflect on moments in their lives that show how reading and writing have affected their experiences and sense of self. Authors of literacy narratives convey their experiences, framing their interactions with the world in terms of reading and writing. They also use personal anecdotes and autobiographical details to re-create their experiences for the reader.

Like memoirs, most literacy narratives are written in the first person. Authors of literacy narratives tell stories not just for the sake of recounting events; rather, their goal is for the narrative to culminate in a larger idea or theme. Writers also use literary elements such as setting, character development, dialogue, vivid descriptions and details, symbols, and metaphors.

Style   Authors use detail to re-create their literacy experiences for readers. For example, in her literacy narrative, Helen Keller shows readers, through specific examples, what it was like to be a blind and deaf child:

WRITE

Think of the stories, memoirs, and other narratives you've read, viewed, or listened to in your life. What details stand out from these stories? How do they affect the ways you think about and remember each story? Jot some notes down to answer these questions. Then turn to a classmate and share your memories.

EXCERPT FROM A LITERACY NARRATIVE

My aunt made me a big doll out of towels. It was the most comical, shapeless thing, this improvised doll, with no nose, mouth, ears or eyes—nothing that even the imagination of a child could convert into a face. Curiously enough, the absence of eyes struck me more than all the other defects put together. I pointed this out to everybody with provoking persistency, but no one seemed equal to the task of providing the doll with eyes. A bright idea, however, shot into my mind, and the problem was solved. I tumbled off the seat and searched under it until I found my aunt's cape, which was trimmed with large beads. I pulled two beads off and indicated to her that I wanted her to sew them on my doll. She raised my hand to her eyes in a questioning way, and I nodded energetically. The beads were sewed in the right place and I could not contain myself for joy.

Helen Keller, from *The Story of My Life*

Most authors of this genre take literacy seriously, which is why they want to write about it and share their experiences with readers; however, each author of a literacy narrative conveys his or her story in a unique voice. Keller's voice emphasizes that, in many ways, she was just like any other child, playing with dolls. Her matter-of-fact tone helps readers identify with and understand her childhood experiences.

Design   The literacy narrative usually takes an essay format: It has an introduction, body paragraphs, and a conclusion. However, literacy narratives can take different forms, including audio essay and documentary. In their written form, literacy narratives use typography to emphasize certain points or language. For example, in the Rodriguez's excerpt, Spanish words are in italics to call attention to them.

Sources   Like print and graphic memoirs, literacy narratives seldom cite outside sources because the source of information is almost always just the writer's memories of his or her own life.

Guided Reading | Literacy Narrative

Richard Rodriguez's *Hunger of Memory* is a collection of autobiographical essays. In the following excerpt, which he calls a memoir and which is also a literacy narrative (genres sometimes overlap), Rodriguez focuses on the power of language as he explores his childhood experiences in a bilingual world. He relates the struggles he faced living in between a Spanish-speaking world and an English-speaking world.

The notes in the margins point out Rodriguez's goals as a writer and his strategies for connecting with his readers. They also show how he works with the genre's conventions to tell a compelling story about literacy.

▶ **BOOK COVER**

Richard Rodriguez on the cover of his autobiography.

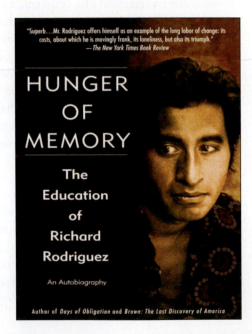

"Superb...Mr. Rodriguez offers himself as an example of the long labor of change: its costs, about which he is movingly frank, its loneliness, but also its triumph."
— *The New York Times Book Review*

HUNGER OF MEMORY

The Education of Richard Rodriguez

An Autobiography

Author of *Days of Obligation* and *Brown: The Last Discovery of America*

Richard Rodriguez, From *Hunger of Memory: The Education of Richard Rodriguez*

RHETORICAL SITUATION & CHOICES

GENRE CONVENTIONS

PURPOSE
Rodriguez aims to share the story of how he came to speak both English and Spanish.

AUDIENCE
The author knows his primary readers care about language and identity. They are bilingual or native English speakers interested in themes of education, family, and coming-of-age.

RHETORICAL APPEALS
Rodriguez begins with a brief story about his parents being willing to do anything for their children, an appeal to pathos. The teachers' connecting of Rodriguez's behavior to his lack of English is an example of logos.

MODES & MEDIA

Mode = written:
This literacy narrative is written. Because Rodriguez's topic is language, his choice to convey his story in written words makes sense. If he were to adapt this narrative using digital technology, he might embed audio so his readers could hear what he experienced.

Medium = print:
Rodriguez's book is intended to be read in hard-copy format or as an e-book. In either case, it's intended

◀ What is the composer, Richard Rodriguez, doing?

How do I know that this ▶ is a literacy narrative?

Three months. Five. Half a year passed. Unsmiling, ever watchful, my teachers noted my silence. They began to connect my behavior with the difficult progress my older sister and brother were making. Until one Saturday morning three nuns arrived at the house to talk to our parents. Stiffly, they sat on the blue living room sofa. From the doorway of another room, spying the visitors, I noted the incongruity— the clash of two worlds, the faces and voices of school intruding upon the familiar setting of home. I overheard one voice gently wondering, "Do your children speak only Spanish at home, Mrs. Rodriguez?" While another voice added, "That Richard especially seems so timid and shy."

That Rich-heard!

With great tact the visitors continued, "Is it possible for you and your husband to encourage your children to practice their English when they are home?" Of course, my parents complied. What would they not do for their children's well-being? And how could they have questioned the Church's authority which those women represented? In an instant, they agreed to give up the language (the sounds) that had revealed and accentuated our family's closeness.

The moment after the visitors left, the change was observed. "*Ahora*, speak to us *en inglés*," my father and mother united to tell us.

At first, it seemed a kind of game. After dinner each night, the family gathered to practice "our" English. (It was still then *inglés*, a language foreign to us, so we felt drawn as strangers to it.) Laughing, we would try to define words we could not pronounce. We played with strange English sounds, often over-anglicizing our pronunciations. And we filled the smiling gaps of our sentences with familiar Spanish sounds. But that was cheating, somebody shouted. Everyone laughed. In school, meanwhile, like my brother and sister, I was required to attend a daily tutoring session. I needed a full year of special attention. I also needed my teachers to keep my attention from straying in class by calling out, Rich-heard—their English voices slowly prying loose my ties to my other name, its three notes, Ri-car-do. Most of all I needed to hear my mother and father speak to me in a moment of seriousness in broken—suddenly heartbreaking—English.

ELEMENTS OF THE GENRE
This is an **autobiographical account about literacy**. Rodriguez shares childhood experiences of learning to speak, read, and write.

He uses **anecdotes** to advance a central idea; for example, with the brief, personal story in paragraph 1, Rodriguez prepares readers for his ideas about language and identity and for his argument about bilingual education.

He writes in the **first person** and **describes settings** to connect readers with his experience. He contrasts his home setting with his classroom (where he is an outsider) to **emphasize the difference in his private and public encounters with literacy.**

STYLE
Rodriguez **uses rich detail** to re-create his experience for readers. Because his essay centers on how he hears language, he focuses on bringing the **dialogue** alive and uses phonetic spelling so that readers hear exactly what he hears.

His **tone and voice reflect his personality**

(Continues on next page)

to be read from beginning to end, one page at a time, unlike online literacy narratives, which can be read in a nonlinear fashion.

The scene was inevitable: One Saturday morning I entered the kitchen where my parents were talking in Spanish. I did not realize that they were talking in Spanish, however, until at the moment they saw me, I heard their voices change to speak English. Those gringo sounds they uttered startled me. Pushed me away. In that moment of trivial misunderstanding and profound insight, I felt my throat twisted by unsounded grief. I turned quickly and left the room. But I had no place to escape to with Spanish. (The spell was broken.) My brother and sisters were speaking English in another part of the house.

Again and again in the days following, increasingly angry, I was obliged to hear my mother and father: "*Speak to us en inglés*" (*Speak*). Only then did I determine to learn classroom English. Weeks afterward, it happened: One day in school I raised my hand to volunteer an answer. I spoke out in a loud voice. And I did not think it remarkable when the entire class understood. That day, I moved very far from the disadvantaged child I had been only days earlier. The belief, the calming assurance that I belonged in public, had at last taken hold.

and speech. He quotes the nuns to emphasize how they enunciate and "Americanize" words.

DESIGN
Rodriguez uses italics to highlight Spanish and English words, and also to emphasize certain passages and sounds ("*That Rich-heard!*").

SOURCES
Rodriguez does not cite outside sources because he is the source of his story.

Credit: From Hunger of Memory: The Education of Richard Rodriguez by Richard Rodriguez. Reprinted by permission of David R. Godine, Publisher, Inc. Copyright © 1982 by Richard Rodriguez.

QUESTIONS | Analyzing Rodriguez's Literacy Narrative

RHETORICAL SITUATION & CHOICES

1. **Purpose.** Rodriguez not only tells a story about his experiences with language but also makes an argument regarding bilingual education. What is his argument? How persuasive is he?

2. **Purpose.** Reread the final paragraph of the essay. Why do you think Rodriguez chose to conclude this way?

3. **Audience.** What techniques does Rodriguez use to connect with his audience? Is an audience that has experienced bilingual education his target audience? Why or why not?

4. **Rhetorical appeals.** How does Rodriguez develop his ethos as someone who speaks about education with authority? How does his

GENRE CONVENTIONS

6. **Elements of the genre.** What are some similarities between Rodriguez's literacy narrative and memoirs that you may be familiar with (e.g., see Alison Bechdel's graphic memoir on p. 255)?

7. **Style.** Given that writers of literacy narratives tell stories about how they learned to speak, read, or write, why might many of them include dialogue? What role does dialogue play in Rodriguez's literacy narrative?

8. **Style.** Rodriguez includes some Spanish words in his narrative. How do the Spanish words contribute to the essay's effect?

phonetic spelling of "Rich-heard" contribute to the pathos of the piece?

5. **Modes & media.** Imagine Rodriguez's literacy narrative as a digital text online. Which words of the excerpt could be linked to other Web sites? For example, perhaps the word "Rich-heard" could be linked to a YouTube video in which someone says the name as Rodriguez's family would say it; this might emphasize how strange the Americanized pronunciation sounded to Rodriguez.

9. **Design.** Rodriguez italicizes bits of dialogue. What do you think is his purpose for doing so?

10. **Sources.** The source for this literacy narrative excerpt is Rodriguez's own memory. Do you think a narrative written by one of the nuns would differ significantly from Rodriguez's? Why or why not?

CHECKLIST | Drafting a Literacy Narrative

Are you thinking of writing about how you learned to speak, read, and write? Ask yourself the following questions.

RHETORICAL SITUATION & CHOICES

☐ **Purpose.** What specific moment in my life as a reader or writer do I want to write about? Why? What questions do I have about that moment? How might I interpret that moment? What insights do I want to share with others? How did that moment shape me as a reader or writer?

☐ **Audience.** How would I describe my readers? Why will my experience with reading or writing matter to my readers? What do I want them to get out of my story? And how will I reach them?

☐ **Rhetorical appeals.** How will I establish my authority as a writer? How reliable will I be as a narrator? To what extent will I appeal to my readers' emotions? To what extent will I rely on logic to support my interpretations of my experiences?

☐ **Modes & media.** Do I want readers to experience my story in written, audio, or visual form? Do I want my literacy narrative to be print, electronic, or presented face-to-face?

GENRE CONVENTIONS MATTER

☐ **Elements of the genre.** I'm writing about my own life: How will I keep my writing true and accurate? How much will I disclose about myself (and others) in my literacy memoir? Will I write in the first person? What anecdotes will I use to tell the story of myself as a reader or writer, and why? Also, what literary elements might I use? For example, will I use dialogue (as Rodriguez does) or a metaphor to help readers compare my experience to something else?

☐ **Style.** What tone will I take in my writing? Will my literacy narrative be serious or funny? Academic or down-to-earth? What kind of language will I use? How much detail will I include?

☐ **Design.** What format will my literacy narrative take? Do I want to compose a standard literacy narrative, focusing on words, or do I want to create a graphic literacy narrative that includes illustrations?

☐ **Sources.** What memories will I draw on? Will I need to check my story with others from my life, or will I rely on my own recollections and interpretations?

PRACTICE

Drawing on Memory & Experience

Think of a single moment from your early life, one that has to do with how you read, see, and experience the world through language. Or, perhaps you want to draw on a recent experience that has shaped you in terms of language, reading, and writing. Freewrite about the experience and how it has shaped your attitudes toward language. Draft a narrative in which you tell the story of your experience; be sure to make specific points about how it shaped you as a reader, writer, and/or speaker. Include anecdotes, details, and quotations from conversations, as Rodriguez does.

Digital Stories

Digital stories are short narratives composed with digital tools. They usually include a combination of digital images, recorded narration, video clips, text, and/or music. Much like other types of stories, digital stories tend to focus on a particular topic and are told from a specific point of view. These finished stories are often shared on the Internet, hosted on such sites as YouTube or Vimeo, or published on digital storytelling sites such as StoryCenter. They can also be shared in the classroom as a culminating presentation of an assignment.

One of the early pioneers of digital storytelling is the documentary filmmaker Ken Burns. In his documentary *The Civil War*, he combined first-person accounts of events with narration, music, and photographs. In the 1990s, digital stories began to be integrated into academia. They are used in a variety of subject areas, such as humanities, science, sociology, and composition.

WRITE

What are some stories you might tell that would be enhanced by using pictures and music? Make a list of those stories and next to each story, jot down what types of pictures and/or music might enhance the story.

Analyzing Digital Stories

Purpose   Writers often compose digital stories to share an experience with their audience. Like a memoirist, digital story composers believe that their insights might help others who have found themselves in similar situations. Sometimes digital storytellers want to share a piece of their family history or help others travel to distant lands in order to experience the wonder and discoveries of their journey. Other times, a digital story might be told to help someone care about or understand an issue, as when a person who has struggled with depression tells his story, hoping to help people who have never experienced depression understand the illness.

Audience   Digital storytellers often compose for a wide audience. However, some might imagine that their audience will be someone who has shared a similar experience.

If a digital story is related to a particular cause, then the audience might be someone who wants to learn about that issue or is already involved in the movement. When a digital story is part of an academic class, the audience is your classmates and professor.

Rhetorical appeals   In order for their story to be believed, digital storytellers need to be reliable narrators. They develop ethos through the anecdotes they share from their own experience. Photographs from the narrator's archives also help convey the truth of the story. Pathos is also central in a digital story, since most digital stories have an emotional layer to help the audience connect with the experience.

Modes & media   Digital stories combine audio and visuals. The audio almost always includes the story's narration. Other audio elements commonly included in a digital story are a soundtrack and sound from any included video. The visuals are usually a series of photographs. Sometimes a digital story might also include some video. Although text is often a part of the story, usually it is only a minor part, in the form of captions or as a title or closing screen. Digital stories are always presented through a digital medium.

Elements of the genre   Following are some of the most common elements of the digital story. Composers of this genre provide:

- *A central, dramatic question.* The story has at its core a particular question that is ultimately answered by the end of the story. This is not always an actual question, but rather a statement that provides the arc for the story.

- *A point of view.* Every story has a particular point of view. This is the vantage point of the narrator. Digital stories use first-person narration (*I did this*) to help the audience connect with the narrative.

- *Emotional content.* Since digital stories tend to use pathos to connect with their audience, the content of the story usually has some type of emotional pull. Content might elicit laughter, tears, shock, or sympathy.

- *Economy.* Digital stories are usually two to five minutes long. The focus should be limited in scope, using just enough detail to get the central point across.

- *Voice.* Since digital stories are usually narrated by the story's writer, the voice can help deliver emotional meaning. By changing the pitch, the narrator can illustrate emotions such as curiosity or anger.

- *Pacing.* A digital story is neither rushed nor told at a crawling pace. Instead, it tends to vary, speeding up to help build tension and slowing down for emphasis (such as by lingering on a particular visual). Varying the pacing helps hold the audience's attention.

- *Soundtrack.* Music and other sounds are often included to help build the story. Music can help establish the mood. It's important that the music doesn't compete with the story by being too loud or having lyrics run over the narration. Also, any music that is added needs to adhere to copyright laws.

Style   Composers of digital stories make stylistic choices based on the following:

- *Detail.* Digital stories usually provide details through narrated anecdotes and visuals. The details help develop the central character (usually the narrator) and her situation. Since economy is a key element of a digital story, details are kept to a minimum (just enough to convey the central point).
- *Tone.* The overall tone of the story is usually informal. It contains language that is natural to the speaker, rather than the elevated diction that might characterize a peer-reviewed journal article. It may include colloquialisms, such as "y'all."
- *Organization.* A digital story is usually organized around a sequence of events that are ordered in a way that helps build tension and that illustrates the experience of the narrator.

Design   When designing their digital stories, composers consider the following:

- *Framing.* Much like films, a digital story uses framing to help a viewer see what to focus on. Zooming can be used to highlight a particular aspect of a photograph, such as a face. Panning from one side of the visual can simulate the reading of a storyboard, revealing pieces of the photograph slowly to the viewer.
- *Duration of images.* When a digital story is assembled, the creator decides how much time a visual should be on-screen. The amount of time is usually varied throughout so that the pacing of the visuals is not monotonous.
- *Transitions between images.* Composers need to decide how to transition between different visuals. Sometimes there is a fade-in, while other times there might be a dissolve of one photo before the next one appears. Whatever transitions are chosen, it's important to avoid distracting the viewer with techniques such as swirling, where a visual spins around into focus.

Sources   The primary source of information for a digital story is usually the composer's life. Any other material that is included is usually attributed in the closing credits with a list of where the visuals/audio were found (while paying close attention to copyright laws).

Guided Reading | Digital Story

In her digital story *Writing the Music Train*, Amy documents her days as a punk rocker. She presents herself as a writer who was stunted by a teacher's comments on her early writing; she tells how she succeeded as a writer by composing songs and lyrics in a punk rock band. Here, Amy establishes her ethos as a memoirist by presenting original lyrics, a piece of writing "corrected" by her teacher, and a series of punk-inspired self-portraits.

Amy Braziller, *Writing the Music Train*

RHETORICAL SITUATION & CHOICES	GENRE CONVENTIONS

PURPOSE

Amy shares a story of how she triumphed over an early writing injury. She uses her musical journey to show how she never stopped writing. Besides telling the story, she hopes that viewers can relate to her journey and find ways to overcome their own perceived failures.

AUDIENCE

Amy creates the digital story primarily for other writers who might have had an experience that made them question their ability to write. She also hopes that other artists might view this and be able to relate.

RHETORICAL APPEALS

Amy establishes her ethos by conveying specifics about her experience. Including visuals, such as comments on her writing and footage from her band, she establishes her credibility as the narrator of this event. She appeals to her audience's emotions (pathos) throughout the story, hoping that they can empathize with her challenges and ultimate triumph. She also includes a blank screen to show the darkness of her experience.

◄ **What is the composer, Amy Braziller, doing?**

How do I know that this is ► a digital story?

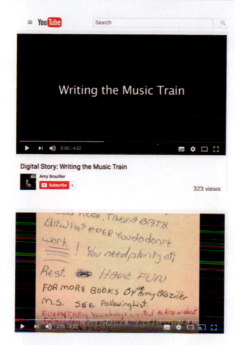

The one thing I always wanted to be was a writer. In first grade, Mrs. Kaylor would brag to my parents about my stories. When cousins would come to town, I was the playwright, assigning roles.

My brother was always the dog. I'd summon all the adults to take their seats in the den, thrilled by the applause.

ELEMENTS OF THE GENRE

Central, dramatic question: Amy's central question revolves around how one overcomes being told that you cannot be a writer. The story moves from her beginnings as a writer, hearing that perhaps she is not a writer, and then ultimately reclaiming her writing voice through playing music in a band.

Point of view: Amy uses first person throughout. She tells the story from her own experiences. Many of the visuals included feature Amy in the picture to help emphasize that this is her story.

Economy: The digital story is just a little over 4 minutes. Details included relate specifically to her dramatic question rather than showing the entire evolution of her band.

Soundtrack: Since the story illustrates how Amy's musical career helped her feel more secure as a writer, she includes some of the songs so that the audience can hear her lyrics. She includes several different pieces of music to help show that it wasn't just one

(Continues on next page)

MODES & MEDIA

Mode = visual, audio, text: Visuals are a combination of photos taken from Amy's life, along with video footage from her time playing in a band. Audio includes not only the narration of the story, but also music from her band that she helped compose. Text is used to provide opening titles and attribute her sources at the end.

Media = digital: *Writing the Music Train* was composed to be seen in a digital form. Even though screenshots are here in print, the original story resides on Amy's YouTube channel at: https://www .youtube.com/ watch?v=yic7 z84YDBk.

In the dark of my teen years, I wrote my way through anger. When I was a sophomore creative writing major, the response to my final portfolio, uttered by the almighty program director, was: "You can't write."

I don't know what his last name was, but his first name was Stuart.

What I do remember, though, was sitting in a laundromat, clothes spinning, me strumming, composing on the guitar, deciding that I would trade college for the music scene in New York City.

song that helped her transform.

STYLE

Tone: Amy uses an informal tone to tell her story. She tells it as if she was sitting down with you and relating a bit of her past.

Organization: The events in the story are presented chronologically since Amy wants to illustrate how one event led to the next and to the next.

DESIGN

Throughout the digital story, Amy **zooms** in to help the reader focus on a particular aspect of the visual. The **duration of visuals** is varied throughout. The video of her performance is on-screen for the longest amount of time.

SOURCES

The visuals come from Amy's own life, and she includes photos of her writing and band days. In the closing title, she lists the songs played in the video, attributing them to their composers.

At the close of the semester, I packed a car, tossing the isolation of Oberlin aside for a straight shot on I-80 to the city.

I traded the guitar for the steady beat of a bass, spending hours teaching myself to play.

With three other women, we formed The Sirens, playing music with an edge of punk-meets-new-wave.

I spent my nights writing music and lyrics, putting voice to ideas I couldn't abandon.

(Continues on next page)

There were no longer comments on the page asking me "what the point" was. "Whose ideas are these? Why is the voice changing here?"

Instead, there were thrashing guitars and a steady beat behind lyrics.

"Your daddy was a 44 magnum" would seg[ue] into "Lisa wanted Robin, but Robin wanted Billy. But Billy wanted somebody else."

With the help of a well-connected CBGB soundman, who became our manager, we got our "fifteen minutes" of Andy Warhol fame opening for The Clash in May of 1981 at Bond's. We were told to play our songs without any chitchat. Get on and get off. So with the crowd screaming: "We want The Clash," I played it loud, thrilled in the moment of performing.

It didn't matter if my words weren't heard. They were sung. For the next eight years, I played in different bands, traveled in and out of different music circles, always composing. Still writing.

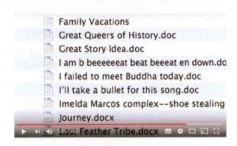

Big sheets of yellow paper found their way back into my college typewriter, spilling lyrics, spilling characters, spilling images. All mine.

QUESTIONS | Analyzing Braziller's Digital Story

RHETORICAL SITUATION & CHOICES

1. **Purpose.** What do you think Amy's main purpose is in telling this story? To simply share an experience? To help others understand an issue? Or something else?

2. **Purpose.** Are there particular images or sounds that help convey Amy's purpose? Are there any that distract from her purpose?

3. **Audience.** Do you feel like you are part of Amy's intended audience? Why or why not?

4. **Rhetorical appeals.** How do the images help convey Amy's credibility as a writer of different kinds of texts?

5. **Modes & media.** Imagine Amy had decided to tell this story only in written form. What might she have to do to make up for the lack of images and sound?

GENRE CONVENTIONS

6. **Elements of the genre.** Because this is Amy's story, it is told from her point of view. Can you imagine how the story might differ if told from someone else's point of view, such as perhaps her sophomore creative writing teacher, Stuart? Or her first-grade teacher, Mrs. Kaylor? Or one of her bandmates?

7. **Style.** How consistent are the images with the tone of Amy's narration? Are there some images that seem more consistent than others?

8. **Style.** Amy chose to tell her story chronologically, beginning with her in the first grade. How might her story have come across differently if she had chosen to begin with herself as a textbook author and then told about her past experiences as flashbacks?

9. **Design.** How do framing, duration of images, and transitions between images heighten the drama of the story Amy tells?

10. **Sources.** Luckily, Amy had kept old papers, photos, and videos from her past. Can you think of sources she might have used for visuals if she hadn't kept those artifacts from her past?

CHECKLIST | Drafting a Digital Story

Are you thinking of writing a story about an important aspect of your life? Ask yourself the following questions.

RHETORICAL SITUATION & CHOICES

☐ **Purpose.** What is your purpose in telling your story? Do you want to share an experience you had? Help people understand something you have struggled with?

GENRE CONVENTIONS

☐ **Elements of the genre.** What is my dramatic question? What is the heart of my story? Have I kept the story between 2–5 minutes? What types of music do I want to include? Have I made sure I'm not breaking any copyright laws? Is the pacing of the narration appropriate for my purpose? Have I used tone to help my viewer feel the emotion?

- **Audience.** Who do you want to tell your story to? Which details of your story will appeal to them the most? Are there details of your story you might leave out because they will confuse your audience?

- **Rhetorical appeals.** How will I establish my credibility? What are some ways I can appeal to my viewers' emotions? Do I want to include humor? Do I want my viewer to feel sad?

- **Modes & media.** Do I want to use just photographs or are there video pieces that make sense to include? What types of audio do I want to include? Does it make sense to include sounds and/or music? Do I want to use any text captioning throughout?

- **Style.** How do I want to organize my story? Do I want to tell the events chronologically? Is there a reason to tell it out of sequence such as starting from the end and moving to the beginning? Or perhaps starting in the middle? What are the details I want to include? Which details should I omit? How do I want to convey my own personal tone? How can I help the reader feel as though she were sitting with me and listening to my story?

- **Design.** How do I want to transition between images? Do I want particular images to fade into another? Are there any images I want to linger on-screen for longer than others? Are there any places where I want a blank screen to emphasize a particular emotion? What aspects of photographs do I want to zoom into? Are there places in the story where panning from one part of a photo to another makes sense?

- **Sources.** What personal photos will I use for my digital story? Do I have any video I want to include? Would interviews help with my story? What sources am I using that aren't my own? How will I cite those sources at the end of my digital story?

Telling a Digital Story

Create a three- to five-minute digital story that recounts an event or tale from your life. Alternatively, you could create a story that tells about a historical moment and why it matters to you, or reflects on a hero in your life. Before you begin drafting your story, view some digital stories on the Web to get an idea of the scope that writers cover in their story. Then, draft a written script that tells your story. Consider what your main dramatic question is and who your audience is to help you focus your ideas. Read this script aloud to others to get feedback about where you need to add or delete details. Once your script is finalized, record it, making sure to pause in places where you want your viewers and listeners to rest on an idea. Gather photos and other visuals that will help tell your story. Put it all together using movie-making software such as iMovie or online software such as YouTube video editor.

8 WORKPLACE GENRES

Cover Letters & Resumes

A cover letter, sometimes called a job application letter, is a persuasive piece of business writing that accompanies a resume (and sometimes other documents). When you're applying for a job, always send your resume—the document that outlines your skills, education, and experience—with a cover letter tailored to the job you're interested in.

At just a page or less, a cover letter is a tool that allows you to introduce yourself, identify the job you'd like to interview for, and make a case for why you are a great candidate. Unless you've exchanged some preliminary e-mails, your cover letter is usually your first written communication with a potential employer. This means you need to make a good impression.

When organizations advertise available positions, they may receive applications from many more people than they could possibly interview. That's why the persuasive aspect of the cover letter is so important. Imagine a hiring manager faced with a stack of thirty resumes to read. She's probably very busy and wants a clean, simple way to turn that stack of thirty resumes into a more manageable pile of five or six. Skimming cover letters is a good way to do that. So keep in mind that when you write a cover letter, your main goal is to persuade readers to invite you in for an interview.

A resume is a document that lists and highlights a person's credentials for a job. When you write a resume, you're writing to convince a potential employer that you have the right education, experience, and skills to succeed in the job you're applying for. A resume typically begins with the writer's name and contact information and a statement about the kind of position he or she is looking for, followed by specific academic and employment information relevant to the particular job being sought. It's crucial for applicants to portray their qualifications accurately and to keep all resume information up-to-date.

Like cover letters, resumes are usually very brief. A good practice is to limit your resume to one page until you have at least ten years of experience in the field in which you're applying for a job. Like cover letters, resumes are read quickly by busy people, so they need to be extremely clear and match your experiences precisely with the qualifications listed in the job posting. Be sure to carefully tailor your resume to each job you apply for, paying particular attention to the section that states the kind of job you're looking for. It would be embarrassing, for example, to send out a resume that focuses on how you are a "people person" and thrive in team environments when you're applying for a job that requires you to work alone. Additionally, resumes focus on the positive only—projects managed successfully, sales goals met, increased responsibility, and the like.

WRITE

When did you last write a cover letter to apply for a job? What was the job? What did you emphasize in the letter? How persuasive was it? Ultimately, was it successful? Why or why not? Write for five minutes about these questions. Include details in your answers.

ATTENTION, JOB APPLICANTS

Another important letter that job applicants write is the postinterview thank-you letter. *Always* send a thank-you note, card, or e-mail after any interview, and as soon as possible. In this correspondence, point out a few specific details from the interview to reinforce your professionalism, your interest in the job, and your potential as the candidate for the job. This letter is not only another tool for being persuasive—it's a great opportunity to ask any questions you wish you'd asked when you were face-to-face with your interviewer.

Analyzing Cover Letters & Resumes

Purpose

- *Cover letters.* People write cover letters, or job application letters, to persuade potential employers to read their resumes and contact them for an interview for the job they want. Employers use resumes and cover letters, in part, as screening devices, to help them sift through a large number of applications to a smaller, more manageable number. A cover letter must capture the attention of the person reading it.

- *Resumes.* Resume writers need to demonstrate to potential employers that their experience and skills align with the employer's needs. The resume needs to be organized and worded in a way that persuades an employer to consider the applicant seriously.

Audience

- *Cover letters.* Writers need to take into account several potential readers: the person who will supervise the new hire, a human resources employee, and members of a screening committee made up of supervisors and employees at the hiring organization. Successful cover letters:

  - » *Convey personality.* Readers want to get a sense of the person they may work with. They'll want to know: Will he or she be interesting as a colleague?

  - » *Communicate a strong work ethic.* Readers want to know: Will this person do his or her share of the work?

  - » *Highlight qualifications.* Readers want a quick sense of what the applicant has done that makes him or her a good candidate for the job. What specific experiences connect up with the job in question? What stands out about this person and his or her experience?

  - » *Get to the point.* Writers should keep in mind that their potential employers usually read cover letters *in addition to* their usual workload. That means readers are moving fast; they want to get an immediate sense of whether the applicant may be a good fit.

- *Resumes.* When composing a resume, writers need to keep the same factors in mind as when they write a cover letter (see above). Their readers are busy and want a quick and clear case for how fit the applicant is for the position.

Rhetorical Appeals

- *Cover letters.* Writers need to establish ethos by conveying their ethics and professionalism, noting related past successes, experiences, and aptitudes that qualify them for the job, and showing that they're genuinely interested in working for the organization, perhaps by mentioning something specific about it that they

WRITE

Have you ever created different versions of your resume for different jobs? If so, what types of edits did you make? What did you do to tailor your message to a specific audience? Jot down the answers to these questions and then share your responses with a classmate.

especially like. Writers also need to appeal to readers' sense of logos by making logical connections between their resume and the organization's values and the requirements of the position.

- *Resumes.* Resume writers need to develop ethos too. They need to be accurate and ethical in everything listed on their resumes. The stakes are high: You've probably seen news stories about people being fired for lying on their resumes, such as Yahoo CEO Scott Thompson, who was fired in 2012 for listing a degree on his resume that he didn't actually hold.

Modes & media

- *Cover letters.* Cover letters can be sent by e-mail, uploaded to an employment site, and printed out and delivered in person. Traditional cover letters are written documents and rarely contain any visual elements. However, LinkedIn and other career-related networking options are causing standards to change. Talk

▼ **VISUAL RESUME**

Kevin Burton, disaster recovery professional.

Credit: By permission of Kevin Burton.

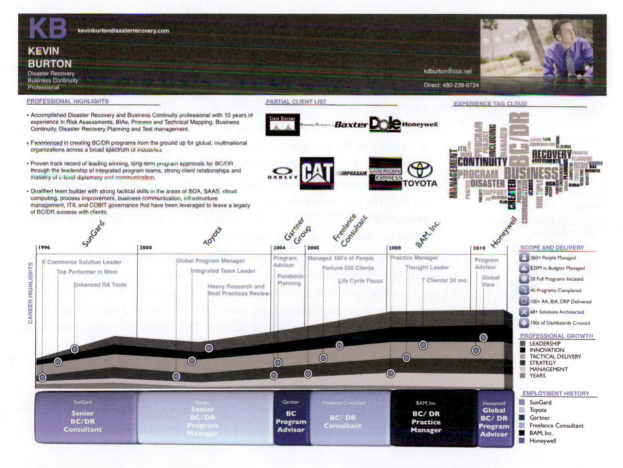

to people in the industry you're interested in to find out what the standard is for that audience. Creative industries, such as publishing and advertising, may allow more flexibility, while other industries may want a text-only cover letter.

- *Resumes.* As with cover letters, resume standards vary from industry to industry. Social networking sites have made digital resumes that incorporate visuals much more acceptable in some industries. For example, Kevin Burton, who works in disaster recovery, created the visual resume on page 169 for the Internet.

Elements of the Genre   In their resumes and cover letters, job seekers do the following:

- *Introduce themselves as applicants.*
  - » *Cover letters.* This is usually the first communication a job applicant will have with a potential employer, so it's important for writers to present themselves as competent and engaged. See the letter by Julia Nollen on page 176 for an example. Nollen provides context for why she's applying for the job she's writing about.
  - » *Resumes.* Writers provide their names and objectives at or near the top of their resumes, highlighting the details that would be highlighted in a traditional, face-to-face introduction. Think about how you normally introduce yourself to people; you probably say something like "Hi, my name is John. I'm a student at XYZ College." A resume communicates the same information.
- *Refer specifically to the position they're applying to.*
  - » *Cover letters.* So that readers can instantly identify which position the writer is applying for, writers need to state the specific job title and reference number (if applicable) near the beginning of the letter.
  - » *Resumes.* Writers need to tailor their objectives to the position they are applying for. This is probably the most important thing to keep in mind each time you apply for a job. Your resume should be a flexible document that you revise as needed for different audiences.
- *Explain why the job and organization are appealing.* The cover letter should be personalized for the specific job and organization being applied to. Candidates applying for a position with Red Rocks Community College, where Amy teaches, would do well to mention something in their cover letter about their experience with or appreciation of the community college mission. This shows that they share values with the organization.
- *Organize content so it's persuasive and reader-friendly.*
  - » *Cover letters.* Cover letters usually begin with a reference to the position being applied for and a brief summary of the writer's qualifications. One to three paragraphs elaborating on qualifications follow, and then the letter closes with a request for an interview.

WRITE

When you are interested in a job, do you research it before applying for it? If so, what things do you look for? Have you ever included any of that information in your cover letter? What are some ways that including these specifics could assist you in your job search? Answer these questions on paper.

» *Resumes.* Job seekers typically organize their experiences either chronologically, working backward from their most recent employment experiences, or according to skill sets, such as by listing all their project management experience under one heading and then all their budget management experience under another. Writers should think about the job they are applying for and which organizational pattern will best highlight their qualifications.

- *Present a clear argument about their qualifications.*

  » *Cover letters.* Writers summarize their qualifications in one or two sentences near the beginning of the letter. They specify the experiences that make them ideal candidates for the job.

  » *Resumes.* Resume writers continue building their arguments by listing specific experiences that illustrate how qualified they are for the position. A student applying for a position might list relevant classes he or she has taken.

- *Make connections between the cover letter and resume and between different personal experiences.* In their cover letters, applicants refer to the specific experiences listed in their resumes. They draw connections between those experiences and the qualifications that the employer has noted in the job listing. If the job listing states that candidates need to have strong customer service skills, the applicant should address that in her letter. A cover letter is also a good tool for showing relationships between seemingly unrelated experiences or tasks. If an applicant has worked as a swim coach and a café manager, she might say that these jobs tied together because they allowed her to develop as a communicator and a leader.

- *Use concise language.* A cover letter should be no more than one page long. The purpose of the cover letter is not to tell the entire story of the writer, but to whet the appetite of the reader. A resume should also be limited to one page until the applicant has at least ten years' experience in a particular field. You can provide your list of references, writing samples, or other portfolio of work separately from the resume.

- *Request an interview.* Cover letters should end with a polite direct request for an interview, such as "I would welcome the opportunity for an interview and hope to hear from you."

Style   When creating a resume and cover letter, writers do the following:

- *Use professional language.* Just as applicants dress formally for a job interview, they also write their cover letters using business- and workplace-appropriate language. That said, because writers are writing about themselves, the use of the first person (I) is appropriate. Use language that is formal enough to be respectful but that is not stilted or boring. In your resume, use professional, specific language to describe your accomplishments.

What are some ways
you can personalize
your cover letter
to reflect your
personality? How
about your resume?
Write a list of the
different ways you
might do this.

- *Give a sense of their personalities.*
  - » *Cover letters.* Just because this is formal correspondence doesn't mean it has to be lackluster. It's okay for a writer to use a voice and tone that let readers know something about who the writer is and why he or she is special. Use the active voice and verb construction. For example, "A degree was earned in history from XYZ University" could be written in the active voice this way: "I earned a degree in history from XYZ University."
  - » *Resumes.* Writers need to convey attributes of their personality and work ethic through the details they provide in their resumes. The voice and tone of a resume, regardless of the voice and tone in the cover letter, need to be professional and businesslike.
- *Provide specific relevant details.* In cover letters, readers will be persuaded by specific statements ("I exceeded sales goals by 15 percent at the Limited") than by *generalizations* ("I am a good salesperson"). Resumes should be precise.
- *Proofread and make sure their documents are error-free.*
  - » *Cover letters.* While proofreading is important for all compositions, it is particularly important when you're reviewing a cover letter; even one typo can cause a reader to dismiss you completely as a job applicant. Recently, Elizabeth received a cover letter and resume from someone who wanted to work in the writing center she directs on campus. One sentence in the cover letter read, "I kept my death clean." The word *death* was probably a simple typo, but Elizabeth could not bring herself to schedule an interview with the writer.
  - » *Resumes.* As with cover letters, it's crucial to proofread your resume so readers will see you as professional. Make sure to keep tenses consistent, place periods at the end of sentences, and carefully check for any misuse of words. Always have someone else proofread your resume to be sure you haven't overlooked anything. Make sure your verbs are parallel in construction in all sections of your resume, including your lists of tasks.

Design   Writers of cover letters and resumes:

- *Use standard business formatting and personalized headings.*
  - » *Cover letters.* Like any other business letter, a cover letter includes the complete contact information of both the recipient and the sender. It also includes a date, a salutation, and a signature. With word processors and online cover letter templates, writers can easily create personalized letterhead that includes their name and contact information at the top or bottom of the page.

» *Resumes.* Job seekers place their contact information at the top of their resumes. They also include standard sections such as Objective, Education, and Experience.

- *Use standard spacing and plenty of white space.*

  » *Cover letters.* Writers single-space their cover letters but insert an extra space between paragraphs. They do not use indents.

  » *Resumes.* Within each section, writers use single spacing. Between sections, they add an extra space. Margins are usually one inch. Make sure to use some white space to separate different areas of the resume in order to keep it from appearing too cluttered. In the sample on page 174, the writer uses white space by indenting the copy.

- *Choose simple, classic fonts.*

  » *Cover letter.* In keeping with the formality of a cover letter, the font should be a simple, classic one like Arial, Calibri, or Times New Roman in 11 or 12 point. This makes the cover letter easy for most readers to read.

  » *Resumes.* Use fonts consistently throughout your resume. Sans serif fonts (such as Arial) are typically used for headings, while serif fonts (such as Times New Roman) are typically used for the text. If you use more than two fonts, you run the risk of distracting your reader.

- *Adhere to any design specifications given by employers or online resources.* When creating a cover letter, follow any specifications supplied by the potential employer, especially the file formats requested. As for your resume, see how others in your industry present their resumes. For example, a visual resume can work for some industries; see Kevin Burton's resume on page 169.

Sources The main source of a cover letter is the resume, which is referred to throughout, and the writer's experiences. The main source of a resume is the applicant's own experiences. When you create a resume, you may want to use other resumes as models for your own.

1936 Elm St.
Atlanta, GA 30098

July 9, 2013

Amy Downs
PricewaterhouseCoopers
1 Park Place
Atlanta, GA 30303

Dear Ms. Downs:

◄ **BUSINESS LETTER**
Standard letter templates are available on the Internet and as part of Microsoft Office. Shown here is the typical styling that precedes the message of a business letter.

◄ **ATTENTION, OVERACHIEVERS**
Wondering how you can get ahead in the job search? Gather some letters of recommendation from former employers, professors, and colleagues. You can submit these shining references—along with writing or other portfolio samples tailored to the position—to a future employer and distinguish yourself from the throng.

William Watson
4460 Main St., Sacramento, CA 95818
(916) 555-0684
williamwatson@email.com

◄ **RESUME (EXCERPT)**

William Watson.

Objective	A full-time position in youth counseling.
Education	**California State University**, Sacramento B.A., **Psychology.** May 2017. GPA: 3.4
Related Experience	<u>Volunteer</u>, Sacramento Community Mental Health Center July 2015–present • Organize mentoring events with local schools and organizations. • Hold regular tutoring sessions. • Lead monthly group discussions with teens, under supervision of staff psychologist.

Guided Reading | Cover Letter & Resume

Julia Nollen is a graduate of the University of Delaware, where she studied English, film, art, and Web design. She then completed a Certificate in Publishing program at New York University. Nollen wrote a cover letter to accompany her resume when she applied for a marketing assistant position at Bedford/St. Martin's, the publisher of this textbook. After introducing herself and naming the position she is applying for, Nollen summarizes her qualifications and her reasons for wanting to work for Bedford/St. Martin's. As you read, notice how Nollen tailors her letter for the specific position and employer. Why do you think she's chosen to mention the name of an executive editor? How does her description of projects she's worked on shape your impression of her?

▶ APPLICANT PHOTO &
JOB DESCRIPTION

Julia Nollen submitted a cover letter and resume for a marketing assistant job with Bedford/St. Martin's, an imprint of Macmillan Learning. **Macmillan Learning** posted the job description shown here, the one that Nollen responded to.

Credit: Photo, by courtesy of Julia Nollen. Screenshot of job description by courtesy of Macmillan Learning.

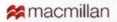

☎ macmillan

Careers | Contact

ABOUT MACMILLAN ▸ | OUR PUBLISHERS ▸ | BOOKSELLER SERVICES ▸ | ACADEMIC & LIBRARY SERVICES ▸

CAREERS

▸ Browse Open Jobs
▸ Search Open Jobs
▸ Submit Your Resume
▸ Edit Your Profile
▸ Privacy Notice
▸ Terms of Use

Job Details

Requisition Number	11-0110
Post Date	6/22/2011
Title	Marketing Assistant
Organization Name	Bedford St. Martins
City	Boston
State	MA
Description	Bedford/St. Martin's is a leading publisher of college textbooks in the disciplines of English, History, Communication, Business and Technical Writing, Philosophy, Religion, and Music. Please visit us on the web at www.bedfordstmartins.com for additional information. Bedford/St. Martin's was originally two separate divisions of St. Martin's Press, Inc. consisting of the St. Martin's Press College Division and Bedford Books of St. Martin's Press. The two companies merged and became Bedford/St. Martin's in 1998. Bedford Books was founded in 1981 by Charles Christensen. The St. Martin's Press College Division was founded much earlier. We are an Equal Opportunity Employer.
Requirements	Position Description:

This is an administrative, entry-level job that supports the Director of Marketing and the Associate Director of Marketing at a college textbook publisher in the humanities. This marketing assistant will be in direct contact with everyone in the marketing department, in other departments at Bedford/St. Martin's, and the sales force.

Major Responsibilities:

- administrative tasks
- handling conference arrangements
- maintaining marketing materials for use by the sales force
- entering and maintaining information in our customer relationship database
- responding to special requests from sales people and customers
- generally helping with the smooth running of the department

Required Skills / Knowledge:

- excellent communication skills
- excellent computer skills
- attention to detail

Experience Needed:
- Please submit a letter of interest, a resume, and a writing sample (a persuasive writing sample is preferred).
Educational Background Required:
- A college degree, preferably in the liberal arts

Apply On-line
Send This Job to a Friend

Julia Nollen, *Application for Marketing Assistant Job*

RHETORICAL SITUATION & CHOICES		GENRE CONVENTIONS	

PURPOSE
Nollen writes her cover letter to persuade the director of marketing that her background makes her an ideal fit for a marketing assistant position.

AUDIENCE
Nollen's primary audience is Karen Soeltz, the director of marketing. Secondary readers might be other supervisors and employees who work with the marketing department.

RHETORICAL APPEALS
Nollen establishes her ethos by describing the variety of her work experience in the publishing industry, such as writing and designing press releases. Nollen appeals to logos by making logical connections between experience mentioned on her resume and her desired place of employment, Bedford. She connects digital publishing trends with part of Bedford's mission statement.

MODES & MEDIA
Mode = written: Nollen relies on text for her cover letter. She does mention a visual in her ending summary of samples included, but the visuals are not an

◄ **What is the composer, Julia Nollen, doing?**

How do I know this is a ► cover letter?

July 6, 2013

Karen Soeltz
Director of Marketing
Bedford/St. Martin's
75 Arlington St.
Boston, MA 02116

Dear Ms. Soeltz:

My name is Julia Nollen, and I am writing at the suggestion of Executive Editor Ellen Thibault, who recommended I apply for the open Marketing Assistant position at Bedford/St. Martin's. I am currently attending New York University's Summer Publishing Institute until July 16 but am available to interview in Boston at your convenience. I've been a longtime fan of Bedford's titles and have even contributed to one of your books. Further, during a recent informational interview at your Boston office, I was impressed by the creative energy and commitment of the people working there. I'd love to be a part of that.

What interests me most about Bedford is its mission to publish educational products across several platforms. At NYU I've studied the publishing industry and confirmed that I want to work for a company that blends established practices and innovative technology to create the best educational tools. I've learned that a firm understanding of both digital and print publishing best addresses the changing currents in pedagogy; Bedford reflects this hybrid approach to content development in its mission to publish texts that stem from "where our disciplines are, where they're going, and what they need," as your Web site states.

While at the University of Delaware, I contributed four student essays to Bedford's textbook *Mirror on America: Essays and Images from Popular Culture*. I was also lucky enough to gain practical editorial and marketing experience for both print and Web products by interning for three very different companies: a Web design studio (Bright

ELEMENTS OF THE GENRE

Introduces herself as an applicant: Nollen names the position she's interested in and mentions that she is currently attending NYU's Summer Publishing Institute, which indicates engagement.

Uses standard business letter formatting: Nollen includes the address and name of the recipient, the date, a salutation, and a signature.

Refers specifically to the position: Nollen mentions the position, marketing assistant, in the opening sentence of her cover letter.

Explains why this job and organization are appealing: In the opening of the letter, and throughout, Nollen discusses Bedford, making the reader aware that she has not only researched the company, but also sees how she fits as a potential employee.

Refers to the resume: On Nollen's resume, she lists the different internships she has had. By explaining some of the work she did during the internship, she gives the reader detailed information that is not available

actual part of her
cover letter.
Medium = digital:
This cover letter was
sent digitally, by
e-mail.

Orange Thread), a freelance columnist (MSNBC.com's Eve Tahmincioglu), and a niche publishing house (Oak Knoll Press). At all three companies, I designed press releases using Adobe InDesign; wrote persuasive copy for mailers, flyers, blog posts, and articles; and posted these materials online. My recent experience at NYU has been even more multifaceted. For the first half of the program, I was appointed Art Director of my group's magazine and won the "Best Art Director" award by professionals, including the Editor in Chief of *People*. In my current appointed role as Marketing Director, my job is to develop a marketing strategy for a mock book imprint and its digital extension, including a pre- and post-publication campaign for each of our first three titles. After presenting my campaign to the VP Associate Publisher of Simon & Schuster, later today, I will devise a budget to present to a panel of marketing experts next week. From writing and designing press releases to updating book and social media sites, I want to learn as much as I can about the present publishing industry, as well as where it's going in the future.

Whether by e-mail, by phone, or in person, I would love to find out more about the open Marketing Assistant position at Bedford and the responsibilities it entails. I've included my contact information at the bottom of this e-mail and attached my resume and writing samples to this e-mail. Thank you for your time and consideration, and I look forward to hearing from you.

Sincerely,

Julia Nollen

0000 Newark Drive
Newark, DE 19711
19711julianollen@000.com
(C) 302.555.0000
(H) 302.555.0000

Enclosed are the following writing samples.

1. Cover for *Expresión* magazine, a bimonthly arts and culture magazine that targets young Latin Americans living in the United States. My cover was awarded "Best Art Design" at New York University's Summer

on the resume, such as mentioning that she wrote "persuasive copy for mailers," something she might do as a marketing assistant.

Is brief: Nollen's cover letter gives enough details to expand on the resume, yet doesn't give so many extraneous details that the reader is bogged down with a long letter.

Closes with a request for an interview: Nollen's final paragraph discusses her availability and desire to meet for an interview.

STYLE

Technique: Nollen uses the first person throughout. For example, she writes, "I want to learn as much as I can about the present publishing industry. . . ."

Voice and tone: While Nollen keeps the tone professional, detailing her accomplishments and fit for the job, she also infuses the letter with part of her personality, such as when she says, "I'd love to be a part of that."

Detail: Nollen uses specific details throughout. Rather than just mentioning that she is a marketing director for a project in the NYU publishing program, she details what that position entails.

(Continues on next page)

Publishing Institute and was designed using Adobe Photoshop and InDesign.

2. Research paper written for a film class at the University of Delaware, titled "Reflecting on Manufactured Masculinity and Motherhood in Brett Ratner's *Red Dragon*."

3. Book review on Shawn Achor's *The Happiness Advantage*, as published on careerdiva.net, which has up to 20,000 unique visits monthly.

DESIGN
Nollen follows cover letter design conventions by using single-spaced paragraphs with spaces between each paragraph.

SOURCES
Nollen draws on her own experiences throughout the cover letter.

◄ **RESUME**

Julia Nollen submitted this resume along with the cover letter shown on p. 176 when she applied for a job with Macmillan as a marketing assistant.

Credit: Used with permission of Julia Nollen.

JULIA NOLLEN

julianollen@000.com • 0000 Newark Drive, Newark, DE 19711 •
(C) 302.555.0000 • (H) 302.555.0000

EDUCATION

Certificate in Publishing, New York University, July 2013

BA of English and Film, Interactive Media minor, University of Delaware, May 2013

Study Abroad Programs:

- London—literature, film, political science and theater (Fall 2011)
- Athens—art history, Greek language and literature (Summer 2010)
- Caen—contemporary and conversational French (Winter 2010)

RELATED EXPERIENCE

Intern, Oak Knoll Press & Books, New Castle, DE (Winter, Spring 2013)

Proofread manuscripts, designed press releases using Adobe InDesign, wrote and edited book descriptions, and cataloged rare books for sale on the Web. 360+ hours.

Intern, **MSNBC.com** columnist Eve Tahmincioglu, Wilmington, DE (Fall 2012)

Wrote, researched, and edited articles and videos for **CareerDiva.net**. Also featured on **MSNBC.com, Excelle.monster.com, thedailybrainstorm.com**, and others. 180+ hours.

Intern, Bright Orange Thread Web Design Studio, Lincoln University, PA (Summer 2012)

Wrote and published articles and coupons for the Web site and blog. Used Basecamp daily, wrote and posted tweets, and helped design a wireframe. 180+ hours.

Student Writer, Bedford/St. Martin's, Boston, MA (2007–Present)

Research material for upcoming editions of *Mirror on America: Essays and Images from Popular Culture*, attend meetings with the editor, and write and edit student essays (four published so far). 100+ hours.

Nonfiction Editor, *Caesura Literary Magazine*, University of Delaware (Fall 2012–May 2013)

Edit submissions, design cover and layout, advertise, and update social media sites. 30 hours.

SKILLS

- Adobe Creative Suite 5 and 6 (Dreamweaver, Photoshop, InDesign, and Bridge)
- Working knowledge of HTML
- Practiced photographer (Nikon D5100, EOS Rebel) and published video editor (Final Cut Pro X, iMovie '11)

ACCOMPLISHMENTS

Published in *Mirror on America: Essays and Images from Popular Culture*, Bedford/St. Martin's

Published four essays on popular culture in the third, fourth, and fifth editions (2006, 2009, and 2011).

Presented research at the English Association of Pennsylvania Undergraduate Conference, West Chester (2009)

Presented "The Best of Both Worlds: Ofelia as Gender Role Revisionary in del Toro's *Pan's Labyrinth*."

Presented research at the National Popular Culture Association Conference (St. Louis 2010, New Orleans 2009)

Presented "One Last 'Memo from Turner': Gender Roles Revisioned in Performance."

QUESTIONS | Analyzing Nollen's Cover Letter & Resume

RHETORICAL SITUATION & CHOICES

1. **Purpose.** Nollen mentions her familiarity with Bedford several times in the letter. Is this an effective strategy for persuading her reader to interview her for the position? Why or why not?

2. **Audience.** Is the letter appropriately tailored to the director of marketing? What information does Nollen include that shows she realizes this is her audience?

3. **Rhetorical appeals.** How does the cover letter demonstrate that the writer would make a desirable employee? How does the resume do this?

4. **Rhetorical appeals.** How does the cover letter use ethos and logos to persuade the recipient to schedule an interview?

5. **Modes & media.** Read Nollen's cover letter out loud and notice how well it flows as a kind of audio essay. What might be some of the benefits—and drawbacks—of reaching an audience through an "audio cover letter"?

GENRES CONVENTIONS

6. **Elements of the genre.** Are there items on Nollen's resume that she should have elaborated on in the cover letter? If so, which items and why?

7. **Elements of the genre.** Nollen includes a summarized list of her writing samples at the end of her cover letter. Is this necessary? Why or why not?

8. **Style.** How does the author convey her personality while still maintaining a formal tone?

9. **Design.** How does the cover letter's design make it easily and quickly readable?

10. **Sources.** How does Nollen draw on her resume as a source for the cover letter?

CHECKLIST | Drafting a Cover Letter & Resume

Are you thinking of drafting a cover letter and resume? Ask yourself the following questions.

RHETORICAL SITUATION & CHOICES

☐ **Purpose.** I need to remember that the main purpose of my cover letter is to persuade the reader to schedule an interview with me. How can I draw on my experiences to best position myself as a good candidate for an interview? Does my resume illustrate how my experiences and skills align with my potential employer?

☐ **Audience.** When I sit down to write my cover letter, I need to think about what my reader's concerns

GENRE CONVENTIONS

☐ **Elements of the genre.** In my cover letter, what aspects of my resume will I want to elaborate on to highlight my qualifications for the specific job I'm applying for? What makes this particular position and organization appealing to me? What about my experiences connects up with what the employer is looking for?

☐ **Style.** In my cover letter, how can I use specific details to support and develop generalizations that I make about myself? Does my resume support the case I make for myself in my letter?

will be. How can I appeal to those concerns in my letter and resume? To what extent does my resume provide a quick snapshot of my skills for my reader?

☐ **Rhetorical appeals.** How can I establish myself as reliable and responsible? How can I logically connect my experiences and skills with the reader's needs and the position's requirements?

☐ **Modes & media.** Will my cover letter and resume be delivered in print form or digitally? Would it be appropriate for me to include a visual(s)?

And, for both documents, is my tone inviting yet professional? Is my language formal enough? Did I proofread carefully?

☐ **Design.** Will I create personalized letterhead for my letter? And how will I lay out my resume? Is it consistent in design? Am I using no more than two fonts? Am I using headings and white space to direct my reader's attention to certain parts of the resume?

☐ **Sources.** Did I remember to use my resume as a source for the details and anecdotes in my cover letter?

Responding to a Specific Job Description

Want to experiment? Draft your own cover letter and resume.

Locate a description for a job in your field that you are interested in. Working with that job description and your own experience, respond to the individual qualifications in both your resume and cover letter. Create a new resume or revise an existing one using the advice and models in this chapter. Draft a cover letter that expresses your interest in the job and that makes explicit connections between what the employer's stated needs are and what you have to offer. Remember to close with a request for an interview. Be sure that your cover letter expands on the details in your resume that show how you are an excellent fit for the job.

Business Memos

The word *memo* is short for *memorandum*, a document used for communicating within a business or organization, so the authors of and audience for memos are colleagues in a workplace. Memos are generally brief, seldom running more than a few pages long when printed out. Some memos are formatted as the document on page 182: The "professional design" memo template offered by Microsoft Office. Others are sent as e-mails or attachments to e-mails. (See Microsoft Office for templates for memos, e-mails, and more.)

In the workplace, we write and read memos for a variety of reasons, such as:

- To provide (or receive) information for specific plans, meetings, events, policies, and so on
- To provide (or receive) instructions for specific tasks
- To persuade others (or be persuaded) to take a specific action or make a decision

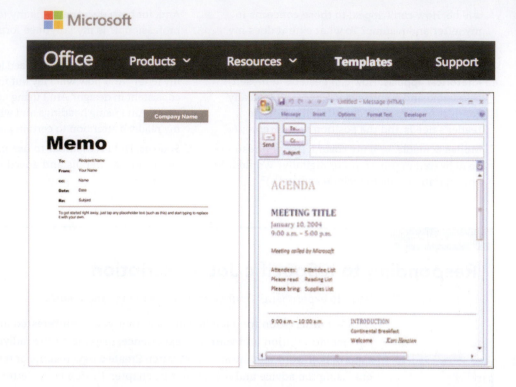

The information in memos is often time sensitive and related to specific tasks or events, so people usually read them when they receive them or in preparation for a specific meeting, discussion, or decision. For example, a company president trying to decide whether to create a new position for a director of sales and marketing might read the company's year-end report and the memos about sales, competition, and the larger marketplace as part of his or her decision-making process.

Analyzing Business Memos

Purpose   We write memos to share data, summarize events, give instructions, lay out a plan, and explain and get buy-in for our ideas. In some cases, a colleague or manager may ask you to write a memo that provides an update on a project you're working on, a problem you're solving, or a schedule you're planning. Other times, you may decide to write a memo to a specific reader (or readers) with a proposal for getting something done or a plan for making an improvement to a process or product. Often our memos have multiple purposes—not just to inform but also to convince our readers to agree with something or to do something specific. Memos are often written collaboratively by a group of people who worked on a project together. For instance, a college committee charged with exploring ways to better serve alumni might write a memo to the administrator responsible for alumni communications with its recommendations.

Audience   In the workplace, memo writers know that their readers need information in order to take specific actions or make decisions. Readers of instructional memos—or any correspondence that provides instruction—want to learn quickly what needs to be done—and why, when, how, and in what order.

Workplace writers need to keep in mind that they always have multiple audiences. Their primary readers are the people they've addressed the memo to; they are the ones who will use the information and/or take action based on the content of the memo. Writers' secondary audiences might include the supervisor(s) of the primary audience. Finally, memos and e-mails can have unforeseen audiences, as is the case when an e-mail is accidentally sent to the wrong person or forwarded by the recipient to people the author may not have intended as readers. Sometimes a memo or e-mail is leaked to the press, as happens with company or government scandals. Internal memos are often presented as evidence in court when companies are charged with crimes. Amid the scandal of the extensive 2009–10 safety recall of Toyota cars, internal memos came to light in which Toyota executives boasted of saving millions in 2007 by putting off U.S. safety regulations they knew would improve their cars' safety.

Rhetorical appeals   Memo writers appeal most often to readers' senses of ethos and logos, and sometimes to pathos. Because readers will use the information in the memo to formulate plans, make decisions, and take action, it's important that they feel that the information contained in the memo is accurate and true. Sometimes an appeal to pathos can help you develop a rapport with your readers.

Modes & media   Memos are text based, and writers sometimes include images. For example, if you need to discuss sales figures, you might present them in a chart. Memos can be in print or digital format. Many organizations ask their employees to send memos as e-mails to reduce paper usage. Sending memos digitally also allows readers to archive memos, which saves space and makes it easier to search for particular memos.

Elements of the genre   Business memos are characterized by the following qualities. They:

- *Are written to specific recipients.* As discussed above, memos always have multiple audiences. When writing a memo, identify your primary and secondary audiences. To determine if a person is part of your secondary audience, think about (1) to what degree that person would be interested in the information you're presenting, and (2) what his or her connection is to your primary audience.
- *Answers the questions who, what, when, where, why, and how.* Be sure to provide recipients with the information they'll need to understand your context and purpose. If you're reporting on a client visit, for example, include the name of the client and his or her company; the date of the visit; a clear statement about the purpose of the visit; a summary of the visit; an explanation of whether or to what extent

WRITE

Think of the last memo you read, whether at work or school. How well did the writer succeed in connecting with you? How clear and informative was the memo? Were you persuaded to do something specific? What could the writer have done differently or better? Spend five minutes writing answers to these questions. Use specific details when answering.

the purpose of the visit was achieved, and how the purpose was achieved; and an explanation of the next steps. If any of this information is missing, the reader will need to contact the author for more information.

- *Includes important information in subject line and first paragraph.* Use your memo's subject line to concisely and specifically state what the e-mail is about. "Client visit" is too vague in a company that might make hundreds of client visits every month; "Simpson follow-up visit, June 2011" gives more information for the reader who wants to quickly determine what the memo is about. Use your first paragraph to convey the most important points; many readers will only have time to read the first paragraph carefully and will then skim the rest of the memo.

Style   Business writers make sure that their memos are:

- *Accurate and clear.* Whether you are writing to inform, instruct, or persuade, the information in your memo must be correct and easy to understand. This is crucial when providing instructions to a colleague or when supplying information that will be used as the basis for plans and decisions.

- *Concise and precise.* Readers want data, steps to specific tasks, and any arguments for taking action presented succinctly; they also need to be able to skim your memo or e-mail quickly to find what they need. Information must be precise. For example, telling a company president that "sales are up" may not be enough information for him or her to make an informed decision; the president needs to know that sales are up by 0.5 percent or 3 percent.

- *As brief as possible.* Writers of memos and e-mails strive to be as brief as their subject allows, especially in a busy workplace.

- *Informal yet professional in tone and voice.* Memos are internal business documents; colleagues write them to each other. This allows for a certain level of informality; the writing can be friendly yet professional.

- *As detailed as required for the situation.* Use details to help your readers understand your purpose. Stating that there "were problems" at a client site won't be particularly illuminating to your audience. However, if you write, "I encountered problem X. I resolved problem X by doing A, B, and C," you give readers enough detail to understand the situation.

Design   Business writers use these design elements:

- *Headings.* Memo headings include the date, recipients' names, sender's name, and a descriptive subject line. The names of anyone receiving a copy of the memo (secondary readers) are listed after "CC." ("CC" stands for "carbon copy," an old-fashioned way of producing an instant copy by using carbon paper between two sheets of regular paper.) In e-mailed memos, the e-mail's "To," "CC," "From," and subject lines serve the purpose of a heading. E-mail also makes possible blind CCing, in which an e-mail is CCed to someone who is not listed in the heading. However, blind CCing can be seen as unfair or deceptive, so it's best to avoid this practice.

- *Spacing.* Memos are usually single-spaced within paragraphs, with an extra line break between paragraphs (rather than indenting paragraphs). This extra white space between paragraphs makes it easier for memos to be read quickly, which is often necessary in a business or organizational setting. E-mailed memos are generally formatted in the same way.

- *Numbered and bulleted lists.* Because memos are usually read very quickly (or skimmed), format important information so that readers can grasp it quickly. Use numbered and bulleted lists to present brief points of information: A numbered list indicates that order matters; a bulleted list indicates that order is not as important. In a memo about steps taken to solve a client's printer issues, for example, a numbered list would give which steps were taken and in what order.

Sources Include sources as needed to back up and support your points—and to credit others who have contributed to the ideas you're presenting. If you're sending a memo about sales figures to your company's president, you might refer to a recent sales report. You wouldn't include a Works Cited page as you would for a research or scholarly article; instead you might refer to the specific report in the body of the memo and attach the report as a separate document. Alternatively, you could copy and paste it directly into your memo.

WRITE

Review a piece of workplace writing that you or someone else composed. Does it include detailed paragraphs that you wish were in list form? If so, revise the memo or e-mail so that the details or steps are presented in a succinct bulleted list. Is it easier to read? How might you apply this practice to future business correspondence?

Guided Reading | Business Memo

The memo below was written by Ellen Thibault, the editor for the first edition of this book at Bedford/St. Martin's, an imprint of Macmillan Learning. In it, Thibault asks her assistant to track down some information related to a project she's working on. She sent the memo as an e-mail with an attachment.

Ellen Thibault, *Video Project*

RHETORICAL SITUATION & CHOICES	GENRE CONVENTIONS

PURPOSE
Thibault's purpose is to outline specific tasks for her assistant, Mallory Moore, to complete. The specific tasks are (1) to find contact information for a list of authors provided and (2) to find additional authors.

AUDIENCE
The primary audience is Moore, Thibault's assistant, who must perform the tasks outlined. The secondary audience is Sophia Snyder, who might be called upon to provide advice. Other audiences might include others at the company; also, all work e-mails and memos are stored in an organization's archive.

RHETORICAL APPEALS
Thibault appeals to Moore's sense of logos by organizing the tasks described in the memo in an orderly fashion. Thibault develops her ethos by indicating that she is well informed about the project she's working on and has a clear and

◄ **What is the composer, Ellen Thibault, doing?**

How do I know this is ▶ a business memo?

From: Thibault, Ellen
Sent: Tuesday, June 06, 2013 4:12 PM
To: Moore, Mallory
CC: Snyder, Sophia

Subject: Video Project: Need your help finding authors to interview

Mallory,

I am writing to you about an upcoming project. This summer I'm working with a video producer on a project to interview local literary authors. You and I need to begin identifying interviewees and inviting them to participate. We plan to conduct interviews in July and August. Note: I'm CCing Sophia because she's helped me with a similar project in the past and might have some helpful tips for you.

1. I've attached a list of authors that I'd like to invite. Could you please find their contact information— e-mails, addresses, and phone numbers—and those of their literary agents and add that information to the list? I will take it from there.
2. Next, could you please check the following local university writing programs and organizations to see if you can find an additional six or so literary authors who are currently teaching?
   • Brown; UMass Boston and Amherst; Emerson; and Boston University
   • Pen/Faulkner Foundation and other literary groups

ELEMENTS OF THE GENRE
Important information is given up front: The subject line and first paragraph summarize the project the e-mail relates to.

Writing is clear, precise, and directive: Thibault states clearly what she would like Moore to do. She also states the order in which she'd like Moore to complete the tasks. She doesn't provide her opinions or say more than she needs to: She sticks to the information relevant to the tasks at hand.

Brief: This e-mail is only three paragraphs long but conveys enough instruction and information for Moore to take action. Thibault does not include irrelevant detail; she sticks to the point. Also, Thibault sends a list of author names as an attachment. Including them in the body of the e-mail might have made the message too long and difficult to skim.

systematic approach to the project in mind.

MODES & MEDIA
Mode = written: The memo is text based and does not include images, though some memos benefit from images. Because the document is a written text (and not, say, a voice mail), the recipient, Moore, will be able to reread the memo (even print it out as a to-do list) as she completes the tasks to make sure she has done everything asked of her, or to check the names of the universities listed.

Medium = digital: Thibault and Moore's company, Bedford/St. Martin's, like most companies in the twenty-first century, encourages employees to use e-mail to send memos. E-mails allow colleagues to communicate quickly—and also allow for easy tracking of the memo. If Thibault wants to double-check when she sent the memo, she can simply check her "sent" or "Moore" folder and look at the time stamp on the e-mail. She could even enable her e-mail to request a "read receipt," which is an automatically generated e-mail from the recipient to the sender confirming that the e-mail has been received and opened.

> If you could send me this information by Friday, June 11, at noon, that would be great. Thanks, Mallory, and let me know if you have questions.
>
> Ellen Thibault
> Executive Editor * Bedford/St. Martin's
> 75 Arlington St., Boston MA 02116

STYLE
Detail: Thibault lists specific universities and organizations for Moore to focus on. She also indicates a specific due date for the research to be completed by.

Informal yet professional tone and voice: Although Thibault comes across as approachable ("let me know if you have questions") and polite, she takes a very professional tone in the memo, explaining the tasks to be completed in an organized and methodical way. The firm deadline indicates that Thibault will take action based on the tasks Moore is being asked to perform.

DESIGN
Clear headings: The headings indicate the memo's sender and recipient, who is getting a copy (CC) of the memo; the date; and the subject of the memo.

Lists: Thibault provides a numbered list of tasks to be completed and a bulleted list of resources for finding additional authors.

SOURCES
Thibault's e-mail doesn't require sources because Thibault herself is the source of the information. However, she does give credit to her colleague Sophia Snyder by naming her as a contributor to a similar project.

QUESTIONS | Analyzing Thibault's Business Memo

RHETORICAL SITUATION & CHOICES

1. **Purpose.** What is the main purpose of Thibault's e-mail? To inform? To persuade?

2. **Audience.** To what degree does Thibault's e-mail anticipate her reader's questions about who, what, when, where, why, and how?

GENRE CONVENTIONS

5. **Elements of the genre.** How does the subject line "Video Project: Need your help finding authors to interview" give the memo a context and describe the tasks for the reader? What purpose does the first paragraph of the memo

3. **Rhetorical appeals.** What does Thibault do to develop her ethos? How does she come across?

4. **Modes & media.** Smartphones and computer programs often offer "voice memos" as an option. Do you think Thibault's memo would be more or less effective if recorded as a voice memo? Why?

serve? Would the memo be more or less effective without the first paragraph? Why?

6. **Elements of the genre.** Notice how specific Thibault is about the information she needs Moore to gather. Does the order in which tasks are presented make sense? Is there another order or organization that might make more sense?

7. **Style.** How would you characterize the tone of the memo? Which words and phrases contribute to the tone? How does the tone contribute to the development of Thibault's ethos?

8. **Design.** Thibault uses two different types of lists in the memo: numbered and bulleted. How do the different types of lists organize the material?

9. **Sources.** This particular memo does not use sources except to note Sophia Snyder as a potential adviser. Snyder is also CCed on the e-mail. What are some reasons to CC a source on a memo?

CHECKLIST | Drafting a Business Memo

Are you thinking of drafting a business memo or e-mail? Ask yourself the following questions.

RHETORICAL SITUATION & CHOICES

☐ **Purpose.** What is the purpose of the memo I am writing? What kind of information do I need to provide? Will the information be used to inform a decision or action? Do I want to persuade my reader to take action? Am I collaborating with others? If so, do we all have a similar purpose in writing the memo?

GENRE CONVENTIONS

☐ **Elements of the genre.** How will I convey information about who, what, when, where, why, and how? How will my subject line indicate as precisely as possible my purpose in writing the memo? How will my first paragraph neatly summarize my most important points? How can I convey information precisely, accurately, and clearly, while still being brief?

☐ **Audience.** Who will use the information in my memo, and how will he or she use the information? Is there anyone else who needs to be "in the loop"? How would the organization or company I represent look if the memo were leaked or blind copied to unintended readers?

☐ **Rhetorical appeals.** How will I establish my credibility as a writer? How can I organize my information and use lists to appeal to readers' sense of logos? If appropriate to the context of the memo, how will I appeal to my readers based on pathos? Will an emotional appeal give me a rapport with my readers?

☐ **Modes & media.** Will my text-based memo benefit from images to convey my point(s) quickly and clearly? Will my memo be more effective in print or digital form? What is the best way to reach my readers? Are they working in the office with me or are they working remotely?

☐ **Style.** How much detail will I need to include to allow readers to fully understand and contextualize the information in the memo? How can I come across as friendly yet professional?

☐ **Design.** How will I use lists to make my information clear and easy to understand? Would numbered lists, which indicate order, make more sense, or would bulleted lists work better?

☐ **Sources.** Will I need to cite sources to back up the information in my memo? Are there attachments I might include to assist readers in understanding the memo better?

PRACTICE

Communicating in the Workplace

Think about where you currently work or where you worked most recently. Make a list of the different policies/practices that employees had to follow. Look over your list and underline those that were perhaps controversial or were ones employees often disregarded. Choose one of those policies and brainstorm a list of reasons why that policy/practice needs to be eliminated. Then, draft a memo to your boss addressing that policy. In your memo, be sure to include a heading with the date, your recipient's name, your name, and a descriptive subject line. Organize your memo logically and be as specific and precise as you can.

Infographics: Visual Instructions

Infographics, like charts, are visual representations of information. Infographics can help you simplify complicated information by providing graphics that consolidate the information into several captivating visuals. In the workplace, infographics can be used to help convey material prior to a training session, to illustrate results of a campaign, to reinforce a company's message, and to illustrate the features of a new product.

Analyzing Infographics

Purpose   Composers create infographics to explain complex information concisely by using engaging visuals. When people view an infographic, they should be able to understand the information presented with a simple glance. Infographics can be designed to communicate messages, show relationships between things, and/or clarify complex processes.

Audience   Composers of infographics know that their readers want information in a concise, easy-to read format. They know readers might consult their infographic for data that will help them make a decision.

Rhetorical appeals   To gain readers' confidence in the content and establish ethos, composers of infographics need to conduct research and present correct information. They can also appeal to audiences through logos by using logical organization and smart, digestible design.

Modes & media   Infographics use visuals and text to convey information. Often the visual content dominates and text is used mainly for labels. Infographics can be communicated in print and digitally, although most infographics are distributed digitally.

Elements of the genre   Infographics are:

- *Based on facts and data.* The information presented in infographics is based on research that others have done (such as existing statistics) or that the composer has collected personally (through primary research such as interviews).
- *Precise and clearly labeled and titled.* The elements in infographics are labeled so that readers know what they represent.
- *Illustrated with symbols that convey information.* Visual devices, such as icons, represent ideas.
- *Focused on relevant data.* Only data that is relevant to the information being presented is included.

Style   Creators of infographics make the following stylistic choices:

- *What details to present.* Infographics only include the details necessary to convey the message. Since the goal of an infographic is to make it easy for readers to absorb data quickly, too much detail might make it difficult for readers to see what's most important.
- *What techniques, tone, and voice to use.* The best infographics use simple, direct language. Text is used judiciously, providing just enough information to clarify the visuals. Tone is neutral and objective.

Design   When designing an infographic, remember the following:

- *Simple is best.* Infographics make information accessible and digestible.
- *Color is key.* Colors are used to help separate and highlight different pieces of information. However, too many colors can be distracting.
- *The parts need to be arranged logically and spatially.* Infographics lay out information and visuals in a way that shows readers what is most important. When there are multiple visuals, designers add white space between the elements to show separation or place the elements near each other to show connections.

Sources   Infographics are based on composers' knowledge or research. Readers assume that the infographic is presenting reliable data based on specific sources. Many infographics include a source or list of sources, which adds to their credibility and authority.

Guided Reading | Infographic

Susanne Jacobs, an employee motivation specialist, created a model (the Jacobs Model) to help employees and employers build trust. The model examines the relationship between eight intrinsic drivers that can be affected by someone's internal psychological well-being and external work environment with two performance paths (positive or negative). UNUM, a UK employee benefits provider, created an infographic to illustrate Jacobs's principles.

UNUM, From *The Jacobs Model: "8 Ways to Build Trust in the Workplace"*

RHETORICAL SITUATION & CHOICES

GENRE CONVENTIONS

PURPOSE
UNUM's purpose is to illustrate the Jacobs Model in a simple, digestible format. UNUM is also showing employers how to cultivate trust in the workplace.

AUDIENCE
Readers of this infographic are most likely supervisors who want to create an atmosphere where workers feel trusted and ultimately perform well. Another audience might be the employees.

RHETORICAL APPEALS
The composers establish their ethos by showing that their ideas are based on a researched model by an expert in the field (Susanne Jacobs). They further support that ethos by providing precise information. The composers use logic (logos) by organizing the information to illustrate cause and effect.

MODES & MEDIA
Mode = written and visual: UNUM uses a combination of visuals and text to convey information about the Jacobs Model. At the top of the infographic, the composers use visual symbols that are then explained with text below. They also

◀ What is the composer, UNUM, doing?

How do I know this is an ▶ instructional infographic?

ELEMENTS OF THE GENRE
Based on data: UNUM draws on Susanne Jacobs's model for the information provided

Precise: The exact language of Jacobs's model is used in the infographic. For example, she uses the phrase "8 Intrinsic Drivers."

Clearly titled: The words in the title convey the main point of the infographic: Workplace Trust.

Uses symbols: At the top of the infographic, a series of icons are used to represent the eight different intrinsic drivers.

STYLE
Minimal detail: Just enough detail is used to make the information clear and authoritative. The upper portion of the infographic illustrates the different drivers and potential outcomes, while the bottom portion further defines the intrinsic drivers. The text provides concise information about the model.

Objective tone: All information is presented as fact.

DESIGN
In the top half of the infographic,

WORKPLACE TRUST

The Jacobs Model
The Jacobs Model links eight intrinsic drivers of trust, each of which is impacted by an individual's psychological wellbeing and work environment, to two paths of performance, leading to either positive or negative outcomes. When each of the drivers is satisfied, this leads to the positive outcome path – engagement, energy release, boosted wellbeing and improved performance

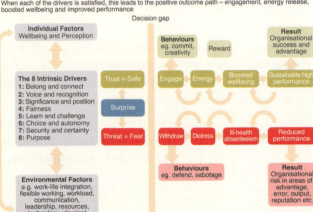

Decision gap

Individual Factors
Wellbeing and Perception

The 8 Intrinsic Drivers
1: Belong and connect
2: Voice and recognition
3: Significance and position
4: Fairness
5: Learn and challenge
6: Choice and autonomy
7: Security and certainty
8: Purpose

Trust = Safe

Surprise

Threat = Fear

Behaviours eg. commit, creativity

Reward

Result Organisational success and advantage

Engage   Energy   Boosted wellbeing   Sustainable high performance

Withdraw   Distress   Ill-health absenteeism   Reduced performance

Behaviours eg. defend, sabotage

Result Organisational risk in areas of: advantage, error, output, reputation etc.

Environmental Factors
e.g. work-life integration, flexible working, workload, communication, leadership, resources, technology, physical environment, reward and performance, other people strategies

The Jacobs Model 2012 Susanne Jacobs

The Eight Intrinsic Drivers

Belong & connect
If people feel excluded in the workplace they feel threatened and it can affect their health and wellbeing. It's important to make sure individuals feel connected to their team

Voice & recognition
People should be encouraged to put their views and ideas across in the workplace so they feel that their contributions are recognised and appreciated

Significance & position
People are continually assessing their role within their organisation and what contribution they are making. If people do not feel valued, they can feel threatened, which will negatively impact their performance

Fairness
It is critical for an organisation to treat its employees fairly and consistently. If employees feel they are being treated unfairly it can cause high stress levels and low productivity

Learn & challenge
Workers need to be continually learning so they can adapt to the ever-changing modern work environment. Research has shown that employees who feel challenged are more productive

Choice & autonomy
Giving workers a degree of control and the ability to make their own choices can help them balance their work and homes lives more effectively, helping to improve their performance

Security & certainty
If workers aren't secure in their position then they can feel threatened which has a negative effect on their performance and productivity levels

Purpose
If workers have a clear sense of purpose and are aware of exactly what their contribution to an organisation is, they are more likely to be engaged and productive

unum
Because everyone needs a back-up plan

use arrows to show how one behavior leads to potential outcomes.

Medium = digital: This information is published online. Even though UNUM developed the infographic, it is reproduced on other workplace online sites, such as Recruiter.com.

color indicates two different paths of performance. Olive green illustrates positive outcomes, while red illustrates negative outcomes.

Arrows show the relationship between items.

SOURCES

UNUM names the source with a source line midway through the infographic: "The Jacobs Model 2012 Susanne Jacobs."

Credit: Workplace Trust: The Jacob's Model. Copyright by UNUM. Used with permission.

QUESTIONS | Analyzing UNUM's Infographic

RHETORICAL SITUATION & CHOICES

1. **Purpose.** How does the infographic convey information about ways to manifest trust in the workplace? To what extent does the infographic present its information as an argument?

2. **Audience.** If the infographic were designed primarily for employees, how would the information need to change?

3. **Rhetorical appeals.** There is only one attribution to the source: "The Jacobs Model 2012 Suzanne Jacobs." Is this enough to establish ethos? How else might the creators of the infographic convey their credibility?

4. **Modes & media.** What are the advantages of making the infographic available digitally? How could the infographic be revised to take better advantage of a digital medium?

5. **Elements of the genre.** What do the symbols or icons add to the infographic? Do the symbols correspond effectively with the text they're representing? Which symbols would you change? How would you change them?

GENRE CONVENTIONS

6. **Elements of the genre.** How does the infographic show how ideas are related? What could be changed to make the relationships clearer?

7. **Style.** Describe the level of detail in the infographic. Why do you think UNUM included the explanations of all the steps at the bottom of the infographic? Is it too much text? Would there be a better way to represent the ideas?

8. **Design.** How does the use of color relate to the information presented in the infographic?

9. **Design.** The infographic includes a lot of information, separated with some subheads. What are some other ways the designers might have separated sections?

10. **Sources.** What kinds of additional research and sources would strengthen the infographic?

Are you thinking of creating an infographic? Ask yourself the following questions.

RHETORICAL SITUATION & CHOICES

☐ **Purpose.** What complex information might be explained more easily using engaging visuals? Is there a complex process I want to illustrate visually? How can I make sure the information presented is easily digestible? What message do I want to communicate?

☐ **Audience.** Who are my readers? Why should/will my infographic matter to them? What do I want them to get out of it? Does my audience consist of specialists or general readers? What level of visual detail will my infographic need to communicate my message to my readers?

☐ **Rhetorical appeals.** How will I establish my authority and reliability? How will I convey my information so my readers believe my data? To what extent will I rely on logic to support my interpretations? How will I organize the information to convey this logic?

☐ **Modes & media.** What balance of visuals and text do I want to use? Do I want readers to access my infographic digitally or in print? If digital, how can I make use of the digital environment? Should I have links to other digital material?

GENRE CONVENTIONS

☐ **Elements of the genre.** What types of data will I use to create my infographic? Is my data focused? Do I want to include symbols? Do I want my title to indicate my ultimate findings or present a question?

☐ **Style.** How will I keep my tone objective? What level of detail will I include in the infographic?

☐ **Design.** How do I want to organize my infographic spatially? Are there multiple visuals I need to include? Does each visual have accompanying text? How will I use colors in the infographic? What colors will help me convey my information?

☐ **Sources.** Is the infographic based on my own knowledge or do I need to do research to gather data and statistics? How many sources do I need to draw on in order to present the information effectively?

Conveying Information Visually

Think about a relationship you have with another person (friend, family, partner). How does trust factor into the ways you relate? What are some of the situations that occur where trust derails the relationship? How might you visually represent this information in an infographic? Using the infographic about workplace trust as your model, create an infographic entitled "Relationship Trust." As you create your infographic, consider what you want to convey and why, how you can best establish your ethos, and how to best use images, text, color, and design.

Proposals

A proposal is a persuasive document that suggests a plan or purchase. As with memos, proposals are often written collaboratively by a group of people. For example, a group of people who manage purchases for a company might collaborate to propose a new purchasing system that will save time and money.

Analyzing Proposals

Purpose   We write proposals to suggest that something be purchased or an action be taken in the workplace. A proposal clearly states what is being proposed, why it is being proposed, what actions need to be taken and by whom to achieve the proposed idea, and how much the proposed item or plan will cost.

Audience   Proposals are usually written to the person who can make the decision to adopt the proposed plan. Proposal readers will reach a decision based entirely on the information included in the proposal, so it is important to anticipate exactly what they will need to know to make that decision. Secondary readers might include people who will be affected by the proposed plan or who might be consulted by the decision maker.

Rhetorical appeals   Proposal writers need to appeal primarily to readers' senses of ethos and logos. Because proposal readers make decisions based on proposals, the proposal writer must come across as ethical and trustworthy, and the plan proposed must logically grow out of a need (to save money, to make things more efficient, to improve quality, or the like).

Modes & media   Proposals are text based and may include images that help build the case for the proposed plan, such as a chart that compares the current cost of making copies with the cost of making copies with the fancy new copy machine the proposal suggests purchasing. Proposals can be in print or digital format; they are often sent out as e-mail attachments.

Elements of the genre   Proposals are characterized by the following. They:

- *Are written to specific recipients.* Like a memo, a proposal usually begins with the specific recipient(s) listed.
- *Provide context.* The proposal must establish that there is a need for the proposed plan, either a problem that the proposed plan will solve or another need, such as improving quality or cutting costs.
- *Make a clear statement of what is being proposed.* The proposal must precisely state what is being proposed so decision makers know exactly what they are saying yes or no to, such as the purchase of a new copy machine, a new policy on who can use the copy machine, or a new plan for training employees in using the copy machine.

- *Give information about the advantages of adopting the proposed plan and possible obstacles.* A proposal should explain what will be gained by adopting the proposed plan or acknowledge that there are obstacles to adopting it. For example, if use of the copy machine will be restricted, people who are accustomed to being able to make copies whenever they want may become disgruntled; the proposal should explain how to mitigate that disgruntlement.

- *Provide an implementation plan, including the costs of adopting the proposed plan.* The steps that would need to be taken to implement the plan should be defined. If there are costs associated with it, those should be clearly spelled out in the proposal.

Style   Proposal writers make the following stylistic choices. Their work is:

- *Accurate and clear.* To enable the decision maker to make a good decision, the proposal must include accurate and clear information.

- *Detailed.* Details are important to help the reader understand exactly what is being proposed. Outlining a problem and then saying "something has to change" isn't helpful to the reader, but "we can mitigate this problem with a new three-step procedure," and then outlining the three steps, is helpful.

Design   When designing a proposal, you will make choices about the following:

- *Headings.* Proposals are organized with headings for the different sections, such as "Background," "Plan," and "Budget." This allows busy readers to quickly identify what kind of information will be discussed in the section. It also helps a reader returning to the document to quickly find the information he or she needs; for example, if the decision maker has decided to greenlight a proposed plan, he may need to quickly flip to the budget section while on a phone call with the company financial manager.

- *Numbered and bulleted lists.* Like memos, proposals are often read very quickly, so the use of numbered and bulleted lists helps readers absorb important points.

Sources   Proposals may cite sources that support the proposed plan or help build the argument for the existence of a problem. A source that explains how older copy machines contribute to workplace toxins may help convince readers to consider replacing a machine that seems to be working just fine.

Guided Reading | Proposal

Kelly Ratajczak, *Proposal to Add a Wellness Program*

| RHETORICAL SITUATION & CHOICES | | GENRE CONVENTIONS |

RHETORICAL SITUATION & CHOICES

PURPOSE
Ratajczak's purpose is to convince the head of Human Resources to implement a wellness program at their organization.

AUDIENCE
As the head of Human Resources, the reader is the person who will make the decision on whether to implement the wellness plan Ratajczak proposes.

RHETORICAL APPEALS
By citing reputable sources, Ratajczak appeals to ethos. Those sources help create the logical chain that supports her proposal to create a wellness program (logos).

MODES & MEDIA
Mode = written: Ratajczak opted not to include any visuals and relied solely on words to make her argument.

Medium = digital: The proposal was e-mailed to the decision maker as an attachment.

◄ What is the composer, Kelly Ratajczak, doing?

GENRE CONVENTIONS

How do I know this is ► a proposal?

To: Jay Crosson, Senior Vice President, Human Resources
From: Kelly Ratajczak, Intern, Purchasing Department
Subject: Proposal to Add a Wellness Program
Date: April 24, 2017

Health care costs are rising. In the long run, implementing a wellness program in our corporate culture will decrease the company's health care costs.

Research indicates that nearly 70% of health care costs are from common illnesses related to high blood pressure, overweight, lack of exercise, high cholesterol, stress, poor nutrition, and other preventable health issues (Hall, 2006). Health care costs are a major expense for most businesses, and they do not reflect costs due to the loss of productivity or absenteeism. A wellness program would address most, if not all, of these health care issues and related costs.

BENEFITS OF HEALTHIER EMPLOYEES

A wellness program would substantially reduce costs associated with employee health care, and in addition our company would prosper through many other benefits. Businesses that have wellness programs show a lower cost in production, fewer sick days, and healthier employees ("Workplace Health," 2006). Our healthier employees will help to cut not only our production and absenteeism costs but also potential costs such as higher turnover because of low employee morale.

IMPLEMENTING THE PROGRAM

Implementing a good wellness program means making small changes to the work environment, starting with a series of information sessions. Simple changes to our work environment should include healthier food selections in vending machines and in the employee cafeteria. A smoke-free environment, inside and outside the building, could be a new company policy. An important step is to educate our

(Continues on next page)

ELEMENTS OF THE GENRE

Specific audience: The proposal is addressed specifically to the head of Human Resources.

Context for the proposal: The proposal opens with information about how a wellness program could help reduce healthcare costs.

A clear statement of what is being proposed: The subject line is "Proposal to Add a Wellness Program."

Information about advantages of the plan and obstacles to adopting it. The proposal discusses both individual and financial obstacles to implementing a wellness program.

Implementation plan: The implementation plan is loosely described because several types of plans could be adopted. Ratajczak assumes her audience will decide what kind of plan to implement and that will then dictate the costs.

STYLE
Accurate and clear: Ratajczak carefully refers to specific research studies that

employees through information seminars and provide health care guides and pamphlets for work and home. In addition, the human resources department could expand the current employee assistance program by developing online materials that help employees and their families to assess their individual health goals.

Each health program is different in its own way, and there are a number of programs that can be designed to meet the needs of our individual employees. Some programs that are becoming increasingly popular in the workplace are the following ("Workplace Health," 2006):

- health promotion program
- subsidized health club membership
- return-to-work programs
- health-risk appraisals and screenings

OBSTACLES: INDIVIDUAL AND FINANCIAL

The largest barrier in a wellness program is changing the habits and behaviors of our employees. Various incentives such as monetary bonuses, vacation days, merchandise rewards, recognition, and appreciation help to instill new habits and attitudes. Providing a healthy environment and including family in certain programs also help to encourage healthier choices and behaviors (Hall, 2006).

In the long run, the costs of incorporating a wellness program will be far less than rising costs associated with health care. An employee's sense of recognition, appreciation, or accomplishment is an incentive that has relatively low or no costs. The owner of Natural Ovens Bakery, Paul Sitt, has stated that his company gained financially after providing programs including free healthy lunches for employees (Springer, 2005). Sitt said he believes that higher morale and keeping valuable employees have helped his business tremendously.

It is important that our company be healthy in every way possible. Research shows that 41% of businesses already have some type of wellness program in progress and that 32% will incorporate programs within the next year ("Workplace Health," 2006). Our company should always be ahead of our competitors. I want to thank you for your time, and I look forward to discussing this proposal with you further next week.

support her argument that the company would benefit from a wellness program.

Detailed: Ratajczak names specific benefits of an employee wellness program and gives the percentage of companies that already have wellness programs.

DESIGN

Headings: Each section ("Benefits," "Obstacles," etc.) begins with a heading.

Numbered and bulleted lists: The implementation section includes a bulleted list of the types of wellness programs.

SOURCES

Sources are cited throughout the text and in the references list in APA format.

References

Hall, B. (2006). Good health pays off! Fundamentals of health promotion incentives. *Journal of Deferred Compensation 11*(2), 16–26. Retrieved from http://www.aspenpublishers.com/

Springer, D. (2005, October 28). Key to business success? *La Crosse Tribune*. Retrieved from http://lacrossetribune.com/

Workplace health and productivity programs lower absenteeism, costs. (2006). *Managing Benefit Plans 6*(2), 1–4. Retrieved from http://www.ioma.com/

QUESTIONS | Analyzing Ratajczak's Proposal

RHETORICAL SITUATION & CHOICES

1. **Purpose.** Aside from the fact that Ratajczak's text has the word "proposal" in the subject line, how can you identify this document quickly as a proposal?

2. **Audience.** Is the proposal appropriately tailored to the head of Human Resources? What information does Ratajczak include that shows she knows the organization's culture?

3. **Rhetorical appeals.** How does Ratajczak establish her ethos as a concerned employee? Can you think of additional ways Ratajczak could have developed her ethos?

4. **Rhetorical appeals.** How does the proposal logically connect the proposed wellness program to an existing problem?

5. **Elements of the genre.** Are you convinced by the first two paragraphs of the proposal that the organization would benefit from a wellness program? Why or why not? If not, is there a point later in the proposal that convinces you that the organization would benefit from a wellness program?

GENRE CONVENTIONS

6. **Elements of the genre.** Do you think Ratajczak adequately deals with the obstacles to implementing a wellness program? Why or why not?

7. **Modes & media.** Ratajczak did not include any visuals in this proposal. Can you think of a chart or infographic that might have been helpful?

8. **Style.** Is one section of the proposal more or less accurate and clear than other sections? What advice would you give Ratajczak about making the proposal more accurate and clear?

9. **Design.** How does the proposal's design make it easily and quickly readable?

10. **Sources.** How do the sources used reflect upon Ratajczak?

Are you thinking of drafting a proposal? Ask yourself the following questions.

RHETORICAL SITUATION & CHOICES

☐ **Purpose.** How can I convince the decision maker that there is a problem that my proposal will address? How can I persuade the decision-maker that my proposed plan will address the problem?

☐ **Audience.** Who is the person who will make a decision about my proposal? How can I show the decision maker that my proposed plan will address his or her priorities?

☐ **Rhetorical appeals.** How can I establish myself as reliable and responsible? How can I logically connect my proposed plan with a problem that exists?

☐ **Modes & media.** Will my proposal be delivered in print form or digitally? Would it be appropriate for me to include a visual(s)?

GENRE CONVENTIONS

☐ **Elements of the genre.** Have I clearly explained the context for my proposal? Have I expressed my proposed plan clearly and succinctly? Have I provided information about advantages and/or obstacles to implementing my proposed plan? Have I suggested a plan for implementation?

☐ **Style.** How can I use specific details to support and develop generalizations that I make? Does my proposal state clearly exactly what I am proposing? Does my proposal clearly explain what it would take to implement my plan?

☐ **Design.** How can I use headings to organize the material in my proposal? How can I use bulleted or numbered lists to organize my material? How can I ensure that someone who reads my proposal quickly will understand what I am proposing and how it will address a problem?

☐ **Sources.** What sources can I use to establish myself as professional and knowledgeable? Have I properly cited any sources I do use both in the text and in a Works Cited list?

PRACTICE

Proposing Ideas & Solutions in the Workplace

Think about a current or former job. Brainstorm a list of all the current problems you face or others face at that job. For each problem, generate potential solutions. For example, perhaps the cafeteria is too crowded at lunchtime. A possible solution might be to have staggered lunch hours. Look over your list and choose the problem you find most important/compelling. Who would be the person who could affect change? Draft a proposal to that person that establishes the problem, describes the need for change, makes an argument for a solution, acknowledges any obstacles, and includes an implementation plan. Make sure to include specific details/evidence to support your ideas.

9 PUBLIC GENRES

Presentations

Most presentations are brief talks about a particular topic delivered by a knowledge-able speaker to a specific public audience, such as neighborhood associations and school boards. Often they are persuasive—aimed at getting audience members to agree with the speaker about something or to take action. For example, a speaker at a TED event might give a presentation to try to convince the audience to understand an aspect of human nature differently. Even though presentations usually occur in public spaces, they also are a part of academia and the workplace. You might give a presentation to persuade your classmates to agree with you about a specific topic or issue.

With software available on the Web, you can reach more viewers and listeners and also make your presentation more visual and multimodal. For example, you might use online products such as Skype, WebEx, Microsoft Live Meeting, or Elluminate to reach people at other locations. You can also record a presentation and then post it online for future viewing.

To put a presentation together, you can use software to organize your ideas. For years, PowerPoint, part of Microsoft Office, was the standard in many workplaces and class-rooms. However, some presenters are now turning to more visually engaging tools, such as Prezi.

Analyzing Presentations

Purpose   Presenters always have a goal for their presentations. In a neighborhood meeting, you might give a presentation about a problem to persuade your audience that your solutions are the best route to take. Over the last several years, a presenta-tion series called Ignite talks has sprung up in cities around the world. The tagline for Ignite is "Enlighten us, but make it quick." Presenters persuade public audiences about their ideas and passions within a very small time frame. They can use only twenty slides that automatically advance every fifteen seconds. A similar phenomenon is the PechaKucha, which involves twenty slides that show for twenty seconds each.

Audience   Presenters know their audiences; they know what kind of background information they'll need to present, what terminology is useful, and what cultural ref-erences their listeners will connect with. For example, writer and professional speaker Scott Berkun gave a talk "How and Why to Give an Ignite Talk." He knew that his audi-ence would be potential Ignite performers, so he geared his talk to persuade them that they all have a story to tell, something worth sharing on the Ignite stage.

Rhetorical appeals   Any time you want to persuade you need to establish your ethos in order to get your audience to embrace your ideas. Berkun establishes his ethos by showing he knows how to present within the constraints of Ignite—he uses twenty

How To Produce an Ignite Event

Thanks for bringing Ignite to your community. Here's some information on how to get started.

What is Ignite?

Imagine that you're in front of an audience made up of your friends, family, and people from your community, about to present a 5-minute talk on the thing you're most passionate about. You've brought 20 slides, which advance every 15 seconds whether you're ready or not. You have a few last-minute butterflies, but off you go—and the crowd loves it. Welcome to Ignite.

Ignite is a fast-paced geek event started by Brady Forrest, Technology Evangelist for O'Reilly Media, and Bre Pettis of Makerbot.com, formerly of MAKE Magazine. Speakers are given 20 slides, each shown for 15 seconds, giving each speaker 5 minutes of fame. The first Ignite took place in Seattle in 2006, and since then the event has become an international phenomenon, with gatherings in Helsinki, Finland; Paris, France; New York, New York; and many other locations.

Ignite has two parts: the Ignite contest, where people make things, and Ignite talks, where presenters get 20 slides and five minutes to make their point. You can opt to only have talks, but the contest is fun and can serve as a great warm-up for the talks.

Below is all sorts of information that will help you get started. Once you've picked your date and venue, let us know and we'll provide you with logos and more information on setting up your blog and creating supporting materials.

self advancing slides within five minutes. If you are giving a persuasive talk some ways to build ethos are to state your argument clearly, support it with accurate data and appropriate evidence. If you're working with slides, provide well-designed slides that are free of spelling and grammatical errors. When presenting you can boost your ethos through good posture and eye contact. To be persuasive you'll also need to appeal to your audience's sense of logic. If you want to convince a client to purchase a product then you need to provide the reasons and benefits in a logical order. You might also appeal to pathos by being funny or surprising. The humorous and unexpected can work well depending on your audience.

Modes & media   Presenters use a combination of audio, visual, and text. If slides are involved, they may include text, visuals, and even hyperlinks to multimedia, such as

Web pages, animated visuals, movie clips, music, and audio clips. Some speakers use physical props (for example, in the guided reading/viewing in this chapter, the speaker holds up a doll). Some provide their listeners with printouts of their slides. Some deliver their presentations face-to-face or in a digital environment (such as WebEx) where the talk can be replayed anytime, anywhere. Scott Berkun gave his presentation live at a conference; it was recorded and is now available on YouTube.

Elements of the genre Effective presenters do the following:

- *Give a bold introduction to capture their audience's attention.* For example, Scott Berkun opens with "I think storytelling is everything," which prepares his audience for the persuasive claims he will make later in the presentation. Presenters also:

  » Introduce themselves

  » Establish credibility and their relationship to the topic

  » Preview what they will cover during their talk

- The introduction is where speakers make a first impression on their audience—and also where they need to persuade the audience that the presentation is worth listening to.

- *Provide enough background so that the audience can understand the content of the presentation.* Presenters must clarify acronyms and define unfamiliar terminology.

- *Present their information and arguments in the body of their talks.* This is where speakers make claims and back them up with facts, data, personal stories, and quotes from experts.

- *Address objections and counterarguments to make the best case possible.*

- *Conclude with a summary and solid message.* This ensures that the audiences have understood the argument presented, have gotten a clear message, and know what the speaker is asking of them in terms of agreeing and/or taking action (for example, against a particular injustice). Many speakers end by inviting the audience to ask questions.

- *Use visuals, video, audio, and other media to support their arguments.* Most presenters use slides as a way to present key points, infographics, photos, and links to various multimedia—and to provide context and support for their arguments. For example, if a presenter wants to persuade listeners of the need for a program to reduce childhood obesity, he might include an image of obese children, or a chart that shows the relationship between childhood weight and diabetes. To take another example, when Berkun mentions famous people who were "lousy speakers," he backs this up with a visual of Abraham Lincoln. However, visuals and other media should not distract the audience. And it's a good idea to bring handouts of slides so audiences have something to refer to.

- *Make transitions to move the audience from one point to the next.* Presenters can do this by advancing slides or by cuing listeners through speech (for example, "This brings me to my second point . . .").

Style Effective presenters do the following:

- *Organize their material so that it's clear and persuasive.* Presenters must make it easy for audiences to follow what they're saying and to accept their claims and arguments. Some speakers may arrange their talks into three or so main parts built around separate but related concepts. Others might use a chronological organization, which is especially useful for laying out the history of an idea or movement. A speaker arguing about the factors that led to the AIDS crisis might organize his talk chronologically, while a speaker arguing about possible ways to curb the spread of the disease might organize her talk by first focusing on the problem and then focusing on potential solutions and actions.

- *Tailor their level of detail.* Presenters consider their subjects and audiences when deciding on the level of information to share. For an introduction to a topic, a speaker doesn't need to provide as much complex detail as he or she would for a more advanced approach to a subject. Similarly, for an audience of experts, a presenter would provide more depth and detail, such as a speaker talking about climate change and changing geologic formations to a group of geologists.

- *Make eye contact with the whole room and stand tall.* These nonverbal cues connect speakers with audiences and convey their confidence, knowledge, and persuasiveness.

- *Vary their delivery and show emotion.* Speakers vary the volume of their voices, speaking softer at some points and louder at others to stress certain aspects of what they have to say. For example, a speaker may raise his voice to show anger at a situation or excitement about a future possibility. Speakers also vary their pacing between speaking slowly and more quickly, depending on their content and what they want to stress. However, it's important to not speak too quickly, as Scott Berkun demonstrates, and to pause so that audiences can digest information. Many speakers work in a few funny stories or anecdotes: Humor can connect them with the audiences they want to persuade.

Design For presenters creating slides, a smart, clean, nondistracting design will persuade audiences by allowing them to focus on content. Most successful slides reflect the following design features:

- Fonts are usually sans serif—at 20 points or larger for easy reading.

- There is contrast between backgrounds and text. Light-colored text on dark backgrounds or dark-colored text on light backgrounds works best. It's best to avoid clashing colors such as pink text on an orange background.

- Slides are not crowded with lots of points and images. Each slide should have only one main point with a few supporting points.

Sources To persuade their listeners, presenters, like anyone building an argument, may do the following:

- Draw on their own expertise of a subject

- Confer with others who are knowledgeable in the field or subject

- Read articles, reports, books, or other reference material
- Provide a Works Cited list on a slide at the end of the presentation (and/or provide brief citations throughout the slides)
- Credit charts, photos, or any other graphics, usually on the slide where the visual appears, underneath the visual

Guided Reading | Presentation

Sunni Brown is a visual thinker, researcher, and self-described "large-scale Info-doodler and Leader of the Doodle Revolution" who believes in the power of doodling. She argues that focused doodling, in any scenario, gets our minds and memories working better. Brown's academic background is in journalism and linguistics, and she holds a master's degree in public affairs. She lives in Austin, Texas, owns a design company, works as a consultant and creative director, and is the coauthor of *Gamestorming*, a book on innovation and visual thinking.

Brown gave a talk at an Ignite event in which she makes her case for the Doodle Revolution. Ignite hosts events around the country where speakers talk about things (in their lives, in their work, etc.) that they care about most. An Ignite talk can be no longer than five minutes. In her presentation, Brown uses images and statistics to support her points on the value of doodling.

▶ **PRESENTATION**

Ignite, *The Doodle Revolution,* introductory page for Sunni Brown's presentation.

Credit: Courtesy of igniteshow.com/howto.

Sunni Brown, *Ignite Talk: "The Doodle Revolution"*

RHETORICAL SITUATION & CHOICES	GENRE CONVENTIONS

PURPOSE

Sunni Brown wants to persuade her audience that doodling, though considered socially unacceptable in many settings, is actually a very effective tool for recording, absorbing, and retaining information. As she seeks to persuade, she also seeks to entertain her audience and hold their interest with visuals, humor, focused statements, and brisk pacing.

AUDIENCE

Brown's audience is composed of information geeks, designers, writers, and doodle enthusiasts who appreciate irony, comedy, comics, and pop culture.

RHETORICAL APPEALS

Brown builds **ethos** as a creator of doodles and expert on visual thinking. As a professional, scholar, and coauthor of a book on innovation and visual thinking, she is recognized by her viewers as an authority on her topic.

Brown appeals to her audience using **logos** by presenting specific examples in an orderly way.

She connects with viewers' sense of **pathos** through her use of humor—both in what she's saying

◄ What is the composer/ presenter, Sunni Brown, doing?

How do I know this is a ► presentation?

"I am what I refer to as a large-scale strategic doodler. So people pay me to track auditory content and display it to them in a visual language format. And I have a series of 'whoa' moments when I do this."

"I have a significantly high level of comprehension of the information that I doodle. I also have increased attention and recall of that content, weeks and months later, and I can easily immerse myself back into it. Additionally, I've noticed that when I do strategic doodling, I have increased creativity

ELEMENTS OF THE GENRE

Ethos-building introduction to her argument: Brown establishes her ethos by explaining that people pay her to doodle, and she makes clear that she will argue for a "Doodle Revolution" and lay out the reasons that focused doodling should be taken seriously. Brown sets a tone that indicates she's knowledgeable; at the same time she uses humor, even before the presentation officially begins, that has her audience listening and laughing.

Thoughtful conclusion: Her ending sums up the essence of her presentation—and the humor of her delivery, her slides, and the statistics she shares—with clear statements on why and how doodling should be used.

Interesting visuals: Each of Brown's slides relates to a specific part of her argument for doodling. Her visuals include hand-drawn text, cartoons, the doodles of other people (including Ronald Reagan and Alexander Graham Bell), as well as statistical information. The

(Continues on next page)

and what she's showing.

MODES & MEDIA

Mode = audio and visual: Brown uses a combination of audio and visuals throughout her presentation. The audio is her voice presenting ideas, along with laughter from the audience. Her visuals are the images on her slides, which include doodles, comics, and hand-drawn infographics.

Medium = face-to-face and video: This talk was originally delivered before a live audience. In the example given, the presentation is digital, since it is a recording of the original talk that can be found on the Ignite Web site.

and I can make solutions to problems that are even surprising to me. And finally, my listening skills are like, ninja-like. I can discern immediately what's relevant and what's not relevant."

"So I have this series of 'whoa' moments, and simultaneously I notice that our society frowns on doodling in learning environments. In the boardroom, in the situation room, and in the classroom. So, I find that problematic. . . ."

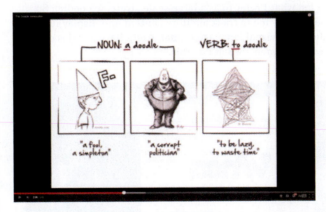

"I discovered five interesting things. One of them is that there is no flattering definition of a doodle. In the seventeenth century, a 'doodle' was a fool; in the eighteenth century, a 'doodle' was a corrupt politician; and in the modern-day society, in the 1930s we see the emergence of our verb 'to doodle,' and it means to be lazy or waste time. . . . [Later] there was a period in time when the ballpoint pen came into play, and people had access to mass-produced pulp paper. So they actually were kind of like flipping around, just like, 'wee, look at these tools we have!' But [doodling] wasn't necessarily meaningful at that point in time."

slides are designed for readability and for persuasive and humorous impact.

Clear transitions: Brown uses the slides themselves to advance the points of her talk. She also uses verbal cues to lay out the structure of her ideas and to transition from one idea to the next ("I discovered five interesting things. One of them . . ." and "finally").

Use of supporting examples: Throughout the presentation, Brown shows an example to support her pro-doodle argument. In fact, she uses twenty examples (each slide is one idea).

STYLE

Smart use of detail: Brown offers just enough detail to illustrate her ideas. She chooses specific images, each for a reason. For example, to support her claim that scientists use doodles to work out solutions to complex problems, she shows a doodle by Alexander Graham Bell and moves on.

Delivery technique: Throughout her talk, Brown faces the audience comfortably (she does not fidget). Her facial expression and hand gestures are not distracting, but rather make the audience feel as though she is just

"In the 1930s, Freudianism was at its height, and people believed that you could actually psychoanalyze someone based on their doodles, and dig into the recesses of their freaky psyches. And naturally, people have an aversion to that." [laughter]

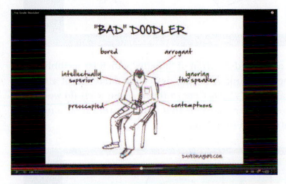

"And finally . . . the physical gesture of doodling gives people the impression that you're not present, right? So, whenever there's a speaker, um, not me, but if there were another speaker [up here] they would think that it was rude and that you're not paying attention."

having a casual (and funny) chat with them.

Persuasive, friendly voice and tone: Brown speaks with an even pace throughout, never rushing through any parts of the talk. Her pacing works with her humor; for example, after she's laid out considerable evidence supporting her claims that doodling should be taken seriously, she says, "So doodling isn't a joke. Okay?" The audience laughs as she reinforces her points.

DESIGN
The speaker does not use traditional slides with text; rather, she uses specific visuals to support the points she's making.

SOURCES
Brown's sources for her presentation are her own experience and background, as well as information that she's gathered as a researcher on doodling, visual thinking, and memory. If this were a research paper and not a presentation, she would have a References list or Works Cited page that would include, for example, a source for her information on the phenomenon of "picture superiority effect," and the film *Mr. Deeds Goes to Town*, which she mentions in her talk.

(Continues on next page)

". . . Also, in our society, we don't think that national leaders doodle. We don't think it's appropriate. But that's patently false. These are Ronald Reagan's doodles. . . . Every president, ever, in our history has been a doodler. Republicans are actually more prolific doodlers than Democrats, which I find interesting."

"Here's a better definition of 'doodle,' which is: scribblings to help a person think. And that definition came out of a 1936 movie called *Mr. Deeds Goes to Town*. . . . So what do we know about the doodle? We know that doodlers retain 30% more information than non-doodlers."

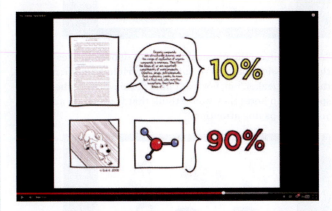

"We also know that there's a phenomenon called the 'picture superiority effect,' which means that after this event is over, you're only going to remember 10% of what I say, but you're going to remember 90% of what I showed you. And so when you're doodling and you're creating pictures that you get to reflect back on, it actually is a way of processing and retaining information. . . . So the doodle's not a joke, okay? Ya get it?" [laughter]

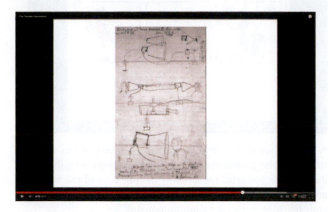

"We also know that almost every genius inventor and innovator and scientist and screenwriter and poet, they all use sketches and doodles in order to get to a solution they wouldn't otherwise have gotten to. This is Alexander Graham Bell's sketches of the telephone."

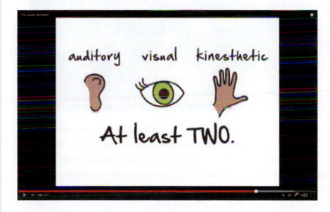

"There are three learning pathways, primarily, that we all have. . . . In order to lock in information, you have to engage at least two. . . . Or, you have to have an emotional experience coupled with one of those things."

(Continues on next page)

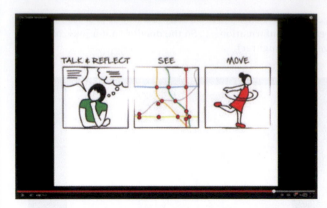

"... These are the three things that you have to do in order to engage the pathways. And I think the reason why the doodle is so powerful for so many people around the world and throughout time is that it actually employs all three of your learning pathways simultaneously."

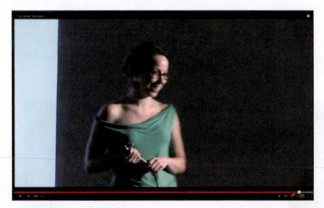

"... I think that the doodle is actually most appropriate in those situations where society actually believes it to be the least appropriate, which is where you have an informationally dense situation, and people are accountable for learning that information. So I say bring on the freaking doodle revolution." [laughter, applause].

Note from editors: The annotations in the Guided Reading above refer to the full video, available at igniteshow.com.

Credit: Sunni Bown, Infodoodler-in-Chief, Author and Leader of the Doodle Revolution.

RHETORICAL SITUATION & CHOICES

1. **Purpose.** How does Brown use examples to support her central argument and purpose? Why does she choose to incorporate these specific examples in her talk, "Doodle Revolution"?

2. **Audience.** What assumptions do you think Brown holds about her audience at Ignite? Why do you think that?

3. **Rhetorical appeals.** One way Brown establishes her ethos is through her demeanor. How else does she establish ethos throughout the presentation?

4. **Rhetorical appeals.** What does Brown's appeal to pathos and use of humor add to the presentation? To what extent does it make it more (or less) persuasive?

5. **Modes & media.** What effect would it have had on the presentation if, rather than using illustrations, doodles, and infographics, Brown had used traditional slides with headings and explanatory text? Also, how is the experience of watching the talk digitally different from experiencing it as a live audience?

GENRE CONVENTIONS

6. **Elements of the genre.** At the start of the presentation, Brown mentions that as a professional strategic doodler she has lots of "whoa moments," and that, thanks to strategic doodling, she has "ninja-like" listening skills. What effects do you think these statements have on her audience? Is this a good strategy for beginning her talk? Why or why not?

7. **Elements of the genre.** What are some of the choices that Brown makes to present her argument? Why does she make those choices, and which parts of her talk are most convincing? To what extent does she persuade you that a "Doodle Revolution" would be a good idea?

8. **Style.** How does Brown create a sense of a personal conversation throughout the talk? How do her delivery, tone, and pacing foster this sense?

9. **Design.** Brown says that most people remember 10 percent of what they hear and 90 percent of what they see or are shown in a presentation. Does this seem right to you? How does this apply to your experience of her talk?

10. **Sources.** Why do you think Brown chose the specific evidence (and visuals) that she uses in her talk (aside from Ignite's parameters of twenty slides)? Do the slides work? Why or why not?

CHECKLIST | Drafting a Presentation

Thinking of drafting a presentation? Ask yourself the following questions.

RHETORICAL SITUATION & CHOICES

☐ **Purpose.** What subjects am I passionate about? What current issues are most important to me? Do I want to motivate my audience to action? Do I want to persuade them to think differently about an idea? Do I want them to see things from a different perspective?

☐ **Audience.** When I deliver my presentation, will I be speaking to experts in the field? Or, will I want to persuade a more general audience? What do I expect is my audience's attitude toward my topic? How will I inspire and persuade my audience? Will I post my presentation online to attract a wider audience?

☐ **Rhetorical appeals.** How will I establish my ethos? Do I want to use emotion to appeal to my audience? If so, how will I make sure my audience continues to see my approach to the subject as reasonable? Will I use logic in my appeal? How can I use logic to persuade my audience to accept my claim?

☐ **Modes & media.** Will I prepare slides with text to accompany my presentation? What visuals might I add to the slides? Should I embed video clips from YouTube? Should I provide handouts? Would audio enhance my presentation? Do I want my presentation to be viewed live (face-to-face)? Do I want it available for future viewing online?

GENRE CONVENTIONS

☐ **Elements of the genre.** How will I grab my audience's attention at the start of my presentation? What background information or terminology do I need to cover first in my presentation? How will I anticipate and address my audience's opposition to any of my persuasive claims? How could slides and visuals enhance my presentation? Will they clarify concepts? Expand ideas? Persuade?

☐ **Style.** What organization is best for my presentation? Do I want to examine a problem and persuade my audience to adopt a solution? To what extent do I need to examine causes and effects? How much time have I allotted to practicing my delivery? What strategies can I use to make sure I stay composed while presenting? Do I want to incorporate humor? Shock?

☐ **Design.** Are my slides simple, uncluttered, and readable? Is my font size large enough for the room and screen? Do I have enough contrast between my font and the background? Is each slide focused around one main point?

☐ **Style.** What organization is best for my presentation? Do I want to examine a problem and persuade my audience to adopt a solution? To what extent do I need to examine causes and effects? How much time have I allotted to practicing my delivery? What strategies can I use to make sure I stay composed while presenting? Do I want to incorporate humor? Shock?

☐ **Sources.** Will my sources help me develop my ethos? Are my sources cited properly?

Presenting Ideas to Boost Creativity

In the presentation featured in this unit, Sunni Brown argues that visualizing ideas—in a variety of contexts, including the workplace—boosts creativity and memory. What ideas do you have about boosting creativity and memory or for improving a process or learning environment? Plan out your argument and gather supporting evidence, and then put together an Ignite-style talk that:

- Is no longer than five minutes

- Is supported by twenty slides (that will advance every fifteen seconds)

As you plan your presentation, review the annotations provided in the Guided Reading of Sunni Brown's talk and keep the following in mind:

- Think about your rhetorical situation—your purpose, audience, and how you will use rhetorical appeals and media. For example, will you be most persuasive if you are also funny?

- Think about the genre's conventions—the elements of a presentation such as a strong introduction and conclusion, interesting visuals, and clear transitions, as well as appropriate style, design, and use of sources. For a five-minute talk, you'll want to streamline your major points, perhaps sticking to only three or so, and be sure to support each one.

- Ask yourself: What do I most want my audience to remember about my presentation?

News Articles

The first newspapers were handwritten pages that reported on economic and social issues in Europe in the 1400s. The first successful English-language paper was *The Weekly Newes*, established in the 1620s; a little later, *The London Gazette* became the official newspaper of Great Britain (1666). In 1704, a bookseller and postmaster named John Campbell kicked off newspapers in America with *The Boston News-Letter*, an effort that was followed up more successfully in 1728 by Benjamin Franklin, who published *The Pennsylvania Gazette*, a paper considered to be *The New York Times* of the eighteenth century.

Today, most cities have at least one local daily newspaper; Chicago, for example, has the *Chicago Sun-Times* and the *Chicago Tribune*. Daily newspapers are divided into sections on world, domestic, and local news; sports; business; science; health; obituaries;

and weather. Many have sections dedicated to editorials/opinions, food, travel, education, entertainment, and fashion, along with advice columns, comics, puzzles, and horoscopes. Smaller communities and colleges also publish newspapers on topics of interest to more specific audiences. Many publications are available online and include links to related stories and topics, as well as social media features that allow readers to post reactions to published stories.

Before the Internet, major newspapers were published once or twice a day. However, now that readers can check news headlines and follow stories online throughout the day, they expect constant updates. News reporting and publishing is now a 24/7 occupation.

While newspapers publish many kinds of writing—persuasive editorials, letters to the editor, advice columns, ads—at their core are factual news articles written by reporters. Reporters research their writing: They gather information for a story by conducting interviews, serving as eyewitnesses (reporting from the scene, for example), checking public records, and working with library and online sources. News journalists need to be able to back up the accuracy of their writing with facts from several reliable sources.

Analyzing New Articles

Purpose   Journalists research and write news articles to inform readers of facts and events. Their purpose is to present true and fair accounts of issues and happenings, and to do so while adhering to ethical standards, such as those outlined by the Society of Professional Journalists. Like any organization, each news provider has its own policies, agenda, and built-in biases. That said, the news articles that providers publish or air should be as fact based and objective as possible.

Audience   Journalists who write news articles know that readers want to be informed about world events and issues and to be kept up-to-date, especially online. They know that some readers will scan the first few paragraphs to get the main idea, so they need to include the most important material up front. Some readers who are especially interested—personally or professionally—in a given topic, however, will read for depth. They will read the entire article and also turn to related articles. Journalists keep that audience in mind as well.

Rhetorical appeals   Journalists use ethos and logos to reach their audiences. A news publisher's reputation for "getting the story right" is crucial, as are the reputations of reporters associated with the publisher. If a reporter's credibility is seriously tarnished, his or her career in journalism will quickly end. In 2003, for example, promising *New York Times* reporter Jayson Blair was fired for plagiarizing parts of several news reports he had written. The *Times* called it "a low point in the 152-year history of the newspaper" and apologized profusely to its readers. In 2016, the *Guardian* dismissed reporter Joseph Mayton for fabricating stories.

Modes & media   News articles can take many forms. Here, we're highlighting written news articles because text can appear in print or digital formats. With the rise of digital news sites such as *The Huffington Post*, many print newspapers have moved online (see also "Purpose" on p. 216). Most traditional print newspapers have companion Web sites; for example, you can read many of the same stories in both the print and online versions of *The New York Times*, the *Wall Street Journal*, *The Washington Post*, and the *Los Angeles Times*, although some online content requires a subscription. The advantages of the online news article are that it can be updated instantly, can link to related articles and sources, and can be accompanied by video. Online publications also allow readers to post comments, making these sources much more interactive than print newspapers.

In addition to appearing in print and in digital formats, news stories can take the form of audio and video reports. National Public Radio covers all the top stories that print and digital news outlets cover, but in audio form. Many digital news outlets, such as MSNBC, also make videos of news coverage available online.

Elements of the genre   Following are some of features that define news articles. They:

- *Are well researched and fact-checked.* As previously discussed, the authority (or ethos) of the reporter, publisher, and content is crucial. Writers must be scrupulous in their research and fact-checking. A rule of thumb in journalism is to verify a report with at least three reliable sources. When an error is discovered in an article, journalists and publishers are usually quick to make a correction and apologize.

- *Usually aim at a broad audience.* Most newspapers, news magazines, and news sites have a very broad readership with varying degrees of education, so the level of vocabulary in a news article must be appropriate for all. Most are written with a ninth- or tenth-grade vocabulary. *The New York Times*, however, is written at a twelfth-grade level of vocabulary and comprehension.

- *Open with a concise summary in a lead (or lede) paragraph.* Most journalists begin their news articles with a paragraph that states the most important aspects of their story and grabs the reader's attention. In the rest of the article, reporters elaborate on what was presented in the opening paragraph. Because many readers skim rather than read a full article, the content of the lead paragraph is especially important.

- *Present information in order of importance.* Paragraphs that follow the lead and make up the body of the article provide details and supporting evidence from sources. Paragraphs closer to the beginning of the story provide details that are more important in understanding the essence of the story; those closer to the end, however, provide information that is less essential, given that some readers may not read the whole article to the end. As explained in the "Style" section on page 218,

Think of the
sources where you
get your news.
Freewrite about
the news sources
you turn to most
often, considering
the following:
How would you
characterize the
writing? The
vocabulary level?
How do a journalist's
style and word
choice contribute
to your reading
experience?

news journalists tend to structure their articles with an overview of the important information at the beginning so that readers can get information quickly.

- *Include quotations.* Journalists often quote sources directly to add flavor to their articles and to maintain the feel of "just the facts, ma'am." No one can accuse a reporter of misinterpreting what someone said if the reporter includes direct quotations.

- *Are written in short paragraphs.* Journalists often write in short paragraphs because they're easier to read than long ones. They're also easier on the eyes, especially considering the formats news articles are generally published in—either in narrow columns in print newspapers or online.

Style   News articles are characterized by the following stylistic features. They demonstrate:

- *A neutral tone and absence of personal opinion.* The goal of writing a news article is to report information. It's appropriate for news journalists to use a serious and fairly formal tone in their writing; of course, "formal" doesn't have to mean dry. It's also appropriate for journalists to refrain from editorializing, unless they are writing an editorial or hosting an opinion column, for example.

- *An objective, third-person voice.* An objective stance conveys the cut-and-dry, fact-based nature of news articles. News journalists also use precise language to clearly communicate facts and details, and they use the third person (*he/she/they*) rather than the first person (*I/we*).

- *Just enough detail for the general reader.* In the annotated article by Nicholas Wade (p. 220), you'll notice that the writer is very specific about his subject: how cats lap water. However, Wade doesn't offer the level of detail that a specialist such as a scientist or veterinarian might want.

Design   News articles feature the following design elements, which also have editorial functions, including:

- *An attention-grabbing title or headline.* The title of a news article is called a headline. It is usually presented in much larger or bolder type than the story itself and is brief and descriptive. Headlines are used to attract readers and are sometimes provocative.

- *A byline.* A byline is the presentation of the author's name, usually below the headline and above the text of the article.

- *A serif typeface.* A serif font has a very small flare at the stroke ends and corners of letters, while a sans serif font lacks these strokes. Print articles are often presented in serif fonts (such as in the print edition of *The New York Times*), while sans serif fonts, such as those used by BBC News (below), are a good choice for the readability of digital content. Compare a serif **A** to a sans serif **A**.

- *Use of columns or chunking.* News sites such as the BBC's present articles in chunked sections that have their own headings. Digital content may be presented in multiple columns or on different sections of the grid with various ways to navigate the content. Print newspapers are limited to columns of no more than fifty-two characters wide.

- *Images: photos, charts, and multimedia components.* Many news articles, especially breaking news on a Web site or a front-page story in a print paper, are contextualized with photos, charts, and graphs, and when published online, they can include video and other multimedia. A piece with a video or audio component usually includes an arrow icon or other visual element to indicate this; sometimes the video or audio itself is the news story. News publishers use visual and multimedia to grab readers' attention, provide context, and enrich the content of print articles.

- *Headers, footers, and tabs.* Designers of online news sites provide tabs and navigational menus and search boxes to keep readers oriented. The designers use repeated design features to reinforce the agency's identity. For example, a print newspaper's title appears on every page and in other elements, and titles, headers, and footers (which include the date and section, for example) help readers find what they need on the page.

- *Use of color.* Online news sites include color images and video. Designers also use color typographically to direct attention toward particular content. Blue is sometimes used for hyperlinks (which turn a different color once you select them), red is sometimes used for breaking news headlines, and gray shading is sometimes used to orient readers as to their location within the content. Images and videos are shown in full color. Print newspapers, which are published on a thin paper called newsprint, are printed in black ink (such as *The New York Times*) or in color (such as *USA Today*).

Sources   News reports are based on eyewitness accounts, authoritative published documents, interviews, and records. Most journalists indicate their sources within their news articles, using attribution phrases such as "according to" and linking directly to their sources. In his article on how cats drink (see p. 220 of this chapter), *New York Times* reporter Nicholas Wade writes:

> Cats, both big and little, are so much classier, according to new research by Pedro M. Reis and Roman Stocker of the Massachusetts Institute of Technology, joined by Sunghwan Jung of the Virginia Polytechnic Institute and Jeffrey M. Aristoff of Princeton. Writing in the Thursday issue of *Science*, the four engineers report. . . .

Wade makes it clear that the information he draws on is a researched article from the journal *Science* and from the four researchers he names. Journalists, unlike the authors of peer-reviewed journal articles (see Chapter 7, "Academic Genres," p. 103), do not use academic documentation styles such as MLA or APA. Because news journalism is a popular genre and not a scholarly genre, it has a different set of conventions for documenting sources, such as the phrasing that Wade uses on page 220. In news journalism, the thinking is that the reader doesn't need the same level of detail about sources that scholarly audiences need. That said, online news providers and journalists can boost their ethos by linking to their sources.

Guided Reading | News Article

The New York Times, which has been publishing since 1851, is considered highly accurate and is regarded as one of the most authoritative newspapers available. Its Web site and print circulation make it one of the most widely read newspapers in the world. It has won over one hundred Pulitzer Prizes, the most prestigious reporting award given. Nicholas Wade is a science reporter for *The New York Times*. He has written several science books, including 2009's *The Faith Instinct*, about the scientific basis of religious faith. The following article appeared in the Science section of the *Times*; the online version includes links to sources, infographics, and video that support the text.

Nicholas Wade, *For Cats, a Big Gulp with a Touch of the Tongue*

RHETORICAL SITUATION & CHOICES	GENRE CONVENTIONS

PURPOSE
As a science news reporter, Wade aims to explain recent findings about how cats drink.

AUDIENCE Wade's audience includes general news readers, online readers, *Times* fans, animal lovers, and science enthusiasts. Also, as a science journalist, Wade may have his own following, so some readers may be his fans.

RHETORICAL APPEALS
Wade appeals to readers' sense of **ethos** through specific references to the work of four scientists who published an article in the journal *Science*. He appeals to **pathos** by using humor, especially at the start of the article. He begins with a tongue-in-cheek statement: "It has taken four

◄ **What is the composer, Nicholas Wade, doing?**

How do I know this is ► a news article?

It has taken four highly qualified engineers and a bunch of integral equations to figure it out, but we now know how cats drink. The answer is: very elegantly, and not at all the way you might suppose.

Cats lap water so fast that the human eye cannot follow what is happening, which is why the trick had apparently escaped attention until now. With the use of high-speed photography, the neatness of the feline solution has been captured.

The act of drinking may seem like no big deal for anyone who can fully close his mouth to create suction, as people can. But the various species that cannot do so—and that includes most adult carnivores—must resort to some other mechanism.

Dog owners are familiar with the unseemly lapping noises that ensue when their thirsty pet meets a bowl of water. The dog is thrusting its tongue into the water, forming a crude cup with it and hauling the liquid back into the muzzle.

Cats, both big and little, are so much classier, according to new research by Pedro M. Reis and Roman Stocker of the Massachusetts Institute of Technology, joined by Sunghwan Jung of the Virginia Polytechnic Institute and Jeffrey M. Aristoff of Princeton.

Writing in the Thursday issue of *Science*, the four engineers report that the cat's lapping method depends on its

ELEMENTS OF THE GENRE

Is well researched and accurate: Wade read a research report in *Science* and talked to the scientists who wrote it. He found out how the research was inspired, funded, and conducted.

Opens with a lead paragraph: This paragraph sets up the article's subject: "[W]e now know how cats drink."

Presents information in order of importance: Wade begins with the researchers' findings: They discovered how cats drink, something previously unknown. "Cats lap water so fast that the human eye cannot follow what is happening, which is why the trick had apparently escaped attention until now." Wade ends with

highly qualified engineers and a bunch of integral equations to figure it out."

He also appeals to readers' sense of logic (logos) by beginning with general statements about cats drinking water and then continuing with more specific details.

MODES & MEDIA
Mode = written, visual, and video: Wade shares most information in words, but photos of Cutta Cutta and a video in the piece as it was published in the *Times* illustrate his most important points (note: scroll down to the video box on the *Times* page). Some news sites, such as *The Huffington Post*, present articles as videos that are introduced by a small amount of text.

Medium = digital: Wade's article was published at *The New York Times* online and also in print. Among the advantages of the digital version of the article are the addition of video and the links to other information, including the researched article that was Wade's source.

instinctive ability to calculate the point at which gravitational force would overcome inertia and cause the water to fall.

What happens is that the cat darts its tongue, curving the upper side downward so that the tip lightly touches the surface of the water.

The tongue is then pulled upward at high speed, drawing a column of water behind it.

Just at the moment that gravity finally overcomes the rush of the water and starts to pull the column down—snap! The cat's jaws have closed over the jet of water and swallowed it.

The cat laps four times a second—too fast for the human eye to see anything but a blur—and its tongue moves at a speed of one meter per second.

Being engineers, the cat-lapping team next tested its findings with a machine that mimicked a cat's tongue, using a glass disk at the end of a piston to serve as the tip. After calculating things like the Froude number and the aspect ratio, they were able to figure out how fast a cat should lap to get the greatest amount of water into its mouth. The cats, it turns out, were way ahead of them—they lap at just that speed.

To the scientific mind, the next obvious question is whether bigger cats should lap at different speeds.

The engineers worked out a formula: the lapping frequency should be the weight of the cat species, raised to the power of minus one-sixth and multiplied by 4.6. They then made friends with a curator at Zoo New England, the nonprofit group that operates the Franklin Park Zoo in Boston and the Stone Zoo in Stoneham, Mass., who let them videotape his big cats. Lions, leopards, jaguars and ocelots turned out to lap at the speeds predicted by the engineers.

The animal who inspired this exercise of the engineer's art is a black cat named Cutta Cutta, who belongs to Dr. Stocker and his family. Cutta Cutta's name comes from the word for "many stars" in Jawoyn, a language of the Australian aborigines.

Dr. Stocker's day job at M.I.T. is applying physics to biological problems, like how plankton move in the ocean. "Three and a half years ago, I was watching Cutta Cutta lap over breakfast," Dr. Stocker said. Naturally, he wondered what hydrodynamic problems the cat might be solving. He consulted Dr. Reis, an expert in fluid mechanics, and the study was under way.

At first, Dr. Stocker and his colleagues assumed that the raspy hairs on a cat's tongue, so useful for grooming, must also be involved in drawing water into its mouth. But the tip

information on how the research was funded, something fewer readers will be interested in.

Includes quotations to personalize the information: The quote from Dr. Stocker shows what inspired his research: "Three and a half years ago, I was watching Cutta Cutta lap over breakfast."

Uses short paragraphs to hold readers' attention.

STYLE
Neutral perspective, no opinions: Wade doesn't indicate his personal opinion about how cats drink.

Objective, third-person voice: Wade reports what researchers discovered, leaving himself out of the article. Though he may be a dog owner himself, instead of writing "My dog," he writes, "Dog owners are familiar. . . ."

Just enough detail for the general reader: Wade relates relevant details precisely, such as the formula used to calculate the drinking speed of cats: "The lapping frequency should be the weight of the cat species, raised to the power of minus one-sixth and multiplied by 4.6."

(Continues on next page)

of the tongue, which is smooth, turned out to be all that was needed.

The project required no financing. The robot that mimicked the cat's tongue was built for an experiment on the International Space Station, and the engineers simply borrowed it from a neighboring lab.

Note from editors: Explore the article and multimedia in their original published form on nytimes.com

DESIGN

Appealing headline: The title interests readers and conveys the gist of the article in a few words. Also, the page presents the newspaper's title, the name of the section, and the date of publication.

Byline: As published in the *Times*, Wade's name (rather than "staff writer") appears under the headline, which adds to his **ethos**.

Friendly typeface: *The New York Times* online uses a clean Georgia serif font designed specifically for easy screen reading.

Columns and chunking: The *Times* divides its Web page into columns. In this case the content and images are in one area; advertising is on the right.

Images and multimedia: A photo of Cutta Cutta gives readers a visual of the cat that inspired the research, and a series of photos shows how cats drink. A video features the researchers explaining why they decided to study cats drinking.

SOURCES

Sources are acknowledged.

Wade and the *Times* use hyperlinks to acknowledge sources. The names of the four engineers who wrote the report on cats are linked so readers can learn more about them. Linking to sources further conveys Wade's reliability and objectivity.

QUESTIONS | Analyzing Wade's News Article

RHETORICAL SITUATION & CHOICES

1. **Purpose.** What is Wade's main purpose in writing this article? What are some of his secondary purposes? Identify passages in the article where these purposes are apparent.

2. **Purpose.** Notice how Wade uses a slightly humorous title for his science- and research-based article. Why does he do this?

3. **Audience.** How does Wade appeal to people who are not cat lovers?

4. **Rhetorical appeals.** The online version of Wade's article includes hyperlinks that connect readers with additional information, including a researched article in *Science* and the biographical profiles of the scientists who wrote it, which contributes to the ethos of Wade and his article. How else does Wade convey a sense of ethos?

5. **Rhetorical appeals.** Cats and kittens can be extremely cute, and there are many online videos devoted to celebrating how adorable they can be. How does Wade approach the subject from a different angle? Are there any spots where Wade emphasizes their cuteness? If so, where—and to what end?

GENRE CONVENTIONS

6. **Modes & media.** Do you read news primarily online, or do you read print newspapers? Why?

7. **Elements of the genre.** How does the lead paragraph set the stage for the rest of the article?

8. **Style.** How does Wade convey scientific information in a way that a general audience can understand? If possible, watch the video embedded in the article. How does its content connect with Wade's article? What stylistic differences, if any, do you see between Wade's writing and the voice-over of the video?

9. **Design.** Notice that the images and video are neatly lined up on the left side of the article rather than interspersed within the article where they are mentioned. Why did the designers at *The New York Times* lay them out this way?

10. **Sources.** Make a list of all the sources Nicholas Wade consulted while writing this article. Are there any sources that surprise you? How can you categorize the sources? Are they primary? Secondary? Tertiary? (See Chapter 13 for support with sources.)

Are you thinking of drafting a news article? Ask yourself the following questions.

RHETORICAL SITUATION & CHOICES

☐ **Purpose.** What newsworthy event or issue do I want to report? Of all the people involved with the story, which person will be my focus? How can I bring the story and people to life for my readers?

☐ **Audience.** Who will read my article? How carefully will they read it? Why will they read it? What will they do with the information?

☐ **Rhetorical appeals.** How will I establish my authority as a writer? How will I logically connect ideas and details? How will I make sure that my use of pathos does not undercut my ethos?

☐ **Modes & media.** Will readers experience my article in print form or online? Do I want to include images or videos?

GENRE CONVENTIONS

☐ **Elements of the genre.** Which information is important enough to my readers that I should present it first? Which information is interesting but not as important?

☐ **Style.** How will I keep my tone objective and neutral? What level of detail will I include in my article?

☐ **Design.** How will I use headers and footers, titles, headlines, tabs, and other design features to keep my readers oriented? Will my article appear online? If so, what information will I hyperlink? How might I embed photos or videos into the layout?

☐ **Sources.** How much research will I need to do to compose this article? Are there people I'll need to talk to? Where will I need to go? Will I need to locate documents or records in a library or online?

PRACTICE

Writing to Inform General Readers

Think of an animal behavior you are curious about—for example, you might wonder why bees sting or why dogs assume certain distinct postures (like the play bow). Search for YouTube videos that explore the animal behavior in depth. Find out if there is a faculty expert on that animal on your campus, and if so, arrange to interview them. Then, think about how to convey what you've learned to a general audience. Which quotations from the videos and/or interview will do the most to bring your article to life? Next, draft a short article for an online newspaper that conveys the big picture of the topic, as well as relevant details that will interest your readers. Be sure to create a catchy headline and to hyperlink to any sources you use (including the people you interview and the videos you reference).

Editorials & Opinion Pieces

Editorials and other opinion pieces are texts that convey a writer's views on a particular topic, sometimes a controversial topic. This type of writing can be called by different names, such as *opinions*, *perspectives*, *commentaries*, and *viewpoints*, and can take the form of a letter to the editor or an online comment in response to an issue or other piece of writing.

Editorials and opinion pieces appear in newspapers and magazines, on TV and radio, and in blogs and other online publications. Editorials also include editorial cartoons. An editorial represents the opinion of a news agency's editorial board, and therefore represents the opinion of the publisher. An opinion piece, on the other hand, could take the form of opinion columns by regular featured writers, and letters from readers in which they share their views. If your school publishes a newspaper, it probably also includes a section dedicated to editorials or opinions.

Analyzing Editorials & Opinion Pieces

Purpose   The purpose may vary depending on whether the writer is an individual or an editorial board writer.

- *Individual writers*. An average citizen or student who writes an opinion piece or letter to the editor does so to convey his or her view on a specific issue, with the intent of persuading other readers. For example, in one issue of the *Oregon Daily Emerald*, a University of Oregon student wrote a column titled "Students Should Have Wider Gun Liberties" in response to an article discussing how the university campus prepares for a campus shooting. The student's purpose is clear—as is his opinion.

- The same is true for an individual columnist—a staff or syndicated writer for a specific newspaper, magazine, or other news organization; that is, the columnist conveys his or her own opinion in the editorial and not the opinion of a publisher, though there is some gray area here because the writers are usually employed by the publisher.

- *Editorial board writers*. Texts that are written by the editorial board of a newspaper or magazine convey the opinion of the publisher. These editorials are intended to educate and persuade readers to agree with a specific idea and/or to take a specific action. The editorial boards of most newspapers reflect a conservative or liberal point of view through their editorials; for example, the editorial board of *The New York Times* has a reputation for being fairly liberal, while the editorial board of the *News-Gazette* of Champaign-Urbana, Illinois, has a reputation for being conservative.

Audience   Anyone with access to newspapers, magazines, television, radio, or the Internet can read or watch editorials and opinion pieces. You might scan the opinion pages of newspapers regularly, or mainly during an election or controversy, in order to read the opinions, analysis, and interpretations of others on various issues. Writers of editorials keep their readers—primary and secondary audiences—in mind as they compose.

Rhetorical appeals   Editorial and opinion piece writers rely most on ethos and logos to persuade readers of the validity of their positions. Writers are careful to avoid exaggeration and oversimplification to come across as credible (ethos), and they use evidence to appeal to readers' sense of logic (logos).

Modes & media   Newspaper editorials and opinion pieces are usually presented as written texts; sometimes they're accompanied by a small photo of the writer to establish the writer's credibility. Some editorials include charts or other infographics. Some editorials are presented as audio texts, such as the commentaries offered by National Public Radio. Editorials and opinion pieces can be found both in print, such as in newspapers and magazines, and digitally, such as on the sites for *The New York Times* and NPR.

Elements of the genre   Editorial and opinion piece writers do the following:

- *Clearly present their work as opinion writing.* The distinction between an editorial or opinion piece and a news article is important: Editorials or opinion pieces are opinions based on research and analysis, whereas news articles are objective reporting based on research. That is, editorials reflect a personal view, while news articles are supposed to be totally free of opinion. Editorials or opinion pieces are usually clearly labeled as *editorials* (or *opinion*, *viewpoint*, or *commentary*).

- *Write concisely.* An editorial or opinion piece is typically about five or so paragraphs long, which means the author needs to make his or her point quickly.

- *Identify and address counterarguments.* Editorial and opinion piece writers make their strongest cases when they anticipate objections and opposition to their views.

- *Offer potential solutions.* Often after explaining a problem, writers will examine potential solutions and suggest one over another.

- *Close with a simple but memorable statement.* For example, the editorial on page 228 by Grecia Sanchez closes with "It is an imperative for young people to acknowledge themselves for who and what they are, according to their own personal opinions."

- *Invite readers to respond.* Many online editorials become discussion starters in which hundreds or even thousands of readers post replies to the original editorial and to other posts.

Style   Editorial and opinion piece writers do the following:

- *Include concise detail.* Writers use specific facts throughout their editorials to support their position. Because they are making a case, they need to use enough evidence to convince readers, but they still need to keep the entire piece fairly brief.

- *Use sound reasoning and avoid logical fallacies.* Opinion writers support their claims with quotations from experts. They also strive to avoid errors in reasoning known as logical fallacies. Here are some of the most common types:
    - » *Red herring*: Distracting the reader from the real issue being argued: for example, "Global warming needs to be addressed, but people are struggling with gas prices."

- » *Ad hominem*: Attacking the person making an argument instead of addressing the argument: for example, "She says women should have equal rights, but look at how ugly she is."
- » *Hasty generalization*: Extrapolating unrealistically from one example: for example, "He lied; therefore all men are liars."
- » *Slippery slope*: Assuming that if one step is taken, then all sorts of catastrophic results will inevitably follow: for example, "If we increase taxes by 1 percent today, tomorrow our children will be paying more in taxes than they take home."
- » *Circular reasoning*: Defining a word by using the word, where the start is the same as the ending: for example, "The reason we should outlaw guns is that guns should be made illegal."
- » *Post hoc*: Confusing chronology with causality: for example, "The cat peed on the bedspread because I just washed it."

- *Use analogies and refer to cultural and historical events.* Writers use comparisons to clarify the issue and refer to other events to help readers identify with it.
- *Use interesting language.* Opinion writers avoid jargon and instead use language that will appeal to readers who may not be familiar with the issue. They may also use rhetorical questions to spark readers' attention.
- *Convey a clear, personable voice and tone.* Writers use clear, persuasive language as they present their opinions and support them with facts. Editorial writers often write in the first person (I) and in a friendly and inviting tone to reach a wide readership.

Design   Editorial and opinion piece writers and the designers they work with do the following. They:

- *Write clear, interesting headlines.* Whether they're published in print or online, editorials, like news articles, are presented with a headline designed to get readers' attention and to make it clear what the editorialist is writing about. Editorials and opinion pieces are also clearly labeled as such, or with other terms, such as *opinions* or *commentaries*, that denote subjective writing.
- *Repeat design features on the page.* Whether you're reading an editorial or opinion piece in print or online, you'll see certain design elements on every page; these elements include the name of the newspaper, perhaps presented as a logo or otherwise branded, at the top and bottom of the page. This helps the writers and designers establish the news organization's identity. You might also find a heading indicating what part of the paper or site you've navigated to ("Editorial," "Opinion," etc.). The date also appears in these spots for easy reference.

Sources   Opinion writers refer to specific examples. They back up their generalizations by offering a variety of support from credible sources. They present evidence with attribution phrases that let readers know where the data came from.

Guided Reading | Editorial

When she wrote this editorial, Grecia Sanchez was a student double-majoring in Philosophy and Multimedia Journalism at the University of Texas at El Paso. Her career goal was to work for a newspaper promoting ideas about social humanities. This opinion piece was published in *The Prospector*, the University of Texas at El Paso's student newspaper. Sanchez was a staff reporter for *The Prospector*. This editorial was published on September 13, 2016, and filed under the "Opinion" section of the site.

Grecia Sanchez, *¿Es que acaso soy hispana?*

RHETORICAL SITUATION & CHOICES	GENRE CONVENTIONS

PURPOSE
Sanchez wants to convince readers that it should be up to individuals to decide how they want to identify their race or ethnicity.

AUDIENCE
Sanchez is writing for a college newspaper, so she knows her readers are college students. Her university is a Hispanic Serving Institution, which means that at least 25 percent of its students are Hispanic, so she knows that many of the paper's readers will be interested in her topic.

RHETORICAL APPEALS
Sanchez establishes her **ethos** by sharing that she was born in Mexico and that her first language was Spanish. She appeals to **logos** by presenting facts about the history of terms like *Latino*, *Hispanic*, and *Chicano*.

MODES & MEDIA
Mode = written: Most editorials and opinion pieces are

◄ **What is the composer, Grecia Sanchez, doing?**

**How do I know this is ►
an opinion piece?**

Grecia Sanchez, Staff Reporter
September 13, 2016
Filed under Opinion

Defining identity at an adolescent age can be a challenge, especially to those who are constantly interacting with a different culture than their own.

I was born and raised in Ciudad Juàrez, Mexico. My first language is Spanish and my only label in Juàrez was that of a Mexican girl. I only had to deal with one nationality and one term to define myself. I didn't realize that just across the border I was defined as something more than just Mexican.

My struggle began at the time I was applying to UTEP. Among the documents I had to deliver for my admission process was a requirement for a meningitis vaccine. I remember going to the pharmacy and having to fill out this form with the question "How do you identify yourself?" It even had optional answers showing Hispanic/Latino, Latinx, Chicano, Asian American, African American, among others.

The overall experience of it was overwhelming. I had to ask the pharmacist to define these terms for me because I had literally no idea what all of these meant. At the end, I just put "Mexican" with my own handwriting in the "Other" space.

Many Mexican students can relate to my experience since we are constantly labeled as Hispanic or Latino students, and though many of us think these terms are the same thing, in reality, they have differences regarding cultural, historical, political and social contexts.

According to the Pais Latino Web site, the term "Hispano" is used for all the people who come from countries that were once conquered by Hispania, or España (using modern

ELEMENTS OF THE GENRE
Is clearly presented as opinion writing: Throughout her piece, Sanchez often asserts her opinions. For example, she says, "I shouldn't be pushed to decide," "one word invented by a large group of disrespectful people," and "it is important for other people to think about who they are."
Is concisely written: Sanchez's sentences and language clearly convey her points. She uses only enough information to support her opinions. Although she has more paragraphs than one might typically see in an opinion piece, her paragraphs are short and follow journalistic conventions.
Invites readers to respond: In her closing statement, Sanchez asks her readers to "think about who they are and which term they identify with the most."

written or audio pieces. Words are vital to editorialists or opinion columnists if they want to make their point because the specificity and clarity of the writer's position is so important.

Medium = digital: The column is available online, and at the bottom there's an option for a print-friendly version, which is formatted specifically to be printed on a standard 8.5″ × 11″ sheet of paper.

terminology). These countries include all the American countries from Mexico all the way down to South America, with the exception of Brazil, since it was conquered by Portugal.

The U.S. Census Bureau imposed the term in 1980 to define the people who would be later called Mexican Americans, unlike the term "Latino," which refers to the geography of Latin America and its inhabitants. This is used for people belonging to countries where the Romance languages are spoken (Spanish, Portuguese and French).

Both of these terms are politically and socially correct to use, as long as one has its definition and correct context in mind. However, Chicano is often used to depict Mexican Americans. It describes those who have Mexican heritage, and although it is a term that is recently accepted nowadays, there are still people who think of this term as a disrespectful one.

Alongside the LGBT movement in recent years, the term "Latinx" has been introduced into our society to refer to the gender-neutral alternative for Latino, Latina and Latin@. According to the Huffington Post's Latino Voices article, "Why People are Using the Term Latinx," it is used as an inclusive term for intersecting identities of Latin American descendants.

Now that I know the differences between these words, I honestly do not consider them as part of my identity. I know I can be considered Hispana because I speak Spanish and I come from Mexico, which was conquered by España during colonial American times. I realize I can be a Latina because I belong to a Latin American country and I speak one of the Romance languages, and I also acknowledge I can be called Chicana because I have Mexican ascendency. But neither of these terms define me because of the simple fact that I was born and raised in Mexico.

Above all the differences, I am Mexican and I believe I shouldn't be pushed to decide whether I am Chicana, but not a Latina, or that I am Latinx, but not Hispanic; I am just a Mexican girl. I've heard that a lot of these terms were introduced by the U.S. government, which was driven by racism and disrespectful jokes toward Mexicans. This is another reason why I do not wish to recognize myself as one word invented by a large group of disrespectful people.

Although I do not identify myself with those terms, I do feel it is important for other people to think about who they are and which term they identify with the most, if they do at all. It is an imperative for young people to acknowledge themselves for who and what they are, according to their own personal opinions.

Note from editors: ¿Es que acaso soy hispana? translates to "Is it that I am Hispanic?"

STYLE
Specific facts used as support: Sanchez provides details from the U.S. Census Bureau and the Pais Latino Web site.

Personal, informal tone: Sanchez writes, "I just put 'Mexican' with my own handwriting in the 'Other' space."

DESIGN
Clear, interesting headline: The headline ¿"Es que acaso soy hispana?" immediately signals that the subject of the opinion piece will relate to Hispanic identity.

Byline, date of publication, and type of article at top.

SOURCES
Sanchez refers to specific sources (Pais Latino Web site, U.S. Census Bureau, and Huffington Post). She also uses her own experiences throughout to help support her opinions.

RHETORICAL SITUATION & CHOICES

1. **Purpose.** Does Sanchez convince you that individuals should be able to make their own choices about their racial and ethnic identity? Why or why not?

2. **Audience.** How do you think a Caucasian person whose family has lived in the United States for many generations might respond to Sanchez's piece?

3. **Rhetorical appeals.** How effective do you think Sanchez's references to the origins of terms like *Hispanic*, *Latino*, and *Chicano* are?

4. **Rhetorical appeals.** How does Sanchez make her case? How does she appeal to her audience using ethos?

5. **Rhetorical appeals.** To what extent does Sanchez come across as authoritative and knowledgeable? What does she do to convince you that she is authoritative and knowledgeable, or alternatively, what does she do that makes you question her authority or knowledge?

GENRE CONVENTIONS

6. **Modes & media.** Imagine that Sanchez had included a map of Central and South America with each country labeled with the different terms the U.S. Census Bureau uses to identify people from that country. How would the addition of this image add to or detract from the effectiveness of this opinion piece?

7. **Elements of the genre.** Sanchez's piece doesn't have a clear, concise statement of her position until the very end. Where did you feel that you had a clear sense of her position? Why there? How would you characterize the tone of Sanchez's piece? How does it affect you as a reader?

8. **Style.** Would you consider Sanchez's language inflammatory? Why or why not?

9. **Style.** How does the fact that the title is in Spanish affect you? Do you think using Spanish for the title is appropriate for her subject and audience? Why or why not?

10. **Design.** If you go online to the piece, there is a button at the bottom to make the article print-friendly. How do the additional options benefit the audience?

11. **Sources.** While Sanchez does mention other sources, most of her piece relies on her own experiences as evidence. Are there areas where she might include more external sources to help convince the reader? What types of sources might help strengthen her position?

CHECKLIST | Drafting an Editorial or Opinion Piece

Thinking of writing an editorial? Ask yourself the following questions.

RHETORICAL SITUATION & CHOICES

☐ **Purpose.** What is my purpose? And what do I want to persuade others to think or do? Do I want readers to see things from a different perspective? To take action? Do I want them to completely change their minds on an issue? How feasible is it to try to change a person's mind?

☐ **Audience.** Who am I trying to persuade? What are my audience's concerns about the issue I'm writing about? What do they fear? What is their stake in the issue (what do they personally have to risk losing if they do what I want)?

☐ **Rhetorical appeals.** How will I establish myself as reasonable and authoritative on this issue? How can I use organization to appeal to my audience's sense of logos? Will my audience respond to emotional appeals or will I seem manipulative if I appeal to pathos?

☐ **Modes & media.** Will I use written words or audio or video to convey my point? Based on the audience I have in mind—are they more likely to read or listen to an editorial in print, on the radio, or on the Internet?

GENRE CONVENTIONS

☐ **Elements of the genre.** How can I make it clear that I'm writing an opinion piece? How can I get my audience's attention immediately and show them how important and relevant this issue is to their lives? Which potential objections and counterarguments should I address? How can I make the closing of my editorial memorable?

☐ **Style.** Would it help to support my case by bringing in quotations from experts? Are there analogies that I could use that would appeal to my readers? What types of rhetorical questions would be most compelling for my editorial? How will I keep my language persuasive yet friendly?

☐ **Design.** Do I want to design a heading or logo for my column to identify myself as the author? How can I use a heading, logo, or other design element to develop my ethos?

☐ **Sources.** What kinds of sources will be most useful and most interesting and persuasive to my audience? How might I bring in sources to address potential objections and opposing arguments?

Writing to Persuade Fellow Citizens

Think about your position on an issue related to an aspect of identity, such as religion, sexual orientation, class, or ethnicity. Brainstorm a list of reasons you hold the position you do, and then consider the reasons someone might take a position different from yours. You might want to do additional research so that you can bring in and respond to the perspectives of others. Then combine your research and ideas into an editorial or opinion piece that convinces your audience that your position is a valid one.

Advertisements

An advertisement is any text created to persuade consumers to purchase a product or service. Print advertising is as old as the first newspapers, which appeared in England in the 1600s. Today, ads are everywhere and are presented in a variety of print and digital media. Advertisers spend large amounts of money to research potential customers and then tailor and distribute sales messages that will appeal to those consumers and translate into sales. The money they spend on Web advertising, in particular, is on the rise, especially for display ads (banners and video ads).

Analyzing Advertisements

Purpose   To sell their products and services, companies need to publicize information about what they're offering. They also need to win business from competitors. Ultimately, an advertisement tries to persuade potential customers to use the company's product or service.

Audience   When advertising firms such as Havas Worldwide create ads, they have a clear picture of their target market, and they aim their branding, visuals, messages, and other persuasive tools squarely at that market. Havas created the ad for Evian water shown on page 235.

Rhetorical appeals   Advertisers use appeals to ethos (authority), logos (logic), and pathos (emotion). Many ads that feature expert testimonials or celebrity endorsements, for example, do so to establish ethos. If you trust the expert giving the testimonial, you are more likely to trust the product. A product that has been long established may have its own built-in ethos, but advertisers may want to freshen that with a modern perspective or testimonial on a traditional brand. Advertisers also appeal to consumers' sense of pathos, tapping into their desire to buy the product, even though it may be a nonessential item.

Modes & media   As more reading and viewing happen online, more advertising will happen there too. A digital ad has the potential to spread through social media and YouTube, giving advertisers more "bang for the buck." In terms of the medium, some online ads are static (e.g., display ads that don't move), while others are videos or animations that incorporate sound. There are even reports of a new medium called "smell-vertising": a product's scent is broadcast in an area with potential consumers of the product.

Elements of the genre   Following are some features shared by advertisements. They present:

- *Headlines*. Advertisers use headlines to immediately attract the reader's attention. The headline often conveys the product's benefits through concise language. Additionally, advertisers pay special attention to the placement of the headline, ensuring that it is not obscured or overwhelmed by a visual element. In the case of some electronic ads, a headline may be read aloud by a narrator.

- *Visuals.* Graphics work together with the headline to attract the reader. They also illustrate the point or provide visual evidence that supports the product's claim. In television commercials, advertisers edit the visuals to hold viewers' attention, maintaining a quick pace and not lingering for too long on one image.

- *Ad copy.* Advertisers use the words of an advertisement, or ad copy, for specific purposes. They use a headline to get a consumer's attention and then draw the reader in further with an intriguing subheading. Copy that is not a headline or heading is called body text, and it tells about the benefits of the product or service and either implicitly or explicitly tells the consumer to make a purchase. Digital and TV ads also feature ad copy that can be spoken or animated on the screen.

- *Advertising slogans.* Advertisers often associate sayings or phrases with a product. For example, Nike's slogan is "Just Do It."

- *A signature.* Usually found toward the bottom of a print ad, the signature includes the advertiser name and contact information. In digital and TV ads, contact information is not normally provided, but the brand and product name is made clear.

Style Advertisers make stylistic choices concerning the following:

- *Technique.* The writing tends to be brief and directive. For example, in the original Smokey the Bear advertisements, Smokey addresses the reader: "Only YOU can prevent forest fires!" Words are usually secondary to visuals. Visuals are carefully selected as persuasive tools (see "Design" below). Because digital and TV ads are very short (usually thirty seconds or less), words are limited.

- *Details.* Advertisers usually keep details (and words, in general) to a minimum.

- *Voice and tone.* In a commercial, voice and tone can give the viewer an impression of the product's benefits. For example, if a company is promoting its product's ability to relieve stress, then the tone of the ad is usually soothing. If a financial company is advertising its services, then the tone is usually reassuring. Written ad copy conveys its tone through word choice and phrasing, while digital and TV ads convey tone through vocal intonation, pacing, and the qualities of the voice itself (male or female, deep or high, etc.).

Design Creators of advertisements use design to reach audiences, including the following elements:

- *A visual of the product.* Advertisers need to provide an image of what they're selling so consumers can identify and purchase it. If the product is less tangible (or not an object), such as an auto insurance policy, then some kind of visual emphasizes the message. For example, in some Geico ads, a caveman is the main visual, emphasizing how easy it is to purchase auto insurance.

- *Additional pathos-building images.* Advertisers use visuals to convey ideas and tap into viewers' emotions. For example, in a commercial for Abilify (a drug used mainly to treat depression), the advertiser presents "before" and "after" images. The commercial begins with a series of people looking stressed, sad, and unable to do anything. The drug is introduced, followed by a series of visuals showing the same people engaged with life and smiling.

- *Color.* Advertisers can further appeal to pathos by using images and colors associated with particular emotions.

- *Product logos.* Advertisers carefully design product logos to convey particular ideas and values about a product. For example, the Nike swoosh indicates speed and movement. All Nike products and advertisements feature the swoosh, which is instantly identifiable and long established.

- *Layout.* In a print-based ad (or a static Web ad), the layout orients the reader and establishes the most important pieces of information. The main visual and head-line are the most prominent parts of the advertisement; contact info and fine print are usually somewhere toward the bottom of the piece. Advertisers use sim-ilar principles in digital and TV commercials to make the featured product and message clear and conspicuous.

Sources   Advertising agencies conduct market research before creating ad cam-paigns so they can most efficiently identify and target their main audience and tailor their overall message accordingly. Once they've identified some possible directions for the content and design, they may ask a test audience to determine which ad will be most successful. Sources noted within an ad can include a company Web site where consumers can find more information about the product.

Guided Reading | Advertisement

The Evian brand of spring water is promoted as a natural product "from the heart of the French Alps." The Danone company introduced Evian to the United States in the 1970s, mostly in luxury hotels and expensive restaurants. Since then, it has associ-ated the brand with luxury and has often used celebrities and people from the fashion industry to build its appeal.

Among the many ads for Evian is the notable "Detox" campaign of 2006. This campaign stressed the health benefits of drinking Evian, arguing that the water helps people maintain youthfulness and purity. Youthfulness is a theme that recurs in Evian's cam-paigns, including their current "Live Young" campaign that invites customers to post photos and participate in a video campaign.

Danone/Evian & Havas Worldwide, *Detox with Evian*

What are the ▶
composers of
the ad, Havas
Worldwide, doing?

How do I know ▶
this is an
advertisement?

The ad copy reads: "Return to purity with water from the French Alps that's been naturally filtered for over 15 years."

(Continues on next page)

PURPOSE

Havas Worldwide, the creators of this ad (hired by Danone/Evian), hope to persuade consumers to buy Evian water.

AUDIENCE

The ad creators are aiming at people looking for health benefits and/or people who want to "detoxify." (Note that this ad appeared right after New Year's Eve 2006, and the idea of detoxifying had been very popular that year.) The audience reads magazines (where the print ad appeared) and spends time online (notice the Evian URL in the ad copy).

RHETORICAL APPEALS

The ad appeals mainly to readers' pathos (emotion)—by displaying a beautiful landscape and model, and by equating both with Evian. The model's nudity implies snow-angel-grade purity. It also—in combination with the giant falling drop—suggests sex. The idea of "detoxing" also plays on readers' worries about health and an "impure" lifestyle.

The ad also conveys Evian's **ethos** through the presentation of the bottle and the emphasis on branding.

MODES & MEDIA

Mode = written and visual: The advertisers use visuals and a small amount of text to persuade viewers to purchase Evian water. Evian's "Detox" campaign stresses the purity and health benefits of the water, so both the visuals and text convey this point. The text emphasizes this through the headline ("Detox with Evian") and also the body copy ("Return to purity"). The visuals make the claim with pictures of snow-covered Alps and a beautiful woman.

Medium = print and digital: While this ad appeared in print magazines, it can also be found digitally. Evian's campaigns are designed not only for print but also for TV and the Internet.

ELEMENTS OF THE GENRE

Argument: This ad presents an argument (which is visual and textual) for purchasing a product.

Action: The headline, "Detox with Evian," is brief, direct, and directive. The ad copy, "Return to purity with water from the French Alps that's been naturally filtered for over 15 years," suggests the benefits of the water and the process used to filter it; the writers also used directive language (i.e., "Return").

Color is used to create drama and focus attention. The writers and designers chose cool tones—blue and white—for the snow and water to suggest purity, and chose bright colors—red and pink—for the product name and product shot to highlight the brand.

The layout focuses on the woman's body; the composition suggests purity but also sexuality to entice consumers.

The spatial arrangement emphasizes the Alps, where the water originates. The placement of the woman below the mountain suggests that drinking water that comes from the mountain can make you young and beautiful.

The use of a sans serif typeface and lowercase letters suggests freshness and a contemporary quality. The clean lines of the font reinforce the pure/natural message.

SOURCES

Havas Worldwide most likely researched a variety of images before choosing the final one. The source of the water itself (the Alps) also plays into the choice of setting for the ad.

RHETORICAL SITUATION & CHOICES

1. **Purpose.** What information did the creators of the ad provide (textually and visually) about Evian water? How interesting is the information? How persuasive is it? Explain.

2. **Audience.** How do the various images in the ad speak to its audience? Who is the primary target audience for this ad? Is there only one audience, or are several audiences being addressed? Why do you think so?

3. **Rhetorical appeals.** How many different ways is the concept of "purity" conveyed in the ad? How is this used to persuade the audience?

4. **Rhetorical appeals.** Why do the ad's creators focus on Evian water's "detoxifying" properties? What does this suggest about Evian's target audience?

5. **Rhetorical appeals.** Look up the word *detox* in a dictionary. Which of the definitions listed seems most appropriate in the case of the ad? Why?

GENRE CONVENTIONS

6. **Modes & media.** The ad copy mentions the French Alps but does not mention the woman, although both are central visuals in the ad. Why do you think the creators chose not to include the woman in the ad copy?

7. **Elements of the genre.** The ad headline is very brief and directive. Does it have the same catchiness as the Nike slogan "Just Do It"? Why or why not?

8. **Elements of the genre.** What is the relationship between the visual images and the text? If the bottom portion of the ad with the text were eliminated, what would your reaction to the image be? How does your reaction change when you see the text?

9. **Style.** How would you characterize the tone of the ad copy? Does the tone fit the advertisement's purpose? Why or why not?

10. **Design.** Describe the visuals in the ad. What do the visuals suggest about what the advertisers want consumers to think, believe, or feel about Evian?

11. **Design.** Water drops are used twice in the ad. What purpose do they serve?

12. **Sources.** Is it effective to use an image of the mountains where Evian water comes from as a backdrop in the ad? Why or why not?

Thinking of creating an ad? Ask yourself the following questions.

RHETORICAL SITUATION & CHOICES

☐ **Purpose.** What product do I use that I want to convince others to use? What are the reasons to use that product? Why would someone besides me want to use the product?

☐ **Audience.** Who are the people in my target audience? Who will use the product? When will they use the product? Where will they use the product? How will they use the product?

☐ **Rhetorical appeals.** How will I establish my credibility in my advertisement? How will I illustrate the product's reliability and ethos? How will I use emotions to persuade my reader to use the product? To what extent will I use logic to support my claim about the product?

☐ **Modes & media.** Will my ad be print-based or digital or made for TV? How will I use visual images to persuade? Will I use one primary image or others that are secondary? How will my text work with my images? Will text explain visuals? Complement them? Will I use animation?

GENRE CONVENTIONS

☐ **Elements of the genre.** Will my visuals be literal or symbolic? What type of catchy slogan can I create to make my product memorable? Will I use the slogan as my headline or within the ad copy?

☐ **Style.** What tone will work best for selling my product? How will my intended audience respond to my tone?

☐ **Design.** What typeface should I use? What size type will work best with my visuals? How can I use layout in order to feature the most important elements and leave the least important for final viewing? How can I use color and other design elements to guide my viewers' experience?

☐ **Sources.** What kind of market research will I conduct? Will I test out my headline/slogan on a potential audience? Will I show them a series of visuals to see which is most persuasive?

PRACTICE

Selling a Product

Think of a product you consume or use, such as an energy drink, candy bar, computer, or article of clothing. Create a draft of a print advertisement that highlights a specific property or aspect of that product, such as the detoxifying properties of Evian. Use symbolic visuals to sell your product, just as the Evian ad uses the model's nudity to convey purity. Use color to create the mood and focus viewers' attention. Alternatively, create a digital or TV ad in which you use images, sound, and text.

Wikipedia Entries

Collecting facts has been a human pursuit for a long time. In the first century CE, a Roman author, naturalist, and military man named Pliny the Elder tried to record everything known about the natural world in his thirty-seven-volume *Naturalis Historia*, the world's first wiki-like document. (You can read it at the Perseus Digital Library, in English or the original Latin.)

Pliny, like all wiki and encyclopedia authors, aimed to provide what was known about a specific or general topic in a way that worked best for his target audience. The *Encyclopaedia Britannica* is a source of general information on many topics; it's geared toward readers who want to gain a broad understanding of a given subject. More specialized encyclopedias, such as *The Encyclopedia of Women's History in America* by Kathryn Cullen-DuPont, may cover topics in more depth, assuming readers already have some understanding of the topic.

Wikipedia is a kind of encyclopedia, thus the "pedia" part of the name. "Wiki" refers to the fact that entries are collaboratively produced online.

- *Wikipedia* entries exhibit many characteristics of typical encyclopedias: They are a general (or sometimes specialized) reference.
- They provide information that is considered true (meaning it is agreed upon by experts on the topic).
- They are compilations and syntheses of what others have said, rather than original research (that is, they are tertiary sources).
- They are organized into individual articles that are well researched and written by content experts, typically people with an academic degree related to the subject they're writing about.

However, *Wikipedia* differs from other encyclopedias in one key way: Instead of entries being written by scholars, entries can be written by anyone. *Wikipedia* is open-access, meaning almost all of its entries can be edited by anyone who registers with the site.

Analyzing *Wikipedia* Entries

Purpose   Encyclopedists, including those writing for *Wikipedia* (often referred to as *Wikipedians*), provide an overview of a subject so that readers can gain a general understanding of it. Some serve as a general reference source. Others are more specialized; they tend to be aimed at readers interested in a particular field.

Audience   Encyclopedists know that their primary audience is general readers looking for a reliable but quick snapshot of a topic. For example, writers for *Wikipedia* know their readers are mainly nonprofessionals. They know they must be accurate and fairly brief; they can link to additional resources with more in-depth information. Although

WRITE
_____

How often do you refer to encyclopedias? What are the benefits and limitations of using an encyclopedia as a source? How often is the encyclopedia you refer to *Wikipedia*? What are the benefits and limitations of using *Wikipedia* as a source? How reliable do you consider *Wikipedia* to be? Make a list of the pros and cons of using *Wikipedia*.

they can write on specialized topics, they are not considered a final authority by the academic world on any of the topics.

Rhetorical appeals   Encyclopedists appeal to readers through ethos; they aim to present accurate information that will inform the reader. Readers can assume that a wiki entry is the result of someone's study and knowledge. Encyclopedists also appeal through logos, presenting content in a logical manner, often moving from general to more specific information. Writers begin by defining the topic and then often break it out into subtopics. The fact that keywords and subtopics are hyperlinked also contributes to the logos of the entry.

Modes & media   Wiki entries are written texts that appear in digital format. Before the digital age, a family would purchase an entire set of print encyclopedias; it's now more common to use free online resources such as *Encyclopedia.com* or *Wikipedia*.

Elements of the genre   Encyclopedia entries, including *Wikipedia* entries, are:

- *Well researched*. Encyclopedists gather, scrutinize, and synthesize information from many reliable sources to create an entry on a given topic. They convey information as objectively as possible (without the interference of opinion). In the case of *Wikipedia*, because anyone can edit what is in an entry, a kind of informal peer review process takes place; when a reader encounters information in a *Wikipedia* entry that they think is inaccurate, they can correct it instantly.
- *Written by experts*. Most encyclopedists are knowledgeable of the topic of the entry to be written. In the case of *Wikipedia*, volunteer editors read new entries and new contributions to existing entries to check that sources are cited and when sources are not, they add a note to the entry that is visible to all readers indicating that source citations are needed.
- *Clear*. Encyclopedists provide basic information in a direct and straightforward manner.
- *Brief*. Entries are not exhaustive; rather, they are intended as jumping-off points for further research. While some entries can be relatively long, they are still extremely short compared with the length of a book on the subject.
- *Accompanied by clear visuals*. Most wiki entries include visuals. An entry on the Grand Canal in China, for example, includes a photo and a map of the canal. Biographical entries include a photo of the person with the person's birth and death dates clearly indicated below.

Style   Encyclopedia entries use the following:

- *Just enough detail to inform general readers*. However, in a given entry, they mention related topics, concepts, and keywords that readers may want to pursue with further research.

- *Precise language and word choice.* Encyclopedists are specific and exact writers. Encyclopedists often use formal, academic language to bolster their authority and emphasize their seriousness. That means they avoid contractions, slang, and abbreviated forms such as "info" for "information."

- *The third person and a serious tone.* Encyclopedists write in the third person, which reinforces their ethos and reminds readers that the entries are based on shared knowledge, not just the perspective of one person. They use a serious tone to project credibility (ethos) to readers. Although the information in an entry might be informative *and also* funny, using humor as a rhetorical strategy in a wiki entry might undermine your authority and trustworthiness.

Design Encyclopedia entries are:

- *Accessible and consistent.* Wiki entries are designed so that readers can quickly identify the parts of the entry. The introduction is followed by an outline of the different parts or headings, which are all hyperlinked so that readers can reach those parts quickly and choose which parts to read.

- *Clearly titled.* The name or title of the entry is in large letters at the top of the entry to clearly indicate the topic.

- *Hyperlinked to other entries.* The use of hyperlinks in an entry allows encyclopedists to provide more information without lengthening the entry itself. These links identify terminology (see "Just enough detail" on the previous page) and provide additional search terms to assist readers in narrowing their investigation of a broad subject.

Sources *Wikipedia* entries contain documentation attributing the information to particular sources. At the end of the entry are sections entitled "Notes" and "References," which the reader can use to learn more about the subject.

Guided Reading | Wiki Entry

The "Therapy Dog" entry on *Wikipedia* gives an overview of what a therapy dog is, presents information in a clear and accessible way to a general audience, and includes links to outside source material. You can see who has contributed to a *Wikipedia* entry by clicking on the "View history" tab at the top of the entry. Composers on *Wikipedia* are known by their usernames, which are generally not their real names, so you won't always be able to discover their credentials, but you can see which other entries they've contributed to. *Wikipedia* has a page devoted to how to read the "View history" page (visit wikipedia.org).

Wikipedia contributors, *Therapy Dog*

RHETORICAL SITUATION & CHOICES

◄ What are the composers doing?

PURPOSE
The composers write to inform readers with documentable facts and uncontested ideas. Their writing is businesslike and factual.

AUDIENCE
The audience for *Wikipedia* and this entry is readers who want an overview on a topic, in this case therapy dogs. Readers are most likely from a general rather than an expert audience. They may use this entry as a jumping-off point for further research.

RHETORICAL APPEALS
The composers establish their ethos as experts through their clear writing, authoritative tone, and bibliography of sources.

The composers appeal to readers' sense of logos (logic) by presenting the information in an accessible way.

NOTE: Some *Wikipedia* entries, including this one, may have a notice posted at the top that asks readers who can contribute to add specific types of sources for credibility. In this case, the notice asks for medical references, which would be appropriate because "therapy" is a medical concept.

GENRE CONVENTIONS

How do I know this is a *Wikipedia* entry? ►

Credit: Courtesy of Wikimedia Foundation, Inc. All rights reserved.

ELEMENTS OF THE GENRE
Gives an overview of the topic: The entry provides established facts (e.g., facts about who originated the idea of therapy dogs and the contexts in which they are used).

Serves as a starting point for further research: The entry introduces related concepts (e.g., the distinction between therapy dogs and service dogs), but it does not get into detail.

Is well researched: The composers provide specific details and cite sources.

STYLE
The authors are precise, naming specific organizations and college campuses that have used therapy dogs.

The authors use specific language, referring to "golden retrievers" rather than "certain breeds."

The tone is neutral and the voice is professional; the entry is written in the third person.

DESIGN
The entry has a clear title and an organized layout. It includes images and is hyperlinked to other *Wikipedia* entries.

MODES & MEDIA

Mode = written and visual: The authors convey information in words, but also with images. For example, they use a photo of two golden retrievers to illustrate the type of dog typically trained as a therapy dog.

Medium = digital: There are pros and cons to providing information digitally. The pros are the many options for providing information. Digital encyclopedias also allow readers to connect through social media or other options. For example, *Wikipedia* readers can select the "talk" tab at the top of the entry to post comments about the entry. One con is the ads.

SOURCES

There is a References list and a list of related links.

Credit: WMF Marks are trademarks of WMF. WMF Marks are used under license from WMF. Text is licensed under Creative Commons.

QUESTIONS | Analyzing a *Wikipedia* Entry

RHETORICAL SITUATION & CHOICES

1. **Purpose.** Although the value of therapy dogs is somewhat controversial, encyclopedists aim to inform—to take a neutral stance rather than try to persuade. What are some strategies the authors of the "therapy dog" entry use to avoid taking a position?

2. **Audience.** Who do you imagine is most likely to look up "therapy dog" in an online encyclopedia: a student, a businessperson, a therapist, or a scientist? What do you imagine his or her purpose might be?

3. **Rhetorical appeals.** Read an entry on a topic of your choice in *Wikipedia* and then read an entry on the same topic in another online encyclopedia.

GENRE CONVENTIONS

6. **Elements of the genre.** A wiki entry about therapy dogs is briefer than a book on the topic. As you read the *Wikipedia* entry, was there information you wished had been expanded upon? Why?

7. **Style.** Notice the neutral, third-person voice. How might your reading of this entry be different if the authors had written it in the first person?

RHETORICAL SITUATION & CHOICES

Compare the authors' techniques in the two entries. Do they use similar methods to develop their ethos? What differences do you notice? Which entry sounds more authoritative, in your opinion? Why?

4. **Modes & media.** In what modes and media have you used encyclopedias? Do you have a preference for one mode or medium over another? Why?

5. **Elements of the genre.** As pointed out in the "Therapy Dog" annotations, encyclopedia entries serve as starting points for research. After reading the entry, what questions do you have about the topic? What might you want to research through more in-depth sources?

GENRE CONVENTIONS

8. **Design.** The entry is consistently formatted and designed so that readers stay oriented. How important is it to you that information be easy to find in a reference work? Why? Can you think of examples of reference works that are not well designed?

9. **Sources.** In the *Wikipedia* entry, the authors rarely use attribution phrases such as "according to." How does this affect your reading of the entry? How might your experience as a reader be different if the entry were peppered with parenthetical notes and attribution phrases?

CHECKLIST | Drafting a *Wikipedia* Entry

Are you thinking of drafting a *Wikipedia* entry? Ask yourself the following questions.

RHETORICAL SITUATION & CHOICES

☐ **Purpose.** What specific topic do I want to write about? Which subtopics do I want to write about? How will I define my topic and subtopics? Writing an entry about "fashion" implies that I will cover fashion over the course of history. Writing about "street fashion," however, significantly narrows the time period I would need to cover.

☐ **Audience.** Who are my readers? How many of them are experts on my topic? Nonexperts who have a mild interest in my topic? What questions will they expect my entry to answer? Are there technical terms I may need to define (or hyperlink to definitions)? What kinds of examples will my readers relate to?

☐ **Rhetorical appeals.** How will I establish my authority as a writer? What kinds of vocabulary, diction, and examples will I use to convey authority?

☐ **Modes & media.** Do I want readers to experience my entry in print or digital format? Do I want to include images or videos? What should I provide hyperlinks to?

GENRE CONVENTIONS

☐ **Elements of the genre.** To keep my entry relatively brief, I will need to summarize other, longer works on the topic. Which works will I summarize? How will I make sure my writing is extremely precise? What terms might I need to carefully define?

☐ **Style.** How can I present everything in a neutral, third-person voice?

☐ **Design.** How can I use titles and subtitles to make my entry easy to access for readers? If I create a digital entry, how will I use hyperlinks to direct readers to other entries?

☐ **Sources.** In addition to a list of sources, will I want to include a list of "additional resources" for readers who want to do their own research?

Contributing to a Public Reference

Are you an expert on a particular subject? Choose one that you're well versed in, and draft a *Wikipedia* entry on that topic based on what you already know and what you can learn by doing some research (that does not involve *Wikipedia* or any encyclopedia). Remember to include only facts that are largely uncontested by others who are well versed in the subject. You may want to include visual features to illustrate key concepts. You'll find a helpful guide for *Wikipedia* authors on wikipedia.org. Note that the guide provides information about conventions that most *Wikipedia* entries follow—and yours should too.

Photo Essays

A photo essay is a group of photos that tells a unified story or makes a unified argument. Some photo essayists provide supplementary text or brief captions for their images; others choose to present the images without words. Some photo essayists are journalists whose purpose is to convey a news or human interest story or offer commentary on an event.

Photo essays can also be viewed as works of art that express ideas and evoke emotional responses in the viewer. You can find them online, in galleries and museums, and also in magazines such as *Life*, *Time*, and *National Geographic*. Photo essayists generally aim to make a particular point or argument; some make specific social commentaries.

Analyzing Photo Essays

Purpose   Photo essayists aim to tell a story and/or to make a point. Usually their work is focused on a specific theme and intended to evoke an emotional response in the viewer.

Audience   Photo essayists know that their audiences are drawn to visual storytelling—and to the issues and themes of their works, which may be social and cultural, journalistic, and/or artistic. For example, photo essayist and documentarian Brenda Ann Kenneally, creator of an ongoing project called "Upstate Girls," aims her work at those interested in her intimate look at working-class women and their families. Norbert Wu targets his essay "Life Beneath Antarctic Ice" at an audience interested in nature.

Rhetorical Appeals   Depending on their subject matter and composition, photo essayists may emphasize logos, pathos, or ethos to make their point. For instance, Andrew Testa's disturbing photo essays of Bangladeshi women who were scarred by acid for refusing to accept marriage proposals emphasize pathos by showing the women's scars close up; ethos is also important because viewers must trust that Testa has not used lighting or perspective to distort reality.

Modes & media   While photo essayists usually combine visuals with some written text, some also incorporate bits of audio, such as in *The New York Times* photo essay "One in 8 Million," which highlights the lives of ordinary New Yorkers. Photo essays can be print based, but they are also offered digitally, as is "Let Us Now Praise Famous Men"; or they can be created mainly for online publication, such as *Time* magazine's photo essays.

Elements of the genre   A photo essay can be used to tell a simple story, but the genre is often used to persuade viewers to sympathize with a point of view or to take a specific action. For example, through "Upstate Girls," Brenda Ann Kenneally hopes that viewers connect with the subjects' struggles and triumphs.

Some photo essayists include captions to provide context; others include more text, with a 50:50 text-to-image ratio. Photo essayists make rhetorical choices about their purpose and audience, and they choose images carefully, in the same way a writer chooses words, paragraphs, and structure. The photo essayist chooses each image with the viewer's intellectual, emotional, or other responses in mind. Similarly, a photo essay can be structured much like any persuasive essay. For example, the introductory images, which function like a written essay's introduction, need to establish the subject matter and further the purposes of the piece — to push the narrative or argument forward.

Photo essayists use some techniques that narrative essayists, storytellers, and persuasive writers do. They select and sequence their content in a way that will spark their readers' interest, keep them reading or viewing, and ultimately convince them of a particular point of view. Initial images may serve as an introduction, while those that follow may build in intensity to support the argument the photo essayist wants to make. (See "Design," below.)

Style   Photo essayists make the following stylistic choices. They consider:

- *Detail*. Most photo essayists do not provide much detail in the text of their essays. Usually captions give just enough information for readers to understand the story behind (and location of) the related photo. The photos themselves can show varying degrees of detail — in some cases, capturing one element up close, such as a person's face, while in others, showing a panoramic view of a landscape.
- *Tone*. Photo essayists choose images that reflect the mood they want to convey. For example, a photo essayist who wants to stir readers to take action in response to an environmental disaster such as an oil spill might feature an image of someone rescuing and rehabilitating an oil-soaked bird.

Design   A successful photo essayist usually presents a variety of images (from different perspectives) and arranges the images in an order that builds emotion, furthers an argument, or advances a story. For example, a photo essayist who wants to tell a story might sequence the images from one event to the next, much like a narrative essayist would. In other cases, the photo essayist might not choose a linear progression but might instead order images for maximum impact, especially when presenting an argument.

Sources   Photo essays always involve primary research, as the photographer is always witnessing the subject of the photos firsthand. Brenda Ann Kenneally's photo essay on working-class women, for example, is entirely informed by Kenneally's interviews with the women she photographed. Sometimes secondary research must be conducted as well, to fill in historical details or other information.

Guided Reading | Photo Essay

Time, a weekly news and current events magazine, often features photo essays related to world events. In February 2006 the magazine commissioned and published an online photo essay titled "Life in the Googleplex." Presented as a slide show, the essay was created by photojournalist Eros Hoagland of Redux Pictures. Hoagland, who began his career reporting on the fallout of El Salvador's civil war, is also interested in showing the subtleties of place, something he clearly brought to the Googleplex project. Given the range of his subject matter, the quality of his work, and the publications he calls his clients (including *The New York Times* and *Newsweek*), Hoagland, like *Time* magazine, has some good ethos.

Hoagland's purpose in creating "Life in the Googleplex" was to give readers an inside look at what it's like to work at Google. By highlighting gadgets and leisure opportunities, Hoagland suggests that employees do serious work but also have plenty of time to play. Further, by showing the human side (and human faces) of Google, Hoagland establishes that the company is more than a search engine.

Eros Hoagland, From *Life in the Googleplex*

RHETORICAL SITUATION & CHOICES		GENRE CONVENTIONS	

PURPOSE

Hoagland (perhaps with the help of *Time* editors) set out to illustrate how a high-tech work environment, such as Google, can be filled with creativity and fun.

AUDIENCE

The audience for the photo essay is *Time* magazine readers, Google fans, and people interested in cultural trends related to technology and the workplace.

RHETORICAL APPEALS

Hoagland uses logos to appeal to readers by building a logical case about how a creative work environment inspires workers' creativity. He establishes the essay's

◀ What is the composer, Eros Hoagland, doing?

How do I know this is ▶ a photo essay?

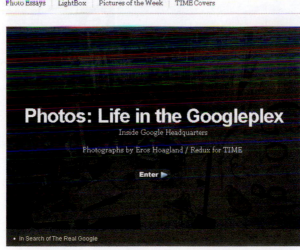

ELEMENTS OF THE GENRE

Is composed mainly of photos: The photos are accompanied with some text.

Is focused on a topic: In this case, the topic is workers' play and leisure time at Google's offices.

Tells a story: This story is about a typical workday at Google.

Makes an argument: The photo essay wants to show that Google's workers are productive and inspired by creativity and recreation.

Includes captions that explain the photos: For example, the caption with the first image reads, "Be Yourself." Without it,

(Continues on next page)

ethos by using photos of Google workers.

MODES & MEDIA

Mode = written and visual: Hoagland's primary goal was to visually portray a typical workday at Google. Adding written details tells a more complete story; it also provides a commentary about what is taking place, to persuade viewers that the workplace atmosphere is pleasant.

Medium = digital: Although *Time* publishes photo essays in their print edition, "Life in the Googleplex" was published digitally at *Time's* Web site. Publishing this essay online is especially appropriate because Google is a digital company; further, the advantages of publishing online are obvious. As long as viewers have an Internet connection, they can see and share the essay; if it were only in print form, they would need to locate a copy of that edition of the magazine.

Photos: Life in the Googleplex   1 of 12   ◄ BACK   NEXT ►

◄ BACK   NEXT ►

EROS HOAGLAND / REDUX FOR TIME

BE YOURSELF
Desktop gizmos and lava lamps express Google's laid-back ethos.

• In Search of The Real Google

Photos: Life in the Googleplex   2 of 12   ◄ BACK   NEXT ►

◄ BACK   NEXT ►

EROS HOAGLAND / REDUX FOR TIME

ASK THE HELP DESK
Laptop on the fritz? Google keeps experts on site to fix computers and other digital gadgets.

• In Search of The Real Google

viewers could assume the message is that the office is crowded and cluttered rather than supportive of individuality and expression.

STYLE

Present tense: The present tense reinforces the "this is happening now" feeling of the piece.

Playful tone: A light tone emphasizes that Google is a fun place to work. For example, the swimmer is referred to as a "Googler with Goggles."

DESIGN

The variety of the photos suggests the breadth of activities that can take place in the Googleplex. Elements of the text are highlighted by typeface choice and color. Captions consistently appear below the photos, and each caption has a pithy heading.

SOURCES

Hoagland conducted primary research—spending time at Google, following around employees, trying to capture the elements of a typical day and different aspects of work and play.

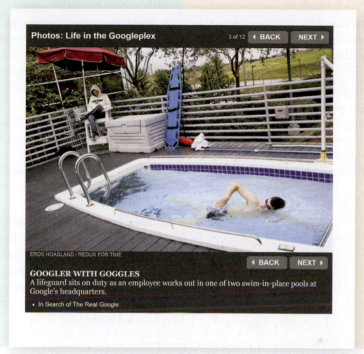

EROS HOAGLAND / REDUX FOR TIME

◀ BACK   NEXT ▶

GOOGLER WITH GOGGLES
A lifeguard sits on duty as an employee works out in one of two swim-in-place pools at Google's headquarters.

• In Search of The Real Google

Credit. All images on pp. 247–249: Eros Hoagland/Redux Pictures.

QUESTIONS | Analyzing Hoagland's Photo Essay

RHETORICAL SITUATION & CHOICES

1. **Purpose.** What is the unifying message of the three photos shown? Explain in one sentence.

2. **Purpose.** Do the photos tend to focus more on people or objects? Why do you think Hoagland chose that emphasis?

3. **Audience.** What techniques did Hoagland use so that viewers would see the playful nature of working at Google?

GENRE CONVENTIONS

6. **Elements of the genre.** In "Life in the Googleplex," do the photos illustrate the captions, or do the captions describe the photos? Explain your answer.

7. **Elements of the genre.** View the entire "Googleplex" slide show. Now that you've seen the whole thing, would you say that this essay is primarily telling a story or making an argument? Why?

4. **Rhetorical appeals.** Based on the three photos shown, what is your impression of the ethos of Hoagland and the *Time* editors he most likely worked with?

5. **Modes & media.** If there were no captions, what assumptions might you make about life at Google? Are there places where the image is able to fully convey its message without the text? Where and how? Why is this essay best viewed digitally, rather than in print?

8. **Style.** How does the tone and voice of the writing emphasize the working environment at Google? How does the selection and presentation of photographs contribute to that tone? Use specific examples to illustrate your answer.

9. **Design.** View the entire "Googleplex" slide show again. Pay attention to how Hoagland and *Time* ordered the images. How might a different ordering of images impact the narrative? How do Hoagland and *Time* use organization of the images to build logic?

10. **Sources.** The photos were taken by Eros Hoagland, a professional photographer commissioned by *Time* magazine (Hoagland is the source of the images). Do you think someone working at Google would choose to highlight different aspects of working there? How?

CHECKLIST | Sketching Out a Photo Essay

Are you thinking of composing a photo essay? Ask yourself the following questions.

RHETORICAL SITUATION & CHOICES

☐ **Purpose.** What is my story, and why do I want to tell it? Or do I want to do more than tell a story? If so, what main point or argument do I want to make, and why?

☐ **Audience.** Who are my readers/viewers that I want to attract to my photo essay? Why will my photo essay matter to them? What do I want them to get out of it? And how will I reach them?

☐ **Rhetorical appeals.** How will I use ethos, pathos, and logos to reach my audience? How will I establish my authority as a photographer and writer? Will I rely more on pathos or logos? How will my photos and text work together to appeal to my readers' sense of ethos, pathos, and/or logos?

GENRE CONVENTIONS

☐ **Elements of the genre.** I know that the best photo essays tell a story but also put forth some type of argument. For example, in his "Googleplex" essay, Eros Hoagland asks viewers to see Google as a successful company in part because the workplace itself encourages creativity. How does this compare to what I want to do? What argument will I make in my photo essay—and how will I do it?

☐ **Style.** What tone do I want to strike? Playful, like in "Life in the Googleplex"? Or more serious, like in Kenneally's photo essay?

☐ **Design.** What order will I arrange the photos in, and how will the order affect how my viewers understand my story?

☐ **Modes & media.** Do I want to present my photo essay in hard-copy format, as in a photo album; or electronically, as on a Web site; or in some other way? How will these choices impact how my viewers experience my photo essay? For example, would it be better to present it online or as a collection of large photos matted and framed on the wall?

☐ **Sources.** Where will I need to go to take my photos? Will I want to photograph individuals and their possessions? Or perhaps historical sites? Will I need to request special permission to do so?

PRACTICE

Making a Point with a Photo Essay

Just as Eros Hoagland conveys a sense of work life at Google in his photo essay, you might want to do something similar. What do you have to say about your own work-place, campus, or residence? Brainstorm about how people at one or more of those locations feel about that place; then take three to five photos of the place that convey that feeling. Your draft photo essay should offer some kind of commentary on the place you've chosen as your subject; it should not simply show it. Add brief captions similar to the ones in the "Googleplex" essay that help tell a story and offer perspective.

Graphic Memoirs

WRITE

What are your favorite graphic memoirs or novels? What aspects of the story are most memorable? Why?

The graphic memoir is an autobiographical or semi-autobiographical story told through text and images, usually drawings. Sometimes there are more words than images, but usually it's the other way around. The graphic memoirist Alison Bechdel (p. 254) has described her process in interviews: First she writes her text; then she inks the images. Other graphic memoirists use different techniques, foregrounding the images in the panels and writing the text in later. You may already be familiar with graphic memoirs, a genre first made popular by Art Spiegelman's *Maus*, a graphic memoir about surviving the Holocaust. Graphic narratives now have a place as respected literary texts: They're the focus of college courses; they've won Pulitzer Prizes; and they've inspired successful movies, including *A History of Violence* and *Sin City*.

Analyzing Graphic Memoirs

Purpose   Like other memoirists, graphic memoirists tell the story of (or a story from) a writer's life. Using such literary devices as character (in this case, real people rather than fictional ones), dialogue, and setting, graphic memoirists connect their readers with their work. Graphic memoirs, which look something like extended comic strips, focus on transporting the reader to a world that is very different from everyday reality. Sometimes a graphic narrative, such as Marjane Satrapi's *Persepolis*, discloses elements of a culture—Satrapi's life growing up in Iran and later as an expatriate—showing readers a world that may be outside their own experience.

Audience   Graphic memoirists know that their audiences want a look into someone else's life, as told by that person. They know that their audiences are particularly drawn toward the visual, and perhaps grew up reading comic books, or really like illustrated texts or alternative narrative forms. As graphic memoirs are becoming more popular in academic settings, with instructors assigning them as part of their reading lists or as an alternative to the print memoir in composition classes—more students are creating and reading them.

WRITE

Consider Art Spiegelman's graphic memoir *Maus,* which is a Holocaust narrative (the story of Spiegelman's father). Freewrite about to what extent you think the graphic memoir is an appropriate genre for dealing with traumatic experiences.

Rhetorical appeals   The play between visuals and text helps graphic memoirists emphasize certain aspects of the narrative to readers. Because memoirists want their readers to empathize with their experiences, they often use appeals to emotion to draw readers into their world. For example, when a story is meant to elicit shock, the shape of the letters and the use of bold graphics, along with the expressions on the character's face, can guide the reader's emotional response, emphasizing pathos. In a graphic memoir, ethos is a central concern because the audience must trust that the writer is accurately representing experience and events.

Modes & media   Graphic memoirs usually take print form but are sometimes digitized for the Web. Graphic memoirs and novels are often adapted for film, reimagined as animated stories.

Elements of the genre   Like all memoirs, the graphic memoir has a real-life plot that revolves around a series of events, or a story line. The story line hinges on a central conflict driven by real people who function as characters do in fiction. The central conflict of Marjane Satrapi's *Persepolis*, for example, is her (and her family's) struggle to survive the Iranian Revolution of 1979, also known as the Islamic Revolution; at that time, the country's monarchy was overthrown and Iran became an Islamic republic with an increasingly repressive government.

To tell their stories, graphic memoirists use words—usually organized into short, simple sentences—that provide dialogue and move the plot along toward the conflict and its resolution. The visuals (usually inked drawings) move the plot too, but also assist in creating the setting, atmosphere, and emotion of the memoir.

The written content of the graphic memoir often appears in boxes or in sentences interspersed among the visuals. Dialogue is usually placed in a bubble or box linked to the character's mouth. Most graphic composers do not present words and sentences in traditional paragraphs. The advantage is that by isolating a sentence in a box, the author creates a snapshot of a moment or of a series of moments, adding to the power of the story. Further, though the graphic narrative may not provide traditional transitions between ideas and scenes, there are some transitional expressions that help the visual memoirist move from one idea to the next.

Just as in comic strips, the visuals of a graphic memoir do a lot to relate the story and reinforce aspects of the written narrative. The visuals, which can focus in on a detail and pan out like a movie camera, for example, emphasize certain moments and allow readers to see what is happening. See the "Design" section below for more on how drawings function in a graphic memoir.

Style The reader's experience depends on the written and visual style of the graphic memoirist—how much (and what kind of) detail and specific techniques he or she uses, and the quality of the visual story's voice and tone.

- *Tone and voice.* Graphic memoirists communicate the tone of their stories and their voices as storytellers through word choice, diction, visuals, and the choice of typeface and other graphics. For example, if a character is feeling exasperated, the writer might choose a font (such as Impact) to illustrate that mood.

- *Detail.* Depending on their target audience, graphic memoirists may use intricate, almost lifelike detail, as in Bechdel's *Fun Home* (p. 255). Other times, graphic memoirists might take a more cartoon/superhero approach, such as that of DC Comics' *Watchmen.* Typically, graphic memoirists limit their reliance on text, using it primarily to keep the plot moving. Sentences in a given panel tend to be short, without much embellishment.

Design Like comic strips, graphic memoirs are organized into visual panels, usually squares or rectangles that essentially freeze a moment in its own individual space. Like all graphic composers, graphic memoirists make choices about where to place panels, how large to make them, and what words from the written narrative to emphasize. They also decide how and where to place figures and objects within a panel in order to direct the reader. The size of one object next to another (scale), the direction an object is facing in relation to the page, and the cutting off of part of an object in a frame are all careful choices that create meaning for readers.

Other design choices include whether to use a font, real handwriting or lettering, or a font that mimics handwriting. Many graphic composers use block lettering, boldface, and italics when they want to show emphasis, and they use different graphical styles when needed (such as Courier or other distinctive fonts). Graphic memoirists also need to make decisions about the style, shape, and size of boxes, balloons, or other word-framing devices. Sometimes they assign specific shapes for specific speakers in the story. They also make choices about white space from panel to panel and within a frame of text. White space is used for aesthetic reasons but also to call attention to certain parts of the text, to provide a visual pause, or to represent the absence of something or someone.

Sources   Most graphic memoirs are based on personal observation and experience. For this reason, graphic memoirists seldom cite outside sources. However, if someone were to write a graphic memoir of a group or an organization, that person would, no doubt, draw on historical documents, interviews, and other sources of information.

Guided Reading | Graphic Memoir

▲ **BOOK COVER & AUTHOR PHOTO**

Alison Bechdel, *Fun Home: A Family Tragicomic.* Author photo: Liza Cowan.

Credit: From FUN HOME: A Family Tragicomic by Alison Bechdel. Copyright © 2006. Reprinted by permission of Houghton Mifflin Harcourt Publishing Company. All rights reserved.

Alison Bechdel gained notoriety in the comics scene in 1983 with her syndicated strip *Dykes to Watch Out For.* In her comic strip, Bechdel combined political commentary with the daily lives of mostly lesbian characters, narrating their love affairs, breakups, and adventures as attendees at such lesbian festivals as the Michigan Womyn's Music Festival. Bechdel wrote a graphic memoir, *Fun Home: A Family Tragicomic,* published in 2006. This was later adapted into a Broadway musical, which won the 2015 Tony Award for best musical. In *Fun Home,* Bechdel tells the story of growing up with a closeted father who ran a funeral parlor and taught English. In this work, she conveys the importance of her father in her life. The section that we've excerpted here is from the book's first chapter. In it, Bechdel's own coming-out story is overshadowed by the death of her father.

As a graphic memoirist, Bechdel makes plenty of decisions about her purposes and how she will draw in her readers. She also works with many of the conventions of the graphic narrative, while using a style that is all her own.

Alison Bechdel, From *Fun Home: A Family Tragicomic*

RHETORICAL SITUATION & CHOICES

PURPOSE
Bechdel's goal is to tell a story about her life, which includes childhood, coming out, and coming to terms with her father's identity and death.

AUDIENCE
Bechdel knows her readers enjoy memoirs and are especially drawn to comics and graphic novels. They are also interested in the coming-of-age and sexual identity themes in *Fun Home.*

RHETORICAL APPEALS
Bechdel appeals to readers' emotions (pathos) by showing how her father's "queer death" caused her to feel "qualmish, faint, and, on occasion, drunk." The author uses events from her life to establish her ethos. Announcing "I am a lesbian" helps establish her ethos in what is partly a coming-out story.

MODES & MEDIA
Mode = written and visual: Bechdel uses both the written and visual texts to communicate her story about coming out. Bechdel's use of visuals—such as when she mails a letter to her parents or talks on the phone with her mother—shows readers how Bechdel wants us to view her at that moment.

Medium = print: Just like traditional memoirs, graphic memoirs are available in both print and digital media. Bookstores, these days, have sections devoted to graphic

◄ What is the composer, Alison Bechdel, doing?

How do I know this is ► a graphic memoir?

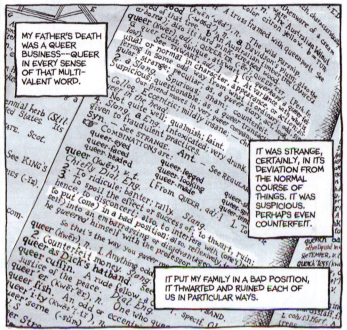

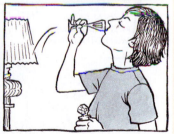

GENRE CONVENTIONS

DESIGN
Handwriting effect: Bechdel's text font mimics handwriting, and she uses bold, italics, and other type effects to convey emotion.

Varied layout: For example, some panels are parallel to each other, while others are not aligned evenly.

Varied frame shapes: These shapes around the text indicate what is thought, spoken, or narrated. Different shapes indicate who is speaking. In the last frame, the mother's dialogue appears in a jagged box that comes out of the phone.

Different graphical styles: Bechtel varies the graphical style to approximate reality. When the narrator types out, "I am a lesbian," Bechdel switches to Courier to approximate typing.

SOURCES
Bechdel's source is her own memory, so there are no citations to outside materials.

(Continues on next page)

novels, where you can also find graphic memoirs such as Bechdel's. There are, however, digital graphic novels and memoirs that are often created online. Web sites such as Comic Master allow you to create your own short graphic novel or memoir online using their free software.

ONLY FOUR MONTHS EARLIER, I HAD MADE AN ANNOUNCEMENT TO MY PARENTS.

I am a lesbian.

MY HOMOSEXUALITY REMAINED AT THAT POINT PURELY THEORETICAL, AN UNTESTED HYPOTHESIS.

BUT IT WAS A HYPOTHESIS SO THOROUGH AND CONVINCING THAT I SAW NO REASON NOT TO SHARE IT IMMEDIATELY.

THE NEWS WAS NOT RECEIVED AS WELL AS I HAD HOPED. THERE WAS AN EXCHANGE OF DIFFICULT LETTERS WITH MY MOTHER.

THEN A PHONE CALL IN WHICH SHE DEALT A STAGGERING BLOW.

YOUR FATHER HAS HAD AFFAIRS WITH OTHER MEN.

WHAT?

I'D BEEN UPSTAGED, DEMOTED FROM PROTAGONIST IN MY OWN DRAMA TO COMIC RELIEF IN MY PARENTS' TRAGEDY.

HE...HE WAS MOLESTED BY A FARM HAND WHEN HE WAS YOUNG.

I HAD IMAGINED MY CONFESSION AS AN EMANCIPATION FROM MY PARENTS, BUT INSTEAD I WAS PULLED BACK INTO THEIR ORBIT.

AND WITH MY FATHER'S DEATH FOLLOWING SO HARD ON THE HEELS OF THIS DOLEFUL COMING-OUT PARTY, I COULD NOT HELP BUT ASSUME A CAUSE-AND-EFFECT RELATIONSHIP.

IF I HAD NOT FELT COMPELLED TO SHARE MY LITTLE SEXUAL DISCOVERY, PERHAPS THE SEMI WOULD HAVE PASSED WITHOUT INCIDENT FOUR MONTHS LATER.

(YES, IT REALLY WAS A SUNBEAM BREAD TRUCK.)

WHY HAD I TOLD THEM? I HADN'T EVEN HAD SEX WITH ANYONE YET. CONVERSELY, MY FATHER HAD BEEN HAVING SEX WITH MEN FOR YEARS AND NOT TELLING ANYONE.

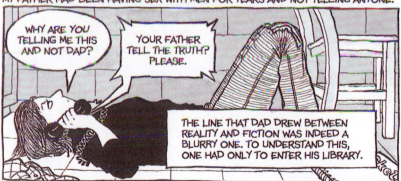

WHY ARE YOU TELLING ME THIS AND NOT DAD?

YOUR FATHER TELL THE TRUTH? PLEASE.

THE LINE THAT DAD DREW BETWEEN REALITY AND FICTION WAS INDEED A BLURRY ONE. TO UNDERSTAND THIS, ONE HAD ONLY TO ENTER HIS LIBRARY.

RHETORICAL SITUATION & CHOICES

1. **Purpose.** What parallels does Bechdel draw between her father's homosexuality and her own coming out?

2. **Audience.** Based on the short excerpt, who would you say is the audience for this graphic memoir? Why?

3. **Rhetorical appeals.** How do the visuals emphasize the main character's emotional state?

4. **Modes & media.** What different elements of the plot do the text and visuals emphasize?

5. **Elements of the genre.** Are there any places where the visuals and words seem to contradict each other or seem to be in tension with each other? If so, why do you think there is a contradiction or tension?

GENRE CONVENTIONS

6. **Elements of the genre.** How much time is covered in the pages shown? How does Bechdel show the passage of time?

7. **Elements of the genre.** Only three pages of the graphic memoir are represented here. Even though it is a small snapshot of the book, what sense do you get of Bechdel as the narrator of her own story? How do the different graphic elements, combined with words, give you that sense of her?

8. **Style.** How would you describe the level of detail Bechdel uses in her visuals? In her text? Does the level of detail serve different purposes? If so, how?

9. **Design.** Sometimes Bechdel chooses to sandwich the narrative text between the visual panels. Other times, she places the narrative text within its own box. What reasons might she have for this? Are the narrative pieces that are in a box more significant? Why?

10. **Sources.** The main source for the graphic memoir is Alison Bechdel's life and experience. How does this influence your reading of the work?

CHECKLIST | Drafting a Graphic Memoir

Are you thinking of composing a graphic memoir? Ask yourself the following questions.

RHETORICAL SITUATION & CHOICES

☐ **Purpose.** What specific moment in my life do I want to write about? Why? What questions do I have about that moment? How might I interpret that moment? What insights do I want to share with others? How would visuals illustrate the moment and make my experience more tangible for my reader?

☐ **Audience.** Who are my potential readers? Why will my memoir matter to them? What do I want them to get out of it? How old are they and how will I reach them? How will I use visuals to do that?

☐ **Rhetorical appeals.** How will I establish my authority as a writer? How reliable will I be as a narrator? To what extent will I appeal to my readers' emotions? How might I use logic?

☐ **Modes & media.** Do I want to create my story first with graphics or text? What aspects will I represent visually, and what aspects will I represent in written form? Would my graphic memoir be appropriate to translate into a film? Do I want to create my story using ink on paper or using a digital program?

GENRE CONVENTIONS

☐ **Elements of the genre.** How will I keep my writing true and accurate? How much will I disclose about myself (and others) in my graphic memoir? Will I write in the first person? What anecdotes will I use to tell my story, and why? How will I visually represent my characters? Will they be true to life or exaggerated? How will I balance the narrative with dialogue?

☐ **Style.** What tone will I take in my writing? Will my graphic memoir be funny? Serious? Tragic? What kind of language will I use? How much detail will I provide? How will I use the visuals to convey my tone?

☐ **Design.** What fonts will I use? How might I use shapes of boxes to indicate specific character voices? Will I vary the shapes of my panels?

☐ **Sources.** What specific memories will I draw on? Will I need to check my story with others from my life, or will I rely on my own recollections and interpretations? Will I need to research historical and cultural events related to the time period of my story?

Sharing Experience Through a Graphic Memoir

Identify a pivotal moment in your life. Sketch out a few panels of a graphic memoir that convey the moment and its importance. Think about how you want the key people who participated in the event to come across to readers and how you can convey those characteristics with visual details. Think about what you want to convey through dialogue and what you want to convey through internal reflection.

Fairy Tales

A fairy tale, in the simplest terms, is a story that conveys a moral or lesson, typically to children. Most have historical connections to folklore and oral tales; they are about magic and magical creatures and feature houses made of gingerbread, godmothers with magic wands, and animals that talk and wear human clothing. Many traditional fairy tales, such as "Cinderella," "Snow White," and "Sleeping Beauty," feature princesses in peril and princes saving the day. However, modern tales, such as Margaret Atwood's *The Handmaid's Tale*, offer a critique of society (in Atwood's novel, it's a feminist critique), and sometimes a grim view of the future.

As a child, you probably read or saw film versions of traditional fairy tales and learned social lessons from them. "Hansel and Gretel" and "Little Red Riding Hood" warn children of the dangers of going into the dark woods without a grown-up and reinforce the rule "don't talk to strangers." "The Three Little Pigs" enforces the idea that if something is worth doing, it's worth doing right.

As an adult—and as a reader and writer—you most likely encounter fairy tales from a different, more analytic angle. Use the guidelines that follow to read fairy tales and related genres critically. Understanding their conventions and rhetorical contexts are key to composing in them.

Analyzing Fairy Tales

Purpose   Traditionally authors write fairy tales to entertain their readers and to teach morals or lessons to young audiences. Authors achieve these purposes in part through characters—often stock characters such as imperiled princesses and dangerous wolves that are easily identifiable and generic enough that a wide audience can relate to them. Authors of fairy tales entertain by keeping their stories brief and their pacing brisk and instruct by using every detail sentence and line of dialogue so it leads to the moral or lesson.

Audience   Authors of fairy tales create stories for children and, secondarily, for the adults who read to them at home or at school. Authors bring in fantasy elements, such as magic and talking animals, because these elements captivate children. The stories are written so that they're easy for young readers to understand and remember; authors tend to focus on universal human themes (curiosity, fear, coming of age) to connect with as many readers as possible.

Rhetorical appeals   Authors of fairy tales most often rely on appeals based on pathos. Because their purpose is to teach a lesson to a young audience, writers rely on emotion to move the reader. In "Little Red Riding Hood," the reader needs to feel the danger of wolves in order to heed the warning of the tale. Authors also establish their credibility (ethos) by using the conventions of the genre, such as the stock opening of "Once upon a time" and a voice that sounds very assured.

Modes & media   Most often, we encounter fairy tales in anthologies such as *Grimm's* and *Mother Goose*. These print-based collections of tales are usually illustrated; sometimes individual tales are translated into film, such as Disney's *Snow White and the Seven Dwarfs* and *Sleeping Beauty*, or recorded as audiobooks.

Elements of the genre   Fairy tales are characterized by the following:

- *Typical elements of fiction*. Fairy tales are works of fiction, and like other works of fiction, they are typically structured around a few main elements. The plot is an arrangement of incidents that shape the action of a story. Authors also employ characters (the people involved in the story), a setting (the time, place, and atmosphere in which the story takes place), symbolism (the use of a person, object, image, word, or action that has a range of meaning beyond the literal), a point of view (who tells the story and how), and a theme (the story's central meaning or main idea).

- *Magical or fantasy elements*. Unlike most other types of fiction, fairy tales, as the genre's name implies, also feature fairies and magical creatures, such as the fairy godmother in "Cinderella"; magical elements, such as the decades-long naps in "Sleeping Beauty" and "Rip Van Winkle"; and/or magical objects, such as the talking mirror in "Snow White."

- *Stock characters*. Fairy-tale characters are usually one-dimensional, defined by only a few exaggerated details, such as greed, intelligence, or beauty. In "The Three Little Pigs," each pig is defined by one particular trait: One builds a house of straw, one a house of sticks, and one a house of bricks. Fairy-tale characters are usually completely good or completely evil (such as the "big bad" wolf in "Little Red Riding Hood"). They are often animals that the author has anthropomorphized—that is, the animals have human capabilities, such as being able to speak and wear clothing.

- *Conflict*. In most fairy tales, main characters have a task to fulfill or a journey to complete; often they are in danger.

- *Moral or lesson*. Conveying a moral or lesson—which is usually direct and obvious—is the main purpose of most fairy tales (don't go into the woods alone).

Style   Fairy tales are characterized by:

- *A conversational but often didactic tone*. Authors often use an informal tone (e.g., "Grandma, what big teeth you have"), but because they are writing to teach children a lesson, the tone can also be preachy. Traditional fairy tales do not feature irony or humor, though some modern versions do.

- *Simple prose.* Most authors of fairy tales use very straightforward language and sentence structure (e.g., "Once upon a time").
- *Repetition and rhythm.* Like poems or songs, fairy tales often include specific patterns of language and refrains (e.g., "I'll huff and I'll puff and I'll blow your house down.")
- *Sparse detail.* Authors tend to rely on just a few details, for example, describing a castle simply as "gloomy" or a forest as "dark." Details such as how large or old the castle is, or what kinds of trees grow in the forest, are usually not revealed.

Design   Although the details in the fairy tales themselves are usually spare, many are lavishly illustrated. Some are illustrated with realistic images, such as the Gustave Doré engravings that accompany some editions of Charles Perrault's version of "Little Red Riding Hood." In more modern books of fairy tales, illustrations are often colorful and fanciful looking; in *The Random House Book of Fairy Tales*, for example, each tale includes full-color images that illustrate key moments.

Sources   Fairy tales do not include footnotes or Works Cited pages, although most modern-day fairy tales are based on older stories that have been circulating in either oral or written form for generations. "Little Red Riding Hood," for instance, is connected to many European peasant tales that go back as far as the 1300s.

Guided Reading | Fairy Tale

Charles Perrault (1628–1703) was a French writer during the reign of Louis XIV, and he told stories and tales, in part, to entertain the king and the royal court. Perrault's work did much to promote the fairy tale as a literary genre, and many of his versions of tales have been retold by other writers, including the Brothers Grimm. Presented here is Perrault's telling of "Little Red Riding Hood." Drawing on existing tales that had been passed on verbally through generations, he published the tale, originally titled "Le Petit Chaperon Rouge," in a collection of fairy tales in 1697. Our source for the Perrault text is a library of folklore and mythology at the University of Pittsburgh, hosted by Professor D. L. Ashliman, who has also gathered a collection of critical essays for each tale. The illustration on page 263 was created by Gustave Doré and is from a Perrault edition of "Le Petit Chaperon Rouge."

In the annotations that are shown, we've applied a possible analysis of the tale in terms of the author's rhetorical situation and the fairy tale's conventions as a genre. The analysis is meant not as an interpretation of the story, but as a tool for reading fairy tales and other narrative genres critically.

Charles Perrault, *Little Red Riding Hood*

RHETORICAL SITUATION & CHOICES	GENRE CONVENTIONS

PURPOSE
Perrault's purpose is to convey a message or moral.

AUDIENCE
Readers of fairy tales are usually children who are learning about how the world works.

RHETORICAL APPEALS
Perrault establishes the tale's credibility by beginning with "Once upon a time," associating the tale with a venerable past (ethos). The author appeals to readers' pathos by implying that the child is in danger.

MODES & MEDIA
Mode = written:
Author Charles Perrault might have assumed two things about the audiences for his collected fairy tales: (1) that adults would read the stories silently to themselves, and (2) that adults would read the stories aloud for their children. Further, given the long oral tradition of telling tales and the limited options for entertainment (seventeenth century), it is also likely that the story would have been read aloud as a source of amusement for adults. So there are both written and verbal aspects to fairy tale modes.

◄ What is the composer, Charles Perrault, doing?

How do I know this is ▶ a fairy tale?

ELEMENTS OF THE GENRE
This is a made-up story, geared toward children.
It has a moral, which, in this case, is spelled out in the final paragraph.
It includes magical elements, such as a talking animal.
The main character has a task or journey to complete and is in potential danger.
The tale features symbolism, in this case, a red cloak.

STYLE
The story is set in the past; the author begins with the much-used opening "Once upon a time."
Perrault tells the story simply but builds tension as he moves toward the conflict and the closing lesson that he wants to impart.
The tale features a stock character (the big bad wolf).
The setting has little detail.

DESIGN
Perrault wrote text; editors of some editions of his text added illustrations, such as the one shown here.

SOURCES
There are no footnotes or Works Cited list. There are many different sources and versions of this

Credit: Gustave Doré illustration from "Le Petit Chaperon Rouge."

Once upon a time there lived in a certain village a little country girl, the prettiest creature who was ever seen. Her mother was excessively fond of her; and her grandmother doted on her still more. This good woman had a little red riding hood made for her. It suited the girl so extremely well that everybody called her Little Red Riding Hood.

One day her mother, having made some cakes, said to her, "Go, my dear, and see how your grandmother is doing, for I hear she has been very ill. Take her a cake, and this little pot of butter."

Little Red Riding Hood set out immediately to go to her grandmother, who lived in another village.

As she was going through the wood, she met with a wolf, who had a very great mind to eat her up, but he dared not, because of some woodcutters working nearby in the forest. He asked her where she was going. The poor child, who did not know that it was dangerous to stay and talk to a wolf, said to him, "I am going to see my grandmother and carry her a cake and a little pot of butter from my mother."

"Does she live far off?" said the wolf.

"Oh I say," answered Little Red Riding Hood; "it is beyond that mill you see there, at the first house in the village."

"Well," said the wolf, "and I'll go and see her too. I'll go this way and you go that, and we shall see who will be there first."

(Continues on next page)

Medium = print:
"Little Red Riding Hood" is presented here in print, and the assumption is that you will read it linearly, that is, from beginning to end. (In this case, you might be noticing the annotations in the margins as well.) Printed media are usually presented as pages that you turn; this gives an author the opportunity to create a mini-cliffhanger at the end of a page so that readers will turn the page and stay hooked. In contrast, a digital rendering of this tale might include hyperlinks that would allow you to skip around and read the story in whatever order you like.

The wolf ran as fast as he could, taking the shortest path, and the little girl took a roundabout way, entertaining herself by gathering nuts, running after butterflies, and gathering bouquets of little flowers. It was not long before the wolf arrived at the old woman's house. He knocked at the door: tap, tap.

"Who's there?"

"Your grandchild, Little Red Riding Hood," replied the wolf, counterfeiting her voice; "who has brought you a cake and a little pot of butter sent you by mother."

The good grandmother, who was in bed, because she was somewhat ill, cried out, "Pull the bobbin, and the latch will go up."

The wolf pulled the bobbin, and the door opened, and then he immediately fell upon the good woman and ate her up in a moment, for it been more than three days since he had eaten. He then shut the door and got into the grandmother's bed, expecting Little Red Riding Hood, who came some time afterwards and knocked at the door: tap, tap.

"Who's there?"

Little Red Riding Hood, hearing the big voice of the wolf, was at first afraid; but believing her grandmother had a cold and was hoarse, answered, "It is your grandchild Little Red Riding Hood, who has brought you a cake and a little pot of butter mother sends you."

The wolf cried out to her, softening his voice as much as he could, "Pull the bobbin, and the latch will go up."

Little Red Riding Hood pulled the bobbin, and the door opened.

The wolf, seeing her come in, said to her, hiding himself under the bedclothes, "Put the cake and the little pot of butter upon the stool, and come get into bed with me."

Little Red Riding Hood took off her clothes and got into bed. She was greatly amazed to see how her grandmother looked in her nightclothes, and said to her, "Grandmother, what big arms you have!"

"All the better to hug you with, my dear."

"Grandmother, what big legs you have!"

"All the better to run with, my child."

"Grandmother, what big ears you have!"

"All the better to hear with, my child."

"Grandmother, what big eyes you have!"

"All the better to see with, my child."

"Grandmother, what big teeth you have got!"

"All the better to eat you up with."

And, saying these words, this wicked wolf fell upon Little Red Riding Hood, and ate her all up.

story. This one is the popular seventeenth-century Charles Perrault version, and its sources, in turn, probably date back to the fourteenth century. He is credited with being the first person to gather tales that had only been told orally in the past and to treat them as literature.

> Moral: Children, especially attractive, well-bred young ladies, should never talk to strangers, for if they should do so, they may well provide dinner for a wolf. I say "wolf," but there are various kinds of wolves. There are also those who are charming, quiet, polite, unassuming, complacent, and sweet, who pursue young women at home and in the streets. And unfortunately, it is these gentle wolves who are the most dangerous ones of all.

QUESTIONS | Analyzing Perrault's Fairy Tale

RHETORICAL SITUATION & CHOICES

1. **Purpose.** Charles Perrault, in his telling of "Little Red Riding Hood," seeks to entertain and provide a lesson—in fact, he states the official moral at the end of the story. However, what other interpretations could be reached about the main character, the story, and the story's lessons? Which details support these alternative interpretations?

2. **Audience.** To what degree does Perrault gear his version of the tale toward children—and to what degree toward adults? What makes you think so? What are the ages of the children who are the primary targets of this tale, and how do you know? Which details or aspects of the story would appeal to different age groups?

3. **Rhetorical appeals.** Little Red Riding Hood seems to be an extremely naïve character, not quite recognizing that the creature in her grandmother's bed is not her grandmother. How does Little Red's naïveté function in terms of ethos, pathos, and logos?

4. **Rhetorical appeals.** How would the ethos of the tale be affected if, instead of beginning with "Once upon a time," it opened with a specific time and place, such as "Stockholm, Sweden; January 12, 1960"?

5. **Modes & media.** If you were to adapt "Little Red Riding Hood" for a digital format, what changes would you make? What might you hyperlink? Why?

GENRE CONVENTIONS

6. **Elements of the genre.** Why is a wolf a fitting animal to play the role of the villain in this story? What other animals might adequately fulfill the role?

7. **Elements of the genre.** What is the significance of Little Red Riding Hood's red cape? What abstract or symbolic meaning might it have? Why do you think so?

8. **Style.** Sometimes the moral in a fairy tale is made explicit, as in this tale, and other times it's implied but not explicitly stated. What is the effect of the author stating the moral explicitly? And why does Perrault say that gentle wolves are the most dangerous?

9. **Style.** Identify the details of the story that convey the setting. To what extent do they contribute to your visualization of the story? To what extent do they add to the story's universality?

10. **Design.** How does Gustave Doré's woodblock illustration included with the text influence your reading of the story?

11. **Sources.** It's possible that oral stories served as inspiration for Perrault's tale and other similar tales. Can you think of more modern stories or films that may use this story as a source?

Thinking of drafting a fairy tale? Ask yourself the following questions.

RHETORICAL SITUATION & CHOICES

☐ **Purpose.** What is my story, and why do I want to tell it? What message, main idea, or moral do I want to convey? What makes my message so important?

☐ **Audience.** Who are my readers? Why will my story matter to them? And how will I reach them?

☐ **Rhetorical appeals.** How will I use ethos, pathos, and logos to tell my tale and reach my audience? How will I establish my authority as a writer? To what extent will I appeal to my readers' emotions? What role, if any, will logic play in my tale?

☐ **Modes & media.** Will I compose my fairy tale in written, audio, or visual form? Will I present it in print, electronically, or face-to-face?

GENRE CONVENTIONS

☐ **Elements of the genre.** How will I structure my plot? Who are my characters? What is going to happen to them? What is my story's setting? Who will narrate the story, and how? To what extent will I use symbols to convey meaning? How about magical objects? Talking animals? What is the central conflict of my tale? How will I get to my moral?

☐ **Style.** What tone will I take in my writing? Will my tale be funny? Preachy? Both? What kind of language will I use? How much detail?

☐ **Design.** How will I format my story? Will I include illustrations? If so, what kind? And for what key scenes? Why?

☐ **Sources.** Will my fairy tale connect to an existing tale? Will it connect with actual events in history? What sources, if any, will I draw on for my story? Why will I use those sources?

PRACTICE

Telling a Tale

Draft a brief fairy tale of your own in which a generic character defined by one trait (old man, poor woman, silly boy, vain girl) experiences something that teaches a lesson. The lesson should connect in some way to a main trait of your character, just as Little Red's naïveté is connected to her ultimate demise. Alternatively, write your own version of "Little Red Riding Hood" or another popular traditional tale. What will be your main goal in rewriting the tale (perhaps you want to improve on it or make it more modern)? How will your rhetorical situation differ from that of the earlier authors of the tale? What conventions will you adhere to or adapt? How will your writing style compare to the original?

10 REVISING & REMIXING

While feedback can help during any stage of your composing process, once you have a solid draft of your work, it's an ideal time to get some advice on how to make it even better. In this chapter, we pick up where we left off with Gwen Ganow (remember her from Chapter 4?). She's finished her genre piece—a film review of the movie *X-Men*—and has a first draft of her accompanying Author's Statement, which still needs work. In the first part of this chapter, she revises two drafts and polishes her final Statement, working with her own ideas and those she gets from peer review.

Later, Gwen decides she wants to remix her genre project: to repurpose her film review and create something entirely new. Later in this chapter, we provide guidelines for remixing any genre project—that is, advice for how to work with your topic, research, and any composing you've already done, to make something totally different.

Revising Your Work

▲ **STUDENT AUTHOR PHOTO**

Gwen Ganow.

Credit: Gwen Dalynn Ganow.

Why revise, you ask? Because your first draft is geared toward getting your ideas out of your head and onto the page. Some people call this a writer-based draft. A writer-based draft usually has gaps in development and logic. The purpose and sense of audience are usually unclear. They become clear through revision and as you move toward a more audience-focused composition.

Revising Based on Your Own Observations

Gwen has a solid first draft of her Author's Statement to accompany her film review. Now she wants some input from others—from her instructor and classmates—on how to revise her Statement so it's more analytical and persuasive. Gwen's Author's Statement gives her an opportunity to explain the choices she made in addressing her rhetorical situation and working with her genre. But it's also a document in which she can reflect on and learn from her own process.

◀ **DRAFT AUTHOR'S STATEMENT & FILM REVIEW**

Gwen Ganow.

Draft 1 (left);
Final draft (right)
(Gwen's film review appears in Chapter 4.)

Credit: Gwen Dalynn Ganow; Everett Collection.

When you create an Author's or Artist's Statement, you develop skills that will transfer into other settings. You learn to reflect critically on your own work—so that you can improve on it. This is a skill, a habit, even, that you (and all of us) can use in other coursework and outside of school—in future professions or when creating for any audience.

Need another reason why reflecting on your genre project (and revising your Author's or Artist's Statement) is a good idea? Here's an example. In art school, students hardly ever create the "perfect" painting or sculpture or installation in one course or semester. Often, they'll sketch, paint drafts, or create models that they'll use later, as maps or inspiration when they can flesh out their vision for the composition in a different or fuller way. Drafting, thinking critically, and revising go a long way in making great authors and artists truly great. Why not be great?

Revising Based on Peer Review

Let's say that, like Gwen, you've created your genre piece and/or your Author's or Artist's Statement. You've done some revising, and you feel that you've done the best you can. Maybe you can no longer review the content objectively because you've been working on it for a while. Asking others for feedback on your draft is an excellent way to find out how well you've met your purposes or reached your audience. Readers/viewers/listeners will experience your composition with fresh eyes and ears. They can help you figure out where you need to make connections more explicit, where you need to develop examples, and where the draft could be restructured, among other things.

Respondents to your work can be classmates, a teacher, a tutor, friends, parents, or coworkers. Ideally your respondents are from your intended primary audience. These individuals are most likely to give you solid advice on how well you're doing in terms of your rhetorical situation and chosen genre. The respondents you choose, even if they're not part of your primary audience, should be those whose opinions you value, people whom you can trust to respond constructively. They should be able to articulate clearly their reactions to your draft.

Ask for responses at any point in your composing process. For example, at the beginning, when you're brainstorming, you can ask others to talk with you about your ideas and approach to your topic. Once you have a rough draft or a first solid draft, you can ask others to respond to your focus, development, voice, and organization. Once you have completed your first or second draft, ask respondents to give you feedback on how clearly you convey your purpose, how well you're reaching your audience, and what you might do better or differently. Respondents can also help you see counter-arguments and other perspectives at this stage. Near the end of your composing process, ask respondents to take a finer focus: Ask whether your transitions between ideas are consistent, and whether you need to do any fine-tuning in regard to working in your genre, for example.

To get feedback that will be helpful, ask yourself: What do I want to know from my respondents? What would be most helpful to know at this stage? Here are some questions you might ask respondents:

- Would you take a look at my paper (or watch my video, or listen to my podcast, etc.) and tell me what you think? As someone who isn't (or is) familiar with my topic, how well do you think I am conveying my ideas? How persuasive do you find the writing? I'm looking for "big picture" comments right now.

- I'm really struggling with adding specific details (or some other issue). Can you read my draft and point out some places where I could add more detail?

- Other respondents have found some parts of my composition confusing (or identified some other specific problem). Could you take a look at this and let me know if you're sometimes confused, and at what point you start to feel that way?

Gathering responses doesn't mean you'll implement every change that your respondents suggest. You may ultimately decide not to make a particular recommended change, perhaps because you disagree with the suggestion or think the reader misunderstood your purpose. But even if you disagree with a reader comment, consider why the reader made it. And if more than one person makes the same recommendation, you might want to consider it more seriously.

CHECKLIST | Questions to Ask People Responding to Your Draft

Wherever you are in your composing process, it can be helpful to get feedback. Here are some more questions you might want to ask your respondents.

☐ **What kind of genre does this piece appear to be? How can you tell?**

Possible follow-up questions:

☐ Can you suggest some ways to make it read more like an encyclopedia entry/photo essay/blog/other genre piece?

☐ Can you suggest any areas that are not consistent with the genre?

☐ **What would you say is the purpose of this document? How can you tell?**

Possible follow-up questions:

☐ Can you suggest some ways to make the purpose of the piece clearer?

☐ Can you point to some places where the purpose is not consistent?

☐ **How would you characterize the rhetorical appeals the genre piece uses?**

Possible follow-up questions:

☐ Can you suggest ways to make the appeal to my audience more defined?

☐ Can you suggest some ways to emphasize ethos so that my reader accepts the piece's credibility?

☐ Can you suggest some ways to emphasize pathos so that my reader understands the emotion behind the piece?

☐ **How would you characterize the writing style of this document?**

Possible follow-up questions:

☐ Can you point to some places where that style is particularly apparent?

☐ Can you point to some places where that style is not apparent?

☐ Can you point to some places where the style is inconsistent?

☐ Can you suggest some ways to make the style more consistent with that of an encyclopedia entry/photo essay/blog/other genre piece?

☐ **How would you characterize the tone of this document?**

Possible follow-up questions:

☐ Can you point to some places where that tone is particularly apparent?

☐ Can you point to some places where that tone is not apparent?

☐ Can you point to some places where the tone is inconsistent?

☐ Can you suggest some ways to make the tone more consistent with that of an encyclopedia entry/photo essay/blog/other genre piece?

☐ **How would you characterize the voice in this document?**

Possible follow-up questions:

☐ Can you point to some places where that voice is particularly strong?

☐ Can you point to some places where that voice is not as strong?

☐ Can you point to some places where the voice is inconsistent?

☐ Can you suggest some ways to make the voice more consistent with that of an encyclopedia entry/photo essay/blog/other genre piece?

☐ **How do the design elements direct your attention?**

Possible follow-up questions:

☐ Can you suggest some ways I might better use design to help me get into my topic?

☐ Can you suggest some ways to emphasize the visual elements?

☐ Can you suggest some ways to help the text have more impact on the reader?

☐ Can you suggest some ways design elements might clarify for readers that this is an encyclopedia entry/photo essay/blog/other genre piece?

☐ **How have experience and evidence informed the piece?**

Possible follow-up questions:

☐ Can you suggest some ways I might use experience and evidence to make the piece more credible?

☐ Can you suggest some places where I need to add more evidence?

Guided Process | Integrating Peer Feedback: Draft to Finished Composition

Let's circle back to Gwen Ganow and her draft of the Author's Statement that will accompany her film review.

Draft 1   Gwen asks her respondents—a few of her classmates—the following questions about her Author's Statement:

- Have I made my purpose in writing a film review clear?
- Have I clearly communicated the ways I used rhetorical appeals to reach my audience?
- Is my tone reflective and persuasive enough for an Author's Statement?

Her readers report back that they want more information about how Gwen thinks she demonstrated her passion for the subject. They also suggest that she clearly connect her research and what she incorporated into her review, to make her Statement more reflective and persuasive. Finally, one respondent recommends that Gwen rethink the organization of the second half of her Statement.

DRAFT 1   **Gwen Ganow** (STUDENT), *Superhero Project, Author's Statement with Peer Review*

Author's Statement
Why I Wrote a Film Review of *X-Men*

There are two reasons I chose to write a film review. As a "hard-core" comic book fan, I always considered *X-Men* (Singer) as a good example of what a true comic book movie should be. What sets the movie apart from other comic book movies is that the story behind *X-Men* is not overshadowed by special effects. The second reason I chose to do a film review was to show another perspective on how comic books are interrelated with our modern culture. Superheroes, heroes, antiheroes, and villains don't just come to us through the pop culture pages of a comic book. They have also expanded their influence to include the American silver screen. The stories of these comic book characters are now told by our Hollywood actors and actresses.

Created by Stan Lee and Jack Kirby in 1963, the X-Men are the children of humans who were exposed to atmospheric radiation and became genetically altered. These children are born with "differences" and become outsiders in a world that considers them mutants. Even though they do not show any outward signs of difference, their extrahuman powers evoke the envy and fear of ordinary people (Brewer 134). We can link the alienation of the X-Men to groups of people who have gone through their own form of prejudice in real life. African Americans, Jews, Japanese, and homosexuals have all endured the pain of living in an American society that is quick to respond in fear to someone who may be different from the norm.

In *X-Men*, solutions to the problems of prejudice are explored through the actions of two important mutants. Both of these men are leaders, one being the leader of the X-Men, the other the leader of the Brotherhood of Mutants. Charles Xavier creates a school for the gifted for young ostracized mutants. He teaches his mutant students to use their powers to benefit humanity, even if that same humanity hated and distrusted them (Brewer 142). Xavier's "turn the other cheek" philosophy links him to the Jesus Christ of Christian culture. The fact that Xavier provides a safe house for people rejected by humanity also links him to our real life organizations like NAACP, GLBT resource centers, and some of our churches.

Magneto's perspective on humanity stems from his experiences as a young boy at a WWII concentration camp. This experience left Magneto distrustful of humanity, and he is convinced that mutants are bound to suffer the same fate met by the inmates of the Nazi death camps (Brewer 143). To preserve the survival of his mutant species, Magneto declares war on humankind. We can link the thoughts and actions of Magneto to our own real-world thoughts and actions. We, as humans, have always wanted to put our persecutors into the shoes and lives of the persecuted. If we were given the technology to right the wrongs against us, would we create a machine similar to Magneto's? As humans, why are we quick to return violence with more violence?

Overall, I wanted my readers to see my passion for the subject. I wanted to persuade them, using pathos, to understand that you could read the film as a larger statement on the intolerance GLBT people often face. One of the ways I achieved this was by relying on logos, helping my readers follow the film logically, using strategies employed in other film reviews, such as giving snippets of

(Continues on next page)

the plot and using some of the plot summary to highlight the film's strength.

I studied several film reviews to help me figure out how to best create my review. One of the things that was missing from my initial draft was placing the film in a broader context. Thus, in my revision I began the review by discussing my relationship to comics (even if briefly) and then moved on to the film itself. I also incorporated the theory of punctuated equilibrium to help establish my ethos; I know about the theory because of my zoology/biology major. Another thing I wanted to make sure to achieve in the film review was a clear evaluation of the film. My earlier draft did not really make this clear; it primarily consisted of a retelling of some of the plot. In the revision I made sure to include this, not only in the close of the review but with some word choices in the review, such as "powerful image," "good chemistry," and "fine job."

When comic book fans or superhero film fans finish reading my review, I hope that they will see that *X-Men* is definitely an appealing film. More importantly, though, I want my audience to realize that lessons about ourselves can be learned through the story of the X-Men. By witnessing and learning from the actions of a misguided mutant like Magneto, humankind can learn how to be more understanding and tolerant—like Charles Xavier.

Works Cited

Brewer, H. Michael. *Who Needs a Superhero? Finding Virtue, Vice, and What's Holy in the Comics.* Baker Books, 2004, pp. 134–44.

Singer, Bryan, director. *X-Men.* Performances by Hugh Jackman, Ian McKellen, and Patrick Stewart, Marvel Studios, 2000. Film.

With these factors in mind, Gwen creates a list of what to focus on in her next draft.

Gwen Ganow (STUDENT), *Superhero Project: Author's Statement*

Author's Statement
Revision List

Based on my careful rereading of my draft—and comments from others who have read it—I need to do the following in my next draft:

- In general, use my Author's Statement to make a case for my film review. I need to do a better job of letting readers know what I set out to do, and why, and how.
- Explain how I use rhetorical appeals (or at least intended to use them). In my draft I've listed the appeals I worked with, but have not organized my ideas well enough for readers. Just stating my passion is not enough. I need to include an example or two to back up that claim.
- Connect my evidence to the choices and claims that I make in my review.
- Add signal phrases to clearly separate my research from my own ideas.

Gwen then implements these revisions in the following draft. The blue text in the body of the Statement indicates places where Gwen reworked her Statement.

DRAFT 2 **Gwen Ganow** (STUDENT), *Superhero Project: Author's Statement*

Gwen's notes on draft 2 of her Author's Statement

Author's Statement
Why I Wrote a Film Review of *X-Men*

There are several reasons I chose to write a film review. As a "hard-core" comic book fan, I always considered *X-Men* (Singer) as a good example of what a true comic book movie should be. What sets the movie apart from other comic book movies is that the story behind *X-Men* is not overshadowed by special effects. The second reason I chose to do a film review was to show another perspective on how comic books are interrelated with our modern culture. Superheroes, heroes,

(Continues on next page)

Gwen's notes
on draft 2 of her
Author's Statement

I'm giving readers
more context for why
I chose to write my
film review.

antiheroes, and villains don't just come to us through the pop culture pages of a comic book. They have also expanded their influence to include the American silver screen. The stories of these comic book characters are now told by our Hollywood actors and actresses. My final reason for writing a film review is that I wanted to choose a genre that I felt my peers would be interested in reading. Many of my classmates are movie-goers, and even if they are not comic book fans, they probably would be interested in an action film like *X-Men.*

When writing the film review, I wanted to demonstrate I had a clear understanding of the role of the outsider in the film by using some of my research and my knowledge about the original comic book story. Created by Stan Lee and Jack Kirby in 1963, the X-Men are the children of humans who were exposed to atmospheric radiation and became genet-ically altered. H. Michael Brewer, in his book *Who Needs a Superhero?*, discusses how these children are born with "differences" and become outsiders in a world that considers them mutants. Even though they do not show any outward signs of difference, their extrahuman powers evoke the envy and fear of ordinary people (134). If we think about the movie in terms of a larger context, we can link the alienation of the X-Men to groups of people who have gone through their own form of prejudice in real life. African Americans, Jews, Japa-nese, and homosexuals have all endured the pain of living in an American society that is quick to respond in fear to some-one who may be different from the norm.

Here I connect with
my research—through
citing a specific
source.

Brewer also discusses how in *X-Men* solutions to the problems of prejudice are explored through the actions of two impor-tant mutants. Both of these men are leaders, one being the leader of the X-Men, the other the leader of the Brotherhood of Mutants. Charles Xavier creates a school for the gifted for young ostracized mutants. He teaches his mutant students to use their powers to benefit humanity, even if that same humanity hated and distrusted them (142). Xavier's "turn the other cheek" philosophy links him to the Jesus Christ of Christian culture. The fact that Xavier provides a safe house for people rejected by humanity also links him to our real life organizations like NAACP, GLBT resource centers, and some of our churches.

In his book, Brewer also focuses on how Magneto's perspective on humanity stems from his experiences as a young boy at a WWII concentration camp. This experience left Magneto distrustful of humanity, and he is convinced that mutants are bound to suffer the same fate met by the inmates of the Nazi death camps (143). To preserve the survival of his mutant species, Magneto declares war on humankind. We can link the thoughts and actions of Magneto to our own real-world thoughts and actions. We, as humans, have always wanted to put our persecutors into the shoes and lives of the persecuted. If we were given the technology to right the wrongs against us, would we create a machine similar to Magneto's? As humans, why are we quick to return violence with more violence?

Overall, I wanted my readers to see my passion for the subject. One of the ways I did this was by opening with the fact that I am a "hard-core" comic book fan. Besides demonstrating my passion, I wanted to persuade my readers, by using pathos, to understand that you could read the film as a larger statement on the intolerance GLBT people often face. One of the ways I achieved this was by relying on logos, helping my readers follow the film logically, using strategies employed in other film reviews, such as giving snippets of the plot and using some of the plot summary to highlight the film's strength. While both pathos and logos are important for reaching my audience, I realized that if I did not establish my ethos, people would not care about what I had to say. By incorporating the theory of punctuated equilibrium, which I know about because of my zoology/biology major, and connecting it to the film, I help readers view me as a knowledgeable and informed writer.

I studied several film reviews to help me figure out how to best create my review. One of the things that was missing from my initial draft was placing the film in a broader context. Thus, in my revision I began the review by discussing my relationship to comics (even if briefly) and then moved on to the film itself. Another thing I wanted to make sure to achieve in the film review was a clear evaluation of the film. My earlier draft did not really make this clear; it primarily consisted of a retelling of some of the plot. In the revision I made sure to include this, not only in the close of the review but with some word choices in the review, such as "powerful image," "good chemistry," and "fine job."

Gwen's notes on draft 2 of her Author's Statement

I've worked in signal phrases to make my research more apparent and to make my Statement more readable.

I've made it clearer how I set out to use ethos, pathos, and logos, and backed that up with details.

(Continues on next page)

When comic book fans or superhero film fans finish reading my review, I hope that they will see that *X-Men* is definitely an appealing film. More importantly, though, I want my audience to realize that lessons about ourselves can be learned through the story of the X-Men. By witnessing and learning from the actions of a misguided mutant like Magneto, humankind can learn how to be more understanding and tolerant—like Charles Xavier.

Works Cited

Brewer, H. Michael. *Who Needs a Superhero? Finding Virtue, Vice, and What's Holy in the Comics*. Baker Books, 2004, pp. 134–44.

Singer, Bryan, director. *X-Men*. Performances by Hugh Jackman, Ian McKellen, and Patrick Stewart, Marvel Studios, 2000. Film.

At this point, Gwen asks her respondents to read the above draft with the following questions in mind:

- Is my tone persuasive enough?
- Have I said enough about the film reviews I studied as models?
- What is the single most important revision I can make to strengthen my Author's Statement?

Respondents suggest that Gwen:

- Improve her persuasiveness by looking carefully at the word choices in her Author's Statement
- Make more-specific comments about the film reviews she used as models for her own review
- Refer to more than one outside source

Gwen agrees with the first two suggestions, but feels that adding more sources is not necessary to achieve her purpose. With this feedback and her own ideas in mind, Gwen creates a quick revision list before moving on to her final draft.

Gwen Ganow (STUDENT), *Superhero Project: Author's Statement*

> **Author's Statement**
> **Revision List**
>
> I think I'm making a pretty good case for my review—and am specifically explaining my intentions to my readers. I've incorporated research successfully. Now I just have a little more to do:
>
> - Back up my choices by referring specifically to the film reviews I used as models for my own composition.
> - Fine-tune my writing to make it more persuasive overall; also, make sure I'm choosing the most persuasive words and phrasing.
> - Check my Statement for mechanics, grammar, tense, spelling, and so on. Proofread.

With these points in mind, Gwen revises her Statement a final time. The document below (created in Microsoft Word) shows Gwen's edits as tracked changes.

FINAL Gwen Ganow (STUDENT), *Superhero Project: Author's Statement (shows edits)*

> **Author's Statement**
> **Why I Wrote a Film Review of** *X-Men*
>
> Why did I choose to write a film review—and to write one about *X-Men*? I have several reasons. ~~There are several reasons I chose to write a film review. As~~ First, as a "hard-core" comic book fan, I've always considered *X-Men* (Singer) to be a good example of what a true comic book movie should be. ~~What sets the movie apart from other comic book movies is that the story behind *X-Men* is not overshadowed by special effects.~~ *X-Men*, the film, inspired me to write a review because of what sets it apart from other comic book films: the *X-Men* story itself. The filmmaker clearly understood this, and did not clutter the story with over-the-top special effects. The second reason I chose to ~~do~~ write a film review is a little broader: I wanted to comment on ~~was to show another~~

(Continues on next page)

perspective on ~~how~~ comic books are ~~interrelated~~ intertwined with ~~our~~ modern popular culture. Superheroes, heroes, anti-heroes, and villains don't just come to us through ~~the pop culture pages of a~~ comic books anymore. They ~~have also~~ come to us through Hollywood, brought to life ~~expanded their influence to include the American silver screen. A~~ by the actors and actresses who portray the characters and stories of America's favorite superheroes. ~~The stories of these comic book characters are now told by our Hollywood actors and actresses.~~ My final reason for choosing to write a film review, rather than a researched journal article, for example, is that I wanted to choose a genre that I ~~felt~~ knew my peers would relate to. ~~be interested in reading.~~ Many of my classmates are moviegoers and readers of reviews: ~~, and e~~Even if they are not comic book fans, they are likely to ~~probably would~~ be interested in an action film like *X-Men*, and therefore in a review of the film.

~~When writing the~~ In my ~~film~~ review, I wanted to demonstrate ~~I had~~ a clear understanding of the role of the outsider in *X-Men*. ~~the film.~~ To do this, I drew on ~~by using some of my~~ research and my own knowledge ~~about~~ of the original *X-Men* comic book story. Created by Stan Lee and Jack Kirby in 1963, the X-Men are the children of humans who were exposed to atmospheric radiation and became genetically altered. H. Michael Brewer, in his book *Who Needs a Superhero?*, discusses how these children are born with "differences" and become outsiders in a world that considers them mutants. Even though they do not show any outward signs of difference, their extrahuman powers evoke the envy and fear of ordinary people (134). If we think about the movie in terms of a larger context, we can link the alienation of the X-Men to groups of people who have gone through their own form of prejudice in real life. African Americans, Jews, Japanese, and ~~homosexuals~~ gay men and lesbians have ~~all~~ endured the pain of living in an American society that is quick to respond in fear to someone who may be different from the norm.

Brewer also discusses how in *X-Men* authors Lee and Kirby explore solutions to the problems of prejudice ~~are explored~~ through ~~the actions of~~ two important mutants: Charles Xavier and Magneto. Both of these characters ~~men~~ are leaders; Xavier~~, one being the leader of~~ leads the X-Men, while Magneto ~~the other the leader of~~ leads the Brotherhood of Mutants. ~~Charles~~ Xavier creates a school for the gifted for young ~~ostracized~~ outcast mutants~~.~~, where he ~~He~~ teaches ~~his~~

~~mutant students~~ them to use their powers to benefit humanity, even if that same humanity hate~~d~~s and distrust~~ed~~s them
(142). Xavier's "turn the other cheek" philosophy links him to
the Jesus Christ of Christian culture. The fact that Xavier provides a safe house for people rejected by humanity also links
him to our real-life organizations ~~like~~ such as the NAACP,
GLBT resource centers, and some of our churches.

In his book, Brewer also focuses on how Magneto's perspective on humanity stems from his experiences as a young boy
at a WWII concentration camp. ~~This experience~~ Life in the
camp left Magneto distrustful and despairing of humanity,
and ~~he is~~ convinced that mutants are bound to suffer the
same fate as Jews imprisoned and murdered in ~~met by the
inmates of the~~ Nazi death camps (143). To preserve the survival of his mutant species, Magneto declares war on humankind. ~~We can link~~ I see Magneto's ~~the thoughts and actions~~
distrust and violence as related to contemporary life and the
collective urge to "right wrongs," gain power, or find revenge
through warfare. ~~of Magneto to our own real-world thoughts
and actions. We, as humans, have always wanted to put our
persecutors into the shoes and lives of the persecuted.~~ If we
had the technology available to Magneto in *X-Men*, would
we use it the same way? ~~were given the technology to right
the wrongs against us, would we create a machine similar to
Magneto's? As humans, why are we quick to~~ Would we return
violence with more violence?

In my review, I consciously worked with rhetorical appeals.
Overall, I wanted my readers to see my passion for my topic—
toward superheroes, society, and the film *X-Men*. ~~the subject.~~
I worked to establish ethos ~~One of the ways I did this was
opening with the fact that I am~~ by letting readers know I am
~~"hard-core"~~ a serious comic book fan and think of myself as
somewhat of an expert on the genre. Besides demonstrating
my passion, I wanted to persuade my readers~~;~~ by using pathos,
by appealing to emotion to persuade them to ~~understand that
you could~~ read the film as a larger statement—a statement
on the intolerance that "outsiders," specifically GLBT people,
often face. I supported my argument logically, with ~~One of the
ways I achieved this was by relying on logos, helping my readers follow the film logically,~~ key points from the plot, ~~using~~
and used strategies I learned from other film reviewers, such
as using summary and highlighting particular moments in a
film. ~~employed in other film reviews, such as giving snippets
of the plot and using some of the plot summary to highlight
the film's strength.~~ While both pathos and logos ~~are~~ were
important for reaching my audience, I realized that if I did

(Continues on next page)

not establish my ethos, people would not care about what I had to say. For example, I ~~By~~ incorporating~~ed~~ the theory of punctuated equilibrium that I learned about in my studies as a~~, which I know about because of my~~ zoology/biology major, and used that as a lens for reading ~~and connecting it to~~ the film~~,~~. I believe this perspective, and the fact that I am a long-time and avid comics reader, helped my audience see ~~I help readers view~~ me as a knowledgeable and informed writer.

I studied several film reviews to help me figure out how to best create my own review. ~~One of the things~~ Something that I did not do in ~~was missing from~~ my initial draft was to place ~~placing~~ the film in a broader context. ~~Thus, in my revision~~ In my next draft, I began with a brief discussion of ~~the review by discussing~~ my relationship to comics ~~(even if briefly)~~ and then moved on to the film itself. Another thing I focused on in revisions was ~~wanted~~ to make sure ~~to achieve in the film review was~~ I gave a clear opinion ~~a clear evaluation~~ of the film. I did not do this in ~~My~~ my earlier draft, ~~did not really make this clear; it primarily consisted of a~~ which was also too focused on retelling ~~of some of~~ the plot~~.~~—and not focused enough on evaluating it. In my revised review, ~~the revision~~ I made sure to be more straightforward in my opinion, and to choose words that supported my observations clearly. I sharpened up my language to make it more persuasive and precise, using phrases ~~include this, not only in the close of the review but with some word choices in the review~~, such as "powerful image~~;~~" and "good chemistry~~,~~." ~~and "fine job."~~

When comic book fans ~~finish reading~~ or superhero film fans read my review, I want them to ~~hope that they will~~ see that *X-Men* is ~~definitely an appealing~~ a film worth seeing—and one that offers insight into human experience. ~~More importantly, though,~~ I want my audience to realize that—through the story of the X-Men—we can learn ~~lessons~~ about ourselves. ~~can be learned through the story of the X-Men.~~ Maybe we can learn something from ~~By witnessing and learning from the actions of a~~ the misguided mutant ~~like~~ Magneto~~,~~ ~~humankind can learn how to be more understanding~~ and his tolerant, loving counterpart, ~~—like~~Charles Xavier.

Works Cited

Brewer, H. Michael. *Who Needs a Superhero? Finding Virtue, Vice, and What's Holy in the Comics.* Baker Books, 2004, pp. 134–44.

Singer, Bryan, director. *X-Men.* Performances by Hugh Jackman, Ian McKellen, and Patrick Stewart, Marvel Studios, 2000. Film.

The following document shows Gwen's work with her edits accepted.

Author's Statement

Why I Wrote a Film Review of *X-Men*

Why did I choose to write a film review—and to write one about *X-Men*? I have several reasons. First, as a "hard-core" comic book fan, I've always considered *X-Men* (Singer) to be a good example of what a true comic book movie should be. *X-Men*, the film, inspired me to write a review because of what sets it apart from other comic book films: the *X-Men* story itself. The filmmaker clearly understood this, and did not clutter the story with over-the-top special effects. The second reason I chose to write a film review is a little broader: I wanted to comment on how comic books are intertwined with modern popular culture. Superheroes, heroes, antiheroes, and villains don't just come to us through comic books anymore. They come to us through Hollywood, brought to life by the actors and actresses who portray the characters and stories of America's favorite superheroes. My final reason for choosing to write a film review, rather than a researched journal article, for example, is that I wanted to choose a genre that I knew my peers would relate to. Many of my classmates are moviegoers and readers of reviews: Even if they are not comic book fans, they are likely to be interested in an action film like *X-Men*, and therefore in a review of the film.

In my review, I wanted to demonstrate a clear understanding of the role of the outsider in *X-Men*. To do this, I drew on research and my own knowledge of the original *X-Men* comic book story. Created by Stan Lee and Jack Kirby in 1963, the X-Men are the children of humans who were exposed to atmospheric radiation and became genetically altered. H. Michael Brewer, in his book *Who Needs a Superhero?*, discusses how these children are born with "differences" and become outsiders in a world that considers them mutants. Even though they do not show any outward signs of difference, their extrahuman powers evoke the envy and fear of ordinary people (134). If we think about the movie in terms of a larger context, we can link the alienation of the X-Men to groups of people who have gone through their own form of prejudice in

(Continues on next page)

real life. African Americans, Jews, Japanese, and gay men and lesbians have endured the pain of living in an American society that is quick to respond in fear to someone who may be different from the norm.

Brewer also discusses how in *X-Men* authors Lee and Kirby explore solutions to the problem of prejudice through two important mutants: Charles Xavier and Magneto. Both of these characters are leaders; Xavier leads the X-Men, while Magneto leads the Brotherhood of Mutants. Xavier creates a school for the gifted for young outcast mutants, where he teaches them to use their powers to benefit humanity, even if that same humanity hates and distrusts them (142). Xavier's "turn the other cheek" philosophy links him to the Jesus Christ of Christian culture. The fact that Xavier provides a safe house for people rejected by humanity also links him to our real-life organizations such as the NAACP, GLBT resource centers, and some of our churches.

In his book, Brewer also focuses on how Magneto's perspective on humanity stems from his experiences as a young boy at a WWII concentration camp. Life in the camp left Magneto distrustful and despairing of humanity, and convinced that mutants are bound to suffer the same fate as Jews imprisoned and murdered in Nazi death camps (143). To preserve the survival of his mutant species, Magneto declares war on humankind. I see Magneto's distrust and violence as related to contemporary life and the collective urge to "right wrongs," gain power, or find revenge through warfare. If we had the technology available to Magneto in *X-Men*, would we use it the same way? Would we return violence with more violence?

In my review, I consciously worked with rhetorical appeals. Overall, I wanted my readers to see my passion for my topic—toward superheroes, society, and the film *X-Men*. I worked to establish ethos by letting readers know I am a serious comic book fan and think of myself as somewhat of an expert on the genre. Besides demonstrating my passion, I wanted to persuade my readers by using pathos, by appealing to emotion to persuade them to read the film as a larger statement—a statement on the intolerance that "outsiders," specifically GLBT people, often face. I supported my argument logically, with key points from the plot, and used strategies I learned from other film reviewers, such as using summary and highlighting particular moments in a film. While both pathos and logos were important for reaching my audience, I realized that if I did not establish my ethos, people would not care about what I had to say. For example, I incorporated the theory of punctuated equilibrium that I learned about in my studies as a zoology/biology major, and used that as a lens for reading the film. I believe this perspective, and the fact that I am a longtime and avid comics reader, helped my audience see me as a knowledgeable and informed writer.

I studied several film reviews to help me figure out how to best create my own review. Something that I did not do in my initial draft was to place the film in a broader context. In my next draft, I began with a brief discussion of my relationship to comics and then moved on to the film itself. Another thing I focused on in revisions was to make sure I gave a clear opinion of the film. I did not do this in my earlier draft, which was also too focused on retelling the plot—and not focused enough on evaluating it. In my revised review, I made sure to be more straightforward in my opinion, and to choose words that supported my observations clearly. I sharpened up my language to make it more persuasive and precise, using phrases such as "powerful image" and "good chemistry."

When comic book fans or superhero film fans read my review, I want them to see that *X-Men* is a film worth seeing—and one that offers insight into human experience. I want my audience to realize that—through the story of the X-Men—we can learn about ourselves. Maybe we can learn something from the misguided mutant Magneto and his tolerant, loving counterpart, Charles Xavier.

Works Cited

Brewer, H. Michael. *Who Needs a Superhero? Finding Virtue, Vice, and What's Holy in the Comics.* Baker Books, 2004, pp. 134–44.

Singer, Bryan, director. *X-Men.* Performances by Hugh Jackman, Ian McKellen, and Patrick Stewart, Marvel Studios, 2000. Film.

Remixing Your Work into Different Genres

Sometimes we ask our students to remix their finished genre piece into a different genre. For example, Gwen, who composed a film review on superheroes and justice, thought at one point that she'd create a presentation, animation, or advertisement. Remixing her film review would be an opportunity to work in a different genre on a topic she had already researched and written about—and to think about the different ways of reaching an audience that other genres allow.

Guided Process | Remixing a Genre Project

Gwen wants to shape her film review into something new. When our students create remixes, we ask them to think their projects through as shown in the following assignment.

REMIX **Gwen Ganow** (STUDENT), *Film Review PowerPoint: "We Are All Mutants"*

English 101
Professor Braziller

Assignment: Remix Your Genre Project

What is a remix? When you remix an object or composition, you repurpose it. For example, Martha Stewart might repurpose flowerpots to be utensil holders in her kitchen. Originally intended for outdoor use to hold soil and plants, the pots will need to be overhauled for indoor kitchen use. Stewart would probably wash them, apply a nontoxic sealant, and paint them or decorate them in some way. The finished product—the utensil holder that was formerly a flowerpot—is a remix.

How will you create a remix? Your assignment is to remix one of the genre pieces you've already composed. You will repurpose your creation for a different context. This may involve changing the purpose, audience, and/or message of your original piece. Your energy should go toward revising your original material to fit into a new mode and/or genre appropriate to your new context.

For example, you might remix an editorial you wrote about school funding into a short YouTube video. The editorial was originally geared toward politicians or taxpayers, but you now imagine an audience of college students. Thus, you need to make the editorial interesting and palatable to college students. You also need to take into account the conventions of the new genre.

You might also consider taking parts from other assignments and weaving them together into a new work. Quilters do this when they take scraps of fabric from outgrown clothing and sew them together into a new item: a quilt.

Gwen repurposes her film review to create a PowerPoint presentation that begins with a top 10 list. In this case, her purpose is to persuade an audience of fans who watched the film when it came out in the year 2000 to watch it again. She chooses the genre of the top 10 list because it gives her the opportunity to use humor to persuade. Her plan is to share her list with friends and fans on social media sites, and to ask them to contribute their own lists of reasons for watching the *X-Men* movie again.

Following are her first three slides.

▶ POWERPOINT
SLIDE
Gwen Ganow, Remix of film review.
Credit: Slides: Gwen Dalynn Ganow; X-Men poster; TM and Copyright © 20th Century Fox Film Corp. All rights reserved. Courtesy: Everett Collection.

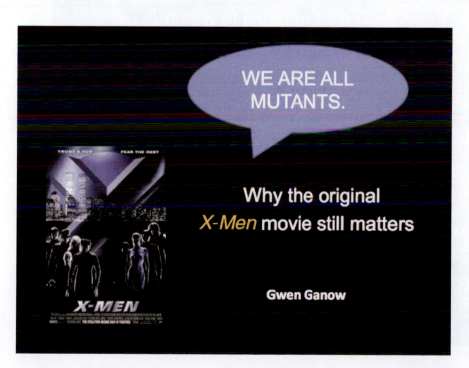

Top **10** reasons to watch
the original *X-Men* movie again

10. The year 2000 was a wicked long time ago.

9. Hugh Jackman cage-fight scenes.

8. Pre *True Blood* Anna Paquin. Halle Berry. Lycra.

7. Need refresher on details of Mutant Registration Act.

6. Xavier School for Gifted Youngsters is way cooler than Hogwarts.

Top **10** reasons to watch
the original *X-Men* movie again

5. That scene where Jackman flips the fork-fingered bird.

4. Far too long since a Holocaust survivor with magnetic-field- control superpowers tried for world domination.

3. "Trust a few and fear the rest" starting to sound like a good idea.

2. Humans (except for Patrick Stewart) still totally overrated.

1. You are *such* a geek.

CHECKLIST | Remixing a Genre Piece?

Keep the following questions in mind.

RHETORICAL SITUATION & CHOICES

☐ **Purpose.** What is the purpose of my new, remixed composition? How can I make that purpose clear?

☐ **Audience.** Who is the targeted audience for my remix? How can I take my new audience's expectations, values, and concerns into account? What kind of vocabulary, examples and details, organization, and other elements should I use to appeal to my new audience?

☐ **Rhetorical appeals.** How can I use rhetorical appeals to connect with my new audience?

☐ **Modes & media.** What mode and medium will be most likely to engage my new audience?

GENRE CONVENTIONS

☐ **Elements of the genre.** How can I use the elements of my new genre to guide my new audience's experience?

☐ **Style.** How can I use word choice, sentence structure, literary devices (like metaphor), and other stylistic techniques to keep my new audience engaged?

☐ **Design.** How can I use design elements, such as color, images, and font, to emphasize my purpose and main point?

☐ **Sources.** What kinds of sources should I use to convince my new audience of my point? How should I cite these sources appropriately in my new genre?

11 EXPLORING TOPICS & CREATING A RESEARCH PROPOSAL

In this chapter, we will follow student Jasmine Huerta through her research process. Note that the process Jasmine uses is a typical research process, but it is not the only process. Many researchers do things in a different order, utilize different strategies, and so on. The more you research, the more you will tailor processes to fit you and what works for you.

Considering Your Rhetorical Situation

As with everything you compose, you should start by thinking about your rhetorical situation—your purpose and audience. If you are responding to a research assignment, your instructor may have stipulated a particular purpose and audience, or you may be able to choose those on your own. Sometimes instructors also stipulate what types of sources need to be used. Be sure you understand what your instructor expects and how much latitude you have to make choices.

Choosing a Topic Through Basic Research

The Internet offers an unlimited source of topics, and beginning your reading can be exciting but overwhelming: You can easily locate millions of resources on any topic simply by doing a quick online search. That's why it's important to go about the process in an orderly fashion. This chapter will show you the steps you need to take.

Whenever you write—as a student in a composition classroom or a professional in a workplace—you focus on a specific topic. Sometimes you may be provided with a general theme or a specific topic or issue. For example, your instructor might ask you to respond to an essay you've read for class, or your manager at work might ask you to share your plans to improve business or increase sales in the next quarter. Other times, most often in the course of college work, you get to start from scratch and choose a topic purely out of your own interest and curiosity.

So how do you choose a topic? Where should you start? One place might be this book. The Index of Themes (p. T-1) organizes every reading in this text by topic, and the Index of Genres (p. G-1) will help you see the relationship between topic choice and genre choice.

1. Brainstorm Topic Ideas | What Are You Curious About?

The best way to get started on identifying a topic that is meaningful to you is to get your ideas flowing. Whether you're composing from your own experience or composing based on research, you can use the same prewriting techniques that we discussed in Chapter 4: talk to people, make a brainstorm list, make a mind map, and freewrite.

In addition to those strategies, find out what others have already said about the topic and discuss those ideas with others.

Do some preliminary reading online, but be disciplined about it.   Google a few things you are interested in to find some potential topics to research. You can find out what's in the news or what others are talking about by going to news sources, like *The New York Times* or CNN, and opinion sources, like *Salon* and *Slate*. If you want to skim scholarly sources, try Google Scholar (scholar.google.com). If you go to *Wikipedia*, be sure to look at the source links for the entries you read. That's where you'll find the best leads. And don't be all day about it: Remember, you're generating ideas, not surfing mindlessly. To come up with a healthy list of topic ideas, try answering the following questions. Keep in mind any topic restrictions built into your assignment.

> **Activity: Generating Ideas for Topics**
> 1. Ideas come out of conversations. What comes up in your talks with friends? What was the topic of your last discussion or disagreement? What are some of your unresolved questions about the topic?
>
> 2. Ideas come out of our passions. What are you passionate about?
>
> 3. Ideas come out of pet peeves. What bothers you on a regular basis? What would you change about your campus, town, state, country, or the world if you were in charge?
>
> 4. Ideas come out of our curiosities. What are you curious about?
>
> 5. Ideas come out of our concerns. What do you worry about?

2. Explore Topic Ideas Through Preliminary Research | Ask Yourself, Who's Saying What?

Once you've identified a topic area, you're ready to dig a little deeper to better understand it. Keep a few possibilities in mind and conduct preliminary research on several related topics (or subtopics) so you can make an informed decision about which one to commit to; the viability of each topic will depend on what you find out at this point. As with the preliminary reading you did during brainstorming, you'll continue to draw on sources written for nonexperts. Later in your process, you'll move on to more specialized sources using scholarly databases. As you conduct preliminary research, focus on the following:

Words and facts.   Ask yourself some questions. Are there terms you need to define? And what are the facts?

Opinions.   Find out what others have to say on the subject, and notice what evidence they use to support their opinions. In addition to facts, what opinions surround your topic? Who writes about the topic, and why are they concerned? On what sources do they base their statements or arguments? What sources do they draw on? And what sources might you want to use, too?

Your perspective.   Form your own arguments in response to others. As you research, you will begin to form your own ideas and opinions about your topic.

Conflicting views.   Notice who disagrees about your topic. When you begin reading sources related to your topic, you might begin to notice that there are viewpoints that stand opposed to each other. Furthermore, as you dig into these disagreements, you might realize that the differing viewpoints are well researched and should not be immediately dismissed. Discovering well-researched, well-reasoned opposing stances related to your topic forces you to accept that there is not necessarily one "correct" viewpoint; reasonable people can disagree.

The irrational.   Avoid arguments that are just too "out there." In the course of your research, you may stumble upon the ideas of people who are unreasonable, ill informed, or both. Keep a critical eye as you read sources.

Key terms.   As you conduct preliminary research, you'll notice that certain terms pop up. Follow up on these key terms by using them in your searches of the Internet and library databases.

Following is an assignment we give our students during their preliminary research phase. It includes the responses of a student, Jasmine Huerta, whose research topic is diabetes. (Note: We will see more of her work on this project later in the chapter.)

Through answering the assigned questions, Jasmine realizes that she has several interesting potential research questions to pursue. The list of key terms helped her continue and refine her research. She realized that the glycemic index is not 100 percent accepted, which surprised and intrigued her. By using the Internet to find key terms, exploring some of these potential subtopics, previewing and reading sources, and then reflecting on her process and discoveries, Jasmine narrows her topic from diabetes to the role of nutrition in the diabetic patient.

▲ **STUDENT AUTHOR**

Jasmine Huerta.
In this chapter, we follow this student as she chooses and investigates a topic (diabetes). Jasmine appears next on page 300.
Credit: Claudelle Girard/ iStock/Getty Images

ASSIGNMENT   **Jasmine Huerta** (STUDENT), *What Is Your Topic?*

English 101
Professor Braziller

September 26, 2017
Respond to the following questions to see how workable your topic may be.

1. What is the general topic area you are considering?

    I am interested in researching and writing about diabetes.

◀ To the left, in blue type, are Jasmine's very early ideas about her diabetes project and some information on what she's discovered during preliminary research.

(Continues on next page)

2. Why? Are you truly fascinated/curious/passionate about the topic? How did you become interested in this topic? (If your answer is no, explain why and then move on to the next topic without answering any more questions.)

Diabetes runs in my family, so it's something I want to understand more about in case I am faced with it at some point. My six-year-old cousin has type 1 diabetes. My mother had gestational diabetes when she was pregnant with me. Most recently, my grandfather, who is a bit overweight (as is my cousin), was diagnosed with diabetes. I'm wondering if I am just destined to develop it at some point because of my family history. I also wonder if perhaps there are things I can do to prevent the disease, since I presently don't have diabetes. I worry about both my cousin and grandfather, so I'd like to see if there are some things they could do to keep their diabetes under control, rather than just relying on traditional medicine.

3. What surprising facts have you gathered so far about your topic? What further questions do you have that you need answered with data?

Surprising facts/data:
- According to *Wikipedia's* entry "Diabetes" (accessed on 9/20/17): "Diabetic patients with neuropathic symptoms such as numbness or tingling in feet or hands are twice as likely to be unemployed as those without the symptoms."
- A link found on the American Diabetes Association to an article on SmartBrief.com stated that those who are exposed to secondhand smoke have a greater risk of contracting diabetes.
- According to an article about lifestyle and home remedies, found on the Mayo Clinic's page, diabetes can contribute to gum infections.

4. Do reasonable people disagree about the topic? If so, what aspects of the topic do they disagree about? Who disagrees with whom? Name names.

There seems to be a bit of a debate about what makes the best approach for a diabetic diet. While surfing around on the Internet, one of the big debates I found discussed the glycemic index and how it relates to managing diabetes. It seems that people used to think you just had to avoid high-sugar foods, but after reading a few articles, I realized that many researchers want to look more closely at using the glycemic index (taking into account carbohydrates) in working with diabetic diets.

In an article titled "Low–Glycemic Index Diets in the Management of Diabetes," Miller et al. argue that this is a positive approach. I found an editorial written by Marion Franz in the publication *Diabetes Care* that argues with this approach: "The Glycemic Index: Not the most effective nutrition therapy intervention." In the Mayo Clinic's advice column, "Ask a Diabetes Specialist," someone wrote to Dr. Maria Collazo-Clavel, asking, "Is the glycemic-index diet useful for people with diabetes?" She responds that it's very complicated to use this as a measure, cautioning that it might not be the best approach for everybody.

5. **Is the topic researchable in the time you have?**

   I don't see any issues with researching the topic this semester. In a short amount of time I was able to find many sources and potential ideas. I have a number of family members who deal with diabetes. I can easily interview them. I also would like to contact a doctor who treats people with diabetes and arrange an interview, perhaps by phone or e-mail.

6. **What are some subtopics that have emerged in your research?**

   Nutrition to manage diabetes, medication to manage diabetes, alternative treatments for diabetes, prevention of diabetes, social issues connected to diabetes.

7. **What questions might you pursue in further research, based on what you've discovered during preliminary research?**

   - What types of diets are best for people with diabetes?
   - How can diet prevent someone from getting diabetes if he or she has a family history of diabetes?
   - How can following certain nutritional guidelines make diabetes go away?
   - How can alternative treatments or natural medications be used instead of insulin?
   - What countries have the highest rate of diabetes? What contributes to the high rate?

8. **What are some key terms that keep coming up in relation to this topic?**

   Glycemic index, metabolism, blood sugar, hypertension, obesity, glucose monitoring, insulin.

3. Commit to a Single Topic | What Are You Most Curious About?

Once you've identified a general topic area, it's time to commit to one specific topic within it. The "What Is Your Topic?" assignment (p. 295) can assist you with this choice, as can the following questions:

Is your topic compatible with your assignment? And can you make a strong argument about it?   If your instructor has given you an assignment, read it carefully and consider the degree to which your topic will work. If you've been asked to make an argument, you might find yourself gravitating toward controversial issues—such as gun control, abortion, and censorship. However, we urge you to consider other, less obvious topics. For example, if you are interested in the subject of gun control, rather than choosing the topic of concealed weapons and constitutional rights, you might take the topic of gun control and examine the power that gun control groups, such as the NRA, hold in the political arena.

Do you like your topic enough to stick with it?   If you are not truly curious about your topic, you probably won't remain interested in your research beyond the first week or so. Choose something you really want to learn about, that has some connection to you and your life.

What is your deadline, and how will it affect your plans for research?   If your completed project is due in two weeks, choose a topic for which there is plenty of information that you can access easily. If you have more time, say an entire fifteen-week semester, you have the luxury of using a range of sources, and conducting interviews or surveys, for example, so you can select your topic accordingly. On the other hand, if your topic is so obscure that your only sources need to be ordered through interlibrary loan (which can take several weeks), it is not a good topic for either a two-week or fifteen-week deadline.

ATTENTION, RESEARCHERS

Looking for something to argue about? Almost any topic offers argumentative angles: The key is to find the angles.

For example, while "reading" may not seem like the most provocative topic, a quick Google search reveals that it's the subject of much debate. Some questions around this debate include: Do college students read more or less than in the past? Is online reading cognitively different from reading books? What is the relationship between how much we read and our development of critical thinking skills?

The point is to keep an open mind to topics that seem vanilla. You may find some spice under the surface.

Will you find appropriate sources for your topic? Some topics are so current that there is little or no published research available. For example, a friend who works in the field of bioengineering might tell you that scientists are developing crops with deeper roots to reduce the amount of carbon dioxide in the atmosphere, but because the research has just begun, there are no published articles about it. In this case, you might want to shift your topic toward an aspect of bioengineering that is more researchable in the present.

4. Form a Working Research Question | Refine as You Go

What's your general topic? What questions will move you from a basic, broad idea to more specific ideas? Creating research questions focuses your attention from a general topic to a specific aspect of the topic, as follows:

GENERAL TOPIC	Diabetes
WORKING RESEARCH QUESTIONS	What causes diabetes?
	What is the latest medical research on diabetes?
	How can people avoid getting diabetes?

While you'll ask (and answer) lots of questions in your research, your "research question" is the big question, the one that you are ultimately interested in answering.

But as you discover more about your topic, you might revise your question to reflect what you're learning, as follows:

REVISED RESEARCH QUESTION	What is the relationship between nutrition and diabetes?

What questions—focused on finding facts and defining terms—can move you toward a final research question? As you begin your research, many of your questions will be focused on gathering facts and defining terms. If, as in the example above, you're researching the general topic of diabetes, you will ask questions at the outset such as the following:

BASIC FACT-FINDING QUESTIONS	What causes diabetes? Who is affected by it, and why?
	What alternative treatments are there (as opposed to insulin)?
	What is the role of glucose and the glycemic index?

WRITE

What is the general topic of your research? What are your questions about it so far?

Which questions have to do with finding facts? Which ones are more about analysis? What, in your early research, has surprised you most?

Your research question, however, should focus on more complex *analysis*. Following are some examples of revised, more final research questions:

RESEARCH QUESTIONS — How can changes in diet help a person manage diabetes?

How can managing sugar and sodium intake help someone avoid taking insulin?

Why does the traditional medical establishment not promote alternatives to insulin injections?

Notice how these questions require extensive research and even speculation, especially the last question. These would make solid research questions, while the first set of questions would not, although they would be useful questions to ask in the course of researching one of the questions in the second list.

CHECKLIST | Refining Your Research Question

What are the qualities of a really good research question? As you refine yours, ask yourself:

☐ **Is it appropriate for your rhetorical situation or assignment?**

☐ **Is it open-ended,** meaning it cannot be answered with a simple yes, no, or maybe, or a single number?

☐ **Are the terms of the question specific enough or too general?**

☐ **Can it be answered in the time you have—and with the resources you have access to?** You might have a fascinating and specific research question, but if you can't feasibly research it in the time you have, it just won't work.

☐ **Is it a question that you really want to find answers to?** The best research grows out of curiosity. No matter how good your research question is, if it isn't backed up by your genuine interest, it won't lead you to rich, interesting research.

Moving from a Research Question to a Proposal

Now that you've got an understanding of how to explore a topic and form working research questions, let's look at some next steps.

While you may not follow every step that Jasmine takes as you work on your own research topic, tracing her process (through p. 309) may give you ideas for how to proceed.

Ultimately, Jasmine moved from a research question to the argument she made in her final paper, which also became her title:

FINAL RESEARCH QUESTION — How can diet help someone with diabetes manage the disease and avoid taking insulin?

Finding Facts About Diabetes

What was Jasmine's process? First, through her early reading, and as a person with a family history of the disease, Jasmine realizes that what interests her most are the dietary concerns of diabetics. With this in mind, she begins to explore a few more sources.

Wikipedia is her starting point. Even though her instructor has cautioned the class against using *Wikipedia* as a source (see our advice about *Wikipedia* on p. 294), Jasmine sees it as a good starting point for general information, and perhaps some leads related to the dietary concerns of diabetics. She begins with the "Diabetes mellitus" page (when she typed in "Diabetes," she was redirected there).

After reading through the overview, Jasmine realizes that she needs information about the differences between type 1 diabetes and type 2 diabetes (which the entry explains is the more common form, and the one that can be treated through diet). She discovers she'll also need to explore diabetes in terms of blood glucose levels, metabolism, body weight, and insulin.

Of particular interest is the "References" section of the "Diabetes mellitus" page, which offers Jasmine a head start on exploring other sources.

▼ **WIKIPEDIA ENTRY**

"Diabetes mellitus." Jasmine reads through this entry with special attention to the "References" section for further resources for information on diet.

Credit: Courtesy of Wikimedia Foundation, Inc. All rights reserved.

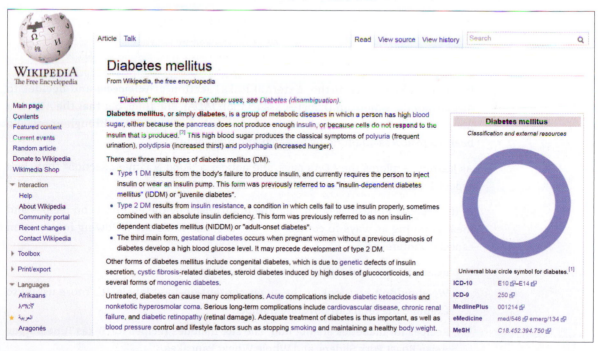

References

1. ^ "Diabetes Blue Circle Symbol" International Diabetes Federation. 17 March 2006.
2. ^ "About diabetes". World Health Organization. Archived from the original on 31 March 2014. Retrieved 4 April 2014.
3. ^ a b c d e f g h i j "Diabetes Fact sheet N°312". *WHO*. October 2013. Archived from the original on 26 August 2013. Retrieved 25 March 2014.
4. ^ Kitabchi, AE; Umpierrez, GE; Miles, JM; Fisher, JN (Jul 2009). "Hyperglycemic crises in adult patients with diabetes." *Diabetes Care*. **32** (7): 1335–43. doi:10.2337/dc09-9032. PMC 2699725. PMID 19564476.
5. ^ a b c d e f Shoback, edited by David G. Gardner, Dolores (2011). "Chapter 17". *Greenspan's basic & clinical endocrinology* (9th ed.). New York: McGraw-Hill Medical. ISBN 0-07-162243-8.
6. ^ *RSSDI textbook of diabetes mellitus*. (Rev. 2nd ed.). New Delhi: Jaypee Brothers Medical Publishers. 2012. p. 235. ISBN 9789350254899.
7. ^ a b c "The top 10 causes of death Fact sheet N°310". *World Health Organization*. Oct 2013.
8. ^ Rippe, edited by Richard S. Irwin, James M. (2010). *Manual of intensive care medicine* (5th ed.). Philadelphia: Wolters Kluwer Health/Lippincott Williams & Wilkins. p. 549. ISBN 9780781799928.
9. ^ Picot, J; Jones, J; Colquitt, JL; Gospodarevskaya, E; Loveman, E; Baxter, L; Clegg, AJ (September 2009). "The clinical effectiveness and cost-effectiveness of bariatric (weight loss) surgery for obesity: a systematic review and economic evaluation". *Health Technology Assessment (Winchester, England)*. **13** (41): 1–190, 215–357, iii–iv. doi:10.3310/hta13410. PMID 19726018.
10. ^ Cash, Jill (2014). *Family Practice Guidelines* (3rd ed.). Springer. p. 396. ISBN 9780826168757.
11. ^ a b "Update 2015". *IDF*. International Diabetes Federation. p. 13. Retrieved 21 Mar 2016.

38. ^ Visser J, Rozing J, Sapone A, Lammers K, Fasano A (2009). "Tight junctions, intestinal permeability, and autoimmunity: celiac disease and type 1 diabetes paradigms." *Ann N Y Acad Sci*. **1165**: 195–205. doi:10.1111/j.1749-6632.2009.04037.x. PMC 2886850. PMID 19538307.
39. ^ a b Risérus U, Willett WC, Hu FB (January 2009). "Dietary fats and prevention of type 2 diabetes". *Progress in Lipid Research*. **48** (1): 44–51. doi:10.1016/j.plipres.2008.10.002. PMC 2654180. PMID 19032965.
40. ^ Malik VS, Popkin BM, Bray GA, Després JP, Hu FB (2010-03-23). "Sugar Sweetened Beverages, Obesity, Type 2 Diabetes and Cardiovascular Disease risk". *Circulation*. **121** (11): 1356–64. doi:10.1161/CIRCULATIONAHA.109.876185. PMC 2862465. PMID 20308626.
41. ^ Malik VS, Popkin BM, Bray GA, Després JP, Willett WC, Hu FB (November 2010). "Sugar-Sweetened Beverages and Risk of Metabolic Syndrome and Type 2 Diabetes: A meta-analysis". *Diabetes Care*. **33** (11): 2477–83. doi:10.2337/dc10-1079. PMC 2963518. PMID 20693348.
42. ^ Hu EA, Pan A, Malik V, Sun Q (2012-03-15). "White rice consumption and risk of type 2 diabetes: meta-analysis and systematic review". *BMJ (Clinical research ed.)*. **344**: e1454. doi:10.1136/bmj.e1454. PMC 3307808. PMID 22422870.
43. ^ Lee IM, Shiroma EJ, Lobelo F, Puska P, Blair SN, Katzmarzyk PT (1 July 2012). "Effect of physical inactivity on major non-communicable diseases worldwide: an analysis of burden of disease and life expectancy". *The Lancet*. **380** (9838): 219–29. doi:10.1016/S0140-6736(12)61031-9. PMC 3645500. PMID 22818936.
44. ^ a b "National Diabetes Clearinghouse (NDIC): National Diabetes Statistics 2011". U.S. Department of Health and Human Services. Retrieved 22 April 2014.

Jasmine looks closely at the "External links" section of *Wikipedia* and decides to investigate the American Diabetes Association (ADA). She finds out that the ADA is a nonprofit group whose purpose is to control diabetes, especially through improving healthcare access and funding research and prevention.

As Jasmine explores the ADA's page, she notices a "Food & Fitness section" that she's especially drawn to because of her interest in nutrition.

In the "Food & Fitness" section, Jasmine is surprised by the emphasis on recipes and meal planning as ways to control the disease. She finds the following information especially interesting:

- Beans, berries, and tomatoes are diabetes "superfoods."
- We shouldn't just look at the sugar content on food labels. It's more useful to examine the total carbohydrate number.
- Recipes for diabetics are not dull. The site includes recipes for Texas Tuna Burger, Asian Roast Pork Sliders, and Whole Wheat Pancakes.

As Jasmine continues to read through the ADA site, she gets more absorbed in the idea that eating specific kinds of foods can assist in managing diabetes. She decides her next step is to find more information on nutrition, maybe even some more recipes designed for diabetics. A hospital or research facility might be another good source, she thinks, and she decides to check out the Mayo Clinic site.

There she finds information on diabetes, along with meal plans and recipes. She gets even more interested in the relationship between diet and diabetes management.

Jasmine notices a recipe for Blackberry Iced Tea. The recipe itself, and the surrounding information, presents Jasmine with a few things to think about. First, the "Dietitian's tip" mentions that most herbal teas are caffeine-free, which makes her wonder about the connection between caffeine and the health of a diabetic. She also notices the use of cinnamon and ginger and wonders how these natural ingredients might benefit a diabetic. In the nutritional analysis of the recipe, Jasmine sees that the drink is low in calories and does not contain any sodium. She wonders if these are important concerns; before she started browsing recipes at the ADA and the Mayo Clinic, Jasmine knew that diabetics should avoid sugar, but she hadn't been taking sodium and calorie content into consideration.

Now that Jasmine has done some exploratory, informational reading, she's ready to see what scholars have to say about managing diabetes through diet. She moves on to look for sources that will offer viewpoints and arguments about diabetes and nutrition.

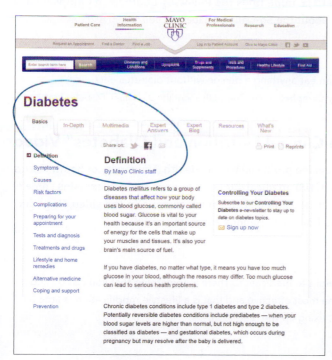

◀ WEB SITE

Mayo Clinic. On their "Diabetes" page, the Mayo Clinic provides a definition of the disease. Jasmine is interested to see how this information compares to that of the ADA.

Credit: Mayo Foundation for Medical Education and Research

Gathering Opinions about Diabetes

Jasmine looks for other sources—including a journal article, a Web site, and a YouTube video—to provide current viewpoints on nutrition as prevention/treatment for diabetes.

1. *Progress in Lipid Research* article

When Jasmine looks at the references on the *Wikipedia* entry, she finds a peer-reviewed journal article entitled "Dietary Fats and Prevention of Type 2 Diabetes." When she goes to the article, she finds in the introduction this statement:

> Dietary composition could play a significant role in improving insulin sensitivity and reducing risk of diabetes and its composition. Risérus, Ulf, Walter C. Willett, and Frank B. Hu. "Dietary Fats and Prevention of Type 2 Diabetes."
>
> *Progress in Lipid Research,* vol. 48, issue 1, 2009, pp. 44–51.

2. The Joslin Diabetes Center

At this site, Jasmine reads the views of Amy Campbell, a Joslin nutritionist and the coauthor of a book titled *16 Myths of a Diabetic Diet.* Campbell states that there is no such thing as a "diabetic diet." Jasmine finds the following quote from Campbell on a Joslin page titled "The Truth about the So-Called 'Diabetes Diet'":

> A person with diabetes can eat anything a person without diabetes eats.
>
> **Amy Campbell,** from "The Truth about the So-Called 'Diabetes Diet'"

3. "Introduction to Clinical Nutrition and Diabetes" Video

On YouTube, Jasmine finds a video produced by USF Health (University of South Florida College of Public Health). In it, USF medical student Candace Haddox explains some of the connections between nutrition and diabetes management. In the video, "Introduction to Clinical Nutrition and Diabetes," Haddox suggests:

> You don't have to go straight to medication. There is something that you can do and it actually happens to be the most effective and that is a lifestyle modification: a little bit of weight loss, you know, fixing up the diet. . . .

CHECKLIST | Narrowing a Topic

As you start your research, consider following these steps:

☐ **Brainstorm topic ideas.**

　☐ Read what others have said.

　☐ Google your topic (but stay focused).

　☐ Discuss what you find with others.

☐ **Start writing informally.**

　☐ Make a list of topics that interest you, then double it, then double it again.

　☐ Freewrite about your topic.

　☐ Sketch out a mind map.

☐ **Do preliminary research.**

　☐ Ask questions of fact and definition so that you will understand the more complex research you do later.

　☐ What arguments have others made about your topic? How do they support their views?

　☐ Note key terms to aid in later research.

☐ **Commit to a topic. Consider these factors:**

　☐ Is the topic compatible with the assignment?

　☐ Have you found an argumentative angle?

　☐ Will you stay interested in this topic?

　☐ Are there enough appropriate sources available for you to research in the time you have?

☐ **Form a research question. Consider these factors:**

　☐ Does your question focus more on stating facts and defining terms? Or are you making an argument? Providing an analysis?

　☐ Is your question open-ended?

　☐ Is your question specific enough? If not, how will you move from a general question to a more specific one?

　☐ Are you truly interested in finding answers to this question?

　☐ What are some challenges you may come up against as you research this question, and how can you deal with these challenges?

Now that she's gathered some facts and arguments about diabetes, Jasmine decides to meet with her instructor to talk about a final research question and plan her research proposal.

Creating a Research Proposal

A research proposal sets forth a writer's rationale for choosing a particular research question. For Jasmine, the proposal gives her an opportunity to fine-tune her research question and her focus. Your instructor may ask you to turn in a proposal or a working bibliography that outlines your sources (pp. 310–312). Or your instructor might simply ask you to think about your research before looking more carefully at sources.

Even if your instructor does not assign a formal research proposal, it can be a great tool for use in planning your project. Following is a research proposal assignment that we give our students.

Research Proposal.
Creating a research proposal is a great way to help you focus and plan. See below for Jasmine's completed assignment.

English 101
Professor Braziller

Research Proposal Assignment: What Is Your Focus?
This proposal will help you solidify your ideas for your semester's research. Your proposal should be approximately two double-spaced pages in MLA manuscript format. Your proposal should include the following:

1. Your research question
2. A working title for your project
3. A summary of your project. Identify your topic and describe what you will be looking at in terms of the topic. Include some key terms and additional questions that will guide your research.
4. A description of your purpose for working on this project. Why did you choose this topic? What do you hope to learn from this project?
5. A discussion of the key challenges you will face or you imagine you will face. What concerns do you have regarding the research/project?

Following is Jasmine's research proposal, in response to the above assignment.

Research Proposal.
Jasmine has explored her topic and gathered facts and opinions from some solid sources, and she is now ready to share her ideas for what she plans to do next.

English 101
Professor Braziller

Research Proposal Assignment: What Is Your Focus?
Jasmine Huerta
English 101
October 6, 2017

Research Proposal
1. Your research question
   How can diet—specifically, monitoring the intake of sugar, calories, and sodium—help someone with diabetes manage the disease and avoid taking insulin?

2. A working title for your project

   The working title for my project is "Living with Diabetes: Diet Is the Answer."

3. A summary of your project. Identify your topic and describe what you will be looking at in terms of the topic. Include some key terms and additional questions that will guide your research.

I plan to research and write about different ways you can control diabetes through nutritional choices. While there are medications used to control the disease, such as insulin, I'm more curious about natural approaches, such as diet. I want my readers to understand that diabetes doesn't have to be a death sentence and that even if you are predisposed to it, there are some simple things you can do to keep it from taking over your life or causing other health issues.

I also think, based on my research, that diet and nutrition might be just as powerful as insulin for some people. I wonder if doctors are too quick to prescribe insulin.

Much of the debate around diabetes has to do with the connection between diabetes and obesity. I wonder to what extent diabetes can be prevented by a healthy diet, one that helps people avoid obesity. Also, are there specific foods that children need to avoid? Are these different from what older people should avoid?

Besides researching different diabetes-related diets, I want to find out how people learn about these diets. Are there specific programs, initiatives, or educational tools used to get this information out to the public? How might schools and doctors share this information?

Following are some **key terms** I've discovered during my preliminary research: *glycemic index, metabolism, blood sugar, hypertension, obesity, glucose monitoring, and insulin.*

Following are some of the **questions that will guide my research:**

- What diets are best for diabetics?
- What foods do diabetics need to avoid?
- Can diet cure diabetes? If so, how?
- Can diet prevent someone from getting diabetes, even if he or she has a family history of the disease? If so, how?
- Can diet prevent someone's diabetes from getting worse? If so, how?
- Can dietary changes prevent or reduce a diabetic's dependence on insulin?

4. **A description of your purpose for working on this project. Why did you choose this topic? What do you hope to learn from this project?**

Diabetes runs in my family, so it's something that is very close to me. My cousin, who is only six years old, has

(Continues on next page)

type 1 diabetes. Just last month, my grandfather, who is somewhat overweight, but definitely not obese, was diagnosed with diabetes. When my mother was pregnant with me, she had gestational diabetes.

I believe I may be predisposed toward the disease, and I want to find out what I can do to avoid it. I also want to help my family by sharing what I learn—especially in terms of natural alternatives rather than traditional medicine.

5. **A discussion of the key challenges you will face or you imagine you will face. What concerns do you have regarding the research/project?**

My biggest challenge so far has been making sense of some terms I've encountered in my research. Some articles go into a lot of detail about the relationship of the glycemic index to insulin levels. Authors of these pieces also use technical terms such as pancreatic *islet cells, resistant starches,* and *macronutrients.*

Another challenge I might face is that my topic may be too narrow. Based on my research so far, it seems that many sources say yes, diet does contribute to diabetes prevention and management. But how might I expand on that? Will I end up just listing foods to eat and not to eat?

I think that trying to figure out if nutritional changes can actually replace insulin as treatment gives my project a good argumentative angle, but I am a little worried that I may end up arguing more strongly against insulin than I really want to.

I am also afraid of getting sidetracked and focusing too much on the obesity problem, especially in regard to children, and losing my focus on diabetes. While obesity is related, I really want to focus on preventing and managing the disease—and not so much on the causes of diabetes. While it's important to understand some of the causes, especially as they relate to nutrition, I'm more interested in prevention and treatment.

Now that Jasmine has written her proposal and submitted it to her instructor, she is ready to begin the next stage of her research.

CHECKLIST | Creating a Research Proposal

What does a good research proposal do?

- ☐ **It assists you in organizing your project,** and includes five major components:
  - ☐ Research question (the main thrust of your research)
  - ☐ Working title
  - ☐ Summary of the project (a sketch of the research you've done, the questions you've raised, and the possible direction you will take, including the potential argument you may make)
  - ☐ Overall purpose (why you want to pursue this topic and project)
  - ☐ Potential challenges

- ☐ **It shows that you have a clear focus for your research.** Your research question and working title are specific, showing your reader the angle you are researching. Throughout the proposal, you include details rather than vague generalities. For example, Jasmine doesn't just write, "I want to learn how people find out about these diets." She adds these details: "Are there specific programs, initiatives, or educational tools. . . ."

- ☐ **It illustrates that you have done some preliminary research.** Your summary includes key terms that you discovered while doing research. While Jasmine might have previously thought of the key terms *obesity* and *insulin*, she probably had not considered such terms as *glycemic index* and *glucose monitoring*.

- ☐ **It gives reasons why you have selected your area of research.** By communicating why you chose your topic, your reader understands your choice, and you see why this research matters to you. By articulating these reasons, you stay more engaged.

- ☐ **It shows that you have considered potential challenges.** Anticipating challenges prepares you for the bumps you might hit during research. Additionally, a good research proposal tells your reader about those challenges so that you might be given assistance. For example, when Jasmine writes that she has encountered technical terms such as *pancreatic islet cells*, her reader might point her to resources where she can get help deciphering these terms.

Organizing Your Sources

ATTENTION, BIBLIOGRAPHERS

The latest MLA guidelines require writers to include source URLs without http:// as is shown in Jasmine's bibliographies. Including URLs (or embedding hyperlinks in your paper) leaves no room for confusion about where you obtained information, and makes it easier and faster for your readers to check your sources. For sources accessed through a database such as JSTOR, provide a DOI, if available, rather than a URL. (See also Chapter 13.)

For online sources that do not include a date, include in your Works Cited list an "Accessed" date, as Jasmine does.

Guided Process | How to Create a Bibliography

Jasmine Huerta (STUDENT), *Diabetes Project: Bibliography*

We highly recommend that you create an annotated working bibliography. A working bibliography is simply a list of the sources you've gathered and plan to refer to. An annotated bibliography is a working bibliography (a list of your sources) that includes your own brief notes about each source. In your annotations, you summarize each source, capturing its essence in a few sentences. If the source is argumentative, you also note the main points of the writer's argument. In addition, note the potential reliability of the source: Is it from a reliable site, news organization, or publication? Was it created by a source you can trust? How well do the source and its author fit with your research? What might the source add? What might be its drawbacks? (For details on evaluating sources, see Chapter 12.)

Here is how Jasmine describes her process:

> I began each entry with a basic summary. In my summaries, I note specific examples, such as unfamiliar terms or important evidence. I've also indicated my evaluation of how dependable each source is. When I quoted exact language from a source, I used quotation marks. I also made connections among my sources.

Huerta 1

Annotated Working Bibliography/Works Cited

Brand-Miller, Jennie, et al. "Low–Glycemic Index Diets in the Management of Diabetes." *Diabetes Care*, vol. 26, no. 8, 2003, pp. 2261–67, care.diabetesjournals.org/content/26/8/2261.long.

The authors explore the controversy about whether a low-glycemic diet actually helps someone manage his or her diabetes. The article presents the research methods used, along with the results. Ultimately, the results of their study show that a low-glycemic diet did help patients manage their diabetes—in contrast to patients whose diets consisted of high-glycemic foods. The article is filled with unfamiliar terms such as "acarbose therapy." At the end is a list of footnotes and references that will be useful as I continue my research. This is a very reliable source because *Diabetes Care* is a peer-reviewed journal; also, the use of documentation reinforces the authors' ethos.

"Glycemic Index and Diabetes." *American Diabetes Association*, www.diabetes.org/food-and-fitness/food/planning-meals/glycemic-index-and-diabetes.html. Accessed 26 Sept. 2017.

The ADA's page on the glycemic index and its relationship to diabetes is an informative summary on the topic. It has three subheads, so readers can immediately find information: "What is the glycemic index?" "What affects the GI of a food?" And, "Is the GI a better tool than carbohydrate counting?" The article discusses how the glycemic index is affected by many things and is not simply determined by a food's type. For example, factors such as length of ripening and cooking time affect a food's glycemic index. The article is written for a general reader, so I found that I could understand all its terms and get a beginning grasp of the glycemic index. This article, too, is very reliable since the American Diabetes Association is a respected and noted organization related to the field.

Risérus, Ulf, Walter C. Willett, and Frank B. Hu. "Dietary Fats and Prevention of Type 2 Diabetes." *Progress in Lipid Research*, vol. 48, issue 1, 2009, pp. 44–51.

This article summarizes the research on the connection between dietary fat and diabetes and then discusses the results of a study of how dietary fats affect insulin resistance. That study found that replacing foods high in saturated fats with foods that do not have hydrogenated or partially hydrogenated fats has a positive effect on diabetes. The article contains a lot of medical jargon and technical terms, but because I am already somewhat familiar with diabetes and the concept of glucose metabolism, I was able to understand most of it. I believe this is the most reliable source I have found so far because it appears in a peer-reviewed scientific journal and the authors have received prestigious grants for their research.

"Simple Steps to Preventing Diabetes." *The Nutrition Source*, Harvard School of Public Health, www.hsph.harvard.edu/nutritionsource/diabetes-prevention/preventing-diabetes-full-story/index.html. Accessed 26 Sept. 2017.

This article focuses on ways to prevent type 2 diabetes. It gives statistics on the number of people affected by the disease and lists illnesses that the disease may cause, such as blindness. Prevention strategies are offered, such as diet and exercise. The writers sum up these strategies by saying, "Stay lean and stay active." This article, like the Brand-Miller piece, also includes a list of references, so I will add that to my potential project sources. Since this piece was published by a Harvard University site, I trust the information presented.

CHECKLIST | Beginning Your Research

As you begin drawing on sources, forming your research questions, drafting your research proposal, and creating a bibliography, ask yourself the following questions.

RHETORICAL SITUATION & CHOICES

☐ **Purpose.** What am I learning as I research? And how can I develop what I'm learning into a solid research question? Does it simply focus on facts (if so, it's not refined enough)? Or is it geared toward analysis and argument (if so, I'm heading in the right direction)?

☐ **Audience.** What expectations will my readers (my instructor, classmates, and any audience beyond) have regarding the quality of my sources? (See Chapter 12 for more on evaluating source quality.) As I gather sources into an annotated bibliography, how can I make certain that my notes on each source show readers its potential usefulness?

☐ **Rhetorical appeals.** How will I know whether to trust an author and source? What about a given author and source gives me confidence, or doubts? What techniques and appeals do authors use that I can adopt for my own purposes? To what degree do they use logos (logic) and pathos (emotion) to reach readers?

☐ **Modes & media.** How do modes and media come into play as I'm reading and choosing sources? Do my sources represent a range of modes and media?

GENRE CONVENTIONS

☐ **Elements of the genre.** Does the author of this source draw on other sources? Does the author document the work of others?

☐ **Style.** When I look at a potential source, how much attention should I pay to the author's style? Are informal first-person pieces the right fit for my topic? Do I need to gather sources written in a variety of styles? To what extent do tone and level of detail contribute to a source's reliability?

☐ **Design.** When I look at a potential source, how important are design considerations?

☐ **Sources.** What documentation style will I use (MLA, APA, *Chicago*, other)?

Organizing Your Sources

Want to experiment? Draft a research proposal. Create an annotated working bibliography.

Find a topic that interests you and work through the points in the Refining Your Research Question checklist until you develop a workable research question. Then do the following:

1. Draft a research proposal for your professor that includes:
   - A working title for your project (you can always change the title later, when you have a better idea of what your finished project will actually cover).
   - A summary of the project, including which aspects of the topic you will research.
   - A list of the keywords you've identified in the research you've done so far.
   - A discussion of your purpose in working on the project. This is where you'll discuss why you are interested in answering the research question.
   - A discussion of the challenges you anticipate facing in your project and strategies you can use to deal with them.
2. Keep an annotated working bibliography of all the sources you use, even ones you think you won't refer to in your final written report. You never know.
3. Annotate three sources you find particularly interesting or thought-provoking. In your annotation, discuss:
   - What the summary is about
   - The argument the source makes
   - How reliable you judge this source to be and why
   - How this source might be used in your project

12

EVALUATING & CHOOSING SOURCES

In Chapter 11, we discussed how to begin your research to explore topics—and ultimately to come up with a research question and proposal. We assume in this chapter that you've done your preliminary research, you have a topic, and you are ready to focus in on an important aspect of that topic. In the following pages, we will discuss research in greater depth, covering how to identify a source that is appropriate, reliable, and useful to you.

Getting Started with Sources

What Are Sources?

The word *source* comes from the Anglo-French word *surse*, which means "to rise or to begin." Think of a source as a starting point. To cook something you've never made before, you might first refer to a cookbook, an online recipe database, or the Food Network for inspiration. To plan a trip, you might begin with sources including maps, photos, and brochures. To begin a research paper, you might refer to Google and online databases such as *EBSCOhost* and *ProQuest*, and consult research librarians and professors to shape and define your ideas and narrow your topic.

In the context of this book, we see everything you read (or view, or listen to, or experience in any way), every text you encounter, every conversation you have, as a potential source for your writing. When you compose—whether in college or on the job—you draw on sources for information and opinions. These sources do more than get you started; they are also the texts that you'll converse with throughout your composing process, from your earliest topic ideas to your final project. (For more on early topic ideas, see Chapter 11. For information on later stages of research and writing, see Chapter 13.)

ATTENTION, RESEARCHERS

What research have you done for other courses? Where did you seek advice? What sources worked especially well? What do you wish you'd done differently or better?

◄ ARTIFACT

Roxy's Gourmet Grilled Cheese is based in Boston. Researching food? A food truck or other eatery can be a valuable source of firsthand information.
Credit: f 1.2/Alamy Stock Photo.

Can a food truck be a source? Sure. Especially if you're researching the trend of food trucks, or the growing number of people who identify themselves as "foodies." Maybe you're interested in comparing the old-time ice-cream truck to the phenomenon of the food truck. Depending on your argument, you might use the truck as a starting point for your research, talking with its chef or operator to learn more about the business: its operation, clientele, and profitability. Or maybe about the food itself: the source of its ingredients and its nutritional value. (See roxysgrilledcheese.com.)

Where Do I Find Sources?

Sources are everywhere. Imagine that a friend tells you about an upcoming debate about women's healthcare on campus; because she has provided you with information, your friend is a source. Let's say you become interested in the debate and decide to search your online campus newspaper for articles and editorials on the topic. Your campus paper and the materials it contains are sources. From there, you could learn

▶ **STUDENT NEWSPAPER: EDITORIAL PAGE**

Accent: The Student Voice of Austin Community College.

Here a student offers a commentary on women's healthcare in the state of Texas, which has some of the most restrictive reproductive health policies in the country. Your own campus publication may provide an excellent source for ideas, facts, and opinions on your topic.

Credit: The Accent

more by talking to a member of the campus health center staff, or a local activist organization supporting women's healthcare. The people you talk with and the discussions you have with them are sources.

What Can Sources Do for Me?

For one thing, they help you make decisions. You use sources all the time—not only to inform your school and work projects, but to aid you in making informed choices. For example, you want to choose a movie to see this weekend. You'd probably consult a variety of sources: Maybe you'd read film reviews, watch current movie trailers, or talk with a film-buff friend. Or imagine you're shopping for a car. You would probably do some research; you would probably visit some manufacturers' sites, talk to your mechanic and other car owners, or visit dealerships for test drives. You might check out the advice at Cars.com.

Now that you have a sense of what sources are, the rest of this chapter will show you how to:

- Locate and preview sources
- Identify sources in terms of general versus specialized academic
- Read sources critically, with attention to author, purpose, audience, and other rhetorical concerns
- Evaluate what sources will be best for your own research and writing

What's a General Source?
What's a Specialized Academic Source?

When you look at a source, think about who created that text, and for what purpose and for what audience. That will guide you as to when and how to use that source.

General Sources General sources are aimed at a general audience; that is, they're written by knowledgeable authors and are meant to be understood by nonexperts. For example, a journalist who regularly covers local politics for your newspaper might write a piece to inform readers about a scandal at city hall. To get the gist of the story, you don't have to know anything about local politics or politicians. General sources help you:

- Begin to understand the overall topic
- Begin to see what the subtopics are
- Discover keywords
- Find the different conversations that are related to the topic
- Begin to explore your research questions

An example of a general source is "The Truth about Beauty," an article written by Amy Alkon, a journalist and writer for the magazine *Psychology Today*. Alkon's purpose is to persuade her audience, primarily middle-aged women, about how men define beauty. Her ultimate goal in the article is to empower women so that they can understand their choices and the effects of their choices when it comes to beauty and landing a man.

Specialized Academic Sources These sources are aimed at (you guessed it!) specialized academic readers. They are usually written by scholars and other experts—professors, scientists, doctors, and researchers—who have studied the subject extensively. An example of a specialized academic source is an article from *JAMA* (*The Journal of the American Medical Association*) on a new clinical trial and its success. Readers of such an article would include doctors interested in new treatments that they can incorporate in their own practice. Although academic articles are aimed at people with expertise on a given subject, that doesn't mean you should avoid these sources. They may include information that you can use—and may become easier to understand as you deepen your research and gain an understanding of your topic (and associated terms and vocabulary). You might turn to these sources once you've built a foundation of understanding with your general sources. Specialized academic sources help you:

- Delve into a topic in depth
- See how experts view the subject
- Access the latest research in the field
- Access critiques of research in the field
- Find other academic sources through Works Cited lists and bibliographies

An example of a specialized academic article is a piece on self-esteem development by Ruth Yasemin Erol and Ulrich Orth (see below), which appeared in the American Psychological Association's publication, the *Journal of Personality and Social Psychology*. In the article, the authors examine the ways that early self-esteem affects health and happiness in later life. The primary audience for this piece consists of psychology and sociology scholars interested in social behavior.

How Do I Preview a Source Critically?

Previewing your sources before committing to them is worth the effort. Ask yourself the following questions to identify what you might expect from a particular source, and whether you will want to use it in your research.

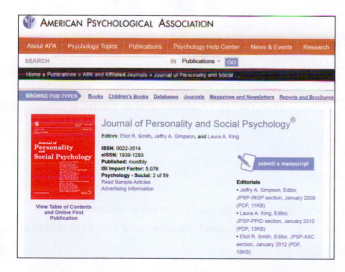

▲ **WEB SITE & ARTICLE: SPECIALIZED ACADEMIC SOURCE** ▶

American Psychological Association. This article from the *Journal of Personality and Social Psychology* is aimed at an audience of experts.

1. What is the overall rhetorical situation?

That is, what is the context of the source? Who wrote this piece, why, for whom, and how? And how does this impact the value of this text as a potential source?

Following is an example that we'll refer to throughout this section. It's an editorial published at Bloomberg.com.

► **EDITORIAL, EXCERPTED**

Bloomberg.com. An opinion piece by the editorial board of Bloomberg has a specific purpose and is written for a specific audience. These factors are important to consider when you are choosing sources.

Illustration by Bloomberg View

Western U.S. Will Keep Burning Unless Fire Policy Changes

By **the Editors** | Jul 16, 2012 6:30 PM ET

💬 22 COMMENTS ⊕ QUEUE

It is only mid-July, and Colorado has already had its most destructive wildfire in history -- some 350 houses in and near Colorado Springs burned, causing more than $110 million in damage.

This broke the previous state record, which was set earlier this summer in a fire farther up the Front Range of the Rockies. In May and June, New Mexico suffered its most devastating blaze ever -- worse than the one last year that threatened Los Alamos.

This is a scary trend.

In the 1960s, Colorado had about 460 fires a year that burned an average of 8,000 acres, according to a report compiled from state forest service records. In the past 10 years, the state averaged about 2,500 fires a year that consumed about 100,000 acres.

Climate change plays a role. Higher average temperatures mean the snowpack recedes earlier, and the fire season is extended in some places by almost two months. A study in Montana found that a rise of one degree in summer temperatures doubles costs of protecting a home against fire.

Yet hand-wringing about global climate patterns shouldn't distract us from dealing with the primary causes of the danger: human development and forest policy.

As more people moved to the so-called Wildland Urban Interface, where houses and forests intersect, the national policy of suppressing fires rather than letting them burn became more entrenched. That has meant fewer natural fires, which burn the underbrush but allow the mature trees to survive and propagate. In recent decades, fuel on the ground has built up, causing today's fires to burn more intensely, leaving a moonscape of ash.

Life and property have been lost in the fires, at unfathomable cost. But this can't be allowed to obscure the burden borne by U.S. taxpayers -- more than $3 billion annually. About half of the Forest Service's entire budget goes into fighting wildfires, up from 13 percent in 1995.

What's the Rhetorical Situation?

Bloomberg Editors, "Western U.S. Will Keep Burning Unless Fire Policy Changes"

To get a sense of the rhetorical situation of this Bloomberg editorial—or any potential source—ask and answer some basic questions:

- **Who wrote this piece?** The editorial board at Bloomberg, an influential news organization focused on business and finance and with clout in both of these areas.
- **Why?** The Bloomberg editors wanted to address the disastrous Colorado fires of the summer of 2012. Their purpose was to persuade readers that the government could adopt a course of action that could prevent future fires—and also save taxpayers money.
- **For whom?** Bloomberg's audience includes general readers with Internet access interested in business news and a "business take" on issues—both in Colorado and across the country—as well as business and government leaders who could do something about the problem.
- **How?** The editors collaborated to come up with their collective view on government policies regarding fires in the Rockies. They published their editorial in the opinion section of their Web site. The editorial includes hyperlinks to related materials, and there are options for commenting and linking to social networking.

As you look at sources, think about the rhetorical context of each by paying attention to the authors and their purposes, their target audiences and how they appeal to them, and the modes and media that they use for delivering their messages.

Purpose   First, ask yourself: Who is the author of this piece? What are his or her reasons for writing? What assumptions does the author make? How does all of this fit in with what I'm looking for? Keep in mind:

- *What is the author's background?* This information will give you a sense of the author's credibility (ethos) and his or her perspective on the topic at hand. Begin by reading any biographical information provided and see if there are links to any other writing the author has done on this topic. The authors of the editorial about fire policy (p. 321) are the members of Bloomberg's editorial board. Bloomberg is a well-respected news group focused on money and the marketplace, part of what makes this source a trustworthy one.

- *Is the author seeking to persuade?* Report information? Tell a story? All of the above? How does this fit with the type of information you're looking for? Begin by examining the title and then skim the piece with a critical eye.

- *What are the author's biases?* While you're skimming, keep an eye out for assumptions built into the text. The Bloomberg editorial represents the viewpoints of editors whose priorities are business growth and other financial concerns rather than the environment and other aspects of fire policy.

Audience   Ask yourself: Where did I find this text? Was it published in a popular magazine? A specialized academic journal? At a particular Web site? If so, who is the main audience for that magazine, journal, or Web site?

- *Am I part of the author's primary audience?* Based on the text's origin and a quick read of its contents, is the author aiming at a general readership or a narrower, more specialized audience? Evaluate the piece in terms of whether you find it readable, challenging, or perhaps oversimplified or condescending. Ask yourself: How much subject knowledge does the author assume readers have? As for the editors at Bloomberg (p. 321), they write for businesspeople, not environmentalists, so their take on fire policy is likely going to mesh better with the concerns of the business community than those of tree huggers.

Rhetorical appeals   In general, what strategies does the author use to build his or her case and connect with readers?

- *Does the author use ethos, logos, and pathos to connect with readers?* How much authority does the author convey in the writing? Is the writing logical? To what extent does it appeal to your emotions? For example, you might realize as you analyze an author's appeal to pathos that his or her argument is not logical. At that point (unless you want a piece that is not logical, perhaps so you can critique it), you might decide not to use the source. In the case of the Bloomberg editorial, the numerical data particularly appeals to their business and government audience.

- *Does the author use humor?* Again, examine the title and skim the composition. If the author uses humor, does it work to strengthen the piece? How well does a humorous piece fit in with your topic and research?

Modes & media

- *Modes* In what mode was the source produced—written, audio, video, or something else? How does the composer's choice of mode contribute to the composition? What assumptions do you have about the mode? For example, it's fair to assume that hearing an audio essay, which features the composer's voice, is a more intimate experience than reading an article online. By considering mode you're more aware of how the author appeals to his or her audience.

- *Media* In what medium is the source delivered—print, digital, or something else? What does the composer's choice of medium tell you about his or her assumptions about the audience? For example, digital sources are used primarily by audiences with access to computers or smartphones. Think, too, about the relationship between medium and the currency of information. A composer who publishes online can make revisions to the piece, adding links to newer articles on the topic at hand.

In Boise, Housing Struggles to Emerge From Its Malaise

1 of 8 ◄ BACK   NEXT ►

LightBox   LIFE   Pictures of the Week   TIME Covers

DANNY WILCOX FRAZIER / REDUX

◄ BACK   NEXT ►

Nice House, But...
Vinny and Karla Trovato, along with their kids, Steven and Ashley enjoy their new home, in a subdivision north of Boise, but they are surrounded by empty lots and unsold homes.

• Why There's Hope About Housing

ATTENTION, RESEARCHERS

Do you think that some modes are more reliable than others? For example, do you assume that printed sources are more authoritative than stories you hear on the radio? Why or why not?

▶ **PHOTO ESSAY**

Time. This photo essay, "In Boise, Housing Struggles to Emerge from Its Malaise," includes photos by Danny Wilcox Frazier of Redux, and captions by *Time* editors. As you consider sources, think about the genre of those sources (see the box on page 321).
Credit: Danny Wilcox Frazier/ Redux

2. What is the genre of the piece?

What are you looking at? What kind of composition is it? What qualities is this genre known for? What makes this text a potentially workable source, or not?

Following is an example that we'll refer to throughout this section. It's a photo essay published at *Time* magazine's Web site. The photos are by Danny Wilcox Frazier of Redux photography, and the text was written by editors at *Time*.

What's the Genre?

***Time* and Danny Wilcox Frazier/Redux, "In Boise, Housing Struggles to Emerge from Its Malaise"**

When you look at a potential source, you want to understand its rhetorical situation (see the Bloomberg editorial on p. 320)—its authorship, purpose, audience, etc.

You also want a sense of the genre that the composer chose—will it work for you?—as well as the style, design, and other sources drawn on. Ask and answer the following questions:

- **What am I looking at?** The image on the facing page is from a photo essay published online, created by *Time* editors and a photographer.

- **What qualities is this genre known for?** Photo essayists combine images and words to tell a story and/or to make an argument. Here, the editors at *Time* show the impact of an economic crisis—and hoped-for recovery—on a community. The title, "In Boise, Housing Struggles to Emerge from Its Malaise," suggests the argument being made.

- **What makes this text a potentially workable source, or not?** The authorship of this photo essay and its publication in a respected magazine make it a promising source. Also promising is that the journalists who composed the piece conducted interviews with residents. The genre makes it useful to a researcher looking for a persuasive visual/textual argument-based on experience.

Elements of the genre   Ask yourself: What do I know about the genre? What can I expect or assume about it? Keep in mind:

- *What is the scope of the information?* Different genres present different amounts and degrees of information: An encyclopedia entry provides an overview of information, while a peer-reviewed journal article provides in-depth treatment.

- *How reliable is the information?* Some genres are known for their reliability and objectivity, others less so. For example, in terms of factual accuracy, a peer-reviewed journal article is probably more reliable than a political ad. (See also Chapter 1, "Rhetorical Situations and Choices.")

- *What is the connection between genre and purpose?* Remember we talked in Chapter 2 about how genre is a social response to a rhetorical situation? For example, the authors of the photo essay (see p. 323) chose that genre for a reason. The *Time* editors and photographer Danny Wilcox Frazier, who collaborated on the photo essay, chose to focus on the human side of the housing crisis in Boise. Consider how differently the business-oriented Bloomberg editorial board might have dealt with the same issue, perhaps writing an opinion piece on the financial aspects of the crisis rather than on how people deal with losing their homes.

Style When evaluating a source, pay attention to the style of the author. Ask yourself:

- *How does the author use language?* As you skim, pay attention to the writer's word choice and vocabulary level. To what extent do they contribute to (or undermine) the author's ethos? How formal or informal is the language? Does the writer use slang? If so, keep in mind that slang is not an indicator of unreliability, just as formal language is not an indicator of reliability.

- *What is the author's tone? How does he or she use voice?* Describe the author's presence in the text. How does he or she use stylistic techniques to create a memorable voice and tone? For any source, pay attention to tone—some authors may be off-putting, while an author with an engaging voice and tone might get you to read a piece that you weren't initially sure about.

- *How well does the author's style work with the chosen genre?* Think of the author's style in the context of the genre the author composed in. For example, if the author has written an editorial, ask yourself: Is the style generally in keeping with other editorials? For example, is it direct and persuasive?

- *What special techniques does the author use? How much detail does he or she provide?* Does the author use literary techniques, such as dialogue, setting, and metaphor? How do these techniques get and keep your attention? And how detailed does the author get? Paying attention to these factors will assist you in deciding whether to commit to the source; in the best cases, other authors provide examples of techniques that you can adapt in your own writing. Consider the *Time*/Frazier photo essay as a source (p. 323). The editors don't go into much detail in the textual part of the essay, but the photos they chose highlight the personal connections people have with their homes.

Design All compositions—from the lowliest e-mail to the biggest-budget film—are designed. Ask yourself: Is the source I'm looking at presented in a way that draws me in?

- *How are text and images laid out?* How does the author use spatial arrangement to guide your reading? How does formatting, such as use of capital letters, bold, or special fonts, direct your attention or shape your understanding of the source's organization? Is color used to highlight information? As with style, you might notice how an author uses design elements to communicate with a reader and decide to try some of the same techniques yourself. Designs that you find annoying or gimmicky may turn you off to a source, and the opposite may happen too: Clever design that resonates with you can draw you in.

- *How are sound and other nontext/nonimage elements arranged?* How does the composer use sound to guide your listening? How does the composer use sound to evoke emotion? How do these elements direct your attention toward or away from aspects of the piece? Note, for example, how in the *Time*/Frazier photo essay (p. 323), the photos stand out against the black background.

ATTENTION, RESEARCHERS

What is the price of drawing on unreliable sources? Have you ever lost faith in an author because of the sources he or she used? What were the sources? What made them seem unreliable?

Sources   When you preview a text, learn what you can about its author's research methods, and therefore the text's validity. Ask yourself:

- *How did the author gather and analyze data?* For example, if you're looking at an article that draws its data from surveys of large groups, you expect to encounter a lot of statistics and charts that compile the data. You'd also hope that the data is dependable. For example, the *Time* editors who created the photo essay on the housing situation in Idaho visited the location and conducted interviews, gathering information firsthand.

- *What types of sources did the author draw on?* Pay attention to where the author obtained the information on which the piece is based. Also, keep in mind the type of information you're looking for. For example, if you want facts on a specific topic and the source you're looking at is anecdotal or only relies on the author's experiences rather than on scientific research, you might decide the source won't be of use to you after all.

- *Did the author document sources?* Are sources listed in a bibliography or Works Cited list? Within the text, are specific details about sources given, such as page numbers and dates of publication for written sources? For example, in the *Time*/Frazier photo essay (p. 323), the writers refer to the names of the homeowners in the text of the piece.

- *Did the author not conduct research?* Not all authors conduct outside research, especially when they compose in particular genres such as the memoir. In the case of the memoir, the source that informs the piece is the author himself or herself—it's based on his or her own experiences.

Previewing a Source

▲ STUDENT AUTHOR
Emily Kahn.
Credit: megamix/Getty Images

Emily Kahn | Women in Comic Books Project

Let's follow a student, Emily Kahn, as she previews a possible source. Emily is interested in comics and graphic novels, and she plans to write an academic argument about the portrayal of women in these works. She locates a promising-looking article on the topic of women in graphic works in *Lightspeed: Science Fiction & Fantasy*, a weekly online magazine for fans of sci-fi and fantasy literature. The article, "The Objectification of Women in Comic Books," is by a writer named Jehanzeb.

Before Emily reads the article in depth or adds it to her working bibliography, she will preview it. This means she'll dig around to better understand the context of the article.

Keeping in mind the factors outlined above, Emily will set out to learn basic information about the publisher and author of the article—in addition to the author's purpose, audience, choice of genre, and more.

1. What Is *Lightspeed* Magazine?

Emily first considers who publishes the magazine in which the article appears. She asks herself:

- What type of magazine is this?
- Who publishes it?
- What is the quality of the work presented there?
- Who is the main audience?
- Are the articles in the magazine peer-reviewed? Scholarly?

On the "About" page, she reads a note from the publisher (see below).

For Emily, the facts that *Lightspeed* has been nominated for a number of awards and that the editor seems to be knowledgeable are important selling points. While at first glance *Lightspeed* might look like a fanzine, she sees when she browses the contents that the nonfiction pieces published there seem sophisticated in terms of subject matter, cultural analysis, and the use of sources and Works Cited lists. *Lightspeed* may be more scholarly than she'd originally thought, though it's very readable for a general audience. She's not sure what to assume about it, so she reads on.

ABOUT

Lightspeed is an online science fiction and fantasy magazine. In its pages, you will find science fiction: from near-future, sociological soft SF, to far-future, star-spanning hard SF—and fantasy: from epic fantasy, sword-and-sorcery, and contemporary urban tales, to magical realism, science-fantasy, and folktales. No subject is off-limits, and we encourage our writers to take chances with their fiction and push the envelope.

Lightspeed was a finalist for the 2011 & 2012 Hugo Awards, and stories from *Lightspeed* have been nominated for the Hugo Award, the Nebula Award, and the Theodore Sturgeon Award.

Edited by bestselling anthologist John Joseph Adams, every month *Lightspeed* brings you a mix of originals and reprints, and featuring a variety of authors—from the bestsellers and award-winners you already know to the best new voices you haven't heard of yet. When you read *Lightspeed*, it is our hope that you'll see where science fiction and fantasy comes from, where it is now, and where it's going.

▲ **MAGAZINE**

Lightspeed.

"About" page. Emily begins her initial research, locating an article, "The Objectification of Women in Comic Books," in an online magazine for sci-fi fans, titled *Lightspeed*. She goes to the "About" page to learn more about the publication and the people behind it.

ATTENTION, RESEARCHERS

A word about previewing. When you find a source, do basic detective work before you commit to it. Start by getting to know its publisher and author. Ask yourself:

1. Where did the piece appear? Was it published by a scholarly journal? A well-known news outlet? An obscure but solid-looking blog? To what extent does the publisher have a specific point of view or agenda (e.g., *The Weekly Standard* states that it is a conservative publication)? How will this perspective fit in (or compare/contrast) with my project?
2. Who is the author? Someone I've heard of? Someone I don't know, but who seems to be a good writer?

2. Who Are the Editors & Staff Members at *Lightspeed* Magazine?

Emily scrolls down to the masthead to find out more about the magazine's editorial staff.

She asks herself:

- What can I learn about who runs the magazine?
- Who is the publisher or main editor? What are his or her credentials? Is this an independent company, or is a parent company in charge?
- Who are the other editors and regular contributors to the magazine? What else have they written, and for what publications?
- Are the editors and contributors scholars? Critics? Fans of the genres of science and fantasy fiction? Authors themselves?

Emily is curious about the publisher and editor-in-chief, John Joseph Adams, and sees that he has won several awards as an anthologist and also is affiliated with Wired.com. She notices that *Lightspeed*'s monthly sponsor is Orbit Books, an imprint of Hachette, which publishes books by authors she has read, so that adds to the magazine's credibility. Reading down the masthead, she sees that many editors are published authors themselves who also write critical articles for other magazines devoted to fantasy, science fiction, horror, culture, and comics. Emily is pleasantly surprised that the editors of *Lightspeed* are more than enthusiastic consumers of science fiction and fantasy: They are experts as well. From the information Emily reads on the "About," "Our Staff," and "Our Sponsor" pages, she finds that *Lightspeed* magazine may be an appropriate source for her paper.

3. Who Is Jehanzeb, the Author of the Article?

Emily sees that *Lightspeed* attributes the article to a writer named Jehanzeb, for whom no last name is given. She asks herself:

- How can I discover the last name of the author, so that I can learn more about this writer?
- Is there a biography somewhere? Maybe a link to a blog or personal Web site?
- What else has this author written—whether on this topic or others? And where has his or her work been published?
- How much credibility does the author convey?

Emily first needs to discover Jehanzeb's full name. She notices a brief biography at the end of the article, which links to Jehanzeb's blog, where the article was first published. She also sees that *Lightspeed* has published three other articles by Jehanzeb on the topic of women in comics. To learn more, Emily follows the link to Jehanzeb's *Broken Mystic* blog, where he posts poems, personal writing, and articles. There she links to a second blog, called *Muslim Reverie*, where Jehanzeb posts about "politics, current events, feminism, and media literacy." Here Emily discovers that his last name is Dar. She notices e-mail links at both blogs, so she can contact him directly. She thinks she might do that if she decides to use his article as a source in her research.

Jehanzeb is a film student who writes about Islam, Feminism, Politics, and Media. This piece was originally published on his blog.

Tagged as: comics

Related Posts

- ○ A Critique of Muslim Women in Comics -- AK Comics' Jalia and Aya
- ○ A Critique of Muslim Women in Comics -- The 99
- ○ Female, Muslim, and Mutant

Now that Emily knows Jehanzeb's full name, she does a quick Google search to learn more about him. She wonders: Has Jehanzeb Dar published elsewhere—besides *Lightspeed* magazine and his blog? To what extent is he considered an expert on comics? A critic? She's interested to discover that Dar was interviewed by the Associated Press about the film *Prince of Persia*.

By tracking down information through the bio that appeared with the article, through Dar's blogs, and through a Google search, Emily has turned up some rich information. As her mental picture of Dar gets clearer—as a writer, and as a thinker and critic who takes part in larger, public conversations about the presentation of race in popular culture— she becomes more interested in his article on women in comics as a source for her paper.

4. What Type of Article Is This? Will It Work for My Topic?

Now that Emily has a better sense of *Lightspeed* magazine and the writer Jehanzeb Dar, she's ready to do a closer reading of the article itself. Below is Dar's article, along with Emily's notes in the margins—you can see how she identifies her assumptions and also begins to read the piece closely and critically. At this point, she is still deciding on whether to use this source. Once she's done some annotating, she's ready to make her final call.

Guided Process | How to Preview a Source

Emily Kahn (STUDENT), *Women in Comic Books Project: Previewing Jehanzeb Dar*

As she reads, Emily asks herself the following questions:

- What is Dar's main purpose? And how does this fit in with my research questions?
- Who is his primary audience? Am I part of it? How does he connect with readers through rhetorical appeals?
- What genre is this piece? Based on what I know about the genre, what assumptions can I make?

- What is Dar's writing style? How do his techniques, voice, and tone affect me as a reader? How much detail does he use?
- Does the design of the article support what Dar seeks to achieve?
- What sources does he draw on? Does he document them? What types of sources are they—and how reliable are they?

Emily's notes on Dar's essay

What genre is this?
Definitely an article/essay. The title indicates the author is making an argument about sexism in comics. I know it's a researched argument because there is a references/Works Cited page at the end.

What can I assume about this genre?
I assume Dar will make claims (and maybe counterarguments) and support them with evidence from outside sources.

What is the author's style?
His style is serious and scholarly, but the tone is kind of entertaining—he uses terms such as "kick-butt." He also uses lots of detail.

How does the author use design?
I like the subheadings. They divide the article into sections on different portrayals of women in comics.

How does the author work with sources?
He cites sources in the text and in a References list. Looks like APA format.

Sources look to be from experts on comics and feminist and cultural critics. He also draws on comics themselves.

Jehanzeb,
The Objectification of Women in Comic Books

During World War II, a handsome American intelligence officer, Colonel Steve Trevor, crash-lands his plane on a mysterious island inhabited by the beautiful Amazons of Greek mythology. This new world is known as "Paradise Island" (what else would an island populated by Amazonian women be called, right?) and changes the course of human destiny. A princess by the name of Diana attends Trevor's wounds and subsequently falls in love with him. When she learns about the U.S. war against the Nazis, she dons a costume of America's red, white, and blue, and departs for the "Man's World." She becomes Wonder Woman—"beautiful as Aphrodite, wise as Athena, stronger than Hercules, and swifter than Mercury." She can fly like Superman and hurl heavy objects like the Hulk, and if you refuse to tell her the truth, she'll crack out her golden lasso and tie you up (especially if you're a heterosexual man).

At first glance, she may look like an empowered, kick-butt, feminist superheroine amidst a realm dominated by white heterosexual male superheroes. But is Wonder Woman really empowered? Is she really a symbol of feminism in comic books? Is her message really all about defending sisterhood, freedom, and democracy?

A historical overview is necessary to examine the role women have played in mainstream comic books as well as how intersecting dynamics of race and gender have impacted the way women are presented.

1. The Damsel in Distress
Originally, the only women that appeared in mainstream American comic books were white women, though they played very small roles. In the late 1930s, superpowered heroes like Superman and Captain Marvel dominated the stage while women scarcely had any presence. If women made

appearances, they were depicted as dependent and "damsels in distress"—victims (typically of male violence) needing to be rescued by the male protagonist (who typically exerts more violence over the male villain). The "damsel in distress" is not only a prize that needs to be won by either the male villain or hero, but also an object that measures the masculinity of the male characters. For example, Superman's "masculinity is defined by what it is not, namely 'feminine,' and by all its associated traits—hard *not* soft, strong *not* weak, reserved *not* emotional, active *not* passive" (Brown, 2001, p. 168). The manner in which women service masculinity is apparent in the first issue of *Superman*, where news reporter and future love interest Lois Lane is kidnapped by criminals and eventually saved by Superman. A romantic relationship is not developed between the two characters and nothing is learned about who Lois is—she is only a weak "feminine" body reinforcing Superman's strong "masculinity" and "savior" role. Superman simply rescues her from villains, flies her to safety, and then flies away. Such one-dimensional portrayals were evident in other ways women were depicted: as the "girl-Friday . . . seductive vamp, or perhaps, the long-suffering girlfriend" (Lavin, 1998, p. 93). The stereotypical gender roles were quite obvious: men alone are capable of succeeding independently and being courageous, while women are dependent and weak beauties relegated to the background. These early attitudes toward women in comic books are quite suggestive of common sexist-defined role patterns where women are thought to be less intelligent than men and only have a place in the house as a caretaker and/or source of emotional support. As New York cartoonist Jules Feiffer states, "The ideal of masculine strength, whether Gary Cooper's, Lil Abner's, or Superman's, was for one to be so virile and handsome, to be in such a position of strength, that he need never go near girls. Except to help them" (1965).

2. Women as Sex Objects

The role of women changed dramatically during World War II when patriotic characters emerged and surprisingly attracted the interest of new readers, who were both men and women. Arguably, the most noteworthy female character was Wonder Woman. As mentioned above, she possesses enormous super-human strength, has the ability to fly, and can overcome any

(Continues on next page)

Emily's notes on Dar's essay

Who is the author?
Dar is a writer concerned with comics and critical of the portrayal of women in them. He also writes about issues related to race and popular culture.

What is the author's purpose?
The title says to me that Dar wants to persuade readers that women are objectified in comic books. As I read further, I see that he argues that even strong female characters are created to be alluring.

obstacle that comes her way. Even more interesting is how her love interest, Colonel Trevor, is constantly being rescued by her, as if he is the male version of the aforementioned Lois Lane. Rather than the male rescuing the female in every episode, it is reversed in the Wonder Woman comics. In the following years, other strong superheroine characters surfaced like Miss America—the female version of Captain America—Mary Marvel, Supergirl, She-Hulk, and many others. They carried the symbolic message that "girls could do anything boys could do, and often better, especially if they stuck together" (Robbins, 2002).

However, despite these new portrayals of strong and powerful female characters like Wonder Woman, something else was occurring: they were being depicted as sex objects. As stated by Michael Lavin: "Powerful super-heroines like DC's Wonder Woman or Marvel's She-Hulk may easily overcome the most overwhelming threats and obstacles, but they are invariably depicted as alluring objects of desire, wearing the scantiest of costumes." The images of women with large bust sizes, hourglass figures, bare legs, and half-naked appearances became enormously popular after the success of Wonder Woman. Believe it or not, comic books were filled with so many sexual images of women that they were known as "headlight comic books" (crudely referring to the female anatomy). Comic book historian Ron Goulart writes: "In the days before the advent of *Playboy* and *Penthouse*, comic books offered one way to girl watch" (quoted in Lavin, p. 93). A prime example of "headlight comics" was in Bill Ward's *Torchy*, a series that ran from 1946 to 1950. The comic books contained dull and uninteresting storylines where the scriptwriters were merely making an excuse to draw Torchy as a tall, bare-legged blonde, who walked around in her underwear.

The escalating amount of sex and violence in comic books eventually led to complaints, particularly by psychologist Fredric Wertham who held a symposium in 1948 on the "Psychopathology of Comic Books." He also wrote a book, *Seduction of the Innocent,* which correlated a connection between "juvenile delinquency and comic book reading" (Lavin, 1998, p. 95). As a result, the Comics Code Authority established a written code that set the guidelines for comic book publishing. During this time, the comic book industry took a remarkable new turn where the constant objectification of women was seized. The brief period where comic books were geared more toward teenage girls wouldn't last long, as superheroes reemerged in the late 1960s, along with their scantily clad superheroines and damsels in distress. Women were drawn in the same stereotypical fashion, but this time, the artists took it one step further on the skimpy scale. Consider the White Queen, a female villain who appeared in the *X-Men* comics during the 1980s. She was "the stuff of male sexual fantasy: a push-up bustier, panties, and high-heel boots, all in white" (Lavin, 1998, p. 94).

Today, women are becoming more and more sexualized. As described by Jones and Jacobs (1995, p. 341):

> Females, perpetually bending over, arching their backs, and heaving their anti-gravity breasts into readers' faces, defied all laws of physics . . . the Victoria's Secret catalogue became the Bible of every super-hero artist, an endless source of stilted poses ripe for swiping by boys who wanted their fantasies of women far removed from any human reality.

One study conducted by Jessica H. Zellers shows an examination of how women are depicted in eighteen comic books. She finds that "of the suggestively clad, partially clad, or naked individuals . . . about three times as many were women (296) than men (107)." From the comic book sample where there were 1,768 male characters and 786 female characters, only 6 percent of all males were suggestively clad, partially clad, or naked; while of all the females, 38 percent were suggestively clad, partially clad, or naked. Additionally, of all males, 2 percent were naked, while of all females, 24 percent were naked. Zellers writes: "It is incredible that almost one out of every four females was, at some point, depicted in the nude" (2005, p. 34). . . .

References

Baughman, L. (1990). A psychoanalytic reading of a female comic book hero: Elektra: Assassin. Women and Language, 13.

Brown, J. A. (2001). Black superheroes, Milestone comics, and their fans. Jackson: University Press of Mississippi.

Brown, J. A. (2011). Dangerous curves: Action heroines, gender, fetishism, and popular culture. Jackson: University Press of Mississippi.

Donald, A., et al. (2003, September 9). The panel: "Why don't 'black books' sell?" Silver Bullet Comic Books. Retrieved from http://www.silverbulletcomicbooks.com/panel/1063121223602.htm. . . ."

Emily's notes on Dar's essay

How do the mode & medium impact readers?
The article appears online, so it probably has a wider potential audience than a print article would. This allows for hyperlinks to sources and other pages. Also, readers can add comments and interact with the author and each other.

5. Should I Add This Source to My Working Bibliography?

Emily is now satisfied that the author of the article is knowledgeable and that the article itself is interesting, readable, and potentially quite useful for her research project. She decides to add it to her working bibliography. She will return to the piece again later. Emily's next step is to create a research plan. (See pp. 305–9 for information on research plans.)

Evaluating a Source

Evaluating a source is much like previewing a source (see pp. 325–28), only with more depth and attention to specifics. Once you've decided that a source is a potential "keeper," it's time to do a closer reading of it and decide whether it fits in with your research plan. Your main questions include:

- Is this a trustworthy source—do the author and publication convey an ethos of credibility?
- Will it work for my assignment—and further my purpose?

Calvin Sweet | Hurricane Katrina Project

In the following pages, we will follow student Calvin Sweet as he looks at three different sources related to his topic, Hurricane Katrina. These sources, which appear on pages 340–347, are:

- **Madison Gray,** "The Press, Race and Katrina," an argument/editorial from *Time* magazine online.
- **Lincoln Shlensky,** "Hurricane Katrina, Race and Class: Part I," an argument/editorial from Shlensky's blog, titled *Aulula.*
- **Ed Gordon and Allison Keyes,** "Katrina Coverage Exposes Race, Class Fault Lines," a news report with analysis from National Public Radio (NPR), *News & Notes* program.

You'll read these sources along with Calvin in the next few pages. For now, here is information on each author and the context in which his or her work appeared.

Madison Gray, "The Press, Race and Katrina"   Madison Gray, a journalist and the Home Page Producer for *Time,* makes choices about the content that appears daily at Time.com. On his LinkedIn page, he describes himself as a "writer, online editor, breaking news monitor, and critical thinker." Gray was educated at Central Michigan University, and his experience includes work with AOL Black Voices and the Knight Digital Media Center. Gray wrote his editorial about Hurricane Katrina in 2006, almost one year after the storm. In it, Gray calls attention to his views on how journalists handled the reporting of Katrina, especially in terms of race. Gray's editorial appears on page 339.

Lincoln Shlensky, "Hurricane Katrina, Race and Class: Part I"   Dr. Lincoln Shlensky, author of the blog *Aulula,* is an assistant professor of English at the University of

Victoria. During Hurricane Katrina, Shlensky was an assistant professor of English at the University of South Alabama. As a resident of Mobile, he was directly affected by Katrina. In his blog entry titled "Hurricane Katrina, Race and Class: Part I," he discusses his perspective on Katrina in relation to how the press covered the event. An excerpt from Shlensky's blog entry appears on page 342.

Ed Gordon and Allison Keyes, "Katrina Coverage Exposes Race, Class Fault Lines"   Ed Gordon is the host and executive producer of *Conversations with Ed Gordon*, a nationally syndicated program, and former host of NPR's *News & Notes*. He is known for his interviews with President Obama and pop culture celebrities. Allison Keyes is a broadcast journalist who covers national news for NPR. A member of the National Association of Black Journalists, Keyes has commented that her work on NPR's *News & Notes* allowed her to focus on national news affecting communities of color.

Gordon and Keyes's news report and analysis of the media coverage of Hurricane Katrina was featured on NPR's *News & Notes* program on September 13, 2005 (the hurricane made landfall in New Orleans on August 29). In this piece, Gordon (host of the program) and Keyes (reporter and commentator of the story) examine ways that race and class may have affected the media's reporting and analysis of the storm and its victims. An excerpt from their news story appears on page 345.

Before we read these sources on Hurricane Katrina in depth, we'll identify some guidelines for evaluating sources.

▲ **AUTHOR PHOTO**
Ed Gordon.
Credit: Ed Gordon Media.

▲ **AUTHOR PHOTO**
Allison Keyes.
Credit: Allison Keyes

How Do I Evaluate a Source? How Is This Different from Previewing?

While some of this overlaps with advice on previewing sources, we are asking you to do a more in-depth analysis of texts than you did earlier in the chapter. To evaluate whether a source is strong enough to draw upon for your own writing, ask yourself the questions posed in the following section.

1. Is this source relevant to my project?   First, determine whether the source you're looking at is related to and useful for your project and research question(s). Ask yourself: Does the information in the source generate additional research questions related to my original question—does it get me deeper into my research? Does the source contribute to my knowledge on the topic—did I learn something new about the subject? In other words, does the author simply rehash what others have said, or does he or she say something new—or provide an alternative perspective? If the author simply duplicates knowledge, then the source is probably not a good choice for your project.

2. What is the author's level of credibility?   When evaluating a source, you need to figure out how trustworthy the author is. Ask yourself:

- *What can I find out by Googling the author?* Learn about the author's education, degrees held, and any institutional, organizational, or professional affiliations.

Find out whether the author is mentioned in other sources on the topic, and to what extent he or she is considered to be an "expert" on the subject by other experts in the field. Research other works by the author: One indicator of expertise is whether someone has published numerous times on the subject. However, don't discount the author's credibility just because this is the author's first piece on the subject—the author could be a rising scholar in the field.

- *What if I can't figure out who the individual author is?* If there is no obvious author, look at the reliability of the organization sponsoring the Web site. For example, if the site is the American Diabetes Association, you can assume that the information presented is researched and reliable because it is an organization that publishes researched articles on diabetes. Additionally, this organization funds research.

No matter how much you might agree with the viewpoint conveyed in a source or how much you might like the way the author has presented information, establishing the author's credibility is absolutely necessary if you are to use this source in your research. If you cannot trust the author, then you should not use the source.

3. What is the author's purpose? To persuade? Inform? Tell a story? Some combination?   Identify the author's purpose by reading the source critically and carefully. As you read, ask yourself the following questions to determine the author's objectives:

- What is the author's purpose?
- Is the author trying to get me to agree with an opinion?
- Is the author presenting facts and information to teach me about the subject?
- Does the author use a narrative structure (include characters, conflict, setting)?

Once you have determined the purpose, ask yourself whether the author's purpose fits with your research question(s). For example, student Calvin Sweet's sources (see p. 333) are three works in which authors seek to inform and persuade readers about Hurricane Katrina. One of these texts, Madison Gray's "The Press, Race and Katrina" (p. 339), presents an argument critiquing the way the press handled the reporting of Katrina in relationship to race. Calvin knows this because as he reads the article, he notes that the author discusses and provides specific examples from the media. He also circles explicit related statements such as "many journalists who monitored the coverage felt in hindsight that African Americans caught in Katrina's wake were misrepresented in the press."

4. Who is the author's target audience? How does the author use rhetorical appeals to reach that audience?   When you preview a source, you determine the author's audience (see "Previewing a Source," p. 325). In order to determine the audience, ask yourself the following questions:

- Does the place of publication offer clues about audience? (For example, an editorial in *Bloomberg Businessweek* is clearly aimed at a business audience.)

- Does the author use a formal or informal tone?
- What level of detail is presented in the piece?
- Does the author include information that assumes previous knowledge?
- Does the author use jargon or vocabulary used by experts?

When Calvin reads Shlensky's blog entry about Katrina (p. 342), he notices that the author uses informal language, such as "I'm doing okay." This tells Calvin that Shlensky's primary audience is people concerned about how Hurricane Katrina affected him.

Once you've determined the audience for the text, take a look at how the author appeals to that audience. Is the author establishing a sense of credibility that speaks to particular readers? Is the author using an emotional appeal to connect with the audience? Calvin notices that Shlensky begins his blog with an emotional appeal to those who know him, discussing the long lines for gas he experiences and his concern for those who live closer to where the hurricane hit.

Besides identifying the audience and analyzing rhetorical appeals, you also need to examine the evidence the author provides and determine whether it is appropriate for his or her intended audience. Pay attention, too, to how the author keeps readers' perspectives in mind so that they will continue to read the piece. For example, when Calvin reads the NPR news report and analysis by Gordon and Keyes, he sees that they begin with a claim about disparities, a claim that they support with an example (the survivors in the Super Dome). This alerts audiences that the piece will draw on specific evidence.

5. What is the source's genre? Does the author make the most of its conventions?   Let's say you're considering using a news and opinion blog as a source. As you evaluate it, look at a few other examples to see how other bloggers typically convey information—and the types of conventions they tend to adhere to. How does your potential source compare with other blogs? Does your blogger take advantage of the conventions of the genre? For example, does he clearly identify himself as the author? Does he embed hyperlinks to additional details or sources? Does he invite feedback? If not, you might want to consider using a different source. When an author chooses to ignore the traditional conventions of a genre, he may also ignore other things, such as using reliable evidence to support opinions.

6. How does the author use evidence—and how reliable is that evidence?   As you evaluate a source, pay close attention to how the author supports his or her claims and arguments. Look at:

- *Sufficient support: Does the author use enough evidence?* If not, that's a problem. A skilled persuasive writer will back up each claim with an appropriate example. Read the source and (1) make a note every time the author makes a claim, and (2) also note whether the claim is supported. Notice also whether the evidence

ATTENTION, READERS
Do you read any blogs regularly? If so, think of two or three that you particularly enjoy. What do they have in common in terms of how the bloggers present information? Do they share design elements, such as headings and lists? Are there things that are done better on one blog than on the others?

A note about
evidence.
Wondering what we
mean by "evidence"?
Evidence is facts,
examples, and source
citations that authors
use to illustrate and
support each point
they make in their
compositions. Skilled
authors use evidence
to develop their
arguments as well as
their ethos. The type
of evidence authors
choose reflects upon
them; for example,
citing a celebrity
gossip magazine as
evidence suggests
shallowness, while
citing the *Wall Street
Journal* suggests
professionalism.

When you're
evaluating a
source, look at how
the author uses
evidence: Think of
the evidence as the
foundation upon
which the argument
is built. A shoddy
foundation can
cause even the most
beautiful building to
crumble.

is vague and general, or specific and detailed. For example, Madison Gray, the author of one of Calvin Sweet's sources on Hurricane Katrina, race, and the media, writes:

CLAIM

"In fact, many journalists who monitored the coverage felt in hindsight that African Americans caught in Katrina's wake were misrepresented in the press."

Gray follows that claim with evidence—a quote from one person—that shows that at least one person believed there was misrepresentation. However, he doesn't sufficiently support his statement that "many journalists" felt that way. He could have made a stronger case by drawing on, say, a study of many journalists, or providing multiple quotes from journalists, for example.

INADEQUATE EVIDENCE

"I don't think African Americans were portrayed in the best light," said Camille Jackson, a staff writer for the Southern Poverty Law Center's Tolerance.org Web site. "It came out just how uncomfortable the media is when it comes to race, with the exception of a few."

- *Timeliness: Is the source and evidence current?* In most cases, you'll want to draw on sources that are as recent as possible.

Timeliness mattered to Calvin Sweet when he conducted research on Hurricane Katrina. He knew he wanted a contemporary account of the hurricane, told by someone who had survived it. He wanted reporting based on actual events that occurred at the moment of the storm—so he looked for sources published on or around the storm date. He was excited to find Shlensky's blog entry, "Hurricane Katrina, Race and Class: Part I," dated September 2, 2005, just a few days after the August 29, 2005, landfall of the hurricane as well as the NPR report dated September 13, 2005.

If Calvin had wanted a source focused on the longer-term aftermath of the storm—perhaps a yearlong study on the impact of the hurricane on people's lives—he'd probably have searched for sources written in 2006 or later. Such a source would likely draw on research conducted over time; the author could report the information provided in a study, or perhaps reflect on the situation, drawing on the study's data as supporting evidence for his claims. Depending on how you plan to use a source, its timeliness could make a difference.

7. Does the author cite sources?   As you evaluate a source, ask yourself: Does the author give credit to others? Does he mention the work of others in the text itself—perhaps with hyperlinks or a list of credits? How easily can I tell where the author obtained his or her information? If you can't tell what sources the author drew on, it's possible that the information isn't well researched or can't be supported.

Citation conventions—and by this we mean the format in which an author identifies his sources—can vary across genres. Before you can judge whether an author has cited sources properly, you need to be aware of the documentation conventions for the genre you are looking at. For example:

- Authors of newspaper articles usually cite sources in the body of the article itself, by using quotations and naming people and publications they've drawn on.
- Authors of blogs usually cite sources by providing hyperlinks to them, assuming the sources are online sources. You can see this in the two blog entries on Katrina featured in this chapter.
- Authors of peer-reviewed journal articles usually use strict source-citing conventions; for example, *The American Journal of Family Therapy*, a peer-reviewed journal on family behavioral health, requires authors to cite sources in accordance with the *Publication Manual of the American Psychological Association*. (See Chapter 13 for information on APA documentation style.)

Once you know something about the citation conventions of a genre, ask yourself: Does the author of the source I'm evaluating cite sources the way she should? For example, a journalist who doesn't mention any sources in an article or editorial should raise eyebrows—but a blogger who uses hyperlinks (rather than an academic style such as APA) should not. In a reliable text, an author makes it clear where she drew from the material of others. The author provides this information in the format that is common to that genre. If the source you're looking at falls short on this score, you may want to look for a different one.

Guided Process | How to Evaluate Sources

Calvin Sweet (STUDENT), *Hurricane Katrina Project: Evaluating 3 Sources*

Let's circle back to Calvin Sweet, who has identified a research question—and three sources that he's thinking of using.

> RESEARCH QUESTION
>
> How did the press treat race and class in their coverage of Hurricane Katrina, and what are the consequences of that treatment?

Using the guidelines on pages 335–339, Calvin now evaluates his sources. His notes in the margins of each source show his thinking. He begins with Madison Gray's editorial for *Time*. (For biographical information on Madison Gray, see p. 334.)

Relevant to my topic?
Yes. I want to look at media coverage of Katrina, as it relates to race and class. Madison Gray's critique of the storm coverage relates directly to my topic.

Credible author?
Yes. Gray writes for *Time*, so I trust he's a reliable journalist. He's also reported for the AP, *The New York Times*, and the *Detroit News*; he's a member of the New York Association of Black Journalists.

I did a search for Gray on Google and found his 2008 article on Rodney King that won a journalism award. Race definitely factors into some of his articles.

Author's purpose?
Gray wants to persuade readers that "African Americans caught in Katrina's wake were misrepresented in the press." He also wants to inform about how journalists dealt with race in reporting the storm.

Audience?
Gray is writing for *Time* readers, especially African Americans who experienced Katrina and whose stories were not properly reflected in the press. His readers are also probably interested in journalism and concerned about media bias. Gray relies on ethos to appeal to readers' concerns.

Madison Gray
The Press, Race, and Katrina

If you watched any television, listened to any radio, picked up a newspaper or visited a news Web site in the days that followed Hurricane Katrina last year, you probably were witness to the result of dozens of on-the-spot editorial decisions made by news managers around the country.

As much as we may have wanted to avoid the issue in those first confusing days, because New Orleans was 67% African American prior to the storm, race played a significant role in criticisms of government, both local and federal, humanitarian aid and not surprisingly, the media. Fortunately, the fourth estate has its own self-policing mechanisms and is much faster than government and other industries at evaluating and scrutinizing itself. But it is only in recent years that the media has taken a look at how it relates to the country's racial divisions, and Katrina provided an opportunity to do just that.

Keith Woods, faculty dean of the Poynter Institute, a St. Petersburg, Florida–based journalism training organization, said many mistakes were made by the media, but in bringing attention to the crisis, the press got it right.

"The media brought a palpable sense of outrage with the coverage from the very beginning," said Woods. "If you looked at NPR, CNN, and scattered sightings of the networks and newspapers, where they did well was to recognize the size of the story and the need to stay with it."

But where race comes in is more difficult, he told me. Where journalism failed is not in any lack of emphasis on how disproportionately blacks were affected, but in how "too many people were making the surface observation that there were lots of blacks affected without spending the time parsing the facts that would make it meaningful or informative."

In fact, many journalists who monitored the coverage felt in hindsight that African Americans caught in Katrina's wake were misrepresented in the press.

"I don't think African Americans were portrayed in the best light," said Camille Jackson, a staff writer for the Southern Poverty Law Center's Tolerance.org Web site. "It came out just how uncomfortable the media is when it comes to race, with the exception of a few."

Jackson authored a series of articles for the Web site that spoke to media outlets referring to victims as "hoodlums," "animals" and "thugs." But she said it comes from cultural insensitivity in the media, which led to false news reports and eventually to a curtailing of emergency response.

She warned that the important lesson to be learned is "to be an honest journalist, to tell the whole story, and be aware of your own personal biases. I know it's scary, but we're going to have to start talking about race so that we can get at the fear."

Buttressing criticisms of the press response to Katrina was a bipartisan Congressional report released in February that outright accuses the media of making a bad situation worse. It does not specify race in its pages, but its accusations implicate press reports that it says contributed to the confusion.

The report from the bipartisan House committee investigated preparations for and responses to Katrina and found that media reports of gunshots fired at rescue helicopters, rapes and murders in the Superdome, and mass rioting in the streets were unsubstantiated at best, and many were simply false. "It's clear accurate reporting was among Katrina's many victims," the report says. "If anyone rioted, it was the media."

But Margaret Engel, managing editor of the Newseum, an Arlington, Virginia–based interactive news museum, said there are more important things to consider, like images that seemingly cast a divide between black and white survivors. Two in particular were now-infamous captions placed with Agence France-Presse and Associated Press photos. The AFP photo caption described two whites as "finding" food, while the AP caption described a black youth as "looting" a store.

"That to me is much more troubling than reporters quoting cops who didn't really know," said Engel. "I think you'll find that some of the stories on that day of looting were wildly overstated. It's not good that the press reported that, but it is a footnote to the overall coverage which riveted the nation over the lack of response." She added: "I think for Congress to cast the media response as rumor-mongering is to miss the forest for the trees."

Despite the varied points of view, two things are clear. First, mistakes were made. As Woods pointed out, there has never

(Continues on next page)

Calvin's notes on Gray's argument

Identifiable genre/mode/media?
This magazine article is an editorial: Gray's column is titled "Viewpoint." Its mode is written and it is published online.

Essentially, Gray's article is an argument. He presents his case in short paragraphs and works in sources and quotes: This technique is common to editorials and other journalistic writing.

Reliable evidence?
Gray's sources include a journalism dean, a journalist, and other media experts; he also refers to a congressional report. That all seems solid.

Gray writes: "many journalists who monitored the coverage felt in hindsight that African Americans caught in Katrina's wake were misrepresented in the press."

He supports this claim by mentioning one specific journalist. Are there others he could mention to back this statement more strongly?

Sources cited?
Gray attributes his information to sources when he quotes people and names them in the body of the editorial.

He also provides hyperlinks so readers can get more information. For example, I clicked on the Keith Woods link and it took me to the Poynter Institute, where Woods was faculty dean (until 2010 when he joined NPR).

been a how-to book on covering a disaster that nearly wipes out a whole city. Secondly, and most importantly, if African Americans in New Orleans are to be fairly served, the story must be told. "Now that the initial event has passed, the problem is maintaining people's attention," said Richard Prince, chairman of the National Association of Black Journalists' Media Monitoring Committee. "People are desperate for media attention because they fear the country will forget them. While a lot of reporters have covered the follow-up, it has not been compelling enough."

Prince said that the way to learn from what happened is for journalists to continually go to the Gulf Coast Region and find new stories, which are abundant. "They call it one of the worst natural disasters in the history of the country. So many people have a story to tell; somehow those stories have to be told."

After reading through the informative and persuasive piece in *Time*, Calvin decided he wanted a more personal lens into the issues of the press and its reporting of Katrina. He found Lincoln Shlensky's blog containing writing about his views related to press coverage of Katrina. Additionally, he found that Shlensky provided the argumentative take on the situation that he was looking for. (For more biographical information on Lincoln Shlensky, see p. 334.)

Calvin's notes on Shlensky's argument

Relevant to my topic?
Yes. Shlensky focuses on issues of race and how they affected the media's response to the disaster. This will be a valuable source for my research.

Credible author?
Yes. Shlensky is a college professor, and I trust that his research and sources are valid. His area of specialty is Caribbean literature (he holds a PhD), and according to his CV, he's presented numerous times on this subject, looking at issues of race in relationship to literature.

Lincoln Shlensky
Hurricane Katrina, Race, and Class: Part I

I have been in Pensacola, Florida, since late Tuesday because my house in Mobile still is without electricity. I'm doing okay here, but I look forward to getting back home as soon as electricity is restored. The University is supposed to reopen on September 6th, but that may change, depending on conditions. Yesterday and today the gas stations here in Pensacola were mainly without gas, and I waited in a long line at the one station that (only briefly) had gas to offer. It's scary to see people begin to panic when basic commodities are in short supply; I can only imagine to what degree such a sense of panic must be magnified nearer to the epicenter, where essential necessities such as water, food, and sanitation are in severe shortage.

From my vantage—geographically and emotionally near the disaster, but safely buffered from its worst deprivations—much of the press coverage has not adequately dealt with the most difficult social issues that mark this still unfolding catastrophe. It is difficult to avoid concluding that one important cause of the slow response to the debacle has to do with the fact that most of the people who are caught up in it are poor and black. Here in Pensacola I keep hearing blame expressed towards the victims: "they should have heeded the call to evacuate." Even the FEMA chief said as much in a news conference today. So where, I must ask, were the buses he should have provided to take them away before Katrina hit? Where were the troops to supervise evacuation? Where were the emergency shelters and health services? People who ought to know better do not seem to understand or acknowledge the enormous differential in available resources—access to transportation, money, information, social services, etc.—that forms the background to this human catastrophe. Terms such as "looting" are tossed about in the press and on TV with no class or race analysis at all. In recent news reports, there is an emerging discussion of the political background to the calamity: the Bush administration's curtailment of federal funding for levee repair in order to pay for the war in Iraq, rampant commercial housing development on environmentally protected wetlands, financial evisceration of FEMA, and so on. But there's been little or no discussion of the economic background that makes New Orleans a kind of "Third World" nation unto itself, with fearsomely deteriorated housing projects, extraordinarily high crime and murder rates, and one of the worst public education systems in the country.

Major newspaper editors and TV producers have prepared very few reports about issues of race in this disaster, and those reports that have appeared so far seem to me deeply insufficient in their analysis of endemic class and race problems. I've been communicating with a national magazine reporter friend of mine since Tuesday night about the issues

(Continues on next page)

Calvin's notes on Shlensky's argument

Because he's regularly subject to the peer review of fellow academics, I'd imagine Shlensky is careful with how he states things. Also, as an educator, he may look at his loss during Katrina through a more analytical than emotional lens.

Author's purpose?
Shlensky writes his post to persuade readers that "much of the press coverage has not adequately dealt with the most difficult social issues that mark this still unfolding catastrophe . . . [because] most of the people who are caught up in it are poor and black."

Audience?
Shlensky writes to those critical of the media. He appeals to his audience with ethos (using quotes and evidence from media coverage) and pathos, hoping his audience gets angry enough to demand attention to the issues of race.

Identifiable genre/mode/medium?
Shlensky mixes information and opinion. He uses blog conventions such as hyperlinks, comments, and an archive of his previous posts.

Sources cited?
Shlensky attributes quotes and information throughout. He also uses hyperlinks to take you to the full source, such as when he discusses the *Washington Post* article.

Reliable evidence?
There is a good amount of evidence and it's varied, including firsthand observations and references to a news report and Michael Moore's letter to President Bush. The entry is timely (he wrote it within days of Katrina making landfall).

Author's purpose?
Shlensky writes his post to persuade readers that "much of the press coverage has not adequately dealt with the most difficult social issues that mark this still unfolding catastrophe . . . [because] most of the people who are caught up in it are poor and black."

Audience?
Shlensky writes to those critical of the media. He appeals to his audience with ethos (using quotes and evidence from media coverage) and pathos, hoping his audience gets angry enough to demand attention to the issues of race.

Identifiable genre/mode/medium?
Shlensky mixes information and opinion. He uses blog conventions such as hyperlinks, comments, and an archive of his previous posts.

Sources cited?
Shlensky attributes quotes and information throughout. He also uses hyperlinks to take you to the full source, such as when he discusses the *Washington Post* article.

Reliable evidence?
There is a good amount of evidence and it's varied, including firsthand observations and references to a news report and Michael Moore's letter to President Bush. The entry is timely (he wrote it within days of Katrina making landfall).

of race and class in this catastrophe; here's my email comment on this topic from earlier today:

CNN addressed the race question today on TV, but only to ask softball questions of Jesse Jackson, who to his discredit didn't exhibit even a modicum of the anger of one Louisiana black political leader, who said: "While the Administration has spoken of 'shock and awe' in the war on terror, the response to this disaster has been 'shockingly awful.'"

The *Washington Post* also ran a puff piece that doesn't ask any of the relevant questions, such as whether the Administration's response would have been faster if these were white people suffering the agonies of a slow motion disaster. Here's the link to the *Post*'s piece.

Michael Moore also had this to say in a letter to President Bush circulated today:

No, Mr. Bush, you just stay the course. It's not your fault that 30 percent of New Orleans lives in poverty or that tens of thousands had no transportation to get out of town. C'mon, they're black! I mean, it's not like this happened to Kennebunkport. Can you imagine leaving white people on their roofs for five days? Don't make me laugh! Race has nothing—NOTHING—to do with this!

(See Michael Moore's full letter here.)

A member of the Congressional Black Caucus had to remind reporters today to stop referring to those displaced by the flooding with the blanket term "refugees" (recalling, of course, the waves of Haitian or Central American or Southeast Asian refugees who sought shelter in the United States): these people are citizens, she said, deserving of the full protections guaranteed to all Americans.

The federal government promised on Wednesday that those receiving food stamps could get their full allotment at the beginning of September, rather than the usual piecemeal distribution throughout the month. How very generous. What these people need is relief money and access to services now—even the 50,000 or so exhausted and traumatized people whose images we've seen at the N.O. Superdome and at the Civic Center are just a few of the far larger number of those residents of the region displaced by the hurricane, many of whom live from monthly paycheck to paycheck. It will be months at the very least before these people can return home; their jobs may be gone for good. The mayor of New Orleans was actually caught off camera crying in frustration today at the slow pace of the federal response.

If there is a hopeful side to this tragedy, it is perhaps that Hurricane Katrina's damage and efforts to relieve those displaced by the storm may spark a wider national discussion about the ongoing and unaddressed issues of race and economic disparity in America. If that doesn't happen, I fear that there will be even further deterioration in the living conditions and economic predicament of those left destitute and homeless by Katrina—a situation in which our own government's years of neglect must be included as a crucial contributing factor. We must not let such a deterioration of conditions for those hardest hit by Katrina occur.

What happens next, when tens or hundreds of thousands of Americans require long-term recovery help, will be an important barometer of our society's ability to heal itself.

After realizing that Shlensky's blog contained a lot of evidence to support the writer's opinion, Calvin decided that a news report might give him an additional perspective on Hurricane Katrina. Even though NPR journalists Ed Gordon and Allison Keyes were not reporting from New Orleans and do not identify themselves as being directly affected by the hurricane, their examination of how the media covered Katrina raises questions that will help Calvin dig deeper into his research. (For biographical information on Gordon and Keyes, see p. 335.)

Ed Gordon and Allison Keyes
Katrina Coverage Exposes Race, Class Fault Lines

Media coverage of Hurricane Katrina and its aftermath have exposed huge race and class disparities among Americans. Desperate survivors at the Superdome in New Orleans, for example, were almost universally black and poor.

ED GORDON, host:

From NPR News, this is NEWS & NOTES. I'm Ed Gordon.

Calvin's notes on Gordon and Keyes's analysis

Relevant to my topic?
Yes. I'm intrigued by the journalists' choice of public figures (Wolf Blitzer, Barbara Bush, Kanye West, etc.) editing in audio clips of comments on the disaster and the media coverage of it. In the transcript of the story, Keyes makes very specific points and backs each one with evidence. This piece adds an angle that is different from the other two sources.

(Continues on next page)

Credible authors?
Like Madison Gray, Gordon (*News & Notes* program host) and Keyes (reporter and commentator) are respected journalists with experience in reporting news and providing analysis. (See the authors' bios.) Also, National Public Radio (NPR) is a news source where reporters are held to high standards. (See npr.org/about.)

Authors' purpose?
Gordon and Keyes want to inform listeners about how the media covered the storm and its victims. They also want to persuade listeners to examine the tragedy of Katrina and to take a critical look at how race and class may have affected the national response to the disaster.

Audience?
The audience for NPR's *News & Notes* program includes a general, popular audience interested in national news and public radio journalism. The program, as Keyes suggests in her NPR biography, is particularly focused on news and events that affect people of color.

Images of the evacuees from Hurricane Katrina, overwhelmingly poor and disproportionately black, have dominated news coverage in the weeks since the storm slammed into the Gulf Coast. NPR's Allison Keyes begins our examination of the way race and social class may have influenced reporting and analysis of the catastrophe.

ALLISON KEYES reporting:

Reporters and anchors, even veterans like CNN's Wolf Blitzer, were stunned by what they saw in the days after the storm hit.

MR. WOLF BLITZER (CNN): So many of these people, almost all of them that we see are so poor, and they are so black, and this is going to raise lots of questions for people who are watching this story unfold.

KEYES: On his first visit, President Bush told reporters that he looked forward to sitting on the porch of Mississippi Senator Trent Lott's new house after it was rebuilt. Critics blasted former first lady Barbara Bush for this comment about the evacuees staying at Houston's Astrodome on the radio program "Marketplace."

(Soundbite of "Marketplace")

MRS. BARBARA BUSH (Former First Lady): So many of the people in the arena here, you know, were underprivileged anyway. This is working very well for them.

KEYES: During a telethon to support Hurricane Katrina victims, rapper Kanye West voiced what seems, at least anecdotally, to be the opinion of many African-Americans.

(Soundbite of telethon)

MR. KANYE WEST (Rapper): I hate the way they portray us in the media.

KEYES: He also said . . .

(Soundbite of telethon)

MR. WEST: George Bush doesn't care about black people.

KEYES: Many people spent the first five days after the storm watching the 24-hour cable channels. They saw Americans, mostly black, wading or swimming through neck-deep water, carrying food, water and clothes. Some carried televisions. On one hand, USC critical studies Professor Todd Boyd says the media helped draw attention to the dire straits victims faced, but on the other, he says, some of the images were problematic.

Professor TODD BOYD (USC): When you look at, you know, just the large number of displaced black people there were, that was a certain image. And then when you start to show images of looting, that, of course, plays into some very old stereotypes in society and, I think, sort of confirms for a lot of people what they believe already.

KEYES: Boyd also says race affects everyone's perception of this coverage.

PROF. BOYD: If you're black, you know, race factors into everything that happens to you. If you're not, then, you know, maybe it seems strange. Maybe you think, ' Oh, this doesn't have anything to do with it,' but it does. It has to do with race. It also has to do with class.

KEYES: Boyd says coverage of this hurricane has exposed a class of people who live in this country under Third World conditions, and Americans don't want to accept that. Nationally syndicated columnist Clarence Page of the Chicago Tribune says the invisible poor haven't taken center stage for years. He calls this coverage the first big racial eruption in the media since the O.J. Simpson trial 10 years ago.

MR. CLARENCE PAGE (Chicago Tribune): We saw a story that already contained enough elements to be a big media stoiy suddenly became this whole allegory about modern America and how we deal with our own divisions around race and class.

KEYES: Gregory Kane, a self-described black conservative who writes for The Baltimore Sun and BlackAmericaWeb.com, says he believes some black leaders were playing the race card more than the media. He cites the controversy over use of the word 'refugee.'

MR. GREGORY KANE (The Baltimore Sun; BlackAmericaWeb .com): Some people saw something racial in that. Well, first of all, the definitions I looked up indicate that it just means someone who seeks refuge, and I assume that means everybody who is trying to get the heck out of New Orleans.

KEYES: Kane doesn't believe the media coverage itself was racist. On the local channels in Baltimore, he says he saw looters of all colors, but Kane says the underlying issues that cause this problem do deal with race and class.

MR. KANE: There are a lot of black folks in New Orleans who are poor, but that's because the poor are disproportionately black. But what you have here is a class issue that apparently some decision was made that we're not going to get the poor folks out of New Orleans.

KEYES: The Tribune's Page says he hopes this disaster and its coverage lead to some serious conversation about how we close some of the gaps. But, he adds, he's too old and pessimistic to think that will happen. Allison Keyes, NPR News.

Calvin's notes on Gordon and Keyes's analysis

Identifiable genre/mode/medium?
Yes. This is a radio news report. The audio content features voices and sound clips from events. The content is also available as a print transcript. It is broadcast by radio and through the Internet and is available to anyone with access to these technologies.

Reliable evidence?
Yes, the journalists cite evidence to support each point. Evidence includes clips of other speakers with various points of view. I'm also confident that this is reliable because NPR holds rigorous standards and I assume someone fact-checks their content.

Sources cited?
The sources for this piece are the journalists and the people they refer to and interview. While there is no Works Cited list for this genre, there are hyperlinks to additional sources and related stories.

Following his evaluation of the works of Gray, Shlensky, and Gordon and Keyes, Calvin maps his research out in a little more detail.

RESEARCH PLAN **Calvin Sweet** (STUDENT), *Hurricane Katrina Project*

English 102

February 1, 2017
Research Plan

1. Your research question.
   My research question is twofold: How did the press treat race and class in their coverage of Katrina, and what are the consequences of that treatment?

2. Your goals.
   My starting point was to find out how the press covered Katrina. I want to be a journalist, and I remember my cousin who interned at a newspaper in 2007 saying that the writers at that paper were still talking about how "slanted" the Katrina coverage was. One of my goals is to discover what the Katrina coverage was. In the research I've done so far, it looks like some people think the coverage treated both race and class unfairly. If my research continues to support this view, I'll argue that press coverage didn't adequately take race and class into account and that there were serious consequences because of that. I believe my research would be considered inductive, because I truly haven't made up my mind and even these thoughts I have now are completely based on the three sources I've read. The next source I read could make me see things differently.

3. Types of sources.
   I will continue reading blogs about Katrina. I think reading about people who experienced it gives me an understanding of what actually happened and how race and class mattered in what happened. I also need to read the press coverage and analysis, which I have just begun with the *Time* article and NPR story. In fact, analyzing the press coverage itself will be a major part of my research. I can do *EBSCOhost* searches to find articles. To make my argument that there are consequences because of the coverage, I need to follow up on things like Shlensky's idea that this could all lead to more discussion of race and class. For example, I need to find out if there have been more discussions of race and class, maybe by comparing how many articles a particular newspaper published on race and class issues in the two years before and the two years after Katrina. I will also watch Spike Lee's documentary *When the Levees Broke*. My assumption is that it will be like all of Lee's other films, in which race and class are examined.

   For primary sources, I will look for YouTube videos by Katrina survivors to see how they portray race and class. I will also interview Professor Hughes in the African American studies department to see if she can share any insights with me.

4. Your timeline.
   - Find and read more blogs: March 20–31
   - Schedule interview with Professor Hughes: April 1
   - Write interview questions: April 5
   - Conduct interview: April 7
   - Watch Spike Lee film on Netflix: April 8–10
   - Find and read press coverage: April 11–25
   - Draft: April 25–May 6
   - Revise: May 7–14
   - Edit: May 14
   - Submit: May 15

13

INTEGRATING & DOCUMENTING SOURCES

BRIEF CONTENTS

In this chapter, we focus on two things: (1) how to integrate sources, and (2) how to cite and document sources using two popular documentation styles. First, we'll show you how to incorporate sources into your own compositions, through quotations, paraphrases, and summaries (pp. 350–71). As you'll discover, there are reasons for choosing one method over the others, or combining methods, depending on your purposes. We'll follow the processes of student writers as they work with their sources (see Guided Processes in this chapter). We will also take a look at the issue of plagiarism. Composers who plagiarize use a source unethically, for example, by using an idea or language from a source without giving credit to that source with an attribution, parenthetical citation, and bibliographical entry. Plagiarism is not always a deliberate act; it can simply be the result of sloppiness. Whether it's intentional or not, plagiarism is a serious offense in any academic setting. However, if you follow the advice in this chapter (especially on pp. 367–71), you can be confident of your integrity and ethos as an author.

In the second part of the chapter, we will show you how to cite sources within the text of your own compositions, and how to document them in lists at the end of your paper. Because the documentation styles of the Modern Language Association (MLA) and American Psychological Association (APA) are the ones most typically used in the humanities and social sciences, we've provided detailed coverage of both (MLA, pp. 374–90; APA, pp. 391–410). There are other popular styles—such as *Chicago* style, used by some of the humanities disciplines, and the American Medical Association (AMA) style, used by health and medical fields. If you are using those styles, we refer you to chicagomanualofstyle.org and amamanualofstyle.com.

Integrating Sources into Your Writing

When we talk about integrating sources, we mean a host of different and related activities. We mean using source material in our own compositions, perhaps to provide context for our ideas or evidence for our claims. We also mean showing how the source material we've used relates to other source material—does it agree with other sources? Does it contradict other sources? Does it provide a perspective missing in other sources? And finally, we mean citing our sources to credit outside sources throughout the text of our papers and documenting them in a Works Cited list (MLA) or References list (APA) so that interested readers can track the sources down for themselves.

Using a Parenthetical Citation or Signal Phrase

Here are examples of how Emily Kahn (the student introduced in Chapter 12) integrated an article into a paper she wrote. She found the article, "The Objectification of Women in Comic Books" by Jehanzeb Dar, online in the fantasy magazine, *Lightspeed*.

In this first example, Emily presents Dar's name in what's called a parenthetical citation. Parenthetical citations must include the author's last name and the page number from the source that the material is taken from. Because Dar's article is from an online magazine, there are no page numbers to list.

EMILY'S IN-TEXT CITATION (MLA style—names author in parentheses)

The writer argues that the comic book industry may begin to attract female readers and readers of color if comics authors reject sexism and racism. He concludes: "As more female writers and artists make contributions to the industry, male writers and artists will need to be inspired to work against sexism, the objectification of women, and the sexualization of women of color" (Dar 000).

author's last name — if there is a page number, it goes here

Alternatively, Emily could have cited Dar's article as follows, by naming him in a signal phrase.

EMILY'S IN-TEXT CITATION (MLA style—names author in a signal phrase)

author named in signal phrase

Jehanzeb Dar argues that if the comic book industry wants to attract female readers, then comic book authors need to reject sexism and racism. He concludes: "As more female writers and artists make contributions to the industry, male writers and artists will need to be inspired to work against sexism, the objectification of women, and the sexualization of women of color" (00–00).

were this a print article, with page numbers, the page or pages referred to would go here

At the end of her paper, Emily provides a bibliographic entry for her references to Dar's article.

EMILY'S WORKS CITED ENTRY (MLA style)

author name: last, first   title of article   title of magazine

Dar, Jehanzeb. "The Objectification of Women in Comic Books." *Lightspeed,*

publisher   publication date   article URL

John Joseph Adams, Aug. 2008, www.fantasy-magazine.com/non-fiction/articles/the-objectification-of-women-in-graphic-novels/.

Using the MLA style of documentation, Emily:

- Cites Dar's article in the text of her paper, using an in-text citation that includes his name (no page number available)
- Documents Dar's article with a corresponding entry in her Works Cited list
- Avoids plagiarism, by citing Dar's article in *both* the text of her paper *and* her Works Cited list

Overview: Quoting, Paraphrasing, & Summarizing

Quoting   In the example on page 351, Emily quotes directly from Dar's article. To signify to her readers that she is using Dar's exact words, she surrounds his words with quotation marks:

> **EMILY'S DIRECT QUOTATION FROM THE SOURCE (Dar)**
> He concludes: "As more female writers and artists make contributions to the industry, male writers and artists will need to be inspired to work against sexism, the objectification of women, and the sexualization of women of color" (Dar).

Emily chooses to include a quotation in order to state the specifics of Dar's argument. The quotation also serves to back up her first sentence, in which she summarizes Dar's main argument.

Paraphrasing   Elsewhere in her paper, Emily paraphrases Dar's argument. To paraphrase, a writer takes the ideas of a source and puts them into his or her own words. A paraphrase rewords without significantly condensing a specific passage.

> **ORIGINAL PASSAGE FROM SOURCE (Dar)**
> The role of women changed dramatically during World War II when patriotic characters emerged and surprisingly attracted the interest of new readers, who were both men and women. Arguably, the most noteworthy female character was Wonder Woman.

> **EMILY'S PARAPHRASE**
> According to Dar, Wonder Woman was the most interesting character to come out of the comics of the World War II era.

Note that Emily rephrases Dar's sentences and condenses them into one. She also attributes the entire idea to Dar by naming him in a signal phrase: "According to Dar . . ." If the article were in print, she would also include a parenthetical note at the end with the page number on which the idea was mentioned.

As you can see in the examples above, Emily always gives credit to Dar when she refers to his ideas, even if she changes his words, as in a summary or paraphrase.

Integrating sources smoothly into your own writing allows you to maintain control over the authorial voice that your readers hear. For example, although the examples above show Emily referring to Dar's ideas, it is clear that she, not Dar, is the author of her paper. Dar's voice never overtakes Emily's. While she draws on the source through quotations, paraphrases, and summary, she does so smoothly. Like Emily, you'll need to decide how and when to use these methods of drawing on sources. You'll also need to decide whether you're going to cite them through signal phrases, such as "According to Dar," or through parenthetical citations, such as "(Dar 000)." And if your instructor has not requested that you use a particular documentation style, you'll need to decide which format to use: MLA, APA, or another method of documentation.

Summarizing   In the example on page 351, Emily summarizes the main point of Dar's entire article in her first sentence:

> **EMILY'S SUMMARY OF ENTIRE SOURCE**
> Jehanzeb Dar argues that if the comic book industry wants to attract female readers, then comic book authors need to reject sexism and racism.

Emily manages to summarize in one sentence a point Dar makes in nine paragraphs. A summary condenses material significantly and focuses only on the point made, not the details that support or illustrate the point. Emily wants to reference Dar's central argument, so summary makes sense.

Quoting

What Does It Mean to Quote from a Source?

When you quote from a source, you provide a passage from that text—in the author's exact language. The best time to quote from a text is when the language from a passage contributes in a crucial way to the argument you are making.

When you quote from a passage, you should:

Use the exact words from the original without alteration   If you do need to alter the words for the sake of agreement of verb tense, use brackets to indicate what you've altered. To shorten a passage, use ellipses.

> **ORIGINAL PASSAGE FROM SOURCE**
> "Sexist undertones and stereotypical images are getting worse and increasingly sleazier."
>
> **EMILY'S ALTERED QUOTE (changes shown in brackets)**
> Dar points out that "[s]exist undertones and stereotypical images [have gotten] worse and increasingly sleaz[y]."

Surround the quoted passage with quotation marks   An exception is long quotes, which should be indented in a block. A long quote, per MLA, is more than four lines long; in APA style, it is more than forty words long.

Give credit to the author of the source being quoted   An attribution phrase, such as "Dar points out that," gives credit and cues readers to hear someone else's voice for a moment or two. Conventions for crediting sources differ. As with summaries and paraphrases, you may need to provide a parenthetical citation and/or a bibliographic entry if that is appropriate for the genre you are composing in.

Quote from other authors to present their specific language for good reasons; for example, if the original language is distinctive enough that paraphrasing would draw the meaning out.

Let's look at an example. Suppose a student named Omar Sadi is writing about the possible connection between extreme weather and global warming. One of his sources is *Yale Environment 360*, published by Yale University and its School of Forestry and Environmental Studies. In that journal, Omar finds an article that gathers the views of eight climate experts.

He decides that the experts' perspectives and voices will support his main argument, and he chooses to quote from the source a passage with memorable word choice.

OMAR'S EFFECTIVE QUOTING

In a recent forum published by *Yale Environment 360*, a panel of experts addressed the question: Is extreme weather linked to global warming? Like many of the panelists, University of Colorado professor Roger A. Pielke Jr. said that because the Intergovernmental Panel on Climate Change defines climate change as a persistent change of weather that takes place over the course of thirty years or more, the question posed cannot be answered now. Instead, Pielke says, we need long-term studies and records to scientifically support a connection. He argues:

> *quotation from a source* — "To suggest that particular extreme weather events are evidence of climate change is not just wrong, but wrongheaded. . . . Weather is not climate and short-term climate variability is not climate change."

So how do scientists explain the extreme weather of recent years? And what are the best ways of evaluating the impact of global warming on the weather? . . .

ATTENTION, WRITERS

A caution against quoting too much.   Remember that every time you quote an author, you are, in effect, turning over the microphone to someone else. So when should you let someone else take the microphone? Perhaps if the author makes a point in language so vivid it deserves a moment in the spotlight. Or if the author's language or phrasing is particularly precise or interesting or humorous. Our point is this: Quote mindfully. Don't use quotations just because you think it will be too much work to paraphrase. Whether you choose to quote, paraphrase, or summarize from a source, be sure to credit it in the text of your paper and list it in your Works Cited (MLA) or References (APA) list.

When Should I Quote from a Source?

A great time to quote from a source is when the ideas or language of the original is so striking that you can't truly capture them in a paraphrase or summary. For example, 9/11 hero Todd Beamer's words "let's roll" could be paraphrased as "we should act now," but such a paraphrase lacks the energy and emotion of the original. It would be best to quote Beamer. Here are some other instances when you might quote rather than paraphrase or summarize:

Quote from a source when a paraphrase or summary would alter the author's meaning   For example, this might be the case when your source is a legal document, as in the following:

> **STUDENT'S QUOTATION FROM A LEGAL DOCUMENT**
> In the Supreme Court's historical ruling on school segregation, Chief Justice Earl Warren offered the court's final opinion in *Brown v. Board of Education*, ruling for the plaintiffs:
>> We conclude that in the field of public education the doctrine of "separate but equal" has no place. Separate educational facilities are inherently unequal. Therefore, we hold that the plaintiffs and others similarly situated for whom the actions have been brought are, by reason of the segregation complained of, deprived of the equal protection of the laws guaranteed by the Fourteenth Amendment.
>
> It was this ruling that changed . . .

— quotation from a source

Note: Because the quoted passage is long, it is "blocked" rather than run in with the text; there are no quotation marks in this case.

Quote from a source when a paraphrase or summary would not capture the essence of the author's clear and memorable words and tone   For example, supermodel Linda Evangelista once famously said, "We don't wake up for less than $10,000 a day." If you were to paraphrase this, you would lose the tone and spirit of her comment.

Quote from a text if your purpose is to analyze that text   For example, if you were writing an analysis of a work of literature, you would include in your paper specific passages to discuss. Let's say you want to comment on mystery writer Agatha Christie's use of an omniscient narrator and want to give an example from her writing to illustrate your point. You might write something like this:

> **STUDENT'S QUOTATION OF A PASSAGE FOR ANALYSIS**
> In *Secret Adversary*, Christie uses her narrator to convey a quick analysis of a character's true nature:
>> Although she was accustomed to take the lead, and to pride herself on her quick-wittedness, in reality she had relied upon Tommy more than she realized at the time. There was something so eminently sober and clear-headed about him, his common sense and soundness of vision were so unvarying, that without him Tuppence felt much like a rudderless ship (88).
>
> The narrator's commentary on Tommy, conveyed through Tuppence's point of view, serves to . . .

— quotation from a source

How Do I Quote from a Source?

To quote a source, do the following:

- Integrate the quote into your prose by providing a context for the quotation. In other words, don't simply plop the quote into the prose, expecting your reader to understand how it fits within the material that precedes and follows it.
- Signal the reader that a quote is coming. This is usually best done by using the author's name (Kleinfeld discusses "...").
- If the quote is shorter than four lines, integrate it into your sentences. If the quote is longer than four lines, use a blocked quote format.

Guided Process | How to Quote from a Source

Paul Pierre (STUDENT), *Nonviolent Protest Project: Quoting Gandhi*

Let's look at the process of student Paul Pierre. He's researching nonviolent protest and has come across some speeches by Mohandas K. Gandhi (commonly known as Gandhi), the philosophical leader of the early twentieth-century independence movement in India. Gandhi became famous for using nonviolent protest strategies.

Paul decides to read some of Gandhi's writings and speeches, and to summarize and paraphrase them within his own writing. However, when he reads "The Doctrine of the Sword," in which Gandhi defines nonviolence, Paul decides that Gandhi's original words are powerful and that he should quote them directly.

Paul located the text of this 1920 article by Gandhi at the Web site of a research foundation dedicated to the author. Gandhi's article was originally published in his weekly journal, *Young India.*

▲ **STUDENT AUTHOR**
Paul Pierre.
*Credit: Svetlana Prikhnenko/
Shutterstock.com.*

M. K. Gandhi
The Doctrine of the Sword

In this age of the rule of brute force, it is almost impossible for anyone to believe that anyone else could possibly reject the law of final supremacy of brute force. . . .

    I do believe that where there is only a choice between cowardice and violence I would advise violence. Thus when my eldest son asked me what he should have done, had he been

Paul's notes on Gandhi's article

1. *I read the whole article* and chose the passage I thought was most significant to my argument about nonviolence.

2. *I thought about how this source works with my other sources.* In my research, I've looked into how well-known political figures define *nonviolence.* Gandhi, probably the best known of these figures, offers a perspective that I think is crucial to present.

present when I was almost fatally assaulted in 1908, whether he should have run away and seen me killed or whether he should have used his physical force which he could and wanted to use, and defended me, I told him that it was his duty to defend me even by using violence. . . .

I am not a visionary. I claim to be a practical idealist. The religion of nonviolence is not meant merely for the Rishis and saints. It is meant for the common people as well. Nonviolence is the law of our species as violence is the law of the brute. The spirit lies dormant in the brute and he knows no law but that of physical might. The dignity of man requires obedience to a higher law to the strength of the spirit.

I have therefore ventured to place before India the ancient law of self sacrifice. For Satyagrah and its off-shoots, non-cooperation and civil resistance are nothing but new names for the law of suffering. The Rishis, who discovered the law of non-violence in the midst of nonviolence, were greater geniuses than Newton. They were themselves greater warriors than Wellington. Having themselves known the use of arms, they realized their uselessness, and taught a weary world that its salvation lay not through violence, but through nonviolence.

Nonviolence in its dynamic condition means conscious suffering. It does not mean meek submission to the will of the evil-doer, but it means the putting of one's whole soul against the will of the tyrant. Working under this law of being, it is possible for a single individual to defy the whole might of an unjust empire to save his honor, his religion, his soul and lay the foundation for the empire's fall or its regeneration.

And so I am not pleading for India to practice nonviolence because it is weak. I want her to practice nonviolence being conscious of her strength and power. . . .

Paul's notes on Gandhi's article

3. *I tried paraphrasing Gandhi's words.* Here's what I came up with:

MY PARAPHRASE

Gandhi named in signal phrase, so no parenthetical citation needed

For Gandhi, nonviolence was a type of active defiance.

I don't think it works. My paraphrase is a lot less powerful than Gandhi's original words.

4. *I decided to quote Gandhi directly.* Here's what I wrote and included in my final audio essay:

MY QUOTATION

Gandhi named in signal phrase, so no parenthetical citation needed

Gandhi was adamant that nonviolence is different from being passive, explaining, "Nonviolence in its dynamic condition means conscious suffering. It does not mean meek submission to the will of the evil-doer, but it means the putting of one's whole soul against the will of the tyrant."

5. *I cited the Gandhi article as a source in my Works Cited list.* Even though I created an audio essay about nonviolent protest, my instructor asked me to formally cite all my sources. I submitted (with my audio essay) an Artist's Statement in which I documented all my research according to MLA style. Here's the entry that corresponds with my in-text citation of the Gandhi article.

MY WORKS CITED ENTRY (MLA style)

author name: last, first | title of short work from a Web site

Gandhi, M. K. "The Doctrine of the Sword."

date | title of site

1920. *Mahatma Gandhi Complete*

publisher

Information Web Site, Bombay Sarvodaya

URL

Mandal and Gandhi Research, www.mkgandhi

date of access

.org/nonviolence/D_sword.htm. Accessed 15

Sept. 2016.

Paul is satisfied that quoting is best in this case. Why? Because Gandhi's words are distinctive and indicate a tone and sensibility that would be lost in a summary or paraphrase.

Paraphrasing

What Does It Mean to Paraphrase a Source?

When you paraphrase a source, you basically restate what you've read from a text or a part of a text. Like when you summarize a source, you capture the author's main idea—usually the main idea behind an entire book or movie, for example—in your own words (for more on summary, see p. 364). However, when you *paraphrase* a source, you capture *all* of the author's ideas in your own words—including details and supporting evidence. Typically you won't paraphrase an entire source; instead you'll probably paraphrase a passage or a sentence or two.

Paraphrasing is handy when you want to share specifics but don't want to use the author's exact original wording. While quoting can be a good option (pp. 353–57), there are times when you want the voice to be all your own. There are still other times when an author's tone is not a good fit for your purpose and audience; in these cases, use paraphrase to present that author's perspective smoothly.

A paraphrase should:

- Provide not only the big-picture message of a source but also the details that the author uses to support his or her argument.
- Be in your own words and voice, with the same level of formality and vocabulary as the rest of your piece.
- Change both the words and the order of the ideas presented in the original.
- Usually end up being close to the same length as the original.
- Give credit to the author of the source being paraphrased. If you are using MLA or APA conventions, be sure to credit your source with an in-text citation and correlating entry for the Works Cited or References list.

Let's look at an example. Shelby Prince, a student writing about therapeutic uses of music (p. 359), found a blog called *The Contrapuntist*, where she read a post by Miguel

---

ATTENTION, WRITERS

How to paraphrase fairly. When you paraphrase a passage from a source, make sure that the details you paraphrase are consistent with the "big picture" of your source; for example, if a source's author is positive overall about an experimental drug treatment, it would be unfair to paraphrase only the few negative details provided. However, it would be okay to mention the negative details, provided that you offer them in the context of the author's main (pro-treatment) argument.

Cano, titled "How Music Saved My Life, and Why Music Education Should Be Taken More Seriously." She wanted to integrate Cano's experience into her writing without shifting over to his voice. She decided to paraphrase.

ORIGINAL PASSAGE FROM SOURCE

That sad instrument became my life; it became my outlet to express my frustration with teenage life. I took it everywhere, practiced everywhere and played for everyone. Like every other 15-year-old, my dream was to become a rock star. I wanted to be like my guitar heroes Alex Skolnick (from Testament), and Marty Friedman (formerly from Megadeth). Eventually, I became introduced to classical guitar music.

SHELBY'S PARAPHRASE

Before classical guitar music entered his life, the blogger fantasized about becoming a rock star like Alex Skolnick or Marty Friedman, and became almost physically attached to the guitar. That guitar enabled him to cope with his teenage angst (Cano).

parenthetical citation
names source

When Should I Paraphrase a Source?

Consider paraphrasing in the following situations:

When you don't want to quote an author directly   You may decide not to quote because you don't want too many competing voices in your piece. In this case, you could paraphrase the sentences from your source, keeping your voice dominant. (See "When Should I Quote from a Source?" on p. 355.)

When *your* audience is very different from your source author's audience   For example, the source you are using may have been written for a specialized or technical audience, and the language might not be suitable for your readers. That is the case in the first example below. A student is writing for an audience of nonexperts about various approaches to treating people convicted of crimes. However, one of her sources is very technical; it was written for criminologists who are familiar with legal terminology. This is an excellent opportunity to paraphrase. The following passage is from an article titled "A Comparative Recidivism Analysis of Releasees from Private and Public Prisons," by Lonn Lanza-Kaduce, Karen F. Parker, and Charles W. Thomas, from the journal *Crime & Delinquency*.

ORIGINAL PASSAGE

Recidivism was operationalized in alternative ways. FDOC records on arrest histories, sentencing, and the movement of inmates in and out of prison were the sources of the data, which were used to develop five different indicators of recidivism.

STUDENT'S PARAPHRASE

authors named in signal phrase; no parenthetical citation needed

Lanza-Kaduce, Parker, and Thomas examined the Florida Department of Correction's records, looking for signs that a prison releasee had returned to prison, such as a record of the releasee's being arrested again or sentenced to another prison term.

You want your writing to flow with your own ideas and words; you want your tone to dominate Paraphrasing allows you to convey all of your source's information, but in your own consistent words and style. For example, imagine you are writing a blog entry in a very informal, snappy tone, and you want to paraphrase the very formal speech Queen Elizabeth II gave in Dublin in 2011.

ORIGINAL PASSAGE

Indeed, so much of this visit reminds us of the complexity of our history, its many layers and traditions, but also the importance of forbearance and conciliation. Of being able to bow to the past, but not be bound by it.

STUDENT'S PARAPHRASE (with humorous intent)

author named in signal phrase; no parenthetical citation needed

The Queen remarked that you gotta remember the past, baby, but you can't let it hold you back. Our relationship's had problems, she told the Irish, but that don't mean it's gotta end.

Note: This paraphrase style can work for nonacademic genres; however, for formal research papers, we do not recommend this technique.

How Do I Paraphrase a Source?

When you want to paraphrase a source, do the following:

Read (or view or listen to) the passage

Put the source away and write down the passage from memory This ensures that you are articulating the ideas in your own words.

Restate the sentence or passage in your own words—while maintaining the sense of the author's original words The following paraphrase retains the meaning of the original passage (from an article by Edison Elementary, "HG/HGT Education") while transforming it into a totally different voice and structure.

ORIGINAL PASSAGE

Giftedness is a collection of certain characteristics that have been displayed by remarkable adults and children past and present. Among the gifted there is great diversity; they are not a homogeneous group.

STUDENT'S PARAPHRASE author named in signal phrase; no parenthetical citation needed
According to educators at Edison Elementary, gifted adults or children are unique individuals who exhibit traits that make them stand out from their peers.

Think of paraphrasing as rephrasing. When you paraphrase, you do more than swap out key words with similar words. Below is an example of an unsuccessful paraphrase created through an inadvisable technique called "patch writing." When people patch write, they simply switch out key words and replace them with synonyms. The result is clunky at best.

The shaded words in the original (again, from the "HG/HGT Education" article by Edison Elementary) are the words the writer replaced with synonyms in the patch-written version.

ORIGINAL PASSAGE
Giftedness is a collection of certain characteristics that have been displayed by remarkable adults and children past and present.

STUDENT'S UNSUCCESSFUL PARAPHRASE (what NOT to do)
According to educators at Edison Elementary, specialness is a group of particular traits that have been shown by extraordinary people of all ages throughout time.

Notice how the patch-written version is not all that different from the original passage—only now it lacks style and voice. The writer chose to switch out words, for example, replacing *collection* with *group*. He also did not change the sentence structure or word order, and kept many of the smaller words (articles and prepositions) as they were in the original. The writer would have done better to use the original quote.

Compare your sentence(s) to the original, making sure that you have altered the language and style enough so that the words are your own

Compare your sentence(s) to the original, making sure that you haven't altered the meaning or intent of the author   Keep in mind that there are some words that you cannot change without changing the meaning of the author's content. Proper nouns and numbers, for example, should not be changed.

Always, always, always attribute your paraphrase to its source   Use the style that is appropriate to the genre you're composing in. For academic genres, see MLA and APA guidelines on pages 372–410.

Guided Process | How to Paraphrase a Source

Paul Pierre (STUDENT), *Nonviolent Protest Project: Paraphrasing Julia Bacha*

Paul, who is writing about nonviolent protest, finds a presentation by documentary filmmaker Julia Bacha. In it, Bacha argues that nonviolent protest is ignored by the media and tells a story about nonviolent protest in a Palestinian town, a story she portrays in her documentary *Budrus*. Following is a step-by-step look at how Paul paraphrased from this source. The image presented on pages 362–63 is a still from Bacha's documentary film.

BUDRUS
Julie Bacha

TRANSCRIPT: I'm a filmmaker. For the last 8 years, I have dedicated my life to documenting the work of Israelis and Palestinians who are trying to end the conflict using peaceful means. When I travel with my work across Europe and the United States, one question always comes up: Where is the Palestinian Gandhi? Why aren't Palestinians using nonviolent resistance?

Credit: Courtesy of Just Vision Media.

The challenge I face when I hear this question is that often I have just returned from the Middle East where I spent my time filming dozens of Palestinians who are using nonviolence to defend their lands and water resources from Israeli soldiers and settlers. These leaders are trying to forge a massive national nonviolent movement to end the occupation and build peace in the region. Yet, most of you have probably never heard about them. This divide between what's happening on the ground and perceptions abroad is one of the key reasons why we don't have yet a Palestinian peaceful resistance movement that has been successful.

I'm [going to] talk about the power of attention, the power of your attention, and the emergence and development of nonviolent movements in the West Bank, Gaza and elsewhere—but . . . my case study is going to be Palestine.

Paul's notes on Bacha's presentation

1. *I watched Bacha's entire presentation.* Then I watched it again. One section of what Bacha said really stood out for me—where she talks about a specific nonviolent protest in Budrus. I think I might want to use some of this in my audio essay. I watched that section of her talk a few times.

2. *Next, I read the transcript.* The entire text of Bacha's talk is available online. I focused especially on the passage that includes the Budrus story.

3. *I put the transcript aside, and paraphrased the passage from memory.* Here is what I came up with:

MY DRAFT PARAPHRASE (of Bacha)

Violent and nonviolent protesters are similar in that to be effective, they need an audience to respond to them. When the media fails to cover nonviolent protest, they deprive nonviolent protestors of an audience (Bacha).

parenthetical citation names author of source

4. *I reread the passage in the transcript and evaluated my draft paraphrase.* I thought I could have done a better job in paraphrasing/restating what Bacha had to say.

5. *I revised and finalized my paraphrase.* I thought the wording of my draft paraphrase was not different enough from Bacha's original text, especially in voice and structure. Here's how I revised to correct those problems:

I believe that what's mostly missing for nonviolence to grow is not for Palestinians to start adopting nonviolence, but for us to start paying attention to those who already are. Allow me to illustrate this point by taking you to this village called Budrus.

About seven years ago, they faced extinction, because Israel announced it would build a separation barrier, and part of this barrier would be built on top of the village. They would lose 40 percent of their land and be surrounded, so they would lose free access to the rest of the West Bank. Through inspired local leadership, they launched a peaceful resistance campaign to stop that from happening.

Let me show you some brief clips, so you have a sense for what that actually looked like on the ground.

FROM THE DOCUMENTARY *BUDRUS*:
Palestinian Woman: We were told the wall would separate Palestine from Israel. Here in Budrus, we realized the wall would steal our land.

Credit: Courtesy of Just Vision Media.

Israeli Man: The fence has, in fact, created a solution to terror.

Man: Today you're invited to a peaceful march. You are joined by dozens of your Israeli brothers and sisters.

Paul's notes on Bacha's presentation

MY IN-TEXT CITATION (paraphrase of Bacha)

Bacha named in signal phrase, so no parenthetical citation needed
Julia Bacha points out that all protesters—including nonviolent ones—need an audience in order to matter. It's a problem that violent protests are the ones we read about, the ones that get attention. When the media fails to cover nonviolent protest, she argues, they deprive peaceful protesters of an audience and of the potential to make a difference.

6. *I cited Bacha as a source in my Works Cited list.* Although audio essays don't usually include a Works Cited list, my instructor asked me to submit one with my Artist's Statement. This caused me some strife because the MLA style for documenting digital sources is confusing to me. However, after consulting a handbook, I cited my source as follows:

MY WORKS CITED ENTRY (MLA style)

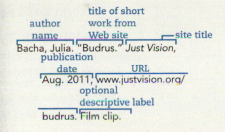

In the paraphrase above (and in his summary on p. 366), Paul strips out references to Palestinians and Israelis. He believes Bacha's idea is relevant to conflicts outside of the Middle East, so he captures Bacha's comparison of violent and nonviolent protest but omits the details of the parties involved.

Summarizing

What Does It Mean to Summarize a Source?

When you summarize a source, you pare the whole thing down to its essence. You eliminate all specific details and give your reader the main point of what the source's author is saying. For example, you might summarize a source in the text of a paper you are writing when you want to investigate or compare the main ideas behind several different sources.

When you summarize, you should:

- Capture the ideas of the source's author.
- Be considerably shorter than the original work. For example, if you are summarizing a two-page article, your summary might be only a paragraph or less. (In the example below, a student writer summarizes twenty-one paragraphs in just one sentence.)
- Write in your own words—not the words of the source's author.
- Give credit to the author of the source summarized. Depending on the genre you compose in, the conventions for crediting sources differ. (In the example below, the student uses a signal phrase to name her source author.)

Let's return to Shelby, the student who is writing about therapeutic uses of music. She finds an article in the blog section of *The Huffington Post* by opera singer Susanne Mentzer, titled "The Catharsis of Song."

Shelby decides she wants to include the opera singer's perspective in her paper, but she wants to do so broadly and briefly, in her Introduction, to draw in her readers. Following are the first few paragraphs from Mentzer's post—as well as Shelby's summary of the post (which she read in its entirety at the *Huffington Post* blog).

> **SHELBY'S SUMMARY OF AN ENTIRE ARTICLE**
> Opera singer Susanne Mentzer has used singing to alleviate both her own stress and tension and the stress and tension of others.

ATTENTION, RESEARCHERS

Summarizing versus paraphrasing. When you summarize a passage from a source, you pick up on *the main points* the author is making and describe them in your own words. When you paraphrase, on the other hand, you do provide a type of summary—but one in which you restate/rephrase the author's words (not just the main points). Summarizing and paraphrasing are both subjective actions, and require you to retain the spirit of the author's meaning and ideas, even if you use them to contrast with your own.

Susanne Mentzer
Opera singer

The Catharsis of Song

Posted: 09/08/11 07:42 PM ET

The human singing voice has the power to release deep emotions. Many know of sounds that give us goosebumps. From the point of view of one who makes sounds, I refer to it as my primal scream therapy. The wonderfulness of singing can be the primal, super-human sound that pours out of one's body. It can also be humbling.

It is thought that hearing is the last sense to leave us when we die. Over the past year, I sang both my parents into the next world. In the ICU, for my mother, an amateur singer who was particularly proud of me, I think I sang my entire repertoire of hymns and arias, toned down to a low dynamic. At one point she awakened with a smile and said, in the slow, whispered voice of one who could barely breathe, "You were singing!" I am not sure if Dad heard me

in his last hours, but I would like to think so. It was a privilege that I would not trade for the world.

Even in my career I have had my own cathartic release of emotion. I once sang a matinee opera performance in Bonn, Germany, after having just put my 10-month old son and his father into a taxi to the airport to fly to the States. It was excruciatingly painful to let my child go but I was contractually obligated to stay. I went to the theater, sang my guts out, and became a blubbering idiot during curtain calls. (Fortunately, it was a dramatic role, the Composer in Strauss's Ariadne auf Naxos.) My colleagues mentioned that I was really "on" that show and that I gave so much emotion. Only then did I share what I was really crying about.

When Should I Summarize a Source?

As a researcher and writer, you might choose to summarize a source when you want to capture the main ideas of a source without going into details. As in the example of Shelby's summary on the previous page, the details of Mentzer's experiences, such as crying during rehearsal, are irrelevant to Shelby's point about the therapeutic nature of music; what matters to Shelby is that Mentzer, a professional singer, has experienced the therapeutic aspects of music in several different contexts.

How Do I Summarize a Source?

To summarize a source, do the following:

- Read (or view or listen to) the source.
- Put the source away and write down the main ideas from memory. This ensures that you are articulating the ideas in your own words.
- Look over the main ideas you wrote down and organize them. For example, begin with a general statement and then move on to the supporting ideas.
- Also, make sure you're simply capturing the main ideas and arguments of the source's author, and not adding any of your own opinions.
- Go back and reread or re-listen to or review the original source. Compare it to what you've written to make sure you haven't distorted any of the points. Make sure you also haven't left out any of the central points.

Attribute your summary to its source. Do this not only in the text of your paper but in your Works Cited or References list as well.

▲ ORIGINAL SOURCE

Susanne Mentzer, "The Catharsis of Song." This article was published at *The Blog*, which is hosted by *The Huffington Post*. Shown here are just the first few paragraphs.

Credit: "The Catharsis of Song" from The Huffington Post *September 8 © 2011. AOL Inc. All right reserved. Used by permission and protected by the Copyright Laws of the United States.*

Guided Process | How to Summarize a Source

Paul Pierre (STUDENT), *Nonviolent Protest Project: Summarizing Julia Bacha*

Paul, who earlier in this chapter paraphrased a passage from a talk by Julia Bacha, decides that he wants to summarize a different passage. Following are the steps he took.

BUDRUS

Julia Bacha

TRANSCRIPT: When I first heard about the story of Budrus, I was surprised that the international media had failed to cover the extraordinary set of events that happened seven years ago, in 2003. What was even more surprising was the fact that Budrus was suc-cessful. The residents, after 10 months of peaceful resistance, convinced the Israeli govern-ment to move the route of the barrier off their lands and to the green line, which is the internationally recognized boundary between Israel and the Palestinian Territories. The resistance in Budrus has since spread to villages across the West Bank and to Palestinian neighborhoods in Jerusalem. Yet the media remains mostly silent on these stories. This silence carries profound consequences for the likelihood that nonviolence can grow, or even survive, in Palestine.

Violent resistance and nonviolent resistance share one very important thing in common; they are both a form of theater seeking an audience to their cause. If violent actors are the only ones constantly getting front-page covers and attracting international attention to the Palestinian issue, it becomes very hard for nonviolent leaders to make the case to their communities that civil disobedience is a viable option in addressing their plight.

Courtesy of Just Vision Media.

Paul's notes on Bacha's presentation

1. *I revisited Bacha's talk*, and was struck by a passage in which she gives a viewpoint on Palestine and nonviolent resistance. I decided to include that material, in some way, in my audio essay.

2. *I reread the transcript*, focusing on the section on Palestine and nonviolent resistance. I decided that it might be best to summarize Bacha's argument.

3. *I drafted a summary of the passage.* To do this, I put the transcript away, and tried to provide an overview of what Bacha said in this part of her talk. Here is what I wrote:

MY DRAFT SUMMARY (of Bacha's passage)

Bacha named in signal phrase, so no parenthetical citation needed

Bacha says that residents of the Palestinian town of Budrus were able to successfully protest against the Israeli building of a fence using nonviolent strategies; however, the news reports of the conflict all focused on a few incidents that involved violence.

4. *Next, I re-viewed Bacha's talk.* I wanted to make sure I had accurately captured her point. Satisfied that I had, I put the summary away for the night.

5. *I revised my summary of Bacha's point.* The next day, when I reread my summary, I decided to cut back on some details of what Bacha had to say. Specifically, I opted not to mention that the Palestinians protested against Israel. For my audio essay, I wanted to stay focused on my main argument—that the media doesn't give enough attention to nonviolent protest—and didn't want to sidetrack my audience with the politics surrounding the protest itself. With this in mind, I revised as follows:

Paul's notes on Bacha's presentation

MY REVISED SUMMARY (of Bacha's passage)

Bacha describes and shows clips of protests in the Middle East that were completely nonviolent. This is in stark contrast to the media reports of the conflict, which failed to mention the nonviolent protests and focused on a handful of violent skirmishes.

6. *Next, I included my summary of Bacha's point in my audio essay.* I drew on Bacha's words to support my argument that nonviolent protest is more powerful than violent protest.

7. *I cited Bacha's talk as a source in my Works Cited list.*

MY WORKS CITED ENTRY (MLA style)

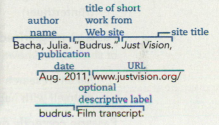

Avoiding Plagiarism

Plagiarism is misrepresenting the ideas or words of others as your own. It includes submitting papers you didn't write, failing to adequately cite sources, and copying small bits and pieces from sources into your own work without properly documenting them. Plagiarism is unethical and committing an act of plagiarism can have serious consequences on your grade, your academic career, and your karma. Your school probably has a statement on academic integrity, defining penalties for acts of academic dishonesty. Be sure to familiarize yourself with the academic integrity policy at your school.

Comparing Passages from a Source

Some plagiarism is unintentional. Writers may read several sources that express similar ideas and only cite one of these sources. Or writers may forget which source they got an idea from and not cite any source at all. Another all-too-common type of unintentional plagiarism occurs when a writer tries to paraphrase a source but doesn't significantly change the original source's language. Here are a couple of examples:

Original passage From a podcast by Adam Hinterthuer, found online at *Scientific American*:

> Want to live a happier life? Try surrounding yourself with happy friends or at least find friends with happy friends. A study published online December 4th in the *British Medical Journal* says happiness can quickly go viral within your social network.

Passage plagiarized The writer misrepresents the source; the source's author, Hinterthuer, is cited, but the writer has gotten the content wrong. Hinterthuer mentions only one study—not "a lot":

> There is a lot of research indicating that happiness is contagious. Simply surrounding yourself with happy friends can make you a happier person (Hinterthuer).

Passage plagiarized In this case, the writer needs to provide an in-text citation. He or she has not shown that this information was obtained from the source, Hinterthuer:

> Recent research indicates that happiness is contagious. Simply surrounding yourself with happy friends can make you a happier person.

Passage correctly presented with an in-text citation

SUMMARY WITH MLA IN-TEXT CITATION

Recent research indicates that happiness is contagious. Simply surrounding yourself with happy friends can make you a happier person (Hinterthuer).

WORKS CITED ENTRY

Hinterthuer, Adam. "Happiness Is Contagious." *Scientific American*, 5 Dec. 2008, www. scientificamerican.com/podcast/episode.cfm?id=happiness-is-contagious-08-12-05 .MP3 file.

SUMMARY WITH APA IN-TEXT CITATION

Recent research indicated that happiness Is contagious. Simply surrounding yourself with happy friends can make you a happier person (Hinterthuer, 2008).

REFERENCES LIST ENTRY

Hinterthuer, Adam. "Happiness Is contagious." *Scientific American*. MP3 audio file. http://www.scientificamerican.com/podcast/episode .cfm?id=happiness-is-contagious-08-12-05.

It's important to realize that whether plagiarism is intentional or unintentional, it is a violation of academic ethics and most schools' codes of conduct. If in doubt about whether to cite a source, cite it. This will prevent you from unintentionally plagiarizing.

CHECKLIST | Getting Help and Avoiding Plagiarism

☐ **Visit your writing center.** If you don't know how to properly summarize or paraphrase a source, consult your instructor or a writing-center tutor for help. It's never a good idea to plagiarize and then plan to apologize if caught. If you're not sure if you're using source material in a way that constitutes plagiarism, get help: Take your draft to your instructor or a tutor and explain what you're having trouble with. As long as you haven't yet turned in the paper, you haven't done anything wrong.

☐ **Use detection software.** If your school subscribes to a plagiarism-detection program like turnitin.com, you can submit a draft of your writing to the program and it will generate a report that indicates what percentage of the draft is from other sources. The report will alert you to places where you've used sources without properly citing them.

☐ **Manage your time.** Allow yourself enough time to complete your writing assignment. Sometimes students accidentally plagiarize because they don't give themselves time to properly double-check all their citations.

☐ **When in doubt, cite that source.** Remember, too, that using an image, audio clip, or video is just like quoting words from someone. These texts need to be cited just as any other source would be.

How to Avoid Plagiarism During Your Research & Composing Process

There are certain crucial moments when researchers and writers can make mistakes that can lead to plagiarism. Please be especially careful at these points:

When taking notes as you conduct research Get in the habit of recording the source's bibliographic information and using quotation marks anytime you use the exact words of a source, even if you use just a few words from the source. For example, you might write in your notes:

> Source: *Our Stressful Lives* site, ourstressfullives.com/pets-and-stress-relief.html
> *About the source:* This site is authored by a "Certified Stress Management Coach," Jill Rheaume, who has also published a stress management workbook. She offers a variety of tips for stress management. I found the following article from the "Pets and Stress Relief: Other Benefits" section of the site, mainly from paragraph 9.

> Notes: Rheaume writes (in paragraph 3) that pets "make great listeners" and help reduce stress in many other ways. In paragraph 9 she writes: "Pets also increase the 'love chemical' oxytocin in our brains. In addition, they can also increase our serotonin, known as the 'happiness chemical.' Both of these things can help to reduce or even prevent stress and prove that our pets can increase our feelings of happiness and help to improve our moods."

Alternatively, you might want to create a screen capture of each source (or otherwise save the original content), so you can refer back to the original as you write.

When quoting as you draft   Always put quotation marks around the words you're using from the source. (In this case, there are quotation marks within quotation marks.)

> **MLA QUOTATION (no in-text cite needed because author is named)**
> Rheaume writes: "Pets also increase the 'love chemical' oxytocin in our brains."

> **WORKS CITED ENTRY**
> Rheaume, Jill. "Pets and Stress Relief: Other Benefits." *Our Stressful Lives*, www
> .ourstressfullives.com/pets-and-stress-relief.html. Accessed 20 Aug. 2013.

> **APA IN-TEXT CITATION**
> Rheaume wrote: "Pets also increase the 'love chemical' oxytocin in our brains."

> **REFERENCES LIST ENTRY**
> Rheaume, Jill. "Pets and stress relief: Other benefits." OurStressfulLives.com. Retrieved
> from http://www.ourstressfullives.com/pets-and-stress-relief.html.

When paraphrasing as you draft   Always credit the source you're paraphrasing. If you aren't sure if you've adequately rephrased the source's idea in your own words, ask a friend, classmate, or writing-center tutor to compare the original passage with your paraphrase. One trick to use when paraphrasing is to read the passage you want to paraphrase and then put the source out of sight and rewrite the idea in your own words. When you do this, you minimize the chance of accidentally using the words of the original. A paraphrase of the above content from Jill Rheaume's site follows. Note that even though we're not using Rheaume's exact words, we still provide the in-text citation.

> **PARAPHRASE WITH MLA IN-TEXT CITATION**
> Pets can make us healthier by raising the levels of oxytocin and serotonin in our brains
> (Rheaume).

> **WORKS CITED ENTRY**
> Rheaume, Jill. "Pets and Stress Relief: Other Benefits." *Our Stressful Lives*, www
> .ourstressfullives.com/pets-and-stress-relief.html. Accessed 20 Aug. 2013.

> **PARAPHRASE WITH APA IN-TEXT CITATION**
> Pets can make us healthier by raising the levels of oxytocin and serotonin in our brains
> (Rheaume).

> **REFERENCES LIST ENTRY**
> Rheaume, Jill. "Pets and stress relief: Other benefits." OurStressfulLives.com. Retrieved
> from http://www.ourstressfullives.com/pets-and-stress-relief.html.

When summarizing as you draft   You can use the same strategies for summarizing that you use for paraphrasing.

> **SUMMARY IN MLA STYLE (no in-text citation needed because author is named)**
> Stress management coach Jill Rheaume writes that interactions with our pets can make
> us happier and more loving by altering levels of certain chemicals in the brain.

WORKS CITED ENTRY

Rheaume, Jill. "Pets and Stress Relief: Other Benefits." *Our Stressful Lives,*
www.ourstressfullives.com/pets-and-stress-relief.html. Accessed 20 Aug. 2013.

SUMMARY WITH APA IN-TEXT CITATION

Stress management coach Jill Rheaume wrote that interactions with our pets can make
us happier and more loving by altering levels of certain chemicals in the brain
(2008–2012, para. 9).

REFERENCES LIST ENTRY

Rheaume, Jill. "Pets and stress relief: Other benefits." OurStressfulLives.com. Retrieved
from http://www.ourstressfullives.com/pets-and-stress-relief.html.

When drafting—without referring to notes   Don't trust your memory! Writers
sometimes don't cite sources in their drafts, thinking they'll go back later and add citations. This is a dangerous practice because if you run out of time and end up not adding
those citations, you've plagiarized. *Always cite your sources,* even in a rough draft.

When integrating sources   When in doubt as to whether or not you should cite a
source, cite it. It's always better to give too much credit with source citations than to
give insufficient credit. You may wonder, for example, if a piece of information counts
as "general knowledge," and therefore doesn't need to be cited. If you're not sure if it
counts as "general knowledge," go ahead and cite a source.

How to Avoid Plagiarism When Using Online Sources

As tempting as it is to copy and paste chunks of online sources into your notes or
drafts, minimize this practice because it greatly increases your chances of accidentally
plagiarizing. Get in the habit of putting quotation marks around every direct quote.
If you paraphrase or summarize, copy the original text into a document and indicate
clearly—with color coding, highlighting, labeling, or some other device—that it is the
original content from your source, and then work on your composition in a separate
document. Another strategy is to create screen captures of each online source, always
accompanied by the URL that will lead you back to that content.

How to Avoid Plagiarism When Composing a Multigenre/ Multimodal Project

All the above guidelines apply to multigenre/multimodal projects: Cite your sources in
drafts, give credit generously, and be meticulous about using quotation marks around
quoted material in your notes. Even if you are composing in a genre or mode that
doesn't use the MLA or APA format for citations, you still need to credit your sources
in ways that are appropriate to the genre or mode of your composition. Additionally,
your instructor may want you to submit a Works Cited list or an Author's or Artist's
Statement that includes MLA or APA citations. (See Chapter 10, p. 285, for example.)

DOCUMENTING SOURCES
A Guide to MLA & APA Styles

Documenting (or citing) a source means giving credit to the authors of any texts—including images, video, sound, or any other composition—that inform your writing, whether you're writing a research paper or creating other types of research-based compositions.

When you document sources, you show your audience where you got your information. You also develop your ethos as an author by showing that you've used reliable source material. Failing to give credit to your sources is a form of dishonesty and is considered plagiarism (pp. 367–71); it leads readers to conclude that all of the ideas and facts that you state come from your own independent thinking or research.

Whether you quote, paraphrase, or summarize from a source, you need to cite it. (For more on quoting, see pp. 353–57; for paraphrasing, see pp. 358–63; for summarizing, see pp. 364–67.)

As composers, when we cite sources, we do so using specific documentation styles. The documentation style you will use depends on the audience you're writing for: Are you writing for an academic audience, your peers, or a general/popular audience? Another factor is the subject matter you're writing about—and the discipline associated with that subject. For example, are your target readers associated with the humanities, social sciences, or sciences? The style you choose also depends on the genre you're composing in (e.g., whether you're writing a straight-up research paper or something else). Following are some guidelines for choosing a documentation style.

ATTENTION, RESEARCHERS

Why don't musicians document their sources when they sample music? Many hip-hop musicians use sampling (taking a part of a song) when they create their songs. For example, Nas's song "Can't Forget About You" includes a sample from Nat King Cole's classic "Unforgettable." Not only does the sample figure in the song, but clearly Nas's title was inspired by Nat King Cole. He doesn't provide formal documentation because it is a convention within the music industry that some sampling is deemed appropriate. This, however, is subject to legal interpretation if the original composer wants to challenge the originality of the composition. To avoid potential legal issues, most musicians will obtain permission prior to including samples in their own compositions—and include some kind of credit in the liner notes. If there *are* liner notes.

Composers of other genres often draw upon other sources; however, because of the conventions of the genres they're working in, they might not use formal academic documentation. Such genres include obituaries, memoirs, sets of instructions, and poems.

How to Choose a Documentation Style

Are you writing a research paper for a specific academic discipline?

- For papers for an English course or other humanities course, you will almost always use the documentation style of the Modern Language Association (MLA; mla.org). However, in some English courses that focus on writing in or across disciplines, you might use the documentation style that is associated with your major area of study.

- For papers for a social science course, you will probably use the format of the American Psychological Association (APA; apastyle.org).

- For papers for a history course, you will likely use *Chicago* style, based on *The Chicago Manual of Style* (chicagomanualofstyle.org).

- For papers for a science course, you will probably use the style specified by the Council of Science Editors in *Scientific Style and Format: The CSE Manual for Authors, Editors, and Publishers* (councilscienceeditors.org).

Are you composing a photo essay, ad, or documentary, or in some other alternative genre? And are your subject and audience based in the humanities, social sciences, or sciences? While MLA tends to be the default documentation style of the English composition course, and is likely the format your instructor may require, you might have the option of deciding for yourself which documentation style would be best for your composition and chosen subject. For example, if your topic involves criminal justice or gender studies, you could make a case for using APA style. And if you are creating a lab report or doctor's notes, you might use the CSE documentation style.

Most of our students submit MLA-style Works Cited lists with their compositions, though some, depending on their chosen genres, subjects, and major areas of study, use APA, *Chicago*, or CSE. If you plan to use one of these styles, you might want to discuss it with your instructor first, and make a case for why that style would be best.

Are you composing an Author's Statement to accompany your genre composition? If you are creating an Author's Statement to accompany your composition (whether it's a research paper or alternative genre project), we recommend the MLA style of documentation, unless you've made a case for using APA, *Chicago*, or CSE. (For more on the Author's Statement—the reflective piece that can be submitted with any genre composition—see pp. 90–102.)

While there are several documentation styles for you to choose from, the following sections of this chapter provide basic guidance for using MLA and APA styles, as these are the styles you are most likely to use in conjunction with this textbook.

MLA Style

The MLA style of documentation is presented in the *MLA Handbook*, 8th ed. (MLA, 2016). It is commonly used in English courses and other courses in the humanities. This style has been around a long time, but it has evolved to take into account the many types of sources we work with today.

The MLA style of documentation has two main components:

1. In-text citations
2. List of Works Cited (a.k.a. Works Cited list)

The in-text citation Each time you cite a source in your paper — whether through a signal phrase or a parenthetical reference — you cue readers to a corresponding entry in your Works Cited list. When you include an in-text citation, you:

- Name the author of your source (or title if author is not provided)
- Provide a page number for that source (if there is one)
- Make sure you have a corresponding entry in your Works Cited list

The list of Works Cited In your Works Cited list, at the end of your paper, you:

- Provide publication information about each source (for Web sources that don't provide publication dates, provide an "Accessed" date)
- Alphabetize your sources by authors' last names (or by title if an author is not provided)
- Include a URL for each online source (for more on this, see the box on p. 377)

Following is an example of an in-text citation along with its corresponding entry in the Works Cited list.

IN-TEXT CITATION

"Parents with this philosophy know there may be things their daughter hides from them, but they don't take it as a personal insult or an indication that their relationship with their daughter is weak" (Wiseman 54).

author · exact page that quotation is from

WORKS CITED ENTRY

author: last name, first name · title of book · publisher · publication year · page number

Wiseman, Rosalind. *Queen Bees and Wannabes.* Three Rivers Press, 2002, p. 54.

In-text citations: General guidelines There are two main ways to handle an in-text citation: by using a signal phrase or a parenthetical reference (or some combination).

SIGNAL PHRASE (author named in phrase)

author

Wiseman suggests that "parents with this philosophy know there may be things their daughter hides from them, but they don't take it as a personal insult or an indication that their relationship with their daughter is weak" (54).

└──── exact page that quotation is from

PARENTHETICAL REFERENCE (author cited in parentheses)

"Parents with this philosophy know there may be things their daughter hides from them, but they don't take it as a personal insult or an indication that their relationship with their daughter is weak" (Wiseman 54).

author └──── exact page that quotation is from

Works Cited entries: General guidelines

For each in-text citation in your paper, you need to provide a corresponding entry in your Works Cited list. The following guidelines provide the basic format for the MLA Works Cited entry.

- Name the author by last name, followed by first name.

| author | book title | publisher | publication year | page range | descriptive label (optional, for clarity) |

King, Stephen. *Full Dark, No Stars.* Pocket Books, 2011, pp. 1–12. Kindle.*

- For works by three or more authors or editors, list the name that appears first on the cover or title page, followed by "et al." (See also page 379, entry 5.) Note that for university presses you should use the abbreviation "UP."

lead author or editor: last name, first name, then et al. — spell out "editors" — book title

Bearman, Peter, et al., editors. *After Tobacco: What Would Happen If Americans*

publisher — publication year — page range

Stopped Smoking? Columbia UP, 2011, pp. 30–36.

- Present the titles of long works—books or entire Web sites—in italics.

author — book title — publisher — publication year — page range

Burroughs, Augusten. *Running with Scissors: A Memoir.* Picador, 2002, pp. 113–17.

author — Web site title — publisher

Sullivan, Andrew. *The Dish: Biased & Balanced.* The Daily Beast, andrewsullivan

URL — in the absence of a publication date, provide an access date

.thedailybeast.com/. Accessed 8 Sept. 2013.

*Provide a page range if your source is an e-book with numbered pages.

- Present the titles of short works—articles or other short pieces from books or periodicals—in quotation marks.

author	article title	periodical title	publication date	page range

Parker, James. "Notes from the Underworld." *The Atlantic*, May 2011, pp. 38–41.

author	article title	periodical and site title	publication date

Acosta, Judith. "Do Guns Make the Man?" *The Huffington Post*, 21 July 2011,

URL

huffingtonpost.com/judith-acosta/do-guns-make-the-man_b_901918.html.

- Present titles with initial capital letters—except in the case of articles (*a, the,* etc.), prepositions (*to, from, with,* etc.), or coordinating conjunctions (*and, but, or, for,* etc.), unless these words come first or last.

author	book title	publisher	publication year	page range

Hemingway, Ernest. *To Have and Have Not.* Scribner's, 1937, pp. 1–4.

author	book title	publisher	publication year	page range	descriptive label (optional, for clarity)

Grafton, Sue. *V Is for Vengeance.* G. P. Putnam's Sons, 2011, pp. 12–13. Kindle.

- For print works, include the publisher's name as it appears on the title page. If no publisher is given on the title page, then see the copyright page.

author	book title	publisher	publication year	page range

Lahiri, Jhumpa. *Unaccustomed Earth.* Bloomsbury Publishing, 2008, pp. 52–56.

- For both print and online works, provide the date that the piece was published. For online sources, if no publication date is provided, include the date you accessed the source. For online sources, provide the URL at the end of the entry (omitting https://).

author	article title	publication title	publisher

Sumners, Christina. "Animal Acumen: Elephantine Intelligence." *NOVA*, PBS,

publication date	URL

26 Aug. 2011, pbs.org/wgbh/nova/insidenova/2011/08/elephants.html.

- When needed to clarify a source, you can include a descriptive label. MLA makes this practice optional. Whatever you decide, be consistent.

  author | book title

  Gates, Henry Louis, Jr. *Life upon These Shores: Looking at African American History:*

  publisher / publication year | page range | descriptive label (optional, for clarity)

  1513–2008. Alfred A. Knopf, 2011, pp. 112–14. Kindle.

  developer | title | publisher | publication year | descriptive label (optional, for clarity)

  Bungie. *Halo: Combat Evolved.* Microsoft Studios, 15 Nov. 2001. Video game.

Organize your Works Cited list alphabetically. For entries of more than one line, indent additional lines five spaces (this is called hanging indentation).

Works Cited

Acosta, Judith. "Do Guns Make the Man?" *The Huffington Post*, 21 July 2011, huffingtonpost.com/judith-acosta/do-guns-make-the -man_b_901918.html.

Bearman, Peter, et al., editors. *After Tobacco: What Would Happen If Americans Stopped Smoking?* Columbia UP, 2011, pp. 30–36.

Bungie. *Halo: Combat Evolved.* Microsoft Studios, 15 Nov. 2001. Video game.

Burroughs, Augusten. *Running with Scissors: A Memoir.* Picador, 2002, pp. 113–17.

Gates, Henry Louis, Jr. *Life upon These Shores: Looking at African American History: 1513–2008.* Alfred A. Knopf, 2011, pp. 112–14. Kindle.

Grafton, Sue. *V Is for Vengeance.* G. P. Putnam's and Sons, 2011, pp. 12–13. Kindle.

Hemingway, Ernest. *To Have and Have Not.* Scribner's, 1937, pp. 1–4.

King, Stephen. *Full Dark, No Stars.* Pocket Books, 2011, pp. 1–12. Kindle.

Lahiri, Jhumpa. *Unaccustomed Earth.* Bloomsbury Publishing, 2008, pp. 52–56.

Parker, James. "Notes from the Underworld." *The Atlantic*, May 2011, pp. 38–41.

Sullivan, Andrew. *The Dish: Biased & Balanced. The Daily Beast*, andrewsullivan.thedailybeast.com/. Accessed 8 Sept. 2013.

Sumners, Christina. "Animal Acumen: Elephantine Intelligence." NOVA, PBS, 26 Aug. 2011, pbs.org/wgbh/nova/insidenova/2011/08/ elephants.html.

MLA Models

Models for Basic Situations

1. Author is named in a signal phrase   When citing a source in the text of your paper, you need to name your author. You can do this in a signal phrase or in a parenthetical reference (along with the source's page number) following your citation. It's simplest to name the author in a signal phrase and keep the parenthetical reference brief. The following citation refers to material from Jonathan Safran Foer's book *Eating Animals* (Little, Brown and Company, 2009).

IN-TEXT CITATION

Jonathan Safran Foer argues that we can't trust language. "When it comes to eating animals," he writes, "words are as often used to misdirect and camouflage as they are to communicate" (45).

WORKS CITED ENTRY

Foer, Jonathan Safran. *Eating Animals.* Little, Brown and Company, 2009, pp. 1–86.

2. Author is named in parentheses   If you decide not to name your author in a signal phrase, then name the author in your parenthetical reference along with the page number; don't use any punctuation between the name and page number.

IN-TEXT CITATION

Others argue that in addition to distrusting factory farming, we should also distrust the words associated with it, such as "natural" and "free range" (Foer 45).

WORKS CITED ENTRY

Foer, Jonathan Safran. *Eating Animals.* Little, Brown and Company, 2009, pp. 1–86.

3. Individual author name is not provided   If you cannot locate an author name for your source, use the title. Provide the complete title of the text (or video, etc.) in a signal phrase—or give a shortened version of the title in the parenthetical reference. (Note: If the author is an organization, see example 6 on p. 380.) Following are sample citations for an article titled "Best Places to Live: 2012" that appears on CNN's *Money Magazine* site.

IN-TEXT CITATION (title in signal phrase; no page number available)

According to a recent *Money Magazine* article, "Best Places to Live: 2012," Carmel, Indiana, is the winner of all American small towns in terms of housing, finances, and overall quality of life.

OR (shortened title in parentheses; no page number available)

Carmel, Indiana, was recently determined to be the best American small town to live in ("Best Places").

WORKS CITED ENTRY

"Best Places to Live: 2012." Money Magazine, CNN, Sept. 2012, money.cnn.com/
magazines/moneymag/best-places/2012/snapshots/PL1810342.html?iid=spl100.

4. Author identified by screen name only   Some online sources identify an author, but not by a traditional first and last name. For example, the author of an eHow article is simply identified as an "eHow Contributor."

IN-TEXT CITATION (no page number available)

Another piece of career-building advice is to ask for extra training and to research and learn more about your industry (eHow Contributor).

WORKS CITED ENTRY

eHow Contributor. "How to Get Along with the Boss." *Demand Media*, 4 Nov. 2010,
ehow.com/how_2057947_get-along-boss.html.

5. More than one author   Some sources have multiple authors. If your source has *two* authors, include both of their names. Following is a reference to *The Worst-Case Scenario Survival Handbook: Life*, a book by Joshua Piven and David Borgenicht (San Francisco: Chronicle Books, 2006).

IN-TEXT CITATION (two authors)

To escape a stampede of giraffes, the best plan of action is to dive or wade into the nearest body of water. Giraffes tend to avoid water unless they are thirsty (Piven and Borgenicht 185).

WORKS CITED ENTRY

Piven, Joshua, and David Borgenicht. *The Worst-Case Scenario Survival Handbook: Life.*
Chronicle Books, 2006, p. 185.

For three or more authors, use the phrase "et al." (short for the Latin phrase *et alia*, which means "and others"). Following is a reference to an article published in *Nutrition Journal* titled "A Survey of Energy Drink Consumption Patterns among College Students." It was written by Brenda M. Malinauskas, Victor G. Aeby, Reginald F. Overton, Tracy Carpenter-Aeby, and Kimberly Barber-Heidal.

IN-TEXT CITATION (four or more authors; no page number available)

According to a 2007 study, college students consume Red Bull and other energy drinks when they feel sleep-deprived (67%), need an energy boost (65%), drink alcohol (54%), study or complete a major project (50%), drive long distances (45%), and have hangovers (17%) (Malinauskas et al.).

WORKS CITED ENTRY

Malinauskas, Brenda M., et al. "A Survey of Energy Drink Consumption Patterns among College Students." *Nutrition Journal*, vol. 6, no. 5, 2007, nutritionj.com/
content/6/1/35.

ATTENTION, RESEARCHERS USING MLA

Does your source have no page numbers?   Many digital sources do not have page numbers. When using these sources, do your best to meet MLA's requirements:

Provide the author, title, publisher/publication title, date of publication, and if no publication date is given, provide your access date. Also, please note: While MLA does not require you to provide descriptive labels such as "photograph," "chart," "map," "cartoon," "episode," etc., you can choose to do so if you think this would be helpful to your readers.

The Works Cited entry for an episode of *The Colbert Report* that you found online could look like this:

WORKS CITED ENTRY (for online clip)

host   episode title   name of show/series   publisher
Colbert, Stephen, host. "Let Them Buy Cake." *The Colbert Report*, Comedy Central,

episode date   URL
13 Dec. 2011, www.colbertnation.com/the-colbert-report-videos/404252/
                                                                    descriptive label
                                                                    (optional for clarity)
december-13-2011/the-word---let-them-buy-cake. Episode.

The Works Cited entry for a film you saw in a theater could look like this:

WORKS CITED ENTRY (for movie)

director   movie title   major performers
Nolan, Christopher, director. *The Dark Knight Rises*. Performances by Christian Bale, Tom

                                    release   descriptive label
                        publisher   date   (optional, for clarity)
Hardy, and Anne Hathaway, Warner Bros., 2012. Film.

6. Author is an organization
Follow the same basic format as for sources with any other type of author.

IN-TEXT CITATION (no page number available)

Mental health is a human and civil rights issue (Mental Health America).

WORKS CITED ENTRY

Mental Health America. "Position Statement 21: Rights of Persons with Mental Health and Substance Use Conditions." *Mental Health America*, nmha.org/go/position -statements/21. Accessed 30 Sept. 2013.

7. No page numbers
Many online sources (unless the source is a PDF) have no page numbers. The box above and examples 3 and 4 (pp. 378–79) show how to handle entries for sources without page numbers.

Another example: A video by *South Park* creators Trey Parker and Matt Stone, which animates a lecture by the philosopher Alan Watts, was found on YouTube.

IN-TEXT CITATION

The animated version of Watts's main arguments about life, music, and how success is measured creates a layered experience for viewers (Parker and Stone).

Parker, Trey, and Matt Stone. "Life and Music." *YouTube*, 18 June 2007, youtube.com/
      watch?v=ERbvKrH-GC4.

8. Source used more than once in a paragraph   If you refer to a source multiple
times in one paragraph, you can provide the author's name(s) just once, as long as it's
clear it's still the same source. For example, see the citation for the article titled "Panic
Disorder" from *The Journal of the American Medical Association*. The authors are Janet M.
Torpy, Alison E. Burke, and Robert M. Golub.

IN-TEXT CITATION

According to research published in *The Journal of the American Medical Association*,
not everyone who has a panic attack gets diagnosed with panic disorder (Torpy et al.).
Still, as the article makes clear, many Americans suffer from mental health issues.

WORKS CITED ENTRY

Torpy, Janet M., et al. "Panic Disorder." *Journal of the American Medical
      Association*, vol. 305, no. 12, 2011, pp. 20–30, jama.jamanetwork.com/article
      .aspx?articleid=646264.

Models for Specific Types of Sources

9. Book   For more in-text citation models for books, see examples 1, 2, and 5
(pp. 378 and 379). The following is from *Unbearable Lightness: A Story of Loss and Gain* by
Portia de Rossi.

IN-TEXT CITATION

In Hollywood, where thinness is demanded at any cost but is extolled as the product
of health and fitness, those who strive for perfection have to lie. As one actress puts it:
"How could I possibly explain my weight maintenance when it was attributed to starving
and bingeing?" (de Rossi 90).

WORKS CITED ENTRY

de Rossi, Portia. *Unbearable Lightness: A Story of Loss and Gain*. Atria Books, 2010,
      p. 90.

10. Article or essay   The following model shows how to cite an article from an
online periodical. In February 2012, *National Geographic* published an article by Tom
O'Neill titled "Lady with a Secret."

IN-TEXT CITATION (article from online magazine)

A chalk-and-ink drawing, titled *La Bella Principessa*, may be the work of Leonardo da
Vinci (O'Neill).

WORKS CITED ENTRY

O'Neill, Tom. "Lady with a Secret." *National Geographic*, Feb. 2012, ngm
      .nationalgeographic.com/2012/02/lost-da-vinci/o-neill-text.

The following model shows how to cite an article from a database.

IN-TEXT CITATION (article from a database)

Some images have the power to "spur a revolution" (Childs).

WORKS CITED ENTRY

Childs, Arcynta Ali. "The Power of Imagery in Advancing Civil Rights." *Smithsonian*,
Oct. 2011, pp. 40–41. *OmniFile Full Text Select*, web.b.ebscohost.com.ezproxy
.bpl.org/.

11. Source quoted in another source   The following models show how to cite a
source that is quoted in another source. "Is Anybody Out There?" by Phil Plait was published by *Discover* magazine (in its November 2010 issue). Plait's article features several quotations from four major astronomers. To cite one of those quotations, use the
phrase "qtd. in" to indicate that you did not read the quoted source itself, but rather
found the quoted material in another source.

IN-TEXT CITATION

According to Gibor Basri, professor of astronomy at Berkeley, proof of whether
"anybody's out there" may come down to a radio signal. "There are about 60 radio
telescopes scanning the skies for these signals right now," he says. "That would be the
definitive answer to the search for life: If you get an intelligent signal, then you know
for sure" (qtd. in Plait).

WORKS CITED ENTRY

Plait, Phil. "Is Anybody Out There?" *Discover*, Kalmbach Publishing, Nov. 2010,
discovermagazine.com/2010/nov/25-is-anybody-out-there/article_view
?b_start:int=0&-C=.

12. Encyclopedia or dictionary entry—or wiki entry   In your signal phrase or
parenthetical reference, provide the word or phrase that you looked up in the dictionary or encyclopedia. If the work or entry has an author, provide that also. For the following example, there is no author provided by *Encyclopaedia Britannica*. Also, because
the source (*Encyclopaedia Britannica*) and publisher (Encyclopaedia Britannica, Inc.) are
essentially the same, MLA does not require that the publisher name be included in the
Works Cited list.

IN-TEXT CITATION (for online encyclopedia)

The phrase "carpe diem," which traces back to an ancient Roman poet, means to seize
or "pluck the day" ("Carpe diem").

WORKS CITED ENTRY

"Carpe diem." *Encyclopaedia Britannica*, britannica.com/EBchecked/
topic/96702/carpe-diem. Accessed 30 Sept. 2013.

IN-TEXT CITATION (for online source)

The wombat is in danger because of destruction to its habitat; meanwhile, a project by a Swiss mining company is experimenting with relocating some of these animals from their native region in Australia to a new colony elsewhere in the country ("Wombat").

WORKS CITED ENTRY

"Wombat." *Wikipedia*, en.wikipedia.org/wiki/Wombat. Accessed 1 Sept. 2013.

ATTENTION, *WIKIPEDIA* LOVERS

Check with your instructor about using *Wikipedia* as a source. It is a public wiki that can be edited by anyone. Tip: *Wikipedia* can be a great place to start your research, especially because the "Reference," "Further Reading," and "External Links" sections can often lead you to excellent and reliable sources to use in your research project. For example, the "Wombat" entry provides links to Australian governmental information, BBC articles, and books authored by wombat experts. See also *Wikipedia's* entry (or go to wikipedia.org and type in "Researching with Wikipedia").

---

13. Entire Web site   In the rare instance that you will want to cite an entire Web site—rather than a specific portion of it, such as an article—use the following model. (For information on citing a short work from a Web site, see example 14 on page 384.) MLA requires that you provide a Web site's author. Note that an author can be an organization such as a library or museum. If no author is provided, begin your Works Cited entry with the title of the site.

Web site with no author

IN-TEXT CITATION

It is possible for an Internet radio station, drawing from a database and using your preferences for artists, songs, and genres, to personalize your experience, playing only the music you want to hear (Pandora).
                                                        Web site title

WORKS CITED ENTRY

Pandora. Music Genome Project and Pandora Media Inc., pandora.com/.
        Accessed 2 Sept. 2013.

Web site with author or editor

IN-TEXT CITATION

One consumer-focused site gives an unflinching critique of big business, addressing the question: What is the worst company in America? (Marco et al.)
                                                        Web site editors

WORKS CITED ENTRY

Marco, Meg, et al., editors. *The Consumerist*, consumerist.com/. Accessed
        30 Sept. 2015.

14. Short work from a Web site   Most of what you cite from the Internet can be categorized as a "short work from a Web site." A short work is any text (of any type and medium) that is not book length or that appears as an internal page or section of a Web site. A short work can be an article, report, poem, song, video, and so on.

Short work with no author

IN-TEXT CITATION

To avoid deep vein thrombosis during air travel, it can help to wear loose clothing and to stroll through the cabin once every hour ("Healthy Travel").

title of short work from a Web site

WORKS CITED ENTRY

"*Healthy Travel Tips.*" *Delta,* www.delta.com/traveling_checkin/travel_tips/health/index .jsp. Accessed 30 Sept. 2013.

Short work with an author

IN-TEXT CITATION

A new genetically engineered salmon produced by a biotech firm will not be labeled as such, according to standards set by the Food and Drug Administration (Bittman).

author

WORKS CITED ENTRY

Bittman, Mark. "Why Aren't GMO Foods Labeled?" *Opinionator,* 15 Feb. 2011, opinionator.blogs.nytimes.com/2011/02/15/why-arent-g-m-o-foods-labeled/.

15. Video, movie, or TV show   In general, cite these sources as you would a short work from a Web site (see example 14). When citing a movie or any work that includes a director, begin with the title and then identify the director, as shown below. NOTE: Although MLA style does not require it, keep in mind that you can add a descriptive label to your Works Cited entry if you think that would be helpful to your readers. For example, you can add words to indicate a source's type, such as "episode," "advertisement," "cartoon," "pamphlet," "photograph," "painting," and so on.

IN-TEXT CITATION

The opening scene of one episode of *Family Guy* is all about consumption: Peter can't resist the cookie dough batter, while Stewie is tempted by the Abercrombie catalog (MacFarlane).

director

WORKS CITED ENTRY (for online episode)

MacFarlane, Seth, director. "The Big Bang Theory." *Family Guy,* Fox, 8 May 2011, hulu.com/watch/237564/family-guy-the-big-bang-theory. Episode.

16. Video game, online game, or software To cite an entire video game, follow the format for an entire Web site (see example 13). For a clip from a video game, follow the format for a short work from a Web site. As noted in example 15, you can include descriptive labels such as *game*, *software*, and so on.

Entire video game

IN-TEXT CITATION

The goal of one popular game is to plow, plant, and harvest on "your own" virtual land (FarmVille 2).

<u>video game title</u>

WORKS CITED ENTRY

FarmVille 2. Zynga, 2012, FarmVille.com. Game.

Clip from video game

IN-TEXT CITATION

Players can build their enterprises by acquiring such animals as the arctic fox and the armadillo ("My Mastery").

<u>video game clip title</u>

WORKS CITED ENTRY

"My Mastery." *FarmVille 2*. Zynga, 2012, FarmVille.com. Game clip.

<u>clip title</u>

17. Visuals (photos, maps, charts, posters) Cite these as you would a short work from a Web site (see example 14) or other, longer work. Include the following, if available: author's or artist's name, title of the work, name of publication, and date of publication. You also have the option to note the type of the composition that your source is, for example, "photograph," "map," "chart," or "poster."

IN-TEXT CITATION

The image is a reminder that among those evicted by the Chicago Housing Authority are families with small children (Reblando).

<u>photographer</u>

WORKS CITED ENTRY

Reblando, Jason. "Jessica Moore's Son Maurice Booker (left), 5, with a Friend." *The New York Times*, 3 Sept. 2011, nytimes.com/2011/09/04/us/04cncfirststrike.html?_r=1. Photograph.

18. Comic strip/graphic work Think of comic strips as short works—from longer works such as Web sites, magazines, and so on—and cite them as you would a short work or article from a Web site (see example 14), online journal, book, or other source.

As an option, you can include the label "cartoon" or "comic strip" at the end of your Works Cited entry if you think that would benefit your readers. For graphic novels (fiction) or memoirs (nonfiction), follow the format that you would for a book. In some cases, the author is also the illustrator; when that is not the case, be sure to include the name of the illustrator, preceded by the phrase "Illustrated by" (see example below).

Comic strip

IN-TEXT CITATION

The comic offers social commentary on issues such as racism, immigration, gay rights, the military, and consumption (Toyoshima).
author/artist

WORKS CITED ENTRY

Toyoshima, Tak. "Why Oppose Openly Gay Soldiers in the Military?" *Secret Asian Man*, 22 Aug. 2010, secretasianman.com/home.htm. Comic strip.

Excerpt from a graphic memoir *(author is also illustrator)*

IN-TEXT CITATION

In 1980, a year after Iran's Islamic Revolution, she and her female classmates were obliged to wear a veil to school (Satrapi 3).
author/artist

WORKS CITED ENTRY

Satrapi, Marjane. *Persepolis*. Pantheon Books, 2004, pp. 1–8. Graphic memoir.

Excerpt from a graphic novel *(with an author and an illustrator)*

IN-TEXT CITATION

The story opens with a journal entry that makes clear the character's obsessions with gore, filth, and death, not to mention Communists and intellectuals (Moore 1).
author

WORKS CITED ENTRY   artist

Moore, Alan. *Watchmen*. Illustrated by Dave Gibbons, DC Comics, 2008, pp. 1–32. Graphic novel.

19. Advertisement   To cite an ad, give the name of the product being advertised. Following are the in-text citation and Works Cited entry for an ad for Dove Visible Care Body Wash, found at the company Web site. For the in-text citation, provide a shortened version of the product name.

IN-TEXT CITATION

A recent ad campaign for body wash claims to renew and soften skin, promising "visible results in just one week" (Dove Visible).
ad title (shortened)

WORKS CITED ENTRY

Dove Visible Care Body Wash. *Dove*. Unilever, www.dovecloseup.com/default
    .aspx#home. Accessed 30 Sept. 2013. Advertisement.

20. Personal e-mail, text message, letter, or interview   To cite an e-mail message (that you've written or received), provide the writer's name and the subject line. Next, provide the words "Received by" followed by the name of the recipient and the date the message was received. It is optional to include the descriptive label "E-mail" at the end. For a text message you've received, provide the writer's name followed by "Received by the author," followed by the date the text was received. For a letter you've received, provide the author's name and the phrase "Received by the author," followed by the date it was received. To cite an interview that you've conducted, provide the interviewee's name and "Interview by the author" followed by the date.

E-mail *(received)*

IN-TEXT CITATION

Once customers search for a flight, hotel, or car, the organization e-mails periodic pricing updates, which can lead to a better deal for the consumer (Hotwire).

author of e-mail

WORKS CITED ENTRY

Hotwire. "Another Way to Save on Portsmouth Hotels." Received by the author,
    15 Sept. 2013. E-mail.

Text Message *(received)*

IN-TEXT CITATION

At the rally, a student was pepper-sprayed (Tamura).

author of text message

WORKS CITED ENTRY

Tamura, Annika. Received by the author, 1 Oct. 2011. Text message.

Letter *(received)*

IN-TEXT CITATION

I received an unsettling report of suspicious activity involving my personal credit information (Experian).

author of letter

WORKS CITED ENTRY

Experian National Consumer Assistance Center. Received by the author, 15 Jan. 2013.
    Letter.

Interview (conducted)

IN-TEXT CITATION

The world-traveling journalist admitted that while she might have wanted to stay home on her couch eating Ben and Jerry's Chunky Monkey, she did not have the time: Moscow, Afghanistan, and Cairo awaited (Amanpour).

person interviewed

WORKS CITED ENTRY

Amanpour, Christiane. Interview with the author, 21 Feb. 2013.

21. Blog post or social media posting   Cite as you would a short work from a Web site (see example 14); if the entry has no title, create a brief title based on the first line of the entry. For Twitter posts, however, MLA requires the full text of the tweet, presented without changes, in place of the title.

IN-TEXT CITATION

One journalist who covered the James "Whitey" Bulger story was surprised by the shabbiness of the mob fugitive's Santa Monica apartment (Brady-Myerov).

author

WORKS CITED ENTRY

Brady-Myerov, Monica. "Whitey Bulger's former hideout." *Facebook*, 24 June 2011,
    facebook.com/bradymyerov.

22. Audio recording or podcast from the Web   Cite audio recordings or podcasts that you've accessed online in the same way you would a short work from a Web site (see example 14).

Podcast

IN-TEXT CITATION

It's holiday time, and an unemployed writer takes a job as a Macy's Christmas elf ("Sedaris Returns").

podcast title

WORKS CITED ENTRY

"Sedaris Returns as Crumpet the Elf on NPR." *Morning Edition*, 24 Dec. 2004, npr.org/
    templates/story/story.php?storyId=4243755. Podcast.

Song

IN-TEXT CITATION

The artist performs her iconic song in "Single Ladies (Put a Ring on It)" as her alter ego, Sasha Fierce (Knowles).

WORKS CITED ENTRY

Knowles, Beyoncé. "Single Ladies (Put a Ring on It)." *I Am . . . Sasha Fierce*, Columbia,
    2008, itunes.apple.com/us/album/i-am...-sasha-fierce/id296016891. Song.

23. Phone app   Cite a phone app as you would a Web site, or if you're referring to part of the app, cite it as you would a short work from a Web site (see example 14). It is optional to include the descriptive label "Phone app."

IN-TEXT CITATION

The creators of the app pitch it as a "one-stop GPS outdoor recreation app," with maps created for the screen—maps that are not simply shrunken versions of outdated USGS maps (AccuTerra).

<u>app title</u>

WORKS CITED ENTRY

AccuTerra. Version 3.1 for iPhone. Intermap Technologies, iTunes, 13 July 2011, itunes.apple.com/us/app/accuterra-unlimited-maps-gps/id355787609?mt=8. Phone app.

24. Government or business document   For a government document, provide the author, title, and date. If there is no author, provide the name of the government agency (and department, if any). Follow the rules for a short work from a longer work (e.g., a book, journal, or Web site). For a historical document, such as the one included below, provide the title in italics.

Government document

IN-TEXT CITATION

He wrote: "[A]ll persons held as slaves within any State or designated part of a State, the people whereof shall then be in rebellion against the United States, shall be then, thenceforward, and forever free" (Lincoln).

<u>author</u>

WORKS CITED ENTRY

<u>title of document</u>

Lincoln, Abraham. Emancipation Proclamation. 1 Jan. 1863. The Library of Congress, loc.gov/pictures/item/97507511/resource/cph.3b53030/?sid=40c1ec586dad 774d8a08ebfbf8cdff07. Accessed 30 Sept. 2013.

Business document (annual report)

IN-TEXT CITATION

Even a major corporation such as Microsoft has felt the sting of the global recession (Ballmer).

<u>author</u>

WORKS CITED ENTRY

<u>title of document</u>

Ballmer, Steven A. "Microsoft Corporation: Annual Report 2012." Microsoft, 10 Oct. 2012, microsoft.com/investor/reports/ar12/index.html.

25. Literary work (novel, poem, fairy tale, etc.)   Provide the author, title, publisher, and date. For Web sources, provide a URL. For e-books, it is optional to include a descriptive label, for example "Kindle" or "Nook," to identify for readers the brand platform.

Novel

WORKS CITED ENTRY

McCarthy, Cormac. *All the Pretty Horses.* Alfred A. Knopf, 1992.

Novel

WORKS CITED ENTRY

McCarthy, Cormac. *All the Pretty Horses.* Vintage International, 11 Aug. 2010. Kindle.

Poem

WORKS CITED ENTRY

Crane, Hart. "At Melville's Tomb." *Poetry Out Loud,* poetryoutloud.org/poem/172021. Accessed 11 Apr. 2013.

26. Selection from an anthology or textbook   Begin with the selection author and title, followed by the anthology or textbook title, editors, publisher, year, and page range.

IN-TEXT CITATION

Advances in DNA testing have complicated commonly held ideas about racial identity (Eubanks).

author of selection (shortened)

WORKS CITED ENTRY
author of selection

information on textbook where selection appears

Eubanks, W. Ralph. "Color Lines." *The Bedford Book of Genres,* edited by Amy Braziller and Elizabeth Kleinfeld, 2nd ed., Bedford/St. Martin's, 2018, p. 457.

27. Object/artifact (cereal box, etc.)   If you find an object or artifact online, cite it as a short work from a Web site (see example 14). As an option, you can include a descriptive label for the item in your Works Cited entry.

IN-TEXT CITATION

Children might be drawn to the sunny yellow box, but parents likely focus on the red heart and the soft claim about lowering cholesterol (Cheerios).

name of object

▲ **OBJECT**
Cheerios box.

Object (found online)

WORKS CITED ENTRY

"Cheerios." General Mills, www.cheerios.com/Products/Cheerios. Accessed 30 Sept. 2013. Cereal box.

Object (found in physical world)

WORKS CITED ENTRY

"Cheerios." General Mills. Cereal box.

APA Style

The APA style of documentation is the style presented in the *Publication Manual of the American Psychological Association*, 6th ed. (Washington: APA, 2010). It is commonly used in the behavioral and social science disciplines, which include courses in psychology and in sociology, and some English and cultural studies courses.

The APA style of documentation has two main components:

1. In-text citations
2. List of References

The in-text citation   Your in-text citations refer your readers to your list. Each time you cite a source in your paper—whether through a signal phrase or a parenthetical reference—you cue readers to a corresponding entry in your References list. When you include an in-text citation, you:

- Name the author of your source
- Provide the source's year of publication—and (if it's a print source) a corresponding page number
- Make sure you have a corresponding entry (for each in-text citation) in your References list

The References list   In your References list, at the end of your paper, you:

- Provide publication information about each source
- Alphabetize your sources by authors' last names (or by title if an author is not provided)

The following example shows an in-text citation along with its corresponding entry in the References list.

IN-TEXT CITATION

As students who visit our writing centers are working with

       author   publication year

multimodal compositions (Sheridan, 2010), it makes sense to open up our idea of what it means to help with the entire composing processes (p. 3).

    exact page where information is from

ATTENTION, RESEARCHERS

A note about APA & tense.   When you use a signal phrase to discuss a source, you must introduce the source by using the past or present perfect tenses. For example: "Lady Gaga (2017) said," or "Lady Gaga (2017) has argued." For more examples, see the APA in-text citation models provided in this chapter (pp. 395–410).

Note that MLA dictates a different approach, and requires you to use the present tense. For example: "Lady Gaga (2017) says," or "Lady Gaga (2017) argues." See pages 378–90 for MLA models.

(Continues on next page)

REFERENCES LIST ENTRY

author — publication year — title of chapter — editors

Sheridan, D. M. (2010). Writing centers and the multimodal turn. In D. M. Sheridan &

title of book

J. A. Inman (Eds.), *Multiliteracy centers: Writing center work, new media, and multimodal rhetoric* (pp. 1–22). Cresskill, NJ: Hampton Press.

page range of chapter — place of publication — publisher

In-text citations: General guidelines There are two main ways to handle an in-text citation: by using a signal phrase or a parenthetical reference (or some combination).

SIGNAL PHRASE (author named in phrase)

authors — publication year

Kingsolver, Kingsolver, and Hopp (2007) explained to readers that they "had come to the farmland to eat deliberately" (p. 23).

exact page that quotation is from

PARENTHETICAL REFERENCE (author named in parentheses)

In discussing psychiatric illnesses, the author argued, "Psychiatry has found a way to medicalize all human behavior and offer a pharmaceutical intervention for everything" (Plante, 2012, para. 3).

author — publication year — for this online source, no page number is available, but source has paragraph numbers

References entries: General guidelines Provide a corresponding entry in your References list for each in-text citation in your paper. The following guidelines provide the basic format for the APA References list entry.

- Give the author's last name, followed by initials for all first and middle names. Provide additional authors' names with each last name followed by initials for first and middle names.

author: last name + initial(s) — publication year — title of book

Ben-Shahar, T. (2007). *Happier: Learn the secrets to daily joy and lasting fulfillment.*

place of publication — publisher

New York, NY: McGraw-Hill.

authors: last name + initial(s) — publication year — title of article

Watkins, P. C., Woodward, K., Stone, T., & Kolts, R. L. (2003). Gratitude and happiness:

title of article

Development of a measure of gratitude, and relationships with subjective well-being.

title of journal — volume

Social Behavior and Personality, 31.

- Present the titles of long works—books or entire Web sites—in italics. Capitalize the first word of the title; other words in the title (except proper nouns) are lowercased. If there is a subtitle, capitalize the first word of the subtitle.

author: last name + initial(s) | publication year | title of book

Deutsch, D. (2011). *The beginning of infinity: Explanations that transform the world.*

place of publication | publisher

New York, NY: Viking Penguin.

- Present the titles of short works from books or Web sites without quotation marks or italics. Capitalize the first word of the title; other words are lowercased (though be sure to retain the capitalization of proper nouns). If there is a subtitle, capitalize the first word of the subtitle. IMPORTANT: For all online sources, include the URL. Although APA suggests you provide the URL for the source's homepage, we recommend that you provide the exact URL for the specific article or other work you're referring to. For example, the article cited below is from Salon.com. The URL takes readers to the page for the article itself, not Salon's homepage.

author: last name + initial(s) | publication year, month, day | title of article | title of magazine

Mustich, E. (2011, June 15). Can students be disciplined for online speech? *Salon*

paragraph range | article URL

(paras. 1–6). Retrieved from http://news.salon.com/2011/06/15/students

_online_speech/singleton

- For print works, present the city and state of publication, and spell out the entire name of the publisher.

author: last name + initial(s) | publication year | title of book

Lieber, L. (2008). *The Einstein theory of relativity: A trip to the fourth dimension.*

place of publication | publisher

Philadelphia, PA: Paul Dry Books.

- For both print and online works, provide the date that the piece was published. For online sources, provide the URL, but not the access date—unless there is a chance the content of the source may change.

author: last name + initial(s) | publication year | title of book

Clark, D. P. (2010). *Germs, genes, and civilization: How epidemics shaped who we are*

place of publication | publisher

today. Upper Saddle River, NJ: Pearson Education, Inc.

author: last — publication year,
name + initial(s) — month, day — title of photo essay

Lewis, T. (2012, August 13). Slimy but cute: 10 newly discovered amphibians

descriptive — title of
label — magazine — photo essay URL

[Photo essay]. *Wired.* Retrieved from http://www.wired.com/wiredscience/2012
/08/new-amphibian-species/

- If your source is a work that would benefit from clarification, provide that term in brackets. (See models for these on pp. 399–410.)

author — publication year,
month, day — title of newspaper editorial

The Denver Post Editorial Board. (2012, January 20). School trans fat ban not needed

descriptive — title of
label — newspaper — editorial URL

[Editorial]. *The Denver Post.* Retrieved from http://www.denverpost.com
/opinion/ci_19778812

Organize your References list alphabetically. For entries of more than one line, indent additional lines five spaces (this is called hanging indentation).

References

Ben-Shahar, T. (2007). *Happier: Learn the secrets to daily joy and lasting fulfillment.* New York, NY: McGraw-Hill.

Clark, D. P. (2010). *Germs, genes, and civilization: How epidemics shaped who we are today.* Upper Saddle River, NJ: Pearson Educational, Inc.

The Denver Post Editorial Board. (2012, January 20). School trans fat ban not needed [Editorial]. *The Denver Post.* Retrieved from http:// www.denverpost.com/opinion/ci_19778812

Deutsch, D. (2011). *The beginning of infinity: Explanations that transform the world.* New York, NY: Viking Penguin.

Kingsolver, B., Kingsolver, C., & Hopp, S. L. (2007). *Animal, vegetable, miracle: A year of food life.* New York, NY: HarperCollins.

Lewis, T. (2012, August 13). Slimy but cute: 10 newly discovered amphibians [Photo essay]. Wired. Retrieved from http://www.wired .com/wiredscience/2012/08/new-amphibian-species/

Lieber, L. (2008). *The Einstein theory of relativity: A trip to the fourth dimension.* Philadelphia, PA: Paul Dry Books.

Mustich, E. (2011, June 15). Can students be disciplined for online speech? *Salon* (paras.1–6). Retrieved from http://news.salon .com/2011/06/15/students_online_speech/singleton

Plante, T. (2012, February 1). The psychopathology of everything [Editorial Weblog post]. *Do the right thing: Spirit, science, and health. Psychology Today*, para. 3. Retrieved from http://www .psychologytoday.com/blog/do-the-right-thing/201202/ the-psychopathology-everything

Sheridan, D. M. (2010). Writing centers and the multimodal turn. In D. M. Sheridan & J. A. Inman (Eds.), *Multiliteracy centers: Writing center work, new media*, and multimodal rhetoric (pp. 1–22). Cresskill, NJ: Hampton Press.

Watkins, P. C., Woodward, K., Stone, T., & Kolts, R. L. (2003). Gratitude and happiness: Development of a measure of gratitude, and relationships with subjective well-being. *Social Behavior and Personality, 31*.

APA Models

Models for Basic Situations

1. Author is named in a signal phrase   When citing a source, name your author in a signal phrase—that is, name the author in the body of your text, and provide the source publication year and page number in parentheses. Or use a parenthetical reference—as shown in the example below—and provide everything in parentheses: the author's last name, the source publication year, and page number.

The simplest, cleanest method is to name the author in a signal phrase and keep the parenthetical reference brief:

IN-TEXT CITATION
David Myers (2011) identified shifts in the study of human behavior. He wrote: "I find myself fascinated by today's psychology, with its studies of the neuroscience of our moods and memories, the reach of our adaptive unconscious, and the shaping power of the social and cultural context" (p. 4).

REFERENCES LIST ENTRY
Myers, D. (2011). *Psychology* (10th ed.). New York, NY: Worth Publishers, 1–4.

2. Author is named in parentheses   If you don't name your author in a signal phrase, then do so in your parenthetical reference along with the publication year and page number; use commas between the name, year, and page number.

IN-TEXT CITATION

Part of what has made the study of psychology so interesting is the current focus on neuroscience, the adaptive unconscious, and social and cultural factors (Myers, 2011, p. 4).

REFERENCES LIST ENTRY

Myers, D. (2011). *Psychology* (10th ed.). New York, NY: Worth. 1–4.

3. Individual author name is not provided   In the rare case that you cannot locate an author name for your source, use the title (or the first word or two of the title) in parentheses. (Note: If the author is an organization, see example 6.) Following are sample citations for a brief article titled "Psych Basics: Charisma" that appears on *Psychology Today*'s site.

IN-TEXT CITATION (title in signal phrase; no page number available)

According to a current *Psychology Today* article, "Psych Basics: Charisma" (2012), charming and influencing others requires "confidence, exuberance, and optimism" (para. 1).

OR (shortened title in parentheses; no page number available)

Charisma is said to be a quality that you either have or you don't ("Charisma," 2012, para. 1).

REFERENCES LIST ENTRY

Psych basics: Charisma. (2012). *Psychology Today*, para. 1. Retrieved from http://www.psychologytoday.com/basics/charisma

ALTERNATIVE APPROACH: If you consider the publisher, *Psychology Today*, as the author, here is how the in-text citation and References list entry would work:

IN-TEXT CITATION (organization treated as author)

There are physical aspects to charisma, as well: smiling, using body language, and speaking with a friendly voice (*Psychology Today*, 2012, para. 1).

REFERENCES LIST ENTRY

Psychology Today. (2012). Psych basics: Charisma. *Psychology Today*, para. 1. Retrieved from http://www.psychologytoday.com/basics/charisma

4. Author identified by screen name only   Some online sources identify an author, but not by a traditional first and last name. For example, the author of an eHow article is simply identified as an "eHow Contributor."

IN-TEXT CITATION (no page number available)

Among the suggestions for improving memory were doing crossword puzzles, reading, and playing word games (eHow Contributor, 2011).

REFERENCES LIST ENTRY
eHow Contributor. (2011, September 6). How to sharpen your memory. *eHow*.
 Retrieved from http://www.ehow.com/how_5594193_sharpen-memory.html

5. More than one author   Some sources have multiple authors. In general, you will list only up to five names in your in-text citations; for your References list, you can list up to seven authors, using an "&" just before the final name. Below is a reference to *The Worst-Case Scenario Survival Handbook: Work*, a book by Joshua Piven and David Borgenicht (San Francisco: Chronicle Books, 2003).

IN-TEXT CITATION (two authors)
To avoid taking a nightmare job, the authors recommended that applicants should schedule a morning interview and observe the mood of workers as they arrive: slouching, pouting, or looking dejected are all signs of low morale (Piven & Borgenicht, 2003, p. 16).

REFERENCES LIST ENTRY
Piven, J., & Borgenicht, D. (2003). *The worst-case scenario survival handbook: Work*.
 San Francisco, CA: Chronicle Books, 1–32.

For three to five authors, identify all authors the first time you use the source in text; afterward, use only the first author's name and the phrase "et al." (short for the Latin phrase *et alia*, which means "and others"). Note: The article cited in the example below is from a database; many databases provide a DOI number for use in your References list entry. If there is no DOI, then use the phrase "Retrieved from" followed by the URL.

IN-TEXT CITATION (three to five authors)
A recent study found a boost in girl power in India, thanks to affirmative action laws that gave women leadership roles in their village councils. In terms of career goals, the gender gap for teen girls in the villages with women leaders closed by 32% (Beaman, Duflo, Pande, & Topalova, 2012, pp. 582–586).

LATER CITATIONS
(Beaman et al., 2012, pp. 582–586)

REFERENCES LIST ENTRY (article retrieved from database with DOI)
Beaman, L., Duflo, E., Pande, R., & Topalova, P. (2012, January 12). Female leadership raises aspirations and educational attainment for girls: A policy experiment in India. *Science, 335,* 582–586. doi:10.1126/science.1212382

REFERENCES LIST ENTRY (article from publisher site, abstract or summary only)
Beaman, L., Duflo, E., Pande, R., & Topalova, P. (2012, January 12). Female leadership raises aspirations and educational attainment for girls: A policy experiment in India [Abstract]. Science, 335, 582–586. Retrieved from http://www.sciencemag .org/content/335/6068/582.abstract

For six or more authors, for your in-text citations, name the first author listed, followed by "et al." In your References list entry, list up to seven authors. If there are more than seven authors, list the first six followed by three ellipsis dots and the last author's name. Following is a reference to an article published in the British journal *Animal Behaviour* titled "Firefly Flashing and Jumping Spider Predation." It was written by Skye M. Long, Sara Lewis, Leo Jean-Louis, George Ramos, Jamie Richmond, and Elizabeth M. Jako.

IN-TEXT CITATION (six or more authors)

Sadly for fireflies, flashing does more than entice mates; it can attract predators, including two species of attacking spiders (Long et al., 2012, pp. 81–86).

REFERENCES LIST ENTRY (up to seven authors)

Long, S. M., Lewis, S., Jean-Louis, L., Ramos, G., Richmond, J., & Jako, E. M. (2012). Firefly flashing and jumping spider predation. Animal Behaviour, 83, 81–86. doi:10.1016/j.anbehav.2011.10.008

6. Author is an organization   Follow the same basic format as for sources with any other type of author.

IN-TEXT CITATION

The American Civil Liberties Union argued that since 9/11, our civil liberties have "undergone constant erosion" thanks to expanded powers of government security agencies (ACLU, 2012, para. 1).

OR

Since 9/11, Americans' civil liberties, especially in the digital realm, have been under attack by security agencies such as the NSA and FBI (American Civil Liberties Union [ACLU], 2012, para. 1).

LATER CITATIONS

(ACLU, 2012)

REFERENCES LIST ENTRY

American Civil Liberties Union. (2012). Protecting civil liberties in the digital age, paras. 1–3. Retrieved from http://www.aclu.org/protecting-civil-liberties-digital-age

7. No page numbers   Most print sources have numbered pages, but unless your online source is provided as a PDF file, it probably will not include page numbers. Examples 3 and 6 show in-text citations for sources that have no page numbers; in those cases we provided paragraph numbers.

IN-TEXT CITATION

Erik Qualman's (2011) video provided a fast-paced barrage of statistics showing the rapid growth of social media.

REFERENCES LIST ENTRY

Qualman, E. [Screen name: Socialnomics09] (2011, June 8). Social media revolution 2011 [Video file]. Retrieved from http://www.youtube.com/watch?v=3SuNx0UrnEo

8. Source used more than once in a paragraph   Let's say that you give the author's name in a signal phrase in the text of your paper (and the publication date and page number in parentheses). To refer to that same source later in the same paragraph, simply provide the page number (or paragraph number).

For a print source

The example below refers to an article by Rob Sheffield about *Mad Men*; it appeared in the print edition of *Rolling Stone* on March 29, 2012.

IN-TEXT CITATION

Sheffield (2012) wrote that Draper built his career by "hustling in the dirty world of American dreams" (p. 36). I've always assumed that, unlike the rest of us, Don Draper, the cool ad man, is immune to the beautiful lies he sells. But as the writers further developed the character, he has become more impulsive, a man looking for Disney happiness and fresh starts. What's clear is this: "[T]his guy believes in Hollywood happy endings" (p. 36).

REFERENCES LIST ENTRY

Sheffield, R. (2012, March 29). More desperate than mad. *Rolling Stone* (1153), p. 36.

ATTENTION, RESEARCHERS

A note about APA style.   Like language, documentation styles are always evolving. APA style changes from edition to edition, of APA's manual, and even daily on the organization's blog. Our best advice:

1. Provide readers with the information they'll need to identify and find your sources.
2. If you aren't sure how to cite a particular source and you don't see a model for it here, find a similar source and adapt the model provided.

For an online source

The example below refers to an article by Miriam Coleman about Madonna's 2012 Super Bowl performance; it was published on *Rolling Stone*'s Web site on February 5, 2012. Note that while there are no page numbers for this source, we have provided paragraph numbers.

IN-TEXT CITATION

Miriam Coleman (2012) detailed how Madonna was "ushered in on a golden chariot pulled by a phalanx of centurions" for the first part of her Super Bowl performance (para. 1). As a high priestess of popular culture, Madonna understands fanfare and branding, not to mention big entrances and exits: "In the final moment of the show, gold beams projected up into the sky as Madonna disappeared from the stage in a massive plume of smoke" (para. 3).

REFERENCES LIST ENTRY

Coleman, M. (2012, February 5). Madonna's glittering Super Bowl spectacle. *Rolling Stone*, paras. 1–3. Retrieved from http://www.rollingstone.com/music/news/madonnas-glittering-super-bowl-spectacle-20120205

ATTENTION, RESEARCHERS USING APA

Does your source have no page numbers? For most online sources (anything that's not a PDF), you will not be able to provide page numbers. However, for online articles and other text-based digital sources, you can provide paragraph numbers. Paragraph numbers help your readers see exactly where you drew from a source.

For sources you cannot provide paragraph numbers for—videos, audio recordings, and many other types of digital media—we recommend that you do your best to provide whatever information will guide your audience to a particular moment in that video or audio recording. You can provide a time range, for example.

Let's look again at the Qualman video presented as part of example 7 (p. 399). Here is how you might cite a particular moment from that source.

IN-TEXT CITATION

According to Erik Qualman's (2011) video on the role of social media, "If Facebook were a country it'd be the world's 3rd largest" (0:42–0:44).

Let's say that elsewhere in your paper you refer to other moments of the video, which is two minutes and thirty-five seconds long. This is what a very precise References list entry would look like.

REFERENCES LIST ENTRY

Qualman, E. (2011, June 8). Social media revolution 2011 [Video file]. Retrieved from http://www.youtube.com/watch?v=3SuNx0UrnEo (0:01–2:35)

Models for Specific Types of Sources

9. Book   For more in-text citation models for books, see examples 1, 2, and 5. The following is from *Just Kids* by Patti Smith.

ATTENTION, RESEARCHERS

Citing entire works is a rarity.   When working with sources, 99.9 percent of the time you refer to specific passages and pages from a source—and include them in both your in-text citation and the corresponding References list entry. In the *extremely* rare instance that you need to summarize an entire work (as shown in the example below), you do not need to provide specific page numbers. Unless you are creating an annotated bibliography, we do not recommend that you make a practice of summarizing entire sources.

IN-TEXT CITATION (that summarizes entire work)
In her memoir, Patti Smith (2010) described numerous adventures with the artist Robert Mapplethorpe, highlighting stories from when they lived in the Chelsea Hotel.

REFERENCES LIST ENTRY
Smith, P. (2010). *Just kids*. New York, NY: HarperCollins.

IN-TEXT CITATION (that quotes from a specific passage)
Smith (2010) writes: "My mother gave me *The Fabulous Life of Diego Rivera* for my sixteenth birthday. I was transported by the scope of his murals, descriptions of his travels and tribulations, his loves and labor" (p. 12).

REFERENCES LIST ENTRY
Smith, P. (2010). *Just kids*. New York, NY: HarperCollins, 1–12.

IN-TEXT CITATION (that paraphrases a specific passage)
She was quite taken by a sixteenth birthday gift from her mother: *The Fabulous Life of Diego Rivera* (Smith, 2010, p. 12).

REFERENCES LIST ENTRY
Smith, P. (2010). *Just kids*. New York, NY: HarperCollins, 1–12.

10. Article or essay   The following models show how to cite online and print articles. In February 2012, a magazine called *5280: The Denver Magazine* published an article by Josh Dean—"The Australian Shepherd Is From"—in two forms: online and in print.

IN-TEXT CITATION (article from an online magazine)
According to Dean (2012), "[D]ogs that appeared to be Aussies were doing their jobs all over the West, but no one seemed interested in documenting their provenance" (para. 1).

REFERENCES LIST ENTRY

Dean, J. (2012, February). The Australian shepherd is from [Electronic version]. *5280: The Denver Magazine*, paras. 1–38. Retrieved from http://www.5280.com /magazine/2012/02/australian-shepherd

IN-TEXT CITATION (article from a print magazine)

In his article, Dean (2012) argued that although the Australian shepherd "isn't Colorado's official state dog . . . it really should be" (p. 75).

REFERENCES LIST ENTRY

Dean, J. (2012, February). The Australian shepherd is from. *5280: The Denver Magazine*, 70–75, 110–118.

11. Source quoted in another source   The following models show how to cite a source that is quoted in another source, whether online or print. "Is Anybody Out There?" by Phil Plait was published by *Discover* magazine in two different forms—in a print edition (in its November 2010 issue) and online at discovermagazine.com (on January 27, 2011). Plait's article features several quotations from four major astronomers. To cite one of those quotations, you need to use the phrase "as cited in" to indicate that you did not read the quoted source itself, but rather found the quoted material in another source.

IN-TEXT CITATION (article from an online magazine)

According to Gibor Basri, professor of astronomy at Berkeley, proof of whether "anybody's out there" may come down to a radio signal. "There are about 60 radio telescopes scanning the skies for these signals right now," he said. "That would be the definitive answer to the search for life: If you get an intelligent signal, then you know for sure" (as cited in Plait).

REFERENCES LIST ENTRY

Plait, P. (2011, January). "Is anybody out there?" *Discover* (paras. 1–3). Retrieved from http://discovermagazine.com/2010/nov/25-is-anybody-out-there/article_view?b _start:int=0&-C=.

IN-TEXT CITATION (article from a print magazine)

According to Gibor Basri, professor of astronomy at Berkeley, proof of whether "anybody's out there" may come down to a radio signal. "There are about 60 radio telescopes scanning the skies for these signals right now," he says. "That would be the definitive answer to the search for life: If you get an intelligent signal, then you know for sure" (as cited in Plait, 2010).

REFERENCES LIST ENTRY

Plait, P. (2010, November). Is anybody out there? *Discover*, 49–51.

Check with your instructor about using Wikipedia as a source. It is a public wiki that can be edited by anyone. Tip: *Wikipedia* can be a great place to start your research, especially because the "Reference," "Further Reading," and "External Links" sections can often lead you to excellent and reliable sources to use in your research project. For example, the "Racial segregation" entry provides links to *The Washington Post, The American Historical Review,* and books authored by experts on apartheid. You can also go to wikipedia.org and type in "Researching with Wikipedia."

12. Encyclopedia or dictionary entry—or wiki entry When the author or authors of an entry are named, follow the format that you would for an article (see example 10). When no author is named, use the name of the publisher or publication—or begin the citation with the title of the entry. If there is a publication date, provide it. If not, then indicate that there is no date by using "n.d." in parentheses following the author's name.

IN-TEXT CITATION (for online dictionary)

publisher name

According to *Merriam-Webster* (2012), psychoanalysis is used to "treat emotional disorders."

REFERENCES LIST ENTRY

Merriam-Webster. (2012). Psychoanalysis. Retrieved from http://www.merriam-webster
.com/dictionary/psychoanalysis

Unlike *Merriam-Webster, Wikipedia* is a multiple-authored wiki: This means that the authors and the content itself change all the time. Following is a model for citing a *Wikipedia* entry. We've included a "Retrieved from" date because any *Wikipedia* entry cited today may be quite different by tomorrow.

IN-TEXT CITATION (for a wiki)

Racial segregation (2012), according to *Wikipedia,* is defined as "the separation of humans into racial groups in daily life" (para. 1).

REFERENCES LIST ENTRY

Wikipedia. (2012, February 6). Racial Segregation. Retrieved February 8, 2012, from
http://en.wikipedia.org/wiki/Racial_segregation (para. 1)

13. Entire Web site In the extremely rare instance that you will want to cite an entire Web site—rather than a specific portion of it, such as an article—use the following model. (For information on citing a short work from a Web site, see example 14 on page 404.) APA requires that for Web sources, you provide the name of the organization that authored the page, the publication date (use "n.d." if there is none), the name of the site, and the URL.

Note: All Web sites have an author—or at least a hosting organization. If an individual person or persons are not named as authors, then consider the organization that hosts or publishes the site to be the author. Similarly, if you find an article at MSNBC.com that does not list an individual author, then you should consider MSNBC.com as the author of that article.

Web site with an organization as author

IN-TEXT CITATION

Web site sponsor/publisher

Fastweb (2012) divided its scholarship links into categories including "Art Scholarships," "Hispanic Scholarships," and "Scholarships for College Freshmen."

REFERENCES LIST ENTRY

Fastweb. (2012). Retrieved from http://www.fastweb.com

14. Short work from a Web site   Most of what you cite from the Internet can be categorized as a "short work from a Web site." A short work is any text (of any type and medium) that is not book length or that appears as an internal page or section of a Web site. A short work can be an article, report, poem, song, video, and so on. In some cases, you will include a descriptive label (see example 15 on p. 405).

Short work with an organization as author

IN-TEXT CITATION

Web site sponsor/publisher

The WebMD entry "Anxiety Disorders" (2009) defined various types of disorders, such as panic disorder and social anxiety disorder.

REFERENCES LIST ENTRY

WebMD (2009). Anxiety disorders. Retrieved from http://www.webmd.com/anxiety
-panic/guide/mental-health-anxiety-disorders

Short work with an individual author

IN-TEXT CITATION

All is not necessarily lost in a relationship if someone cheats. Sometimes, according to Clark-Flory (2012), infidelity might bring couples closer and "[open] new lines of communication" (para. 1).

REFERENCES LIST ENTRY

Clark-Flory, T. (2012, January 23). When infidelity heals. *Salon*. Retrieved from http://
life.salon.com/2012/01/23/when_infidelity_heals/singleton/

15. Video, movie, or TV show   In general, if you find these sources online, cite them as you would a short work from a Web site (see also example 14). Include an identifying label in brackets: "Television series episode," "Film," and so on.

IN-TEXT CITATION

During the *Big Bang Theory* episode "The Friendship Connection," the character Wolowitz spent time trying to choose an astronaut nickname (Lorre, Kaplan, & Reynolds, 2012).

REFERENCES LIST ENTRY (for a TV episode)

Lorre, C., Kaplan, E., & Reynolds, J. (Writers), & Cendrowski, M. (Director). (2012, February 2). The friendship connection [Television series episode]. In Lorre, C., Prady, B., & Molaro, S. (Producers), *Big bang theory*. New York, NY: CBS.

REFERENCES LIST ENTRY (for a different episode, online)

Lorre, C., Kaplan, E., & Reynolds, J. (Writers), & Cendrowski, M. (Director). (2012, January 19). The recombination hypothesis [Television series episode]. In Lorre, C., Prady, B., & Molaro, S. (Producers), *Big bang theory*. Retrieved from http://www .cbs.com/shows/big_bang_theory/video/2188321432/the-big-bang-theory-the -recombination-hypothesis

16. Video game, online game, or software   To cite an entire video game, follow the format for an entire Web site and include a description—"Video game," "Online game," or "Computer software"—in brackets. For a clip from a video game, follow the format for a short work from a Web site (see example 14).

Entire video game

IN-TEXT CITATION

The goal of one popular game was to plow, plant, and harvest on "your own" virtual land (Zynga, 2009).
video game publisher

REFERENCES LIST ENTRY

Zynga. (2009). *FarmVille* 2 [Online game]. Zynga. Retrieved October 13, 2012 from http://www.farmville.com/

Clip from video game

IN-TEXT CITATION

Players can build their enterprises by acquiring such animals as the arctic fox and the armadillo (Zynga, 2009).
video game publisher

REFERENCES LIST ENTRY

Zynga. (2009). My mastery. [Online game clip]. *FarmVille* 2. Zynga. Retrieved February 13, 2012 from http://www.farmville.com/

17. Visuals (photos, maps, charts, posters)   Cite these works as you would a short work from a Web site (see example 14), or other longer work. Include the following, if available: author's or artist's name, date of composition, title of the work, and publication's name. Also note the medium of the composition—"Photograph," "Map," "Chart," "Poster," and so on—in brackets.

IN-TEXT CITATION

Most visitors spend time in the capital city of Kuala Lumpur, located in the southwestern part of the country (Lonely Planet, 2012).

author of map

REFERENCES LIST ENTRY

Lonely Planet. (2012). Malaysia [Map]. Retrieved from http://www.lonelyplanet.com/maps/asia/malaysia/

18. Comic strip/graphic work   Think of comic strips as short works—from longer works such as Web sites, magazines, and so on—and cite them as you would a short work or article from a Web site, online journal, book, or other source. Include the description—"Cartoon" or "Comic strip"—in brackets. For graphic novels (fiction) or memoirs (nonfiction), follow the format that you would for a book. In some cases, the author is also the illustrator; when that is not the case, in parentheses after the title, indicate the illustrator's name followed by the word "illustrator."

Comic strip

IN-TEXT CITATION

author/artist

Thomas's (2012) comic strip offered a commentary on the mentality of social media users.

REFERENCES LIST ENTRY

Thomas, C. (2012, February 5). Watch your head [Comic strip]. *The Washington Post Writer's Group*. Retrieved from http://www.cartoonistgroup.com/properties/wpwg.php?id=106&today=2012-02-05

Excerpt from a graphic memoir *(author is also illustrator)*

IN-TEXT CITATION

author/artist

In her graphic memoir, Crumb (2007, pp. 1–7) chronicled her life journey from New York to the south of France.

REFERENCES LIST ENTRY

Crumb, A. K. (2007). *Need more love: A graphic memoir*. London, United Kingdom: MQ Publications, 1–7.

Excerpt from a graphic novel *(with an author and an illustrator)*

IN-TEXT CITATION

author

Powell (2008) retold the classic story of Little Red Riding Hood in graphic novel form.

artist

Powell, M. (2008). *Red Riding Hood: The graphic novel.* (Victor Rivas, illustrator.) North Mankato, MN: Stone Arch Books, 1–4.

19. Advertisement To cite an ad, name the product being advertised, along with the word "Advertisement" in brackets. Following are the in-text citation and References list entry for an ad created by the BBDO advertising firm for FedEx Kinko's. We found it at the Ads of the World Web site (which is not a publication).

author
of ad

IN-TEXT CITATION

One ad for FedEx Kinko's featured a larger-than-life highlighter (BBDO, 2007).

REFERENCES LIST ENTRY

BBDO advertising firm. (2007, March). FedEx Kinko's Giant Highlighter [Advertisement]. Retrieved from http://adsoftheworld.com/media/ambient /fedex_kinko_giant_highlighter?size=_original

20. Personal e-mail, letter, or interview Even though APA does not require you to list e-mails, personal interviews, letters, memos, or other personal communications in your References list, we recommend you do so for the sake of clarity. To cite an item in the text of your paper, include the author's first and middle initials (if known) and last name and the term "personal communication" (regardless of whether it was an interview, letter, or e-mail), and then the full date of the communication. In your References list, you can indicate in brackets the medium of the item, such as "E-mail."

E-mail (received)

IN-TEXT CITATION

Metro State's first Undergraduate Research Conference was scheduled to take place in April (P. Ansburg, personal communication, February 9, 2012).

author of e-mail

REFERENCES LIST ENTRY

Ansburg, P. (2012, February 9). First annual metro state undergraduate research conference [E-mail].

Interview (conducted)

IN-TEXT CITATION

person interviewed

I spoke to one tutor who described a method known as "glossing" (P. Calzia, personal communication, May 2, 2011).

REFERENCES LIST ENTRY

Calzia, P. (2011, May 2). Writing center discussion [Interview by E. Kleinfeld].

21. Blog post or social media posting   Cite postings as you would any short work from a Web site (see example 14). In your References list entry, add in brackets a brief description of the item: "Web log," "Facebook post," "Twitter post," and so on. Note: APA requires that you use the term "Web log." As with example 4, use the author's screen name if that is all that is provided.

IN-TEXT CITATION

author

Marino (2012) used social media to convey some of the items on his bucket list.

REFERENCES LIST ENTRY

Marino, B. (2012). Bucket list [Facebook post]. Retrieved from http://www.facebook. com/billy.marino1

22. Audio recording or podcast   Cite podcasts that you've accessed online in the same way you would cite a short work from a Web site (see example 14). Audio recordings should be cited similarly to works of art, regardless of whether they are downloaded from the Web or not.

Podcast from Web

IN-TEXT CITATION

Conan (2012) introduced listeners to historian Noah Andre Trudeau and described Trudeau's mission to collect artifacts from President Lincoln's presidency.

REFERENCES LIST ENTRY

Conan, N. (2012, February 9). Historian seeks artifacts from Lincoln's last days [Audio podcast]. Retrieved from National Public Radio Web site: http://www.npr.org/ programs/talk-of-the-nation/

Song from the Web (via iTunes)

IN-TEXT CITATION

Ritter's (2010) song "The Curse" played with the ideas of love at first sight and coming back from the dead.

REFERENCES LIST ENTRY

Ritter, J. (2010). The curse [Song]. On *So Runs the World Away*. Brea, CA: Pytheas Recordings. Retrieved from http://itunes.apple.com/us/album/change-of-time /id362130747?i=362130766&ign-mpt=uo%3D4

23. Phone app   Cite a phone app as you would an advertisement, but include "Phone app" in brackets. Use the date of the most recent iteration of the phone app as the publication date. Put the developer's or publisher's name where you would put an author for a print source.

IN-TEXT CITATION

The social media app called MassUp was created to help bicyclists gather in large groups (Bedno, 2010).

app publisher

REFERENCES LIST ENTRY

Bedno, A. (2010, November 17). MassUp [Phone app]. Retrieved from http://www
.apple.com/webapps/sports/massup.html

24. Government or business document
For a government document, provide the author, government organization and department, title, and date, as well as publication information. If there is no author, provide the name of the government agency (and department, if any).

Government document

IN-TEXT CITATION

One of the top concerns of organizers of farmers' markets was the availability of parking for customers (Ragland & Tropp, 2006, pp. 6–10).

authors

REFERENCES LIST ENTRY

Ragland, E., & Tropp, D. U.S. Department of Agriculture, Agricultural Marketing

title of document

Service. (2006). *USDA national farmers market managers survey*. Washington, DC:
U.S. Department of Agriculture, 6–10.

Business document *(annual report)*

IN-TEXT CITATION (for document found online; no page numbers)

The company that makes Clif Bars had in place a plan that allowed employees to purchase stock in the company (Pham & Hammond, 2010).

authors

REFERENCES LIST ENTRY

title of document

Pham, T., & Hammond, E. (Eds.). Clif Bar & Company (2010). All aspirations: Clif Bar &
Company annual report [PDF file]. Retrieved from http://www.clifbar.com
/uploads/default/ClifBar_AA2010.pdf

25. Literary work (novel, poem, fairy tale, etc.)
Provide the author, date, title, publisher's city, and publisher. For a selection (such as an essay) within a longer work (such as a collection of essays), provide the selection title before the full title.

IN-TEXT CITATION

One technique the author used was simile. For example, she described "bundled dough mounds" as being "as white and round as babies" (McCoy, 2012, p. 1).

Novel (print)

REFERENCES LIST ENTRY

McCoy, S. (2012). *The baker's daughter: A novel.* New York, NY: The Crown Publishing Group, 1–232.

Novel (e-book)

REFERENCES LIST ENTRY

McCoy, S. (2012). *The baker's daughter: A novel* [Kindle version]. Retrieved from http://www.amazon.com/The-Bakers-Daughter-Novel-ebook/dp/B004W3IEI6

26. Selection from an anthology or textbook   Include the selection author, publication date, and selection title, followed by the anthology editors, anthology title, page range of selection, publisher's city, and publisher.

IN-TEXT CITATION

Advances in DNA testing have complicated commonly held ideas about racial identity (Eubanks, 2013).

author of selection (shortened)

REFERENCES LIST ENTRY

author of selection

information on textbook where selection appears ———— Eubanks, W. Ralph. (2013). Color Lines. In A. Braziller & E. Kleinfeld (Eds.), *The Bedford book of genres,* Second Edition (p. 457). Boston, MA: Bedford/St. Martin's.

27. Object/artifact (cereal box, etc.)   If you find an object or artifact online, cite it as a short work from a Web site, but include a description of the item in brackets. If you find such a source in the physical world, cite it as a work with an author and include a descriptor in brackets.

IN-TEXT CITATION

The box is a cheerful sunny yellow meant to attract children, but parents likely focus on the red heart and the soft claim about lowering cholesterol (General Mills, 2012).

author is an organization

Object (found online)

REFERENCES LIST ENTRY

General Mills. (n.d.). Cheerios [Cereal box]. Retrieved from http://www.cheerios.com/Products/Cheerios

Object (found in physical world)

REFERENCES LIST ENTRY

General Mills. (n.d.). Cheerios [Cereal box].

14

COMPOSING:
DRAWING ON IN-DEPTH RESEARCH:
A Student Case Study

In this chapter, Michael Kipp, a writer and artist who studied at Red Rocks Community College and who currently works at the school's Communication Lab, shows how he researched and composed a multimodal project. Michael will walk us through his process of gathering sources; evaluating, annotating, and choosing sources; composing and integrating sources; and documenting those sources in his composition.

Project Overview

▲ STUDENT AUTHOR

Michael Kipp.

Credit: Michael Kipp.

To see Michael Kipp's complete project, go to LaunchPad Solo for *The Bedford Book of Genres* at **launchpadworks.com**.

My Assignment & Topic

"Gratitude for Happiness" is a multimodal, multigenre project that uses positive psychology research to show how gratitude can make us happier and more fulfilled. It looks at the benefits of gratitude, shares a few methods for practicing gratitude, and encourages us to take responsibility for our happiness through conscious gratitude practice.

My Rhetorical Situation

Thinking about hypothetical, real-world applications of audience analysis in the classroom can be hard. We think of our instructors as the only audience because our feedback comes in the form of a grade. But whether it's art, blogs, or business, the audience is a co-creator. They inform our entire process. Because of this, I spent a lot of time considering who I'm speaking to in my work.

Although I am a male author, I recognized that the emotional nature of my topic leans my audience toward a female majority. I also imagined most would be in the college-age and early adult years between eighteen and twenty-eight, when people are struggling with life transitions, moving out, getting jobs, and going to school. They're also developing their sense of identity, and considering difficult, fundamental questions about their desires, direction in life, and survival. Many will have struggles with mental health, as depression, anxiety, and other mental health challenges are common. My audience would also be diverse in ethnic and racial backgrounds, diverse socioeconomically, have had varying educational advantages, and be mostly from city and suburban neighborhoods. This makes my audience similar to myself and many people I know. If my topic were different, this may not be the case.

My purpose varied from genre to genre, but when considered collectively, the project was meant to be persuasive: I wanted my audience to use gratitude to become happier. Individually, the memoir told a story, the online magazine article was informative, and the advertisements were persuasive.

The collage's primary purpose is harder to put in a box. It is intended to inform the audience by showing the concept of gratitude through a visual description of this woman's mind-set. But it also persuades them to think about how gratitude requires changing your frame of mind, and shares her mental and emotional story through symbolism.

Like the collage, the other genres also used all three. The informative, online magazine article, for instance, also tries to persuade the audience to practice gratitude themselves.

My Research Plan & First Steps

After I chose my topic, I began to gather sources. Getting organized at this stage is important. For most of us, the creative process is not linear and can seem chaotic. This is especially true if we are unfamiliar with our personal creative process, which we can adapt to and optimize with practice.

Getting organized seems like extra work, but taking the time in the beginning and maintaining your organization systems throughout the process will save you enormous amounts of time and stress in the long-run. That said, you will not always do this and this is okay. It's important to be realistic and not expect perfection. Procrastination and resistance are mighty foes, and your best weapon next to self-discipline is self-compassion.

Potential Sources

What Information Do I Need?

With any project, I start by looking for potential sources, and I ask, "If I used this source later, what information would I need?" I would want to know:

- The type of source
- How to access that source again
- What that source is about
- How to cite the source

So I create a digital document called "Potential Sources" to store this information. I organize the document by source type (scholarly, book, interview, etc.). Then, I list them alphabetically, as it will be in the Works Cited, under each type and include:

- The title and author
- A link to the source (if it is digital)
- Obvious citation information
- A summary of the source

In the case of a peer-reviewed, scholarly journal source, this process is simple. Most databases have a "citation" feature that allows you to select a citation style (like MLA) and copy the information for an at-a-glance look at the info you will include in your final citation.

However, it's not unusual for these to be out of date or contain errors, so you must double-check these later.

Studies also come with their own summary: the abstract. This can be copied over to the document as well.

Types of Sources

But how do I decide what sources to look for? I create a list of source types to step through:

- Scholarly journals (studies)
- Books (digital and physical)
- News articles
- Interviews (text, audio, or video)
- Videos (documentaries, lectures, talks, etc.)
- Podcasts
- Blogs and opinion pieces
- Infographics and charts
- Other

I begin with the types of sources most likely to be credible, like studies, books, and interviews with experts. If I see an expert or author that shows up more than once, I'll search for other works or research by that person.

Where Do I Look?

Databases   The first place I look is the database resources I can access through my campus. Because my topic used positive psychology research, studies were the first thing I wanted to gather.

After I've used the database(s), I move to both Google Scholar and Google's general search to look for other studies. Sometimes it is a struggle to find free access to the full-text of a study, and after trying to locate it on the school's database(s), you may need to ask a librarian for help.

If I'm struggling to find credible sources, or if I know of someone whose opinion about the topic I value, I may ask for source recommendations from that person or for help from a librarian. This is not something I needed to do for the "Gratitude for Happiness" project.

Books   After I have exhausted peer-reviewed sources, I look at books. I will often start with Google Books, which has previews of many books, so you can quickly check for relevancy.

I also do a general search online to locate books on the topic, as well as through the school and local library. I prefer digital texts I can access anywhere, so I focus on locating those first. Print books have their advantages as well.

Other sources   Then I move to other types of sources. A search-engine, or even library search, can get access to videos, Web sites, news articles, and opinion pieces.

Throughout this process of finding potential sources, I keep anything that seems even remotely relevant. I spend the minimum amount of time determining source relevancy and credibility because I know I'll go back to look at them more closely.

Although I do most of this gathering at the beginning of the project, I usually go back and do this several times. While composing and evaluating, I often find holes in my research, find out sources weren't as relevant as they seemed, or change the way I'm framing my topic. I also look for sources that are cited within other sources. This means I move through this process multiple times during the project.

My Working Bibliography

Below is one scholarly source I chose for my project. In the annotations, you'll see how I kept track of the source and laid the groundwork for integrating it into my project.

The type of source

SCHOLARLY

1. Algoe, Sara B., et al.
    "Putting the 'You' in 'Thank You': Examining Other-Praising Behavior as the Active Relational Ingredient in Expressed Gratitude"
    Link: http://spp.sagepub.com/content/7/7/658

Summary:
"Although positive emotions as a class can build interpersonal resources, recent evidence suggests a unique and direct role for gratitude. In the current research, we shine the spotlight on what happens between a grateful person and the benefactor to illuminate what can build a bridge between them. Specifically, we draw on work calling gratitude an 'other-praising' emotion. In an original study and a conceptual replication that included two independent samples, couples had video-recorded conversations in which one member expressed gratitude to the other ($n = 370$).

Abstract quoted to use for summary. I often go back and edit this to make it easier to understand once I've read the article.

Expresser's other-praising behavior was robustly positively associated with the benefactor's postinteraction perception of expresser responsiveness, personal good feelings in general, and felt loving in particular. Several practical and theoretical alternative explanations are ruled out. By clarifying the specific behavioral and subjective psychological mechanisms through which expressed gratitude promotes relationships, this work advances affective and relationship science, two domains that cut across disciplines within psychology."

Citation Details:
Sara B. Algoe, Laura E. Kurtz, and Nicole M. Hilaire
"Putting the 'You' in 'Thank You': Examining Other-Praising Behavior as the Active Relational Ingredient in Expressed Gratitude"
Social Psychological and Personality Science vol. 7 no. 7
doi:10.1177/1948550616651681

2. Diebel, Tara, et al.
"Establishing the Effectiveness of a Gratitude Diary Intervention on Children's Sense of School Belonging"
Link: https://drive.google.com/open?id=0B-KDbYpALgJPRngxbFZFaTUxYjg

Original Link: https://drive.google.com/open?id=0B-KDbYpALgJPbm1wNDEwOF83Tmc

Basic information taken from the Web site for reference. This is neither all the information nor the correct format for the Works Cited page, and it should always be double-checked.

Sometimes logging into a database is inconvenient. I downloaded the full text PDF and stored it on Google Drive.

I kept the original database link for access and for my citation.

Evaluating, Annotating, & Choosing Sources

Evaluating My Sources

After I've gathered my list of potential sources, I begin to evaluate them. I begin at the top of the "Potential Sources" document and work my way down, starting with digital sources. This means I begin with scholarly articles.

To evaluate scholarly sources, I reread the abstract, focusing on the conclusion, and ask myself whether the results support my claim, or whether it's evidence against my claim that I should acknowledge in my work. I also look at what journal it was published in to see who the journal's audience is (a coaching journal is going to be different from a positive psychology journal), and whether the journal seems credible. There are a surprising number of journals with poor reputations.

Article Excerpt

Although the title of this article seemed relevant, and even the abstract at the top appears to apply, once I began to read the paper I could tell quickly that it wasn't what I needed.

Techniques and Approaches section
Positive psychology techniques – gratitude

Jonathan Passmore & Lindsay G. Oades

This article builds on a descriptive paper on positive psychology coaching and several previous techniques papers. This paper explores the application of gratitude, with its associated benefits, as a part of positive psychology coaching practice.
Keywords: *gratitude; positive psychology coaching.*

Gratitude

This technique can form a regular routine that the coachee can develop and help build positivity and manage workplace stress, challenging times or difficult situations. This can be done through using a 'gratitude diary' or letters. Which of these tools to use will depend on the individual and their situation, with Emmons (2008) suggesting dtat we need to be cautious in offering only one 'gratitude' technique.

Research by Seligman et al. (2005) found individuals who did this task daily become bored, whilst those asked to write down their

Conclusion

This short technique of gratitude can help which can be used to both coaches and coachees in the development of positivity, potentially leading to enhanced wellbeing,

Correspondence
Dr Jonathan Passmore
Email: jonathancpassmore@yahoo.co.uk

References
Emmons, R. (2008). *Thanks. How practicing gratitude can make you happier.* New York: Houghton Mifflin.

McCullough, M.E., Emmons, R. & Tsang. J. (2002).

Article Excerpt

This article is only two pages, and while it does cite research on gratitude, it isn't an experimental research study. Instead, it's a short description of a gratitude technique used by positive psychology coaches.

Once I've considered those, I look at the full text. At this point, I'm not reading the entire thing, but skimming for indications that it's credible and relevant. Sometimes all it takes is a quick glance to realize a text isn't relevant.

If I need to go deeper, I will usually read the conclusion and the section describing limitations. I may also examine the methods, if they aren't clear in the abstract and parts I've already read. If a study was published about a population in a particular culture, I'll evaluate whether it's still relevant to my topic, and if a study is a translation, whether the translation seems clear. I alternate between skimming and reading more carefully. It's likely I'll still eliminate more sources later, but I want to get rid of the obvious ones.

During this, I maintain the organization of my sources document and update the summaries to make things clearer, as needed. If I eliminate a source, I remove it and put it in a separate document called "Eliminated Sources." In the event I change my mind, I can still access it.

Here is an example of a source I decided was useful:

Article Excerpt

The title looks clearly relevant.

Establishing the effectiveness of a gratitude diary intervention on children's sense of school belonging

Tara Diebel, Colin Woodcock, Claire Cooper & Catherine Brignell

Article Excerpt

The abstract explains the goal, method, results, limitations, and concluding thoughts of the study. It tells me immediately that it's a gratitude journal intervention study, and that it looked at school belonging and gratitude after the intervention. The gratitude journal is a common intervention that I want to use in my project, so I know I can use this as a source.

Aim: The promotion of wellbeing in schools using evidence-based interventions from the field of positive psychology is a growing area of interest. These interventions are based on the principle that sustainable changes in wellbeing can be achieved through regularly engaging in simple and intentional activities. This study examines the effectiveness of a school-based gratitude diary intervention to promote school belonging for primary school aged pupils (age range 7 to 11 years).
Method: The intervention took place in a one-form entry primary school for four weeks and involved participants writing a diary about things that they were either grateful for in school that day or about neutral school events.
Findings: Participants who completed the gratitude intervention demonstrated enhanced school belonging and gratitude relative to the control group, although this was moderated by gender with the gratitude diary showing clearer benefits for males. Increases in gratitude were positively correlated with increases in school belonging.
Limitations: The lack of a follow-up measure meant that it was not determined whether positive outcomes were maintained. Participants' diary entries were not analysed for content.
Conclusions: The findings extend the evidence base concerning the use of gratitude diaries with children and indicate that this intervention can be beneficial for children younger than research has previously demonstrated. This study also illustrates how a gratitude diary intervention can be used to build social resources and makes a novel connection between gratitude and sense of belonging. Implications for how this simple intervention has the potential to have a systemic impact on the wellbeing of pupils and staff are discussed.
Keywords: gratitude; gratitude intervention; sense of school belonging.

design. In addition, while the gratitude manipulation appeared to protect female pupils from the fall in gratitude observed in the control group, only males showed a significant increase in gratitude scores following the gratitude diary intervention. This was an unexpected finding insofar as the literature on gender differences in the expression of gratitude suggests that males are less inclined to this activity than females (e.g. Kashdan et al., 2009; Thompson et al., 2015). It is possible gratitude was already at ceiling level in the girls in our study, however there was no evidence that baseline levels of gratitude were effected by gender. Most such effect on both gratitude and SoSB. This would make the control group in the current study comparable to the hassle diary in both Emmons and McCullough (2003) and Froh et al. (2008). However, in these studies significant declines were not observed. A coded analysis of diary entries would be needed to establish the content of the diary entries and explore these hypotheses. Finally, the fact that the gratitude diary intervention and the control intervention were occurring in the same classes could have been an issue, if participants became aware that they were in different groups.

Article Excerpt

The abstract mentions gender differences, so I looked at the "discussion" part of the study to find a summary and thoughts about why the differences existed.

Annotating My Sources

There are several ways I've annotated my sources. I actually used two ways during this project, as I experimented to see what worked best. I haven't settled on a method, and I think each person will be drawn to a different one.

The first method was on paper. I printed off the articles to have physical copies and took a highlighter and pen to them. The benefit of this was readability and retention. The downside was that if I did not have them with me, I couldn't reference my annotations. But I did find it easier to keep track of information and engage with the texts than with digital copies. If you find yourself easily distracted, having trouble keeping track of things, or if your eyes hurt reading digitally, this method may work for you.

The second method was digital. Many of the studies were PDFs, and many PDF-viewing programs have a highlighter feature. So I digitally highlighted them, if the feature was available. Other programs allow you to do this with other kinds of sources, and some allow you to take notes or make comments.

As I highlighted, I also did something a little unusual: I took screenshots. I already have a "Potential Sources" document and an "Eliminated Sources" document at this stage. Now, I added one more: a "Screenshots of Sources" document. In this document, I put the title and author of the source, and below it I included the screenshots of all my highlights. Here, I could take notes if I wanted to or leave comments.

What this allowed me to do was keep everything I found relevant in *one place*. I could look at it at a glance and find the information I wanted. If I needed more context, I had a summary in the "Potential Sources" document or could access the full text. This saved me from having to go back and forth between documents as often, which I find makes it difficult to track information. I also felt like I could make connections between different sources more easily. The one improvement I'd make on this method is using a program that can search text in images, which would make keyword searches possible. But this wasn't necessary.

Digital Highlighting

Here is an example of how I highlighted text I was particularly interested in.

> that aims to gain greater understanding of how positive emotions and character traits can contribute to positive wellbeing (Seligman et al., 2005). Advocates of positive psychology assert that interventions that prompt people to engage in simple intentional activities can be more effective in increase levels of the sense of school belongingness (SoSB).
>
> Gratitude arises following help from others, but is also a process that involves awareness of and appreciation on positive aspects of life (Wood, Froh & Geraghty, 2010). The empirical literature concerning

Digital Highlighting with Notes

And here is an example of how I added notes to the margins once I highlighted the text.

> **Studies:**
>
> 1. "Establishing the Effectiveness of a Gratitude Diary Intervention on Children's Sense of School Belonging"
>
> Diebel, Tara, et al.
>
> Notes and Quotes:
>
> **Discussion**
> The present study represents the first to use a gratitude diary intervention that requires children to write specifically about school. There have also only been two published studies to dale that have used gratitude diaries with primary school aged children. As predicted, the study found the gratitude diary intervention had a beneficial effect on both gratitude towards school and SoSB. Improvements in gratitude due to die grati-
>
> Gratitude diary with children.
>
> Beneficial for:
> * Sense of belonging
> * Gratitude towards school

Annotating and highlighting sources is something I do throughout the process. During my initial evaluation of sources, I may do it as I skim or read portions. Then when I read the full text, this is where the most annotation happens. But as I'm composing and integrating sources, I may reread a source or portions of it, and may add more annotations. The process of engaging with the source is continuous. As I have said, the creative process is not linear.

Choosing My Sources

Once I've gathered sources and done an initial evaluation, I begin to examine them in full. This is where I read the entire text of a study. As mentioned, it's also where the bulk of annotation happens. Often, I end up eliminating sources again. When examined more deeply, I may realize a source isn't as relevant as it seemed, or I may think it's poorer quality than my first examination indicated.

After I've gone through all my sources, I update the "Potential Sources" document with correct MLA citation format. I do this early, so that I can add correct in-text citations as I go to save time. Like the other stages of interacting with sources, I come back to this one often. I don't ever truly know what sources I'm going to choose until I begin the process of composing, when the ideas and knowledge from my research combine with my own ideas.

Composing & Integrating Sources

Drafting

By the time I'm ready to do an initial draft, I've read many or all of my potential sources and eliminated poor quality or irrelevant ones. I've also spent some time annotating, highlighting, and drawing connections between different sources. Because of this, sometimes I have a very clear idea of what I want to talk about and can create an outline to follow. Other times I'm better off doing a brain dump and organizing later.

For "Gratitude for Happiness," I went the brain dump method. I had a purpose, knew my audience, had chosen a genre, and I knew what the research said about my topic. All the pieces were inside my head and only needed to come out. So I would do a first draft where I didn't filter myself. Usually, the organization would come intuitively, and I'd just need to clean it up. This involved several drafts and revisions.

Integrating Sources

As I'm doing my initial draft, because I've read my sources and I'm familiar with them, I find myself drawing on the research naturally. If I want to make a point, I'll back it up with the source or sources I remember that support it. Because I'm doing this during my draft and I want to keep track of what sources I use, I put the in-text citation in immediately. I try to format it correctly, but always check during the revision.

After I've done that first draft, I add more sources as I revise. I'll ask myself if there are other sources to support a point, and if there are other points that I need to make and sources to include with them. Sometimes I feel like there isn't enough support, and I'll start at the beginning of the process, looking for more sources.

Integrating sources in the genre pieces was different than integrating sources in my author's and artist's statements. Not all the genre pieces had references in the genre piece itself. The online magazine article had links, but the memoir, collage, and advertisements don't reference the research in the piece itself. This meant I kept my

Introduction

My highlighted source, as discussed on p. 419.

that aims to gain greater understanding of how positive emotions and character traits can contribute to positive wellbeing (Seligman et al., 2005). Advocates of positive psychology assert that interventions that prompt people to engage in simple intentional activities can be more effective in increase levels of the sense of school belongingness (SoSB).

Gratitude arises following help from others, but is also a process that involves awareness of and appreciation on positive aspects of life (Wood, Froh & Geraghty, 2010). The empirical literature concerning

Integrated Source

Here is an example of how I integrated my source into my project.

One's life" (277).

For Nelson and Lyubomirsky, this difference between gratitude and appreciation lies in interpersonal context (277). They believe that gratitude involves an interpersonal exchange, contrasting it with appreciation as a generalized gratitude for one's life blessings (277). Similarly, Jane Taylor Wilson says that gratitude "refers to an ability to recognize and appreciate the benefits received from others" (2); and Nancy S. Fagley describes a model for appreciation as an umbrella term broken into eight aspects, one of which is gratitude (71). Here it is defined as, "being grateful to others for benefits they provided or tried to provide" (71). However, not all people in the field adhere to the definition of gratitude as a subset of appreciation or as a description limited to an interpersonal context. For example, Tara Diebel, et al. remark that, "Gratitude arises following help from others, but is also a process that involves awareness of and appreciation on positive aspects of life" (117).

Because the definition of gratitude is still being clarified amongst psychological researchers, and because the lay definition includes both interpersonal contexts and an appreciation for the positive aspects of a person's life (Nelson and Lyubomirsky 277), this project will recognize gratitude in both interpersonal exchanges and in general life circumstances, and will not distinguish between appreciation and gratitude.

In this project I decided to use a series of advertisements by a fictional organization called "Gratitude4Happiness" to guide the flow of concepts. The organization's purpose is to persuade the readers to believe that gratitude is one tool for happiness, and that they should take action to improve their well-being by practicing it themselves. These advertisements connect with the genre piece following them, serve to highlight points made in the other genre, and create a thread throughout the project that brings all of the genres together.

Each of the genre pieces, including the last advertisement, has an accompanying

research in mind as I composed it, and then I integrated the research into the author or artist's statement that accompanied it, which explained my thought process. The integration of the research in the genre pieces was indirect—it informed my composition, but wasn't demonstrated in the piece. In contrast, the author's and artist's statements directly integrated the research and it was cited within.

To give an example, the study "Establishing the Effectiveness of a Gratitude Diary Intervention on Children's Sense of School Belonging" by Tara Diebel et al. was used as a source in three sections of my project: the Introduction, Chapter 1 ("The Benefits of Gratitude"), and Chapter 2 ("Ways to Practice Gratitude"). Here's how I did it:

Chapter 1: The Benefits of Gratitude

My highlighted sources, as discussed on p. 419.

iour but did not find any significant outcomes. Finally, Lambert et al. (2010) investigated the impact of a gratitude intervention on communal strength, the sense of responsibility the participant feels for their partner s welfare. The study used a novel intervention and asked participants to increase the frequency that they expressed gratitude to their partner. The results indicated that this intervention yielded significantly higher increases in communal strength compared to paying attention to grateful events or sharing positive events with a partner. No information was reported

Fredrickson). Research has also linked gratitude to wellbeing through the building of social resources such as increasing feelings of connectedness (Froh, Bono & Emmons, 2010), prosocial emotions such as forgiveness, compassion, trust and empathy (Dunn 8c Schweitzer, 2005; Hill & Allemand, 2011; McCullough et al., 2001) and increasing perception of social support (Algoe, Haidt 8c Gable, 2008; Wood et al., 2008).

Findings: Participants who completed the gratitude intervention demonstrated enhanced school belonging and gratitude relative to the control group although this was moderated by gender with the gratitude diary showing clearer benefits for males. Increases in gratit ude were positively correlated with increases in school belonging.

At the beginning of the study, Tara Diebel et al. discuss what gratitude is. I also wanted to talk about how positive psychology defines gratitude in my own project to give my readers a foundation for understanding the rest of it. This study used a definition of gratitude that contrasted with some other studies, and I wanted to highlight that. Tara Diebel et al.'s definition itself drew off past research, which is common in studies that build upon existing literature.

Chapter 2: Ways to Practice Gratitude

My highlighted source, as discussed on p. 419.

> ical feelings of belonging. Research on school belonging has shown it is inversely related to school dropout and linked with engagement and interest in school positive relationships (Bond et al. 2007) intrinsic motivation and academic achievement (Goodenow 1993; Osterman 2000).

Integrated Source

An example of how I integrated my source into my project.

significant others rated the participants in the gratitude group as more helpful than the participants in the other groups (31-32). Emmons and McCullough also say, "In a sample of adults with neuromuscular disease, a 21-day gratitude intervention resulted in ... a greater sense of feeling connected to others . . ." ("Highlights"). Furthermore, Tara Diebel, et al. discuss that research has linked gratitude to increased feelings of connection, pro-social emotions, and sense of social support (118), and that another study showed expressing gratitude to one's partner more often increased communal strength (the level of responsibility a partner feels for the other's welfare) more than noticing grateful events or sharing positive events (119). These findings support the idea that grateful people are more connected, helpful, and involved with others, and I tried to show this in my memoir.

In the second section, I describe the day I dropped out of high school. Tara Diebel, et al.'s study showed students experienced increased feelings of school belonging (117), which has been connected to decreased dropout rates and increased intrinsic motivation and academic achievement (121). Gratitude was something I rarely experienced during this time, and I wanted to show I also had a lack of motivation, energy, and goals; experienced negative physical symptoms; and was disconnected from others. Emmons and McCullough say that study participants who kept gratitude lists made more progress toward personal goals, including academic, interpersonal, and health-based goals, and young adults reported higher levels of positive states, including alertness, enthusiasm, determination, attentiveness, and energy. They also write that participants who kept a weekly gratitude journal "exercised more regularly, reported fewer physical symptoms, felt better about their lives as a whole, and were more optimistic about the upcoming week compared to those who recorded hassles or neutral life events. . . ."

Tying social connection and experiences of poor physical health, one recent study

*Findings: Participants who completed the gratitude intervention demonstrated enhanced
school belonging and gratitude relative to the control group although this was moderated by
gender with the gratitude diary showing clearer benefits for males. Increases in gratitude were
positively correlated with increases in school belonging.*

Integrated Source

An example of how I
integrated my source
into my project.

well as, *Thanks! How the New Science of Gratitude Can Make You Happier,* which details his
study more in depth (27-35). I wanted to highlight the gratitude journal both because its
well-known, and because of its benefits. Emmons' and McCullough's studies found that
people had increased life satisfaction, felt more energetic and alert, and felt more optimistic when doing the exercise ("Highlights"). In support of these findings, a more recent
study on children in school showed the gratitude diary resulted in an increase in gratitude
and sense of belonging, although the findings suggested gender may be a moderating
factor and more research needs to be done exploring this possibility (Diebel. et al. 117).
The quote by Chris Peterson (from Aaronson's *Psychology Today article*), which says the
gratitude exercise "can be done with skepticism, but not with cynicism," reinforces the
ideas discussed above, because it says that it must be done authentically, with genuine
intent. Meditating briefly on the feeling helps achieve this.

In the next section, I referenced *Authentic Happiness* by Martin Seligman. In his
book he describes how to carry out a "gratitude visit," and I paraphrased his instructions
for the visit (74). I also reference a study by Sara B. Algoe, et al., where increased other-praising behavior is shown to be a key component in the expression of gratitude, causing the target to feel more positive emotions, perceive the expresser as more responsive,
and feel more "loving." In contrast, the self-benefit behavior did not have any association
with the target's perception of responsiveness, general positive emotions, or experience
of love (661). This is important, because increasing the positivity of the experience for the
person for whom someone is grateful for encourages social bonds and relational growth
(658, 664), and high-quality relationships are a part of living a happy life.

Here, I paraphrased Tara Diebel et al.'s summaries of previous research. I wanted to
illustrate in my project the connection between gratitude and my involvement in
school. Diebel et al.'s study supported my personal experience in the memoir, and their
summaries provide more evidence of the connection. The research they reference is
also part of the support for their own hypothesis and its results.

et al. 2010). Gratitude is also thought to promote resilience as it provides an adaptive coping mechanism for dealing with negative life events (Lambert et al. 2012; Watkins et al. 2008). These hypotheses

Gratitude has been found to be negatively correlated with stress (Wood et al. 2008) burnout (Chan 2010) and buffer the effect of two suicide risk factors: hopelessness and depressive symptoms (Kleiman et al. 2013).

In the second paragraph, I use Diebel et al.'s research to discuss school belonging and dropouts in the context of my own choice to drop out of school. I want to show that the connection between low gratitude and low sense of school belonging may have been a factor in my choice to drop out.

The first citation (117) is the results of their study. The second citation (121) is a paraphrase of summarized results from a former study that they used to support their own research.

The online article recommends the gratitude journal, so in my author's statement, I expanded on the research supporting it as an effective gratitude intervention. The results of Tara Diebel et al.'s study are in direct support of the exercise.

However, I also wanted to note that the study showed gender may be a moderating factor. It's important to represent the results of a study with as much accuracy as possible, rather than twisting the results to support a claim. Rather than weakening my point, including this adds credibility.

Integrated Source

An example of how I integrated my source into my project.

eye forward and to a higher point. A Spanish study confirmed that positive affect rises in persons who practice gratitude, which validated what was found in a previous study (Martinez-Marti 893). Gratitude has also been tied to resilience, providing a coping mechanism in challenging times, and it buffers the effect of hopelessness and depressive symptoms, which are risk factors for suicide (Diebel, et al. 118). Also, the landscape refers to the fact that grateful people experience a positive memory bias—they are more likely to recall positive memories, similar to the negative memory bias experienced in depression (Watkins, et al. 63). The idea of creation is also shown in the plant, whose roots surround her head. Her efforts to be thankful and practice gratitude are nourishing the plant, who grows upward, changing her reality, subjective and objective, for the better.

In the collage, I'm showing the impact a grateful mind-set and practice has on one's perception of reality, and that this positive shift in perception has objective benefits. In this part, I'm specifically describing the rise of the landscape and rainbow as symbolism for that positivity. Tara Diebel et al. summarize in their study some research linking gratitude and resilience, and its positive effect on depressive symptoms. This supports what I wanted to symbolize in the collage.

Documenting Sources in MLA Style

When I'm wrapping up any project, and it's time to formally document my sources, I'm never sorry that I kept thorough records and notes along the way. As Amy and Elizabeth write on p. 372, "When you document sources, you show your audience where you got your information. You also develop your ethos as an author by showing that you've used reliable source material." Properly and accurately documenting sources—and showing that you've used quality sources in the first place—is worth the work.

For a detailed guide, including models, on documenting in MLA and APA style, see Chapter 13. And to see my whole project, go to LaunchPad Solo for *The Bedford Book of Genres* at launchpadworks.com.

15

ASSEMBLING A MULTIGENRE PROJECT

What is a multigenre project? It's a collection of three or more genre compositions, built around a single topic. A multigenre project is an opportunity to experiment. It also gives you the chance to practice in a variety of rhetorical situations, forms of composition, and types of media.

Let's look at an example. You've conducted research on the topic of, say, the significance of the bond between people and dogs. Through the course of your research, brainstorming, and drafting, you decide that you want to make the case that dogs were essential to the rise of civilization. You also want to present a history of the relationship between humans and canines, and perhaps even tell a story of a particular relationship. You are strong in a variety of genres and media (better at some than others). Your audience is one of general readers; that is, it's an unspecialized audience, but one with some interest in dogs and humanity. A multigenre project for your topic could include a few of these genres and media options:

- An **annotated timeline** tracing human-canine interactions from ancient times to the present
- A brief TED talk–style video **presentation** on how and why dogs were critical to human civilization
- A **story** of how dogs and humans relate now
- A **photo essay** or **slide show** that demonstrates how dogs benefit humans by reducing stress
- An **annotated map** locating where humans first settled and domesticated dogs
- An **interview** with a dog behaviorist, a therapy dog trainer, or a psychologist who uses dogs to treat humans
- An **Author's or Artist's Statement** that brings everything together

The Possibilities of the Multigenre Project

Just like any research endeavor, a genre project allows you to join a conversation about a particular subject or issue. Whether you research and compose a single genre piece or multiple related pieces, you address a research question, make clear arguments, and draw on sources, all while keeping a strong sense of purpose and audience. Unlike more traditional academic projects, genre projects let you break away from (or embrace, if you prefer) the usual forms such as the research paper. Multigenre projects go a step beyond: They open up unlimited channels and formats for you to convey your points. Nothing is out of bounds. Think handmade objects, videos, blogs, animations, photo essays, collages, and other visual arguments. Further, genre projects, and multi-genre projects in particular, offer you the chance to connect with audiences beyond the classroom.

Your Rhetorical Situation

When you begin thinking about creating a multigenre project, consider the following:

Furthering your purpose   You can do this by assembling a coherent collection. Think of each genre piece as a chapter that contributes to a whole. You will unify the pieces by building in relationships among them by choosing a sequence and package (more on this on pp. 431–32)—and by composing an Introduction that pulls everything together. For multigenre projects, we recommend that you compose a separate Author's or Artist's Statement for each of your individual genre pieces, and use the Introduction to discuss how the pieces work together. However, it also works to create one Author's or Artist's Statement for the entire project. Check with your instructor about specific preferences. (For more on Author's and Artist's Statements, see Chapter 6, pp. 90–97)

Reaching your audience   You might do this by providing different *perspectives*. As you decide on the genres to compose in, think about whether you want to convey multiple perspectives on your topic through each piece. For example, if you are presenting an argument, you could address a different point of view in each composition.

Using rhetorical appeals to your advantage   Imagine how you might use each genre piece to make your case through different rhetorical appeals. Maybe in one genre you emphasize ethos; in another, logos; and in another, pathos. Or maybe you want to organize your project around a single rhetorical appeal.

Choosing modes and media   Think about using a mix of modes and media throughout your pieces so that your audience has different ways to connect with your message. Some of the best projects we've seen are a combination of textual, visual, and audio compositions.

The Conventions of the Multigenre Project

Every multigenre project will be different—a culmination of one author's choices about which genres to mix together, which perspectives to represent, which voices or tones to incorporate. There are no "conventions" for a multigenre work beyond the use of multiple genres to convey ideas to an audience. Typically, we ask student composers of multigenre projects to provide an Introduction, a separate Author's or Artist's Statement for each individual piece, or a single statement in which they reflect on each of their genre pieces. The Statement(s) should include Works Cited or References lists.

The Steps to Assembling a Multigenre Project

1. Introduce your project and provide context   Write a one- to two-page Introduction that gives your audience an overview of your topic, your scope, and what sparked your interest in your topic. Provide a brief explanation for your rationale for the sequence of your genre pieces (more on that below). You can provide more details—and cite and document your research—in your Author's or Artist's Statement(s), which is typically longer than the Introduction and includes a list of References or Works Cited. Alternatively, you can combine your Introduction and Statement into one document, as some of our students have done.

Your Introduction should also provide any context that your audience will need to fully understand your project and individual genre pieces. This means you may need to provide a brief history of your topic, the people who are key to its larger discussion, and the main controversies surrounding it.

2. Sequence your genre pieces   Do this in a way that will make sense to your audience. Each piece should prepare your audience for the one that follows it. Sequencing helps orient your audience, and it also helps you methodically achieve your purpose. Here are some scenarios:

- If your goal is to convince your audience to take action on a specific problem, begin with a composition that highlights that problem, and end with a piece that offers a possible solution and/or makes a direct call to action. An alternative approach could be to begin with a visual piece that shows what could happen if no one took action to solve the problem.

- If your purpose is to compare or contrast specific views on your topic, you might arrange your pieces to highlight differences and similarities.

- If one of your goals is to tell a story, sequence your pieces into a narrative structure (consider a beginning, middle, and end), and bring out narrative elements such as character and conflict.

- If you want to emphasize a particular rhetorical appeal, think about how the order of your genre pieces could do that. For example, to emphasize pathos, you could

---

ATTENTION, AUTHORS & ARTISTS

Need some ideas for genres?   Working on a multigenre project? Great. There are lots of genres to choose from. Here are just a few (they can be delivered in digital, print, and/or 3-D physical media): researched arguments, editorials, articles, user manuals, brochures, encyclopedia articles, obituaries, exposés, editorials, letters to the editor, interviews, book reviews, essays, surveys, business letters, poems, personal letters, short stories, scripts, journal entries, memoirs, advice columns, political speeches, eulogies, tabloid articles, restaurant menus, top 10 lists, resumes, directions, syllabi, Web pages, photographs, collages, photo essays, charts, graphs, advertisements, comics, cartoons, posters, movie posters, skit performances, paintings, sketches, musical scores, musical performances, sculptures, audio essays, film clips, and scrapbook pages.

begin and end with the pieces that will evoke the most emotion in your audience. Alternatively, if establishing your ethos is more important, you might begin with a piece that establishes your expertise and credibility, such as a researched journal article.

3. Title your project   Your title should reflect your topic and your "take" on your topic. Create a title that will spark the interest of your target audience, a title that is memorable and provocative. The title should reflect your project's message but can go beyond simply stating it. Consider how the tone and word choice of the title will build expectations in readers' minds about what the project will or will not do.

Here are some titles our students have come up with:

- Dawson Swan's project on nature and mental health: "The Threat of Nature Deficit Disorder" (p. 441)
- Gwen Ganow's project on how the concept of superheroes intersects with "real life": "When Worlds Collide: Why Superheroes Matter" (p. 438)
- Scarlet Moody's project on Rwanda radio: "The Rwandan Genocide and Radio-Television's Libre des Milles Collines"
- Emma Jones's project on Alzheimer's disease: "The Road of Life"

4. Create an Author's or Artist's Statement   Use your Statement to discuss your research, explain your rhetorical choices, and evaluate your project overall. (See Chapter 4, pp. 47–54, and Chapter 6, pp. 90–102, for advice and examples.) We encourage our students to write a Statement for each genre piece, and provide an Introduction or project-wide Statement to unify their work.

5. Package your project creatively   While a standard research paper is generally packaged quite simply, with a cover page or perhaps in a folder, a multigenre project can be packaged more imaginatively. As with every other aspect of your project, your package and delivery will impact your audience and indicate your tone and angle on your subject. For example, a multigenre project packaged in a miniature black coffin indicates somberness, while a project presented in a miniature pink-polka-dotted coffin suggests a humorous and ironic approach.

Here are some ways students have packaged their projects in the past:

- A project on globalization: All the components were rolled up inside a mailing tube covered with stamps and postal marks from around the world.
- A project on the drinking age: All the genre pieces were presented in a wire wine bottle carrier.
- A project on education: The title page was designed to look like the cover of a teacher's grade book, and all the pieces inside had pale blue columns on the borders (like grade books have).

CHECKLIST | Assembling a Multigenre Project

Keep the following questions in mind. Wherever you are in your composing process, it can be helpful to get feedback. Here are some more questions you might want to ask your respondents.

Note: There are no conventions for multigenre projects. However, there are conventions for individual genres. See Chapters 5–10 for advice and examples.

RHETORICAL SITUATION & CHOICES

☐ **Purpose.** What is the overall purpose of my project? What are the purposes of my individual genre pieces? What is the effect of reading/viewing each piece in isolation versus reading/viewing each piece as a group? When all are experienced together, how is the effect different from reading/viewing each piece in isolation? How can I sequence or package my pieces to best achieve my overarching purpose? What title will signal my overall purpose to my readers?

☐ **Audience.** How does my Introduction and Author's/Artist's Statement work to draw my audience in? If I aim to persuade my audience, how does the sequencing encourage readers/viewers to accept my point of view? What kind of packaging will capture the attention of my audience?

☐ **Rhetorical appeals.** How do my individual genre compositions, Author's/Artist's Statements, and Introduction, taken together, establish my credibility (ethos)? Is there a clear logical aspect to the project (logos)? Is there something that will resonate emotionally (pathos) with readers? Given my audience, should I emphasize one appeal over another, perhaps highlighting it in my Introduction? Given my purpose, can I use sequencing to begin and end my project with a particular appeal?

☐ **Modes & media.** Have I used a mix of modes and media throughout my pieces so that my audience has different ways to connect with my message? Have I balanced one mode/medium with others so that the project overall isn't text-heavy or too visual?

Examples of Multigenre Projects

Let's take a look at some student projects. We've annotated these to highlight the components of each project and how the student assembled them into a whole. We've also indicated how our students handled their rhetorical choices (regarding purpose, audience, rhetorical appeals, and modes and media) and the possibilities of the multigenre project (elements, style, design, and use of sources).

Guided Reading | A Multigenre Project

One multigenre project will look very different from another. Here is student author Neil Carr's multigenre project on video games and violence.

Neil Carr (STUDENT), *Video Games and Violence: Who Should We Blame When Kids Are Violent?*

NEIL'S RHETORICAL SITUATION & CHOICES		MULTIGENRE PIECES	

PURPOSE
Neil wants to persuade his audience that video games and their makers should not be blamed for the violent real-life behavior of some players.

AUDIENCE
Neil identifies his primary audience as general readers who do not have specialized knowledge of video games. He's aiming at regular citizens/taxpayers. He sequences his compositions so that his audience will get a sense of the humanity of gamers themselves, as well as the escape aspects of gaming, before he moves on to more detailed research findings.

◄ **What is the author/artist, *Neil Carr*, doing?**

▲ **STUDENT AUTHOR PHOTO**
Neil Carr.
Credit: Neil Carr.

What are the parts? How do ► **they work together?**

NEIL'S PROJECT CONSISTS OF

A **researched essay** on studies of video games and violence.

An **audio diary** of a truancy officer (see recorder).

A narrative and persuasive **film script** of the story of two boys, one who plays video games and one who doesn't, comparing their tendencies toward violence.

The **film** (on DVD).

To unify his project, Neil provides:

An **Introduction** with contextual information.

RHETORICAL APPEALS

Neil's choice to compose both a film script and an audio diary indicates that appealing to pathos and ethos is important to him.

MODES & MEDIA

Neil chooses film and audio to engage his audience in a narrative, persuasive, and entertaining way. However, he opts to present his own views and research findings on the topic in a traditional research paper.

MULTIGENRE CONVENTIONS

There are no conventions for multigenre projects. However, there are conventions for individual genres. See Chapters 5–10 for examples.

An **Author's Statement** in which he discusses his research, explains his rhetorical choices, and evaluates his project as a whole.

Packaging for his print pieces—a binder with an illustrated cover—and a recorder that contains his audio piece.

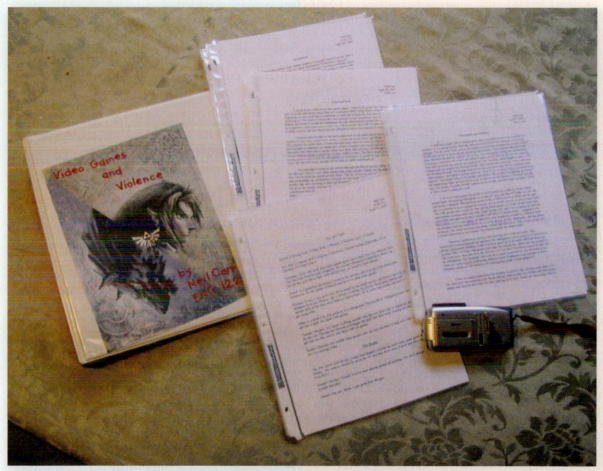

Credit: Neil Carr.

(Continues on next page)

Let's look at the audio diary from Neil's multigenre project.

PURPOSE

Neil channels the voice of a truancy officer to make a point about video gamers. This piece fits in with the broader purpose of his multigenre project: to persuade others that video games and their producers should not be blamed for the violent behavior of some gamers.

AUDIENCE

Neil's audience includes his classmates, his instructor, and a general audience.

If this had been a "real" audio diary by Officer Rendar, the audience could have been the court, if he'd been asked to submit his observations.

◀ What is the author/artist, *Neil Carr*, doing?

What makes this ▶ an *audio diary*?

ELEMENTS OF THE GENRE

A diary entry is a first-person narrative in which the writer records thoughts and observations.

STYLE

A diary entry is very casual; it often reads/ sounds like a person's speaking voice. In this case, Neil has adapted some literary narrative elements, and has written this piece almost like dialogue or even a short scene from a play.

DESIGN

In this case, Neil has provided a transcript of the audio diary. He has formatted it as a Word document; it looks like an essay.

Neil Carr
Audio Diary of a Truancy Officer (transcript)

March 31, 2013. This is truancy officer Mike Rendar, and this is the first entry of my audio diary. I've never done one of these before, but I decided to start because I've been put on a new duty—a pretty strange one. See, as a truancy officer, I usually patrol looking for kids trying to ditch their classes. When I find them, I ticket them—or rather, their parents—and get them to where they need to be. Well, I got called in by Sergeant Purser yesterday, on my day off, so he could tell me about my new assignment.

It seems that some kid named Thomas Miller was expelled from school yesterday for fighting. I guess with everything that's been going on lately . . . the school shootings and violence and all . . . Higher-ups must think the kid is gonna hurt someone.

I looked into the kid's profile, and I can see what they mean, but I just don't think it's gonna happen. Call it a hunch. [sigh] Oh, well. I'll begin my observation today . . . Here we go.

I spent all day yesterday watching this kid . . . nothing. He lives in a crappy little apartment with his dad. They live on the bottom floor, so I can go peek in the window sometime. At first, I waited in my car because the shades were all closed. Finally, the kid's dad opened the shades and left about 7:30 AM. Probably for work.

Once Dad left, I looked in to see what was going on. Nothing. Kid was probably sleeping. A couple hours later, I checked again. Kid was playing some video game. I checked again an hour later—same story. An hour later—no change.

That was when I realized this whole damn thing is political. The chief just doesn't want to get caught with his pants down . . . who can blame him. Anyway, the most exciting thing the kid did all day was switch from playing the video game to surfing the Net. I couldn't see what Web sites he was going to. Coulda been buying knitting needles . . . or looking up a recipe for a bomb.

April 1, 2013. It's morning again and I'm sitting in my car outside the kid's apartment . . . again. I've had way too much

Neil clearly appeals to ethos by choosing a truancy officer to be the speaker in this creative audio diary. The officer has authority and knowledge of teen behavior. Neil also appeals to pathos by presenting the officer as a sympathetic character; he also uses humor.

MODES & MEDIA

Neil created an audio diary, which could just as easily have been a video diary. Either can be delivered in a digital environment. When he submitted his project, he included this paper transcript of the recording.

SOURCES

Typically the source for a diary entry is the writer's own experience. In this case, however, Neil is channeling a truancy officer's voice and experience. He has also based this on his research on how gamers respond to video games, and what video games may or may not have to do with violence.

time to think just sitting here. I'm starting to wonder if what I'm doing is even legal. Course, even if it isn't, I wouldn't bring it up with Sergeant Purser. Up until now, I've enjoyed my job and I'd like to keep it. Besides, there's probably some new amendment to the Patriot Act.

But this kid never leaves the damn house. I wanna go invite him out to Denny's . . . McDonald's, 7-Eleven, anything! Who doesn't leave their house?

It's the end of the day. Another day this kid hasn't moved. Seems to be having fun with his games, though. At least one of us is having a good time. He went online again today. I hope the kid is getting a girlfriend or something. [chuckle]

I wonder if his dad even knows he's been expelled. Wouldn't surprise me if he didn't . . . They never talk to each other.

April 2, 2013. I think I got too many of my personal thoughts in this thing yesterday. I guess I forgot I may have to turn this over to a court someday. Hopefully not. Problem is, it might be the only thing keeping me sane on this job. Hmm, either way I gotta try and keep it more professional today.

I just checked on the Miller kid . . . like I do every hour. He's back at it, playing his game. His father left approximately forty-five minutes ago. I'm going to go approach the window and see what I can see.

Ah geez . . . I went up to the window, and I was being as sneaky as a person can be in daylight, but I think the kid might've seen me . . . [pause] Hmmm, you know, I didn't think about this before, but if he sees me . . . [chuckle] I won't have to do this crappy duty anymore. I'll lie low out here for a while, maybe he didn't notice me after all.

[laughing] Wow, now that was surprising. The kid walks out his door, looks me straight in the eye, and hocks a loogie from his patio to the hood of my car. Man, that kid has got range! Since he didn't pull a gun and blow me away, I doubt the kid's actually gonna hurt anyone. Still, he's got some nerve to go spitting on a cop car.

Anyway, my cover is blown so I'm heading back to Purser's office now . . . He'll probably rip me a new one, but that's better than working this job. What a waste. Rendar out.

Credit: Neil Carr.

Guided Reading | A Multigenre Project

Gwen Ganow (STUDENT), *When Worlds Collide: Why Superheroes Matter*

In her multigenre project, "When Worlds Collide: Why Superheroes Matter," Gwen Ganow represents a variety of genres and media, as her table of contents shows (see below). (To learn more about Gwen's project, see Chapters 4 and 10.)

▲ STUDENT AUTHOR PHOTO
Gwen Ganow.
Credit: Gwen Dalynn Ganow.

GWEN'S RHETORICAL SITUATION & CHOICES

MULTIGENRE PIECES

◄ What is the author/artist, *Gwen Ganow*, doing?

What are the parts? ► How do they work together?

PURPOSE

Gwen's overall purpose is to persuade her audience that superheroes can help convey hope and strength to marginalized people who experience intolerance.

AUDIENCE

Gwen's primary audience is comic book readers; she sequenced the genre pieces to immerse readers in the world of the superhero right away.

RHETORICAL APPEALS

The film review, researched argument, and brochure rely on ethos and logos. The journal entry, memoir, and film review rely on pathos.

MODES & MEDIA

A mix of text and visuals help readers visualize, relate to, and interpret the world of the superhero.

> **When Worlds Collide:**
> **Why Superheroes Matter**
>
> Gwen Ganow
> **Project Contents**
>
> 1. Introduction 2
> 2. The Research: God, Superman, Batman, The Punisher, and Me 3
> 3. The Collage: Superheroes, Strength, Hope, and Justice 6
> 4. The Journal: The Worst Day of My Life 8
> 5. The Brochure: Gay/Straight Alliance: Be a Superhero 19
> 6. The Review: *X-Men*: Mutants R Us 22
> 7. The Presentation: We Are All Mutants: Why the Original *X-Men* Movie Still Matters 26
> 8. The Narrative: The Ties That Bind 29

Credit: Gwen Dalynn Ganow

Gwen's project consists of:

A researched argument

A journal entry

A brochure

A film review

A Power-Point presentation

A memoir

To unify her project, Gwen provides:

An **Introduction** that offers context. In it, she explains her research and rhetorical choices, and evaluates her project (item 1).

Packaging. Gwen puts her project together in a Word document that she can e-mail to her instructor. This format suits her project because some of her genre pieces—such as her film review and PowerPoint—include embedded links to film clips and other media.

Let's examine the brochure from Gwen's multigenre

| GWEN'S RHETORICAL SITUATION & CHOICES | | THE GENRE'S CONVENTIONS |

GWEN'S RHETORICAL SITUATION & CHOICES

PURPOSE
In this brochure, Gwen makes a case for gay marriage, arguing for tolerance and presenting an invitation to a GSA (Gay/Straight Alliance) meeting. The brochure relates to her project on superheroes, "otherness," and acceptance.

AUDIENCE
The audience for this piece is specifically gay teens, but Gwen also makes it relevant for her wider audience of comics/superhero fans as well as her classmates and instructor.

RHETORICAL APPEALS
Gwen uses mainly pathos in this piece, both in her list (e.g., "Secrets hurt" and "You're not alone") and by choosing festive images of kissing couples.

MODES & MEDIA
This piece can be used as a physical flyer or shared on digital media (in which case it can include links to the GSA, for example).

◄ **What is the author/artist, Gwen Ganow, doing?**

What makes this a _persuasive_ brochure? ▶

 Sometimes you are Superman, and sometimes you are just Clark Kent, but your gay identity should never be hidden within yourself.

 If your parents love you even though you're an alien/mutant/superhero, they'll still love you even if you're gay.

 All gay superheroes need a Fortress of Solitude. One can be found in your GLBT (Gay, Lesbian, Bisexual, and Transgender) resource center.

 Superheroes fight for what is right. This includes the coexistence of all religions, all skin colors, and all sexual orientations.

 Sticks and stones will not break your steel bones.

 Secrets hurt everyone, even superheroes.

 Bigotry and hatred can be just as deadly as kryptonite. Always stand up for yourself, and let strength and hope guide your path.

 You're not alone. Superheroes have to struggle and fight for what they believe in.

 Captain America fights for freedom, democracy, and the American way. He desires these things for ALL Americans.

**Superhero GSA Brochure
Gay/Straight Alliance: Be a Superhero**

Hear ye! Hear ye!
The GSA of Metropolis would like to invite all gay and straight superheroes to its first meeting of the year. Come as you are with an open heart and an open mind for a "brown bag" discussion on marriage in the twenty-first century. Through support for each other, we can lead the way for humanity.

The GSA meeting will be held at the time and place stated below:

GSA Headquarters
5655 W. Kent Ave.
Metropolis
Special Guest Speaker, Captain America
5–7 p.m.
Capes and refreshments will be provided.

Credit: Gwen Dalynn Ganow.

THE GENRE'S CONVENTIONS

ELEMENTS OF THE GENRE
Brochures are usually used to inform and/or persuade an audience, which is the case here. They are usually brief, to the point, and visual.

STYLE
Gwen uses a casual but persuasive tone, and plays with the concept of the superhero to move readers/viewers to action.

DESIGN
She works in two columns to present her content. In column 1 she chooses gay pride flags instead of bullets to telegraph the message behind the brochure. In column 2 she presents her eye-catching images and centers the invitation to the meeting.

SOURCES
Gwen draws on the sources she has used in her research. See her Works Cited list in Chapter 10 (p. 285).

Guided Reading | A Multigenre Project

In his multigenre project, Dawson Swan works with a variety of genres and media, as the image below shows.

Dawson Swan (STUDENT), *The Threat of Nature Deficit Disorder*

DAWSON'S RHETORICAL SITUATION & CHOICES

What is the ▶
author/artist,
Dawson Swan,
doing?

MULTIGENRE PIECES

What are the ▶
parts? How do they
work together?

Credit: Dawson Swan.

PURPOSE

Dawson's overall purpose is to persuade his audience that nature deficit disorder is real and that it should be taken seriously by parents, educators, and doctors.

AUDIENCE

Dawson's primary audience is educated adults; his choice for packaging the components reflects his view that exposure to nature is important for all children.

RHETORICAL APPEALS

Dawson's choice of the poster with a small child, the music CD, and the wagon used as packaging indicate that appeals to pathos are most important to him.

MODES & MEDIA

Dawson's project includes print (the magazine article), audio (the CD), and visual pieces (the poster, the artwork with the CD, and the packaging).

MULTIGENRE CONVENTIONS

There are no conventions for multigenre projects. However, there are conventions for individual genres. See Chapters 5–10 for examples.

DAWSON'S PROJECT CONSISTS OF:

A **poster** (staked into a chunk of real dirt and grass, complete with a dandelion).

A **compilation CD**, leaning against a rock, of songs about nature, accompanied by liner notes that identify each song and the message it sends about nature.

A research-based **magazine article**, rolled up and "planted" in a green flowerpot.

To unify his project, Dawson provides:

An **Introduction** that prepares his audience to experience his project and serves as his Author's/Artist's Statement. In it, he explains his research and rhetorical choices and evaluates his project (item 1).

Packaging consisting of a Roadmaster wagon, which represents childhood play and nature.

Let's take a closer look at Dawson's Introduction to his multigenre project.

PURPOSE

Dawson introduces his topic and argues for its importance.

AUDIENCE

The audience for this piece is people who don't understand the gravity of nature deficit disorder, so Dawson takes a serious tone.

RHETORICAL APPEALS

Dawson appeals to logos when he explains his genre choices and the order in which he wants them viewed/read and why.

MODES & MEDIA

The mode and medium were dictated by the assignment, which specified that the Introduction be a print-based essay. Dawson felt that visuals did not need to be part of the Introduction because the project itself was so eye-catching. So he used text exclusively to explain his decisions.

◀ What is the author/artist, *Dawson Swan*, doing?

What makes this an ▶ *Introduction* to a multigenre project?

Dawson Swan
Introduction
The Threat of Nature Deficit Disorder

"Things are not like they used to be." I've heard this said many times in reference to technology, nature, parenting, music, and the world in general. That phrase will always be true because change is inevitable, but there is one change that is occurring unnoticed today that I believe requires our urgent attention. This change has resulted in a condition that has recently been identified as nature deficit disorder (NDD). Richard Louv introduced this condition in his book *Last Child in the Woods: Saving Our Children from Nature-Deficit Disorder*. Most people have never heard of this "disease," and when they do hear about it, their initial reaction is that it is a joke, just a clever play on words. Unfortunately NDD and the misery it causes are very real (pp. 22–24).

In today's society, it seems we no longer have time to relax, to take a walk outside and smell the roses. Instead, we are bombarded by tight schedules, economic pressures, and chronic stress. The former secretary of education Richard Riley was quoted as saying, "The top ten jobs that will be in demand in 2010 didn't exist in 2004. Students are being prepared for jobs that don't exist, using technologies that haven't been invented, to solve problems that we don't know about yet" (qtd. in Fisch). This shows how incredibly overwhelming it can be to simply live in our culture and to plan for the future, let alone find time to be outside.

Due to continually advancing technology, globalization is becoming a reality. The quantity of data created every day is increasing exponentially. Toddlers are learning to use technology scientists wouldn't have dreamed of thirty years ago. As a result, it is becoming vitally important to train our children about technology. Fortunately the young generations are easily able to learn to use technology, but there is always much more to be learned as technology continues to advance. The increasing need for technological "geeks" is drawing more and more of us into cyberspace and shoving nature off into a corner.

ELEMENTS OF THE GENRE

Dawson begins by acknowledging that many people will initially view his topic as a joke; this helps him build rapport with his readers. He gives an overview of the different pieces in the project and prepares readers for what to expect.

STYLE

Dawson writes in a formal tone, which develops his ethos as someone who takes this issue seriously.

DESIGN

The design of Dawson's Introduction is minimal; he formats his Introduction into paragraphs for easy reading.

SOURCES

Dawson incorporates three outside sources: two books and a video that went viral in 2007 about how the world is changing. He uses the MLA style of documentation, which requires parenthetical in-text citations that are, in turn, included in a Works Cited list on page 445. (See also MLA coverage in Chapter 13.)

Ironically, going "green" is becoming increasingly popular. Our culture is reveling in new ways to better the environment and preserve nature, but it is seriously missing the point because the culture, particularly pop culture, has little firsthand knowledge of nature. We would rather stay inside and watch the hit TV show *Planet Earth* on our massive high-definition TVs than take a walk outside. Instead of climbing a mountain or sitting on our porch watching the sunset, we would rather sit in front of a computer monitor and look at beautiful photographs of exotic places. This misguided relationship with nature has created a synthetic environment and a secondhand relationship with the earth—an environment that is convenient and controlled. While those who have generated this environment are supposedly pursuing the natural, they have only created a vague reflection of the real thing. Our culture is sadly lacking in an understanding of the true meaning of "natural."

Now you may ask, "Why should I care? I get enough nature from the Discovery Channel and an occasional ski trip." Well, look at it this way. The generation that is currently approaching, or is already in, the child-rearing stage is the largest generation ever (Tapscott 20). The men and women of this generation are going to begin having children, and the decisions they make about how they raise their children will have a monumental impact on the future.

The logical next question you may ask is, "Is NDD a real threat?" Yes it is, and its effects can be devastating: obesity, ADD, emotional disorders, high blood pressure, and chronic pain that kids develop decades before they should. These conditions have always been there, but now they are disturbingly prevalent.

This project serves a couple of purposes: First, I want to inform people of NDD, and if they already know about it, I want to increase their knowledge and alert them to how urgent it is to take action. Second, I hope that this project gives inspiration to fight NDD. It can be as easy as walking outside, looking up at the stars, or smelling the fragrance of a wildflower in the night air.

I planned each part of the project to fit into a different category of media so I could communicate to more people. My first piece is a poster that can be displayed nearly anywhere, and it quickly draws people in—far more than an essay or a brochure can. A poster evokes emotion and thoughts of

(Continues on next page)

Dawson Swan, *The Threat of Nature Deficit Disorder*

childhoods spent playing outside. This sets them up for my second piece.

The second and third pieces actually merge into a CD album, which can reach people on multiple levels. The artwork for the album is made up of photographs I have taken of nature during the last couple of years. These pictures grab the attention of the viewer and create a relaxing and thought-provoking environment for them to take part in as they experience the second half of the album—the music and lyrics (I searched through hundreds of songs to find specific songs about nature). I wrote an Introduction to the album that describes the purpose of each piece and its message. My fourth piece is a magazine article. It could appear in parenting magazines because my primary audience is people who are moving into, or are in, the childbearing years, and because children are most susceptible to NDD.

I have concluded that these pieces fit together best in a conference setting where the poster in a booth would initially draw people. Then they would see the CD. It could be considered a fund-raiser for my topic or maybe just a sampler. After leafing through the pages of artwork and listening to the music, people would want to know what it's all about, and they could read the magazine article. The article brings everything home and explains NDD in depth. Between these four pieces, a variety of media are used to grab people's attention, engaging both their minds and hearts. NDD is a compelling subject that affects everyone. Although a presentation of the simple facts of NDD would be enough to win people over, the potential of engaging them emotionally just as nature herself does, is fulfilled through photographs, poetry, and music.

Works Cited

Fisch, Karl. "Did You Know 2.0?" YouTube, www.youtube.com/watch?v=pMcfrLYDm2U&feature=related. Accessed 13 Oct. 2012.

Louv, Richard. *Last Child in the Woods: Saving Our Children from Nature-Deficit Disorder.* Algonquin, 2005, pp. 22–24.

Tapscott, Don. *Growing Up Digital: The Rise of the Net Generation.* McGraw-Hill, 1998, p. 20.

Reader

16

IDENTITIES:
WE ARE MULTIPLE

CONTENTS

What do our online profiles, tattoos, or bumper stickers say about who we are? How about the magazines and blogs we read? The things we carry and the things we wear? And how do we define and represent ourselves in other genres and media—such as music, poems, movies, advertisements, or national slogans?

As individuals and as members of a larger community, we may define ourselves based on where we live, our religion, heritage, race, class, gender, and sexual orientation. We may also identify ourselves through favorite activities or sports teams, educational major, or profession, for example.

When we express something about identity, we create. What we create depends on what we want to say and the people we want to say it to—and also on how we say it. In other words, our creative expression depends not only on our choices about our purpose, message, and audience but also on the genres and media that we choose as vehicles for that expression.

For example, if you wanted to share something about your own identity with your friends, you might create a musical mixtape or playlist. As you compile that music, would you choose songs that reflect where you're from? Would the lyrics say something about your likes and dislikes, or some other aspect of you?

Now, imagine that instead you've decided to say something about who you are in the form of a narrative essay, or through a poem, blog, or YouTube video. What might change? What different choices would you need to make in order to represent your ideas about identity through these genres?

In this chapter, you will encounter a range of voices commenting on personal and cultural identity. You'll read a variety of genres: poster, ad, researched essay, editorial, article, blog, and book excerpt. As you read, pay attention to how these authors use different types of compositions and media to present ideas and arguments about identity.

The readings explore such ideas as how our material possessions reflect who we are, with an ad for a luxury car. Consider how many quick judgments you make about others based on their possessions. For example, if you notice your mom has traded in her old phone for a smartphone, you might identify her as a tiny bit cooler today than she was yesterday.

Other readings examine social aspects of identity. How does where we're from, or where we live now, affect who we are? Ted Merwin explores a brief social history of the Jewish American deli and Marisa Kabas details the reasons behind a Muslim woman hiding her identity upon moving to the United States.

Closing the chapter is David Sedaris's humorous examination of how language influences our identity. As you read through all the pieces in this chapter, consider different ways these pieces resonate with your own experiences.

▼ Poster/Ad Campaign

The Fighting-Bigotry-with-Delightful-Posters Campaign!,
Facts About Muslims

The Facts about Muslims poster is part of a humorous ad campaign promoting tolerance of Muslims. These ads were designed by the creators of the 2013 documentary film *The Muslims Are Coming!* and were hung inside more than one hundred New York City subway stations.

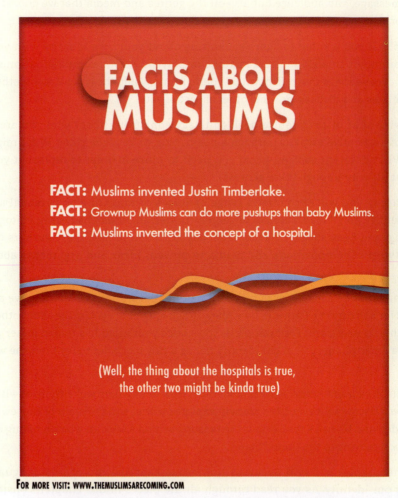

Credit: themuslimsarecoming.com

QUESTIONS

1. How does the poster use humor to combat bigotry?

2. What features in the poster's design make it effective for hanging inside a busy city subway station?

COMPOSING PROJECT | Create a Humorous Political Poster

Think about a current issue that is making headlines. This could be something local or global. Using humor, create your own poster about the issue to its viewers.

▼ Ad

Acura, *The Acura TSX*

The advertisement for the Acura TSX (see p. 454) is available online and was originally obtained from a print issue of *Food & Wine* magazine. Like most ads for luxury goods, this one is selling not only the product itself but a lifestyle. Notice how the people in the ad do not actually appear in or even with the car.

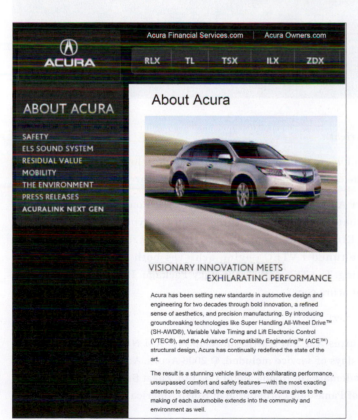

◄ COMPANY HOMEPAGE

Acura's Web site sells the brand as visionary and of high quality.

Credit: Courtesy of American Honda Motor Company, Inc.

Old luxury has a glass of warm milk and turns in early. Modern luxury goes out all night and still makes it into the office by eight. A new generation has arrived.

TSX

>> commercial-archive.com

Introducing the all-new Acura TSX. This is modern luxury. Loaded with innovations like dynamic Traffic Rerouting™ and Zagat® reviews, it can find you an uncrowded road or a crowded club. Its ELS Surround® Sound could turn punk rock into a symphonic experience. And its re-tuned i-VTEC® engine achieves both more power, and an ultra-low emissions rating. The TSX with Technology Package. It's luxury for a whole new generation. See it at acura.com.

ACURA
ADVANCE.

▲ AD ACURA'S TSX

Credit: Courtesy of American Honda Motor Company, Inc.

The text of the ad (left to right):

"Old luxury has a glass of warm milk and turns in early. Modern luxury goes out all night and still makes it into the office by eight. **A new generation has arrived.**

Introducing the all-new Acura TSX. This is modern luxury. Loaded with innovations like dynamic Traffic Routing and Zagat reviews, it can find you an uncrowded road or a crowded club. Its ELS Surround Sound could turn punk rock into a symphonic experience. And its re-tuned i-VTEC engine achieves both more power, and an ultra-low emissions rating. The TSX with Technology Package. It's luxury for a whole new generation. See it at acura.com."

Fine print (upper right corner):

"Traffic Rerouting requires XM NavTraffic subscription. XM NavTraffic available in select markets. First 90 days of service included. © 2008 Acura. Acura, TSX, i-VTEC and Traffic Rerouting are trademarks of Honda Motor Co., Ltd. Zagat Survey. ELS Surround is a registered trademark of Panasonic Corporation of North America. All rights reserved."

1. What are some of the ways the Acura ad conveys that this car is "modern luxury"?
2. How does the ad use lighting, contrast, and framing to convey its message?

COMPOSING PROJECT | Design an Ad

Redesign the Acura ad for a different audience than the one intended in the ad shown here. You might consider redesigning the ad for an older audience, such as people who typify "old luxury."

▼ Editorial

Ted Merwin, *What Makes the Jewish Deli Quintessentially American?*

Ted Merwin is a journalist, author, and professor of religion and Judaic studies at Dickinson College. His articles have appeared in *The New York Times*, the *Washington Post, New York Jewish Week*, and *Haaretz*, the publication in which the following editorial appeared. Merwin is author of a book on New York Jews in the Jazz Age, and *Pastrami on Rye: An Overstuffed History of the Jewish Delicatessen*; he also gives talks on Jewish food, history, and culture.

Credit: Used by permission of Ted Merwin.

When *Haaretz*'s food and wine critic, the late Daniel Rogov, moved from Paris to Tel Aviv in the late 1970s, he discovered a cornucopia of Jewish foods from all over the world, stemming from the manifold cultures from which Jews had emigrated. What he missed was one of his favorite foods from his childhood in Brooklyn: a pastrami sandwich on rye.

Indeed, what is arguably the quintessential American Jewish dish has never played a major role in any other Jewish cuisine in the world. There is something irreducibly American about the deli sandwich, which bespeaks the unique history of American Jews.

Much of the Jewish deli sandwich's popularity in America is tied to the evolution of the sandwich itself, which exploded in popularity after the First World War. Even before the advent of the mechanical bread slicer in Iowa in 1928, the sandwich (originally invented by Rabbi Hillel the Elder, as we commemorate each year during the Passover seder), became one of the most popular of all American foods, with more than 5,000 sandwich shops in New York by the mid 1920s. In a city defined by its manic energy, the sandwich became the perfect fuel for people on the go.

> **The kosher deli became no less than a secular alternative to the synagogue.**

The kosher deli became no less than a secular alternative to the synagogue. The corner kosher deli, which served as the Jewish equivalent of the Irish pub or black barbershop, served a crucial social function; at the height of the Great Depression there were more than 1,500 kosher delis in New York, and after the Second World War, delis began popping up wherever Jews had relocated, from Miami Beach to Los Angeles.

Delis enabled Jews to bridge their Jewish and American identities, and to congratulate themselves on their rising social and economic position in American society. In legendary "kosher style" eateries like Reuben's and Lindy's, Jews devoured skyscraper-high sandwiches named after the stars of the day. The very atmosphere of glamour and celebrity enabled Jews to flatter themselves on their arrival in mainstream American society. The overstuffed deli sandwich symbolized no less than the attainment of the American Dream.

In other countries, the deli sandwich never made it so big. Not that Europeans, for example, were unfamiliar with smoked and pickled meat. In Great Britain, tinned corned beef was served to generations of soldiers from the Boer War to the end of World War II. The French and Italians had their charcuteries and salumerie, respectively, where gourmet sausages and cured meat products (mostly made from pork) were retailed. And every town in Germany, it seemed, was known for the particular kind of sausage that it produced.

Delis did occasionally migrate outside of the United States. Indeed, a handful of Jewish delis prospered for decades in Europe; these included Bloom's in the leafy London suburb of Golders Green and Jo Goldenberg's on the lively Rue des Rosiers in Paris, But for the most part, Europeans never went in for the kind of in-your-face, conspicuous consumption that scarfing down American-style deli sandwiches entailed. European cuisines typically featured small portions, refined atmospheres, elegant presentations, leisurely meals—the opposite of dining in a loud, raucous environment in which people ate with their hands, talked with their mouths full, and rushed through their repast. This uncouth behavior was associated with people who were marginalized, low-class, immigrant.

Nor, as Rogov found, did the deli sandwich tend to appeal to Israelis. As he speculated not long before his death last fall, the pre-eminent critic attributed this palpable absence to a number of factors dating back to the country's formation, including the desert nation's prevailing taste for simpler and lighter foods, the socialist predisposition to spend as little time and money on food as practicable, the substitution of turkey and chicken breasts for beef in making pastrami, and the use (which he deplored) of cows rather than steer for meat.

New delis continue to open in Europe and Israel, from the glatt kosher Reuben's in London (which serves steak and lamb chops along with its salt beef sandwiches) to Ruben's in Tel Aviv (which carries a wide selection of draft beers). But the New York Jewish deli was never just about the food. It fed the soul as much as the stomach. It nourished a faith in America as a land where Jews could finally be free to be both Jewish and American at the same time. It nurtured a sense of confidence and belonging that was as filling as the most pastrami-packed sandwich could be.

1. What is the central purpose of Ted Merwin's editorial, "What Makes the Jewish Deli Quintessentially American?" What evidence does Merwin use to support his point?

2. How does Merwin establish his ethos? What are some of the strategies he uses in his editorial to build his credibility?

COMPOSING PROJECT | Create an Editorial

Think about a food that is related to an aspect of your identity. It might be a food connected to your religion, your ethnicity, or your family's history. Using Merwin's editorial as a model, create your own editorial that makes an argument about food and identity.

▼ Researched Essay

W. Ralph Eubanks, *Color Lines*

W. Ralph Eubanks is an author and journalist. He is perhaps best known for his critically acclaimed 2003 memoir, *Ever Is a Long Time: A Journey into Mississippi's Dark Past*. His researched essay, "Color Lines," which appeared in 2013 in the magazine *The American Scholar*, explores how DNA testing complicates our notions of racial identity.

When I was a young boy, I found a photograph half-hidden in the back of my parents' closet, leaned up behind my mother's stacked boxes of high-heel shoes. A dandyish man in a dark suit and skinny tie stared out at me, bearing a striking resemblance to my mother. Who was he? His hair, parted neatly in the middle, peeked out under a broad-brimmed hat perched jauntily on his head. In time, I learned that the unknown man was my grandfather James Morgan Richardson. But not until I was 16, when I overheard a conversation between my parents in the middle of the night, did I learn that he was white.

My parents kept my grandfather's portrait hidden because in 1960s Mississippi, with all its racial paranoia, displaying the picture in our living room would have been risky, if not impossible. Severe social consequences awaited any black person claiming close kinship with a white person. So the picture stayed hidden, part of my mother's past, and my own—something I knew about but didn't yet feel free to explore.

My mother knew that the portrait fascinated me, and when I got married, she gave it to me. I saw that gift as an invitation to learn more about the man within the borders of the frame. It has taken me 20 years, but I've finally begun to figure things out and better understand my own history as well.

In 21st-century America, my family would be described as multiracial. But in the world I grew up in—the American South of the 1950s and 1960s, where the idea of race and identity determined who you were and your place in the world—you were either black or white. We were first colored, later Negroes, and still later black. Claiming mixed status meant you were either trying to be white (implying that black was inferior) or trying to pass for white (a dangerous business few spoke of openly), and doing so carried the risk of being labeled a racial traitor. Consequently, my identity was shaped by the racial boundaries of the American South as well as the double consciousness that W. E. B. Du Bois speaks of in *The Souls of Black Folk*. I always felt that duality: "an American, a Negro; two souls, two thoughts, two unreconciled strivings; two warring ideals in one dark body, whose dogged strength alone keeps it from being torn asunder."

My mother was seven years old when her mother died. The town doctor who pronounced my grandmother dead offered to help the family start over as a white family, far away from their small town in rural, isolated south Alabama. Even though my grandmother Edna Howell Richardson was black, all her children's birth certificates said they were white. So, this "transformation" would have been easy. But in the end my grandfather, the man whose portrait had been hidden in the closet, chose not to hide his children's mixed race. Instead, my mother and her sister grew up going to black schools and identifying as black. When they married black men, they had to have their race officially changed on their birth certificates in order to get legal marriage licenses.

I grew up hearing my mother say, "You can always tell when someone is passing." Since she could pass for white, my mother spoke from a position of authority. Racial passing, once a common subject of discussion in the black community, has faded from American consciousness with the emergence of racial and multiracial pride. But even today, with six multiracial grandchildren of her own, my mother stands by her statement: "You can always tell."

Once, in 1967, she spotted an old classmate from Tuskegee Institute who was managing the men's furnishings section of a Mississippi department store where, a few years earlier, black people weren't allowed to try on clothes, much less work above the position of elevator operator. Black people couldn't even work as clerks in that store, so the man could not have moved up to this level unless he was passing. When my mother recognized him, he was fussily arranging a display of memorabilia from southern schools. She strolled over to take a look, remarking, "Why, I don't see anything from my school here."

The man replied with steely silence, carefully maintaining his composure.

Then my mother asked him point-blank, "Do you have anything from Tuskegee? I'd like to get something for my husband."

The man turned beet red, quietly said no, and tried to smile his way through my mother's attempt to "out" him. In her inimitable southern manner, my mother responded with fury cloaked in sweetness: "Well, *I thank you so much* for checking." From that day forward, the man avoided my mother whenever she walked into the store, and each time, her eyes shot in his direction, casting that knowing glare upon him.

When I look back on this incident, I realize that my mother reacted the way she did because she saw this man as a traitor of the highest order. He had turned his back on the philosophy of racial uplift he had been taught at Tuskegee; the oppressed had assumed the role of oppressor. And all this during the height of the civil rights movement. Given the times, and my mother's history, I can understand her anger.

In spite of her being mixed race, in spite of having been raised primarily by her white father, being black remains the core of my mother's identity. Perhaps to keep from confusing my siblings and me, she didn't tell us about her father's race until the four of us were all nearly adults. So, for many years, I had to pretend that I hadn't overheard my parents talking in the middle of the night — talking about how hard it had been for my dark-skinned father to ask a white man for his daughter's hand. And I had to pretend, as well, that I hadn't seen the portrait hidden in the closet.

• • •

My family's complex racial history, filled as it is with myths and truths, led me to DNA ancestry testing. I had begun writing a book on the life and times of my maternal grandparents, whose marriage around 1915 was an act of defiance in a part of the South governed by Jim Crow laws. In that book, *The House at the End of the Road,* my purpose had been to tell the little-known story of mixed-race families in the American South, like my mother's, that prevailed in spite of Jim Crow and laws against interracial marriage. As the book took shape, a scientific study caught my eye.

In late 2005, scientists reported the discovery of a gene mutation that had led to the first appearance of white skin in humans. Other than this minor mutation — just one letter of DNA code out of 3.1 billion letters in the human genome — most people are 99.9 percent identical genetically. And yet, what divisions have arisen as a result of such a seemingly inconsequential genetic anomaly. Moreover, this mutation had separated members of my family along tightly demarcated racial lines for three generations. As this discovery became known, I was invited to join a class on race relations at Pennsylvania State University in which all the students participated in DNA ancestry testing as a way of discussing contemporary attitudes about race and cultural identity.

Through the DNA tests, students came to realize that the racial or ethnic identities they grew up with were sometimes in conflict with their genetic material, belying the notion of racial purity. In class, I listened to students talk about racial labels and identities, and whether ancestry testing had changed their perceptions of themselves. Most embraced the newly found diversity that their DNA test revealed, and none felt that ancestry testing had changed their personal identities. Still, the discovery of mixed ancestry was a struggle for a few. One white student wondered whether her African heritage came from "a rape in my past," and another thought that her African DNA must have come from "promiscuous family members." These comments were indicative of the stigma that any hint of African ancestry carries for many white Americans. No one suggested that racial passing — which I'd immediately brought up in the discussion — might explain some of these traces of mixed heritage. Only one student even seemed to understand the idea of racial passing. He grew up in an interracial home, with a father of Jamaican descent and an Irish mother, and he was close to both sides of his family. Although issues of race were discussed openly at home, he told me, no one ever forced him to choose between being black and being white. And in spite of having fair skin, he did not claim to be white, choosing instead to forge his own identity as multiracial, thus embracing his phenotypic ambiguity.

When the instructor, sociologist Sam Richards, asked whether I would be interested in taking my own DNA ancestry test, as part of a larger DNA study being conducted by anthropologist Mark Shriver, I did not hesitate to say yes. Given that I already knew my mixed-race background, the results weren't shocking: 60 percent West African ancestry combined with 32 percent European, six percent East Asian, and two percent Native American. The East Asian ancestry was the only surprise, but Mark explained that Asians and Native Americans are closely related evolutionarily. (Several years later, I took a second and more sophisticated DNA test that revealed slightly different results: 50 percent African, 44 percent European, and six percent Asian. These two sets of results are within the margin of error.)

Outside Mark's office at Penn State, I studied a wall of photographs showing the faces of various people from his DNA study, from Penn State and around the world, each image accompanied by the ethnic designation that person identified with. Beside the photograph was a paper flap, which, when lifted, showed what a DNA sample revealed about that person's ethnic background. As I went through photograph after photograph, few of the personal ethnic identities matched the DNA profiles. Most people had some mixture of DNA from at least two groups; many, like me, had genetic ancestry from Europe, East Asia, West Africa, and Native American groups. Blond people had African and Asian ancestry, and several dark-skinned people had more than half of their DNA from Europe.

What we see when we look at a person may or may not correlate to his or her ancestral and ethnic background. DNA results confirmed for me that identity cannot be constructed based on a "percentage" of African ancestry, and that our society's generally accepted racial categories cannot begin to address the complexity and nuance of our heritage. I soon began to think about race only in terms of culture and biology together. And as race became an abstract rather than a concrete concept, the categorical ways in which I had thought about race in the past were quickly broken down. Once we see how small the differences are that bring about the characteristics we think of as racial—hair, skin color, eyes, facial features—in relation to the entire human genome, it's hard to make a fuss about them. Our differences are astonishingly slight.

• • •

Around this time, I was immersing myself in the work of philosopher Kwame Anthony Appiah and especially his books *Cosmopolitanism* and *The Ethics of Identity*. I'd begun to make distinctions between my personal identity and the collective dimension of identity that comes from society. When you accept that race is socially constructed—that being African American is a collective identity developed outside one's self and is therefore not within one's control—race matters less. DNA ancestry testing made that idea much clearer for me. It highlighted the flawed logic underlying the American concept of race based on standards of purity and superiority, since very few people have DNA that comes from only one part of the world. More important, it confirmed for me how many people have several cultural identities, not just one. The way I saw myself did not change, but DNA ancestry testing helped me abandon the racial myths that had shaped the first part of my life. I was moving away from the very limiting vision that divided the world into "us" and "them."

I began thinking about how firmly my own children's identities were rooted in the post–civil rights era. My three children are multiracial—my wife is of Irish, Swedish, and Swiss-German descent—and they grew up talking openly about race and cultural identity. They knew all about my parents and grandparents. Moreover, we live in Washington, D.C., until recently a majority black city but one with constantly shifting ethnic and social demographics. Given the diversity of our city, my children's identities have been shaped in an environment more rarefied than less-urban parts of the country. What would a DNA ancestry test reveal to them? Excited about my own experience, I asked my eldest son, Patrick, who was born in 1992, to take an ancestry test and to tell me how he felt about the results.

I imagined we'd have a vigorous discussion about how DNA turns the historical concept of race upside down. But for my son, the traditional concept of race had already been overturned, and our discussions revealed a deep generational gulf between us. As in my case, the sources and percentages of my son's ancestry were not surprising: 72 percent European, 25 percent African, and three percent Asian. But when I mentioned how revealing DNA had been to me, Patrick just shrugged his shoulders, as if the numbers meant little to him. "They don't change the way I think of myself or the way I view the world," he said. "When people ask me, 'What are you?' I generally tell them that I am American. And given how diverse my background is, it's in my way of thinking, a background that could only come about in America."

My wife and I had fielded "what is he" questions about Patrick over the years, particularly when he was quite small. Patrick is very fair-skinned, with light brown hair. Up until his teen years, he was so blond that people sometimes assumed that my dark brown–haired wife and I had adopted him. Once, a visitor to my wife's office, glancing at a family picture, asked insistently why we had adopted one of our three children, pointing directly at Patrick. "I gave birth to that child, believe me," my wife responded quite sternly to her incredulous visitor. "No, that one," he insisted, pointing to Patrick, "is definitely adopted." This man believed that a child who looked like Patrick was a genetic impossibility, based on our appearance and my ethnic background. If he had seen the wall of photographs hanging outside Mark Shriver's office at Penn State, he might have better understood how hard it is to judge "identity" on looks alone.

"What I tell people depends on the assumptions someone makes about me," Patrick told me. "Since I am from D.C., people will ask me what it was like for a white kid to grow up in a black city or will launch into a series of stereotypes of black people. I'll tell them it was pretty easy growing up in D.C., since I am black. Then I watch the shocked disbelief on their face. If someone appears to have no real agenda when they ask me, I tell them that my mother is white and my father is black." Patrick said he never gets into the complex racial mix on my side of the family, with a white great-grandfather and a black great-grandmother, both of whom had blond hair and blue eyes. "Still, I always make it clear I am not white. I've tried not to fall into that fear of belonging to a single group that many people have, even though I know race is not a real thing and just something people have made up over time to define themselves."

Since Patrick is a college student, the conversation about "what he is" sometimes moves toward a discussion of science and a belief in evolution, in the context of generational differences. "We're asking ourselves better questions now," he said to me. "The science that drove discussions of race in the last century was conducted to maintain the status quo and affirm stereotypes. That's the one thing DNA changes." And yet, I kept coming back to Patrick's indifference to his DNA ancestry test. "Seeing that I have ancestry that can be traced back to Mesopotamia is pretty cool," he said, "but for the most part, I'd put DNA ancestry testing on the 'meh' list. Your DNA test may have deconstructed race for you, but my DNA test had no real impact because race has already been deconstructed for me—and has been my whole life."

> **What is left once we have deconstructed race, and what does such a concept mean for the present and the future?**

I grew up in a world of racial boundaries; Patrick grew up free of a repressive racial calculus. Therein lies the difference between us. Two sets of test results inside one family; two markedly different responses. And not because of the numbers, but because of what those numbers mean (or do not mean). Because of how we read them, because of the context of our lives, our different moments in history.

According to the 2010 census, the number of multiracial children in the United States has increased in a decade by 50 percent to 4.2 million people, making multiracials the fastest-growing youth group in the country. Across the country, nearly three percent of the population chose more than one race on the last census, a change of about 32 percent since 2000. In the South and parts of the Midwest, the growth of the multiracial population has increased more than the national average. In my native Mississippi, the multiracial population grew by about 70 percent, and the state had the largest increase in interracial marriage of any state since the last census. Still, the multiracial population of Mississippi is only 1.1 percent, and many Mississippians see the legacy of the state's racial inequities as part of the cultural mindset. That's not hard to understand, given that less than half a century ago interracial marriage was illegal in Mississippi. Neighboring Alabama—where my grandparents lived—removed the constitutional prohibition against interracial marriage only in 2000, with 40 percent of Alabamians voting to keep the prohibition in place.

How do we get people such as those who voted against interracial marriage to focus less on the concept of race and more on the concept of humanity? As Mark Shriver remarked when we discussed my DNA test results, "You can defuse traditional thinking about race by making people see these differences as natural and teaching them that the differences are just part of the variety of life. That's the trajectory we are on regardless. How quickly we get there depends on how good a job we do in educating people to this new way of thinking."

• • •

What is left once we have deconstructed race, and what does such a concept mean for the present and the future? Racism is easy when only two races exist in any significant numbers, as has generally been the case throughout American history. Multiple and overlapping ethnicities (with none in the majority) make racism more difficult. In the 19th century, the eventual path to acceptance for the Irish, Italians, Eastern European Jews, and to a certain extent, Asians who immigrated to America, was to become "white." This option was uniquely closed to African Americans. In a more diverse and racially mixed America, "becoming white" may no longer be a key to equality. That may be the biggest, most significant change in American culture over the next generation.

Demographically, we are becoming less white and more multiracial, and have a larger population of Hispanics and Asians. Moreover, Hispanics complicate America's simplistic black-white dichotomy: they do not fit neatly into either racial category. As Amitai Etzioni pointed out in a 2006 essay that appeared in these pages, if "Hispanics continue to see themselves as members of one or more ethnic groups, then race in America might be pushed to the margins." And yet, American cultural discourse on race is still stymied by a tainted racial past largely divided between black and white. For more than a century, America built a racial caste system, a concept originally invented to categorize perceived biological, social, and cultural differences. Though that system has been eroding for decades, our changing demographics require a swifter transformation. Our rapidly expanding multiracial and Hispanic populations do not signal the end of race as a concept, but they do open up new possibilities for how we think, talk, and understand the subject. And talking about race—engaging in the sort of frank and open discussions that I witnessed at Penn State—is precisely what we need more of at the moment.

Such dialogues will, alas, likely take place only within a small part of our population. Too many people are still in the thrall of cultural myths. Having grown up with many of those myths, I recognize their power to divide and to cause harm. And yet, I no longer look at a person and think I can presume to know his race, ethnicity, or background, or whether he is claiming a race other than the one into which he was born. Increasingly, I believe that it is unethical to engage with another person solely on the basis of race or ethnicity.

Perhaps it all goes back to the man in the portrait at the back of my parents' closet. Before I knew he was white, I thought he was just a cool-looking guy. I didn't know why he'd been relegated to the back of a closet. There was no flap to lift on his portrait, as with the photographs on the wall at Penn State, to reveal what percentage of his makeup came from this part of the world, or that. Maybe part of what appeals to me about DNA testing is that it helps show how much all of our portraits are composites, and reminds us how much better it is to expose those portraits than to hide them away.

I still see myself as a black kid from Mississippi, but first and foremost, I think of myself as a member of the human family. Embracing this idea has allowed me to reconcile ways of feeling and of comprehending race previously clouded by my personal history. I like to think that W. E. B. Du Bois would be pleased that I no longer feel held back by unreconciled strivings. As Du Bois wrote in 1909 in his biography of John Brown, "the cost of liberty is less than the price of repression."

QUESTIONS

1. Eubanks tells several stories within his essay. Do you find these to be a central part of his argument or a distraction? Why?

2. Do you trust Eubanks as an authority on racial identity and the science behind it? Why or why not?

COMPOSING PROJECT | Conduct a Survey or Interview

Eubanks suggests, "Our rapidly expanding multiracial and Hispanic populations do not signal the end of race as a concept, but they do open up new possibilities for how we think, talk, and understand the subject. And talking about race—engaging in the sort of frank and open discussions that I witnessed at Penn State—is precisely what we need more of at the moment." Survey or interview several professors from departments on your campus that engage directly with racial and/or ethnic identity, such as Ethnic Studies, Africana Studies, and Chicano Studies, to find out where they stand on this issue.

▼ **Article**

Marisa Kabas, *She Hid Her Muslim Identity for 15 Years*

Marisa Kabas is a freelance writer and blogger. She often writes for Fusion, an online media outlet that describes itself as "the media brand for a young, diverse, and inclusive world." Fusion is where the story below appeared. In it, Kabas tells the story of a Somali immigrant to the United States who kept her Muslim identity a secret from even her closest friends for fifteen years.

Credit: "This Woman Hid her Muslim Identity for 15 Years. Here's Why She Came Out." By Marisa Kabas, Gawker, May 20, 2016. Copyrighted 2017. Gawker Media. 128690:0717PF

When Elhan moved to Washington, D.C. from Somalia, the United States was not at war with Iraq and Afghanistan and the Twin Towers still dominated the New York skyline. But just a few weeks later, on September 11, 2001, everything changed. Overnight, "Muslim" became a dirty word—and Elhan became "Amy."

With this one day of terror, the nation's attitudes toward followers of Islam went from fairly neutral to vitriolic, after the perpetrators of the most deadly terrorist attack on U.S. soil were revealed to be Muslim. Elhan, a high school freshman at the time, could see the change happening before her eyes.

That's when she decided that in public she'd be "Amy," a normal American teenager.

For the next 15 years, Amy would go to school, hang out with her friends, and go to parties, never letting on that she was deeply attached to her religion. When she wasn't at school, though, she was at her mosque, where she prayed regularly and engaged with a close-knit community as Elhan. Never did these two lives meet, she said—not even any close calls.

That all changed earlier this year, however, when Elhan finally worked up the courage to come clean to her friends about her double life—and the entire world.

"It felt like a very heavy rock was on my chest. I just didn't know how to get out of it," Elhan, now 32, told me in a phone conversation last week. "I was stuck. I got so used to it being my daily routine and it became a normal thing to be 'Amy' once I was outside the door."

Not only did Elhan decide she was going to finally share her secret, but she elected to do it on the season two premiere of the Pivot network docu-series *Secret Life of Americans*. Each week on the show, a different subject reveals something personal they've been hiding from loved ones. On Friday's episode, viewers follow Elhan on her self-filmed journey toward revealing her religious, Muslim self to her friends—and her secular identity as "Amy" to her family.

"My whole adult life, I've been living in fear," she tells the camera, set in selfie mode. "Fear of rejection from society. Fear of being labeled as a terrorist. Fear that someone might hurt me because I'm Muslim. That fear is still there."

While not all Muslims go to the lengths Elhan did to hide their religious identity, her story provides a vivid example of the conflict many Muslims feel in simply navigating daily life in this country. In the years since 9/11, racial tensions have arguably gotten worse, not better. This climate of intolerance has forced many, like Elhan, to hide in shame. But perhaps leading by example will encourage others to come out from the shadow of hate.

In the days following 9/11, Elhan made a few practical decisions that would affect her life and identity for the decade-and-a-half to come: She asked school administrators to officially address her as Amy and she began changing out of her traditional garments and into jeans and t-shirts before school. Once she began hearing mean-spirited jokes in the wake of 9/11, including insults about how Muslims look and dress, she became convinced this superficial assimilation was the only way to live a peaceful existence in this country.

> " **Never did these two lives meet, she said—not even any close calls.** "

"It's not like I had two different personalities," she tells me. "I was still the same girl." But one of those girls—the real her—was only seen within the safety of her home and at her mosque. It was never a question of her commitment or love of her faith, but rather a paralyzing fear that left her, and so many like her, she says, feeling like she would be put in harm's way by simply being herself.

This fear was not unfounded. According to 2015 numbers from the FBI's Uniform Crime Reports program, the county has seen five times more annual hate crimes against Muslims since 9/11. The group estimates that 100 to 150 have occurred per year, in contrast with 20 to 30 per year before the attacks.

Merely "looking" Muslim isn't the only thing Elhan and fellow followers of Islam need to worry about—so-called "Muslim-sounding" names can also impact how others perceive you. In a 2014 study that analyzed the way employers respond to prospective employees whose resumes indicate a religious affiliation, the researchers found that resumes with one of the seven religions tested "received [on average] 29 percent fewer emails and 33 percent fewer phone calls than the control group." But Muslims fared even worse, receiving 38 percent fewer emails and a staggering 54 percent fewer phone calls.

Despite these discouraging odds, earlier this year Elhan took the bold step of embracing her religion and lifestyle in public after the big reveal to her family and friends. She'd been contemplating it for the past few years since being diagnosed with relapsing Multiple Sclerosis and realized the stress of concealing her true identity was not only bad for her emotionally, but also bad for her health. These days, she can once again be seen everywhere she goes donning the headscarf and traditional garment she had worn in Somalia, from her regular Starbucks to the gas station and over to her friend's places. As far as she's concerned, the hardest part about "coming out" as Muslim is over, which was telling her friends. Before she told them, she feared that not only would they not accept her because of her religion but, above all, they'd be angry she lied to them for all of these years.

When she finally told them, tears streaming down her face, they understandably had some questions. "Why didn't you tell us before?" "How have you been able to party with us when Muslims don't drink?"—a common misconception. But she says that since the initial shock wore off, they've all been accepting and supportive. It's other Americans that still need some help. . . .

"So many communities are being swooped to the side because they want to be free, want to be themselves," she said, pointing to the embattled transgender community as an example. "We're Americans no matter what we are. And all we need is to be loved."

QUESTIONS

1. Sometimes Kabas quotes Elhan, and other times she summarizes what Elhan said. Do you think the quotations Kabas chose to include are effective? Why or why not?

2. How do you think Kabas's article would have to be changed for a media outlet that doesn't gear itself toward a "young, diverse, and inclusive world"?

COMPOSING PROJECT | Write a Researched Essay or Blog Entry

Kabas mentions that Elhan's decision to "come out" was motivated in part by the toll that hiding her identity was taking on her health. Research coming out and the different reasons people give for coming out or not coming out. Present your findings to your classmates in a researched essay or blog entry.

▼ Blog

B. J. Priester, *The Heroine's Journey*

B. J. Priester, also known as "Lex," is a writer for the *FANgirl Blog*, which is devoted to analyzing and critiquing "*Star Wars*, storytelling, and female characters." In this entry, Priester argues that Campbell's model of the Hero's Journey — which you may be familiar with from high school or other college courses — fits only stories that place a male protagonist at the center and doesn't account for the many social changes that have happened in recent decades. Priester proposes a model of the Heroine's Journey that takes into account issues Campbell's model doesn't mention but are paramount in women's lives, such as whether and when to have children.

Credit: Reprinted by permission of FANGirl Blog.

Last year the blog introduced the series Seeking Strong Female Heroines. In the first post, Tricia described the reason for the series — to highlight stories featuring these kinds of characters — and defined some of the core characteristics of strong female heroines. Since then, we've discussed a number of characters as strong female heroines: Princess Leia from the Star Wars movies, her daughter Jaina Solo and her sister-in-law Mara Jade Skywalker from the Expanded Universe, and *Castle*'s Kate Beckett. More Seeking SFH posts are in the works, including Alicia Florrick and the women of *The Good Wife*, Olivia Dunham from *Fringe*, Myka Bering from *Warehouse 13*, and Buffy Summers. Up next, of course, is Katniss Everdeen from *The Hunger Games.* This year we're adding a complementary series: the Heroine's Journey. Inspired by some of our favorite stories, including *The Hunger Games*, as well as the story design and writing of *Wynde*, this series has a slightly different focus. Seeking SFH is mostly descriptive, identifying well-written strong female heroines and why they're effective. The Heroine's Journey series will do some of that, drawing insights from the small number of stories out there that already fit our concepts. But the main purpose of the Heroine's Journey series is prescriptive — to help continue the push for more and better stories with great female leads by thinking about what would constitute the elements of a heroine-centered storytelling model parallel to the well-known Hero's Journey monomyth.

Before we move into tackling that ambitious endeavor, though, we thought it was important to define several of our key concepts.

The Heroine's Journey Is a Mythic, Epic Coming of Age Tale

Many great stories with notable characters are not epic or mythic, and many others are not coming of age tales. Some of them feature female leads, or even strong female heroines, and they can bring hours of enjoyment to readers or an audience. But we have something more specific in mind for the Heroine's Journey.

What Joseph Campbell identified in his research into the world's myths was a particular type of story with a specific kind of resonance throughout numerous human cultures—the transformation of a young man from ordinary to extraordinary, triumphing over his adversaries and leaving him changed forever. This Hero's Journey, also called the monomyth, has a core structure and common elements that still ring true across millennia.

Although grounded primarily in ancient myths and legends, Campbell's Hero's Journey has formed the basis of highly successful coming of age tales written in the modern world, as well. The most famous example, probably, is George Lucas directly consulting with Campbell while writing the first *Star Wars* movie. But there are other examples, too, including Orson Scott Card's *Ender's Game* and the film *The Matrix*. Many elements of Campbell's progression also appear throughout the *Harry Potter* saga.

> "The heroine's transformation is the character development at the core of the tale, and she is the character around whom all the other characters' paths orbit."

The Heroine's Journey retains these two elements of Campbell's model. Characters like Dana Scully, Olivia Dunham, Sarah Connor, and Mara Jade Skywalker participate in tales of epic proportion and mythic resonance, but they begin their stories as adults; while their adventures change them forever, they cannot fairly be called coming of age journeys. Likewise, there are numerous coming of age tales with young women at the center, but which lack mythic or epic qualities—just as there are countless sports movies where the most epic event in the protagonist's life is making the winning play in the championship game at the end.

To qualify as a Heroine's Journey in our formulation, then, the story must have substantial mythic and epic elements, and it must be a coming of age tale. This common ground with Campbell's monomyth explains why some elements of the Heroine's Journey will align with the Hero's Journey. Yet there will be significant differences, as well, as upcoming posts in the series will explore. After all, the Heroine's Journey has one crucial distinction—its primary character is a young woman.

The Heroine's Journey Has a Strong Female Heroine as Its Lead Character

In one respect, the Heroine's Journey is a subset of the Strong Female Heroine category—both require the traits of strength, femininity, and heroism. Strength comes in many forms, especially for women. In upcoming blogs, we'll say more about what it means to ensure that a heroine's female nature carries through in her portrayal. The key point for now is to emphasize that the Heroine's Journey's focus is not on young women as protagonists, but as *heroes*. Stories with dark themes are quite popular these days, and some strong female characters now are best identified with labels like antihero, anti-villain, or morally compromised hero. The "avenging angel" archetype, for example—Aeon

Flux, Nikita, or the Bride from *Kill Bill*, to name a few—is often a strong female character, but she is rarely heroic. The protagonist of the Heroine's Journey is not morally flawless, but she must be, in her heart, profoundly on the *good* side.

On the other hand, the Heroine's Journey also requires something more than the Strong Female Heroine—that the heroine be the center of the story, as its principal character. In the Heroine's Journey, the heroine's transformation is the character development at the core of the tale, and she is the character around whom all the other characters' paths orbit. Many of the popular recent strong female heroines are supporting characters to a young man's Hero's Journey: Princess Leia to Luke Skywalker, Padmé Amidala to Anakin Skywalker, or Hermione Granger to Harry Potter. In *Pirates of the Caribbean: The Curse of the Black Pearl*, Elizabeth Swann sets the story in motion, but by the end her character development becomes secondary to Will Turner and Jack Sparrow. Yet each of these characters was vibrant enough to have supported a Heroine's Journey, had the storytellers been willing to commit to developing their character arcs as fully as the male lead's. In the Heroine's Journey, the story is the heroine's—and everyone else's character arcs support hers.

Unfortunately, very few existing stories meet both of these criteria. Two that do meet them have proven highly successful: *The Hunger Games* and *Buffy the Vampire Slayer*. As we discuss the Heroine's Journey model further, Katniss and Buffy will be major touchstones for how to execute this kind of story effectively.

The Heroine's Journey Might—or Might Not—Have a Happy Ending

Just as with the Hero's Journey, nothing in the Heroine's Journey model necessitates any particular type of ending to the character's story. Some heroes triumph and live happily ever after; others sacrifice their lives to ensure victory, or pay a terrible price for succeeding in their quest. The key to the Heroine's Journey is not her reward for victory, but how and why she fights, struggles, and perseveres to the end.

Among stories with strong female heroines, a wide range of fates befall them. Some follow the fairy tale structure and a happy, or hopeful, ending: Princess Leia in the original *Star Wars* trilogy, Hermione in *Harry Potter*, or Rapunzel in *Tangled*. Others face tragedy in the literary sense, and the painful destiny that comes with it: Padmé watches her husband fall to the dark side, betray the Republic, and turn against her in the *Star Wars* prequels; Katniss faces a bittersweet future with everlasting fear and loss by the end of *Mockingjay*. And some characters, especially those with the longer story arcs, end up with elements of both: Buffy's life has both fairy tale highs and tragic lows throughout the seven seasons of her titular television series, as does Sydney Bristow's character arc on *Alias*; in a similar fashion, Elizabeth Swann has a fairy tale arc in *Curse of the Black Pearl* but ends with a bittersweet, tragic fate by the end of *Dead Man's Chest*. In the Heroine's Journey, any one of these fates, or others, is possible.

QUESTIONS

1. Get an overview (or refresh your memory) of Campbell's model by going to the *Wikipedia* entry for "Hero's Journey." Based on what you see there and what Priester has said, are you convinced by his argument that Campbell's model is inadequate for female characters and heroines? Why or why not?

2. Priester uses examples from *Star Wars, The Hunger Games, Buffy the Vampire Slayer*, and other current movies and TV shows to bolster his points. Can you think of movies or TV shows that have come out since this entry was published in 2012 that could be used as examples?

COMPOSING PROJECT | Construct a New Hero's or Heroine's Model

Priester focuses on the differences between men and women in critiquing Campbell's Hero's Journey model. Review Campbell's model and Priester's model, and propose a third model that takes into account ethnicity, religion, sexual orientation, or another marker of identity that neither Campbell nor Priester focuses on.

▼ Humorous Essay

David Sedaris, *Me Talk Pretty One Day*

David Sedaris is a humor writer and author of numerous books and essay collections. He also frequently contributes to radio programs such as National Public Radio's *This American Life.* In his book, *Me Talk Pretty One Day*, Sedaris chronicles his experiences prior to moving to France and his escapades living in France. In the excerpt below, Sedaris recollects the struggles he and others faced in a French class.

Credit: Reprinted by permission of Don Congdon Associates, Inc. Copyright © 1999, 2000 by David Sedaris.

At the age of forty-one, I am returning to school and having to think of myself as what my French textbook calls "a true debutant." After paying my tuition, I was issued a student ID, which allows me a discounted entry fee at movie theaters, puppet shows, and Festyland, a far-flung amusement park that advertises with billboards picturing a cartoon stegosaurus sitting in a canoe and eating what appears to be a ham sandwich.

I've moved to Paris in order to learn the language. My school is the Alliance Française, and on the first day of class, I arrived early, watching as the returning students greeted one another in the school lobby. Vacations were recounted, and questions were raised concerning mutual friends with names like Kang and Vlatnya. Regardless of their nationalities, everyone spoke what sounded to me like excellent French. Some accents were better than others, but the students exhibited an ease and confidence I found intimidating. As an added discomfort, they were all young, attractive, and well dressed, causing me to feel not unlike Pa Kettle trapped backstage after a fashion show.

I remind myself that I am now a full-grown man. No one will ever again card me for a drink or demand that I weave a floor mat out of newspapers. At my age, a reasonable person should have completed his sentence in the prison of the nervous and the insecure—isn't that the great promise of adulthood? I can't help but think that, somewhere along the way, I made a wrong turn. My fears have not vanished. Rather, they have seasoned and multiplied with age. I am now twice as frightened as I was when, at the age of twenty, I allowed a failed nursing student to inject me with a horse tranquilizer, and eight times more anxious than I was the day my kindergarten teacher pried my fingers off my mother's ankle and led me screaming toward my desk. "You'll get used to it," the woman had said.

I'm still waiting.

The first day of class was nerve-racking, because I knew I'd be expected to perform. That's the way they do it here—everyone into the language pool, sink or swim. The teacher marched in, deeply tanned from a recent vacation, and rattled off a series of administrative announcements. I've spent some time in Normandy, and I took a monthlong French class last summer in New York. I'm not completely in the dark, yet I understood only half of what this teacher was saying.

"If you have not meismslsxp by this time, you should not be in this room. Has everybody apzkiubjxow? Everyone? Good, we shall proceed." She spread out her lesson plan and sighed, saying, "All right, then, who knows the alphabet?"

It was startling, because a) I hadn't been asked that question in a while, and b) I realized, while laughing, that I myself did not know the alphabet. They're the same letters, but they're pronounced differently.

"Ahh." The teacher went to the board and sketched the letter a. "Do we have anyone in the room whose first name commences with an ahh?"

Two Polish Annas raised their hands, and the teacher instructed them to present themselves, giving their names, nationalities, occupations, and a list of things they liked and disliked in this world. The first Anna hailed from an industrial town outside of Warsaw and had front teeth the size of tombstones. She worked as a seamstress, enjoyed quiet times with friends, and hated the mosquito.

"Oh, really," the teacher said. "How very interesting. I thought that everyone loved the mosquito, but here, in front of all the world, you claim to detest him. How is it that we've been blessed with someone as unique and original as you? Tell us, please."

The seamstress did not understand what was being said, but she knew that this was an occasion for shame. Her rabbity mouth huffed for breath, and she stared down at her lap as though the appropriate comeback were stitched somewhere alongside the zipper of her slacks.

The second Anna learned from the first and claimed to love sunshine and detest lies. It sounded like a translation of one of those Playmate of the Month data sheets, the answers always written in the same loopy handwriting: "Turn-ons: Mom's famous five-alarm chili! Turnoffs: Insincerity and guys who come on too strong!!!"

The two Polish women surely had clear notions of what they liked and disliked, but, like the rest of us, they were limited in terms of vocabulary, and this made them appear less than sophisticated. The teacher forged on, and we learned that Carlos, the Argentine bandonion player, loved wine, music, and, in his words, "Making sex with the women of the world." Next came a beautiful young Yugoslavian who identified herself as an optimist, saying that she loved everything life had to offer.

The teacher licked her lips, revealing a hint of the sadist we would later come to know. She crouched low for her attack, placed her hands on the young woman's desk, and said, "Oh, yeah? And do you love your little war?"

While the optimist struggled to defend herself, I scrambled to think of an answer to what had obviously become a trick question. How often are you asked what you love in this world? More important, how often are you asked and then publicly ridiculed for your answer? I recalled my mother, flushed with wine, pounding the table late one night, saying, "Love? I love a good steak cooked rare. I love my cat, and I love . . ." My sisters and I leaned forward, waiting to hear our names. "Tums," our mother said. "I love Tums."

The teacher killed some time accusing the Yugoslavian girl of masterminding a program of genocide, and I jotted frantic notes in the margins of my pad. While I can honestly say that I love leafing through medical textbooks devoted to severe dermatological conditions, it is beyond the reach of my French vocabulary, and acting it out would only have invited unwanted attention.

When called upon, I delivered an effortless list of things I detest: blood sausage, intestinal pâté, brain pudding. I'd learned these words the hard way. Having given it some thought, I then declared my love for IBM typewriters, the French word for "bruise," and my electric floor waxer. It was a short list, but still I managed to mispronounce IBM and afford the wrong gender to both the floor waxer and the typewriter. Her reaction led me to believe that these mistakes were capital crimes in the country of France.

"Were you always this palicmkrexjs?" she asked. "Even a fiuscrzsws tociwegixp knows that a typewriter is feminine."

I absorbed as much of her abuse as I could understand, thinking, but not saying, that I find it ridiculous to assign a gender to an inanimate object incapable of disrobing and making an occasional fool of itself. Why refer to Lady Flesh Wound or Good Sir Dishrag when these things could never deliver in the sack?

The teacher proceeded to belittle everyone from German Eva, who hated laziness, to Japanese Yukari, who loved paintbrushes and soap. Italian, Thai, Dutch, Korean, Chinese—we all left class foolishly believing that the worst was over. We didn't know it then, but the coming months would teach us what it is like to spend time in the presence of a wild animal. We soon learned to dodge chalk and to cover our heads and stomachs whenever she approached us with a question. She hadn't yet punched anyone, but it seemed wise to prepare ourselves against the inevitable.

Though we were forbidden to speak anything but French, the teacher would occasionally use us to practice any of her five fluent languages.

"I hate you," she said to me one afternoon. Her English was flawless. "I really, really hate you." Call me sensitive, but I couldn't help taking it personally.

Learning French is a lot like joining a gang in that it involves a long and intensive period of hazing. And it wasn't just my teacher; the entire population seemed to be in on it. Following brutal encounters with my local butcher and the concierge of my building, I'd head off to class, where the teacher would hold my corrected paperwork high above her head, shouting, "Here's proof that David is an ignorant and uninspired ensigiejsokhjx."

Refusing to stand convicted on the teacher's charges of laziness, I'd spend four hours a night on my homework, working even longer whenever we were assigned an essay. I suppose I could have gotten by with less, but I was determined to create some sort of an identity for myself. We'd have one of those "complete the sentence" exercises, and I'd fool with the thing for hours, invariably settling on something like, "A quick run around the lake? I'd love to. Just give me a minute to strap on my wooden leg." The teacher, through word and action, conveyed the message that, if this was my idea of an identity, she wanted nothing to do with it.

> "If you have not meismslsxp by this time, you should not be in this room. Has everybody apzkiubjxow? Everyone? Good, we shall proceed."

My fear and discomfort crept beyond the borders of my classroom and accompanied me out onto the wide boulevards, where, no matter how hard I tried, there was no escaping the feeling of terror I felt whenever anyone asked me a question. I was safe in any kind of a store, as, at least in my neighborhood, one can stand beside the cash register for hours on end without being asked something so trivial as, "May I help you?" or "How would you like to pay for that?"

My only comfort was the knowledge that I was not alone. Huddled in the smoky hallways and making the most of our pathetic French, my fellow students and I engaged in the sort of conversation commonly overheard in refugee camps.

"Sometimes me cry alone at night."

"That is common for me also, but be more strong, you. Much work, and someday you talk pretty. People stop hate you soon. Maybe tomorrow, okay?"

Unlike other classes I have taken, here there was no sense of competition. When the teacher poked a shy Korean woman in the eyelid with a freshly sharpened pencil, we took no comfort in the fact that, unlike Hyeyoon Cho, we all knew the irregular past tense of the verb "to defeat." In all fairness, the teacher hadn't meant to hurt the woman, but neither did she spend much time apologizing, saying only, "Well, you should have been paying more attention."

Over time, it became impossible to believe that any of us would ever improve. Fall arrived, and it rained every day. It was mid-October when the teacher singled me out, saying, "Every day spent with you is like having a cesarean section." And it struck me that, for the first time since arriving in France, I could understand every word that someone was saying.

Understanding doesn't mean that you can suddenly speak the language. Far from it. It's a small step, nothing more, yet its rewards are intoxicating and deceptive. The teacher continued her diatribe, and I settled back, bathing in the subtle beauty of each new curse and insult.

"You exhaust me with your foolishness and reward my efforts with nothing but pain, do you understand me?"

The world opened up, and it was with great joy that I responded, "I know the thing what you speak exact now. Talk me more, plus, please, plus."

QUESTIONS

1. Throughout the essay, Sedaris tries to place us directly in his experience. How does he do this? What are some of the techniques he uses to make us feel as if we are there, learning the language with him and other students?

2. Why do you think we chose to include this essay in a chapter on identity? Give specific examples from the essay to support your answer.

COMPOSING PROJECT | Create a Humorous Comic

Think of a time you felt like you were in over your head—you had no idea what was going on. Create a comic strip poking fun at yourself or someone you perceived to be an antagonist in that situation.

LONG-TERM PROJECTS # Identity

1. **Investigate & analyze a subculture as an outsider.** Identify a subculture group that you are not a member of, perhaps computer nerds, hunters, skateboarders, parents, chess players, organic food eaters, or bluegrass music fans. Then, observe the group. Depending on the group you choose, you might attend an event, such as a bluegrass concert or chess club meeting; visit a retail outlet such as a skateboarding shop, Babies "R" Us, or computer or video game store; or visit a computer lab.

   a. **Conduct three observations of at least 30 minutes each. Take detailed observation notes** that include information about what you see, hear, smell, etc. Consider:

      - What are people wearing? Describe their clothing, hairstyles, jewelry, piercings, tattoos, and so on.

      - How do people position themselves in the space? How close do they stand or sit to each other? Do people move within the space or do they take a position, such as sitting at a table, and maintain it?

      - How does the space look? Describe the furniture and décor.

      - How do people speak to each other? What role does body language play? How loudly or softly do they speak?

      - What kinds of props do people have? Do they bring equipment with them? How do they use their props or equipment?

   b. Once you've completed your three observations, **review all your notes and look for commonalities** that tie the people together as members of the same subculture. What inferences can you make or what conclusions can you draw based on what you've seen? Answer the following questions:

- Why do people come to this space? What needs or desires draw them there?
- What sort of people come to this space? How do they behave within this space?
- What types of behaviors seem to be encouraged or discouraged, based on what you've observed?
- What roles do socializing and consumption seem to play in the gatherings you've observed?

c. **Write an analytical essay** that makes a point about your subculture that might surprise readers, providing photos and quotations and references to details from your observations throughout to support your point. Your finished essay should **include a variety of media, such as a mixture of text, photographs, drawings, sketches**, and so on.

For example, observations of bluegrass fans might indicate that they are much more fashion savvy than stereotypes about them imply. An essay on this might include photos of bluegrass fans wearing designer sunglasses, chic blouses, and trendy heels to support the point. Quotations from overheard conversations about taste, shopping, or fashion might be woven throughout.

2. **Brand your family: create a motto, logo & illustrated history.** Your family reunion is coming up and you've been nominated to put together a family history. The history will ultimately take the form of a paper scrapbook, Web page, or blog. You've also been asked to design a T-shirt that family members will wear for a group portrait. The T-shirt needs to feature a slogan that makes a statement about your family.

- **Brainstorm a motto** signifies your family's identity. For example, Amy might design a T-shirt that says "The Brazillers: Even the Adults Are Children," to reflect the playful nature of her extended family.

- **Interview at least three family members** and ask them to consider your motto. Does it ring true for them? Would they identify your family with some other phrase or slogan? Ask interviewees to recall at least three memorable family episodes that support or refute your motto, and have them share photos with you (and video, if you have multimedia access).

- **Write up the best anecdotes** and/or include transcripts of your family interviews. Illustrate the stories (and/or transcripts) with family photos. If you have multimedia access, include audio and video recordings of your interviews, as well as any multimedia materials you gather from family members.

- **Revise your motto as needed,** based on feedback from interviewees.

- **Design a logo** that complements your family motto. Perhaps you'll use one of the photos you've collected or another image that works for your slogan and family history. For example, Amy could create a logo that portrays stick-figure people playing on a seesaw to illustrate the playful nature of her family, or work with a photo of family members at play.

- **Assemble your motto, logo & illustrated family history** in a paper scrapbook or on a Web page or blog.

- **Write a reflective essay** that explains the choices you made along the way in your project. How did your audience (family) and purpose (to tell family stories and reflect family identity) affect your decisions and revisions? To what extent does what you've created offer a true picture of your family?

- **Alternative project:** Adapt the above assignment so that it's about you and a group of your friends.

17 MIND & BODY: CONNECTIONS

CONTENTS

How do we define ourselves in relation to our minds and bodies? Are we what we eat—the healthy green salad and the late-night extra-cheesy mac and cheese? Are we our muscles? Our belly fat? Our illnesses and addictions? Our physical disabilities? Evidence of our attitudes toward our minds and bodies can be found in various genres of everyday life. Consider these questions: What do our food labels say about how we fortify our bodies? How do we represent our bodies in advertising, and in art and literature? How do our (dis)abilities define us, and how do others use them to define us?

Opening this chapter is a poem celebrating the body by the famous American poet Walt Whitman. Focusing on the brain, a piece by Nicholas Carr looks at how technology might be changing our most important organ.

The next two pieces offer different perspectives on (dis)ability. The Whole Brain Group's infographic celebrates the Americans with Disabilities Act, while Kerry Magro shares his experience living with autism.

The chapter ends with Dwayne Godwin and Jorge Cham's comic about addiction and Emily Sohn's article about the health benefits of having friends.

As you work through this chapter, consider the different perspectives on what a "normal" body or mind is, and how the genre choices of these authors can be seen as responses to social situations.

▼ Poem

Walt Whitman, From "I Sing the Body Electric"

Walt Whitman's poem "I Sing the Body Electric" was originally published in 1855 as part of his collection *Leaves of Grass*, which was labeled obscene by some because of its explicit sexuality. In "I Sing the Body Electric," Whitman celebrates both the male and female body through physical and spiritual imagery.

O my body! I dare not desert the likes of you in other men and women, nor the likes of the parts of you,

I believe the likes of you are to stand or fall with the likes of the soul, (and that they are the soul,)

I believe the likes of you shall stand or fall with my poems—and that they are poems.

Man's, woman's, child's, youth's, wife's, husband's, mother's, father's, young man's, young woman's poems.

Head, neck, hair, ears, drop and tympan of the ears.

Eyes, eye-fringes, iris of the eye, eye-brows, and the waking or sleeping of the lids,

Mouth, tongue, lips, teeth, roof of the mouth, jaws, and the jaw-hinges,

Nose, nostrils of the nose, and the partition,

Cheeks, temples, forehead, chin, throat, back of the neck, neck-slue,

Strong shoulders, manly beard, scapula, hind-shoulders, and the ample side-round of the chest.

Upper-arm, arm-pit, elbow-socket, lower-arm, arm-sinews, arm-bones,

Wrist and wrist-joints, hand, palm, knuckles, thumb, fore-finger, finger-balls, finger-joints, finger-nails,

Broad breast-front, curling hair of the breast, breast-bone, breast-side,

Ribs, belly, back-bone, joints of the back-bone,

Hips, hip-sockets, hip-strength, inward and outward round, man-balls, man-root,

Strong set of thighs, well carrying the trunk above,

Leg-fibers, knee, knee-pan, upper-leg, under-leg,

Ankles, instep, foot-ball, toes, toe-joints, the heel;

All attitudes, all the shapeliness, all the belongings of my or your body or of any one's body, male or female,

The lung-sponges, the stomach-sac, the bowels sweet and clean,

The brain in its folds inside the skull-frame,

Sympathies, heart-valves, palate-valves, sexuality, maternity,

Womanhood, and all that is a woman, and the man that comes from woman,

The womb, the teats, nipples, breast-milk, tears, laughter, weeping, love-looks, love-perturbations and risings,

The voice, articulation, language, whispering, shouting aloud,

Food, drink, pulse, digestion, sweat, sleep, walking, swimming,

Poise on the hips, leaping, reclining, embracing, arm-curving and tightening,

The continual changes of the flex of the mouth, and around the eyes,

The skin, the sun-burnt shade, freckles, hair,

The curious sympathy one feels, when feeling with the hand the naked meat of the body,

The circling rivers, the breath, and breathing it in and out,

The beauty of the waist, and thence of the hips, and thence downward toward the knees,

The thin red jellies within you, or within me, the bones, and the marrow in the bones,

The exquisite realization of health;

O I say these are not the parts and poems of the body only, but of the soul,

O I say now these are the soul!

QUESTIONS

1. In his poem, Walt Whitman compares the body and the soul. In what ways does he find the body similar to the soul? What does he mean by the line "I believe the likes of you are to stand or fall with the likes of the soul, (and that they are the soul)"?

2. In his poem, Whitman lists various parts of the body. Sometimes he is just naming the part of the body ("Ribs, belly, backbone") and sometimes he is more descriptive ("brain in its folds inside the skull-frame"). What effect does this have for the reader?

COMPOSING PROJECT | Revise the Poem

Take several of the lines in Whitman's poem where he just lists the body parts and revise them to read more like the lines "brain in its folds inside the skull-frame" and "the bowels sweet and clean."

▼ Book Excerpt

Nicholas Carr, *The Juggler's Brain*

Nicholas Carr is an author and journalist who writes about technology. The excerpt below is from his book *The Shallows: What the Internet Is Doing to Our Brains*, which was a finalist for the 2011 Pulitzer Prize in nonfiction.

Credit: From The Shallows: What the Internet Is Doing to Our Brains by Nicholas Carr. Copyright © 2010 by Nicholas Carr. Used by permission of W. W. Norton & Company, Inc.

What can science tell us about the actual effects that Internet use is having on the way our minds work? No doubt, this question will be the subject of a great deal of research in the years ahead. Already, though, there is much we know or can surmise. The news is even more disturbing than I had suspected. Dozens of studies by psychologists, neurobiologists, educators, and Web designers point to the same conclusion: when we go online, we enter an environment that promotes cursory reading, hurried and distracted thinking, and superficial learning. It's possible to think deeply while surfing the Net, just as it's possible to think shallowly while reading a book, but that's not the type of thinking the technology encourages and rewards.

One thing is very clear: if, knowing what we know today about the brain's plasticity, you were to set out to invent a medium that would rewire our mental circuits as quickly and thoroughly as possible, you would probably end up designing something that looks and works a lot like the Internet. It's not just that we tend to use the Net regularly, even obsessively. It's that the Net delivers precisely the kind of sensory and cognitive stimuli—repetitive, intensive, interactive, addictive—that have been shown to result in strong and rapid alterations in brain circuits and functions. With the exception of alphabets and number systems, the Net may well be the single most powerful mind-altering technology that has ever come into general use. At the very least, it's the most powerful that has come along since the book.

During the course of a day, most of us with access to the Web spend at least a couple of hours online—sometimes much more—and during that time, we tend to repeat the same or similar actions over and over again, usually at a high rate of speed and often in response to cues delivered through a screen or a speaker. Some of the actions are physical ones. We tap the keys on our PC keyboard. We drag a mouse and click its left and right buttons and spin its scroll wheel. We draw the tips of our fingers across a trackpad. We use our thumbs to punch out text on the real or simulated keypads of our BlackBerrys or mobile phones. We rotate our iPhones, iPods, and iPads to shift between "landscape" and "portrait" modes while manipulating the icons on their touch-sensitive screens.

> **With the exception of alphabets and number systems, the Net may well be the single most powerful mind-altering technology that has ever come into general use.**

As we go through these motions, the Net delivers a steady stream of inputs to our visual, somatosensory, and auditory cortices. There are the sensations that come through our hands and fingers as we click and scroll, type and touch. There are the many audio signals delivered through our ears, such as the chime that announces the arrival of a new e-mail or instant message and the various ringtones that our mobile phones use to alert us to different events. And, of course, there are the myriad visual cues that flash across our retinas as we navigate the online world: not just the ever-changing arrays of text and pictures and videos but also the hyperlinks distinguished by underlining or colored text, the cursors that change shape depending on their function, the new e-mail subject lines highlighted in bold type, the virtual buttons that call out to be clicked, the icons and other screen elements that beg to be dragged and dropped, the forms that require filling out, the pop-up ads and windows that need to be read or dismissed. The Net engages all of our senses—except, so far, those of smell and taste—and it engages them simultaneously.

The Net also provides a high-speed system for delivering responses and rewards—"positive reinforcements," in psychological terms—which encourage the repetition of both physical and mental actions. When we click a link, we get something new to look at and evaluate. When we Google a keyword, we receive, in the blink of an eye, a list of interesting information to appraise. When we send a text or an instant message or an e-mail, we often get a reply in a matter of seconds or minutes. When we use Facebook, we attract new friends or form closer bonds with old ones. When we send a tweet through Twitter, we gain new followers. When we write a blog post, we get comments from readers or links from other bloggers. The Net's interactivity gives us powerful new tools for finding information, expressing ourselves, and conversing with others. It also turns us into lab rats constantly pressing levers to get tiny pellets of social or intellectual nourishment.

QUESTIONS

1. In the last sentence of the excerpt, Carr says that the Internet "turns us into lab rats." What connotations does the term "lab rat" have? What is your reaction to being compared with a lab rat?

2. Carr gives a detailed list of the activities we engage in when we are on the Internet: tapping on keyboards, clicking on links, hearing sounds, and more. Why do you suppose he gives such elaborate descriptions of these activities instead of simply saying that the Internet engages multiple senses?

COMPOSING PROJECT | Create a Tip Guide for Reading on the Internet

Carr writes that "dozens of studies by psychologists, neurobiologists, educators, and Web designers point to the same conclusion: when we go online, we enter an environment that promotes cursory reading, hurried and distracted thinking, and superficial learning." Do some research to find several of these studies (you might start by going to Google Scholar and searching "Internet effects on reading comprehension") and read them. Then create a list of tips for college students to help them read text on the Internet with the same level of concentration and thought that reading offline encourages. You might find that the research articles you read include tips; feel free to use those with citations, but also come up with your own.

▼ Infographic

The Whole Brain Group, *Celebrating Americans with Disabilities Act*

This infographic was created by the Whole Brain Group, a marketing company that specializes in using social media to attract people to a product or concept. It created the infographic because its work in social media made it appreciate accessibility, and it wanted to communicate the importance of accessibility to its clients. The infographic originally appeared on the Whole Brain Group's blog.

Celebrating
Americans
— with —
Disabilities Act

23rd anniversary
1990 - 2013

Americans with Disabilities Act (ADA)
Signed into law on July 26, 1990, this act is a civil rights law that prohibits, under certain circumstances, discrimination based on disability. It was intended to be a flexible set of laws that could only be strengthened, not weakened, by future case law.

We are are excited to continue honoring the Americans with Disabilities Act, now celebrating its 23rd anniversary! As public perception evolves and technology advances, more attempts are being made to address inequality through accessibility legislation and standards. This updated infographic addresses recent legislation enacted to improve digital equality in the US and Canada.

new! ★

How the ADA defines disability:
A physical or mental impairment that substantially limits one or more major life activities, has a record of such an impairment, or is regarded as having such an impairment.

50 Million Americans
are living with a disability

16%

Distribution of age
groups with a disability

5%   10%   38%

age   age   age
5-17   18-64   65+

Types of disability:

Visual	Self-care	Hearing	Independent Living	Cognitive Mental	Ambulatory
3.2 million	3.4 million	3.9 million	6.6 million	7.9 million	9.8 million

American population living with a disability

Education:

Of people over the age of 25:

have a bachelor's degree or higher
with a disability — 13%
without a disability — 31%

have less than a high school education
with a disability — 28%
without a disability — 12%

Employment:

The unemployment rate for people with a disability is typically twice as high as the rate of people without a disability.

10% without   20% with

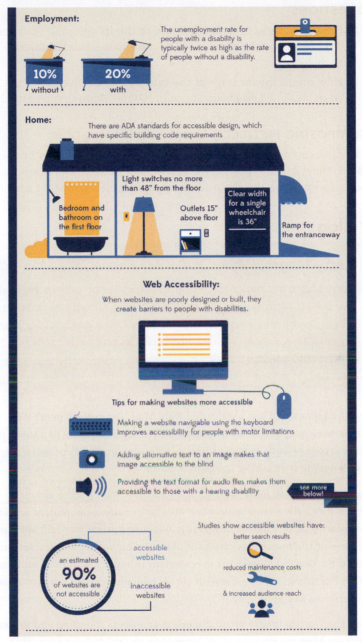

Employment:

The unemployment rate for people with a disability is typically twice as high as the rate of people without a disability.

10% without

20% with

Home:

There are ADA standards for accessible design, which have specific building code requirements

Light switches no more than 48" from the floor

Bedroom and bathroom on the first floor

Outlets 15" above floor

Clear width for a single wheelchair is 36"

Ramp for the entranceway

Web Accessibility:

When websites are poorly designed or built, they create barriers to people with disabilities.

Tips for making websites more accessible

Making a website navigable using the keyboard improves accessibility for people with motor limitations

Adding alternative text to an image makes that image accessible to the blind

Providing the text format for audio files makes them accessible to those with a hearing disability

see more below!

an estimated 90% of websites are not accessible

accessible websites

inaccessible websites

Studies show accessible websites have:

better search results

reduced maintenance costs

& increased audience reach

Credit: The Whole Brain Group, LLC.

QUESTIONS

1. How would you describe the tone of the infographic? Is it serious? Whimsical? Dry? Humorous? Intimidating? Approachable? Something else? What contributes to its tone?

2. How might the message of the infographic be changed if the same information were presented as a memo from the Whole Brain Group to its clients?

COMPOSING PROJECT | Create an Infographic

Choose a law that you support, whether it's slowing down in a school zone, paying taxes, shoveling the snow off the sidewalk in front of your house, picking up after your dog, or something else. Create an infographic celebrating that law.

▼ Blog

Kerry Magro, *When One of My Peers Called Me "Rain Man"*

Kerry Magro is a nationally recognized speaker on autism. He is also the author of two books: *Defining Autism from the Heart* and *Autism and Falling in Love*. Magro also blogs about his experiences with autism. This piece is a blog Magro wrote for the organization Autism Speaks, which has as one of its goals to help people better understand autism.

Credit: Used with permission of Autism Speaks, Inc.

Do you know that I was once called Rain Man by a college peer? Wow. I was furious. When I look back at the reason why anyone would say something like that I think of some of the stereotypes of autism. Some think people with autism lack social interaction and others think people with autism are good at math.

In the 1988 movie *Rain Man*, Actor Dustin Hoffman plays a character that is autistic and shows he's good with numbers but also lacks some communication skills. Because of the popularity of this movie and mainly because autism was still very unknown during the release of the movie it became, for better or for worse, a characterization of what autism could be. But you know what the problem is here? I'm autistic and I'm nothing like Rain Man. I'm now an adult great with verbal communication, I'm not as good in math and the differences keep piling up.

You see, autism is very broad. No one diagnosis is the same and therefore when we think of Rain Man we must think of Rain Man as ONLY Rain Man. He is one symbol of the countless symbols of real people out there that have autism. I think that's what makes our autism community great. We all are unique in our own way and we all have the opportunity to have our "voices" heard. Sometimes that voice is not a verbal one, sometimes it is heard through our art or music or some other skill or talent we have or simply a smile at our family members. Each and every individual with autism is a new and unique symbol of what autism is today and will be for our future. So in keeping with the future . . . To those who are reading . . .

> ❝ He is one symbol of the countless symbols of real people out there that have autism. ❞

Don't call me Rain Man. Call me Kerry. Don't think I'm bad at verbal communication, because in fact in my own way I'm great at communication and I'm getting a Master's Degree in Strategic Communication to boot. Don't think I'll be ready to help when it comes to numbers, because all I'm going to do is pass you a calculator. AND, most importantly, just look at me as me. I'm Kerry and there is only one of me. Just like there is only one of you. Let's embrace the fact that there will only be one Kerry Magro, just like there will only be one Rain Man. We write our own stories based on the biography of life which we are all living through right now.

Let's make sure the chapters we're writing are good ones, by living it just the way we are. So please call me Kerry the next time you see me, because that is someone who I was always meant to be.

QUESTIONS

1. Magro's short blog piece is designed to debunk some myths related to autism. What are some of the myths, and how does Magro disprove them?

2. What tone does Magro use in his blog? Why do you believe he chose this tone to get across his point?

COMPOSING PROJECT | Write a Letter

Go to your campus disability services office and find out what materials it has related to autism. Read over the materials, and if you need more information, interview the head of disability services. Then compose a letter to the chair of the department you're majoring in that offers information and advice about teaching students with autism.

▼ Comic

Dwayne Godwin and Jorge Cham, *Understanding Addiction*

Dwayne Godwin is a neuroscientist and professor at Wake Forest University School of Medicine. Jorge Cham earned his PhD in mechanical engineering from Stanford University and is the creator of the comic strip *Piled High and Deeper*. Together, Godwin and Cham create comic strips related to the brain for *Scientific American*.

ADDICTION

BY DWAYNE GODWIN
& JORGE CHAM

ADDICTION COSTS AMERICANS OVER $700 BILLION EACH YEAR IN LOST WORK, TREATMENT AND DRUG-RELATED CRIME.

BUT WHAT IS ADDICTION... AND HOW DO WE BREAK IT?

ADDICTION HAS ITS ROOTS IN THE BRAIN'S REWARD SYSTEM.

FEEL GOOD   FOOD, SEX

IT'S THE SYSTEM MEANT TO REINFORCE BEHAVIORS NEEDED FOR SURVIVAL SUCH AS EATING AND HAVING SEX.

ONE IMPORTANT COMPONENT IN THIS SYSTEM IS THE MESOLIMBIC PATHWAY ...

... A COLLECTION OF NEURONS THAT PRODUCES AND RELEASES DOPAMINE WHENEVER YOU ENGAGE IN A POSITIVE ACTIVITY.

DOPAMINE IS A NEUROTRANSMITTER THAT, AMONG MANY OTHER THINGS, GIVES YOU THE SENSATION OF PLEASURE WHEN RELEASED IN CERTAIN BRAIN AREAS.

ADDICTION CAN OCCUR WHEN THIS PATHWAY IS HIJACKED REPEATEDLY BY DRUGS OR OTHER STIMULI, CREATING CHANGES IN THE SYNAPTIC CONNECTION THAT ARE HARD TO REVERSE.

DRUGS OR OTHER STIMULI EXAGGERATE DOPAMINE INCREASES ...

RECEIVING NEURON

DOPAMINE RECEPTORS

DOPAMINE

TRANSMITTING NEURON

SYNAPSE

... WHICH ALTERS THE NUMBER OF DOPAMINE RECEPTORS.

THIS CHANGED PATHWAY, ALONG WITH INCREASED STRESS DURING WITHDRAWAL, CAUSES ADDICTS TO COMPULSIVELY SEEK OUT THE STIMULUS ...

... DESPITE LONG-TERM NEGATIVE CONSEQUENCES.

NOT ALL DRUGS OR ADDICTS ARE THE SAME. SOME PEOPLE ARE GENETICALLY MORE SUSCEPTIBLE TO ADDICTION ...

... AND A DRUG'S ADDICTIVENESS SEEMS TO DEPEND ON HOW RAPIDLY IT ACTS ON YOUR SYSTEM.

HEALING ADDICTION IS A DIFFICULT PROCESS, AIDED BY GROUP EFFORT.

THE BEST WAY TO BEAT A HARMFUL DEPENDENCY IS BY DEPENDING ON OTHERS.

Credit: Dwayne Godwin and Jorge Cham.

QUESTIONS

1. The comic illustrates the complicated disease of addiction in several concise panels. How do the creators take a scientific process and make it understandable to someone who doesn't have a scientific background?

2. "Understanding Addiction" is text heavy for a comic. Why do you think the creators chose to include so much text? Could this have less text and convey the same information to the same audience? Why or why not?

COMPOSING PROJECT | Create a Comic

Think about a complicated process you know something about. Perhaps it is in a field you are studying. Maybe it's a skill you have. Then create a comic that illustrates this process to a general audience. Consider how you will use text along with your visuals.

▼ Researched Essay

Emily Sohn, *More and More Research Shows Friends Are Good for Your Health*

Emily Sohn is a freelance journalist whose work has appeared in many newspapers and magazines, including the *Washington Post*, where this article was published. In this piece, Sohn summarizes recent research on the health benefits of having a circle of friends.

Credit: Used with permission of Emily Sohn and Tide Pools LLC.

Overwhelmed recently by the stress of an impending move—along with the usual demands of a busy life — I turned to the people I love.

In small chunks of time between tasks on my to-do list, I called and texted with my sister, my parents, local friends and old friends scattered around the country. Some conversations turned my stress into laughter. Others made me cry. One friend came over to clean out my closet. Then she took our kids for four hours so we could pack without interruption.

With each hug, conversation and gesture of support, I started to feel better. As it turns out, those feelings may be paying long-term dividends, too: According to accumulating evidence, strong relationships breed better health, with benefits that include resilience against heart disease and a longer life.

It's encouraging research that's worth paying attention to. When life gets hectic, making time for friends can be a challenge. And some studies suggest that many of us have fewer friends today than our parents did a generation ago.

Those obstacles make prioritizing relationships all the more important, experts say.

"A good friendship is a wonderful antidepressant," says psychologist Janice Kiecolt-Glaser, director of the Institute for Behavioral Medicine Research at the Ohio State University College of Medicine in Columbus. "Relationships are so powerful, we don't always appreciate the many levels at which they affect us."

Ever since researchers began to make links between loneliness and poor health about twenty-five years ago, the scientific literature on the value of friendship has exploded. Today, the data make a convincing case: Having people who care about us is good for us.

In a 2010 meta-analysis that combined data on more than 308,000 people across 148 studies, for example, researchers found a strong connection between social relationships and life span. The size of the effect rivaled that of better-known health-related behaviors such as smoking and exercise.

Because the studies used different methods, the analysis couldn't say exactly how many more years of life we might gain by having true pals, says lead author Julianne Holt-Lunstad, a psychologist at Brigham Young University in Provo, Utah.

But in a 2015 analysis that compiled data on more than 3.4 million people across seventy studies, she and colleagues found that the absence of social connections carried the same health risk as smoking up to fifteen cigarettes a day. Loneliness led to worse outcomes than obesity. And the findings held true for people of all ages.

Early on, it seemed possible that healthier people might simply make more friends. But a growing body of research suggests instead that good relationships actually lead to better health. One clue comes from studies that begin with a large group of healthy people and follow them for decades. Experimental work on animals has also linked isolation with earlier death.

And plenty of studies have revealed biological theories that may explain what makes us healthier when we feel supported: lower blood pressure, better hormone function, stronger immune systems and possibly lower levels of inflammation.

Meanwhile, friends can influence health-related behaviors through peer pressure that values healthy eating, exercise, taking prescriptions and going to doctor's appointments, Holt-Lunstad adds. True friendships can also give us a sense of purpose, making us more motivated to take care of ourselves.

But even as evidence piles up to support the value of bonding, the nature of friendship seems to be changing, says Glenn Sparks, a communications professor at Purdue University in West Lafayette, Ind., who studies how media affect people. One reason is that people move more frequently than they used to. And for many people, a focus on display screens has replaced a focus on faces.

Sparks remembers arriving at Purdue in 1986 and marveling at a stretch of sidewalk on campus dubbed the "Hello Walk." The point was to smile and say hello to the people you passed there, and that's what students did.

"Today, you walk down that sidewalk and people are staring at their iPhones and iPads and in some cases even their laptops," says Sparks, co-author of "Refrigerator Rights: Creating Connections and Restoring Relationships." "Their ear buds are in and they're gone into some virtual space. We think that really takes a toll on the relational health of any community."

Technology isn't necessarily all bad, he adds. Facebook and Skype can help keep people connected from afar, and science hasn't yet caught up with the nuanced ways that digital devices might alter relationships. But a confluence of factors seems to be threatening the potential for connection.

According to a long-term study published in 2006, people had an average of about three friends they felt they could discuss important things with in 1984. By 2005, the average number of confidants had dropped to about two. At the end of the study, close to 25 percent of respondents said they didn't have anyone they could truly trust, triple the proportion from two decades earlier.

More recently, a 2010 study by AARP surveyed more than 3,000 people age forty-five and older and found that 35 percent scored in the lonely category. Another survey, published this year by researchers at the University of Oxford, included more than 3,300 British people and found that, even though respondents averaged 155 Facebook connections, the number they felt they could approach in times of extreme distress was just four.

It's not necessarily important to have a lot of friends, though some studies suggest that more might be better than fewer. The AARP survey found that loneliness rates were highest in people who had fewer than three close friends, and having five or more was better than having three or four.

What is clear is that quality trumps quantity. Just as strong relationships can improve health measures, toxic or stressful relationships can lead to depression, high blood pressure and other negative outcomes.

In one recent study, Kiecolt-Glaser and colleagues asked married couples to discuss something they disagreed about. Over the next day, pairs that both included someone with a history of depression and had argued with hostility burned fewer calories than did those who talked to each other with more kindness. That suggests that relationship quality can affect metabolism. So how can we cultivate more and stronger relationships? Science can't yet say. Studies that have randomly assigned patients in hospitals to be part of a support group or have sent visitors to sit with lonely people have produced mixed results, probably because of chemistry: There's no guarantee that two people will click.

> "Today, the data make a convincing case: Having people who care about us is good for us."

A better strategy, Holt-Lundstad suspects, is to try volunteering or joining activities that allow for interaction with a wide variety of people. It's also worth making a conscious effort to be the kind of friend you'd like people to be for you, Kiecolt-Glaser says. That includes being supportive, being there when friends need you, having fun together and making an effort to listen, even when you're busy or stressed-out.

In my case, I'm going to try to remember how much it meant to me when friends helped us with our move. And if I can organize a closet or even show up to give a hug, I'll do my best to be there. After all, there's something in it for me, too.

QUESTIONS

1. What do you think Sohn's central argument is? What are the main pieces of support she offers for it? What objections to her central argument can you think of that she doesn't deal with?

2. Sohn is not a researcher or expert on friendship. What does she do to build her ethos? Are there things she doesn't do that you think she should have done to develop her ethos?

COMPOSING PROJECT | Create a Collage

Go through your photos of yourself with friends. Notice which ones document important moments, which ones seem to capture the spirit of a particular friendship, and which ones reflect the personality or values or something else of you or your friend(s). Select your favorites and create a collage that illustrates the role friendship has played in your life.

LONG-TERM PROJECTS | **The Body**

1. **Create a marketing campaign for a law.** Imagine you work for a marketing firm or ad agency hired by your city or state to promote the benefits of a particular law. Perhaps your city has asked you to promote and celebrate the law that requires drivers to slow down in school zones, or maybe your state has hired you to "sell" citizens on the value of the state sales tax.

a. To begin your project, **choose a real, existing law.** Then find the actual law on your city or state's Web site and read it carefully to make sure you understand it.

b. Conduct a survey or several interviews with residents of your city or state to find answers to these questions:

- Who are they, in terms of age, race, education level, income level, etc.?
- Do they typically follow the law, or do they try to find ways around it? Why?
- Do they appreciate the law, or do they find it a nuisance? Why?
- From their perspective, what are the benefits and costs of the law?
- How does the law affect them on a daily or weekly basis?

c. Next, review the survey results or interview notes you collected. **Decide what group of citizens you want to target** with your marketing. **Consider these questions:** How will you entice them to appreciate the law? How can you appeal to their needs and values?

d. Then take this information and create the pieces of your marketing campaign. Your ultimate goal is to sell your campaign in a presentation to your class (who will pose as your peers at the marketing firm or ad agency and/or as the city or state officials who have hired your firm). **Create at least three different pieces for your campaign,** perhaps a series of print ads, storyboards for television ads, scripts for radio ads, slogans for bumper stickers or billboards, or YouTube videos. Your final presentation to your class should include the following:

- A description of your target group
- Your specific goal and message
- A rationale for the marketing campaign (including the needs and wants of the target group)
- A presentation of the pieces of the marketing campaign that you created

2. **Create an illustrated timeline.** Begin by researching advertisements past and present for a particular addictive substance, such as tobacco (cigarettes), alcohol, or prescription drugs (oxycontin, codeine). How has the substance/product been advertised over time?

a. Research and create the timeline:

- **Identify and print out** as many images of ads as you can find online, keeping careful track of the original dates of each. Make sure your ads represent a wide time span, from the nineteenth century to the present if possible. As you search, you might want to use the search terms "Vintage Medicine Ads" or "Vintage Codeine Advertisements" (if you're researching codeine).

- **Choose four or five** of the most interesting ads, again keeping in mind the desired time range. Remember that you want to illustrate the ways this substance/product has been advertised over time.

- **Research the historical, political, and cultural events** that were taking place as your substance/product was advertised.

- **Create a timeline** that incorporates the ads with the corresponding historical, political, and cultural events you have identified.

b. Analyze:

- **Look for ways that history, politics, and culture affected your product's ad campaign.** For example, do ads from the Great Depression reflect the nation's economic desperation in any way? Are certain social or ethnic groups represented in new or different ways? Are products geared toward certain afflictions that reflect the time period? Try to make connections between the ads and what was happening at that time.

- **Write an essay** to accompany your timeline. Be sure to write about each ad and each point in your timeline. **Analyze** how history, politics, and culture impacted the way your product was advertised over time. Alternatively, you can write analytical annotations to accompany your timeline.

CONTENTS

What does it mean to be an activist? Are you writing a letter to the editor urging drivers to be mindful of cyclists on the road? Perhaps you are joining thousands of marchers in your city and around the world protesting for an environmental change. You might even be sitting at a table on your campus on World AIDS Day (December 1), passing out pamphlets and answering questions.

Activism takes on all forms. You might participate in a shopping boycott, choosing only to support small businesses on a particular day rather than support major corporations. You could write a play and perform it to raise awareness about an issue, as Eve Ensler did with *The Vagina Monologues*. Or, you could attend a local open mic and perform a piece of spoken word poetry that challenges the audience's notion of privilege.

Margaret Mead, a U.S. anthropologist, once said, "Never doubt that a small group of committed people can change the world. Indeed, it is the only thing that ever has." This chapter explores different ways activists have expressed their ideas and made their mark on the world. You'll examine photographs and protest signs, analyze fact sheets and speeches, and explore organizational sites and their messages.

The chapter begins with photographs of the activists Martin Luther King Jr., Malala Yousafzai, and Jason Collins. This is followed by two Web sites: the "We the People" page from the White House site, which shows how you can create a petition and congressional testimony; and the United Nations' "Sustainable Development Goals" page, which includes a list entitled "The Lazy Person's Guide to Saving the World."

The chapter then moves on to congressional testimony from Barbara Burnette, a 9/11 responder, a poster and fact sheet from the Mine Safety and Health Administration, and actor/activist Jesse Williams's acceptance speech at the BET awards. This is followed by a series of three protest signs from rallies from three different movements: the Tea Party, Black Lives Matter, and the Women's March.

Ending the chapter are a speech by the actress Ellen Page given at the Human Rights Campaign Foundation Conference and an article celebrating the birthday and accomplishments of the activist Malala Yousafzai.

As you read through the chapter, consider what different forms activism takes and how you might define activism.

Getty Images, *Martin Luther King Jr.*

This photo captures Dr. Martin Luther King Jr. after he delivered his "I Have a Dream" speech in Washington, D.C., on August 28, 1963. The occasion was the March on Washington for Jobs and Freedom, a civil rights event that called for an end to racial discrimination. In his speech, King expressed his hope: "I have a dream that one day this nation will rise up and live out the true meaning of its creed: 'We hold these truths to be self-evident, that all men are created equal.'" While there were many photographs taken that day, this one was taken by an unidentified photographer and provided to us by Getty Images from its database.

Credit: CNP/Contributor/Getty Images.

▼ Photo

Bilawal Arbab, *Malala Yousafzai on* Time *Magazine*

Malala Yousafzai (b. 1997) is a Pakistani student and activist for girls' education. In October 2012, while traveling through the Swat Valley on the way to school, she was shot in the head by a Taliban member. After receiving medical treatment in Britain, she recovered enough to return to school and to make appearances around the world to promote girls' rights to education. Malala won the Nobel Peace Prize in 2014. The photo that follows was taken by photojournalist Bilawal Arbab, whose work is distributed through the European Press Photo Agency (epa) and Corbis. Arbab took the photo on April 23, 2013, in Peshawar, Pakistan. The original caption accompanies the image.

"A copy of *Time* magazine at a newsstand with the cover photo of a Pakistani girl, Malala Yousafzai, who was shot and injured by Taliban militants in Swat valley, in Peshawar [the capital of] Khyber Pakhtunkhwa province. . . . Malala Yousafzai emerged in the list of 100 most influential people in *Time* magazine. Malala was attacked by Taliban on October 9, 2012 for advocating girls' rights to education and [was] wounded along with two schoolmates. After initial treatment, she was sent to Britain where she is recovering."
Credit: BILAWAL ARBAB/EPA/Newscom.

▼ Photo

Rick Friedman, *Jason Collins at Boston Pride*

Jason Collins played in the NBA for thirteen seasons, including for the Boston Celtics and the Washington Wizards, at center position. He wore jersey number 98 in honor of Matthew Shepard, who was killed in 1998 because he was gay. In April 2013, Collins wrote an article for *Sports Illustrated* in which he announced that he is gay. He is the first professional basketball player to do so.

He wrote:

> I'm a 34 year old NBA center. I'm black. And I'm gay. I didn't set out to be the first openly gay athlete playing in a major American team sport. But since I am, I'm happy to start the conversation. . . . I've endured years of misery and gone to enormous lengths to live a lie. I was certain that my world would fall apart if anyone knew. And yet when I acknowledged my sexuality I felt whole for the first time. I still had the same sense of humor, I still had the same mannerisms, and my friends still had my back.

Jason Collins retired from basketball in November 2014. This photo was taken by Rick Friedman, a Boston-based photojournalist whose work has appeared in major publications, including *The New York Times*, *Time* and *Newsweek* magazines, and *The Guardian*. In this image, Jason Collins marches in the Boston Pride Parade in 2013 with his former college roommate, Congressman Joseph Kennedy III.

Credit: Rick Friedman/Getty Images.

QUESTIONS

1. These three photos portray heroic figures. How do the photos emphasize their heroic or historic stature?

2. Do you find one photo more compelling than another? Why?

COMPOSING PROJECT | Create a Photo Essay

Research the civil rights movement of the 1950s and 1960s, the history of women's and girls' rights in Pakistan (where Malala Yousafzai is from) or elsewhere, or the gay-rights movement from the Stonewall Rebellion (1969) to the Supreme Court ruling on same-sex marriage (2015). Find pictures of people and events that display the activism involved in the movement you've chosen to research. Create a photo essay that tells the story and conveys the spirit of one of these movements.

▼ Web Site

The White House, *Petition the White House on the Issues That Matter to You*

"We the People" is a page on the White House's official Web site that allows people to create petitions to be reviewed by the president and other officials. To be reviewed, petitions need to receive 100,000 signatures. The page was created during President Obama's administration.

Credit: Whitehouse.gov.

① **Create a Petition**
Call on the White House to take action on the issue that matters to you.

② **Gather Signatures**
Share your petition with others, build a comunity for change you want to make.

③ **100,00 Signatures in 30 Days**
Get an official update from the White House within 60 days.

QUESTIONS

1. Why do you think the creator of the Web site used an image of the White House's Truman Balcony at the top of the page rather than an image that shows the entire front of the White House? Do you think the image is effective? Would you have chosen a different one? Why or why not?

2. Do you think the three steps beneath "How Petitions Work" (which are listed in the margin) are sufficient for explaining the process? Why or why not?

COMPOSING PROJECT | Create a Web Page

Review some of the many Web sites that give advice on what to say in phone calls, e-mails, and letters to elected officials (just Google "Tips for Talking to elected Officials"). Then create a Web page that invites citizens to call or write a particular elected official. Choose an image or images that will convey a particular notion of democracy and include some explanation, as the "We the People" page does, of how contacting an elected official works.

▼ List

United Nations, *The Lazy Person's Guide to Saving the World*

On the United Nations' "Sustainable Development Goals" page, there is a list of activities people can do that will positively impact the earth. The list is geared toward lazy people, since, according to the site, "Every human on earth — even the most indifferent, laziest person among us — is part of the solution." The list is divided into three categories: Sofa Superstar, Household Hero, and Neighborhood Nice Guy.

Credit: From THE LAZY PERSON'S GUIDE TO SAVING THE WORLD by The United Nations. Copyright © The United Nations. Reprinted with the permission of the United Nations.

End extreme poverty. Fight inequality and injustice. Fix climate change. Whoa. The Global Goals are important, world-changing objectives that will require cooperation among governments, international organizations and world leaders. It seems impossible that the average person can make an impact. Should you just give up?

No! Change starts with you. Seriously. Every human on earth — even the most indifferent, laziest person among us — is part of the solution. Fortunately, there are some super easy things we can adopt into our routines that, if we all do it, will make a big difference.

We've made it easy for you and compiled just a few of the many things you can do to make an impact.

Level 1: Sofa Superstar
Things you can do from your couch

- Save electricity by plugging appliances into a power strip and turning them off completely when not in use, including your computer.

- Stop paper bank statements and pay your bills online or via mobile. No paper, no need for forest destruction.

- Share, don't just like. If you see an interesting social media post about women's rights or climate change, share it so folks in your network see it too.

- Speak up! Ask your local and national authorities to engage in initiatives that don't harm people or the planet. You can also voice your support for the Paris Agreement and ask your country to ratify it or sign it if it hasn't yet.

- Don't print. See something online you need to remember? Jot it down in a note-book or better yet a digital post-it note and spare the paper.
- Turn off the lights. Your TV or computer screen provides a cosy glow, so turn off other lights if you don't need them.
- Do a bit of online research and buy only from companies that you know have sustainable practices and don't harm the environment.
- Report online bullies. If you notice harassment on a message board or in a chat room, flag that person.
- Stay informed. Follow your local news and stay in touch with the Global Goals online or on social media at @GlobalGoalsUN.
- Tell us about your actions to achieve the global goals by using the hashtag #globalgoals on social networks.
- Offset your carbon emissions! You can calculate your carbon footprint and purchase climate credit from Climate Neutral Now. In this way, you help reduce global emissions faster!

Level 2: Household Hero
Things you can do at home

- Air dry. Let your hair and clothes dry naturally instead of running a machine. If you do wash your clothes, make sure the load is full.
- Take short showers. Bathtubs require gallons more water than a 5–10 minute shower.
- Eat less meat, poultry, and fish. More resources are used to provide meat than plants.
- Freeze fresh produce and leftovers if you don't have the chance to eat them before they go bad. You can also do this with take-away or delivered food, if you know you will not feel like eating it the next day. You will save food and money.
- Compost—composting food scraps can reduce climate impact while also recycling nutrients.
- Recycling paper, plastic, glass & aluminium keeps landfills from growing.
- Buy minimally packaged goods.
- Avoid pre-heating the oven. Unless you need a precise baking temperature, start heating your food right when you turn on the oven.
- Plug air leaks in windows and doors to increase energy efficiency.
- Adjust your thermostat, lower in winter, higher in summer.
- Replace old appliances with energy efficient models and light bulbs.
- If you have the option, install solar panels in your house. This will also reduce your electricity bill!
- Get a rug. Carpets and rugs keep your house warm and your thermostat low.

> "Every human on earth—even the most indifferent, laziest person among us—is part of the solution."

- **Don't rinse.** If you use a dishwasher, stop rinsing your plates before you run the machine.
- **Choose a better diaper option.** Swaddle your baby in cloth diapers or a new, environmentally responsible disposable brand.
- **Shovel snow manually.** Avoid the noisy, exhaust-churning snow blower and get some exercise.
- **Use cardboard matches.** They don't require any petroleum, unlike plastic gas-filled lighters.

Level 3: Neighborhood Nice Guy
Things you can do outside your house

- **Shop local.** Supporting neighbourhood businesses keeps people employed and helps prevent trucks from driving far distances.
- **Shop Smart**—plan meals, use shopping lists and avoid impulse buys. Don't succumb to marketing tricks that lead you to buy more food than you need, particularly for perishable items. Though these may be less expensive per ounce, they can be more expensive overall if much of that food is discarded.
- **Buy Funny Fruit**—many fruits and vegetables are thrown out because their size, shape, or color are not "right." Buying these perfectly good funny fruit, at the farmer's market or elsewhere, utilizes food that might otherwise go to waste.
- **When you go to a restaurant and are ordering seafood always ask:** "Do you serve sustainable seafood?" Let your favorite businesses know that ocean-friendly seafood's on your shopping list.
- **Shop only for sustainable seafood.** There are now many apps like this one that will tell you what is safe to consume.
- **Bike, walk or take public transport.** Save the car trips for when you've got a big group.
- **Use a refillable water bottle and coffee cup.** Cut down on waste and maybe even save money at the coffee shop.
- **Bring your own bag when you shop.** Pass on the plastic bag and start carrying your own reusable totes.
- **Take fewer napkins.** You don't need a handful of napkins to eat your takeout. Take just what you need.
- **Shop vintage.** Brand-new isn't necessarily best. See what you can repurpose from second-hand shops.
- **Maintain your car.** A well-tuned car will emit fewer toxic fumes.
- **Donate what you don't use.** Local charities will give your gently used clothes, books and furniture a new life.

- Vaccinate yourself and your kids. Protecting your family from disease also aids public health.
- Take advantage of your right to elect the leaders in your country and local community.

These are only a few of the things you can do. Explore this site to find out more about the goals you care most about and other ways to engage more actively.

QUESTIONS

1. Are the actions organized in a particular way under each category? If so, how would you describe the pattern of organization? If you don't feel they are arranged in a particular order, how might you rearrange them?

2. Are there actions you would add to any of the categories? What are they?

COMPOSING PROJECT | Create an Activism Diary

Take "The Lazy Person's Guide to Saving the World" list and note which actions you already do. Then choose five more that you will do in the course of a week (you can always do more than that). Keep a diary of what you did and when. Note in your entry the date, time, and what you did. Then write a paragraph noting how it felt to take that particular action. Is this something you will continue to do? Why or why not?

▼ Congressional Testimony

Barbara Burnette, *Statement on 9/11 Health and Compensation Reauthorization Act*

Barbara Burnette was a 9/11 first responder. Her work in the debris of the Twin Towers collapse resulted in severe health problems that make it impossible for her to work or live a normal life. She testified in front of Congress about her experience in support of the reauthorization of the James Zadroga 9/11 Health and Compensation Act. The Zadroga Act, which funds health monitoring and financial assistance to first responders like Burnette, was signed into law in 2011 and reauthorized in 2015. James Zadroga was a 9/11 first responder who died from respiratory disease caused by his recovery work at the World Trade Center.

Statement of Barbara Burnette of Bayside, New York

Before the United States House of Representatives

Committee on Energy and Commerce Committee Subcommittee on Health

Regarding H.R. 1786

James Zadroga 9/11 Health and Compensation Reauthorization Act of 2015

June 11, 2015

Thank you, Committee Chairman Upton, Ranking Member Pallone, Subcommittee Chairman Pittman, Ranking Member Green, and Members of the Subcommittee on Health, for inviting me to appear before you today.

My name is Barbara Burnette. I live in Bayside, New York. I am 52 years old, a wife, a mother, and a grandmother. With me here today are my husband, Lebro Sr., and my son, Lebro Jr.

I am a proud, former New York City Police Detective. I retired from the department after 18 and a half years of service. My career came to an end because of illnesses I developed from the time I served at the World Trade Center site. I served there for more than three weeks, about twenty-three days in total.

The morning of September 11, 2001, I was working in Brooklyn, New York. I had been assigned to the Police Department's Gang Intelligence Division. When my fellow officers and I learned that morning of the terrorist attacks in New York City, we rushed to lower Manhattan the fastest way possible. We took boats. We arrived at the piers near the West Side Highway. We arrived around the time the Towers had collapsed.

The air was thick with dust and smoke. I had to place my hands over my-mouth and nose just to breathe. That first day, I worked for about twelve straight hours in these difficult, almost impossible conditions. My fellow officers and I worked all day and well into the night. We evacuated people from around the World Trade Center site. We directed them away from the disaster. There was so much dust, I had to wash my eyes out frequently, with running water.

I was not given any respirator or any kind of protection for my eyes, throat and lungs. To wash dust and debris out of my eyes, mouth and throat throughout the day, my only choice was to pick up a hose and let the muddy, dirty water run out of my mouth and onto the ground. At one point, Emergency Medical Services rinsed out my eyes with bottled water. My eyes were irritated, swollen and dark red in color.

My fellow officers and I, along with all the rescue workers and First Responders, could not stop doing what we had to do. That first night, I finally left the World Trade Center site around 10 P.M.

Five hours later, I reported back to the World Trade Center. I arrived for work at four in the morning on September 12th. We were assigned directly to the debris pile on the second day. I worked until late afternoon, removing debris, by hand and by using buckets and shovels. At no time was I provided with any type of respiratory protection. Like the day before, I had to run water into my mouth and throat to wash away the dust and debris and then spit it out. My eyes needed constant rinsing. If I was not crying over what I was seeing in the ruins, tears streamed down my face from the burning, irritating dust.

I spent weeks at the World Trade Center site in this routine: shoveling; clearing away debris; searching for survivors; and later, sifting for body parts of the dead. We worked side by side and hand in hand with iron workers and construction workers who worked as contractors for the City of New York. The firefighters, the police officers, the construction workers, all of us searched in the dust and removed debris together.

For all of us, no matter what our job was, each day was pretty much the same. We made our way across all parts of the World Trade Center, which was a rectangle in shape, all debris, from north to south, east to west. There were no landmarks or street signs left. All I knew is that we were searching and removing wreckage of the World Trade Center. We were working right on top, on the burning, smoky, hot rubble.

These conditions did not change during my time on the debris pile. The fires never stopped burning. There was constant dust and debris flying around. Air quality, we were told was not a concern. All of us were allowed to continue to work 24/7. The work was tough and dirty, it would cause choking and it was dangerous. But there was never a time when I even thought about quitting and leaving. I thought of the thousands of poor victims, including my fellow Police Officers. I thanked God that I was not one of them. If our energy and toil brought the removal and recovery efforts closer to completion, we were glad to contribute. There were those who should have taken the necessary precautions to protect all of us from the exposure to dust. All I know is that we held up our end of the deal.

I live with the consequences of 9/11 every day. I have been diagnosed with interstitial lung disease, more specifically hypersensitivity pneumonitis with fibrosis in my lungs. I have failed the pulmonary function tests that doctors have given me. The inflammation in my lungs interferes with my breathing and destroys the tissues that get oxygen to my blood. My lungs are permanently scarred. I cannot move around my home without wheezing or gasping for breath. I take large doses of steroids that add to my weight. I start each morning connecting to a nebulizer and inhaling multiple doses of medications. I am told I will eventually need a lung transplant.

Long term steroid use and other prescription medications have caused me to have many additional illnesses. I have been diagnosed with diabetes, high blood pressure, osteoarthritis and rheumatoid arthritis. I have suffered partially detached retinas in both eyes each requiring laser surgery.

Prior to my World Trade Center service, I was in top shape. I had no history of lung disease. I never smoked. I always had a physically demanding lifestyle and career. During my time with the NYPD, I worked for five years in the plainclothes narcotics unit. These assignments required me to walk up to four miles per day, standing ready to make arrests in buy-and-bust operations and the execute search warrants. Making an arrest is tough, intense and physical. I have made over 200 arrests in my career and have assisted in hundreds more. I have been recognized by the NYPD numerous times for Excellent Police Duty. I have also received several medals for Meritorious Police Duty.

I was born and raised in Brooklyn, New York. I played high school and college basketball. I played on the Police League women's team which competed across the United States and internationally. We won four championships.

> ## "We were working right on top, on the burning, smoky, hot rubble."

Life has been very different since I became sick. I cannot walk up the stairs or down the street without gasping for breath. It seems a long time ago that I arrested drug dealers or did most police work. Simply walking is difficult for me now. Because of my illness, sometimes I black out. That is why I avoid driving. I rely on my husband, family and friends to get me where I need to go. In September of 2004, while working full duty, I experienced a blackout at work. There was no explanation for this episode. I underwent many medical tests. In May 2005, having discovered inflammation in my bronchial passages, doctors at the Mount Sinai Medical Center performed two bronchoscopies and an open lung biopsy. Granulomas, abnormal tissue formations were detected in my lungs and I was placed on daily doses of Prednisone to fight the inflammation. My condition worsened.

I soon realized that I would never go back to work full duty as a Detective for the NYPD. On August 11, 2006, the Police Department agreed. Department doctors determined that I was permanently disabled with illnesses resulting from exposure at the World Trade Center site. The James Zadroga 9/11 Health and Compensation Reauthorization Act is a lifesaver for me and thousands of other first responders and 9/11 survivors. Every day we fight serious health issues resulting from our exposure to toxic smoke, dust and debris from the World Trade Center site. Recently, more than sixty types of cancers have been identified by medical researchers as being directly related to the toxins found at Ground Zero. The Zadroga Bill enables me to participate in the Mount Sinai Medical Center's World Trade Center Health Program and medical monitoring.

Every month I see the doctors at Mount Sinai to receive care and to renew my prescriptions. This program saves lives. It is saving my life. It provides a medical structure in my life by coordinating doctors and medications. My family does not have to suffer the financial burden of doctor visits, co-payments, deductibles and the terrible costs of prescription medication which I know would not be available to me without the program.

I would note that our health conditions are worsening. Many of my First Responder colleagues have been diagnosed with cancer. Many colleagues have died of cancer. The amount of dust to which we were exposed was unprecedented. Many, many of us fear cancer and other injuries that may arise late, after toxic exposure.

For these reasons, I would urge the committee to approve the bipartisan legislation before it. I would be happy to answer your questions. Thank you for the hearing.

QUESTIONS

1. Make a reverse outline of the main ideas in Burnette's testimony. Do you see other ways Burnette could have organized her ideas? Do you think she chose the most effective order to present her ideas in? Why or why not?

2. Burnette's primary audience is members of the U.S. Congress. In what ways does she frame her comments to account for the needs and concerns of her audience?

Imagine you have been invited to testify before Congress on an issue that is important to you. Draft the comments you would make, beginning by introducing yourself and explaining your connection to the issue. Then, as Burnette does, explain how the issue has affected you and what you would like to see done about it. The Association for Career and Technical Education Web site (acteonline.org) has helpful information about testifying before policymakers.

▼ Poster & Fact Sheet

Mine Safety and Health Administration, *MSHA's Final Rule to Lower Miners' Exposure to Respirable Coal Mine Dust and End Black Lung*

The Mine Safety and Health Administration (MSHA) is a branch of the U.S. Department of Labor charged with ensuring that mines comply with safety and health standards. Mining is a very dangerous activity for workers; in addition to facing death and dismemberment on the job, miners often suffer from maladies such as black lung or coal workers' pneumoconiosis, an ailment caused by exposure to coal dust. As the poster below indicates, black lung is both fatal and preventable. The fact sheet below describes a new rule designed to help prevent new cases of black lung.

Fact Sheet

MSHA's Final Rule to Lower Miners' Exposure to

Respirable Coal Mine Dust

According to data from the National Institute for Occupational Safety and Health (NIOSH), coal workers' pneumoconiosis (also known as black lung) was a cause or contributing factor in the death of more than 76,000 miners since 1968. Caused by breathing unhealthy coal mine dust, this disease has cost more than $45 billion dollars in federal compensation benefits. Evidence shows that miners continue to get the disease, even younger miners.

The Mine Safety and Health Administration has taken a historic step forward in the effort to end black lung disease by issuing a final rule to reduce miners' exposure to respirable coal dust. The new rule takes effect August 1, 2014 and accomplishes the following:

- Lowers the concentration of dust in the air that miners breathe and improves sampling practices to better reflect actual working conditions and protect all miners from overexposures;

- Increases sampling and makes use of cutting-edge technology developed for the mining environment to provide real-time information about dust levels, allowing miners and operators to identify problems and make necessary adjustments instead of letting overexposures languish. Requires immediate corrective action for excessive levels of dust; and
- Has a common sense phase-in over a two-year period to give the industry the time it needs to adjust to the new requirements, acquire monitoring equipment, and obtain compliance assistance from MSHA.

Highlights of the final rule

Lowers dust concentration levels: Reduces the overall dust standards in coal mines from 2 to 1.5 milligrams per cubic meter of air; Cuts in half the existing standard for air in entries used to ventilate places where miners work, and for Part 90 miners (those who have evidence of pneumoconiosis).

Further lowers dust levels by eliminating loopholes that masked overexposures and improves sampling for more accurate measurements:

> **The persistence of black lung disease has long troubled health researchers, labor advocates and responsible industry leaders.**

- Changes the current practice of averaging dust samples, which allows miners on some shifts to be exposed to levels above the standard;
- Mandates immediate action by mine operators when dust levels are high instead of allowing miners to be exposed to unhealthy dust levels for days or weeks;
- Requires more frequent sampling of areas known to have high dust levels, such as those closest to the production area;
- Requires sampling for the full shift a miner works to ensure protection for all working hours rather than stopping measurement after 8 hours, as is the existing requirement;
- Requires sampling on all shifts;
- Requires dust samples to be taken when mines are operating at 80 percent of production or more, as opposed to the existing 50 percent requirement, so that samples are more representative of actual working conditions; and
- Requires more thorough examinations of the dust controls on mining sections each shift with records of the exams signed by mine officials.

Utilizes cutting-edge technology to measure dust levels: Requires use of the continuous personal dust monitor (CPDM), a device developed with mining industry involvement to provide real-time sampling results. The CPDM is to be worn by miners in high-risk occupations. It continuously evaluates dust levels and provides operators with readings they can use to take immediate action to correct dust conditions, instead of waiting days for lab results, as is necessary with current sampling methods.

Improves the early warning system for the disease: Expands the medical surveillance program to include surface as well as underground coal miners, and adds lung function testing as well as x-rays.

Background

The persistence of black lung disease has long troubled health researchers, labor advocates and responsible industry leaders. In separate reports in the mid-1990s, the Centers for Disease Control's National Institute for Occupational Safety and Health, and a Secretary of Labor's Advisory Committee of industry, labor and government representatives recommended changes to exposure limits and enforcement protocols, many of which are included in the new rule.

The rule builds on years of research and was developed with the input of industry, labor, and health professionals. It is the centerpiece of the agency's campaign to End Black Lung, launched in 2009, which seeks to fulfill a promise originally made by Congress in passing the Federal Coal Mine Health and Safety Act of 1969.

MSHA proposed the rule in October 2010 and followed its announcement with an extensive period of public outreach that included seven hearings in coal-producing regions and at its headquarters in Arlington, VA. About 2,000 pages of comments were received over an 8-month period. The final rule is responsive to the comments.

Extensive training and outreach will prepare miners and operators

MSHA will provide extensive guidance and support to mine operators and miners, including:

- Outreach to all coal mine operators during the implementation period;
- Stakeholders meeting at MSHA headquarters in Arlington, VA;
- Field seminars in coal mining regions, including in Beckley, WV; Washington, PA; Hazard, KY; Birmingham, AL; Evansville, IN; and Grand Junction, CO; and
- Comprehensive compliance assistance material, including distribution of guidance documents.

More outreach sessions will be scheduled. During these sessions, MSHA representatives will highlight the major provisions and effective dates, and describe best practices for controlling dust and reducing exposures. Training will be provided to MSHA enforcement personnel before implementation, and training materials will be available on the MSHA Web site for operators and miners.

For more information, visit www.msha.gov/endblacklung

THE TOLL OF BLACK LUNG CONTINUES

Chester Fike
Born Feb. 3, 1952
Died Dec. 18, 2012
A victim of black lung, Chester died four months after undergoing a double lung transplant.

It is time to end this preventable disease

76,000
deaths since 1968

$45 billion
spent in federal compensation

New cases
being diagnosed, including in young miners

A new rule issued by the U.S. Department of Labor's Mine Safety and Health Administration will greatly improve the protection of America's coal miners from this debilitating disease. The rule is the centerpiece of MSHA's initiative to End Black Lung – Act Now! To learn more, visit **www.msha.gov/endblacklung**.

  MINE SAFETY AND HEALTH ADMINISTRATION
UNITED STATES DEPARTMENT OF LABOR

Credit: Mine Safety and Health Administration.

QUESTIONS

1. These two documents convey the idea that Black Lung can be prevented, but they do it in quite different ways. Who do you think the audience is for each piece and why?

2. The fact sheet uses bulleted lists to convey much of the information. How do the bullets help you read the information? Would you prefer that the bulleted information be conveyed in full paragraphs? Why or why not?

COMPOSING PROJECT | Create an Infographic

Notice that the poster is almost purely visual and the fact sheet is purely text-based. Create a third piece that combines visuals (find or create your own or use the image from the poster) and some of the text from the fact sheet into an infographic designed for college students or an audience other than the ones you identified in question 1 above.

▼ Speech

Jesse Williams, *BET Humanitarian Award Acceptance Speech*

Jesse Williams is an actor and an activist. His best-known acting role is Dr. Jackson on the television show *Grey's Anatomy*. He is a civil rights activist and was the executive producer for the 2016 documentary *Stay Woke: The Black Lives Matter Movement*. The following is a transcript of the speech he made after receiving the Humanitarian Award at the 2016 BET (Black Entertainment Television) Awards.

Credit: Used with permission of Jesse Williams and August Moon.

Peace peace. Thank you, Debra. Thank you, BET. Thank you Nate Parker, Harry and Debbie Allen for participating in that.

Before we get into it, I just want to say I brought my parents out tonight. I just want to thank them for being here, for teaching me to focus on comprehension over career, and that they make sure I learn what the schools were afraid to teach us. And also thank my amazing wife for changing my life.

Now, this award—this is not for me. This is for the real organizers all over the country—the activists, the civil rights attorneys, the struggling parents, the families, the teachers, the students that are realizing that a system built to divide and impoverish and destroy us cannot stand if we do.

It's kind of basic mathematics—the more we learn about who we are and how we got here, the more we will mobilize.

Now, this is also in particular for the black women in particular who have spent their lifetimes dedicated to nurturing everyone before themselves. We can and will do better for you.

Now, what we've been doing is looking at the data and we know that police somehow manage to de-escalate, disarm, and not kill white people everyday. So what's going to happen is we are going to have equal rights and justice in our own country or we will restructure their function and ours.

> **The burden of the brutalized is not to comfort the bystander.**

Now... I got more y'all—yesterday would have been young Tamir Rice's fourteenth birthday so I don't want to hear anymore about how far we've come when paid public servants can pull a drive-by on [a] twelve-year-old playing alone in the park in broad daylight, killing him on television and then going home to make a sandwich. Tell Rekia Boyd how it's so much better than it is to live in 2012 than it is to live in 1612 or 1712. Tell that to Eric Garner. Tell that to Sandra Bland. Tell that to Dorian Hunt.

Now the thing is, though, all of us in here getting money—that alone isn't gonna stop this.

Alright, now dedicating our lives, dedicating our lives to getting money just to give it right back for someone's brand on our body when we spent centuries praying with brands on our bodies, and now we pray to get paid for brands on our bodies.

There has been no war that we have not fought and died on the front lines of. There has been no job we haven't done. There is no tax they haven't leveed against us—and we've paid all of them. But freedom is somehow always conditional here. "You're free," they keep telling us. But she would have been alive if she hadn't acted so . . . free.

Now, freedom is always coming in the hereafter, but you know what, though, the hereafter is a hustle. We want it now.

And let's get a couple things straight, just a little sidenote—the burden of the brutalized is not to comfort the bystander. That's not our job, alright—stop with all that. If you have a critique for the resistance, for our resistance, then you better have an established record of critique of our oppression. If you have no interest, if you have no interest in equal rights for black people then do not make suggestions to those who do. Sit down.

We've been floating this country on credit for centuries, yo, and we're done watching and waiting while this invention called whiteness uses and abuses us, burying black people out of sight and out of mind while extracting our culture, our dollars, our entertainment like oil—black gold, ghettoizing and demeaning our creations then stealing them, gentrifying our genius and then trying us on like costumes before discarding our bodies like rinds of strange fruit. The thing is though . . . the thing is that just because we're magic doesn't mean we're not real.

Thank you.

QUESTIONS

1. In his speech, Williams says, "Now, this award—this is not for me." Who does he believe the award is for? What evidence does he offer to support this?

2. How would you describe the tone of his speech? Why? Does it stay consistent throughout or does it change? If so, what are the changes?

COMPOSING PROJECT | Compose an Activism Speech

Think about something you're passionate about, something you would protest for. This could be an issue on campus or in your community. It might be environmental, political, or sports related. Compose a speech that brings the issue into focus for your audience. Try to use some of the techniques Williams used to evoke the urgency of the situation. After you have written out the speech, read it aloud to a few classmates. You might also consider recording it.

▼ Protest Sign

Darren McCollester, *Tea Party Tax Day Rally (New Hampshire State House)*

On April 15, 2011, several hundred people gathered for a Tea Party rally in Concord, New Hampshire. At the rally, several prospective Republican candidates called for cuts in federal spending and the lowering of taxes. Buddy Roemer, the former governor of Louisiana, told the crowd, "I think it's time for a second revolution." The photo below was taken at the rally.

Credit: Darren McCollester/Getty Images.

▼ **Protest Sign**

Karla Ann Cote, *Black Lives Matter Rally (New York City, July 7, 2016)*

On July 7, 2016, protesters gathered in New York City to protest the recent police shooting deaths of Alton Sterling, a thirty-seven year-old black man, and Philando Castile, a thirty-two year-old black man. People marched up Fifth Avenue from Union Square at rush hour, bringing traffic to a halt. Many chanted, "Black Lives Matter," and "No justice, no peace." Below is a photo from this rally.

Credit: NurPhoto/Getty Images.

▼ Protest Sign

Angela Datre, *The Women's March (New York City, January 21, 2017)*

On January 21, 2017, the day after President Trump's inauguration, millions of women and their allies protested worldwide. In Washington, D.C., where the main march was held, hundreds of thousands gathered. According to the Women's March Web site, "The Women's March on Washington will send a bold message to our new government on their first day in office, and to the world that women's rights are human rights." The photo below is from the New York City Women's March.

Credit: Angela Datre.

QUESTIONS

1. What are some similarities you notice in the protest signs? Besides the message, are there key differences?

2. Do some brief research on each march. Then look at each protest sign. Is it representative of the march's intent? Why or why not?

COMPOSING PROJECT | Create a Collage

Choose a social justice movement (e.g., women's rights, LGBT rights, immigration rights, Black Lives Matter). Find photos from different protests related to that movement (you might want to focus on just one march or several marches). Choose photos that represent different faces of the movement/march. Then assemble them into a collage that conveys the story of the march(es).

Ellen Page, *Speech at Human Rights Campaign Foundation Conference*

Ellen Page is a TV and film actor who has starred in films including *X-Men: The Last Stand*, *Inception*, and *Juno*, for which she was nominated for several awards, including an Oscar. She delivered the speech below at the 2014 Time to THRIVE conference, an event organized by the Human Rights Campaign Foundation. The conference aims to support LGBTQ youth.

Credit: "Ellen Page Comes Out As Gay in a Beautiful Speech at Human Rights Campaign Foundation" by Marlow Stern, from the Daily Beast, February 15, 2014. Reprinted by permission via YGS Group.

Thank you, Chad, for those kind words, and for the even kinder work that you and the Human Rights Campaign Foundation do every day on behalf of the lesbian, gay, bisexual, and transgendered young people here and across America.

It is such an honor to be here at the inaugural Time to THRIVE Conference. But it's a little weird, too. Here I am in this room because of an organization whose work I deeply, deeply admire, and I'm surrounded by people who make it their life's work to make other people's lives better—profoundly better. Some of you teach young people. Some of you help young people to heal and find their voice. Some of you listen. Some of you take action. Some of you are young people yourselves, in which case it's even weirder for a young person like me to be speaking to you.

> **If we took just five minutes to recognize each other's beauty instead of attacking each other for our differences—that's not hard, it's really an easier and better way to live.**

It's weird because here I am, an actress, representing at least in some sense an industry that places crushing standards on all of us—and not just young people, everyone. Standards of beauty, of a good life, of success; standards that I hate to admit have affected me. You have ideas planted in your head—thoughts you never had before—that tell you how you have to act, how you have to dress, and who you have to be. And I've been trying to push back to be authentic and follow my heart, but it can be hard. But that's why I'm here, in this room. All of you, all of us, can do so much more together than any one person can do alone. And I hope that that thought bolsters you as much as it does me. I hope that the workshops you go to over the next few days give you strength, because I can only imagine that there are days when you've worked longer hours than your boss realizes or cares about just to help a kid who you know can make it. Days where you feel completely alone, undermined, or hopeless.

And I know that there are people in this room who go to school every day and get treated like shit for no reason. Or you go home and you feel like you can't tell your parents the whole truth about yourself. And beyond putting yourself in one box or another, you worry about the future, about college, or work, or even your physical safety. And trying to create that mental picture of your life, of what on earth is going to happen to you, can crush you a little bit every day. And it is toxic, and painful, and deeply unfair. And sometimes it's the little, insignificant stuff that can tear you down.

Now, I try not to read gossip as a rule. But the other day, a Web site ran an article with a picture of me wearing sweatpants on the way to the gym. And the writer asked, "Why does this petite beauty insist on dressing like a massive man?" Because I like to be comfortable. There are pervasive stereotypes about masculinity and femininity that define how we're all supposed to act, dress, and speak, and they serve no one. Anyone who defies these so-called "norms" becomes worthy of comment and scrutiny, and the LGBT community knows this all too well. Yet there is courage all around us. The football hero Michael Sam; the actress Laverne Cox; the musicians Tegan and Sara Quinn; the family that supports their daughter or son who has come out. And there is courage in this room. All of you.

And I'm inspired to be in this room because every single one of you is here for the same reason: you're here because you've adopted, as a core motivation, the simple fact that this world would be a whole lot better if we just made an effort to be less horrible to one another.

If we took just five minutes to recognize each other's beauty instead of attacking each other for our differences—that's not hard, it's really an easier and better way to live. And ultimately, it saves lives. Then again, it can be the hardest thing—because loving other people starts with loving ourselves and accepting ourselves. And I know many of you have struggled with this, and I draw upon your strength and your support in ways that you will never know.

And I am here today because I am gay. And because maybe I can make a difference to help others have an easier and more hopeful time. Regardless, for me, I feel a personal obligation and a social responsibility. I also do it selfishly, because I'm tired of hiding. And I'm tired of lying by omission. I suffered for years because I was scared to be out. My spirit suffered, my mental health suffered, and my relationships suffered. And I'm standing here today, with all of you, on the other side of that pain. And I am young, yes. But what I have learned is that love—the beauty of it, the joy of it, and yes, even the pain of it—is the most incredible gift to give and to receive as a human being. And we deserve to experience love fully, equally, without shame, and without compromise. There are too many kids out there suffering from bullying, rejection, or simply being mistreated because of who they are. Too many dropouts. Too much abuse. Too many homeless. Too many suicides. You can change that, and you are changing it. But you never needed me to tell you that, and that's why this was a little bit weird.

The only thing that I can really say is what I have been building up to for the past five minutes: thank you. Thank you for inspiring me. Thank you for giving me hope. And please keep changing the world for people like me. Happy Valentine's Day, I love you all.

QUESTIONS

1. What do you think Page's purpose is? To inspire? To motivate? To share her story? What are some details and examples from her speech that support your idea?

2. Were you surprised to see the phrase "treated like shit" in Page's speech? Why or why not? Why do you think Page decided to use that colloquialism rather than a more formal statement to express her idea?

COMPOSING PROJECT | Write a Speech

Imagine you have been invited to give a speech at a conference on an issue of interest to you. Consider your audience and the point you want to make. Write a speech, carefully considering how much of yourself and your personal story you want to share with a room full of strangers, what kind of language you want to use, and what message you want to send.

▼ Article

Amy Davidson, *Happy Birthday, Malala*

Amy Davidson is a senior editor and writer for *The New Yorker*. She worked as a fact-checker for *The New Yorker* before becoming an editor. Davidson has written about topics such as immigration and politics. In the piece below, she uses the occasion of Malala Yousafzai's sixteenth birthday to remind readers of the difference that educating one child can make.

Credit: From The New Yorker by Amy Davidson, July 12, 2013. © Conde Nast.

A sixteen-year-old girl wearing three shades of pink stood in front of the United Nations on Friday. She was introduced by Gordon Brown, Britain's former Prime Minister — a broad, lumbering man who nonetheless seemed as slight as a pencil sketch next to her. "Let me repeat the words," Brown said. "The words the Taliban never wanted her to hear: happy sixteenth birthday, Malala."

It was Malala Day at the U.N.'s Youth Assembly, in honor of Malala Yousafzai, the girl who wanted to go to school. Less than a year ago, she was on a school bus in Pakistan when a man with a gun got on and said, "Where is Malala?" He shot her in the face; the bullet entered near an eye and ended up near her left shoulder. "They shot my friends, too," Yousafzai told the audience at the United Nations.

> They thought that the bullet would silence us. But they failed. And out of that silence came thousands of voices. The terrorists thought they would change my aims and stop my ambitions, but nothing changed in my life except this: weakness, fear, and hopelessness died. Strength, power, and courage was born.

Those qualities were born in this young woman, one has the sense, the moment she came into the world. They might have been wasted. She had the luck of having parents who believed in her education, and the great barrier of an armed group that thought it would be better if she were dead. Among Yousafzai's many gifts is the ability to convey both how extraordinary she herself is and how many other children might be, too, if someone taught them how to read and write. "So here I stand. So here I stand, one girl among many," she said. "I am here to speak up for the rights of education for every child."

Yousafzai's delivery was as compelling as her words—watch the video. She has an air of control about her, and self-possession, that goes beyond fearlessness. Speaking of the Taliban gunman who tried to kill her, she said that she was not seeking revenge. "Even if there is a gun in my hand, and he stands in front of me, I would not shoot him," she said—and one believed her, not because as a child she would be too meek or gentle but because she knew, intuitively, that it was not the way to impose her will. "The power of education frightens them. They are afraid of women. The power of the voice of women frightens them." She knew that she, in the end, was the stronger one.

> **And out of that silence came thousands of voices.**

And yet Yousafzai can't go home; nor, as the *Times* has reported, has there been a pause in attacks on schools that educate girls in Pakistan. Many have been bombed. British doctors saved Yousafzai's life, and she is now in school in Birmingham.

"I am the same Malala. My ambitions are the same. My hopes are the same. My dreams are the same," Yousafzai said. One hopes that those ambitions will remain limitless. She was wearing a shawl, she said, that Benazir Bhutto, the former Prime Minister of Pakistan, had worn before she was murdered. Yousafzai could run a country someday; she might do almost anything. "One child, one teacher, one book, and one pen can change the world," she said. "Education is the only solution. Education first." With time, perhaps, for a birthday party.

QUESTIONS

1. About midway through the piece, Davidson says, "Yousafzai's delivery was as compelling as the words—watch the video." You can watch the video on YouTube. After watching the video, do you agree with Davidson's assessment of Yousafzai's delivery? What is the effect of having a piece in one mode—print, in this case—refer you to a piece in another mode?

2. Davidson uses several quotations from Yousafzai throughout the short piece and also quotes Britain's former prime minister, Gordon Brown. Despite the liberal use of quotations, does Davidson maintain her own voice as the controlling voice in this piece, or did you forget that the piece was written by someone other than Yousafzai?

COMPOSING PROJECT | Write a Tribute

Think of someone you admire in your life: perhaps a friend, relative, or coworker. Compose a one- to two-page tribute to that person and a particular quality of that person you wish the world had more of. Then try to connect the person and the quality to a bigger issue, just as Davidson connects Yousafzai's fearlessness and self-possession to the importance of education for children.

LONG-TERM PROJECTS   # Activism

1. **Create an activist campaign.** For this project, you will choose an issue you care about. This might be something related to your community, such as fighting against a new highway that is going to be built through a poor neighborhood. Perhaps it's something related to the environment, such as a company's use of nonsustainable palm oil and its connection to deforestation. Or maybe you want to focus more broadly on a topic such as racism, such as fighting mass incarceration of young black males.

   Part I: Preliminary Steps.

   a. To begin your project, **brainstorm a list of causes** you're passionate about. Share this list with classmates, discussing why you chose to put some items on the list.

   b. Choose the cause you want to focus on for the activist campaign. **Research** your cause to find out the various issues related to it. Are there leaders on a global, national, state, or community level? Who are they? What are they doing? Why do some people support the cause? Why are some people opposed to the cause?

   c. **Create a five-minute oral presentation** for your class. In the presentation, you want to describe your issue to students and your teacher, demonstrating why they should care and be involved. Ultimately, you want to persuade them to join you in the movement.

   Part II: The Campaign.

   a. **Design a protest sign.** Do a Google image search for protest signs and see the varying ways people represent causes. You will need cardboard, poster board, glue, markers, and possibly photos/images. Remember that your phrase/text should only be a few words—people will want to be able to read it quickly and remember it.

   b. Choose a place where you would hold a march and/or rally. Research how you would go about getting a permit for your event. If you are holding a rally, decide what speakers you might have. Do you want any musicians/poets? Do you want any religious leaders? Would it be appropriate to have politicians speak?

   c. Decide how you are going to advertise your event. Will you have a hashtag for Twitter? Will there be a Facebook page, and if so, what will you call the page? Are there other ways you might get word out?

   d. **Create a leaflet** to hand out at your march/rally that describes the issues related to your cause.

   e. Put together a **ten-minute oral presentation** for your class. In the presentation, show your protest sign and pass around your leaflet. Describe to the class where you are going to hold your march/rally and why you've chosen that location. Who is going to be present at the march/rally? How are you going to get word out about the event?

f. Write up a one- to two-page paper that describes your cause and campaign for your teacher. Include the information that you are presenting and make sure to articulate why you made certain decisions (such as why you chose the phrase for your protest sign, why you chose particular speakers).

2. **Create a poster and fact sheet for an environmental issue.** Research an environmental issue that interests you, such as overfishing, climate change, deforestation, or ocean pollution.

a. Choose one environmental issue to investigate. Your goal is to formulate an innovative response that helps mitigate the environmental issue's impact. For example, the Coca-Cola company has formed partnerships with the communities their plants are in to protect the water supplies.

b. As you research the issue, consider the following:
   - How has the environmental issue affected local economies?
   - How has the environmental issue shaped legislation?
   - How has tourism been affected by the environmental issue?
   - What business practices have been developed in response to the environmental issue?
   - What have been some innovative responses to the environmental issue?

c. Next, consider what innovative response you might suggest. For example, you might have an idea for a program to prevent overfishing from getting worse, a plan to rebuild the rain forests or a campaign to make the public aware of how they contribute to the problem. Once you decide on your response, produce:
   - A fact sheet that conveys facts about the issue, its impacts, and the innovative response you have come up with.
   - A poster that gets people's attention and highlights a few compelling facts about the issue and its impacts.

19

CREATIVITY:
IT'S COMPLICATED

CONTENTS

What does it mean to be "creative"? While we often associate creativity with artsy types, anyone who creates anything new can be said to be creative. When you think about it that way, doesn't "creative" apply to all of us? Whether you create poems, flower arrangements, baby blankets, grilled specialties, tattoos, hairstyles, or something else, you are making something that did not previously exist—creating.

When we are inspired to create, to combine ingredients in a bold new way or to carve a hunk of wood into some never-before-seen shape, it can feel magical. Perhaps you recall a time when you awoke from a dream, knew your dream had a fantastic story line, and sat down at your computer and furiously typed out a rough plot for a short story. Or maybe you went to the farmers' market, purchased a wide assortment of vegetables, and then went home and invented a new dish with many of them, delighted in the new taste combinations you had created.

Sometimes our creative juices flow. Is it magic? Everyone at some point, though, experiences the frustration of not being able to create. Writers call it Writer's Block, which is defined as the inability to write. We may not have a fancy term to describe the lack of inspiration a flower arranger may feel when he struggles to figure out his next bouquet—Flower Arranger's Block just doesn't have a great ring to it—but we know that every person involved in creative endeavors has that awful feeling occasionally (or more often) of just being completely stumped by what to do next. Sometimes creators even wonder if they will ever be able to create again. Staring at a bare canvas or empty page or collection of ingredients with a blank mind can be intimidating enough to paralyze even the most seasoned creator.

While we typically celebrate success and try to hide our failures, the burgeoning failure movement asks us to not only acknowledge our failures but to recognize them as learning experiences and honor them. By publicizing our failures, we can normalize the idea that defeat is often a precursor to success. Appreciating failure also helps us understand the value of a less-than-smooth process.

The beginning of the chapter focuses on creative impulses and processes. Anne Lamott suggests that the secret to creativity is to not aim for brilliance. A meme expresses what a fine line there is between being blocked and simply lacking motivation. Emily Temple presents the advice of thirteen well-known writers on beating Writer's Block. New York Book Editors suggest that Writer's Block may boil down to procrastination. Andre Grant explores the creative genius of Beyoncé's visual album *Lemonade*.

The chapter ends with a look at forces that crush creativity and ways to free ourselves of those forces. Philosopher Alan Watts suggests that the education system's emphasis on grade completion causes us to not pay attention to the journey, which to his mind, is the inspiration. Johannes Haushofer and the Aalto Entrepreneurship Society urge us to embrace failure as part of the process of getting to success.

▼ Style Book Excerpt

Anne Lamott, *Shitty First Drafts*

Anne Lamott is a nonfiction writer and novelist. In her book *Bird by Bird: Some Instructions on Writing and Life*, she guides writers to move beyond their writing blocks, helping them to get words onto the page. She shares some of her own experiences with the writing process, allowing readers to see that a prolific writer also battles with writing demons. In the excerpt below, Lamott concentrates on ways to get that initial draft out of your head and onto the page.

Now, practically even better news than that of short assignments is the idea of shitty first drafts. All good writers write them. This is how they end up with good second drafts and terrific third drafts. People tend to look at successful writers, writers who are getting their books published and maybe even doing well financially, and think that they sit down at their desks every morning feeling like a million dollars, feeling great about who they are and how much talent they have and what a great story they have to tell; that they take in a few deep breaths, push back their sleeves, roll their necks a few times to get all the cricks out, and dive in, typing fully formed passages as fast as a court reporter. But this is just the fantasy of the uninitiated. I know some very great writers, writers you love who write beautifully and have made a great deal of money, and not *one* of them sits down routinely feeling wildly enthusiastic and confident. Not one of them writes elegant first drafts. All right, one of them does, but we do not like her very much. We do not think that she has a rich inner life or that God likes her or can even stand her. (Although when I mentioned this to my priest friend Tom, he said you can safely assume you've created God in your own image when it turns out that God hates all the same people you do.)

Very few writers really know what they are doing until they've done it. Nor do they go about their business feeling dewy and thrilled. They do not type a few stiff warm-up sentences and then find themselves bounding along like huskies across the snow. One writer I know tells me that he sits down every morning and says to himself nicely, "It's not like you don't have a choice, because you do—you can either type or kill yourself." We all often feel like we are pulling teeth, even those writers whose prose ends up being the most natural and fluid. The right words and sentences just do not come pouring out like ticker tape most of the time. Now, Muriel Spark is said to have felt that she was taking dictation from God every morning—sitting there, one supposes, plugged into a Dicta-phone, typing away, humming. But this is a very hostile and aggressive position. One might hope for bad things to rain down on a person like this.

For me and most of the other writers I know, writing is not rapturous. In fact, the only way I can get anything written at all is to write really, really shitty first drafts.

The first draft is the child's draft, where you let it all pour out and then let it romp all over the place, knowing that no one is going to see it and that you can shape it later. You just let this childlike part of you channel whatever voices and visions come through and onto the page. If one of the characters wants to say, "Well, so what, Mr. Poopy Pants?," you let her. No one is going to see it. If the kid wants to get into really sentimental, weepy, emotional territory, you let him. Just get it all down on paper, because there may be something great in those six crazy pages that you would never have gotten to by more rational, grown-up means. There may be something in the very last line of the very last paragraph on page six that you just love, that is so beautiful or wild that you now know what you're supposed to be writing about, more or less, or in what direction you might go—but there was no way to get to this without first getting through the first five and a half pages.

I used to write food reviews for *California* magazine before it folded. (My writing food reviews had nothing to do with the magazine folding, although every single review did cause a couple of canceled subscriptions. Some readers took umbrage at my comparing mounds of vegetable puree with various ex-presidents' brains.) These reviews always took two days to write. First I'd go to a restaurant several times with a few opinionated, articulate friends in tow. I'd sit there writing down everything anyone said that was at all interesting or funny. Then on the following Monday I'd sit down at my desk with my notes, and try to write the review. Even after I'd been doing this for years, panic would set in. I'd try to write a lead, but instead I'd write a couple of dreadful sentences, xx them out, try again, xx everything out, and then feel despair and worry settle on my chest like an x-ray apron. It's over, I'd think, calmly, I'm not going to be able to get the magic to work this time. I'm ruined. I'm through. I'm toast. Maybe, I'd think, I can get my old job back as a clerk-typist. But probably not. I'd get up and study my teeth in the mirror for a while. Then I'd stop, remember to breathe, make a few phone calls, hit the kitchen and chow down. Eventually I'd go back and sit down at my desk, and sigh for the next ten minutes. Finally I would pick up my one-inch picture frame, stare into it as if for the answer, and every time the answer would come: all I had to do was to write a really shitty first draft of, say, the opening paragraph. And no one was going to see it.

> A friend of mine says that the first draft is the down draft—you just get it down. The second draft is the up draft—you fix it up.

So I'd start writing without reining myself in. It was almost just typing, just making my fingers move. And the writing would be *terrible*. I'd write a lead paragraph that was a whole page, even though the entire review could only be three pages long, and then I'd start writing up descriptions of the food, one dish at a time, bird by bird, and the critics would be sitting on my shoulders, commenting like cartoon characters. They'd be pretending to snore, or rolling their eyes at my overwrought descriptions, no matter how hard I tried to tone those descriptions down, no matter how conscious I was of what a friend said to me gently in my early days of restaurant reviewing. "Annie," she said, "it is just a piece of *chicken*. It is just a bit of *cake*."

But because by then I had been writing for so long, I would eventually let myself trust the process—sort of, more or less. I'd write a first draft that was maybe twice as long as it should be, with a self-indulgent and boring beginning, stupefying descriptions of the meal, lots of quotes from my black-humored friends that made them sound more like the Manson girls than food lovers, and no ending to speak of. The whole thing would be so long and incoherent and hideous that for the rest of the day I'd obsess about getting creamed by a car before I could write a decent second draft. I'd worry that people would read what I'd written and believe that the accident had really been a suicide, that I had panicked because my talent was waning and my mind was shot.

The next day, though, I'd sit down, go through it all with a colored pen, take out everything I possibly could, find a new lead somewhere on the second page, figure out a kicky place to end it, and then write a second draft. It always turned out fine, sometimes even funny and weird and helpful. I'd go over it one more time and mail it in.

Then, a month later, when it was time for another review, the whole process would start again, complete with the fears that people would find my first draft before I could rewrite it.

Almost all good writing begins with terrible first efforts. You need to start somewhere. Start by getting something—anything—down on paper. A friend of mine says that the first draft is the down draft—you just get it down. The second draft is the up draft—you fix it up. You try to say what you have to say more accurately. And the third draft is the dental draft, where you check every tooth, to see if it's loose or cramped or decayed, or even, God help us, healthy.

What I've learned to do when I sit down to work on a shitty first draft is to quiet the voices in my head. First there's the vinegar-lipped Reader Lady, who says primly, "Well, *that's* not very interesting, is it?" And there's the emaciated German male who writes these Orwellian memos detailing your thought crimes. And there are your parents, agonizing over your lack of loyalty and discretion; and there's William Burroughs, dozing off or shooting up because he finds you as bold and articulate as a houseplant; and so on. And there are also the dogs: let's not forget the dogs, the dogs in their pen who will surely hurtle and snarl their way out if you ever *stop* writing, because writing is, for some of us, the latch that keeps the door of the pen closed, keeps those crazy ravenous dogs contained.

Quieting these voices is at least half the battle I fight daily. But this is better than it used to be. It used to be 87 percent. Left to its own devices, my mind spends much of its time having conversations with people who aren't there. I walk along defending myself to people, or exchanging repartee with them, or rationalizing my behavior, or seducing them with gossip, or pretending I'm on their TV talk show or whatever. I speed or run an aging yellow light or don't come to a full stop, and one nanosecond later am explaining to imaginary cops exactly why I had to do what I did, or insisting that I did not in fact do it.

I happened to mention this to a hypnotist I saw many years ago, and he looked at me very nicely. At first I thought he was feeling around on the floor for the silent alarm button, but then he gave me the following exercise, which I still use to this day.

Close your eyes and get quiet for a minute, until the chatter starts up. Then isolate one of the voices and imagine the person speaking as a mouse. Pick it up by the tail and drop it into a mason jar. Then isolate another voice, pick it up by the tail, drop it in the jar. And so on. Drop in any high-maintenance parental units, drop in any contractors, lawyers, colleagues, children, anyone who is whining in your head. Then put the lid on, and watch all these mouse people clawing at the glass, jabbering away, trying to make you feel like shit because you won't do what they want—won't give them more money, won't be more successful, won't see them more often. Then imagine that there is a volume-control button on the bottle. Turn it all the way up for a minute, and listen to the stream of angry, neglected, guilt-mongering voices. Then turn it all the way down and watch the frantic mice lunge at the glass, trying to get to you. Leave it down, and get back to your shitty first draft.

A writer friend of mine suggests opening the jar and shooting them all in the head. But I think he's a little angry, and I'm sure nothing like this would ever occur to you.

QUESTIONS

1. Throughout this excerpt, Anne Lamott attempts to alleviate the frustration a writer encounters when beginning to write. What strategies does she use? Are they effective? Why or why not?

2. How would you characterize Lamott's tone? Why do you believe she chose this particular tone? Use specific examples to support your answer.

COMPOSING PROJECT | Write an Advice Column

You have been given the role of writing an advice column for writers struggling to get words on the page. Write a series of three to four entries for the advice column. Use your own experiences and some of the ideas from Lamott's piece.

▼ Meme

Unknown Author, *Writer's Block*

The meme below depicts Fry, the lead character in the animated TV series *Futurama*, pondering his inability to write. Since memes are easily created, replicated, and modified, many users do not consider themselves the owner of the composition. In the following example, the author is anonymous.

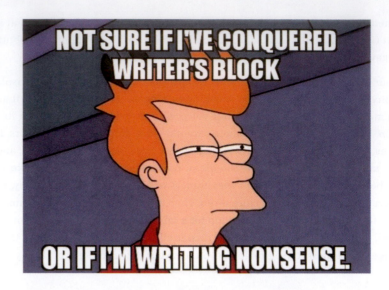

QUESTIONS

1. The creator of this meme is anonymous. How does this anonymity affect the piece's credibility? In what ways does the meme establish its ethos?

2. What makes this meme humorous? Do you have to be familiar with the TV show the character is from to find this funny?

COMPOSING PROJECT | Create a Meme

Using the meme in this chapter, create two new versions. For one of the versions, change the visual. You could use another figure from pop culture, a celebrity, an animal, or any other idea you feel could fit the existing text. For the other version, change the text.

▼ Article

Emily Temple, *13 Famous Writers on Overcoming Writer's Block*

Emily Temple writes fiction and nonfiction. Many of her nonfiction pieces have appeared on *Flavorwire*, an online magazine that focuses on film, art, music, and other culturally relevant topics. In her article "13 Famous Writers on Overcoming Writer's Block," she includes a variety of tips to help inspire writers. Many of the quotes give specific strategies for overcoming writer's block, such as Hilary Mantel's recommendation to "Take a walk, take a bath, go to sleep, make a pie, draw, listen to music, meditate, exercise. . . ."

Credit: Emily Temple, 13 Famous Writers on Overcoming Writer's Block. Used with permission of Falvorpill Media.

It's the first weekend of November, and for all you aspiring writers out there, that might just mean that you're flexing your fingers for your first crack at this year's NaNoWriMo (that's National Novel Writing Month). The philosophy behind NaNoWriMo is pretty simple: get the words—50,000 of them, to be exact—on the page. But what if you experience that dreaded writer's block while you're chipping away at your "Great Frantic Novel"? Never fear, you're not alone. After the jump, take comfort in the words of thirteen famous writers who've been there, done that—and add your own words of encouragement in the comments!

"What I try to do is write. I may write for two weeks 'the cat sat on the mat, that is that, not a rat.' And it might be just the most boring and awful stuff. But I try. When I'm writing, I write. And then it's as if the muse is convinced that I'm serious and says, 'Okay. Okay. I'll come.'"—**Maya Angelou**

"Suggestions? Put it aside for a few days, or longer, do other things, try not to think about it. Then sit down and read it (printouts are best I find, but that's just me) as if you've never seen it before. Start at the beginning. Scribble on the manuscript as you go if you see anything you want to change. And often, when you get to the end you'll be both enthusiastic about it and know what the next few words are. And you do it all one word at a time."—**Neil Gaiman**

"I encourage my students at times like these to get one page of anything written, three hundred words of memories or dreams or stream of consciousness on how much they hate writing—just for the hell of it, just to keep their fingers from becoming too arthritic, just because they have made a commitment to try to write three hundred words every day. Then, on bad days and weeks, let things go at that. . . . Your unconscious can't work when you are breathing down its neck. You'll sit there going, 'Are you done in there yet, are you done in there yet?' But it is trying to tell you nicely, 'Shut up and go away.'"—**Anne Lamott**, *Bird by Bird*

"Now, what I'm thinking of is, people always saying 'Well, what do we do about a sudden blockage in your writing? What if you have a blockage and you don't know what to do about it?' Well, it's obvious you're doing the wrong thing, don't you? In the middle of writing something you go blank and your mind says: 'No, that's it.' Ok. You're being warned, aren't you? Your subconscious is saying 'I don't like you anymore. You're writing about things I don't give a damn for.' You're being political, or you're being socially aware. You're writing things that will benefit the world. To hell with that! I don't write things to benefit the world. If it happens that they do, swell. I didn't set out to do that. I set out to have a hell of a lot of fun.

"I've never worked a day in my life. I've never worked a day in my life. The joy of writing has propelled me from day to day and year to year. I want you to envy me, my joy. Get out of here tonight and say: 'Am I being joyful?' And if you've got a writer's block, you can cure it this evening by stopping whatever you're writing and

> **What you do then is MAKE IT UP.**

doing something else. You picked the wrong subject."—**Ray Bradbury at The Sixth Annual Writer's Symposium by the Sea, 2001**

"The secret of getting ahead is getting started. The secret of getting started is breaking your complex overwhelming tasks into small manageable tasks, and then starting on the first one."—**Mark Twain**

"The best way is always to stop when you are going good and when you know what will happen next. If you do that every day . . . you will never be stuck. Always stop while you are going good and don't think about it or worry about it until you start to write the next day. That way your subconscious will work on it all the time. But if you think about it consciously or worry about it you will kill it and your brain will be tired before you start."—**Ernest Hemingway**

"Writer's block is my unconscious mind telling me that something I've just written is either unbelievable or unimportant to me, and I solve it by going back and reinventing some part of what I've already written so that when I write it again, it is believable and interesting to me. Then I can go on. Writer's block is never solved by forcing oneself to 'write through it,' because you haven't solved the problem that caused your unconscious mind to rebel against the story, so it still won't work—for you or for the reader."—**Orson Scott Card at Fiction**

"Many years ago, I met John Steinbeck at a party in Sag Harbor, and told him that I had writer's block. And he said something which I've always remembered, and which works. He said, 'Pretend that you're writing not to your editor or to an audience or to a readership, but to someone close, like your sister, or your mother, or someone that you like.' And at the time I was enamored of Jean Seberg, the actress, and I had to write an article about taking Marianne Moore to a baseball game, and I started it off, 'Dear Jean . . . ,' and wrote this piece with some ease, I must say. And to my astonishment that's the way it appeared in *Harper's Magazine.* 'Dear Jean . . . ,' Which surprised her, I think, and me, and very likely Marianne Moore."
—**John Steinbeck by way of George Plimpton**

"Over the years, I've found one rule. It is the only one I give on those occasions when I talk about writing. A simple rule. If you tell yourself you are going to be at your desk tomorrow, you are by that declaration asking your unconscious to prepare the material. You are, in effect, contracting to pick up such valuables at a given time. Count on me, you are saying to a few forces below: I will be there to write."
—**Norman Mailer in *The Spooky Art: Some Thoughts on Writing***

"If you get stuck, get away from your desk. Take a walk, take a bath, go to sleep, make a pie, draw, listen to music, meditate, exercise; whatever you do, don't just stick there scowling at the problem. But don't make telephone calls or go to a party; if you do, other people's words will pour in where your lost words should be. Open a gap for them, create a space. Be patient."—**Hilary Mantel**

"[When] the thoughts rise heavily and pass gummous through my pen . . . I never stand conferring with pen and ink one moment; for if a pinch of snuff or a stride or two across the room will not do the business for me— . . . I take a razor at once; and have tried the edge of it upon the palm of my hand, without further ceremony, except that of first lathering my beard, I shave it off, taking care that if I do leave hair, that it not be a grey one: this done, I change my shirt—put on a better coat—send for my last wig—put my topaz ring upon my finger; and in a word, dress myself from one end to the other of me, after my best fashion."
—**Laurence Sterne**

"I learned to produce whether I wanted to or not. It would be easy to say oh, I have writer's block, oh, I have to wait for my muse. I don't. Chain that muse to your desk and get the job done."—**Barbara Kingsolver**

"Writer's block . . . a lot of howling nonsense would be avoided if, in every sentence containing the word WRITER, that word was taken out and the word PLUMBER substituted; and the result examined for the sense it makes. Do plumbers get plumber's block? What would you think of a plumber who used that as an excuse not to do any work that day? The fact is that writing is hard work, and sometimes you don't want to do it, and you can't think of what to write next, and you're fed up with the whole damn business. Do you think plumbers don't feel like that about their work from time to time? Of course there will be days when the stuff is not flowing freely. What you do then is MAKE IT UP. I like the reply of the composer Shostakovich to a student who complained that he couldn't find a theme for his second movement. 'Never mind the theme! Just write the movement!' he said. Writer's block is a condition that affects amateurs and people who aren't serious about writing. So is the opposite, namely inspiration, which amateurs are also very fond of. Putting it another way: a professional writer is someone who writes just as well when they're not inspired as when they are."—**Philip Pullman**

QUESTIONS

1. Emily Temple selected several quotes from famous authors to help convey her point. What is the overall message? How can you tell?

2. Why do you think she chose these particular authors and quotes? Are there other authors/quotes that you would add to her list?

COMPOSING PROJECT | Make a List

Brainstorm what unleashes your creativity. When do you feel most creative? Least creative? Are there places that make you feel more or less creative? Are there activities that seem to bring out your creativity? Are there particular people in your life who make you feel more creative? Make a list that reflects your creative world.

▼ Poster

New York Book Editors, *Got Writer's Block?*

New York Book Editors, a group of experienced editors who have worked for some of New York City's major publishing houses, created an informative visual map to help creative writers extricate themselves from writer's block. The map provides a series of yes/no pathways in response to questions about plot and character. All the paths in the visual lead to one final bit of advice: "Stop procrastinating. Keep writing."

QUESTIONS

1. The creators of this piece used a flowchart approach for their visual. Is this an effective strategy for communicating their ideas? Why or why not? What other approaches might have worked in this poster?

2. How would you characterize the language used in the chart? Do you think it is effective? How might the chart strike you differently if the tone were more formal?

COMPOSING PROJECT | Create a Poster

Using the New York Book Editors' poster as your model, create your own flowchart titled "Need Musical Inspiration?" In the poster, use a series of prompts/questions to help your reader make choices about the types of music to listen to that might inspire the creative process.

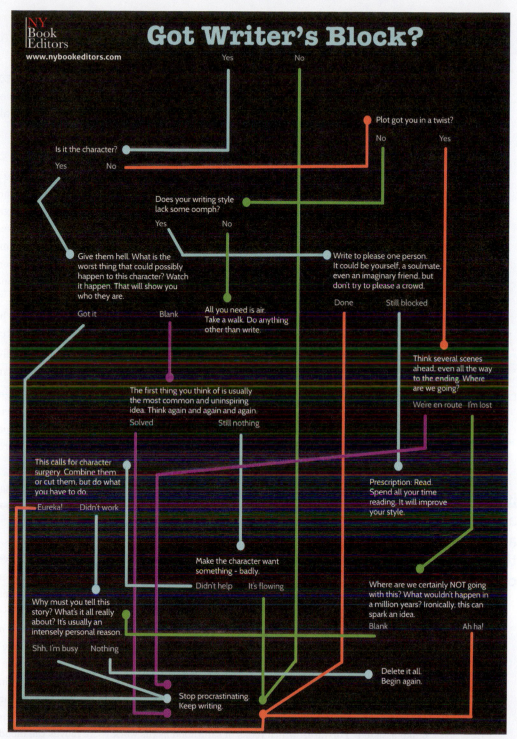

Got Writer's Block?

NY Book Editors
www.nybookeditors.com

Yes   No

Plot got you in a twist?
No   Yes

Is it the character?
Yes   No

Does your writing style lack some oomph?
Yes   No

Give them hell. What is the worst thing that could possibly happen to this character? Watch it happen. That will show you who they are.

Write to please one person. It could be yourself, a soulmate, even an imaginary friend, but don't try to please a crowd.

Done   Still blocked

All you need is air. Take a walk. Do anything other than write.

Think several scenes ahead, even all the way to the ending. Where are we going?

Got it   Blank

We're en route   I'm lost

The first thing you think of is usually the most common and uninspiring idea. Think again and again and again.

Solved   Still nothing

This calls for character surgery. Combine them or cut them, but do what you have to do.

Prescription: Read. Spend all your time reading. It will improve your style.

Eureka!   Didn't work

Make the character want something - badly.

Why must you tell this story? What's it all really about? It's usually an intensely personal reason.

Didn't help   It's flowing

Where are we certainly NOT going with this? What wouldn't happen in a million years? Ironically, this can spark an idea.

Blank   Ah ha!

Shh, I'm busy   Nothing

Delete it all. Begin again.

Stop procrastinating. Keep writing.

Credit: New York Book Editors.

New York Book Editors, *Got Writer's Block?*   531

Andre Grant, *Beyoncé's* Lemonade

Andre Grant is a freelance writer and the former features editor for *HipHopDX*, an online magazine devoted to hip-hop culture and music. His writing focuses on music and fashion. In his review of Beyoncé's visual album *Lemonade*, he analyzes its world premiere on HBO.

Credit: Used by permission of Andre Grant.

Beyoncé is an event. Her projects are black holes, sucking up the space and time around them at a dizzying pace. She's become the rule and the exception. The one pop star with a capital P that can tote the powerful nexus of feminism, America and America's great sin in both of her cosmic hands. Who can encapsulate the struggles of the most disrespected people in America: black women. And yet light a path to reconciliation inside the inner and outer worlds of their shared lineage and narrative. Whether the infidelity comes from Jay Z or Matthew Knowles or whomever; whether the fractured inner-world given as penance to the great tide of women our country has produced but not ever kept. Her second "visual" album, *Lemonade* speaks to those promises unfulfilled, uncounted, waiting to be honored and baptizes itself in the murky poignancy of cheating and being cheated. Out of trust, out of hope, out of the promise of new lives and old moments. All of them now to be rewritten. This, a most personal admission, is strange from Beyoncé and yet it's dazzling.

Everyone remembers the elevator incident. A grainy video showed sister Solange laying H-town hands on the serenely coifed Jigga. The video went viral. Then the theories behind the incident did, too, as everyone wondered whether or not there was trouble in paradise. Whispers of Dame Dash's ex-wife Rachel Roy snuck around the web. Rita Ora's face popped up, too, if only for a moment. Paradise? No. Resilience? Yes.

> **It is both album and manifesto, and illustrates the true power of art.**

Split into three acts, the album opens with her husband's secrets spilled. Each song moves through her courses of grief, from the acceptance and anger that permeates "Pray You Catch Me" on down the rabbit hole to the pillar of strength "Sorry." "Sorry" is particularly ear worming, bells softly chiming around the chorus. But the song does so much, showing how emotions can shift in the blink of an eye. From, "I ain't sorry / Boy, bye" and "He only want me when I'm not there / He better call Becky with the good hair" to "Let's take a toast to the good life / Suicide before you see this tear fall down my eye." Act 2 begins with "6 Inch," enticing The Weeknd's symbolic woman: dazed, unaffected, strong, intoxicating. Someone whose savagery can only be matched by acceptance. In this act, ending in the gorgeous "Sandcastles," Beyoncé finds a way to work through the broken promises of her younger self ("Daddy Lessons"), which sees her reclaim country to great effect, and then reclaim redemption. "Sandcastles" itself is a stunning piano ballad, but the imagery of Jay Z, her adulterous hubby rubbing her ankle as if that is the only space left she trusts him to love, is haunting. The third act crescendo's with the James Blake assisted "Forward," which reeks of sainthood as his work voice moves the mood toward the tabernacle. The reconciliation is complete on "All Night," for now. But Beyoncé's territory is more than just the body of relationship. It's the politics of that body, not only susceptible to defilement by those who count black women as something dangerous and foreign, but by those they count as familiar, whose lines remind them of their fathers and their brothers.

Unfaithfulness, an issue everyone can understand is the album's cause. That single nod sends this album into the stratosphere, as Beyoncé is so tight lipped there have been an army of think pieces devoted to the lack of any real access journalists and their outlets have in the web age with her silence at the center. Yet, that fact does not dominate the record. It's the veracity of the sounds and artistic achievements of the visuals (a marquee that screams "Loveless," a bat named "hot sauce," multiple scenes of loving, simple sisterhood, a Jay Z who's reticent, a speech about turning lemons into lemonade) weighted by her admission but not sunk by it, that stretch into what becomes a feast of genres, both musical and literary, tackled with absolute mastery. She's the most resonant, the most complete and fascinating star in the world.

The video portion of her jaunt through the fragility of promise is layered with yoruba imagery from Laolu Senbanjo, the poetry of belonging and misplacement of Warsan Shire, and the madcap magic of the American south. Beyoncé now is not just from the south, but of it. Painting herself in the regalia of its cultural contradictions and washing herself in the saltwater of its dashed dreams. She turns a tumult of contributors into a tapestry. Boots is once again apart of the fray, but there are many others. From variant collaborations with Brooklyn multi-disciplinary artist Melo X, to more traditional names like Kevin Garrett, Diplo, Wynter Gordon, The Dream, and Mike Dean. Then there are the oddballs. Scraps of undercurrent taken from Ezra Koenig, Father John Misty, and Soulja Boy. Of course, the features: Jack White (The White Stripes), The Weeknd, James Blake and Kendrick Lamar. But there's more and more. Her cup overflows.

It's transcendent not only because it shed a light on the voices and struggles of black women relegated to telling their stories by candlelight, suffering from estrangement, but because it highlights how that voice (through every genre darted through with real grace) is literally everywhere and apart of everything. It is both album and manifesto, and illustrates the true power of art. The power to conjure back from the dark the voice of people the world has chosen to ignore.

QUESTIONS

1. In his review of Beyoncé's visual album *Lemonade*, Grant states, "It is both album and manifesto, and illustrates the true power of art." What evidence does he provide in his review to support this point?

2. Do you have to be familiar with Beyoncé's album to get meaning from this review? Why or why not?

COMPOSING PROJECT | Write an Album Review

Find an album that you believe exemplifies amazing artistry. In your review, highlight what makes this particular musical endeavor worthy of listening and attention. Try to bring the album and its contents to life for a reader that perhaps has not encountered that artist before.

Alan Watts, *Music Is Life*

Alan Watts was a British-born philosopher who wrote many books and articles on Eastern and Western religion. He was most associated with Buddhism. The excerpt below is from *Learning the Human Game*, a recording that captures four of his lectures on the human condition. The excerpt plays with the idea that our schooling system cheats us out of the real experience of education by making us focus on the destination rather than the journey itself.

Credit: Used by permission from Alan Watts.

In music, though, one doesn't make the end of the composition the **point** of the composition. If that were so, the best conductors would be those who played fastest; and there would be composers who only wrote finales. People go to concerts only to hear one crashing chord—because that's the end. Same way in dancing—you don't aim at a particular spot in the room; that's where you should arrive. The whole point of the dancing is the dance.

Now, but we don't see that as something brought by our education into our everyday conduct. We've got a system of schooling which gives a completely different impression. It's all graded—and what we do is we put the child into the corridor of this grade system,

> ❝ **The whole point of the dancing is the dance.** ❞

with a kind of "c'mon kitty kitty kitty . . ." And yeah, you go to kindergarten, and that's a great thing, because when you finish that, you'll get into first grade. And then c'mon, first grade leads to second grade, and so on . . . And then you get out of grade school you go to high school—and it's revving up, the thing is coming . . . Then you're going to go to college, and by jove then you get into graduate school, and when you're through with graduate school, you'll go out to join the world. And then you get into some racket where you're selling insurance. And they've got that quota to make. And you're going to make that.

And all the time, this thing is coming, it's coming, it's coming—that great thing, the success you're working for. Then when you wake up one day about forty years old, you say "My God! I've arrived! I'm there!" And you don't feel very different from what you always felt. And there's a slight letdown, because you feel there's a hoax. And there was a hoax. A dreadful hoax.

They made you miss everything. By expectation. Look at the people who live to retire, and put those savings away. And then when they're sixty-five, and they don't have any energy left, they're more or less impotent, they go and rot in an old people's "senior citizens" community. Because we've simply cheated ourselves, the whole way down the line. We thought of life by analogy was a journey, was a pilgrimage, which had a serious purpose at the end.

And the thing was to get to that end. Success, or whatever it is, or maybe heaven after you're dead. But we missed the point the whole way along. It was a musical thing, and you were supposed to sing, or to dance, while the music was being played.

1. How effective do you think Watts's use of music and dance as metaphors is? Can you think of other metaphors he could have used that would have been more effective?

2. How would you describe Watts's voice in this piece? Does he sound like someone you would like to hang out with? Trust? Why or why not?

COMPOSING PROJECT | Write a Letter to the Principal of Your Former High School

What are some changes that could be made at the high school you went to that would help students there focus on the journey as much as the destination? Write a letter to your high school's principal in which you suggest a few changes that could be implemented.

▼ Curriculum Vitae

Johannes Haushofer, *CV of Failures*

Johannes Haushofer is an assistant professor of psychology and public affairs at Princeton University. His research and publications focus on poverty. Although Haushofer's resume is brimming with impressive successes, his "CV of Failures," below, focuses on his unsuccessful attempts to get grants, jobs, and publications. (Note: CV stands for "curriculum vitae," a form of resume used in academia.)

Credit: Used by permission of Johannes Haushofer.

Most of what I try fails, but these failures are often invisible, while the successes are visible. I have noticed that this sometimes gives others the impression that most things work out for me. As a result, they are more likely to attribute their own failures to themselves, rather than the fact that the world is stochastic, applications are crapshoots, and selection committees and referees have bad days. This CV of Failures is an attempt to balance the record and provide some perspective.

This idea is not mine, but due to a wonderful article in *Nature* by **Melanie I. Stefan**, who is a Lecturer in the School of Biomedical Sciences at the University of Edinburgh. You can find her original article here, her Web site here, her publications here, and follow her on Twitter under *@MelanieIStefan*.

I am also not the first academic to post their CV of failures. Earlier examples are here, here, here, and here.

This CV is unlikely to be complete—it was written from memory and probably omits a lot of stuff. So if it's shorter than yours, it's likely because you have better memory, or because you're better at trying things than me.

Degree Programs I Did Not Get Into

2008   PhD Program in Economics, Stockholm School of Economics

2003   Graduate Course in Medicine, Cambridge University
        Graduate Course in Medicine, UCL
        PhD Program in Psychology, Harvard University
        PhD Program in Neuroscience and Psychology, Stanford University

1999   BA in International Relations, London School of Economics

Academic Positions and Fellowships I Did Not Get

2014   Harvard Kennedy School Assistant Professorship
        UC Berkeley Agricultural and Resource Economics Assistant Professorship
        MIT Brain & Cognitive Sciences Assistant Professorship
        This list is restricted to institutions where I had campus visits; the list of places
        where I had first-round interviews but wasn't invited for a campus visit, and
        where I wasn't invited to interview in the first place, is much longer and I will
        write it up when I get a chance. The list also shrouds the fact that I didn't apply to
        most of the top economics departments (Harvard, MIT, Yale, Stanford, Princeton,
        Chicago, Berkeley, LSE) because one of my advisors felt they could not write a
        strong letter for them.

Awards and Scholarships I Did Not Get

2011   Swiss Network for International Studies PhD Award

2010   Society of Fellows, Harvard University
        Society in Science Scholarship
        University of Zurich Research Scholarship

2009   Human Frontiers Fellowship

2007   Mind-Brain-Behavior Award (Harvard University)

2006   Mind-Brain-Behavior Award (Harvard University)

2003   Fulbright Scholarship
        Haniel Scholarship (German National Merit Foundation)

Paper Rejections from Academic Journals

2016   QJE, Experimental Economics

2015   AER × 2

2013   PNAS, Experimental Economics, Science, Neuron

2009	AER
2008	Science, Neuron, Nature Neuroscience, Journal of Neuroscience, Journal of Vision

Research Funding I Did Not Get

2016	MQ Mental Health Research Grant
2015	Russell Sage Research Grant (two separate ones)
2013	National Science Foundation Research Grant
2010	University of Zurich Research Grant Swiss National Science Foundation Research Grant
2009	Financial Innovation Grant International Labor Organization Research Grant 3ie Research Grant

Meta-Failures

2016	This darn CV of Failures has received way more attention than my entire body of academic work

QUESTIONS

1. Who do you think Haushofer sees as the audience for his "CV of Failures"—students, faculty, or someone else? Why do you think so?

2. What purpose do you think the introductory note on the "CV of Failures" serves? How would you read and understand the piece differently if it didn't have the introductory note?

COMPOSING PROJECT | Create a CV of Failures

List jobs you've applied for but not gotten, colleges that rejected you, perhaps courses or assignments you've failed, relationships that have ended, scholarships you didn't get, fraternities or sororities that rejected you, and other disappointments. What can you learn about yourself by looking at this list?

▼ Blog

Aalto Entrepreneurship Society, *International Day for Failure*

The first official Day for Failure was celebrated in Finland on October 13, 2010. The day calls attention to all the ways we learn and grow from being unsuccessful at something. The "Day for Failure" Web page invites people to share their failure stories via social media. The day is sponsored by the Aalto Entrepreneurship Society, a Finnish student organization that encourages start-up culture.

Credit: Used by permission of Aalto Entrepreneurship Society.

Quotes

"Only those who dare to fail greatly can ever achieve greatly." —**Robert F. Kennedy**

"A person who never made a mistake never tried anything new." —**Albert Einstein**

"There is only one thing that makes a dream impossible to achieve: fear of failure." —**Paulo Coelho**

The Steps

1. Fail. How? You'll find your own personal way to do it.

2. Tweet your failure with hashtag #dayforfailure or read a bunch of fails from other human beings. We human beings are used to failing.

3. Buy great ingredients, read recipe, prepare everything, and burn your food. Serve when you (and the food) are cooled down.

4. Share your failphoto on Instagram. On the 13th, #skateboardingbruises, #blush, and #faces will be paired with #dayforfailure.

5. Do a bankruptcy. Money isn't everything, they say. Right?

6. Ask that boy/girl/anyone out.

7. Go to YouTube and search "fail." Remember, no one on the videos planned failing. It's just something that usually occurs after trying. Still, why so many videos?

8. Use Facebook as you use it every day. Share a story about your day. The more embarrassing, the more likes it usually gains. People are weird.

9. Don't share this awesome ACTIONBOOK.

10. Learn from your failure.

QUESTIONS

1. Go to dayforfailure.com, which is where the steps are from. How does the layout of the "Day for Failure" Web page direct your attention? What did you notice first? Why do you think the creators might have wanted your attention to go there first?

2. Are there steps for failing listed here that you think are not really in the spirit of celebrating failure? Which one(s)? What sets those steps apart from others?

COMPOSING PROJECT | Conduct an Interview

Interview a very successful person you know to find out what role failure has played in that person's life. How has he or she built upon failures or learned from them? Does the person consider some failures as turning points?

Creativity

1. **Conduct a poster session in your class.** Conferences held by many disciplines and organizations feature discussion panels and presentations; they also include poster sessions. In a poster session, researchers present their research methods and findings on a poster that combines text and images to quickly convey information to people walking around the poster session venue. You can find examples of posters used in poster sessions at projects.ncsu.edu/project/posters/ExamplePosters.html.

a. For this project, pair up with a classmate to create a poster for a poster session on strategies for alleviating creative blocks. Your task will be to test a theory or piece of advice about overcoming writer's block or finding inspiration, such as Hilary Mantel's suggestion that you should get away from your desk and bake a pie. To gather a reasonable amount of data for analysis, you will need to implement the advice on at least three occasions, so if you are baking a pie to spur your creativity, you will need to bake a pie on at least three separate occasions and track how that affected your ability to write. Ultimately, you will present a poster detailing the results of your experiments to the class.

b. Begin by choosing a particular strategy to try. You might select one from the readings in this chapter, or you can do further research to find out about other strategies. For example, Elizabeth Gilbert, author of the best-selling memoir *Eat, Pray, Love*, has a popular TED talk, "Your Elusive Creative Genius," in which she suggests that creative types could relieve a lot of the pressure on themselves by reframing where inspiration comes from.

c. Next, decide what your measure of success will be for the strategy. For example, if you test the idea that baking a pie can help with writer's block, the measure of success needs to relate to your ability after baking the pie to write productively, rather than to show delicious the pie is.

d. Then, conduct your test. Take detailed notes. For example, in the case of baking the pie, note whether your attitude toward your creative endeavor changed as you baked the pie and to what extent and exactly when. Remember that you'll need to conduct your test at least three times to make sure that the results are consistent.

e. After you've conducted your test, analyze the results and create a three-panel poster for the class poster session. In your analysis, you might consider:
   - How effective the strategy was
   - Pros and cons of the strategy
   - Changes you might make to your experimental protocol to get more accurate results

2. **Conduct a study of your creative processes.** For this project, you and your creativity are the subject. To better understand patterns in your own creative processes, carefully and systematically study yourself. What makes you productive? Are there specific activities that help spur your creativity? Are there times during the day that you are most creative?

a. To begin your project, devote a section of a notebook or purchase a journal to detail your creativity. Alternatively, you can create a spreadsheet on your computer or phone.

b. Observe and take detailed notes daily over the course of three weeks about the following:
   - What creative acts did you do that day? Write down as many details as you can about what you did, where you were, and how you felt at the moment. Include even seemingly unrelated details, such as what you ate or drank and how well rested you were.
   - Note the times that you engaged in creative endeavors. If you are a writer, when did you produce writing? If you act, when did an idea for a performance capture your imagination? If you cook, what time of day did you feel most inspired to try something new?

- Were there any things that happened during the day that seemed to impede your creative juices? What occurred? For example, were you coming down with a cold? Stressed out about bills? Distracted by an upcoming event?

c. After three weeks, review your notes. What patterns do you notice about your creativity? Are there particular days and times when you were more creative? Do you see any variables that tend to make you more or less productive? Are there things that occurred right before you were inspired? Are there things that occurred that gave you a creative block? What conclusions might you draw about your creative process?

d. Take all the information and compose a written draft of your study. Use these categories: Introduction, Materials and Methods, Results.

INDEX OF GENRES

Student Work

Visual Arguments/Collages/Scrapbooks

Web Sites

Wiki Entries

INDEX OF THEMES

Literacy & Language

Literature & Creative Nonfiction

Money, Economics, Poverty

Multigenre Projects

Sexual Identity, LGBT

Slavery

Sports & Games

Violence & Crime

Work, Job Search, Business

INDEX